GW00724692

New Trends in Grammaticalization and Language Change

Studies in Language Companion Series (SLCS)

ISSN 0165-7763

This series has been established as a companion series to the periodical *Studies in Language.*

For an overview of all books published in this series, please see *http://benjamins.com/catalog/slcs*

Founding Editor

Werner Abraham
University of Vienna / University of Munich

Editors

Werner Abraham
University of Vienna / University of Munich

Elly van Gelderen
Arizona State University

Editorial Board

Bernard Comrie
University of California, Santa Barbara

William Croft
University of New Mexico

Östen Dahl
University of Stockholm

Gerrit J. Dimmendaal
University of Cologne

Ekkehard König
Free University of Berlin

Christian Lehmann
University of Erfurt

Elisabeth Leiss
University of Munich

Marianne Mithun
University of California, Santa Barbara

Heiko Narrog
Tohuku University

Johanna L. Wood
University of Aarhus

Debra Ziegeler
University of Paris III

Volume 202

New Trends in Grammaticalization and Language Change
Edited by Sylvie Hancil, Tine Breban and José Vicente Lozano

New Trends in Grammaticalization and Language Change

Edited by

Sylvie Hancil
University of Rouen

Tine Breban
The University of Manchester

José Vicente Lozano
University of Rouen

John Benjamins Publishing Company
Amsterdam / Philadelphia

The paper used in this publication meets the minimum requirements of the American National Standard for Information Sciences – Permanence of Paper for Printed Library Materials, ANSI Z39.48-1984.

DOI 10.1075/slcs.202

Cataloging-in-Publication Data available from Library of Congress:
LCCN 2018027603 (PRINT) / 2018050144 (E-BOOK)

ISBN 978 90 272 0163 8 (HB)
ISBN 978 90 272 6343 8 (E-BOOK)

© 2018 – John Benjamins B.V.
No part of this book may be reproduced in any form, by print, photoprint, microfilm, or any other means, without written permission from the publisher.

John Benjamins Publishing Company · https://benjamins.com

Table of contents

The verbal phrase

Discourse markers

Introduction

Grammaticalization in the 2010s – A dialogue between the old and the new

Tine Breban and Sylvie Hancil
The University of Manchester / University of Rouen

This volume brings together a selection of papers first presented at the *Second International Conference on Grammaticalization Theory and Data* organized by Sylvie Hancil in Rouen in April 2016. Together they reflect the current state of the art in grammaticalization studies: they present the application of new models, e.g constructionalization, to grammaticalization, the ongoing debate about the status and modelling of the development of discourse markers in grammaticalization, and reveal a renewed interest in the typological application of grammaticalization and in the cognitive motivations for unidirectionality. As such, they characterise grammaticalization studies in the 2010s as a dialogue between the new and the old.

In this introduction, we will first briefly review the history of grammaticalization in order to frame the papers in this volume and show how old interests and questions are given a new lease of life. The next sections introduce the four key themes running through this volume. We take the point of view that two books are in particular instrumental in shaping the current debates and interests, the *Oxford Handbook of Grammaticalization* (Narrog & Heine 2011), with its emphasis on typology and language variety, and *Constructionalization and Constructional Changes* (Traugott & Trousdale 2013) as the most referred to book on diachronic construction grammar.

1. Grammaticalization from 1980s–2000s

In the 1980s, work under the banner of grammaticalization gave the study of language change a new impetus. Even though the term *grammaticalization* dates back to Meillet (1912) and the ideas perhaps even to the 19th century (Narrog &

https://doi.org.10.1075/slcs.202.01bre
© 2018 John Benjamins Publishing Company

Heine 2011: 1), it's the 1980s that see the birth of grammaticalization studies in its modern form. The work was typically data-rich, including both synchronic and diachronic investigations, and bridged subdisciplines and models of linguistics such as historical linguistics and typology, syntax and pragmatics, cognitive and generative linguistics. Seminal works in the 1980s, amongst many others Givón (1979), Lehmann (1982, 1985), Traugott (1982), Heine & Reh (1984), answered questions about the recurrent pathways of development between lexical and grammatical items in a functional, typological perspective.[1]

The late 1980s and 1990s were an extremely productive and conceptually fruitful period in which the formal and semantic characteristics of these pathways were analysed in great detail by notably Traugott & Heine (1991), Hopper & Traugott (1993), Bybee et al. (1994), Lehmann (1995), and integrated with cognitive theories of conceptual semantics (e.g. Sweetser 1990; Heine et al. 1991; Heine 1993) and pragmatics (Traugott 1989; Traugott & König 1991). By this time, grammaticalization had become a household term in historical linguistics and many students of language change developed their studies within its conceptual framework.

It was also at this time that the status of grammaticalization as a theory or even as a phenomenon in its own right were questioned (Newmeyer 1998; Campbell 2001; see Joseph 2011 for a good summary). Other linguists queried the hypothesis of unidirectionality of grammatical change, starting with Ramat (1992) and culminating in Norde (2009) (see Haspelmath 1999 and Börjars & Vincent 2011 for critical discussions).

Despite – and perhaps partially also thanks to – these ongoing healthy challenges, the notion of grammaticalization continued to appeal and to develop. After tentative attempts in the 1990s (e.g. Abraham 1991; van Gelderen 1993; Roberts 1993), fully fleshed out models of grammaticalization within generative theories of morphosyntax were developed by most notably Roberts & Roussou (2003) and van Gelderen (2004, 2011) (see also Fischer 2007). New foci around the turn of century were the interactions with other – unidirectional – paths of semantic-pragmatic change, subjectification and intersubjectification (e.g. Traugott & Dasher 2002; Davidse et al. 2010; Brems et al. 2014); the classification of contexts via which grammaticalization happens, e.g. Heine (2002) and Diewald (2002) on bridging and switch contexts, and later Traugott (2008a) on dialogic/dialogual contexts and Waltereit (2011) on discourse strategies in general.

1. Within the short space of this overview, the works cited as illustrations cannot in any way be exhaustive. We have tried to cite the first work (as known to us) and some key references the reader can take as a starting point for exploring the topics. I trust the reader understand this does not at all reflect our opinion of the quality of many omitted references.

While the field of grammaticalization studies expanded, critical voices asked whether it was possible and, more importantly opportune in view of a principled definition of grammar, to include changes leading to elements below the word and beyond the clause level, which often flaunted traditional parameters associated with grammaticalization. The demarcation with lexicalization (among many others Moreno-Cabrera 1998; Himmelmann 2004; Brinton & Traugott 2005; Boye & Harder 2012; Traugott & Trousdale 2013) and the in/exclusion of discourse markers (see several papers in this volume and Heine this volume for an overview of the discussion) are a case in point. The discussion led to the proliferation of diachronic processes, grammaticalization, lexicalization, subjectification, pragmaticalization, degrammaticalization, etc. which can perhaps be seen as the hallmark of grammaticalization in this first decade of the years 2000.

2. Grammaticalization in the 2010s as reflected in this volume

2.1 A revival of typological explorations of grammaticalization

The year 2011 saw the publication of the first major dedicated handbook of grammaticalization, *Oxford Handbook of Grammaticalization* edited by Heiko Narrog and Bernd Heine. The handbook provided an important opportunity to "take stock" after 30 years of grammaticalization studies, but also set itself the aim of uncovering "possible directions for future research in the field" (Narrog & Heine 2011: 2). One topic which the handbook foregrounded in this respect was the typological application of grammaticalization. As pointed out above, the development of (modern) grammaticalization started from studies discussing recurrent changes in a typological perspective. But very quickly the balance shifted towards the diachronic study of languages that had richly documented historical data, such as English, French, Spanish, etc. (but see López-Couso & Seoane 2008). One of the most important contributions of the Oxford handbook, in our opinion, is that it revived the interest in typological studies and urged the extension of grammaticalization studies in as many varied languages as possible. Its editors would no doubt be happy to see the balance of five studies on Germanic/Romance versus seven on other languages in this volume.

Studies that prominently discuss questions related to the application of grammaticalization in non-Germanic/Romance languages are those by Yang Huang and Fuxiang Wu, Ophelie Gandon, Maris Camilleri and Ekkehard König and Jingying Li. The questions they seek to answer range from the descriptive, i.e. modelling previously unfamiliar processes of change, exotic to a literature that has focused on Germanic-Romance languages, to the theoretical. They provide new data and discussion of topics related to parallel paths of grammaticalization (e.g. Heine & Kuteva 2002), such as internal versus contact-induced grammaticalization in genetically related languages, contact-induced grammaticalization in non-related but geographically close languages (see Matras 2011 and Heine & Kuteva 2011 for overviews) and even identify parallel grammaticalization in non-related geographically distant languages.

Huang and Wu explore a specific case of areal grammaticalization in their paper *Central Southern Guangxi as a grammaticalization area.* They focus on the Mainland Southeast Asia (MSEA), which has been well-established as a macro linguistic/grammaticalization area on the basis of areal grammaticalization, but make the innovative claim that, within this area, a smaller micro-area of grammaticalization should be distinguished involving the Zhuang Tai-Kadai and Sinitic languages in the Central Southern Guangxi Region. They show that these languages display uncommon convergent linguistic features, as well as four uncommon homogenous grammaticalization paradigms. They identify Zhuang as responsible for the diffusion of all grammaticalization models.

Gandon in the paper *The grammaticalization of interrogative pronouns into relative pronouns in South-Caucasian languages: internal development or replica?* investigates the South Caucasian languages, Georgian, Mingrelian and Svan, which all three have relative pronouns that developed out of interrogative pronouns. Gandon carefully weighs up arguments in favour of explaining this similarity as a case of parallel internal developments, for which a.o. identifiable interim steps lend plausibility, or as contact-induced grammaticalization, for which, most strikingly, the absence of the pattern in Laz, a fourth South Caucasian language, but one which is only found in a geographically separate region, provides support. The conclusion she reaches is that both suggestions seem equally conceivable and may actually have occurred jointly: one can conceive of a development through correlative constructions promoted by language contact.

Camilleri (*The avertive and proximative grams in Maltese using the auxiliary* għodd) focuses on Maltese, an Arabic vernacular. She is specifically concerned with the pseudo-verb *għodd,* which derived from the imperative form of the transitive lexical verb *għadd.* As a pseudo-verb, *għodd* can convey two meanings, avertive and proximative. Camilleri discusses how Lexical Functional Grammar can capture the morphological, syntactic and argument structure features of the different uses (lexical versus pseudo-verb, avertive versus proximative), as well as suggest further grammaticalization based on dual syntactic behaviour of *għodd* as an auxiliary.

In their paper *Functional similarity despite geographical distance: On the grammaticalization of German* mal *and Chinese* yíxià, König and Li investigate the surprising similarities between the meanings of German *(ein)mal* and Chinese *yixià*. They show how both elements undergo semantic extension from expressing 'minimal frequency' to acting as a marker of politeness/hedging 'minimal effort/commitment' via strikingly similar processes of change. The change, which is not attested for any languages closely related to German, e.g. English, French, is argued to be motivated by the same pragmatic inferences: "A service requested with minimal frequency and minimal commitment cannot be 'a big deal' and an assertion made with a minimal commitment cannot be authoritative" (König & Li this volume). They conclude that processes of grammaticalization and semantic change that are clearly based on cognitive and interactional principles are likely to occur in several languages, even in cases where those languages are neither geographically, culturally nor genealogically closely related.

2.2 Accounting for the distinctive features of the development of discourse markers as grammaticalization

In the 1990s, grammaticalization scholars turned their attention to the development of discourse markers and modal particles (Abraham 1991; Traugott 1995; Onodera 1995; Brinton 1996). Almost immediately, a (fierce) debate arose as to whether or not the development of discourse markers (including modal particles) could and should be considered as grammaticalization. The debate has its origins in contemporaneous critical observations concerning structural and semantic differences between the process of grammaticalization as defined in the 1980s and early 1990s and the development of discourse markers. On the one hand, studies pointed out that rather than scope-decrease and fixation (Lehmann 1982, 1985), their development typically displayed scope-increase and syntactic flexibility (a.o. Nordlinger & Traugott 1997; Tabor & Traugott 1998). On the other hand, scholars raised the question whether it can be taken for granted that, semantically, discourse markers are part of 'grammar' and that their development involves similar semantic processes of change. This separatist view started with Erman and Kotsinas (1993), who introduced the term *pragmaticalization* (see also Aijmer 1997 for an early discussion of the issue). The debate resulted in opposing 'narrow' and 'wide' views of grammar and as a result on what grammaticalization is. Taking a broad-brush approach, one could say that, for people expounding the former, narrow view, discourse markers develop via a distinctive process of change, pragmaticalization, whereas under the latter, broad view, their development is a (non-prototypical type of) grammaticalization (e.g. Brinton 2001; Barth-Weingarten & Couper-Kuhlen 2002). A complicating factor is that the latter view is by no means homogenous as to how its exponents perceive and hence model the differing features of the development of discourse markers: is the development grammaticalization plain and simple, is it a development at the periphery of a prototypical model, is it a separate type? For a comprehensive and recent discussion of the debate, see Degand and Evers-Vermeul (2015) and also Heine (this volume).

The papers by Bernd Heine, Diana Lewis, Elise Louviot and Sylvie Hancil, which deal with the development of discourse markers in this volume take the latter (inclusive) view – perhaps not unexpectedly given that they stem from a conference on grammaticalization, but they do this with a critical eye and aim to finetune the modelling of the development of discourse markers within grammaticalization and to account for its individual behaviours.

Heine takes up with the discussion of wide versus narrow grammaticalization directly in a theoretical positioning paper titled *Are there two different ways of approaching grammaticalization?* In the first part of his paper, Heine addresses whether, within the inclusive view of grammaticalization, it is necessary to talk about a narrow versus a wide *sub*type of grammaticalization. He does this by taking on the arguments provided in one specific proposal, namely the distinction between GR (grammaticalization as reduction) and GE (grammaticalization as expansion) made by Traugott and Trousdale (2013) as part of their constructionalization model. In a second step, after having refuted the 'two type' approach, he goes on to discuss an alternative explanation for the issues presented by the development of discourse markers for grammaticalization. The differences are a result of the differing input to the grammaticalization process: in the case of discourse markers this is extra-clausal material, 'theticals' in a term borrowed from Discourse Grammar (Dik 1997, as first discussed in Kaltenböck et al. 2011), which can themselves be the result of cooptation, a cognitive-communicative operation whereby some segment of linguistic discourse is transferred from one domain of discourse to another. Heine shows in detail how the combination of coopotation + grammaticalization explains the special features of the development of discourse markers in a principled way whilst 'preserving' a unified view of grammaticalization.

The other papers in this volume position themselves in a more traditional inclusive, wide view of grammaticalization, with one author, Lewis, noting explicitly that cooptation because of its abrupt nature cannot account for the gradual nature of the changes she investigated. Instead the papers focus on other ways in which the grammaticalization analysis of (specific) discourse markers can be enhanced or refined.

Lewis' paper *Grammaticalizing connectives in English and discourse information structure* is concerned with discourse markers that occur both in the left and right peripheries (LP and RP). Previous research has suggested that the different positions are associated with different functions (e.g. Aijmer 2002). Lewis' case study of *in fact* and *after all* suggests a different explanation. LP and RP connectives *in fact* and *after all* each express a particular rhetorical relation independently of position. The different positions are instead motivated by different informational structural contributions: In LP, the connective links its host to the previous idea while also putting the following idea(s) into focus, like a presentative. In RP, the connective has the same linking function, but closes a sequence of at least two ideas, and marks the second one as pragmatically backgrounded, as a comment on (or a modification of) the previous idea. In the cases of *in fact* and *after all*, the pattern with a RP connective constitutes a more complex and arguably more grammaticalized construction than the LP pattern. Lewis concurs with Lehmann (2008) that (further) grammaticalization may be at least partly motivated by information structure. Lewis' paper can also be seen as part of a trend in historical linguistics in general to explore the role of information structure in morphosyntactic change, e.g. Hinterhölzl and Petrova (2009) and Meurman-Solin et al. (2012).

The paper *Pragmatic uses of* nu *in Old Saxon and Old English* by Louviot starts off from quite traditional questions: in which syntactic and pragmatic contexts does the adverb *nu* 'now' develop discourse marker and modal particle uses and is it possible to determine a directionality of change from one to the other? However, after her fine-grained qualitative analysis, she reaches the nuanced and, far more interesting, conclusion that the historical data present a continuum of meanings engaging in a complex interplay with word order patterns and changes, and suggests a scenario whereby a single marker develops a variety of more or less conventionalized pragmatic uses, which, for a long period, still show important similarities and can likely still influence each other, but which may eventually become distinct enough (both formally and functionally) to deserve different labels. As a reader of this volume in its entirety, one might wonder whether a construction grammar approach would offer the technical apparatus to model such a scenario.

Hancil (*(Inter)subjectification and paradigmaticization: The case study of the final particle* but) draws (renewed) attention to several notions proposed in relation to grammaticalization that have not previously been explicitly linked to the development of discourse markers. Firstly, Hancil argues that the development of further discourse meanings of final *but* evidences (lexical) persistence as defined by Hopper (1991), as well as structural persistence (Breban 2009) and 'procedural persistence', i.e. "a linguistic expression has a semantically abstract invariant that illustrates the underlying mechanism of the particle and constrains its evolution" (Hancil this volume). Secondly, Hancil endorses Ghesquière's (2010) and Narrog's (2014) proposals for the uncoupling of subjectification and intersubjectification, as well as for the possible further development from intersubjective to truly 'interactive' (Fitzmaurice 2004, see also Ghesquière et al. 2014). A final notion that she applies in her analysis is paradigmaticization (Lehmann 1982), arguing that final *but* cannot be fully understood by looking at processes of development, but that a complementary perspective of the paradigm of final particles in which it becomes (more) integrated is equally important.

2.3 Modelling grammaticalization: Diachronic construction grammar and lexical functional grammar

As discussed earlier, it was typologists with a functionalist approach to language, such as Talmy Givón, Christian Lehmann, Bernd Heine, Paul Hopper, (and Elizabeth Traugott if we consider the Systemic Functional Grammar distinctions underlying her foundational 1982 paper), who (re)introduced grammaticalization into modern (historical) linguistics. Quite quickly, other cognitive-functional concepts were incorporated to explain the meaning changes observed in cases of grammaticalization: e.g. metaphor, metonymy, subjectivity, pragmatic inferencing (Sweetser 1990; Heine et al. 1991; Traugott 1989; Traugott & König 1991). Even though modern grammaticalization was very much indebted to its cognitive-functional background, it was not associated with a single model within these traditions.[2] As discussed by Narrog and Heine (2011: 2–3) and illustrated in Part I (Grammaticalization and Linguistic Theory) of the *Handbook*, the phenomenon grammaticalization lends itself to different views and to combination with a wide range of approaches. This is at once a strength, as it allows us to see the similarities between a wide range of synchronic and diachronic language phenomena, but also a weakness, as there is a proliferation of definitions and no uniform concept of grammaticalization. Explicit attempts to 'model' grammaticalization within a specific theory have been limited in the past within the generative tradition, with the works of Roberts & Roussou (2003) and van Gelderen (2004, 2011).

One of the most prominent new trends in grammaticalization studies in the 2010s has been its reconceptualization within a particular type of cognitive grammar, Construction Grammar. Construction grammars (see Croft 2007 for an overview and a more detailed description) are synchronic models, whose central tenet is that languages are networks of conventionalized form-meaning pairings (i.e. constructions) of varying sizes and degrees of schematicity. Several aspects of Construction Grammar identified in this description tie in closely with findings of grammaticalization, and it is therefore not a surprise that the two have been brought together. Firstly, from the 1980s already, researchers emphasised that grammaticalization not only affected single words, but also larger multi-word items and items as part of larger structures; which can be captured by the single notion of 'construction'. Secondly, grammaticalization affects both the semantics of an item and its morphosyntactic features; which fits in with the characterization of constructions as 'form-meaning pairs'. More recently it has been argued that changes to meaning and form process incrementally but do so, not necessarily, in

2. There is of course the notorious debate as to whether grammaticalization is a 'theory' in its own right, see a.o. Newmeyer (1998), Haspelmath (2004) and more recently Bybee (2015).

unison (e.g. Traugott & Trousdale 2010); such small step changes can be modelled at all (independent) levels of form (syntax, morphology, phonology) and meaning (semantic, pragmatics, discourse function) in a construction (see e.g. Fried 2009). Finally, grammaticalization has been argued to involve semantic generalization; which can be captured by the different levels of schematicity awarded to different constructions. Within a construction grammar model, grammaticalization is then reconceptualised as the gradual development of a new more schematic form-meaning pairing which serves a grammatical function.

The first proposals for a diachronic construction grammar were made by Noël (2007) and Bergs and Diewald (2008).[3] There are two monographs on the topic, Hilpert (2013) and (probably most influentially) Traugott and Trousdale (2013). The model of Traugott and Trousdale (2013) incorporates both grammaticalization and lexicalization, and distinguishes between constructionalization, i.e. the development of a new construction combining a new meaning and a new form, and constructional changes, whereby only one aspect of a construction changes. It is especially the models and proposals of Traugott and Trousdale (2013) and Hilpert (2013) that are taken up and discussed in this volume. The papers by Yueh Hsin Kuo, Bing Zhu and Kaoru Horie, Mitsuko Narita Izutsu and Katsunobu Izutsu, Reijirou Shibasaki all develop case studies covering a range of phenomena in a range of languages within a Traugott and Trousdale (2013) style constructionalization framework and several of them take the opportunity to argue the advantages of this type of constructionalization approach over a more traditional grammaticalization analysis.

Kuo's paper *The development of three classifiers into degree modifier constructions in Chinese* uses constructionalization to show how the (parallel) grammaticalization of the classifiers *yi xie* 'some', *yi dian* 'one bit', and *yi xia* 'one downward motion' into degree modifiers creates a new productive mesoconstruction (subschema) within the Chinese degree modifier construction (in a similar way to English *N of N* constructions such as *a bit of*, *a lot of* as described by a.o. Traugott 2008b; Brems 2011; Traugott & Trousdale 2013). His detailed corpus analysis shows how a construction grammar model captures change both at the individual level, highlighting differences between the classifiers, and at the schematic (mesoconstruction) level, showing how similarities feed the gradual development of the new construction, which in turn sanctions novel constructs. Within a constructional spirit, his case study also emphasizes that both source meaning and source form (in this case the particular pragmatically-motivated syntagmatic position of these classifiers) are essential in making possible their semantic and functional reinterpretation.

3. Note that Noël (2007) in fact argues that grammaticalization and diachronic construction grammar cannot be conflated.

In their paper *The development of the Chinese scalar additive coordinators derived from prohibitives: A constructionist perspective*, Zhu and Horie also focus on the development of a new more schematic construction. They show how instances of the type 'prohibitive + SAY verb' in specific contexts and via gradual semantic extensions developed into scalar additive coordinators, and subsequently posit the association of 'prohibitive + SAY verb' and scalar additive meaning as a new form-meaning pair (or construction). More recent instances of the schema, they argue were derived through analogical extraction by the schema (rather than by the same constructionalization process) and they include a detailed diachronic overview of new microconstructions sanctioned in this way by the new schematic construction, in order to trace the growth of the construction through increases in both type and token frequency.

Izutsu and Izutsu (*Cross-varietal diversity in constructional entrenchment: The final-tag construction in Irish and American English*) in a similar way employ token and type frequency to assess the degree of constructionalization, but they do this with the aim of comparing the entrenchment of the same construction, the final-tag construction, in different varieties of English, Irish and American English. They interpret the higher type and token frequencies in Irish English in terms of two of three characteristics of grammatical constructionalization given by Traugott and Trousdale (2013), increase in schematicity and in productivity, and provide further evidence for the third, decrease in compositionality. They speculate on the influence of language contact as motivating the strength of the Irish final tag construction, but conclude that it is also likely that the success of the construction is a self-motivating force.

In the paper *From the inside to the outside of the sentence: Forming a larger discourse unit with* jijitsu *'fact' in Japanese*, Shibasaki puts forward that the change of *jijitsu* from nominal in a predicate construction into stand-alone discourse marker, more specifically a 'projector', which anticipates the upcoming discourse (Hopper & Thompson 2008: 105), is most suitably analysed in a constructionalization framework. Shibasaki describes how in the course of the change, examples are found that cannot fully be defined either as a projector or as a predicate, and thus do not allow classification as either lexical or grammatical. While for grammaticalization, the lexical-grammatical dichotomy is "definitional" (Narrog & Heine 2017: 22, cited by Shibasaki), construction grammars hold that the distinction is blurred and meaning is viewed on a lexical-grammatical continuum, which is a better fit for his data. An additional advantage, Shibasaki finds, is the distinction of 'constructional changes' which only affect the semantics of the *jijitsu*-predicate paving the way for the constructionalization.

The prominence of Construction Grammar approaches (and in particular Traugott and Trousdale's constructionalization) in the current debate is obvious not only from these four papers, but also from the fact that they feature prominently in the theoretically oriented papers of Heine (Section 2.2) and Fischer (Section 2.4). Despite the omnipresence of Construction Grammar as a new model for grammaticalization, there is in fact another paper that could have been included under this general heading, Camilleri's paper on avertive and approximative *għodd* in Maltese (see Section 2.1). She constructs her analysis in a Lexical Functional Grammar model. In fact, the advantages of the LFG architecture are not dissimilar to those attributed to Construction Grammar, that is, LFG captures non-simultaneous changes/differences at the morphological, syntactic and argument structure levels. Thinking about Börjars et al.'s (2015) criticism that diachronic construction grammars in their current form lack explicit articulation of form and meaning and the relation between them, it would be interesting to see to what extent studies in LFG can provide an example of good practice. However, the task at hand is much more comprehensive in view of the range of phenomena that have been discussed under the heading of grammaticalization, the range of languages it has been applied to and the range of linguistic levels if affects, as is stressed by Narrog and Heine (2011).

2.4 Revisiting the cognitive principles underlying and motivating grammaticalization

The combination of cognitive linguistics and grammaticalization in the 1990s brought with it a desire to understand how such a change happened and was motivated in the actual mind of the language user. Most cognitive approaches are usage-based and as such believe that language structure emerges through use (e.g. Hopper's (1987) notion of 'emergent grammar'). The mechanisms underlying grammaticalization and motivating unidirectionality are therefore expected to be related to those operational in language use. Several such processes have been identified. Bybee (2003 and other work) emphasises repetition and increases in frequency as a crucial factor in many of the morphophonological processes commonly attested in grammaticalization, i.e. morphophonological reduction, coalescence or chunking, gain in autonomy and subsequent decategorialization, and even in semantic generalization. It's the rise in frequency typically associated with grammatical as opposed to lexical meanings that is responsible for the unidirectionality observed in these processes. The recognition of pragmatic inferences as trigger for semantic change (Traugott & König 1991; Traugott & Dasher 2002; and König & Li this volume) is another one.

Other scholars have sought to connect pathways of grammaticalization with general processes observed in human cognition. Examples here are the discussions of metaphor and metonymy as underlying the semantic changes in grammaticalization (e.g. Sweetser 1990; Heine et al. 1991; Hopper & Traugott 1993). The most drawn out debate in this respect is that on the possible roles of reanalysis and analogy as mechanisms of grammaticalization (see the back to back chapters by Elizabeth Traugott and Olga Fischer in Narrog & Heine 2011). It seems fair to say that in grammaticalization studies in general reanalysis has won out, and is viewed as the most important principle involved in grammaticalization (e.g. Hopper & Traugott 2003; Lehmann 2004; Traugott & Trousdale 2010). We think this is partly due to 'inherited ideas' in (historical) linguistics: Reanalysis has traditionally been associated with syntactic change (e.g. Langacker 1977), whereas analogy is particularly associated with the domain of morphology. In addition, it is often claimed, amongst others by Meillet (1912), that analogy cannot lead to true innovations, but is instead restricted to levelling/pattern matching and generalization/pattern extension. Analogy is then at most awarded a secondary role, as mechanism driving extension of a new meaning to other contexts (actualization), while reanalysis is viewed as creating the actual change. More recently, Traugott and Trousdale (2010) make a distinction between analogization, i.e. the mechanism, and analogical thinking, which they recognize can motivate a reanalysis.

Olga Fischer has been a (lone) advocate for awarding analogy a central role (e.g. Fischer 2007, 2011). She draws attention to the central role analogy plays in language acquisition and language learning and to its status as basic principle in human cognition (the ability to see similarities, and to categorize on the basis of this). Reanalysis is what is observable in the output of change, but from a processing perspective, she argues, analogy is at work in the change. The new alliance between grammaticalization and Construction Grammar has put fuel onto the fire of the old debate concerning the role of analogy as a mechanism underlying grammaticalization. Analogy plays an important role in Construction Grammar in that constructions in the constructional network are related through similarities and 'inherit' features from other constructions. It is precisely from this perspective that Fischer revisits the issue of analogy in grammaticalization in this volume in her paper *Analogy: Its role in language learning, categorization, and in models of language change such as grammaticalization and constructionalization.*

Fischer starts by explaining that a diachronic construction grammar model has a strong advantage over the grammaticalization model, which is hampered by the fact that only one construction undergoing change is usually looked at. Other constructions that may have influenced the development are generally not considered unless they are of a clearly parallel type (e.g. the study of *N of N* constructions, see Section 2.3). As a notable exception, she discusses Traugott's (2008a) study of the development of negative attitudinal '*all*-clefts', which takes into account the rise of cleft constructions in general, the increase in dialogic *wh*-clefts, and the fact that both clefts occur most frequently with the same verbs *say* and *do* (which provides a concrete form of analogy) as factors. However, by and large, the current diachronic construction grammar approaches are still wedded to earlier work on grammaticalization and focus on reanalysis of a single construction. Fischer also identifies a range of issues that would need to be addressed if we want to understand the role analogy plays in constructionalization and by extension language change, including at which levels of schematicity does analogy apply, noting that the influence of highly abstract structures in language processing is in particular difficult to gauge. In the main part of her paper, Fischer proposes that an improved understanding of analogy will be instructive in this respect, and discusses on the one hand the historical ideas of Hermann Paul and on the other hand current studies in cognitive science, which present remarkably similar conclusions. She concludes that these new theoretical insights need to combined with detailed corpus studies of actual changes, because "the more we look at historical cases with analogy in mind, [...] the more we may learn about what is probable and what not".

In addition to Fischer's paper, there are three other papers that investigate possible cognitive motivations for the cases of grammaticalization they describe, by Ekkehard König and Jingying Li, by Susana Rodríguez-Rosique and by Naoaki Wada. As discussed in Section 2.1, König and Li reach the conclusion that certain pragmatic inferences can be shared by speakers of non-related languages and can therefore lead to similar processes of grammaticalization in these languages. The proposals of Rodríguez-Rosique and Wada are more closely tied to the specific phenomena they are concerned with.

Rodríguez-Rosique in *From time to surprise: The case of* será posible *in Spanish* proposes a cognitive analysis of 'future' that can explain the synchrony and diachrony of the different meanings of *será posible* 'it will be possible'. Her analysis reveals *será posible* has two distinct structural behaviors which can be related through grammaticalization, the original compositional one and a non-transparent one, and a range of meanings covering posteriority, conjecture and other epistemic meanings (all associated with the compositional form) and mirativity (expressed by the non-transparent form). She proposes these different meanings can be conceptualised as unified in a cognitive model that views 'future' as a deictic relation of 'pointing/distance forward', working at different levels of meaning, namely, the event level (posteriority), the epistemic level (evidentiality/conjecture) and the utterance level (mirativity). Diachronically, semantic progression via these levels can be viewed as instantiating subjectification and intersubjectification (Traugott & Dasher 2002; Traugott 2010) respectively.

In the paper *C-gravitation and the grammaticalization degree of "present progressives" in English, French and Dutch*, Wada employs the concept of C-gravitation to explain the differing degrees of grammaticalization displayed by the present progressive in English (most grammaticalized), French and Dutch (least grammaticalized). As 'public self'-centred languages (Hirose 2000), the unmarked deictic centre for the consciousness of the speaker in all three languages is the time of speech. In C-gravitation (or gravitation towards the consciousness of the speaker), the consciousness of the speaker as public self at speech time augments its power of influence in the grammatical system. Wada's argument is that the more grammaticalized uses of the English and, to a lesser extent French, present progressive are also more strongly oriented to the speech event (even including it in their reference time), and as such the further grammaticalization of the English and French present progressive can be said to be triggered by C-gravitation.

Brief summary and outlook

In this introduction, we have sought to identify four major themes running through this volume. Some papers are concerned with only one of these areas of interests, but most stride, and, more importantly, contribute critically to, multiple. Grammaticalization studies in the 2010s combine a return to their roots with a renewed interest in typological variation and a new cognitive turn. Grammaticalization studies are enriched by new models, such as diachronic construction grammar, thetical grammar, and the application of LFG. What is clear is that scholars in the current age are not just taking grammaticalization for granted: they want to understand and explain (better) how grammaticalization works. Overall the papers in this volume testify to the continuing quest to explain and model grammaticalization theoretically and empirically. As such, this volume illustrates that grammaticalization studies have plenty of life left to move into the 2020s.

References

Abraham, Werner. 1991. The grammaticalization of the German modal particles. In *Approaches to Grammaticalization, Vol. II: Focus on Types of Grammatical Markers* [Typological Studies in Language 19:2], Elizabeth Closs Traugott & Bernd Heine (eds), 331–380. Amsterdam: John Benjamins. https://doi.org/10.1075/tsl.19.2.17abr

Abraham, Werner. 2010. Methodologische Überlegungen zu Grammatikalisierung, zyklischem Wandel und dem Wechsel von Analytik zu Synthetik – und zyklisch weiter zu Analytik (?). In *Kodierungstechniken im Wandel: Das Zusammenspiel von Analytik und Synthese in Gegenwartsdeutschen*, Dagmar Bittner & Livio Gaeta (eds), 249–274. Berlin: De Gruyter. https://doi.org/10.1515/9783110228458.249

Aijmer, Karin. 1997. *I think* – an English modal particle. In *Modality in Germanic Languages: Historical and Comparative Perspectives*, Toril Swan & Olaf Jansen-Westvik (eds), 1–47. Berlin: Mouton de Gruyter. https://doi.org/10.1515/9783110889932.1

Aijmer, Karin. 2002. *English Discourse Particles: Evidence from a Corpus* [Studies in Corpus Linguistic 10]. Amsterdam: John Benjamins. https://doi.org/10.1075/scl.10

Barth-Weingarten, Dagmar & Couper-Kuhlen, Elisabeth. 2002. On the development of final 'though': A case of grammaticalization? In Wischer & Diewald (eds), 345–361.

Bergs, Alexander & Diewald, Gabriele (eds). 2008. *Constructions and Language Change*. Berlin: Mouton de Gruyter. https://doi.org/10.1515/9783110211757

Börjars, Kersti & Vincent, Nigel. 2011. Grammaticalization and directionality. In Narrog & Heine (eds), 163–176.

Börjars, Kersti, Vincent, Nigel & Walkden, George. 2015. On constructing a theory of grammatical change. *Transactions of the Philological Society* 113: 363–382. https://doi.org/10.1111/1467-968X.12068

Boye, Kasper & Harder, Peter. 2012. A usage-based theory of grammatical status and grammaticalization. *Language* 88: 1–44. https://doi.org/10.1353/lan.2012.0020

Breban, Tine. 2009. Structural persistence: A case based on the grammaticalization of English adjectives of difference. *English Language and Linguistics* 13: 77–96. https://doi.org/10.1017/S1360674308002888

Brems, Lieselotte. 2011. *Layering of Size and Type Noun Constructions in English*. Berlin: Mouton de Gruyter. https://doi.org/10.1515/9783110252927

Brems, Lieselotte, Ghesquière, Lobke & Van de Velde, Freek (eds). 2014. *Intersubjectivity and Intersubjectification in Grammar and Discourse. Theoretical and Descriptive Advances* [Benjamins Current Topics 65]. Amsterdam: John Benjamins.

Brinton, Laurel J. 1996. *Pragmatic Markers in English: Grammaticalization and Discourse Function*. Berlin: Mouton de Gruyter. https://doi.org/10.1515/9783110907582

Brinton, Laurel J. 2001. From matrix clause to pragmatic marker: The history of *look*-forms. *Journal of Historical Pragmatics* 2: 177–199. https://doi.org/10.1075/jhp.2.2.02bri

Brinton, Laurel J. 2002. Grammaticalization versus lexicalization reconsidered: On the late use of temporal adverbs. In *English Historical Syntax and Morphology* [Current Issues in Linguistic Theory 223], Teresa Fanego, Javier Pérez-Guerra & María José López-Couso (eds), 67–97. Amsterdam: John Benjamins. https://doi.org/10.1075/cilt.223.07bri

Brinton, Laurel J. & Traugott, Elizabeth Closs. 2005. *Lexicalization and Language Change*. Cambridge: CUP. https://doi.org/10.1017/CBO9780511615962

Bybee, Joan L. 2003. Mechanisms of change in grammaticalization: The role of frequency. In *The Handbook of Historical Linguistics*, Brian D. Joseph & Richard D. Janda (eds), 602–623. Oxford: Blackwell. https://doi.org/10.1002/9780470756393.ch19

Bybee, Joan L. 2015. *Language Change*. Cambridge: CUP.

Bybee, Joan L., Perkins, Revere Dale & Pagliuca, William. 1994. *The Evolution of Grammar: Tense, Aspect, and Modality in the Languages of the World*. Chicago IL: University of Chicago Press.

Campbell, Lyle (ed.). 2001. *Grammaticalization: A Critical Assessment*. Special issue of *Language Sciences* 23(2–3).

Croft, William, 2007. Construction Grammar. In *The Oxford Handbook of Cognitive Linguistics*, Dirk Geeraerts & Hubert Cuyckens (eds), 463–508. Oxford: OUP.

Davidse, Kristin, Vandelanotte, Lieven & Cuyckens, Hubert (eds). 2010. *Subjectification, Intersubjectification and Grammaticalization*. Berlin: Mouton de Gruyter. https://doi.org/10.1515/9783110226102

Degand, Liesbeth & Evers-Vermeul, Jacqueline. 2015. Grammaticalization or pragmaticalization of discourse markers? More than a terminological issue. *Journal of Historical Pragmatics* 16: 59–85. https://doi.org/10.1075/jhp.16.1.03deg

Diewald, Gabriele. 1997. *Grammatikalisierung: Eine Einführung in Sein und Werden Grammatischer Formen*. Tübingen: Niemeyer. https://doi.org/10.1515/9783110946673

Diewald, Gabriele. 2002. *A model for relevant types of contexts in grammaticalization*. In Wischer & Diewald (eds), 103–120.

Dik, Simon C. 1997. *The Theory of Functional Grammar, Part 2: Complex and Derived Constructions*. Berlin: Mouton de Gruyter.

Erman, Britt & Kotsinas, Ulla-Britt. 1993. Pragmaticalization: The case of *ba'* and *you know*. *Studier i Modern Sprakvetenskap* 10: 76–92.

Fischer, Olga. 2007. *Morphosyntactic Change: Functional and Formal Perspectives*. Oxford: OUP.

Fischer, Olga. 2011. Grammaticalization as analogy-driven change. In Narrog & Heine (eds), 31–42.

Fischer, Olga, Rosenbach, Anette & Stein, Dieter (eds). 2000. *Pathways of Change: Grammaticalization in English* [Studies in Language Companion Series 53]. Amsterdam: John Benjamins.

Fitzmaurice, Susan. 2004. Subjectivity, intersubjectivity and the historical construction of interlocutor stance: From stance markers to discourse markers. *Discourse Studies* 6: 427–448. https://doi.org/10.1177/1461445604046585

Fried, Mirjam. 2009. Construction Grammar as a tool for diachronic analysis. *Constructions and Frames* 1: 261–290. https://doi.org/10.1075/cf.1.2.04fri

van Gelderen, Elly. 1993. *The Rise of Functional Categories* [Linguistik Aktuell/Linguistics Today 9]. Amsterdam: John Benjamins. https://doi.org/10.1075/la.9

van Gelderen, Elly. 2004. *Grammaticalization as Economy* [Linguistik Aktuell/Linguistics Today 71]. Amsterdam: John Benjamins. https://doi.org/10.1075/la.71

van Gelderen, Elly. 2011. *The Linguistic Cycle: Language Change and the Language Faculty*. Oxford: OUP. https://doi.org/10.1093/acprof:oso/9780199756056.001.0001

Ghesquière, Lobke. 2010. On the subjectification and intersubjectification paths followed by the adjectives of completeness. In Davidse, Vandelanotte & Cuyckens (eds), 277–314. https://doi.org/10.1515/9783110226102.3.277

Ghesquière, Lobke, Brems, Lieselotte & Van de Velde, Freek. 2014. Intersubjectivity and intersubjectification: Typology and operationalization. In Brems, Ghesquière & Van de Velde (eds), 129–153.

Giacalone Ramat, Anna & Hopper, Paul J. 1998. *The Limits of Grammaticalization* [Typological Studies in Language 37]. Amsterdam: John Benjamins.

Gisborne, Nikolas & Patten, Amanda. 2011. Construction grammar and grammaticalization. In Narrog & Heine (eds), 92–104.

Givón, Talmy. 1979. *On Understanding Grammar*. New York NY: Academic Press.

Haspelmath, Martin. 1999. Why is grammaticalization irreversible? *Linguistics* 37: 1043–1068.

Haspelmath, Martin. 2004. On directionality in language change with particular reference to grammaticalization. In *Up and Down the Cline – The Nature of Grammaticalization* [Typological Studies in Language 59], Olga Fischer, Muriel Norde & Harry Perridon (eds), 17–44. Amsterdam: John Benjamins. https://doi.org/10.1075/tsl.59.03has

Heine, Bernd. 1993. *Auxiliaries: Cognitive Forces and Grammaticalization*. Oxford: OUP.

Heine, Bernd. 2002. On the role of context in grammaticalization. In Wischer & Diewald (eds), 83–101.

Heine, Bernd, Claudi, Ulrike & Hünnemeyer, Friederike. 1991. *Grammaticalization: A Conceptual Framework*. Chicago IL: University of Chicago Press.

Heine, Bernd & Kuteva, Tania. 2002. World Lexicon of Grammaticalization. Cambridge: CUP. https://doi.org/10.1017/CBO9780511613463

Heine, Bernd & Kuteva, Tania. 2011. The areal dimension of grammaticalization. In Narrog & Heine (eds), 291–301.

Heine, Bernd & Reh, Mechthild. 1984. *Grammaticalization and Reanalysis in African Languages*. Hamburg: Buske.

Hilpert, Martin. 2013. *Constructional Change in English: Developments in Allomorphy, Word Formation, and Syntax*. Cambridge: CUP. https://doi.org/10.1017/CBO9781139004206

Himmelmann, Nikolaus P. 2004. Lexicalization and grammaticization: Opposite or orthogonal? In *What Makes Grammaticalization? A Look from its Fringes and its Components*, Walter Bisang, Nikolaus P. Himmelmann & Björn Wiemer (eds), 21–42. Berlin: Mouton de Gruyter.

Hinterhölzl, Roland & Petrova, Svetlana. 2009. *Information Structure and Language Change: New Approaches to Word Order Variation in Germanic*. Berlin: Mouton de Gruyter. https://doi.org/10.1515/9783110216110

Hirose, Yukio. 2000. Public and private self as two aspects of the speaker: A contrastive study of Japanese and English. *Journal of Pragmatics* 32: 1623–1656. https://doi.org/10.1016/S0378-2166(99)00111-3

Hopper, Paul J. 1987. Emergent grammar. *Proceedings of the 13th Annual Meeting of the Berkeley Linguistics Society*, 139–157.

Hopper, Paul J. 1991. On some principles of grammaticization. In *Approaches to Grammaticalization, Vol. I: Focus on Theoretical and Methodological Issues* [Typological Studies in Language 19:1], Elizabeth Closs Traugott & Bernd Heine (eds), 17–35. Amsterdam: John Benjamins. https://doi.org/10.1075/tsl.19.1.04hop

Hopper, Paul J. & Thompson, Sandra A. 2008. Projectability and clause combining in interaction. In *Cross-Linguistic Studies of Clause Combining: The Multi-Functionality of Conjunctions* [Typological Studies in Language 80], Ritva Laury (ed.), 99–123. Amsterdam: John Benjamins. https://doi.org/10.1075/tsl.80.06hop

Hopper, Paul J. & Traugott, Elizabeth Closs. 2003[1993]. *Grammaticalization*, 2nd edn. Cambridge: CUP. https://doi.org/10.1017/CBO9781139165525

Joseph, Brian D. 2011. Grammaticalization: A general critique. In Narrog & Heine (eds), 193–205.

Kaltenböck, Gunther, Heine, Bernd & Kuteva, Tania. 2011. On thetical grammar. *Studies in Language* 35: 848–893. https://doi.org/10.1075/sl.35.4.03kal

Langacker, Ronald W. 1977. Syntactic reanalysis. In *Mechanisms of Syntactic Change*, Charles N. Li (ed.), 57–139. Austin TX: University of Texas Press.

Lehmann, Christian. 1985. Grammaticalization: Synchronic variation and diachronic change. *Lingua e Stile* 20: 303–318.

Lehmann, Christian. 1995[1982]. *Thoughts on Grammaticalization*. Munich: Lincom. First published in 1982 as *Thoughts on Grammaticalization: A Programmatic Sketch*. [Arbeiten des Kölner Universalien-Projektes]. University of Cologne, Institut für Sprachwissenschaft.

Lehmann, Christian. 2002. New reflections on grammaticalization and lexicalization. In Wischer & Diewald (eds), 1–18.

Lehmann, Christian. 2004. Theory and method in grammaticalization. *Zeitschrift für Germanistische Linguistik* 32: 152–187.

Lehmann, Christian. 2008. Information structure and grammaticalisation. In *Theoretical and Empirical Issues in Grammaticalization* [Typological Studies in Language 77], Elena Seoane & María José López-Couso (eds), 207–229. Amsterdam: John Benjamins. https://doi.org/10.1075/tsl.77.12leh

López-Couso, María José & Seoane, Elena (eds). 2008. *Rethinking Grammaticalization. New Perspectives & Theoretical Issues in Grammaticalization* [Typological Studies in Language 76–77]. Amsterdam: John Benjamins. https://doi.org/10.1075/tsl.76

Matras, Yaron. 2011. Grammaticalization and language contact. In Narrog & Heine (eds), 279–290.

Meillet, Antoine. 1912. L'évolution des formes grammaticales. *Scientia* 12: 6. Reprinted in Meillet, Antoine. 1921[1948, 1965]. *Linguistique Historique et Linguistique Générale*, 130–148. Paris: Champion.

Meurman-Solin, Anneli, López-Couso, María José & Los, Bettelou. 2012. *Information Structure and Syntactic Change in the History of English*. Oxford: OUP. https://doi.org/10.1093/acprof:oso/9780199860210.001.0001

Moreno Cabrera, Juan C. 1998. On the relationship between grammaticalization and lexicalization. In Giacalone Ramat & Hopper (eds), 211–227. https://doi.org/10.1075/tsl.37.10mor

Narrog, Heiko. 2014. Beyond intersubjectification: Textual uses of modality and mood in subordinate clauses as part of *speech-act orientation*. In Brems, Ghesquière & Van de Velde (eds), 29–51.

Narrog, Heiko & Heine, Bernd. 2011. *The Oxford Handbook of Grammaticalization*. Oxford: OUP.

Narrog, Heiko & Heine, Bernd. 2017. Grammaticalization. In *The Cambridge Handbook of Historical Syntax*, Adam Ledgeway & Ian Roberts (eds), 7–27. Cambridge: CUP.

Newmeyer, Frederick. 1998. *Language Form and Language Function*. Cambridge MA: The MIT Press.

Noël, Dirk. 2007. Diachronic construction grammar and grammaticalization theory. *Functions of Language* 14: 177–202. https://doi.org/10.1075/fol.14.2.04noe

Norde, Muriel. 2009. *Degrammaticalization*. Oxford: OUP. https://doi.org/10.1093/acprof:oso/9780199207923.001.0001

Nordlinger, Rachel & Traugott, Elizabeth Closs. 1997. Scope and the development of epistemic modality: Evidence from *ought to*. *English Language and Linguistics* 1: 295–317. https://doi.org/10.1017/S1360674300000551

Onodera, Noriko. 1995. Diachronic analysis of Japanese discourse markers. In *Historical Pragmatics. Pragmatic Developments in the History of English* [Pragmatics & Beyond New Series 35], Andreas H. Jucker (ed.), 393–437. Amsterdam: John Benjamins. https://doi.org/10.1075/pbns.35.22ono

Ramat, Paolo. 1992. Thoughts on degrammaticalization. *Linguistics* 30: 549–560. https://doi.org/10.1515/ling.1992.30.3.549

Roberts, Ian. 1993. A formal account of grammaticalization in the history of Romance futures. *Folia Linguistica Historica* 13: 219–258.

Roberts, Ian & Roussou, Anna. 2003. *Syntactic Change: A Minimalist Approach to Grammaticalization*. Cambridge: CUP. https://doi.org/10.1017/CBO9780511486326

Sweetser, Eve. 1990. *From Etymology to Pragmatics: Metaphorical and Cultural Aspects of Semantic Structure*. Cambridge: CUP. https://doi.org/10.1017/CBO9780511620904

Tabor, Whitney & Traugott, Elizabeth Closs. 1998. Structural scope expansion and grammaticalization. In Giacalone Ramat & Hopper (eds), 229–272. https://doi.org/10.1075/tsl.37.11tab

Traugott, Elizabeth Closs. 1982. From propositional to textual to expressive meanings: Some semantic-pragmatic aspects of grammaticalization. In *Perspectives on Historical Linguistics* [Current Issues in Linguistic Theory 24], Winfred P. Lehmann & Yakov Malkiel (eds), 245–271. Amsterdam: John Benjamins. https://doi.org/10.1075/cilt.24.09clo

Traugott, Elizabeth Closs. 1989. On the rise of epistemic meanings in English: An example of subjectification in semantic change. *Language* 65: 31–55. https://doi.org/10.2307/414841

Traugott, Elizabeth Closs. 1995. Subjectification in grammaticalisation. In *Subjectivity and Subjectivisation: Linguistic Perspectives*, Dieter Stein & Susan Wright (eds), 31–54. Cambridge: CUP. https://doi.org/10.1017/CBO9780511554469.003

Traugott, Elizabeth Closs. 2008a. "All that he endeavoured to prove was …": On the emergence of grammatical constructions in dialogic contexts. In *Language in Flux: Dialogue Coordination, Language Variation, Change and Evolution*, Ruth Kempson & Robin Cooper (eds), 143–177. London: King's College Publications.

Traugott, Elizabeth Closs. 2008b. The grammaticalization of *NP of NP* patterns. In *Constructions and Language Change*, Alexander Bergs & Gabriele Diewald (eds), 21–43. Berlin: Mouton de Gruyter.

Traugott, Elizabeth Closs. 2010. (Inter)subjectivity and (inter)subjectification: A reassessment. In Davidse, Vandelanotte & Cuyckens (eds), 29–69. https://doi.org/10.1515/9783110226102.1.29

Traugott, Elizabeth Closs. 2011. Grammaticalization and mechanisms of change. In Narrog & Heine (eds), 19–30.

Traugott, Elizabeth Closs & Dasher, Richard B. 2002. *Regularity in Semantic Change*. Cambridge: CUP.

Traugott, Elizabeth Closs & Heine, Bernd (eds). 1991. *Approaches to Grammaticalization*, Vols. I & II [Typological Studies in Language 19]. Amsterdam: John Benjamins.

Traugott, Elizabeth Closs & König, Ekkehard. 1991. The semantics-pragmatics of grammaticalization revisited. In *Approaches to Grammaticalization, Vol. I: Focus on Theoretical and Methodological Issues* [Typological Studies in Language 19], Elizabeth Closs Traugott & Bernd Heine (eds), 189–218. Amsterdam: John Benjamins. https://doi.org/10.1075/tsl.19.1.10clo

Traugott, Elizabeth Closs & Trousdale, Graeme (eds). 2010. *Gradualness, Gradience, and Grammaticalization* [Typological Studies in Language 90]. Amsterdam: John Benjamins. https://doi.org/10.1075/tsl.90

Traugott, Elizabeth & Trousdale, Graeme. 2013. *Constructionalization and Constructional Changes*. Oxford: OUP. https://doi.org/10.1093/acprof:oso/9780199679898.001.0001

Waltereit, Richard. 2011. Grammaticalization and discourse. In Narrog & Heine (eds), 413–423.

Wischer, Ilse. 2000. Grammaticalization versus lexicalization: 'Methinks' there is some confusion. In Fischer, Rosenbach & Stein (eds), 355–370. https://doi.org/10.1075/slcs.53.17wis

Wischer, Ilse & Diewald, Gabriele (eds). 2002. *New Reflections on Grammaticalization* [Typological Studies in Language 49]. Amsterdam: John Benjamins. https://doi.org/10.1075/tsl.49

PART 1

General issues

Are there two different ways of approaching grammaticalization?

Bernd Heine
University of Cologne

Grammaticalization as a framework of linguistic analysis developed a fairly stable format in the course of the 1980s and 1990s (Lehmann 1982; Heine & Reh 1984; Traugott & Heine 1991a, 1991b; Heine et al. 1991; Hopper & Traugott 1993; Bybee et al. 1994; Haspelmath 1999). Around the turn of the century one of the basic principles of the framework, namely the unidirectionality hypothesis, was challenged (e.g., Newmeyer 1998), leading to refinements of the hypothesis (e.g., Norde 2009).[1]

A more dramatic challenge arose when the framework was extended to the analysis of discourse markers and related discourse material, which suggests that grammaticalization approaches are hard-pressed when applied to such material. Two main kinds of solutions were proposed. On the one hand, it was argued that the grammaticalization framework is inadequate to account for the development of discourse markers. On the other hand, an expanded notion of grammaticalization was proposed (see Degand & Evers-Vermeul 2015 for an overview of this research). That there is need to distinguish two different approaches to grammaticalization is propounded in detail by Traugott and Trousdale (2013: 99–112).

The main concern of the present paper is to determine the status of grammaticalization studies in light of recent work on discourse markers. It is argued that the justification for distinguishing two kinds of approaches to grammaticalization is questionable. Drawing attention to the cognitive-communicative principle of cooptation, the paper suggests that the development of discourse markers and related metatextual material cannot be reduced to effects of grammaticalization of any kind.

Keywords: cooptation, discourse marker, grammaticalization, pragmaticalization, thetical, unidirectionality

1. Concerning the limits of the unidirectionality hypothesis, see, e.g., Newmeyer (1998), Norde (2009), Börjars & Vincent (2011).

https://doi.org.10.1075/slcs.202.02hei
© 2018 John Benjamins Publishing Company

1. Discourse markers: A problem for grammaticalization

In the course of its history, work on grammaticalization has produced a range of different views on how the genesis and further development of grammatical (or functional) categories is to be approached. More recently, this work has been confronted with the problem of how to deal with discourse markers (or pragmatic markers) and related discourse material.[2]

Observing that discourse markers (DMs) are hard to reconcile with grammaticalization, a number of scholars argue that grammaticalization describes the development of sentence-internal grammatical markers while pragmaticalization describes that of DMs and other metatextual devices[3] – that is, pragmaticalization tends to be viewed as a distinct process of some kind (e.g., Erman & Kotsidas 1993; Aijmer 1997; Günthner 1999; Dostie 2004; Frank-Job 2006; Ocampo 2006; Hansen 2008: 58; Claridge & Arnovick 2010: 21–23; Arroyo 2011; Haselow 2011; Beijering 2012: 56–9).

Thus, for Ocampo (2006: 317), grammaticalization is movement towards syntax and morphology whereas DMs move "precisely to the opposite end: outside of syntax and towards discourse." And Norde (2009: 23) concludes: "[M]ovement towards discourse is genuinely different from movement towards grammar, and the two are therefore best kept separate." Ocampo (2006: 316–7), distinguishes the four hypotheses in (1) that have been proposed for the movement towards discourse characteristic of DMs.

(1) Factors shaping the development of discourse markers (Ocampo 2006: 317)
   a. Grammaticalization (Onodera 1995; Brinton 1996; Pinto de Lima 2002)
   b. An expanded notion of grammaticalization (Traugott 1995; Lenker 2000)
   c. A separate kind of grammaticalization (Wischer 2000)
   d. A distinct pathway, called pragmaticalization (Erman & Kotsinas 1993; Aijmer 1997; Günthner & Mutz 2004)

The classification in (1) is not the only one that has been volunteered on the development of DMs (see, e.g., Norde 2009: 22–3; Heine 2013: 1217–20; Degand &

2. We follow Detges & Waltereit (2007) in distinguishing between discourse markers and modal particles and refer to both of them summarily as pragmatic particles.

3. For the purposes of the present paper we will assume that discourse markers are non-compositional and as a rule short linguistic forms that are (a) syntactically independent from their environment, (b) frequently set off prosodically from the rest of the utterance, and (c) serve metatextual functions (cf. Heine 2013: 1209). Thus, they differ, e.g., from modal particles (such as German *denn, ja, schon, wohl,* etc.), which are associated mostly with (c) but not clearly with (a) nor with (b) (see also Traugott 2007: 141–2 and Waltereit 2001; Detges & Waltereit 2007).

Evers-Vermeul 2015: 62); mention may be made, for example, of lexicalization as an additional pathway for the development of DMs. What most have in common is, first, that there are two contrasting views, represented by (1a) and (1d), according to which this development is or is not an instance of grammaticalization, respectively. And, second, there are also views that can be interpreted as compromises of some kind or other between the two contrasting views.

For an understanding of what 'grammaticalization' is about it is most of all (1b) that is of interest, especially since it has been the subject of a range of studies devoted to DMs. Most of these studies concern DMs in English and a few other European languages, as well as Japanese and Korean (e.g., Onodera 2011). Languages in other parts of the world, such as Australia, Africa, or the Americas play hardly any role in this debate.

2. Two approaches to grammaticalization

2.1 Reduction vs. expansion

Research carried out in accordance with (1b) of Section 1 has frequently been in the direction of (1c) in arguing for a differential view of the notion of grammaticalization. To this end, two kinds of views of grammaticalization tend to be distinguished, referred to, respectively, as the 'narrow' and the 'wider' view.

According to the 'narrow', or 'restricted' view, grammaticalization is compatible with the criteria proposed by Lehmann (1982, 1995) but does not deal with, or has problems with accounting for DMs (Degand & Simon-Vandenbergen 2011: 290). The 'wider' view, by contrast, takes care of DMs, perhaps also of other kinds of discourse material (Traugott 1995; Hansen 1998b; Lenker 2000; Traugott & Dasher 2002; Brinton & Traugott 2005: 136–140; Prévost 2011; Diewald 2011a, 2011b; van Bogaert 2011; Degand & Evers-Vermeul 2015: 67).

A more pronounced position along these lines surfaces in the study of Traugott and Trousdale (2013). Rejecting the term 'pragmaticalization' (cf. Traugott 1995, 2007), they propose a distinction between two kinds of approaches, referred to as 'GR' and 'GE'. In GR approaches, grammaticalization is viewed as reduction and increase in dependency. Examples of such approaches are Givón (1979), Heine & Reh (1984), Heine et al. (1991), Lehmann (1995; 2004), Bybee et al. (1991), Haspelmath (2004), and Boye & Harder (2012).

In GE approaches, by contrast, grammaticalization is viewed as expansion. No particular information is provided on which studies represent this view, other than a discussion of Himmelmann (2004) and a definition of grammaticalization taken from Brinton & Traugott (2005: 99, 106–7).[4] We will return to this definition in Section 2.2.

It would seem that the distinction between the two kinds of approaches raises some problems, which are the topic of the next section.

2.2 Problems with the GR/GE distinction

Like Hilpert (2013), Traugott and Trousdale (2013) is a seminal study demonstrating how Construction Grammar operates in a diachronic space, and how our understanding of grammatical change can be enriched by means of a constructional analysis.[5] Nevertheless, we mentioned in the preceding section that there are problems with the distinction made in the latter study between two approaches, namely between grammaticalization as reduction and increase in dependency (GR) and as expansion (GE). The problems concern most of all some claims made by Traugott and Trousdale (2013), and these claims are now looked at in turn.

Claim A: The authors argue that the "concept of grammar adopted by many of the founders of the GR approach [...] until recently typically did not embrace such grammatical categories as topic and focus" (Traugott & Trousdale 2013: 101).

The claim is somewhat surprising considering that issues of information structure formed an important part in the work of these founders (in particular Givón 1979). Another early 'founder' study (Heine & Reh 1984) discusses not only the grammaticalization of both topic (theme) and focus categories but also the syntactic implications that these processes have for the languages concerned. A paradigm example is provided by a process observed in genetically and areally unrelated languages whereby a cleft construction [main clause + subordinate clause] is reinterpreted and develops into a mono-clausal focus construction (Heine & Reh 1984: 147–82).

What appears to be ignored in Claim A in particular is that these 'founder' studies themselves were building on the pioneering work on information structure by T. Givón, who had demonstrated already in the 1970s how grammatical categories for topic and focus marking can be accounted for with reference to principles of grammaticalization (e.g., Givón 1975b; see Givón 2015 for more details).

4. Elizabeth Traugott (p.c.) adds, however, that in Traugott (2010), a number of references are provided, such as Bybee, Roberts and Roussou, and van Gelderen, plus anything she has written from 1995 on.

5. The main differences between the approaches employed in the two studies are aptly summarized in Traugott and Trousdale (2013: 238). Concerning problems associated with the term 'constructionalization' as used in Traugott and Trousdale (2013), see Börjars et al. (2015).

Claim B: Among the features argued to be characteristic of expansion, that is, GE, is 'multidirectionality', better known as polygrammaticalization. Referring to Craig (1991) and Robert (2005), the authors say:

> Rather than unidirectionality, what we find here is multifunctionality, a phenomenon known in the grammaticalization literature as 'polygrammaticalization'. (Traugott & Trousdale 2013: 108)

This claim raises two problems, namely on the notions of unidirectionality and of polygrammaticalization, respectively. The former will be discussed under Claim C below, while the latter is looked into now. Both the term and the concept of polygrammaticalization were first proposed and developed in the GR tradition (Craig 1991).[6] Numerous cases of polygrammaticalization were already identified in the 1980s by "founders of the GR approach". For example, the study by Heine and Reh (1984) shows that

- demonstratives may grammaticalize on the one hand into copulas and on the other hand into personal pronouns, definite articles, relative clause markers, or conjunctions, and
- adverbs may on the one hand grammaticalize into adpositions and on the other hand into tense markers.

A possible outcome of polygrammaticalization is heterosemy: Etymologically related meanings are associated with different morphosyntactic categories in that, e.g., one meaning is associated with the noun phrase and the other with the verb phrase. Traugott and Trousdale (2013: 107) relate heterosemy to GE approaches but, once again, the term was proposed in the tradition of GR approaches (Lichtenberk 1991). Note further that Traugott and Trousdale's (2013: 60) definition of heterosemy is not exactly the same as that of Lichtenberk (1991), even though they say that they "follow Lichtenberk (1991) and use the term 'heterosemy' for the diachronic association between two meanings."[7]

6. We follow Craig (1991: 486) in defining polygrammaticalization "as a multiplicity of grammaticalization chains that may originate in one particular lexical morpheme". Elizabeth Traugott (p.c.), by contrast, says that "to include that in **uni**directionality would seem to me to be stretching the term too much". Given the fact that 'polygrammaticalization' and 'unidirectionality' appear to be two well-entrenched terms in the grammaticalization literature, re-thinking them runs the risk of introducing more terminological confusion than retaining them.

7. According to Lichtenberk (1991: 476), heterosemy obtains when within a single language "two or more meanings that are historically related, in the sense of deriving from the same ultimate source, are borne by reflexes of the common source element that belong in different morphosyntactic categories."

Claim C: The quotation above implies that polygrammaticalization (or multidirectionality) is different from or incompatible with unidirectionality (Traugott & Trousdale 2013: 108).

This claim is hard to reconcile with the evidence we are familiar with. The classical case of *bang* in the Chibchan language Rama of Nicaragua, analyzed in the GR tradition, is a case in point (Craig 1991): It involves one source item giving rise to unidirectional pathways within the argument-marking domain on the one hand, and within the tense-aspect-modality domain on the other.[8]

Claim D: Furthermore, Traugott and Trousdale (2013: 105–6) argue that the loss-and-gain model is a characteristic of GE rather than of GR.

Both the term 'loss-and-gain model' and the concept were developed in a study that is portrayed by Traugott and Trousdale (2013) as paradigm examples of GR, namely in Heine et al. (1991: 110). According to this model, grammaticalization cannot be reduced to losses of linguistic material but also tends to gain new meanings resulting from context-induced reinterpretation (see below).

Claim E: Traugott and Trousdale (2013: 109) suggest that, unlike GR, "GE asks questions […] about how grammaticalization occurs in context".

Already in Bybee et al. (1994) it was argued in detail that context-induced reinterpretation accounts for much of what happens in grammaticalization, and in Heine et al. (1991) one chapter is devoted exactly to this issue. The significance of context in grammaticalization was later expounded in the context model of Heine (2002) and surfaces in generalizations such as the following:

> In the same way that linguistic items undergoing grammaticalization lose in semantic, morphosyntactic, and phonetic substance, they also gain in properties characteristic of their uses in new contexts. (Heine & Kuteva 2002: 2)

Thus, it is hard to see on which evidence claim E is based.[9] A possible difference between GR and GE can be seen in the fact that works written in the GR tradition were not satisfied with describing how grammaticalization occurs in context but also with *why* this is so. To this end, cognitive-communicative explanations were

8. Unidirectionality as a probabilistic generalization is central to grammaticalization studies but not to Construction Grammar. Accordingly, Traugott and Trousdale (2013: 148) say that directionality is not criterial for grammatical constructionalization.

9. Elizabeth Traugott (p.c.) argues, however, that only with actual historical texts is it possible to show that context is important. If this claim were correct then this would mean that in more than 95 per cent of all languages of the world it is not really possible to study (context-induced) grammaticalization. It would seem that even without access to historical documents, given that there is appropriate contextual information, it is possible to reconstruct mechanisms of context-induced change such as hyperanalysis and hypoanalysis (cf. Croft 2000: 117–44).

proposed to understand some of the motivations underlying grammaticalization (see especially Heine 1997; Haspelmath 1999).

Claim F: Traugott and Trousdale (2013: 109) maintain that GE differs from GR in that it is able to deal with context expansion. For example, "a form that is reduced semantically and has paradigmatic functions … will also be available for a larger range of syntactic uses, and therefore its syntactic contexts may expand."

The way grammaticalization and syntax are intertwined was already a much discussed topic in grammaticalization studies of the 1970s, resulting in a range of seminal publications by T. Givón, Charles Li and others (e.g., Givón 1971, 1975a, 1975b; Li & Thompson 1974; see also the contributions in Li 1975 and Givón 2015).

Context extension (or expansion) was in fact one of the central topics of GR research. Especially Heine et al. (1991) and Bybee et al. (1994) describe examples of a number of semantically reduced forms undergoing context extension. Such examples, which are not only found in Europe but also in other parts of the world, include but are not restricted to new syntactic contexts. As has been shown in Heine & Reh (1984: 183–212), for example, semantic reduction (desemanticization) may even be responsible for the rise of new word order patterns. Crosslinguistically more widespread examples include verbs meaning 'say' in direct speech constructions: Once these verbs are semantically reduced they may in fact develop a range of syntactic functions such as quotatives, complementizers, purpose and cause markers, giving rise to new forms of complement clauses and adverbial clauses (e.g., Saxena 1988; Heine et al. 1991: 158–9; Klamer 2000). In sum, as pointed out in the GR tradition, grammaticalization cannot be reduced to expansion or extension; rather, the methodology employed "rests on the assumption that grammaticalization is based on the interaction of pragmatic, semantic, morphosyntactic, and phonetic factors" (Heine & Kuteva 2007: 33–4).

Once again, a difference between GR and GE can be seen in the fact that whereas the latter focuses mainly on European languages, GR insists that any generalizations on grammaticalization must be supported by crosslinguistic evidence based on data from a wider range of genetically and areally unrelated languages.

Claim G: Traugott and Trousdale (2013: 101) furthermore note "that the concept of grammar adopted by many of the founders of the GR approach … also does not include pragmatic markers such as *well, moreover* … ".

While pragmatic (or discourse) markers in fact played only a minor role in GR studies, they have never been excluded from the work of these 'founders'. For example, in their discussion of discourse functions, Heine et al. (1991: 187) say that "wherever it is possible to trace the etymology of discourse markers, they are likely to originate from lexical material within the "real world".

Claim H: Finally, Traugott and Trousdale (2013: 108) maintain that the difference in perspective between GR and GE also surfaces in the following definition adopted in the GE approach:

> Grammaticalization is the change whereby in certain contexts speakers use parts of a construction with a grammatical function. Over time, the resulting grammatical item may become more grammatical by acquiring more grammatical functions and expanding its host-classes. (Brinton & Traugott 2005: 99)

This definition is not only compatible but is also in accordance with research carried out using GR approaches: First, it assumes that use in context and context extension (or host-class expansion) are crucial for the rise of new grammatical functions (see under Claim E). And second, both kinds of approaches use the notion 'construction' and in both, this notion is used in a pre-theoretical sense.[10]

In sum, it is hard to see how the two kinds of approaches differ essentially from one another and what justification there is for a distinction between GR and GE (but see also Section 3).

2.3 Conclusions

The observations made in Section 2.2 are summarized in Table 1. The table suggests that on the basis of the features examined there appears to be no noteworthy difference between the two kinds of approaches distinguished by Traugott and Trousdale (2013).

In the list of Table 1 we are ignoring other features that are said to be relevant to the distinction GR vs. GE, suffice it to mention two of them. One concerns the status of DMs. Traugott and Trousdale (2013: 108) assume that the grammatical status of pragmatic markers (*well, I think*) or German modal particles (*doch, ja*) has been questioned in the GR tradition (that is, in "restrictive theories of grammar"). We are not aware of any work written in this tradition that would question the grammatical status of these elements.

Another feature concerns 'modularity'. No definition of the term is provided by Traugott and Trousdale (2013: 101), but the authors argue that "the concept of grammar adopted by many of the founders of the GR approach, with the notable

10. With reference to the definition of Brinton and Traugott (2005: 99), Traugott and Trousdale (2013: 108) say that "'construction' is here used in the pre-theoretical sense of string, constituent."

Heine and Kuteva (2002: 2) proposed the following definition: "Grammaticalization is defined as the development from lexical to grammatical forms and from grammatical to even more grammatical forms. And since the development of grammatical forms is not independent of the constructions to which they belong, the study of grammaticalization is also concerned with constructions and with even larger discourse segments."

Table 1. Features distinguishing GR from GE according to Traugott and Trousdale (2013) and the analysis proposed here

	Feature discussed	Feature present in	
		GR (Reduction)	**GE (Expansion)**
A	Grammaticalization of topic and focus categories	+	+
B	Polygrammaticalization	+	+
C	Unidirectionality in polygrammaticalization	+	+*
D	Loss-and-gain model	+	+
E	Grammaticalization occurs in context	+	+
F	Expansion of syntactic contexts	+	+
G	Discourse markers belong to grammar	+	+
H	Same kind of definition of grammaticalization	+	+

* This "+" must be taken with care, it is based on the assumption that Traugott and Trousdale (2013: 100) do not question the analysis proposed by Craig (1991). They note, for example, that both GR and GE are associated with the unidirectonality hypothesis though GE in a weaker form

exception of Givón, was modular". This statement implies that the two kinds of approaches are different, but the authors add:

> Grammaticalization as GR was developed assuming a modular theory of grammar. So was GE, but assuming a less restrictive view of grammar.
> (Traugott & Trousdale 2013: 148)

It does not become entirely clear whether or how "assuming a less restrictive view of grammar" relates to the notion of modularity. If it does not relate to modularity then there would be no difference between GR and GE. But if it does then this statement would seem to suggest that both GR and GE approaches use modularity but GE less so. If in fact this feature is relevant for the distinction then more information would be desirable on what modularity exactly means with reference to GR approaches.[11]

11. Traugott and Trousdale (2013: 150) observe that in modular frameworks a distinction is typically made between lexicon and grammar. One may wonder whether the distinction as it is made in 'GR approaches' really qualifies as modular. If the term is meant, e.g., in the widely held understanding of information encapsulation then one may hesitate to call these approaches modular. As is pointed out in a number of studies classified as GR, for example, the transition from lexicon to grammar is gradual rather than discontinuous – that is, there is no discrete boundary between lexicon and grammar (cf. the notion of *chain of grammaticalization* of Heine et al. 1991: 133 and Heine 1992).

3. Problematic features of discourse markers

As argued in the preceding section, more research is needed on what exactly the distinction between GR and GE and its relevance to the analysis of DMs is about, assuming that such a distinction exists. But in addition there are also features found in DMs, some mentioned in Traugott and Trousdale (2013: 109–12), that were shown by students of pragmaticalization to be problematic for any analysis based on grammaticalization. These features induce authors like Ocampo (2006: 317) and Norde (2009: 23) to argue that grammaticalization is movement towards syntax and morphology whereas discourse markers move precisely to the opposite end, namely outside of syntax and towards discourse. A survey of studies on this issue suggests that it is most of all the following changes to be observed in the development of discourse markers that are hard to reconcile with observations commonly made in grammaticalization:

3.1 Movement outside of the syntax of a sentence
3.2 From prosodically integrated to non-integrated status
3.3 From meaning as part of a sentence to metatextual function
3.4 From restricted structural scope to scope beyond the sentence.

This catalog does not exhaust the number of features that have been pointed out in the rich literature on pragmaticalization but 3.1–3.4 are presumably among the ones most frequently mentioned in that literature. The four changes are now looked at in turn. In Section 4 then, a perspective is proposed that allows dealing with them in a way that does not involve grammaticalization.

3.1 Movement outside of the morphosyntax of a sentence

DMs have been described as being syntactically isolated, extrasyntactic (Brinton 2010: 64), or syntactically invisible in that they do not interact with their host in terms of c-command-based relations (de Vries 2007: 207). Furthermore, they are not part of sentence questions, they cannot become the focus of a cleft sentence, and they are not in the scope of a negated sentence (cf. Haegeman 1991; Espinal 1991).

For some authors, syntactic independence, detachment, or freedom is therefore one of the most conspicuous features of DMs (Schiffrin 1987: 328; Traugott 1995: 1; Martín Zorraquino & Portolés 1999: 4057; Furkó 2005: 20; Frank-Job 2006: 400; Brinton 2008: 241). Accordingly, the growth of DMs has been described as involving "an increase in syntactic freedom instead of syntactic fixation" (Norde 2009: 22; Beijering 2012). Being syntactically unattached, they tend to be positionally flexible, "they can occur in multiple positions in the clause" (Tabor & Traugott 1998: 254).

Increase in syntactic freedom and movement outside of the sentence are features that are not compatible with any of the criteria that have been proposed for grammaticalization (e.g., Lehmann 1982; Heine & Kuteva 2002: 2–4): Grammaticalization entails decategorialization, which almost invariably involves loss rather than gain of morphosyntactic independence (see Table 3).

3.2 From prosodically integrated to non-integrated status

In a number of studies it has been pointed out that DMs tend to be prosodically set off from their host utterance (e.g., Schiffrin 1987: 328; Brinton 1996: 33; Hansen 1998a: 66; Tabor & Traugott 1998: 254; Jucker & Ziv 1998: 3; de Vries 2007: 205–6; Traugott & Trousdale 2013: 110; Romero-Trillo 2015; Gonen et al. 2015), exhibiting a separate intonational contour (Onodera 2011: 620), requiring 'comma intonation' (Tabor & Traugott 1998: 254), and often occurring "in an independent breath unit carrying a special intonation and stress pattern" (Traugott 1995: 6).

The hedge "tend to be" indicates that distinct prosody is not consistently observed or even missing in DMs (Hirschberg & Litman 1993: 516; Wichmann 2011: 335–6; but see also Dér 2010: 15–6; Wichmann et al. 2010; Heine 2013: 1210 for discussion), and Dér and Marko (2010) show that DMs do not need to be preceded and/or followed by a pause. What is obvious, however, is that DMs are more likely to be separated prosodically from their environment than the expressions from which they are historically derived.

In this respect, DMs differ from grammaticalizing items, which almost invariably lose features of prosodic distinctiveness on the way from lexical to grammatical elements: They tend to be typically integrated in the prosodic structure of their host.[12] Loss of prosodic independence "leading to an item's inability to form a prosodic word of its own" (Haspelmath 2011: 347) has been pointed out to be one of the processes commonly associated with grammaticalization. Thus, Wichmann concludes:

> [G]rammaticalization involves not only (and not always) the attrition of phonetic substance but more importantly the loss of prosodic prominence with concomitant loss of independence in intonational structure. Wichmann (2011: 341)

12. As Wichmann (2011: 335–6) shows, this can also happen with frequently used DMs like English *of course* and *sorry*.

3.3 From meaning as part of a sentence to metatextual function

The functions of DMs are described as introducing a higher-level speech act (cf. Schourup 2011), as being extradiscursory (cf. Kac 1970: 627), metatextual (Traugott 1995: 6), metacommunicative (Frank-Job 2006: 397), nonrestrictive (Heine 2013: 1209), discourse-interactional (Frank-Job 2006: 397), as operating on the textual or discourse level (Wischer 2000: 64; Kaltenböck 2010), to serve as text structuring devices at different levels of discourse (Erman & Kotsinas 1993: 79), or as contributing to the interpretation of an utterance rather than to its propositional content (Fraser 1999: 946). And in relevance-theoretic studies, the function of DMs is portrayed as serving to guide the hearer's linkage of an utterance to an appropriate context (Blass 1990: 77–9; Rouchota 1996, Blakemore 2002: 170; Schourup 2011). Furthermore, it is pointed out that DMs cannot be analyzed in terms of truth conditions (cf. Aijmer 1997: 2).

Such features contrast sharply with those captured in accounts that have been proposed for grammaticalization processes of any kind, in particular in cross-linguistic typological accounts (e.g., Heine & Kuteva 2002). Rather than being metatextual, functions arising in grammaticalization shape the meaning of sentences, be that within a phrase or a clause, or between clauses, but not normally beyond the level of sentences. As we will see in Section 4, many of the functions just listed have been used to describe parentheticals.

3.4 From restricted structural scope to scope beyond the sentence

The term 'scope' has been used in a variety of different theoretical works, and in many of its uses it is not really compatible with the way it is employed in discussions on the development of DMs, where it is based on Lehmann's (1995: 164) notion of 'structural scope'. Following other authors in this tradition for the purposes of the present paper we are restricted here to the latter use of the term, referring to it as 'structural scope'.

This means that we will have to ignore treatments of scope as they can be found in particular in some formal models. Thus, in the model of Role and Reference Grammar, grammaticalization-induced change corresponds to a shift from being an element with scope over the nucleus of a clause to scope over the whole clause (Matasovic 2008: 49; Nicolle 2012). And in the model of Functional Discourse Grammar (Hengeveld & Mackenzie 2008, 2011), phenomena falling under the rubric of grammaticalization have been analyzed as involving increase rather than reduction of scope; cf. the C-command Scope Increase Hypothesis of Tabor & Traugott (1998).

It would seem that for many students of DMs it is fairly uncontroversial to assume that DMs are the result of a process leading to a 'wider interpretation' (Lewis 2011: 440) and an expansion in structural scope (Thompson & Mulac 1991; Traugott 1995: 1; Brinton 1996: 253; 2001: 194; 2008; Gohl & Günthner 1999: 59–63; Tabor & Traugott 1998: 254; Lewis 2011: 419; Traugott & Trousdale 2013: 109), their scope extending beyond the clause over the entire speech act (Hansen 1998b: 236).

Accordingly, rather than as reduction in 'structural scope', the development of DMs is described as one leading to scope extension (e.g., Auer & Günthner 2005: 338; Brinton & Traugott 2005: 138; Norde 2009: 22).

DMs thus are said to violate the condensation principle of grammaticalization (Lehmann 1995: 143–7) because they expand rather than shrink in structural scope (Brinton 2001: 194). As the hundreds of pathways of grammaticalization that have been reconstructed so far suggest, extension of 'structural scope' is not a characteristic of these pathways (cf. the data in Lehmann 1982; Heine & Reh 1984; Heine et al. 1991; Bybee et al. 1994; Heine & Kuteva 2002; Hopper & Traugott 2003).

3.5 Conclusion

DMs are not only hard to reconcile with, but even contradict what has commonly been observed crosslinguistically in grammaticalization. We are thus left in particular with questions such as the ones in (3).

(3) Questions on DMs
   a. How to account for the problematic features discussed in Sections 3.1 to 3.4?
   b. Are these features restricted to DMs or can they also be observed elsewhere?

Our concern in Section 4 will be first with question (3b), which – we hope – will be helpful for subsequently turning to (3a).

4. A two-stage scenario

4.1 Discourse markers as theticals

Since the turn of the last century, parenthetical expressions became a new field of research (e.g., Burton-Roberts 2005; Brinton 2008; Dehé 2014; Schneider et al. 2015; see also the contributions to Dehé & Kavalova 2007 and Kaltenböck, Keizer

& Lohmann 2016).[13] An example is provided in (4), retrieved from the British component of the *International Corpus of English* (ICE-GB for short), where the parenthetical *I hope you don't entirely disapprove* is interpolated in the utterance (4),

(4) *What I've done here* ***I hope you don't entirely disapprove*** *is try and limit the time taken on this item by putting it in writing.* (ICE-GB: s1b-075–180)

This research was developed further in the framework of Discourse Grammar (Kaltenböck et al. 2011; Heine et al. 2013). Research findings on parentheticals and Discourse Grammar have the following assumptions in common. Like DMs, parenheticals, referred to by the shortened form *theticals* in Discourse Grammar, are 'extra-clausal constituents' in the sense of Dik (1997: 384). Thus, in the constructed examples of (5), the theticals (printed in bold) are linguistic expressions that are not syntactic parts of the sentence, they tend to be set off prosodically, and express meanings that do not belong to the semantic structure of a sentence. In the framework of Heine et al. (2013), they belong to the category of conceptual theticals.[14]

(5) Constructed examples of theticals
  a. *This is,* ***if I may say so,*** *not exactly what I had expected.*
  b. *This is,* ***and I ask for your understanding,*** *not exactly what I had expected.*
  c. *This is,* ***please forgive me if I am impolite,*** *not exactly what I had expected.*

DMs exhibit much the same features as conceptual theticals, and they have in fact been defined as parentheticals (Brinton 2008: 1).[15] Compare the examples in (5) with those of (6), where instead of theticals, the DMs *well, as it were*, and *in fact* are used.

13. While the parenthetical in (4) is interpolated within the utterance this does not necessarily have to be the case: Depending on their function in discourse, many parentheticals may as well be placed at the left or right periphery of an utterance.

14. This interpretation, while providing a different stance on linguistic categorization, is compatible with that of Functional Discourse Grammar (FDG) to the extent that the material in bold in (4) and (5) corresponds in each case correspond to a Discourse Act (DA) performed by suspending an ongoing DA, uttering the thetical, and then resuming the initial DA (Lachlan Mackenzie, p.c.).

15. Brinton (2008: 1) defines DMs (pragmatic markers in her terminology) thus: "A pragmatic marker is defined as a phonologically short item that is not syntactically connected to the rest of the clause (i.e., is parenthetical), and has little or no referential meaning but serves pragmatic or procedural purposes."

(6) Constructed examples of discourse markers
  a. *This is,* ***well,*** *not exactly what I had expected.*
  b. *This is,* ***as it were,*** *not exactly what I had expected.*
  c. *This is,* ***in fact,*** *not exactly what I had expected.*

The units printed in bold in (5) and (6) exhibit essentially the features listed in (7). Accordingly, DMs have been treated as parentheticals (Peterson 1999: 231; Kaltenböck 2007: 47; Brinton 2008: 1; Dehé 2014: 5–6) or theticals (Heine 2013; Chen 2015). As Table 2 suggests in fact, DMs are far from forming an isolated unit; rather, they seem to be part of a larger group of discourse categories summarily called theticals (or parentheticals).

Table 2. Types of linguistic expressions belonging to the same category as discourse markers (DMs = discourse markers, FSEs = formulae of social exchange)

Authors proposing the category	**Term used for the category**	**Categories**						
		Conceptual theticals	**DMs**	**Comment clauses**	**Interjections**	**Vocatives**	**FSEs**	**Question tags**
Espinal 1991	Disjunct constituents	+	+	+		+		
Dik 1997	Extra-clausal constituents	+	+		+	+	+	+
Kaltenböck 2007	Parentheticals	+	+	+	+	+		+
Heine et al. 2013	Theticals	+	+	+	+	+	+	+
Dehé 2014	Parentheticals	+	+	+	+	+		+

(7) Features typically exhibited by theticals (Kaltenböck et al. 2011)
  a. They are not part of the syntax of the sentence
  b. They are as a rule not integrated prosodically
  c. They have metatextual functions
  d. They have semantic-pragmatic scope beyond the sentence

(7d) is not necessarily restricted to the sentence or some other text piece but rather concerns or includes the situation of discourse as a whole or parts of it.[16] For example, theticals such as vocatives (*waiter!*), formulae of social exchange (*please*) and question tags (*isn't it?*) relate primarily to speaker-hearer interaction whereas

16. The situation of discourse consists of a network of linkages between the following components: Text organization, source of information, attitudes of the speaker, speaker-hearer interaction, discourse setting, and world knowledge (Heine et al. 2013: Section 5).

interjections (*wow!*) concern most of all the attitudes of the speaker (Heine et al. 2013: 163–73).

As we saw in Section 3, the features listed in (7) are also the ones commonly observed in DMs. Accordingly, Tabor and Traugott (1998: 254) note that English DMs "not only have the widest syntactic scope but they also can occur in multiple positions in the clause, and furthermore, they require comma intonation."

This account of DMs as theticals raises a number of questions, in particular on how theticals arise, and how to distinguish DMs from theticals such as the ones in (5). Answers to these questions have been volunteered in Heine (2013), based on the hypotheses in (8). The following notes summarize these answers with reference to the account presented in the preceding sections.

(8) Hypotheses on the development of DMs (Heine 2013)
   a. Theticals arise via cooptation.
   b. Once coopted, some theticals develop further into DMs via subsequent grammaticalization.

Cooptation is defined as a discourse strategy (Heine et al. 2017), more specifically as a cognitive-communicative operation whereby some segment of linguistic discourse is transferred from one domain of discourse to another (Kaltenböck et al. 2011: 874–5; Heine 2013: 1221; Heine et al. 2013: 204–5; Heine 2015). In accordance with this strategy, a unit of Sentence Grammar,[17] such as a clause, a phrase, a word, or any other text piece, is transferred for use as a thetical, either interpolated in an utterance or placed at its periphery, or else used as a syntactic stand-alone. This operation resembles to some extent notions such as discoursivization, leading, e.g., from adjective to discourse particle (Ocampo 2006: 317), and category change (Dostie 2009), both phrased in terms of pragmaticalization:[18]

> The term [pragmaticalization] refers to a process of linguistic change in which a full lexical item [...] or grammatical item [...] changes category and status and becomes a pragmatic item, that is, an item which is not fully integrated into the syntactic structure of the utterance and which has a textual or interpersonal meaning. (Dostie 2009: 203)

There is one main difference between pragmaticalization and cooptation: Whereas the former is conceived as "a process of linguistic change", cooptation is a spontaneous operation (see below).

17. On the notion of Sentence Grammar vs. Thetical Grammar see Kaltenböck et al. (2011) and Heine et al. (2013); see also below.

18. See also the notion of 'post-grammaticalization' of Vincent et al. (1993).

In accordance with its new status, the coopted unit is now an autonomous information unit set off from the clause syntactically, prosodically, and semantically – that is, it is a thetical exhibiting the features in (7). No longer serving a sentence grammatical function, it is a device of metatextual planning (Traugott 1995: 6), its main function being that of relating the text to the situation of discourse. Thus, an English adverb like *sadly* in (9a) can be coopted as a thetical, as in (9b). As a result, it no longer modifies the meaning of the sentence or a part of it; rather, its meaning now relates to the situation of discourse, in this case more specifically to the attitudes of the speaker.[19]

(9) a. *Penelope sadly stayed at home all by herself.*
  b. *Penelope,* ***sadly****, stayed at home all by herself.*

A thetical need not be a full-fledged clause or phrase, it may have the appearance of an 'elliptic' text piece. What matters is that 'missing' syntactic constituents be recoverable from the context or the co-text shaping the situation of discourse.

That the development of DMs involved a stage of use as a (paren)thetical surfaces in some of the reconstructions of the history of English DMs. For example, Simon-Vandenbergen (2007: 17) observes on the usage of the DM *no doubt*: "Summing up, the syntactic positions that *no doubt* takes point to its development into a parenthetical marker."

4.2 Grammaticalization

It has been established in the literature mentioned in Section 4.1 that DMs are parentheticals, or theticals in the terminology of Discourse Grammar (Kaltenböck et al. 2011; Heine et al. 2013). But DMs differ from conceptual theticals such as the ones illustrated in (4), especially in the features listed in (10).

(10) Features distinguishing DMs from conceptual theticals
  a. Rather than being formed spontaneously, they are conventionalized grammatical markers (see Section 5).[20]

19. This case of cooptation thus can be described as an instance of discourse-based subjectification. To establish how this kind of subjectification, which also surfaces, e.g., in the cooptation of interjections (e.g., *Jesus!, Shit!*), differs from grammaticalization-based subjectification remains a task for future research.

20. For example, the conceptual thetical *please forgive me if I am impolite* in (5c) can be said to be "formed spontaneously" in that it may have been produced once and never again. DMs, by contrast, such as *well, as it were* and *in fact* in (6), are "conventionalized" in the sense that they are recurrently used fixed markers.

b. Rather than having semantic (or 'conceptual') content, they serve discourse grammatical functions relating to the situation of discourse.
c. Rather than compositional, they are invariable frozen forms.
d. They may be phonologically reduced.

As is argued in Heine (2013), DMs are grammaticalized theticals: They owe the features in (10) to their recurrent use and gradual grammaticalization – a process that may be enhanced by the 'ancillary' discourse functions they assume (see Boye & Harder 2012).[21] Table 3 lists the most salient changes that grammaticalization is likely to entail – changes that have frequently been observed in DMs (e.g., Brinton 2010: 61–2; Kaltenböck 2013).[22]

Table 3. Subsequent grammaticalization observed in DMs

Domain of grammar	**Type of change**	**Parameter of gramaticalization (Heine & Kuteva 2002: 2–4)**
Semantics	Loss of (lexical) semantic features	Desemanticization
Morphosyntax	Change in morpheme status (open class > closed class category)	Decategorialization
Internal morphosyntax	Freezing of form (univerbation)	Internal decategorialization
(Morpho)phon-ology	Loss of phonetic features	Erosion

To be sure, not all of the parameters listed in Table 3 necessarily apply in a given case. Obviously, internal decategorialization is relevant to DMs such as *I think, what else,* or *you know* but not to *so, then* or *well* since no univerbation is involved. And erosion, which is not an obligatory parameter anyway, is rarely found in grammaticalization following cooptation.

In sum, on the hypothesis expounded in Heine (2013), DMs are the result of a two-stage history. This history involves, first, cooptation, that is, an instantaneous transfer of clausal, phrasal, or other pieces of Sentence Grammar to Thetical Grammar for metatextual functions, giving rise to the features in (7) (see Heine et al. 2017). And subsequently, this involves grammaticalization in accordance with parameters such as the ones listed in Table 3 (see also Brinton 2010: 61–2) and with the context model of Heine (2002). Accordingly, the morphosyntactic, phonological and semantic features of DMs cannot be reduced to or be explained

21. I am grateful to Gunther Kaltenböck for having drawn my attention to this point.

22. For a catalog of ten parameters of grammaticalization relevant to DMs, see Brinton (2010: 61–2).

with reference to only one of these two mechanisms – be that grammaticalization or cooptation.[23]

Note that there may also have been grammaticalization *prior* to cooptation in addition, so that the scenario that we propose for the development of DMs can be sketched as in (11). Nevertheless, we hypothesize that cooptation as a thetical must have been involved, accounting for features of DMs such as the ones listed in (7), while grammaticalization accounts for features like those in (10).

(11) Hypothesized development of discourse markers
(Grammaticalization >) cooptation > grammaticalization

Evidence for (11) can be found in Heine (2013: 1224–36), using the English items *what else, I mean, look, indeed, in fact,* and *besides*. The following sketch illustrates the development with the French item *alors* 'now' as discussed by Degand and Evers-Vermeul (2015: 75; see also Degand & Fagard 2011).[24] This item appears to have been grammaticalized at the end of the thirteenth century from a sentence adverbial adjunct to a temporal, causal or conditional connective. At some later stage, the exact date of which is unclear, cooptation must have taken place, turning *alors* into a conjunct, exhibiting features of a thetical such as being located outside the core syntactic clause. In a second step then, *alors* appears to have been grammaticalized into a DM serving as a discourse-structuring device.

The effects of cooptation can be seen most transparently in cases of transcategoriality, where one and the same kind of linguistic expression is used simultaneously on two different planes of linguistic organization (Robert 2003, 2004; Do-Hurinville & Hancil 2015; Heine & Kaltenböck 2016). For example, once adverbs such as French *alors,* German *nun* 'now', or English *actually, now, then,* and *well* have given rise to DMs, there likely will be doublets with each member of the transcategoriality set being associated with a different plane of linguistic organization, namely as an adverb on the plane of Sentence Grammar and as a DM on the plane of discourse organization (Thetical Grammar).[25]

23. Degand and Evers-Vermeul (2015: 72) say that Kaltenböck et al. (2011), Heine et al. (2013), and Heine (2013: 1222) reduce the development of DMs to cooptation. This statement is in need of correction: The former two studies do not mention the development of DMs while Heine (2013) does but makes it clear that this development involves *both* cooptation and grammaticalization.

24. The following account is based on the data of these authors but the interpretation is ours.

25. For an insightful analysis of English *actually*, see Taglicht (2001).

5. Discussion

The main concern of the preceding analysis was with whether there is need for two kinds of grammaticalization, or else for one that embraces these two kinds, that is, whether a wider concept of grammaticalization should be added to take care of the evolution of discourse markers and perhaps other discourse material, as has been argued in some form or other by some authors (e.g., Traugott 1995: 7; Pinto de Lima 2002: 273; Degand & Evers-Vermeul 2015). To be sure, the history of DMs *does* involve grammaticalization but, as we argued in Section 3, it cannot be reduced to it. What is needed in addition is an account that takes care of properties of DMs that are incompatible with or would contradict principles of grammaticalization. Such properties are in particular the movement outside of the syntax of a sentence, from prosodically integrated to non-integrated status, and from meaning as part of a sentence to metatextual meanings or functions. We argued that exactly these are the properties commonly observed in research on parentheticals (e.g., Dehé & Kavalova 2007) or theticals in the framework of Discourse Grammar (Heine et al. 2013) – that is, theticals that differ from many other ones in having undergone grammaticalization.

A question that we did not deal with is whether discourse markers are to be considered a part of grammar or of something else. This is an issue that has found some attention in work that distinguishes in some form or other between a narrow or restricted and a wider or expanded view of grammaticalization (e.g., Traugott 1995; Degand & Simon-Vandenbergen 2011: 290; Degand & Evers-Vermeul 2015: 75). Degand and Simon-Vandenbergen (2011: 290) plead for "a more comprehensive view of what constitutes grammar", and Traugott and Trousdale (2013: 108) propose to adopt "a broad definition of grammar". With reference to the discourse markers (pragmatic markers) *well, moreover*, the British English tag *innit*, clause final *but* and other metatextual markers they say:

> These are sometimes considered to be on a separate 'discourse' level (see e.g. Wischer 2000; Kaltenböck, Heine & Kuteva 2011). In a construction grammar framework, however, they are part of language …
>
> (Traugott & Trousdale (2013: 101)

This assumption is somehow surprising since it implies that Wischer (2000) and Kaltenböck et al. (2011) view these items as not being part of language. In the framework of Discourse Grammar (Kaltenböck et al. 2011; Heine et al. 2013) in particular, all these items are classified as indubitably belonging to grammar and, of course, to language.[26] More specifically, they belong to the domain of Thetical

26. Since the authors do not say what "other metatextual markers" exactly stands for, this generalization must be taken with care.

Grammar rather than Sentence Grammar; treatments of discourse markers in this framework are found in Heine (2013), of final particles in Heine et al. (2015), of imperatives in Heine (2016), and of insubordination in Heine et al. (2016a).

Discourse Grammar "is composed of all the linguistic resources that are available for designing texts, irrespective of whether these are spoken, written, or signed texts" (Heine et al. 2013: 176). In this framework, grammar includes discourse markers, question tags, clause-final particles and all other units such as the ones distinguished in Table 2. The framework thus does not differ in this respect, e.g., from standard grammars of English like those by Quirk et al. (1985), Biber et al. (1999), or Huddleston & Pullum (2002), where all these units are also treated as part of grammar.[27]

To our knowledge, such a treatment of grammar has not been questioned in any of the works classified by Traugott and Trousdale (2013) as representing a GR view of grammar. It would seem therefore that whether DMs belong to grammar is of limited import considering that neither in GR approaches nor in discourse-oriented approaches on parentheticals or theticals has this question been answered in the negative. Thus, we have no problems calling DMs grammatical markers. Nevertheless, as we saw in Sections 4 and 5, these markers differ from many other grammatical markers with reference to thetical features such as the ones summarized in (7).

But it would seem that there is another difference in addition. Presumably on account of their important role in speaker-hearer interaction, DMs are amongst the first grammatical material that speakers code-switch or borrow in situations of intense language contact (Matras 1998; Grant 2012; Heine 2016b). The following are a few examples taken from a wider corpus of data on language contact situations (see Heine 2016b for more details; see also Maschler 1994, 2000):

- In a study of code-switching of Puerto-Rican Spanish-English bilinguals in New York City, Poplack (1980: 602) found that 29% of all code switches in her corpus, that is the majority of all switches, were DMs.
- In second generation Dutch of Turkish immigrants in the Netherlands, it is in particular Turkish DMs, such as *ama* 'but', *falan* 'etc.', *doğru* 'right', *sey* 'thing', and *niye* 'why', that are commonly switched into Dutch discourse (Backus 1996: 316).
- In American Israeli family interactions, the largest category of code-mixes (60%) was found to be that of nouns, but the second largest category was what

27. The term 'discourse marker' is used only in one of the three works mentioned, namely Biber et al. (1999: 1086–8), whereas in Quirk et al. (1985: 631–46) DMs are mainly referred to as conjuncts and in Huddleston and Pullum (2002: 1356ff.) as supplements.

Olshtain and Blum-Kulka (1989: 68–9) term 'discourse fillers', accounting for 14% of the code-mixes.
- In Siberian Yupik, an Eskimo-Aleut language, DMs and other function words account for more than half the total of loans from the more prestigious Chukchi language (Grant 2012: 311).
- Speakers of immigrant languages in long-term contact with English in the USA lost much of their own native DM systems but borrowed key English DMs (Goss & Salmons 2000: 482; see also Flores-Ferrán 2014: 78).
- The Spanish discourse marker *entonces* 'then, therefore, thus' has been borrowed in a wide range of languages spoken in the former Spanish empire. In a simiar fashion, the Italian discourse marker *allora* 'then' was borrowed in language regions where Italian is spoken as a dominant language, found, e.g., in Maltese, (Italo-)Albanian, Cimbrian, and Molise Slavic (Stolz 2007; see also Stolz & Stolz 1996).

To conclude, next to nouns and other lexical items, DMs appear to be the linguistic items most frequently transferred from one language to another in situations of language contact. DMs thus differ dramatically from grammatical material such as markers for tense, aspect, modality, case, number, gender, (in)definiteness, etc. While there are essentially no limits as to what can be borrowed, grammatical markers of the latter kind are distinctly less likely to be borrowed than DMs.

Looking for an explanation for this observation would be beyond the scope of this paper. But such an explanation would need to consider the particular genesis of DMs as (paren)thetical discourse material, which appears to account for much of their present-day functions.

6. Conclusions

Grammaticalization is a ubiquitous cognitive-communicative activity, but the output of this activity is shaped by what serves as its input. Thus, when the input is provided by discourse material, the outcome is not necessarily the same as the one to be expected when the input is provided by clausal constituents: Theticals are extra-clausal constituents (Dik 1997) and so are discourse markers, their grammaticalized output.

The paper was centrally concerned with the question of whether there really is need for two different approaches, or for a wider, or expanded concept of grammaticalization to take care of certain features characterizing the evolution of discourse markers, as was suggested by some authors (see Section 2.1). It was argued here that these features are beyond the scope of *any* approach to grammaticalization

(Section 4). On this view, it must remain questionable whether a distinction between GR and GE is needed or justified.

Grammaticalization is concerned with development towards (non-lexical) grammatical material and, to our knowledge, it is the only approach that exists to account for directionality in the evolution of grammatical (or functional) categories (see, e.g., Heine et al. 2016). As we hope to have shown in this paper, discourse markers do not challenge the unidirectionality principle: Problems that have been pointed out in the literature on this subject (e.g., Waltereit 2006), especially those listed in Section 2.2, are the product of cooptation rather than of grammaticalization.

The book which was the main concern of this paper was written in the framework of Construction Grammar, and we fully agree with the authors when they say that "a constructional approach can enrich ways to think about the transition from more lexical to more grammatical expressions" (Traugott & Trousdale 2013: 13). Construction Grammar offers an invaluable tool for reconstructing the dynamics leading to the rise and development of grammatical categories. Nevertheless, as is argued in Heine et al. (2016), both the goal and the perspective adopted in this model are different from those of grammaticalization theory and the two frameworks are therefore best kept apart.[28]

It is thanks to the work of students of pragmaticalization that problems such as the ones discussed in Section 3 have become a subject of academic discourse, and that the development of DMs cannot be reduced to effects of grammaticalization (see Section 1). To the extent that the distinction between two kinds of mechanisms made here is taken into account, the interpretation proffered in this paper is compatible with most of the uses that the term 'pragmaticalization' has received.

Acknowledgements

The present paper has benefitted greatly from comments by Ulrike Claudi, Gunther Kaltenböck, Christa König, Tania Kuteva, Lachlan Mackenzie, Heiko Narrog and Elizabeth Traugott, as well as by two anonymous reviewers. We would also like to thank Haiping Long for his cooperation within the project on Mandarin Thetical and Reconstruction of Discourse Grammar (National Social Sciences Fund; 15BYY107), and to Guangdong University of Foreign Studies and the University of Cape Town and Matthias Brenzinger for the academic hospitality we received while working there on this paper.

28. To the extent that an approach to the study of grammaticalization as a diachronic phenomenon, such as the one proposed in Heine et al. (1991) and Heine (1997), provides a tool for understanding in a principled way how and why grammatical (or functional) categories evolve we have no problems with referring to it as a 'theory'.

References

Aijmer, Karin. 1997. *I think* – an English modal particle. In *Modality in Germanic Languages: Historical and Comparative Perspectives*, Toril Swan & Olaf Jansen-Westvik (eds), 1–47. Berlin: Mouton de Gruyter. https://doi.org/10.1515/9783110889932.1

Aijmer, Karin. 2002. *English Discourse Particles: Evidence from a Corpus* [Studies in Corpus Linguistics 10]. Amsterdam: John Benjamins. https://doi.org/10.1075/scl.10

Arroyo, José Luis Blas. 2011. From politeness to discourse marking: The process of pragmaticalization of *muy bien* in vernacular Spanish. *Journal of Pragmatics* 43: 855–874. https://doi.org/10.1016/j.pragma.2010.10.002

Auer, Peter & Günthner, Susanne. 2005. Die Entstehung von Diskursmarkern im Deutschen: Ein Fall von Grammatikalisierung? In *Grammatikalisierung im Deutschen* [Linguistik – Impulse & Tendenzen 9], Torsten Leuschner, Tanja Mortelmans & Sarah De Groodt (eds), 335–362. Berlin: Walter de Gruyter. https://doi.org/10.1515/9783110925364.335

Backus, Angus. 1996. *Two in One. Bilingual Speech of Turkisch Immigrants in the Netherlands.* Tilburg: Tilburg University Press.

Beijering, Karin. 2012. Expressions of Epistemic Modality in Mainland Scandinavian: A Study into the Lexicalization-grammaticalization-pragmaticalization Interface. PhD dissertation, Rijksuniversiteit Groningen.

Biber, Douglas, Johansson, Stig, Leech, Geoffrey, Conrad, Susan & Finegan, Edward. 1999. *Longman Grammar of Spoken and Written English.* London: Longman.

Blakemore, Diane 2002. Relevance and Linguistic Meaning: The Semantics and Pragmatics of Discourse Markers [Cambridge Studies in Linguistics 99]. Cambridge: CUP. https://doi.org/10.1017/CBO9780511486456

Blass, Regina 1990. *Relevance Relations in Discourse: A Study with Special Reference to Sissala.* Cambridge: CUP. https://doi.org/10.1017/CBO9780511586293

Börjars, Kerstin & Vincent, Nigel. 2011. Grammaticalization and directionality. In Narrog & Heine (eds), 162–176.

Börjars, Kersti, Vincent, Nigel & Walkden, George. 2015. On constructing a theory of grammatical change. *Transactions of the Philological Society* 113(3): 363–382. https://doi.org/10.1111/1467-968X.12068

Boye, Kasper & Harder, Peter. 2012. A usage-based theory of grammatical status and grammaticalization. *Language* 88: 1–44. https://doi.org/10.1353/lan.2012.0020

Brinton, Laurel J. 1996. *Pragmatic markers in English: Grammaticalization and Discourse Functions* [Topics in English Linguistics 19]. Berlin: Mouton de Gruyter. https://doi.org/10.1515/9783110907582

Brinton, Laurel J. 2001. From matrix clause to pragmatic marker: The history of look-forms. *Journal of Historical Pragmatics* 2(2): 177–199. https://doi.org/10.1075/jhp.2.2.02bri

Brinton, Laurel J. 2008. *The Comment Clause in English: Syntactic Origins and Pragmatic Development.* Cambridge: CUP. https://doi.org/10.1017/CBO9780511551789

Brinton, Laurel J. 2010. The development of I mean: Implications for the study of historical pragmatics. In *Methods in Historical Pragmatics*, Susan M. Fitzmaurice & Irma Taavitsainen (eds), 37–80. Berlin: Mouton de Gruyter.

Brinton, Laurel J. & Traugott, Elizabeth Closs. 2005. *Lexicalization and Language Change.* Cambridge: CUP. https://doi.org/10.1017/CBO9780511615962

Burton-Roberts, Noel. 2005. Parentheticals. In *Encyclopedia of Language and Linguistics*. 2nd edition, volume 9, 179–182. Amsterdam: Elsevier.

Bybee, Joan L. & Pagliuca, William. 1985. Cross linguistic comparison and the development of grammatical meaning. In *Historical Semantics – Historical Word-formation* [Trends in Linguistics. Studies and Monographs 29], Jacek Fisiak (ed.), 59–83. Berlin: Mouton de Gruyter. https://doi.org/10.1515/9783110850178.59

Bybee, Joan L., Pagliuca, William & Perkins, Revere Dale. 1991. Back to the future. In Traugott & Heine (eds), Vol. 2, 17–58.

Bybee, Joan L., Perkins, Revere Dale & Pagliuca, William. 1994. *The Evolution of Grammar: Tense, Aspect, and Modality in the Languages of the World*. Chicago IL: University of Chicago Press.

Chen, Jiajun 2015. The genesis and development of vio ka ('don't say') in Shanghainese. Ms, Singapore.

Claridge, Claudia & Arnovick, Leslie. 2010. Pragmaticalisation and discursisation. In *Historical Pragmatics* [Handbook of Pragmatics 8], Andreas H. Jucker & Irma Taavitsainen (eds), 165–192. Berlin: De Gruyter Mouton.

Craig, Colette G. 1991. Ways to go in Rama: A case study in polygrammaticalization. In Traugott & Heine (eds), Vol. 2, 455–492.

Croft, William. 2000. *Explaining Language Change: An Evolutionary Approach*. Harlow: Longman.

Croft, William. 2003. *Typology and Universals*, 2nd edn. Cambridge: CUP.

Degand, Liesbeth & Evers-Vermeul, Jacqueline. 2015. Grammaticalization or pragmaticalization of discourse markers? More than a terminological issue. *Journal of Historical Pragmatics* 16(1): 59–85. https://doi.org/10.1075/jhp.16.1.03deg

Degand, Liesbeth & Fagard, Benjamin. 2011. *Alors* between discourse and grammar: The role of syntactic position. *Functions of Language* 18(1): 29–56. https://doi.org/10.1075/fol.18.1.02deg

Degand, Liesbeth & Simon-Vandenbergen, Anne-Marie. 2011. Introduction: Grammaticalization and (inter)subjectification of discourse markers. *Linguistics*. 49(2): 287–294. https://doi.org/10.1515/ling.2011.008

Dehé, Nicole 2014. *Parentheticals in Spoken English: The Syntax-Prosody Relation*. Cambridge: CUP. https://doi.org/10.1017/CBO9781139032391

Dehé, Nicole & Kavalova, Yordanka (eds). 2007. *Parentheticals* [Linguistik Aktuell/Linguistics Today 106]. Amsterdam: John Benjamins. https://doi.org/10.1075/la.106

Dér, Csilla Ilona. 2010. On the status of discourse markers. *Acta Linguistica Hungarica* 57(1): 3–28. https://doi.org/10.1556/ALing.57.2010.1.1

Dér, Csilla Ilona & Marko, Alexandra. 2010. A pilot study of Hungarian discourse markers. *Language and Speech* 53(2): 135–180. https://doi.org/10.1177/0023830909357162

Detges, Ulrich & Waltereit, Richard. 2007. Different functions, different histories: Modal particles and discourse markers from a diachronic point of view. *Catalan Journal of Linguistics* 6: 61–81.

Diewald, Gabriele. 2011a. Grammaticalization and pragmaticalization. In Narrog & Heine (eds.), 450–461.

Diewald, Gabriele. 2011b. Pragmaticalization (defined) as grammaticalization of discourse functions. *Linguistics* 49(2): 365–390. https://doi.org/10.1515/ling.2011.011

Dik, Simon C. 1997. *The Theory of Functional Grammar, Part 2: Complex and Derived Constructions* [Functional Grammar Series 21]. Berlin: Mouton de Gruyter.

Do-Hurinville, Thành & Hancil, Sylvie. 2015. La transcatégorialité à travers les langues. Ms, University of Rouen.

Dostie, Gaetane. 2004. *Pragmaticalisation et Marqueurs Discursifs: Analyse Sémantique et Traitement Lexicographique*. Brussels: De Boeck & Larcier.

Dostie, Gaetane. 2009. Discourse markers and regional variation in French: A lexico-semantic approach. In *Sociolinguistic Variation in Contemporary French*, Kate Beeching, Nigel Armstrong & Francoise Gadet (eds), 201–214. Amsterdam: John Benjamins.

Erman, Britt & Kotsinas, Ulla-Britt. 1993. Pragmaticalization: The case of *ba* and *you know*. *Studier i Modern Sprakvetenskap* 10: 76–92.

Espinal, M. Teresa. 1991. The representation of disjunct constituents. *Language* 67: 726–762. https://doi.org/10.2307/415075

Fischer, Olga 2007. *Morphosyntactic Change*. Oxford: OUP.

Flores-Ferrán, Nydia 2014. So *pues entonces:* An examination of bilingual discourse markers in Spanish oral narratives of personal experience of New York City-born Puerto Ricans. *Sociolinguistic Studies* 8(1): 57–83. https://doi.org/10.1558/sols.v8i1.57

Frank-Job, Barbara. 2006. A dynamic-interactional approach to discourse markers. In *Approaches to Discourse Particles* [Studies in Pragmatics 1], Kerstin Fischer (ed.), 395–413. Amsterdam: Elsevier.

Fraser, Bruce. 1999. What are discourse markers? *Journal of Pragmatics* 31(7): 931–952. https://doi.org/10.1016/S0378-2166(98)00101-5

Furkó, Bálint Péter. 2005. *The Pragmatic Marker: Discourse Marker Dichotomy Reconsidered: The Case of* well *and* of course. PhD dissertation, Bölcsészettudományi Kar, Debreceni Egyetem.

Giacalone Ramat, Anna & Hopper, Paul J. (eds). 1998. *The Limits of Grammaticalization* [Typological Studies in Language 37]. Amsterdam: John Benjamins. https://doi.org/10.1075/tsl.37

Givón, T. 1971. Historical syntax and synchronic morphology: An archaeologist's field trip. *Chicago Linguistic Society* 7: 394–415.

Givón, T. 1975a. Serial verbs and syntactic change: Niger-Congo. In Li (ed.), 47–112.

Givón, T. 1975b. Focus and the scope of assertion: Some Bantu evidence. *Studies in African Linguistics* 6(2): 185–207.

Givón, T. 1979. *On Understanding Grammar*. New York NY: Academic Press.

Givón, T. 2015. *The Diachrony of Grammar*, 2 Vols. Amsterdam: John Benjamins. https://doi.org/10.1075/z.192

Gohl, Christine & Günthner, Susanne. 1999. Grammatikalisierung von *weil* als Diskursmarker in der gesprochenen Sprache. *Zeitschrift für Sprachwissenschaft* 18(1): 39–75. https://doi.org/10.1515/zfsw.1999.18.1.39

Gonen, Einat, Livnat, Zohar & Amir, Noam. 2015. The discourse marker *axshav* ('now') in spontaneous spoken Hebrew: Discursive and prosodic features. *Journal of Pragmatics* 89(1): 69–84. https://doi.org/10.1016/j.pragma.2015.09.005

Goss, Emily L. & Salmons, Joseph C. 2000. The evolution of a bilingual discourse marking system: Modal particles and English markers in German-American dialects. *International Journal of Bilingualism* 4: 469–484. https://doi.org/10.1177/13670069000040040501

Grant, Anthony P. 2012. Contact, convergence, and conjunctions: A cross-linguistic study of borrowing correlations among certain kinds of discourse, phasal adverbial, and dependent clause markers. In *Dynamics of Contact-induced Language Change*, Claudine Chamoreau & Isabelle Léglise (eds), 311–358. Berlin: Mouton de Gruyter. https://doi.org/10.1515/9783110271430.311

Grenoble, Lenore. 2004. Parentheticals in Russian. *Journal of Pragmatics* 36(11): 1953–1974. https://doi.org/10.1016/j.pragma.2004.02.008

Günthner, Susanne. 1999. Entwickelt sich der Konzessivkonnektor *obwohl* zum Diskursmarker? Grammatikalisierungstendenzen im gesprochenen Deutsch. *Linguistische Berichte* 180: 409–446.

Günthner, Susanne & Mutz, Katrin. 2004. Grammaticalization vs. pragmaticalization? The development of pragmatic markers in German and Italian. In *What Makes Grammaticalization? A Look from its Fringes and its Components*, Walter Bisang, Nikolaus Himmelmann & Björn Wiemer (eds), 77–107. Berlin: Mouton de Gruyter.

Haegeman, Liliane. 1991. Parenthetical adverbials: The radical orphanage approach. In *Aspects of Modern Linguistics: Papers Presented to Masatomo Ukaji on his 60th Birthday*, Shuki Chiba, Akira Ogawa, Yasuaki Fuiwara, Norio Yamada, Osama Koma & Takao Yagi (eds), 232–254. Tokyo: Kaitakushi.

Haselow, Alexander. 2011. Discourse marker and modal particle: The functions of utterance final *then* in spoken English. *Journal of Pragmatics* 43(14): 3603–3623. https://doi.org/10.1016/j.pragma.2011.09.002

Haspelmath, Martin. 1999. Why is grammaticalization irreversible? *Linguistics* 37(6): 1043–1068. https://doi.org/10.1515/ling.37.6.1043

Haspelmath, Martin 2004. On directionality in language change with particular reference to grammaticalization. In *Up and Down the Cline – The Nature of Grammaticalization* [Typological Studies in Language 59], Olga Fischer, Muriel Norde & Harry Perridon (eds), 17–44. Amsterdam: John Benjamins. https://doi.org/10.1075/tsl.59.03has

Haspelmath, Martin. 2011. The gradual coalescence into 'words' in grammaticalization. In Narrog & Heine (eds), 342–355.

Heine, Bernd. 1992. Grammaticalization chains. *Studies in Language* 16(2): 335–368. https://doi.org/10.1075/sl.16.2.05hei

Heine, Bernd. 1997. *Cognitive Foundations of Grammar*. Oxford: OUP.

Heine, Bernd. 2002. On the role of context in grammaticalization. In *New Reflections on Grammaticalization* [Typological Studies in Language 49], Ilse Wischer & Gabriele Diewald (eds), 83–101. Amsterdam: John Benjamins. https://doi.org/10.1075/tsl.49.08hei

Heine, Bernd. 2013. On discourse markers: Grammaticalization, pragmaticalization, or something else? *Linguistics* 51(6): 1205–1247. https://doi.org/10.1515/ling-2013-0048

Heine, Bernd. 2016a. On non-finiteness and canonical imperatives. In *Finiteness and Nominalization* [Typological Studies in Language 113], Claudine Chamoreau & Zarina Estrada-Fernández (eds), 245–270. Amsterdam: John Benjamins.

Heine, Bernd. 2016b. Language contact and extra-clausal constituents: The case of discourse markers. In *Outside the Clause. Form and Function of Extra-Clausal Constituents* [Studies in Language Companion Series 178], Gunther Kaltenböck, Evelien Keizer & Arne Lohmann (eds), 243–272. Amsterdam: John Benjamins.

Heine, Bernd, Claudi, Ulrike & Hünnemeyer, Friederike. 1991. *Grammaticalization: A Conceptual Framework*. Chicago IL: University of Chicago Press.

Heine, Bernd & Kaltenböck, Gunther. 2016. Ways leading to transcategoriality. Paper presented at the Workshop on Transcategoriality, Université de Rouen, 27 April.

Heine, Bernd, Kaltenböck, Gunther & Kuteva, Tania 2016a. On insubordination and cooptation. In *Insubordination* [Typological Studies in Language 115], Nicholas Evans & Honoré Watanabe (eds), 39–64. Amsterdam: John Benjamins. https://doi.org/10.1075/tsl.115.02hei

Heine, Bernd, Kaltenböck, Gunther & Kuteva, Tania. 2015. Some observations on the evolution of utterance-final particles. In *Final Particles*, Sylvie Hancil, Alexander Haselow & Margje Post (eds), 111–140. Berlin: De Gruyter.

Heine, Bernd, Kaltenböck, Gunther, Kuteva, Tania & Long, Haiping. 2013. An outline of discourse grammar. In *Functional Approaches to Language*. Shannon Bischoff & Carmen Jany (eds), 175–233. Berlin: Mouton de Gruyter. https://doi.org/10.1515/9783110285321.155

Heine, Bernd, Kaltenböck, Gunther, Kuteva, Tania & Long, Haiping. 2017. Cooptation as a discourse strategy. *Linguistics* 55: 1–43.

Heine, Bernd & Kuteva, Tania. 2002. *World Lexicon of Grammaticalization*. Cambridge: CUP. https://doi.org/10.1017/CBO9780511613463

Heine, Bernd & Kuteva, Tania. 2007. *The Genesis of Grammar: A Reconstruction* [Studies in the Evolution of Language 9]. Oxford: OUP.

Heine, Bernd, Kuteva, Tania & Narrog, Heiko. Forthcoming. Back again to the future: How to account for directionality in grammatical change? In *Unity and Diversity in Grammaticalization Scenarios: Eight Typological Contributions*, Walter Bisang & Andrej Malchukov (eds).

Heine, Bernd, Narrog, Heiko & Long, Haiping. 2016b. Constructional change vs. grammaticalization: From compounding to derivation. *Studies in Language* 40(1): 137–175.

Heine, Bernd & Reh, Mechtild. 1984. *Grammaticalization and Reanalysis in African Languages*. Hamburg: Buske.

Hengeveld, Kees & Mackenzie, J. Lachlan. 2008. *Functional Discourse Grammar: A Typologically-based Theory of Language Structure*. Oxford: OUP. https://doi.org/10.1093/acprof:oso/9780199278107.001.0001

Hengeveld, Kees & Mackenzie, J. Lachlan. 2011. *Functional Discourse Grammar*. In Narrog & Heine (eds), 367–400.

Hilpert, Martin 2013. *Constructional Change in English: Developments in Allomorphy, Word-Formation, and Syntax*. Cambridge: CUP. https://doi.org/10.1017/CBO9781139004206

Himmelmann, Nikolaus P. 2004. Lexicalization and grammaticalization: Opposite or orthogonal? In *What Makes Grammaticalization? A Look from its Fringes and its Components*, Walter Bisang, Nikolaus Himmelmann & Björn Wiemer (eds), 19–40. Berlin: Mouton de Gruyter.

Hirschberg, Julia & Litman, Diane. 1993. Empirical studies on disambiguation of cue phrases. *Computational Linguistics* 19: 501–503.

Hopper, Paul J. & Traugott, Elizabeth Closs. 1993. *Grammaticalization*. Cambridge: CUP.

Hopper, Paul J. & Traugott, Elizabeth Closs. 2003. *Grammaticalization*, 2nd edn. Cambridge: CUP. https://doi.org/10.1017/CBO9781139165525

Huddleston, Rodney & Pullum, Geoffrey K. 2002. *The Cambridge Grammar of the English Language*. Cambridge: CUP.

Jucker, Andreas H. & Ziv, Yael (eds). 1998. *Discourse Markers: Description and Theory* [Pragmatics & Beyond New Series 57]. Amsterdam: John Benjamins. https://doi.org/10.1075/pbns.57

Kac, Michael B. 1970. Clauses of saying and the interpretation of *because*. *Language* 48(3): 626–632. https://doi.org/10.2307/412038

Kaltenböck, Gunther. 2007. Spoken parenthetical clauses in English. In Dehé & Kavalova (eds), 25–52.

Kaltenböck, Gunther. 2010. Pragmatic functions of parenthetical *I think*. In *New Approaches to Hedging*, Gunther Kaltenböck, Wiltrud Mihatsch & Stefan Schneider (eds), 243–272. Bingley: Emerald. https://doi.org/10.1163/9789004253247_012

Kaltenböck, Gunther. 2013. The development of comment clauses. In *The Verb Phrase in English: Investigating Recent Language Change with Corpora*, Bas Aarts, Joanne Close, Geoffrey Leech & Sean Wallis (eds), 286–317. Cambridge: CUP. https://doi.org/10.1017/CBO9781139060998.013

Kaltenböck, Gunther, Heine, Bernd & Kuteva, Tania. 2011. On thetical grammar. *Studies in Language* 35(4): 848–893.

Kaltenböck, Gunther, Keizer, Evelien & Lohmann, Arne (eds). 2016. *Outside the Clause*. [Studies in Language Companion Series 178]. Amsterdam: John Benjamins.

Klamer, Marian. 2000. How report verbs become quote markers and complementisers. *Lingua* 110: 69–98. https://doi.org/10.1016/S0024-3841(99)00032-7

Lehmann, Christian 1982. *Thoughts on Grammaticalization. A Programmatic Sketch*, Vol.1 [Arbeiten des Kölner Universalien-Projekts 48]. Cologne: Universität zu Köln, Institut für Sprachwissenschaft.

Lehmann, Christian. 1995. *Thoughts on Grammaticalization*, 2nd rev. edn. Munich: Lincom.

Lenker, Ursula. 2000. *Soþlice* and *witodlice*: Discourse markers in Old English. In *Pathways of Change. Grammaticalization in English* [Studies in Language Companion Series 53], Olga Fischer, Anette Rosenbach & Dieter Stein (eds), 229–249. Amsterdam: John Benjamins. https://doi.org/10.1075/slcs.53.12len

Lewis, Diana M. 2011. A discourse-constructional approach to the emergence of discourse markers in English. *Linguistics* 49(2): 415–443. https://doi.org/10.1515/ling.2011.013

Li, Charles N. (ed.). 1975. *Word Order and Word Order Change*. Austin TX: University of Texas Press.

Li, Charles N. & Thompson, Sandra A. 1974. An explanation of word order change SVO > SOV. *Foundations of Language* 12: 201–214.

Lichtenberk, Frantisek. 1991. Semantic change and heterosemy in grammaticalization. *Language* 67(3): 475–509.

Martín Zorraquino, María Antonia & Portolés, José. 1999. Los marcadores del discurso. In *Gramática Descriptiva de la Lengua Española*, Ignacio Bosque & Violeta Demonte (eds), 4051–4215. Madrid: Espasa Calpe.

Maschler, Yael. 1994. Metalanguaging and discourse markers in bilingual conversation. *Language in Society* 23: 325–366. https://doi.org/10.1017/S0047404500018017

Maschler, Yael. 2000. What can bilingual conversation tell us about discourse markers? *International Journal of Bilingualism* 4(4): 437–445. https://doi.org/10.1177/13670069000040040101

Matasović, Rolf. 2008. Patterns of grammaticalization and the layered structure of the clause. In *New applications of Role and Reference Grammar: Diachrony, Grammaticalization, Romance Languages*, Rolf Kailuweit, Björn Wiemer, E. Staudinger & Rolf Matasović (eds), 45–57. Newcastle upon Tyne: Cambridge Scholars.

Matras, Yaron. 1998. Utterance modifiers and universals of grammatical borrowing. *Linguistics* 36: 281–331. https://doi.org/10.1515/ling.1998.36.2.281

Mosegaard Hansen, Maj-Britt. 1998a. *The Function of Discourse Particles. A Study with Special Reference to Spoken Standard French* [Pragmatics & Beyond New Series 53]. Amsterdam: John Benjamins. https://doi.org/10.1075/pbns.53

Mosegaard Hansen, Maj-Britt. 1998b. The semantic status of discourse markers. *Lingua* 104(3–4): 235–260. https://doi.org/10.1016/S0024-3841(98)00003-5

Mosegaard Hansen, Maj-Britt. 2008. *Particles at the Semantics/Pragmatics Interface: Synchronic and Diachronic Issues*. Oxford: Elsevier.

Narrog, Heiko & Heine, Bernd (eds). 2011. *The Oxford Handbook of Grammaticalization*. Oxford: OUP.

Newmeyer, Frederick J. 1998. *Language Form and Language Function*. Cambridge, MA: MIT Press.

Newmeyer, Frederick J. 2012. Parentheticals, 'fragments', and the grammar of complementation. Paper presented at the conference on Les verbes parenthétiques: Hypotaxe, parataxe or parenthèse? Université Paris Ouest Nanterre, 24–26 May.

Nicolle, Steve 2012. Diachrony and grammaticalization. In *The Oxford Handbook of Tense and Aspect*, Robert Binnick (ed.), 370–397. Oxford: OUP.

Norde, Muriel. 2009. *Degrammaticalization*. Oxford: OUP. https://doi.org/10.1093/acprof:oso/9780199207923.001.0001

Nosek, Jirí. 1973. Parenthesis in Modern Colloquial English. *Prague Studies in English* 15: 99–116.

Ocampo, Francisco. 2006. Movement towards discourse is not grammaticalization: The evolution of */claro/* from adjective to discourse particle in spoken Spanish. In *Selected Proceedings of the 9th Hispanic Linguistics Symposium*, Nura Sagarra & Almeida Jacqueline Toribio (eds), 308–319. Somerville MA: Cascadilla Proceedings Project.

Olshtain, Elite & Blum-Kulka, Shoshana. 1989. Happy Hebrish: Mixing and switching in American Israeli family interaction. In *Variation in Second Language Acquisition*. Susan Gass, Carolyn Madden, Dennis Preston & Larry Selinker (eds), 59–83. Clevedon: Multilingual Matters.

Onodera, Noriko. 1995. Diachronic analysis of Japanese discourse markers. In *Historical Pragmatics. Pragmatic Developments in the History of English* [Pragmatics & Beyond New Series 35] Andreas H. Jucker (ed.), 393–437. Amsterdam: John Benjamins. https://doi.org/10.1075/pbns.35.22ono

Onodera, Noriko. 2011. The grammaticalization of discourse markers. In Narrog & Heine (eds), 611–620.

Peterson, Peter. 1999. On the boundaries of syntax: Non-syntagmatic relations. In *The Clause in English: In Honour of Rodney Huddleston*, Peter Collins & David Lee (eds), 229–250. Amsterdam: John Benjamins.

Pinto de Lima, José. 2002. Grammaticalization, subjectification and the origin of phatic markers. In *New Reflections on Grammaticalization* [Typological Studies in Language 49], Ilse Wischer & Gabriele Diewald (eds), 363–378. Amsterdam: John Benjamins. https://doi.org/10.1075/tsl.49.23pin

Poplack, Shana. 1980. Sometimes I'll start a sentence in Spanish y termino en español: Toward a typology of code-switching. *Linguistics* 18: 581–618. https://doi.org/10.1515/ling.1980.18.7-8.581

Prévost, Sophie. 2011. *A propos* from verbal complement to discourse marker: A case of grammaticalization? *Linguistics* 49(2): 391–413. https://doi.org/10.1515/ling.2011.012

Quirk, Randolph, Greenbaum, Sidney, Leech, Geoffrey & Svartvik, Jan. 1985. *A Comprehensive Grammar of the English Language*. London: Longman.

Rhee, Seongha. 2004. From discourse to grammar: Grammaticalization and lexicalization of rhetorical questions in Korean. In *LACUS: Forum XXX: Language, Thought and Reality*, Gordon Fulton, William J. Sullivan & Arle R. Lommel (eds), 413–423. Houston TX: Lacus.

Robert, Stéphane. 2003. Vers une typologie de la transcatégorialité. In *Perspectives Synchroniques sur la Grammaticalisation* [Afrique et Langage 5], Stéphane Robert (eds), 255–270. Louvain: Peeters.

Robert, Stéphane. 2004. The challenge of polygrammaticalization for linguistic theory: Fractal grammar and transcategorial functioning. In *Linguistic Diversity and Language Theories* [Studies in Language Companion Series 72], Zygmunt Frajzyngier, Adam Hodges & David S. Rood (eds), 119–142. Amsterdam: John Benjamins.
Romero-Trillo, Jesús. 2015. 'It is a truth universally acknowledged' …, you know? The role of adaptive management and prosody to start a turn in conversation. *Pragmatics and Society* 6(1): 117–145.
Rouchota, Villy. 1996. Discourse connectives: What do they link? *UCL Working Papers in Linguistics* 8: 1–15.
Saxena, Anju. 1988. The case of the verb 'say' in Tibeto-Burman. *Berkeley Linguistics Society* 14: 375–388.
Schiffrin, Deborah. 1987. *Discourse Markers* [Studies in Interactional Sociolinguistics 5]. Cambridge: CUP. https://doi.org/10.1017/CBO9780511611841
Schneider, Stefan, Glikman, Julie & Avanzi, Mathieu (eds). 2015. *Parenthetical Verbs*. Berlin: De Gruyter.
Schourup, Lawrence. 2011. The discourse marker *now*: A relevance-theoretic approach. *Journal of Pragmatics* 43: 2110–2129. https://doi.org/10.1016/j.pragma.2011.01.005
Schwenter, Scott A. & Traugott, Elizabeth Closs. 1995. The semantic and pragmatic development of substitutive complex prepositions in English. In *Historical Pragmatics* [Pragmatics & Beyond New Series 35], Andreas H. Jucker (ed.), 244–173. Amsterdam: John Benjamins. https://doi.org/10.1075/pbns.35.16sch
Simon-Vandenbergen, Anne-Marie. 2007. *No doubt* and related expresssions. In *Structural-Functional Studies in English Grammar: In Honour of Lachlan Mackenzie* [Studies in Language Companion Series 83], Mike Hannay & Gerard J. Steen (eds), 9–34. Amsterdam: John Benjamins. https://doi.org/10.1075/slcs.83.03sim
Stolz, Thomas. 2007. *Allora*: On the recurrence of function-word borrowing in contact situations with Italian as donor language. In *Connectivity in Grammar and Discourse* [Hamburg Series on Multilingualism 5], Jochen Rehbein, Christiane Hohenstein & Lukas Pietsch (eds), 75–99. Amsterdam: John Benjamins. https://doi.org/10.1075/hsm.5.06sto
Stolz, Christel & Stolz, Thomas. 1996. Funktionswortentlehnung in Mesoamerika: Spanisch-amerindischer Sprachkontakt [Hispanoindiana II]. *Sprachtypologie und Universalienforschung* 49(1): 86–123.
Tabor, Whitney & Traugott, Elizabeth Closs. 1998. Structural scope expansion and grammaticalization. In Giacalone Ramat & Hopper (eds), 229–272.
Taglicht, Josef. 2001. *Actually,* there's more to it than meets the eye. *English Language and Linguistics* 5(1): 1–16. https://doi.org/10.1017/S1360674301000119
Thompson, Sandra A. & Mulac, Anthony. 1991. A quantitative perspective on the grammaticization of epistemic parentheticals in English. In Traugott & Heine (eds),Vol. 1, 313–329.
Traugott, Elizabeth Closs. 1995. The role of the development of discourse markers in a theory of grammaticalization. Paper presented at the International Conference of Historical Linguistics XII, Manchester.
Traugott, Elizabeth Closs. 2007. Discussion article: Discourse markers, modal particles, and contrastive analysis, synchronic and diachronic. *Catalan Journal of Linguistics* 6: 139–157.
Traugott, Elizabeth Closs. 2010. Grammaticalization. In *Continuum Companium to Historical Linguistics*, Silvia Luraghi & Vit Bubenik (eds), 269–283. London: Continuum.
Traugott, Elizabeth Closs & Dasher, Richard B. 2002. *Regularity in Semantic Change* [Cambridge Studies in Linguistics 96]. Cambridge: CUP.

Traugott, Elizabeth Closs & Heine, Bernd (eds). 1991a. *Approaches to Grammaticalization*, Vol. 1: *Theoretical and Methodological Issues* [Typological Studies in Language 19:1]. Amsterdam: John Benjamins.

Traugott, Elizabeth Closs & Heine, Bernd (eds). 1991b. *Approaches to Grammaticalization*, Vol. 2: *Types of Grammatical Markers* [Typological Studies in Language 19:2]. Amsterdam: John Benjamins. https://doi.org/10.1075/tsl.19.2

Traugott, Elizabeth C. & Trousdale, Graeme. 2013. *Constructionalization and Constructional Changes*. Oxford: OUP. https://doi.org/10.1093/acprof:oso/9780199679898.001.0001

Van Bogaert, Julie. 2011. *I think* and other complement-taking mental predicates: A case of and for constructional grammaticalization. *Linguistics* 49(2): 295–332.

Vincent, Diane, Votre, Sebastiao & LaForest, Marty. 1993. Grammaticalisation et post-grammaticalisation. *Langues et Linguistique* 19: 71–103.

de Vries, Mark. 2007. Invisible constituents? Parentheses as B-merged adverbial phrases. In Dehé & Kavalova (eds), 203–234.

Waltereit, Richard. 2001. Modal particles and their functional equivalents: A speech-act-theoretic approach. *Journal of Pragmatics* 33(9): 1391–1417. https://doi.org/10.1016/S0378-2166(00)00057-6

Waltereit, Richard. 2006. The rise of discourse markers in Italian: A specific type of language change. In *Approaches to Discourse Markers* [Studies in Pragmatics 1], Kerstin Fischer (ed.), 61–76. Amsterdam: Elsevier.

Wichmann, Anne. 2011. Grammaticalization and prosody. In Narrog & Heine (eds), 331–341.

Wichmann, Anne, Simon-Vandenbergen, Anne-Marie & Aijmer, Karin. 2010. How prosody reflects semantic change: A synchronic case study of *of course*. In *Subjectification, Intersubjectification and Grammaticalization*, Kristin Davidse, Lieven Vandelanotte & Hubert Cuyckens (eds), 103–154. Berlin: De Gruyter Mouton. https://doi.org/10.1515/9783110226102.2.103

Wischer, Ilse. 2000. Grammaticalization versus lexicalization: *Methinks* there is some confusion. In *Pathways of Change: Grammaticalization in English* [Studies in Language Companion Series 53], Olga Fischer, Anette Rosenbach & Dieter Stein (eds), 355–370. Amsterdam: Benjamins. https://doi.org/10.1075/slcs.53.17wis

Functional similarity despite geographical distance

On the grammaticalization of German *mal* and Chinese *yíxià*

Ekkehard König[1,2] and Jingying Li[2]
[1]FU Berlin / [2]Universität Freiburg

German *mal* is the reduced version of *einmal*, i.e. of a construction combining the numeral 'one' with a noun originally denoting a salient local unit and later salient temporal units (occasions, frequency). The final stage of the development was a process of desemanticization of the frequency use from 'minimal frequency' to 'minimal effort'.

This article pursues the following goals:

i. to analyze a discourse marker in German (i.e. *mal*), both diachronically and synchronically, that has never received a coherent and convincing analysis so far and has no clear counterpart in neighboring languages;
ii. to show that a highly similar pattern and target of grammaticalization can be found in Mandarin Chinese (i.e. *yíxià*);
iii. to argue that similarities in processes of grammaticalization may be due to cognitive principles, rather than to contact or genealogical affiliation.

Keywords: grammaticalization, discourse markers, cognitive principles, German, Mandarin, semantic change

1. Introduction[1]

'Modal particles' (e.g. German *aber*, *auch*, *bloß*, *denn*, *doch*, *eben*, *etwa*, *einfach*, *halt*, *ja*, *ruhig*, *wohl*, etc.) are generally considered as a characteristic feature of Germanic languages (Abraham 1988, 1991, 1995). Such a subclass of 'discourse

1. We would like to thank two anonymous reviewers for pointing out mistakes and making helpful suggestions. All remaining errors are our own responsibility.

https://doi.org.10.1075/slcs.202.03koe
© 2018 John Benjamins Publishing Company

markers' is clearly identifiable in German, Dutch and in Scandinavian languages, though not in English (cf. Bublitz 1978), and whether there is an analogous subclass in other European languages is a matter of some dispute. The expression *mal* shows up as a member of the relevant set in all descriptions of modal particles in German, since it meets all the, largely negative, syntactic and prosodic criteria essential for the identification of the relevant subset of discourse markers (cf. Weydt 1969, 1983, 1989). As far as its contribution to the meaning of an utterance is concerned, the effect of *mal* can certainly be subsumed under the general terms *Abtönung* or *Abschwächung* 'hedging', which are generally used in descriptive studies for characterizing the non-truth-conditional meaning of modal particles since Weydt's seminal study (Weydt 1969). On the other hand, this label does not fit various attempts, made within the framework of pragmatic theories and formal semantics, to characterize the meaning of such expressions in more precise terms, such as 'illocutionary modifiers', 'epistemic indicators' or 'metapragmatic instructions' (cf. Jacobs 1991; König 1997, 2010). The goal of this paper is to re-examine the contribution made by *mal* to the meaning of a construction and an utterance type from two perspectives: (a) a reconstruction of the historical development and its relationship to the homonymous noun *das Mal* and (b) a comparison with the semantically related expression yíxià in Mandarin Chinese. Whereas no vaguely related counterpart to German *mal* can be found in languages closely related to German, the basic and extended meanings of this expression and those of Mandarin *yíxià* are strikingly similar and this suggests that they have undergone similar developments. Our contrastive study will start out by analyzing the relevant facts of German and move on to an analysis of analogous data of Mandarin Chinese. The final section will be dedicated to summarizing similarities and contrasts and to discussing the significance of our findings for theories of grammaticalization. The most important implication and claim of our analysis is that highly similar or even identical processes of grammaticalization may also show up in languages that are neither genealogically related nor in close geographic contact and that such phenomena can only be the result of cognitive principles.

2. German *mal*: A historical reconstruction

The particle ***mal*** is a reduced form of ***einmal*** and this bi-morphemic expression is an instance of a construction combining a cardinal number with the noun *Mal*. The nominal status of the second component is no longer clearly visible in the standard orthography in combination with cardinal numbers, but is obvious when pluralized or in combination with ordinal numbers, articles and adjectival modifiers like (ein *anderes*/*weiteres Mal* 'another time', *zum wiederholten Male* 'repeatedly', etc.):

(1) a. einmal, zweimal,... hundertmal, hunderte Male
b. das erste Mal, ein weiteres Mal, zum wiederholten Male

As far as the etymology of the noun *Mal* is concerned, the relevant sources of information (e.g. DWB, DWDS, Kluge, 1983 s.v. *Mal*) agree that the meaning of the noun *māl* in Old High German and Middle High German is quite close to the meaning of its counterparts in Modern German and can be glossed as 'spot, dot, point, mark'. This noun still occurs in the old meaning mainly in compounds like the following:

(2) *Mahnmal* 'memorial', *Identifikationsmal* 'memorial for identification', *Denkmal*, *Ehrenmal* 'monument', *Grabmal* 'tomb' *Muttermal* 'birthmark, mole', *Schandmal* 'brand, stigma', *Brandmal* 'brand', *Kainsmal* 'mark of Cain', *Nägelmal* 'scar caused by nails', Würgemale 'stragulation marks', *Wundmal* 'scar';

Generalizing over the meaning of the nouns listed as possible translations, we can say that *Mal* denotes a small, salient local unit, typically identified as figure against some ground. In the compounds listed above, the ground is the skin surrounding a salient spot or the territory surrounding us and the figure denotes a cause, a result or a building erected for the purpose of reminding people of memorable events. On the basis of the examples listed in (2), we can also say that some kind of negative prosody is attached to this meaning, as is particularly evident in contrasts like *Wundmal* 'scar' vs. *Schönheitsfleck* 'beauty spot'. The verb *malen* 'paint, create salient marks on some surface' is clearly related to this noun.

Whether the homonym *Mahl* 'meal' and the related verbs *mahlen* 'grind' are in any way related to their homophonous counterparts, distinguished orthographically in Modern German, is a matter of some dispute and of no interest at this point. What is of interest for us is that the use of the local sense of the noun *Mal* has almost disappeared outside of compounds of type (2) and has acquired a temporal sense: 'a short salient temporal unit, defined by some event, activity, time or occasion' (cf. DWB, DWDS, Kluge 1983, s.v. *Mal*). The semantic change in question (place > time) is a very general and widespread one (cf. Haspelmath 1997). In combination with cardinal numbers, this temporal noun *Mal* has two uses and may denote 'frequency' or 'a temporal frame'. The relevant uses are typically found in adjuncts and may co-occur:

(3) a. Ich habe es ihm hundert Mal gesagt. 'I told him a hundred times'.
b. Dieses Mal war ich vorsichtiger. 'This time I was more careful'.
c. Einmal habe ich fünfmal getroffen. 'On one occasion I hit the target five times.'

The two meanings are closely related and there are vague and ambiguous examples. The crucial question is whether relevant occasions or times are defined and delimited by the predicate whose adjunct the temporal expression is or independently given by the co-text (anaphoric use) or a modifier of some kind (cataphoric use). If the events or occasions are specified by the main predicate, we find the frequency use; the event(s) specified by the main predicate are assessed in terms of their frequency. If the occasions are given independently of the main predication; they are also counted but specify a time frame for the predication. A frequency interpretation is possible for all combinations of cardinal numbers with *Mal*, provided there is no definite determiner (*diesmal* 'this time', *damals* 'at that time'). The possibility of a time-frame interpretation is clearest for *einmal* and combinations of *mal* with quantifiers (*jedes Mal* 'every time', *viele Male, einige Male, jemals* 'ever', etc.) and ordinal numbers (*das erste Mal* 'the first time', *ein zweites Mal* 'a second time', abermals 'a second time, again', etc.):

(4) a. Einmal hatte ich große Angst. 'On one occasion I was really scared.'
b. Manchester United hat den Pokal dreimal gewonnen. 'ManU has won the cup three times.'

(5) a. Jedes Mal, wenn ich ihn treffe, ist Karl krank. 'Every time I see him, Charles is sick.'
b. Einmal, als ich in London war, hatte ich meinen Pass verloren. 'Once, when I was in London, I had lost my passport.'

A clear contrast is also visible in certain combinations: *manchmal* 'sometimes', *oftmals, vielmals* 'often' encode frequency, *irgend einmal* 'some time', *jemals* 'ever', *zunächst mal* 'first of all', etc. are time-frame adverbials. An analysis of the exact distinction between these two uses, their status as two contextual variants of one univocal meanings or as a genuine case of polysemy, their co-occurrence with other expressions as well as their disambiguation in context would be a worthwhile exercise in itself, but cannot be pursued further in this paper.

The German adverb *einmal* can be reduced to *mal* in both of its uses. This reduction is first found in Early New High German (cf. Kluge, s.v. 2. *mal*) and its use is described in the *DWB* as occurring in informal, colloquial speech, especially that of children (*DWB*, s.v. mal, 4e). It is this reduction which changes the adverb into a particle that can no longer occur in the forefield, i.e. in the position before the finite verb, and that can neither be focused, nor negated:

(6) a. Einmal wirst du das noch bereuen. 'One day you will regret that.'
b. Das wirst du noch mal bereuen. (same translation)

(7) a. Manchester United hat den Pokal EINmal gewonnen. 'ManU won the cup once.'
b. Manchester United hat (halt) mal den Pokal gewonnen. 'ManU won the cup. So what?'

Note that (7b) is not a clear example of a frequency use, but seems to allow both interpretations and has the additional implication 'So what's the big deal'. Since frequency adverbials are typically rhematic and typically bear focal stress, that aspect is lost when the non-focusable particle *mal* rather than the adverb *einmal* occurs. This is a first piece of evidence that there was some change of meaning accompanying the formal reduction of *einmal* to *mal*. The change in question, in our view, can be described as follows: An expression denoting minimal frequency has incorporated the contextual implication that the service asked for requires minimal time and minimal effort. This description applies primarily to imperatives and interrogatives used for requests. As far as assertive speech act are concerned, the relevant implicature is best described as 'requiring a minimal commitment from the speaker'. Before we present further evidence for this hypothesis by examining previous descriptions and by carrying out a comparison with some similar expression in Mandarin Chinese, let us summarize the changes we have assumed so far:

(8) a. Mal [salient local unit(s)] > Mal [salient temporal unit(s)]
b. cardinal numbers + mal > 'frequency' or 'time frame'
c. einmal > mal
d. mal: 'minimal frequency' > 'minimal effort' or 'minimal commitment'

3. Previous views on *mal*

In the rich descriptive literature on modal particles, various attempts have been made to subsume the meaning of these particles, or at least of a subset thereof, under a general semantic or pragmatic category, rather than looking for a specific description in each individual case. Among the relevant descriptive labels, the following have been used for a characterization of the contribution made by *mal* and other modal particles to the meaning of an utterance: indicators of illocutionary force (cf. Jacobs 1991; Abraham 1995; Coniglio 2009, etc.), indicators of strength of commitment (Bublitz 2003; Thaler 2010), indicator of politeness (cf. Bublitz 2003). Let us consider how illuminating these labels are when applied to the use of *mal*.

That *mal* may have an effect on the illocutionary force of an utterance is most obvious in minimal pairs like the following:

(9) a. Kannst du diesen Koffer hochheben? (question) 'Could you lift this suitcase?'
b. Kannst du mal diesen Koffer hochheben? (request) 'Could you please lift this suitcase.'

The particle *mal* may obviously map an interrogative speech act onto a directive one. This, however, is only the case if the question we start out from concerns an activity of the addressee, i.e. if it is a question that could be used by itself as an indirect request. In examples like the following, the relevant effect is not visible:

(10) a. Wird Karl mal nach London reisen? (question) 'Will Charles go to London?'
b. Wirst du mal genug Geld besitzen, um dir ein Haus zu kaufen? (question) 'Will you ever have enough money to buy a house?'

Nor do we find a change of illocutionary type in declarative sentences even if an action of the addressee is under discussion:

(11) Du gehst jetzt (mal) einkaufen. 'You will now go to do some shopping.'

Another frequently found analysis characterizes *mal* as an indicator of strength, expressing a weak commitment of the speaker to the truth of a declarative sentence (cf. (12)) and a weak directive force ('Abschwächung') in an imperative (cf. (13)):

(12) Ich will es mal so sagen: „Die Situation ist verfahren. "Ich nehme mal an, dass…

(13) Kannst du mir mal etwas Geld leihen? Leih mir mal etwas Geld!

In (12) the speaker indicates that his/her formulation is tentative and not the optimal way of describing the situation in question and (13) asks for a minor service. Statements with *mal* are characterized as casual remarks and imperatives with *mal* reduce the commitment of the hearer, i. e. a request with *mal* has no urgency and a certain casualness (cf. Bublitz 2003). A similar point is made by Burkhardt (1989: 366), who characterizes the service requested by imperatives with *mal* as a minor one. Casual requests, characterized by a speaker as not urgent, have a concomitant effect of politeness and it should therefore not come as a surprise that *mal* is often analyzed as a marker of politeness. As in the case of the influence of *mal* on the illocutionary force of an utterance, certain other conditions have to be met for the politeness effect to come about. Consider the following examples:

(14) a. Du kannst mich mal gern haben! 'Go away!'
b. Das wirst du noch mal bereuen. 'You will regret this (one day).'
c. Nimm dir mal ein Beispiel an deinem Bruder! 'Take a leaf out of your brother's book.'

The first example is a euphemistic version of a very rude remark in German and does not get any politer by using *mal*. Example (14b) would typically be used as a threat, which cannot be weakened or made polite through the addition of *mal* and the same applies to the criticism expressed by (14c). What these examples also show is that a distinction needs to be drawn between the two possible meanings of *einmal*, viz, 'frequency' and 'temporal frame', which are relevant for the further development of its reduced form *mal*.

4. From 'minimal frequency' to 'minimal effort'

The observations made above certainly capture some relevant facts of the use of the modal particle *mal* and will find their place in the following more coherent reconstruction. The first relevant point is that the use we are investigating developed from the use of *einmal* referring to minimal frequency and, as it was shown by examples like (10), that the use of *mal* going back to the time-frame use of *einmal* does not manifest the relevant effects. The assumption that it is only one use of *mal* that manifests the effects described in the preceding section is clearly confirmed by paraphrases with their source *einmal*:

(15) Ich werde mir ihn mal (= '(irgendwann) einmal') vorknöpfen. 'I will call him on the carpet before long.

(16) Könntest du endlich mal (= 'EINmal, ein einziges Mal') dein Zimmer aufräumen. 'Could you for once tidy up your room?'

As already pointed out above, the addition of *irgendwann* always gives us the temporal interpretation of *einmal* and *mal*, which never leads to the pragmatic effect associated with the frequency use in (9b). Our analysis of this pragmatic effect roughly as 'the speaker's evaluation of an action as involving a minimal effort' predicts that this use of *mal* should be incompatible with contexts where something outrageously expensive is asked of the addressee. Compare the following examples:

(17) a. Könntest du mir mal € 10 leihen? 'Could you lend me € 10?'
b. ?Könntest Du mir mal (kurz) ein Haus schenken?
'Could you give me a house as a present.'
c. ?Schenk mir doch mal ein Haus! 'Why don't you give me a house?'
d. Haben Sie mal etwas Kleingeld für mich. 'Do you have a few coins for me?'

(18) Ich werde (dies–/jetzt/irgendwann) mal € 50 000 abheben. 'This time I will withdraw € 50 000 from my account.'

The first example could be addressed to a friend and (17d) is what street people use in addressing complete strangers in cities. In (17b)–(17c), by contrast, the co-text of *mal* is totally in conflict with the contextual implications of the particle *mal* and these sentences are therefore extremely odd. If, by contrast, *mal* has the time-interval interpretation there is no incompatibility between particle meaning and an analogous co-text (18).

So far we have corrected and modified previous views on the particle *mal* by (a) drawing a distinction between two different uses of this particle continuing the two uses of the bi-morphemic expression *einmal* they are derived from and by (b) showing that these two uses are (in)compatible with different contexts. These observations show that it is pointless to look for a univocal pragmatic meaning of the particle *mal*; at least two uses have to be distinguished. Finally, we have also spelt out a specific rule of semantic change that accompanied the formal reduction of *einmal* in its frequency use. Let us now look at this process of grammaticalization in more detail.

It is a well-established fact that what is grammaticalized are not simply lexical expressions, but lexical expressions in specific constructions. The English verb *get* has developed into an auxiliary verb not across the board, but only in passive constructions, especially in passive imperatives (*I got stung by a bee. Don't get run over by a car*!). Analogously, *mal*, as a reduction of the frequency use of *einmal*, has been grammaticalized only in specific constructions, such as imperatives and interrogatives, requiring actions from addressees. These are the most obvious cases, frequently noted in the literature, but there are also several other contexts manifesting the same use of *mal* as a marker of minimal effort. A plausible case are declaratives expressing hesitant assertions with weak commitments of the speaker to the truth or strength of a proposition (cf. Bublitz 2003: 185):

(19) Karl hat, sagen wir mal, ganz gute Chancen das Examen zu bestehen. 'Let's say that Charles has got reasonable chances to pass the exam.'

The characterization as 'minimal effort' does not quite fit such cases and a formulation like 'minimal commitment (to the truth of the assertion)' seems to be more appropriate for such examples. A further case that could be subsumed under our analysis with a slight extension is the construction type with *nicht…einmal*. This expression can be analyzed as a complex focus marker, roughly paraphrasable by *sogar…nicht*.

(20) a. Karl hat mich nicht (ein)mal gegrüßt. 'Charles did not even say 'hallo''
b. Die SPD hat nicht (ein)mal 20% der Stimmen erreicht. 'The Social Democrats did not even get 20% of the vote.'

Like all focus markers, *nicht…einmal* evokes contextually given alternatives which are ranked higher within the scope of the negation, i.e. some value like 'talk to me' in (20a) or '25% of the vote' in (20b). Overall, declarative sentences like (20) express weak assertions and the values focused on are low or minimal values compared to the ones they are contrasted with. Again, 'minimal effort', the characterization appropriate for imperatives or directive speech acts, in general, does not quite fit that use.

Let us, finally, conclude the section on German by raising the question in how far the change described in (8d) is an instance of grammaticalization. Of the criteria considered as definitional for grammaticalization we find both formal simplication (*einmal* > *mal*) and semantic change ('minimal frequency' > 'minimal effort'), to begin with. Moreover, the relevant change occurs in specific constructions only. A close look at the semantic change reveals, moreover, another typical property of grammaticalization, viz. the change is from an objective assessment of frequency to a subjective assessment of effort, from a semantic implication to a contextual implicature, thus leading to greater subjectivity. Moreover, the original meaning of frequency has disappeared and combinations like the following, where the frequency adverb and the modal particle co-occur, are perhaps marginal, but not totally excluded:

(21) a. Kannst Du mir mal zum zweiten Mal helfen? 'Could you help me a second time for once.'
b. Hilf mir doch mal zweimal! 'Why don't you help me twice?'

Note that all the observations made in the previous literature can be easily integrated into this coherent picture. They follow more or less from our analysis. The change from 'minimal frequency' to 'minimal effort' or 'minimal commitment' is obviously based on a general inference: A service requested with minimal frequency and minimal commitment cannot be 'a big deal' and an assertion made with a minimal commitment cannot be authoritative.

Grammaticalization is language-specific and construction-specific. There are general and pervasive channels of grammaticalization that are found in a wide variety of languages. Processes of grammaticalization starting out from demonstratives or interrogatives as sources are a clear case in point (cf. Diessel 1999; König 2015) and a variety of such pervasive channels have been compiled in Heine & Kuteva (2002). The change described in this paper, by contrast, is extremely rare and cannot be identified in other European or Indo-European languages. No use of French *pour une fois* (*Pourriez-vous m'aider pour une fois*?) or English *this once* (*Could you help me this once*?) has the pragmatic effect in question. In order to be firmly established as a relevant case, the change under discussion is in need of supporting evidence from other languages and we will now show that a more or less parallel development can be found in Mandarin Chinese.

5. Mandarin *yíxià*

According to the lexicon *Eight Hundred Words from Modern Chinese* (Lü Shuxiang 1999: 565) and the *Practical Modern Chinese Grammar* (Liu Yuehua 2001: 135), the lexeme 一下 *yíxià* has two basic uses: In its first use, 一下 ($yíxià_1$) is analyzed as a combination of "numeral + classifier" phrase, denoting the frequency of an action or event, which is usually of short duration. In its second use, 一下 ($yíxià_2$) is regarded as a temporal adverbial, indicating a short duration of an action and a softening tone of an utterance. (Yang Jiechun 2006; Gao Pin 2008).

As far as its syntactic position is concerned, *yíxià* can be used either as an adverbial after the verb, thus quantifying an action. i.e. indicating minimal frequency or short duration of an action in the sequence V+ *yíxià*, or as an adverbial modifier before the verb in the structure *yíxià* + V, indicating a short duration of an action (Liu Yuehua 2001). Here are two pertinent examples:

(22) Tā qīngqīng de diǎn le yíxià tóu.
He lightly PART nod AUX one CLF head.
'He nodded once lightly.'

(23) Tā yíxià jiù kàn wán le.
He one CLF just read finish AUX.
'He finished his reading quickly.'

Let us now look at these two uses in more detail. As already indicated briefly, *yíxià* has two meanings. On the one hand, *yíxià* can refer to the frequency of a quick short-duration action, as in:

(24) Tā qiāo le yíxià zhuō zi.
He knock AUX once CLF table.
'He has knocked on the table once.'

In this first use, the numeral could be any number, such as '一 *yī*, 两 *èr*, 三 *sān*, 四 *sì*, one, two, three, four…', as in the following example:

(25) Tā tī le sān xià mén.
He kick already three CLF door.
'He has kicked the door three times.'

Note, however, that $yíxià_1$ is only used for quick, short-duration actions. The expression is thus in contrast to many other classifiers for different verbs in Chinese: 顿 dùn, for example, is used for having dinner or for scolding, 场 chǎng is used for performances or sports activities, 趟 tàng is used for a go-and-return actions and 番 fān is for an action requiring a lot of time and energy.

Yíxià₂, by contrast, is not used to indicate exact frequency, but minimal frequency or short duration of an action. In this usage, combinations with numerals other than *yí*, i.e. 两下 *liǎngxià*, 三下 *sānxià*, etc. are not admissible. In contrast to 一下 *yíxià₁*, this use is not restricted to quick actions, as is shown by the following examples:

(26) Qǐng shuō yíxià nǐ de xìngqù.
Please talk ADV your hobby.
'Please talk about your hobbies a little.'

(27) Nǐ guò lái yíxià.
You come ADV.
'Please come here.'

(28) Nǐ néng jiè wǒ yíxià nǐ de bǐ ma?
You could lend me ADV your pen AUX?
'Could you lend me your pen please?'

In Example (26), (27), and (28), the activities '说 talk', '过来 come' and '借 lend' could take up a long or short time. When they are combined with 一下 *yíxià*, however, these activities are described as not taking up much time. As a consequence of this, i.e. by indicating a short duration of the service required, 一下 yíxià₂ is used to make the tone of the utterance sound more polite (Liu Yuehua, 2001), quite analogously to the uses for German *mal* discussed above:

(29) Nǐ lái yíxià.
You come ADV.
'Please come here.' (cf. Germ. Komm mal her.)

(30) Ràng wǒmen tǎo lùn yíxià.
Let us discuss ADV.
'Just let us have a discussion.' (cf. Germ. Lass uns mal darüber reden.)

(31) Nǐ yīnggāi fù xí yíxià.
You should review ADV.
'You should just have a review.'

In the preceding examples (29), (30), and (31), a request, a suggestion and a piece of advice are expressed in a polite manner. Without 一下 yíxià, the sentences would sound very direct and more like a command.

6. Historical development of 一下 *yíxià*

Many linguists have been interested in the historical development of 一下 *yíxià*, (cf. Liu Shiru 1962; Yang Jiechun 2006; Jin Guitao 2007; Gao Pin 2008; Zhou Juan 2012) and previous research shows that '一下 *yíxià*' has undergone a process of grammaticalization. The following part will illustrate the process with examples of Modern and Old Chinese taken from the Center for Chinese Linguistics Corpus Peking University (Zhan, Weidong; Guo, Rui; Chen, Yirong 2003, CCLCorpus: <http://ccl.pku.edu.cn:8080/ccl_corpus/index.jsp>. The name of the literature which the examples come from, the time or the period that the literature was produced are included in the parentheses at the end of the examples.

The character 下 *xià* in 一下 *yíxià* is originally a noun, meaning 'the lower location, bottom', as the vertical stroke under the horizontal line in the character indicates. It is opposite to the noun 上shàng 'the upper location, top'. Here are some examples from Old Chinese,

(32) Shān xià chū quán. (*Zhōu yì*)
'There is a stream at the foot of the mountain.'
(*Changes of Zhou,* The South Zhou Dynasty, B.C. 1046–B.C. 771)

(33) Guāng bèi sì biǎo, gé yú shàngxià. (Jīnwén shàngshū)
'The light covers all directions, to the sky (top) and to the ground (bottom).'
(*Jinwen Shangshu*, The Han Dynasty, B.C.202–220)

In the examples (32) and (33), 下 *xià* is a noun meaning the lower or bottom part.

The verb 下 *xià* developed from the noun *xià*, and came to mean 'move from a higher location to a lower location', as in (34), for example:

(34) Yīn yáng biàn huà, yíshàng yíxià, hé ér chéng zhāng. (*Lǚ shì chūn qiū*)
'The change of yin and yang, one is moving upward, the other is moving downward, so the combination composes a chapter of music.'
(*Lüshi Chunqiu,* Warring States Period, B.C. 239)

下 *xià* in Example (34) is used as a verb, in opposition to the verb 上*shàng* and means 'moving downward'.

The classifier 下 *xià* was derived from the verb 下 *xià*. According to research on classifiers for verbs conducted by many scholars (Liu Shiru 1962; Jin Guitao 2007; Zhou Juan 2012) and research on 一下 *yíxià* by Yang Jiechun (2006), the expression 下 xià began to be used as a classifier for downward short-duration actions, mainly for verbs like, '击打 hit', indicating the frequency of actions, since Wei, Jin, Southern and Northern Dynasties. Since the late Southern and Northern Dynasties, it could also be used for short-duration actions that were not downward-directed. 一下 *yíxià* (represented as 一下 *yíxià*$_1$) was quite often used with short-duration verbs, indicating the frequency in Sui, Tang, and Five Dynasties. For example,

(35) Rén búdé gāoshēng chàng hào, hángzhě qiāo gōng yíxià, zuòzhě kòu shuò sān xià, fāng zhì junhào, yǐ xiàng yīng huì. (*Tōng diǎn*)
'Men should not sing or shout loudly, those who stand knock the bow once, those who sit knock the lance three times, then the bugle is played as a response.' (*Tongdian*, Tang Dynasty, 618–907, in 801)

(36) Shī tánzhǐ yíxià, què zhǎn shǒu. (*Zǔ táng jí*)
'The teacher snapped his fingers once, walked back and opened his hands.' (*Zutangji*, Five Dynasties, 907–960)

The verb 敲 *qiāo* ('knock'), 扣 *kòu* ('knock') and 弹 *tán* ('fillip') in Example (35) and (36) are punctual verbs and typically denote actions of quick and short duration. The composite lexeme 一下 *yíxià* expresses the exact frequency of the actions.

During the Song and Yuan Dynasties, some non-punctual verbs, which neither denoted actions of short duration or downward movements, came to be used with 一下 *yíxià*, showing that the expression 一下 *yíxià* gradually extended its contexts and frequency of use from a classifier to a temporal adverbial use expressing short-duration objectively and subjectively (identified above as 一下 *yíxià*$_2$). In this use, 一下 *yíxià* has become lexicalized, and the numeral *yi* (一) can no longer alternate with other numerals. This development continued during the Ming and Qing Dynasties. Since then 一下 *yíxià* can be used both as a construction 'number + classifier' denoting frequency and as a temporal adverbial expressing short-duration. Later, the original numeral 一*yi* of 一下 *yíxià*$_2$ became omissible and the expression is reduced to 下 *xià*. The following two examples provide illustration:

(37) Ruòyíxià biàn yào lǐ huì dé, yě wú cǐ lǐ. (*Yǔ lù zhū zǐ yǔ lèi*)
'There is no such a principle that just takes a little while to understand.' (*Yulu Zhuzi Yulei*, The North Song dynasty, 960–1127, in 1270)

(38) Xiàng nà shítóu měng jī yíxià. (*Yīng liè zhuàn*)
'(He) hit the stone once fiercely.' (*Yingliezhuan*, Ming Dynasty, 1368–1644)

(39) Wǒ yě xiǎng shāowēi xiūxī yíxià. (*Zéng guó fān jiā shū*)
'I want to have a rest.'
(*Zengguofan Family Letter*, Qing Dynasty, 1644–1912, in mid 19th century)

(40) Érzi xīwàng dàrén gàosùyíxià. (*Zéng guó fān jiā shū*)
'The son hopes his father will tell him (about it).'
(*Zengguofan Family Letter*, Qing Dynasty, 1644–1912, in mid 19th century)

一下 *yíxià* in Example (37) means 'a short time'. Example (38) describes the frequency of action *jī* ('hit') as 'once'. In the Examples (39) and (40), 一下 *yíxià* expresses that the activities of 'resting' (*xiūxī*) and 'telling' (*gàosù*) do not take up a long time. In Example (40), *yíxià* expresses the son's hope for further information from his father in a polite and deferential way. These examples show that both uses have existed since the Song Dynasty.

The preceding examples illustrate a process of grammaticalization that can briefly be summarized as follows: The expression 下 *xià* in 一下 *yíxià*, originally a noun meaning 'bottom, lower end', developed into a verb meaning moving from a higher place to a lower place. Subsequently, it developed into a classifier for quick actions, indicating how many times the relevant action happens. Combined with the numeral 一 *yí*, the phrase 一下 *yíxià* denoted a single occurrence of the quick action (*yíxià*$_1$). Gradually, the phrase 一下 *yíxià* lost its concrete meaning in certain contexts and was also used as an adverb or temporal adverbial, indicating from minimum frequency to the short duration of an action (*yíxià*$_2$) (Yang Jiechun 2006; Gao Pin 2008). Thus 一下 *yíxià*$_2$ expressed the minimum effort through short duration. The numeral 一 *yí* was often omitted when the expression was used as a temporal adverbial (Yang Jiechu 2006; Gao Pin 2008). It can be seen that *xià* in *yíxià* developed from locality to temporal frame, which is similar to German *mal*. Like German *mal*, *yíxià* changed from minimal frequency to minimal duration and extended to minimal effort. All the different uses of *yíxià* exist nowadays. The following table provides a condensed summary of the relevant steps in this grammaticalization process:

Table 1.

a. xià (noun) > xià (verb) > xià (classifier)
b. yí (numeral) + xià (classifier) > yíxià$_1$ (frequency) > yíxià$_2$ (short duration)
c. yíxià$_2$ (short duration) > yíxià (minimal effort)
d. yíxià > xià
e. minimal frequency > minimal duration/time > minimal effort

7. Previous views on *yíxià*

Previous research on *yíxià*' has focused on verb collocations, on the sequential order of object and *yíxià*, on semantic and syntactic features of contexts, the expression itself, as well as on pragmatic functions. The expression *yíxià*$_2$ has been the object of a number of studies which have led to some interesting conclusions.

Xiangyuan mao (1984) observes that 一下 yíxià means 'small amount of time' and gives a casual tone to the utterance. Lü Shuxiang (1999) analyzes the construction [V + 一下 yíxià$_2$] as denoting a quick and short-duration action. Liu Yuehua (2001) points out that the expression can be used as a euphemism moderating the tone of a sentence. Gan Zhilin (2004) *yíxià* presents a subjective view, showing the speaker's attempt to make the utterance casual and relaxing. Jiang Xiangping (2012) analyzes [V + 一下 yíxià$_2$] according to speech act types and concludes that it serves as a politeness strategy in directives by softening the directive force, in assertions by subjective minimization, in offers by minimizing the commitment of speakers, and in the act of criticizing and blaming by protecting the listener's face. Based on the Leech's (1983) Politeness Principles and Brown & Levinson's strategies of negative politeness (1987), Shan Baoshun (2009, 2013), Shan Baoshun and Qi Huyang (2014) point out that minimal quantity is related to politeness, calling it 'a small quantity strategy'. This strategy is manifested not only in the use of 一下 *yíxià*, but also in some other expressions, such as *yidianer* 'a little', *youdianer* etc. This analysis is further supported by the fact that 一下 *yíxià* is not used in combination with derogatory words or in interactions with interlocutors where politeness is not called for, such as criminals.

8. From 'minimal frequency' to 'minimal duration/effort'

All of the above research sheds light on the use of 一下 *yíxià* in Mandarin. Let us now take a more detailed look at how exactly 一下 *yíxià*$_2$ expresses politeness on the basis of subjective minimal quantity (time duration). Consider the following examples:

(41) a. Nǐ néng bāng wǒ (yí)xià ma?
You can help me ADV AUX?
'Can you help me (a while, short duration)?'
b. Nǐ néng bāng wǒ ma?
You can help me AUX?
'Can you help me?'

Both examples in (41) express a speaker's request. 一下 *yíxià* in (41a) literally means 'a while'. Minimizing the duration of the service required, the expression shows that the speaker does not want to impose on the hearer and only needs a small amount of time and effort from the listener. Depending on the context, the service can take a short or longer time in reality, which both the listener and the speaker usually can understand. *Yíxià* does not denote a concrete time interval but is used in accordance with the politeness principle. In requests, minimizing the quantity or effort can soften the tone and thus the imposition and express politeness. Compared with (41b), (41a) is less blunt and more polite.

A similar contrast can be observed in the following minimal pair of imperatives:

(42) a. Nǐ guòlái (yí)xià.
You come ADV.
'Please come here.'
b. Nǐ guòlái.
You come.
'Come.'

The examples in (42) are commands. In (42a) *yíxià* vaguely express that the activity will not take a long time or cost great effort. Using minimal duration reduces the imposition on the listener, thus creating a polite and casual tone. Without 一下 *yíxià*, the utterance has a strong, unmitigated directive force and is thus used as a command, allowing no disobedience. An analogous contrast shows up in the following minimal pair:

(43) a. Wǒ men yīnggāi zǐxì kǎolǜ (yí)xià.
We should carefully think ADV.
'We should think about it carefully.'
b. Wǒ men yīnggāi zǐxì kǎolǜ.
We should carefully think.
'We should think about it carefully.'

In the Examples (43a–b), the activity *zǐxì kǎolǜ* ('think about it carefully') normally demands considerable time, but it does not conflict with 一下 yíxià in a polite sentence. *Yíxià* subjectively reduces the duration and effort to a minimal amount, causing less imposition on the listener. This use fully represents the subjectivity that has come to be encapsulated in 一下 *yíxià*.

However, the use of *yíxià* will not be appropriate in contexts where services involve high costs obviously and require extreme efforts, as the speakers' request should conform to the normal evaluation of minimal effort. The following examples provide the relevant contrasts:

(44) a. Nǐ néng jiè yíxià 10 yuán gěi wǒ ma?
You can lend ADV €10 to me AUX?
'Can you lend me €10 please?'
b. Nǐ néng bāng wǒ mǎi yíxià kāfēi ma?
You can help me buy ADV coffee AUX?
'Can you help me buy coffee?'
c. Nǐ néng bāng wǒ mǎi yíxià fángzi ma?
You can help me buy ADV house AUX?
'Can you help me buy a house?'

(45) Nǐ néng jiè wǒ yíxià 10 000 yuán ma? Wǒ míngtiān jiù hái gěi nǐ.
You can lend me ADV €10 000 AUX? I tomorrow just return to you.
'Can you lend me €10 000? I will return it to you tomorrow.'

Example (44a–b) express requests which do not require a great effort and so the context is compatible with the use of *yíxià*, while in (44c), yíxià is in conflict with the context, since buying a house costs a lot. In (45), by contrast, when the relevant service only involves a short duration, the use of yíxià is acceptable.

9. Summary and conclusions

In its development from 'minimal frequency' to 'minimal duration' and 'minimal effort' and an 'indicator of politeness', *yíxià* manifests some typical grammaticalization features. It changes from a 'numeral + classifier' phrase to a time adverbial, from a meaning of 'limited to downward and short duration actions' to 'short-duration actions' in general and from an objective assessment of frequency to a subjective assessment of time duration and effort. On the formal side, we can observe that 一下 *yíxià* is frequently reduced to 下 *xià*, as a result of morphological erosion. The historical development of *yíxià* thus manifests the typical aspects of grammaticalization, in its semantic changes, in its contextual expansion and in its formal simplification. Most importantly from our comparative perspective, however, we may note that, in contrast to all the languages surrounding German, Mandarin Chinese, a language totally unrelated to German, manifests a process of grammaticalization leading from 'minimal frequency' to 'minimal duration/minimal effort' that finds a clear analogy in German. A general conclusion that can be drawn from these comparative observations is that processes of grammaticalization and semantic change that are clearly based on cognitive and interactional principles, as the one discussed above, are likely to occur in several languages, even in cases where those languages are neither geographically, culturally nor genealogically closely related.[2]

2. One reviewer has drawn our attention to the fact that the expression *ham* (derived from *han bun* 'one [numeral] time [classifier]' has exactly the same semantic and pragmatic properties as *mal* and *yíxià*. This could be a case of contact-induced change or an independent development, but it is interesting to note that the process of change is even more wide-spread than we had assumed.

References

Abraham, Werner. 1988. Vorbemerkungen zur Modalpartikelsyntax im Deutschen. *Linguistische Berichte* 118: 443–465.

Abraham, Werner. 1991. The grammaticization of German modal particles. *Studies in Language* 19(2): 331–380.

Abraham, Werner. 1995. Wieso stehen nicht alle Modalpartikeln in allen Satzformen? *Zeitschrift für deutsche Muttersprache* 23(2): 124–146.

Brown, Penelope & Stephen Levinson. 1987. *Politeness: Some Universals of Language Usage.* Cambridge: CUP.

Bublitz, Wolfram. 1978. *Ausdrucksweisen der Sprechereinstellung im Deutschen und Englischen.* Tübingen: Niemeyer. https://doi.org/10.1515/9783111712369

Bublitz, Wolfram. 2003. Nur ganz kurz mal. Abschwächungsintensivierung durch feste Muster mit *mal.* In *Partikeln und Höflichkeit,* Gudrun Bachleitner Held (ed.), 179–201. Frankfurt: Peter Lang.

Burkhardt, Arnim. 1989. Partikelsemantik. In *Sprechen mit Partikeln,* Harald Weydt (ed.), 354–369. Berlin: De Gruyter.

Coniglio, Marco. 2009. *Deutsche Modalpartikeln in Haupt- und Nebensätzen.* In *Modalität, Epistemik und Evidentialität bei Modalverb, Adverb, Modalpartikel und Modus,* Werner Abraham & Elisabeth Leiss (eds), 191–222. Tübingen: Stauffenburg.

Diessel, Holger. 1999. *Demonstratives. Form, Function and Grammaticalization* [Typologial Studies in Language 42]. Amsterdam: John Benjamins. https://doi.org/10.1075/tsl.42

DWB (*Deutsches Wörterbuch*). Von Jacob und Wilhelm Grimm, 16 Vols. Leipzig 1854–1961. Online-version, 2017.

DWDS (*Das digitale Wörterbuch der deutschen Sprache*). Ein Projekt der BBAW.

Gan, Zhilin. 2004. The grammar meaning of 'V + yixia 2'. *Journal of Hunan University of Arts and Science* (Social Science Edition) 29(5).

Gao, Pin. 2008. Research on grammaticalization of 'yixia'. *Gansu Sociology* 4: 58–61.

Haspelmath, Martin. 1997. *From Space to Time. Temporal Adverbs in the World's Languages.* Munich: Lincom.

Heine, Bernd & Tania Kuteva. 2002. *World Lexicon of Grammaticalization.* Cambridge: CUP.

Jacobs, Joachim. 1991. On the semantics of modal particles. In *Discourse Particles. Descriptive and Theoretical Investigations on the Logical, Syntactic and Pragmatic Properties of Discourse Particles in German* [Pragmatics & Beyond New Series 12], Werner Abraham (ed.), 141–162. Amsterdam: John Benjamins. https://doi.org/10.1075/pbns.12.06jac

Jiang, Xiangping. 2012. A pragmatic analysis of V + yixia in Mandarin Chinese. *Journal of Pragmatics* 44: 1888–1901. https://doi.org/10.1016/j.pragma.2012.08.004

Jin, Guitao. 2007. Research on Classifiers for Verbs in Song Yuan Ming and Qing Dynasties. *Changjiang Academics* 1: 91–91.

Kluge, Friedrich. 1883. *Etymologisches Wörterbuch.* Straßburg: Trübner.

König, Ekkehard. 1997. Zur Bedeutung von Modalpartikeln im Deutschen: Ein Neuansatz im Rahmen der Relevanztheorie. *Germanistische Linguistik* 136: 57–75.

König, Ekkehard. 2010. Dimensionen der Bedeutung und Verwendung von Modalpartikeln im Deutschen: Grundlagen einer Bestandsaufnahme. In *40 Jahre Partikelforschung,* Theo Harden & Elke Hentschel (eds), 11–32. Tübingen: Stauffenburg.

König, Ekkehard. 2015. Manner deixis as source of grammaticalization markers in Indo-European Languages. In *Perspectives on Historical Syntax* [Studies in Language Companion Series 169], Carlotta Viti (ed.), 35–60. Amsterdam: John Benjamins.

Leech, Geoffrey N. 1983. *Principles of Pragmatics*. London: Taylor & Francis.

Liu, Yuehua. 2001. *Practical Modern Chinese Grammar*. Beijing: The Commercial Press.

Liu, Shiru. 1962. Research on classifiers for verbs in Wei Jin southern and northern dynasties. *Chinese Language* 4: 154–161.

Lü, Shuxiang. 1999. *Eight Hundred Words from Modern Chinese*. Beijing: The Commercial Press.

Shan, Baoshun & Qi, Huyang. 2014. On the implicit expression of 'Politeness Principle' in Chinese from the 'Little' meaning. *Chinese Language Learning* (5): 11–17.

Shan, Baoshun & Xiao, Ling. 2009. 一下yixia and Politeness Principle. *Journal of Liaodong College* 11(2): 52–55.

Shan, Baoshun. 2013. Pragmatics of 'V yixia. *Writers 03X*: 189–190.

Thaler, Verena. 2010. Abtönung als Ausdruck von Unsicherheit bei Fremdsprachenlernern und Muttersprachlern. In *40 Jahre Partikelforschung*, Theo Harden & Elke Hentschel (eds), 151–167. Tübingen: Stauffenburg.

Weydt, Harald. 1969. *Abtönungspartikeln: Die deutschen Modalwörter und ihre französischen Entsprechungen*. Homburg: Gehlen.

Weydt, Harald. 1983. *Partikeln und Interaktion*. Tübingen: Niemeyer. https://doi.org/10.1515/9783111661643

Weydt, Harald. 1989. *Sprechen mit Partikeln*. Berlin: Walter de Gruyter.

Xiangyuan, Mao & Shaye. 1984. Quantity Complement 'Yixia'. *Chinese Language Learning* 4: 20–31.

Yang, Jiechun. 2006. On the emergence and development of the quantifier phrase 'yixia'. *Journal of Yunnan Normal University* 4(6): 38–45.

Zhan, Weidong, Guo, Rui & Chen, Yirong. 2003. The CCL Corpus of Chinese Texts: 700 million Chinese Characters, the 11th Century B.C. –present, Available online at the website of Center for Chinese Linguistics (abbreviated as CCL) of Peking University. <http://ccl.pku.edu.cn:8080/ccl_corpus>

Zhou, Juan. 2012. *A Study on the Combination of Verbs and Verbal Classifiers in Mandarin Chinese*. Guangzhou: Jinan University Press.

Examples in Chinese characters

(22) 他轻轻地点了一下头。

(23) 他一下就看完了。

(24) 他敲了一下桌子。

(25) 他踢了三下门。

(26) 请说一下你的兴趣。

(27) 你过来一下。

(28) 你能借我一下你的笔吗?

(29) 你来一下。

(30) 让我们讨论一下。

(31) 你应该复习一下。

(32) 山下出泉。(周 周易)

(33) 光被四表,格于上下。(周 今文尚书)

(34) 阴阳变化,一上一下,合而成章。(战国 吕氏春秋)

(35) 人不得高声唱號,行者敲弓一下,坐者扣槊三下,方擲軍號,以相應會。(唐 通典)

(36) 师弹指一下,却展手。(五代 祖堂集)

(37) 若一下便要理会得,也无此理。(北宋 语录 朱子语类)

(38) 向那石头猛击一下。(明 英烈传)

(39) 我也想稍微休息一下。(清 曾国藩家书)

(40) 儿子希望大人告诉一下。(清 曾国藩家书)

(41) a. 你能帮我(一)下吗?
b. 你能帮我吗?

(42) a. 你过来(一)下。
b. 你过来。

(43) a. 我们应该仔细考虑(一)下。
b. 我们应该仔细考虑。

(44) a. 你能借一下10元给我吗?
b. 你能帮我买一下咖啡吗?c.你能帮我买一下房子吗?

(45) 你能借我一下10 000元吗?我明天就还给你。

Analogy

Its role in language learning, categorization, and in models of language change such as grammaticalization and constructionalization

Olga Fischer
University of Amsterdam

This paper investigates and surveys the role played by analogy in language learning and processing, and its position in models of change such as grammaticalization and diachronic construction grammar. I will illustrate the importance of analogy by looking at Hermann Paul's *Prinzipien der Sprachgeschichte* (1880), indicating that his ideas on how languages are learned and change are closely connected and pervaded by analogical notions. These ideas have recently become current again, after long neglect within linguistic models since the 1950s, and now form the basis for experiments and recent work in cognitive science. The presence of analogy in change will be highlighted through a review of a number of recent diachronic studies, where I will argue that analogy helps to explain the development of the new constructions there investigated.

Keywords: analogy, categorization, constructionalization, language learning, networks, system mapping

> "Categorization and analogy are flipsides of the very same mental process"
> (Douglas Hofstadter 2013)

1. Introduction

In this paper I will broadly consider what the role is of analogy in the way we learn language (including grammatical categories), what its place is in the system of grammar that each individual adult language user develops, and finally how analogy helps to explain what happens in language change, including processes of grammaticalization and constructionalization. Foundational in my thinking

https://doi.org.10.1075/slcs.202.04fis
© 2018 John Benjamins Publishing Company

about analogy are a number of assumptions that are generally acknowledged in the greater part of the linguistic community, such as (i) the idea that the principles and/or constraints that operate in language acquisition also operate in language change; (ii) that linguistics should be concerned with the production and comprehension of language by speakers/hearers, and that, therefore, linguists should concentrate on language *processing*, and on language output – which, of course, first and foremost provides our data – only as a product that is *not* separate from processing (see e.g. Noël 2017); (iii) that all human beings are born with a propensity for language, whatever that propensity entails.

As a historical linguist and syntactician, I will concentrate on how analogy may help explain how categories and constructions emerge and change. In this I will take quite a broad view of constructions, including not only traditional lexical categories such as nouns, verbs, adjectives when they play a syntactic role, or more complex syntactic categories (constituents) such as NP, VP, PP etc., but also larger constructions involving relational categories (such as subject, object etc.), functional categories (agent, theme etc.), and more broadly the position and word order of linguistic elements in the clause.[1] Constructions combine form and meaning, which, I would argue, always form a whole and cannot be treated as separate in linguistic processing.[2] Meaning, of course, also involves pragmatic and discourse aspects, as well as prosody.[3] The grammar thus consists of a collection (or better a 'network') of form and function pairings that can be present or may arise on all possible linguistic levels, from morphophonology to syntax and discourse. The constructions may be quite concrete (micro) or quite abstract (macro), or combinations of the two. Just as with the traditional categories, constructions can be distinguished from each other and be put into categories in so far as they share a number of features (both formal and functional) which distinguish them from other constructions. Also, as in the grammaticalization model and differently from the formal generative model, I will consider constructions to have fuzzy edges:[4] there is no clear distinction between the lexical and grammatical levels,

1. In this I follow Croft (2001), who writes: "everything from words to the most general syntactic and semantic rules can be represented as constructions" (p. 17), and "constructions are the primitive units of syntactic representation" (p. 18).

2. Pace Vincent and Börjars (2010: 290), who argue for a model which does not assume that "form and content are structurally tied together"; they likewise claim that "linguistic form and function do not necessarily change together" (ibid.: 296).

3. As proposed in thetical grammar in Kaltenböck et al. (2011); Kaltenböck & Heine (2014); Heine (this volume).

4. Probably not on the utterance level as part of actual discourse, but on a metalinguistic level.

they can shift but also be relatively firm or isolated, depending on their frequency, their place in the larger structure and the level of abstraction of the structure itself.

The purpose of this paper is first of all to provide insight into the role played by analogy in language learning and processing, and, secondly, to put in a plea for a more central role for analogy in an explanation of how language changes. Analogy is prominent in usage-based approaches to language, i.e. in models such as construction grammar and to a somewhat lesser extent in traditional studies of grammaticalization (cf. Fischer 2011), where form and meaning are deemed equally important. In Section 2, I will therefore first consider the place given to analogy in these two models. Section 3 will then explore the phenomenon of analogy itself. It will pay attention (Section 3.1) to the interesting ideas that Hermann Paul, one of the Neogrammarians, voiced with respect to analogy, emphasizing the importance he attached to it for both language learning and change. His writings on analogy were largely forgotten in the new grammatical models that developed in the second half of the 20th century. Section 3.2 next shows how analogy was given a new lease of life in cognitive science, echoing many of Paul's ideas almost a hundred years after his work was first published. Section 4 will address the question of how the 'reborn' notion of analogy may help historical linguists to acquire a better understanding of the forces at work in language change. Section 5 concludes.

2. Analogy in usage-based models: Construction grammar and grammaticalization

Construction grammar [CxG] is first and foremost concerned with providing an inventory of all the possible constructions in a grammar, and elucidating the connections and differences between them. In this wider approach, it differs from the standard grammaticalization model in that the latter usually concentrates on just one construction centered around a lexical item, which grammaticalizes (cf. De Smet & Fischer 2017). Most CxG linguists follow a usage-based model to explain how constructions are learned and produced, making use of corpora and corpus-based methodologies for their constructional analysis. Most of their work so far has been in synchrony but they have more recently also moved to a diachronic approach, cf. e.g. Bergs & Diewald (2008), Traugott & Trousdale (2013), Hilpert (2013), and Barðdal et al. (2015).

One of the problems within the diachronic construction approach is to decide on what hierarchical level constructions may play a role in change, and how many constructions may be involved in any change. In the discussion of synchronic construction models, all possible structures are included, from isolated words to the most abstract word orders, such as the English P NP order in prepositional phrases and the SVO order of transitive declarative clauses (cf. e.g. Goldberg 2013; Hoffmann 2013). Hilpert (2013), however, clearly hesitates to include such abstract constructions in his diachronic construction approach, presumably because there is little specific lexical or semantic content attached to these. He writes:

> If a highly general macro-construction is posited, there needs to be evidence that speakers actually entertain the generalization that is captured by that macro-construction. The process of paradigm formation, of what one might call the genesis of a macro-construction, is viewed here as the sum total of several individual, low-level constructional changes that result in mutual formal assimilation.
> (Hilpert 2013: 11)

He adds that the above-mentioned generalizations are *epiphenomenal*; they are subject to change, but they cannot cause change themselves (p. 15). Similarly Traugott (2008a: 235, 236) notes that "overarching macro-abstractions" are "linguists' extrapolations"; they are "the overarching frame within which particular changes can be described"; she adds that "the macro-constructions are highly abstract schemas, and it is not here that such *attraction* operates"; rather, speakers "match parts of constructs (tokens) based on one construction (…) to parts of a (…) different construction, given pragmatic and other contexts that make such a match plausible" (p. 238, emphasis added). Traugott (2008b: 33–34) further clarifies the concept of "attraction" (/"attractor sets") and seems to have shifted somewhat in that here more attention is paid to the possible influence of more abstract constructions: "constructions highlight the force of analogy rather than reanalysis"; more precisely "each entering item undergoes local reanalysis [these are 'constructs', on a concrete level, OF] but the attracting force is analogy, alignment with an already existing pattern" (p. 33). She also still notes, however, that "[i]t appears (…) that the 'imposition' by a construction is only partial. A question to be researched then is at what hierarchic level this imposition (to the extent that it occurs) is most likely to occur" (ibid.).

This constructionist way of thinking about reanalysis and analogy can be seen as a left-over of earlier ideas current in grammaticalization studies. Thus, for Hopper and Traugott (2003: 39; 63–9) analogy was a secondary force, something that follows reanalysis but does not drive it. Recent studies on diachronic construction grammar still prioritize the "pragmatic", the "local" and the "immediate" linguistic context (Traugott & Trousdale 2013: 203, 207, 206 respectively). They emphasize the syntagmatic plane in terms of pragmatic inferencing and reanalysis, rather than the paradigmatic plane on which analogy works (for the latter view, see Fischer 2011). Traugott (2013: 230) writes:

> [T]he contribution of contexts is different prior to and after constructionalization. […] prior to constructionalization pragmatic modulation and use with preferred

> lexical subclasses (host class sets) occur. The context here may be understood to be the local network context [...]. Post-constructionalization new construction-types may be formed on the schematic template;

And cf. also Traugott (2015: 51): "Since reanalysis can occur independently of analogy and accompanies analogy understood as a mechanism (analogization), it encompasses more changes and is therefore primary". We see the same ideas in Barðdal and Gildea (2015: 17–8), who discuss "three common steps in the creation of a new construction". These steps involve: (i) a change in the semantics of a construction due to its being used in certain contexts; (ii) the innovative semantic function then motivates a change in the analysis of the syntactic component of the structure; (iii) this is followed by subsequent analogical extensions.[5]

A different view, giving much more space to analogy, is found in De Smet (2012: 604, and see also De Smet 2016):

> traditionally conceived reanalysis has been criticized as a mechanism of change on the grounds that it cannot explain how exactly language users home in on the target of change (Fischer 2007, De Smet 2009). One solution proposed is that *reanalysis often hinges on an underlying analogy*, since a new structural representation can only be assigned to an existing surface sequence if that representation is already available in the grammar. (emphasis added)

Returning now to Traugott's (2008b) question quoted above, we indeed need to find out "at what hierarchic level this imposition" (i.e. analogical influence imposed by one construction on another) "is most likely to occur". The big question concerning the role of analogy is, in other words, not only how strong the force of analogy is, but also what exactly makes a match plausible.

It is difficult to see where in Traugott's continuum of constructions (micro-, meso-, macro-),[6] an abstract structure would become 'too macro' for Traugott

5. Two of the editors further mention in their introduction that all the instances discussed in the papers included in the volume follow this particular scheme, with the exception of the contribution by Lotte Sommerer on the development of the definite article in Old English. Sommerer (2015) argues that the development is shaped first and foremost by the presence of an already existent abstract Determiner NP structure.

Similar observations are also found in Fried (2013: 424), who likewise emphasizes the immediate "local context, which is characterized by a confluence of factors (semantic-pragmatic, syntagmatic, etc.)" in cases of change, with *the constructional dimension only becoming relevant at a later stage of the change* (p. 427, emphasis added), and cf. also Trousdale (2016: 76), who likewise privileges reanalysis over analogy.

6. Trousdale (2012: 171) gives a convenient overview of what the various types of constructions involve. Macro-constructions are the most abstract, which Traugott (2008a) considers primitive sets, probably universal in terms of their function, while meso-constructions involve sets

to be able to still consider it a possible crucial construction operating in change. The problem, of course, is that the influence of highly abstract structures in language processing is as yet difficult to gauge. We need to study in greater depth how language acquisition and language change take place to see what kind of influence macro-constructions may indeed have on the development of language in individual learning and, more generally in change.[7]

As to method, one way to explain the emergence of a new construction or the disappearance of an existing one, is the use of quantitative techniques with which the various constructions involved in a constructional change or generalization can be compared and elucidated.[8] This is what Hilpert advocates for the diachronic approach:

> The starting point of such a procedure would be a complex data set of examples that may vary along multiple dimensions [such as position, lexical category, collocational characteristics, function, relative frequency etc. OF]. In order to find 'a construction,' that is, a generalization that speakers make, it is necessary to find *islands of regularity* in the *variation of the data set* [...]. By searching the data for subsets of examples that share characteristic traits, candidates for constructionhood can be selected and investigated. (Hilpert 2013: 203, emphasis added)

The advantage of such a method is that one gets a fairly precise picture (ideally) of the changes taking place, because the results are presented in easily interpretable figures and schemas, which the high-tech digital programs provide. It makes the change look convincing because it is nicely visualized and because it is based on large and increasingly larger corpora, on proven computational methods and the statistics carried out on them. But there is also a disadvantage. The outcome all depends on what one puts into it, i.e. what "variation in the data set" is crucial,

---

of constructions similar in behaviour, such as 'a type of/a sort of/ a kind of' (see below), with micro-constructions representing any individual type, e.g. all instances of 'kind of x'.

7. Evidence from substratum influence shows that broader syntactic constructions may be involved, i.e. word-order patterns from the substrate may be used in the grammar of imperfect learners. An interesting case in this connection is the influence of Mandarin Chinese on Singapore English described by Bao (2010). He shows how "English grammatical features acquire [...] usage patterns from their Chinese counterparts" (p. 1736) through formal and functional similarities between English and the Chinese substratum dialects. In other words, language contact, which must be considered a frequent phenomenon, may lead to change by means of abstract/macro-constructions.

8. Such as HCFA or Hierarchical Configural Frequency Analysis (which can "determine the prototype structure of a construction and its variants" (Hilpert 2013: 57), e.g. the interaction between variants across registers, or syntactic contexts or time periods) or MDS (Multidimensional Scaling, used to "analyze different entities in terms of their mutual variables" (ibid.: 66).

how many "islands of regularity" are needed? It has been shown, for instance, that quite abstract word-order changes (where there are few 'islands of regularity', that is regularity in the recurrence of the same concrete elements) may have a direct effect on the emergence of new constructions (see further Section 4).

For synchronic purposes, Steels (2011, 2013) has developed an intricate framework containing preliminary or "transient structures" against which each actual construction can be matched.[9] These transient structures represent all the information necessary to produce or interpret a sentence or construction. Thus, each one contains a syntactic as well as a semantic unit, with boxes containing all the relevant features, as shown in Figure 1.

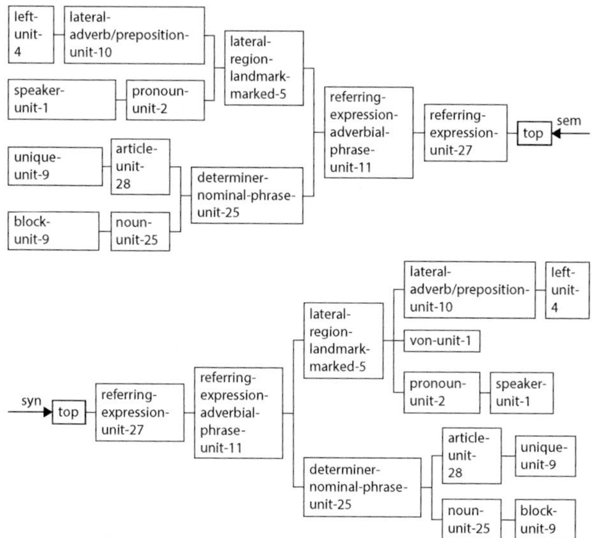

Figure 1. Transient structure created during the production or parsing of the German phrase *der Block links von mir* 'the block on my left'. The top of the figure shows the semantic pole and the bottom one the syntactic pole (from Steels 2013: 155)

The system Steels has developed is ingenious. With the configurations of all possible features, existing constructions can be matched and merged in a *fluid* way, and through the separation of syntactic and semantic mappings, transient (temporary) structures can be used fluidly to understand what elements may play a role in both the production as well as the interpretation process. Other advantages of the model are (i) that the constructions receive "an associated score that reflects their past success" when actually used by speakers/hearers (ibid.: 159) so that frequency and entrenchment can be measured over time; (ii) that the system allows backtracking

9. These transient structures are themselves based on existing constructions but can be used to produce and interpret future constructions.

to help interpret such things as garden-path sentences; (iii) that it organizes the constructions in sets and networks; and (iv) that the system can take into account the influence of quite abstract macro-structures, which Steels perceptively notes "may not be immediately obvious to the grammar designer" (ibid.: 163).

Such a system of transient structures (rather than rules), which are derived from actual usage, would be of great advantage also to the diachronic linguist who wishes to find out which macro- and micro-structures in one period may have contributed to the development of a new construction in another period. However, Steels' fluid synchronic processing system needs more testing and development before it can be adequately applied to the diachronic situation. We need to know more about the range of possibilities at work in synchronic processing in order to gain an idea of the set of constructions that may be involved in any particular change. It is not clear for instance, how much pragmatic information is in fact included in his model, and how much phonological detail. Also, is the system fluid enough to allow connections between phonetics and semantics (these areas look unconnected in Steel's schema, given in Figure 2), i.e. can it deal with onomatopoeia and sound symbolism, and, within semantics, will it be able to take account of the influence of antonyms, next to synonyms and ambiguity, which *are* part of the deal according to Steels?

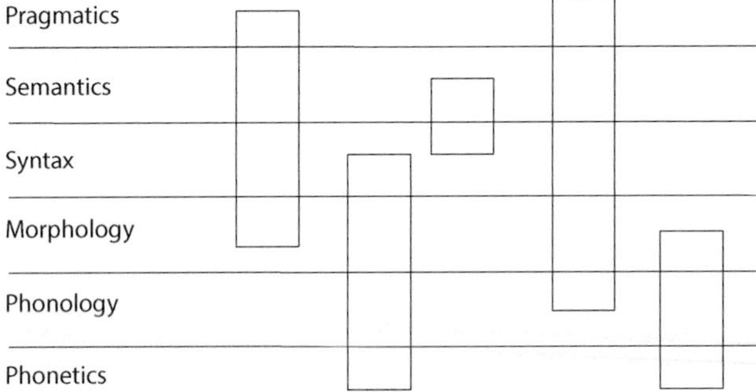

Figure 2. Constructions package constraints that potentially concern any level of linguistic description cutting the traditional levels of linguistic analysis vertically (after Steels 2011: 8)

Another question is how metaphorical or metonymic shifts are accounted for, since these depend to a great extent on encyclopedic knowledge.

Ideally, synchronic and diachronic work should cross-fertilize one another in these attempts. By looking at what may happen in diachronic change with an open mind, we may be able to discover more about the kinds of principles and the level and type of constructions that may play a role in the way language learning takes place in both production and interpretation.

In spite of these difficulties, it is clear that the CxG model has a strong advantage over the grammaticalization model, which is hampered by the fact that only one construction is usually looked at, which is normally seen as undergoing a unidirectional development from a more lexical to a more grammatical construction/function. Other constructions that may have influenced the development are generally not considered unless they are of a clearly parallel type (as is for instance the case in the study of *sort of/kind of/type of* in Denison 2002, Traugott 2008b; for more discussion of this aspect, see the articles in De Smet et al. 2015, and also Fischer & De Smet 2017). The grammaticalization model almost forces one to look for only typical instances of grammaticalization clines that have run enough of their course to become visible as such. When it takes other constructions into account, these usually strongly depend on Hilpert's 'islands of regularity' i.e. sharing quite similar lexical elements and fixed structures, as is the case in the *sort/type of* NP structure referred to above. The construction approach is a big step forward, because the input may consist of a number of independent constructions that may form a family, even if the 'regularity' is not immediately obvious.

A good example of the advantages of the construction approach is Traugott (2008c), which deals with the development of negative attitudinal '*all*-clefts', as in *All he said was thanks*. It takes into account, next to the special dialogic contexts in which the cleft develops, a number of other constructions that must have led to its development, such as the rise of cleft constructions in general, the increase in dialogic *wh*-clefts, as in *What he did was unacceptable* (which evince a similarly negative attitude), and the fact that both clefts occur most frequently with the same verbs *say* and *do* (which provides a concrete form of analogy). Other factors, that Traugott does not mention, but which may well have contributed to the development of the *all*-cleft, are found in the fact that both the *wh*-cleft and the attitudinal *all*-cleft do *not* show a *that*-relative pronoun on the surface. This is grammatically conditioned in the *wh*-cleft because the *what* element contains its own relative (e.g. *What he did was* ... = 'that which' *he did was* ...), but this was a later development in the *all*-cleft, only possible after the macro-construction without a relative *that* in object position became entrenched in Middle English (see Fischer et al. 2017: 102). The absence of this relative led to the loss of *all* being interpreted as a quantified noun, thus preparing the way for a degree reading. Other constructions that may have played a role are similar negative attitudinal expressions also containing *all*, which likewise "occur in contexts of adversativity and refutation" (Traugott 2008c: 161), such as *for all that ever* (see (1)), very frequent since Middle English, and *for all* + NP (in (2)), already frequently found in Old English:

(1) *Lo argus which þat had an hundred eyen / **For al þat euer** he couþe poure or prien / 3et was he blent* (Chaucer, Clerk's Prol. 2111–13)
'Lo Argus, who had one hundred eyes, yet, for all he could pore over or pry into, he was still deceived'

(2) a. OE: *naþelæs **for eallum þissum griðe & gafole** hi ferdon æghweder flocmælum & heregodon ure earme folc, & hi rypton & slogon.* (*ChronC* (O'Brien O'Keeffe) 1006.7)
'nevertheless **for all/in spite of this truce and tribute**, they went everywhere in troops and harried our poor people, and robbed and killed them'

b. ME: *Reseamiradie was taken þat ilk yere, / In Wales þorgh a spie, **for all his powere** .* (Peter Langtoft's Chronicle, p. 247, 14th cent.)
'Reseamiradie was captured that same year/in Wales through a spy, **in spite of all his power**'

In other words, what we need to find out in more detail is what constructions may be part of the 'family', how families arise. For this, it is essential that historical linguists cast their net as widely as possible when they go through corpora to find out what constructions may have contributed to the formation of a new one. We need to find out how many 'islands of regularity' may have been involved, and what may this regularity consist of. We need to know more about the kind of associations that can occur in the way constructions get linked to each other. I hope to show in this paper that a better understanding of analogy is useful in this attempt. It is time therefore to take a closer look at analogy to see how it works.

3. Analogy

The concept of analogy has a very long history, but it is only recently that is becoming more fashionable again after having been swept away by the generative avalanche when analogy was thrown out of the window as being too loose to be put into formal rules (cf. e.g. Kiparsky 1974; Lightfoot 1979: 358ff.).[10] In a way this relegation to the back benches of linguistics started with the Neogrammarians when the new empirical scientific approach entered linguistics. For linguists concerned with the construction of language families via sound change, analogy was awkward, an exception, something to fall back on only when the rules or laws did not apply. Most Neogrammarians saw analogy only in terms of diachrony, not

10. Lightfoot writes (1979: 371): "analogy is [...] in no sense directly represented in those grammars [i.e. of speakers]". Instead he proposes the so-called Transparency Principle, which *is* said to be present in grammars.

in terms of synchrony as in the classical age. In this light, it is remarkable that a number of Neogrammarians, notably Paul, Brugmann and Von der Gabelenz (for the latter, see Willems 2016), gave analogy a much more prominent place both in language change *and* in language learning and language use. The link between these two domains, change and learning, now seems generally accepted, but, interestingly enough, for Hermann Paul this was already quite obvious. In this section, I will first very briefly look at Paul's ideas on analogy, showing how 'modern' he already was, and then make a connection with what is happening today in cognitive science.

3.1 Analogy and Herman Paul's *Prinzipien der Sprachgeschichte* (1880 [1909])

Chapter 4 on semantic change and Chapter 5 on analogy in Paul's *Prinzipien* are the most relevant for us here. In both chapters Paul strongly emphasizes a number of facts connected with analogy that now seem to be accepted as common knowledge in usage-based models and cognitive science. These are indicated under (a) to (g) below. I will briefly refer to each case he brings forward, adding extra information where necessary; the original German text will be given in footnotes.[11]

a. The importance of situational learning, i.e. learning from experience through the recurrence of similar forms/constructions in similar situations.[12]
b. The importance of frequency; the more frequent, the more entrenched an item or construction becomes.[13]

11. I refer to the original German in the notes because an earlier translation by H.A. Strong (1889), is a free and in places totally inadequate translation. Recently a new translation appeared – no doubt due to the renewed interest in analogy – by Auer & Murray (2015), but this only covers parts of a small number of chapters, the important Chapter 4 was not included.

12. "Für das Individuum ist der Anfang zum Übergang einer okkasionellen Bedeutung in das Usuelle gemacht, wenn bei dem Anwenden oder Verstehen derselben *die Erinnerung an ein früheres Anwenden oder Verstehen mitwirkend wird*; der vollständige Abschluss des Überganges ist erreicht, wenn nur diese Erinnerung wirkt, wenn Anwendung und Verständnis ohne jede Beziehung auf die sonstige usuelle Bedeutung des Wortes erfolgt" (Paul 1909 [4th edn.]: 84, emphasis added).

13. "Denn zum Wesen des Prozesses gehört es ja eben, dass er durch wiederholte gleichmässige Anwendung der anfänglich nur okkasionellen Bedeutung zu Stande kommt und dieser muss ein Verstehen wenigstens von Seiten eines Teiles der Verkehrsgenossen entsprechen, und das Verstehen ist für diese wiederum mindestens ein Anfang des Prozesses" (Paul, ibid.: 84).

c. Learning leading to categorization: similar (objects in) similar situations are given the same word/sign.[14]
d. The centrality of our body leading to the use of personification and metaphor.[15] Here Paul provides examples such as: *Die Sonne zieht Wasser, der Baum treibt Knospen* (lit. 'the sun draws water, the tree drives buds' = is sprouting); *schreiende Farben, das Gewehr versagt* (lit. 'crying (= loud) colours, the gun refuses = misfires').
e. The use of metonymy made possible by learning from experience. As an example he mentions the fact that when someone notices a sail on the horizon, he knows from experience that there will be a boat attached to the sail because he has never in his experience seen a sail without a boat (see Paul, ibid.: 98).
f. The building up of patterns/groupings into larger networks (Paul, ibid.: 106). Esper (1973: 39) neatly summarizes Paul's ideas on 'networks':

> There is hardly a word in any language which is not a member of one or more associatively related groups; the ease of formation and the strength of the connections depend upon the degree to which the units have been impressed by virtue of the *frequencies of occurrence* of the individual words and *the number of possible analogies*. These proportional equations are not only operative in linguistic change; they serve also in the analogical creation of all those forms – words and syntactic collocations – which a speaker has never or seldom heard.
> (emphasis added)

Single words, Paul (ibid.: 106) writes, get connected in the *Seele* 'soul', and through this arises a multitude of bigger and smaller groupings, all interconnected. Paul refers all the time to the *Seele*, but it is not difficult to transfer this in modern terms to the neural network in our brains, with its billions of neurons connected by synapses as described for instance in Pulvermüller (2002). Paul also notes (ibid.: 109) that words occur in constructions, which may be concrete (*stofflich*) as well as structural (*formal*), that those words or constructions are all interconnected on various levels via both their form or their function or both at the same time. As concrete examples he gives the similarities of sound and function, as in the Latin datives *libro* and *anno*, or *mensae-rosae*, or the German past tenses *gab/nahm* or

14. "So bildet sich vom Beginn der Spracherlernung an die Gewohnheit nicht bloss einen, sondern mehrere Gegenstände oder Vorgänge, nicht bloss gleiche, sondern auch nur irgendwie ähnliche gegenstände oder Vorgänge mit dem gleichen Worte zu bezeichnen, und diese Gewohnheit bleibt, auch wenn Anfangs übersehene Unterschiede später bemerkt werden, da sie fortwährend durch den Vorgang der Erwachsenen unterstützt wird" (Paul ibid.: 85–86).

15. "Die Gewohnheit des Menschen die Vorgänge an den leblosen Dingen *nach Analogie der eigenen Tätigkeit* aufzufassen hat in der Sprache viele Spuren hinterlassen" (Paul, ibid.: 97, emphasis added).

sagte/liebte. He also notes that the importance of similarity in sound decreases when more structural connections are concerned so that we discover the pattern DATIVE behind *libro/anno* and *mensae-rosae*, and the positive/comparative pattern: *good/better* through more formally concrete examples such as *nice/nicer*. And in a similar fashion, without any similarity in sound, we will discover that the construction *spricht Karl* 'speaks Karl' is similar to *schreibt Fritz* 'writes Fritz'. It is here that function becomes more and more important. This process would later, in cognitive science come to be described as the development from 'clang'-constructions to structure or system mapping (see Section 3.2, note 25).

g. The role of frequency in connection with formal and semantic saliency.

Paul (ibid: 109)[16] emphasizes that the strength of the connections not only depends on frequency but also on the formal and semantic strength of the analogies, which simultaneously make the process more and more automatic. He discusses here the gradual loss of the double object construction with two accusatives in German due to the fact that the double object pattern with a dative and accusative is much stronger (both in frequency and in semantic coherence)[17] so that *Er lehrt mich*[ACC] *die Kunst*[ACC] is now normally *Er lehrt mir*[DAT] *die Kunst*. (Paul, ibid.: 112). This is reminiscent of Barðdal (2008: 167) who writes:

> Whether or not a low type frequency construction is productive depends entirely on the semantic coherence found between the types occurring in the relevant construction. In the history of Icelandic, the Dative subject construction became productive in the latter part of the 19th century, due to its increase in semantic coherence, while the semantically low-coherent Nom-Gen construction, for instance, has not shown signs of productivity in the history of Icelandic.

Because of the strength of this analogical way of learning, and of the importance of the connections, it is not surprising, as Paul notes, that those patterns that are not supported by connections and/or do not occur frequently enough (or, we could add, are not semantically salient enough), will not be able to withstand the power of the better connected groups or patterns. Hence they tend to disappear. Others may increase as shown in Barðdal's Icelandic study.

16. "Die Gruppierung vollzieht sich um so leichter und wird um so fester einerseits, je grösser die Übereinstimmung in Bedeutung und Lautgestaltung ist, anderseits, je intensive die Elemente eingeprägt sind, die zur Gruppenbildung befähigt sind."

17. This is in fact rather similar to the situation with double object constructions in English, which were originally formed with a dative and an accusative. They could survive in English without a preposition because formally and semantically they form a very coherent group in that the pattern is always one involving a beneficiary, the finite verb as a rule contains only one syllable (*give, send, buy* etc.), and is usually of Germanic rather than Latinate origin.

Paul also pays attention to more idiosyncratic instances of 'paradigmatic regrouping' on the lexical level. A word may change its sound shape through analogy if the sounds of an analogous word are close enough, as has happened for instance in vulgar Latin where classical *gravis-levis* became *grevis-levis* (but note not in German *leicht-schwer*, where there is no sound overlap) and Latin *prendere – reddere* became *prendere – rendere* in modern French (cf. Esper 1973: 68, 71). Quite clearly the sound-shape changes through the word being regrouped in another, very small, set. Something similar we see in current English in the pronunciation of *covert*, which is now often pronounced as [kəu'vɜ:t] like its antonym *overt*, rather than earlier ['kʌvət]. The phenomenon of folk etymology is essentially the same process, as when OE *angnægl* 'painful nail' becomes 'hangnail', or OE *brideguma* becomes *bridegroom* changing one of the morphemes (which for some reason has become infrequent, or is opaque) to a more familiar word similar in sound.[18] The similarity in sound or form in these cases is often more important than the similarity in meaning or function so that quite big 'jumps' in meaning are not unusual, as happened for instance in the Dutch word *gijzelaar* 'hostage', which has been changing into the meaning of 'terrorist' or 'hostage taker', under the influence of other words ending in *-aar*, which mostly had active meaning as in *wandelaar* 'walker', *verzamelaar* 'collector', *moordenaar* 'murderer' etc. In a similar way, Dutch *oubollig*, which originally meant 'comical, droll', now usually refers to something being old fashioned because of the association of *ou* (an opaque word) with *oud* 'old'.

A recent example in Dutch of paradigmatic regrouping on the lexico-syntactic level concerns so-called 'psych verbs'. These verbs can be used as causatives, and a number of them occur in a non-causative pattern with a reflexive pronoun, e.g. *zich herinneren* 'to remember', *zich realiseren* 'to realise', *zich ergeren* 'to be irritated'. It is not surprising to find that some other verbs close in meaning also start using that pattern, so that the reflexive is now very frequent with the non-causative verb *beseffen* 'realise', which is becoming *zich beseffen*, while the causative verb *irriteren* (*iets irriteert mij* 'something irritates me') can now also be used as a reflexive, i.e. *zich irriteren*, on analogy of (*zich*) *ergeren* which can be both causative and reflexive. Using Google I found the reflexive pattern *ik irriteer me* 317.000 times and causative *het irriteert me* only 70.900 times, while *ik besef me dat …* occurs in

18. One anonymous reviewer notes that "widespread illiteracy in the past" may have a role to play in cases of folk etymology. It is possible that some instances of folk etymology are stopped in this way, but it is a well-known fact that it still occurs even in standard written languages as an often successful attempt at de-obscuring words, as Malkiel (1993) has convincingly shown.

10% of cases where *ik besef dat …* was once the norm.[19] Similarly in French *se rappeler* acquired the preposition *de* through its relation with *se souvenir de*.

Note that what happens here in processing is not reanalysis (as there is no reanalysis on a syntagmatic plane), but a form of re-grouping: A structure or word may become part of another group or paradigm through analogical thinking because it shares certain features with this group.[20] Important is that these features (Hilpert's 'islands of regularity') may be quite loose. The above examples in fact show that analogy need not be strictly proportional, i.e. that it involves more than analogical extension or its opposite 'levelling', which represent the two forms of analogy to which most linguists have restricted the phenomenon (as if language follows some mathematical equation, cf. Hofstadter & Sander 2013: 15).

I would argue that such analogical 'jumps' are also possible on a higher, more abstract level in syntax, where the composite parts in a similar way may be associated with other elements in other constructions, even when the constructions do not fully match in meaning but are somehow loosely connected in discourse or experience.[21] Before we look at some examples in syntax in Section 4, we will first consider the force of analogy as a deep-seated cognitive principle in language learning.

3.2 Analogy and cognitive science

I will concentrate on the most important findings supporting analogy as a fundamental principle in language learning and language use. These are:

i. the idea that all our utterances involve analogy;
ii. the distinction between low-level and high-level perception;
iii. analogy as a tool in learning (including language acquisition) involving progressive alignment or system mapping.

The important point made in (i) is that analogy is not something odd or different or creative, but it is what we do all the time. It is useful to follow Croft's biological

---

19. It is interesting to note that King Willem Alexander in a recent interview (26 April 2017) on Dutch television used '*ik besef me dat …* twice, and the form without the reflexive once. As in this case, it occurs most frequently in the first person, maybe also because of a possible association with the so-called ethical dative *me*, which occurs quite frequently in constructions involving personal emotion, such as *Daar heeft hij* **me** *toch een smak gemaakt* 'There made he *me* a big fall!'

20. Note that this is quite different from the standard grammaticalization model, where changes are usually considered to be driven by *syntagmatic* pragmatic inferencing (i.e. reanalysis).

21. Kahneman (2011) also refers to the fact that people tend to make 'illogical jumps' in their thinking because, when thinking fast, they often use their intuition and experience rather than their ratio.

metaphor (2000: 3ff.) here. Croft writes that all linguistic utterances involve replication. *Normal replication* preserves the system as is, it provides for the system's stability. *Altered replication* occurs when a form or structure is replicated with a small change, leading to language variation. This could next lead to *differential replication* by a shift in the frequencies of the variants found, causing the earlier form to die out. Replication in all three cases is done by imitation i.e. analogy. A variant form on the sound level may occur when a speaker produces a form with a slightly higher vowel (for whatever reason: emotion, emphasis, physical condition etc.). A variant form on the lexical or structural level may occur in communication through the fact that the hearer thinks the form has meaning *x* while in fact the speaker uses it with meaning *y*, or someone interprets the construction as belonging to category *x* while in fact it was produced as category *y*. In all cases the difference is usually so slight that the language user notes no difference.

The idea then is that all our utterances and interpretations are based on comparison, on the experience of earlier forms used in earlier situations. We learn words that way, and we learn constructions that way, both concrete and abstract. Comparison is the key. And therein lies the snag! Our comparative faculties are not perfect, and small misalignments are easy to make, causing ripples in the network. However, this imperfection of our comparative faculties is now seen as an advantage because comparison across forms and situations can never reach the 100 per cent mark; almost each case is in some small way different from the other (cf. Hofstadter 1995, 2001; Hofstadter & Sander 2013). So, in order not to clutter up our brains, we learn to ignore irrelevant details for our own good.[22] Deacon (1997: 76) emphasizes this *inattentiveness* as the essential point in the workings of analogy. He writes that we often do not notice a new variant because of some limitation involving the interpreter (due to surrounding noise, boredom, lack of knowledge or interest, etc.). In other words, recognizing a new variant as indeed a *new* form, is *not* the norm.[23] This is how new forms or new interpretations may sneak in without us being aware.

22. We see this clearly, for instance, in the way our phonological system develops: we only remember/distinguish those 'sounds' (phonemes) which make a semantic difference. E.g. in English, speakers distinguish /r/ and /l/ as phonemes because words like *lung* and *rung* refer to two different things. For Japanese and Chinese speakers /r/ and /l/ are allophones because they are not used to make a distinction in meaning; hence they also find it hard to distinguish them when speaking English.

23. He illustrates this with the example of a moth camouflaged like the bark of a tree. The moth may escape being eaten by a bird if the bird is inattentive and interprets the moth's wings as being part of the tree: "What makes the moth's wings iconic, is an interpretive process produced by the bird, not something about the moth's wings. Their coloration was *taken* to be an icon

It is clear that perception plays an important role here, an aspect which has also received more attention of late, especially in connection with research in Artificial Intelligence. This concerns point (ii) above. (Note that both (i) and (ii) emphasize fluidity rather than fixed rules or categories). Chalmers et al. (1992: 1–2) distinguish low-level perception (perception of raw sensory information by the sense organs, eye, ear etc., i.e. purely physical perception) from high-level perception, and they situate both on a (conceptual) cline. High-level perception is extremely flexible (ibid.: 2) and is achieved through filtering and organization (ibid.: 1). High-level perception involves first of all object recognition by being able to see similarities (e.g. between an apple and another apple), followed by grasping physical relations (*a* is above/under/inside *b*), and next abstract relations (metaphorical shift from: *in the pool* to *in the party*), leading to a network of relations within a complex situation (ibid.: 2). They state that the distinction of high-level perception leads to mental representation, which may be long-term and short-term (cf. long- and short-term memory) (ibid.: 4), and in this way, these mental representations become part of a speaker's network system. In all this, frequency plays an enormously important role. The authors add that analogical thinking not only guides our perception, it in turn affects our perception (ibid.: 11ff.). Because it has become part of our experience, it affects our next experience.

Chalmers et al. also focus attention on the fact that humans have different understandings (representations) depending on experience, belief, culture, context etc. We have different representations of an object or situation at different times; paper for instance may mean combustible material when we sit in front of a fire, but it may also be sheets to write on.[24] In other words, conventional words or categories arise through usage and experience. These objects thus occur with different functions and hence are represented by different relations within our system (Paul's different groupings). This means that rigid representations (rules etc.) may be fine for stereotypes i.e. for macro-structural patterns that occur very frequently and thus have become conventional, but in the long run they will prove to be a dead end. Chalmers et al. emphasize, therefore, that "flexible, context-dependent, easily adaptable representations will be recognized as an essential part of any accurate model of cognition" (ibid.: 20).

Turning to (iii), it is useful to point to the work of Gentner, Holyoak, Hofstadter and many others on the role of analogy in learning. Their work is supported all along by psychological experiments, and it also follows neurological research.

because of something the bird *didn't* do. (…) It applied the same interpretive perceptual process to the moth as it did to the bark", even though in reality they are *not* the same" (1997: 76).

24. Chalmers et al. refer here to an example used by the philosopher William James in his *Psychology. The Briefer Course* (1892: 222).

What is interesting is that the results that come out of this corroborate in essence many of the intuitions voiced by Hermann Paul. A central claim in their work is that a process of 'progressive alignment', from concrete similarity to abstract relational similarity, is an important bootstrapping process in children's learning. Various aspects are discussed in their articles, from which I will highlight two main points, namely that children indeed proceed from object learning to relational learning, from surface commonalities to more abstract ones, and secondly, from syntagmatic association to paradigmatic association.

The first process is described by Gentner and Namy (2006: 298) as follows:

> From early in development, children believe that if two things have the same name, they share some common properties. But in order to use the name themselves and apply it to new exemplars, children must work out which common properties matter. Early in development, children often focus on perceptual similarity, particularly shape similarity [...]. But children clearly move beyond salient perceptual properties and come to appreciate the deeper commonalities that underlie word meanings. We suggest that *comparison processes are fundamental to this ability*, ... words are invitations to compare. Children spontaneously compare things that have the same name. ... [T]his simple act of comparing two things can lead to an enriched understanding of the word's meaning, by elevating the salience of relational commonalities among its referents that might otherwise not be noticed. *This process enables children to override compelling perceptual commonalities in favor of deeper conceptual ones.* (emphasis added)

Thus, instead of focusing on an object match between the circles in Figure 3 (a) and (b) as indicated by the black arrow, they begin to focus on the relational match indicated by the grey arrow,

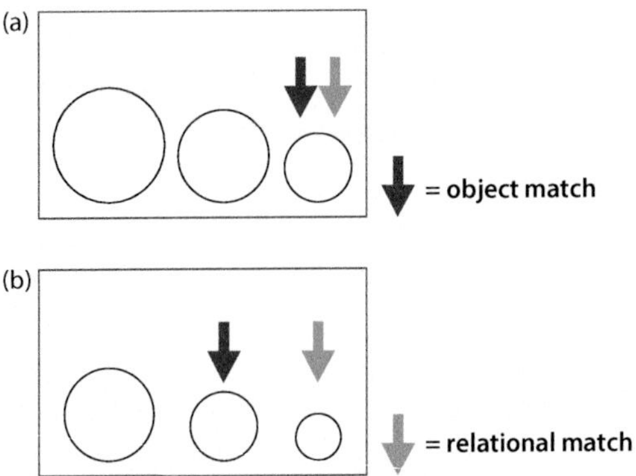

Figure 3. From Gentner & Smith (2012: 131)

They also experimented with adults and found similar results (ibid.: 297–8). According to structure-mapping theory, this relational functional focus arises because when people compare two things, they implicitly seek to find correspondences between their *conceptual* representations, between two situations, a process referred to as structural alignment (cf. Gentner 2003).

The stages that children go through in learning can be summarized as follows, with stages i, ii representing the concrete taxonomic conceptual stage, and stages iii-iv the thematic (structural) conceptual stage (cf. Gentner et al. 2011):

i. Plain object recognition comes first, seeing that one object is like another (a taxonomic, purely perceptual stage cf. Kalénine et al. 2009: 1153)
ii. Learning the symbolic conventional name attached to a concrete object, enables seeing the similarity between them. Comparison across similar objects enables word learning; object nouns are the earliest words acquired [25]
iii. At age 3, children in experiments begin to see relations between objects via progressive structural alignment, first by comparing quite similar structures ('close' pairs) e.g. from seeing the relation between 'orange and knife' and 'apple and knife', up to a similar relation between 'tree and axe' ('far' pairs) (cf. Gentner 2010: 763; Gentner et al. 2011: 1176). Through the labelling of concrete objects, children are able to build up more abstract taxonomies, through lower order categorization (perceptually similar *dog/goat*) via less perceptually similar categories (*dog/tiger*), and with the help of associative (functional, contiguous) connections (*dog/cat; slippers/payamas*), children begin to 'recognize' a concrete object (noun) category
iv. At age 4–5, children can see the relation due to progressive alignment (comparison of similar relational situations) *without* the need for a relational noun (Gentner et al. 2011). They later (age 6) also see the relation when only a *single* exemplar of the relational category was shown. Through structural alignment of relational activities, from 'close pairs' to 'far pairs' children develop a more abstract 'recognition' of relational categories: "thematic relations are extracted from event schemas" (Kalénine et al. 2009: 1159). Children 'recognize' a concrete activity (verb) category.

We now return to the second important process in learning: the change from syntagmatic to paradigmatic association. Again, I have simply collected a number of important points:

- The learning of abstract categories like noun and verb is important for the shift from syntagmatic to paradigmatic association.

25. When objects become attached to labels (acquisition of word meaning), the similarity in the *form* of the label may also lead to grouping (i.e. similarity in sound-form representing object similarity). These are called 'clang-responses' (Ervin 1961: 363), and are found only with young children (Ervin 1961: 372).

- With age "there is an increase in the length and variety of sentences, so that the relative strength of the average syntagmatic association is less" (Ervin 1961: 362). In other words, because context variety increases, the association between contiguous words becomes less strong.
- At the same time there is "an increase in paradigmatic responses" in word-association experiments because "paradigmatic associates are more likely when the variety of verbal contexts of a stimulus-term is high relative to its frequency" (ibid.).
- "As vocabulary increases, children have more contextually similar responses in antonyms, synonyms and words drawn from the abstraction-hierarchy of the stimulus-word" (ibid.).
- Generally, paradigmatic (also called taxonomic) responses increase with age, with a definite shift "from a syntactic response to a paradigmatic response … between ages 6 and 8" (Entwisle et al. 1964: 28, cf. Hashimoto et al. 2007: 172).

From the above we may conclude that analogy is at work both on a very basic category (or construction) level, where form and meaning (function/situation) are still quite similar, to a more and more abstract level (by means of system mapping). Thus, the basis for analogical thinking may range from quite concrete to quite abstract, and all the shades in between. If this is the case in language learning, it will also be the case in language change. Their connection was already clearly made by Hermann Paul, as shown in Section 3.1. When looking at cases of morphosyntactic change in the next section, one of the difficulties will be to decide what constructions may be involved in the formation of a new one, or the loss of an old one. In addition, the more elements the construction that one is considering contains, the more different constructions (with their formal and functional similarities) may play a role in the emergence of that construction. That brings in another difficulty: how to weigh the influence of all these possible variants? Even so, since analogy is such an important basic principle, it should not deter us from seriously investigating the possible effects it may have on change.

4. The influence of analogy in morphosyntactic change

As argued above, analogy plays a role in processing all the time, and is most visible in the mistakes children make in language acquisition and in the synchronic variations that occur in language, which may affect the way it changes.[26] Analogy may

26. In principle, analogy plays the same role in child and adult processing, but since children are still in the process of learning as many constructions as possible and trying hard to make distinctions between them – whereas adults are confronted with a plethora of constructions that

cause the system of language to change imperceptibly from day to day, not in its most basic abstract schemas (macro-constructions), but in its more concrete and superficial (micro-)constructions. But of course the high-level abstract schemas may play a role in the change even when they don't change themselves because they are the overall frame within which the low-level or more concrete constructs change. Variation or variable forms contained in the individual systems of users may thus continuously provide the seeds for change.

I would now like to take a closer, but necessarily brief, look at a study concerning change where analogy is *not* invoked in order to find out whether analogy may have been involved after all, and then finally refer to two studies, where analogy is considered basic to the change.

4.1 A case study where analogy is not given a primary role

Hilpert in his book on *Constructional Change* (2013) is interested in finding out or showing to what extent certain low-level constructions form or begin to form one higher level construction or category, and what the forces are behind such a situation or development. A case he discusses in detail concerns the development of concessive parentheticals with *(al)though*. His three alternative hypotheses about their development are (i) did these parentheticals develop out of full clauses by means of morphosyntactic reduction and clause fusion, (ii) were they originally independent free adjuncts which are augmented with a subordinating conjunction, or (iii) "could it be that [they] were formed 'on the fly' as the products of analogy" (ibid.: 157).[27]

The possibility of analogy is studied on the basis of parallel parenthetical constructions with *if* and *while*, which, like *(al)though*, may be used concessively (as in 10b-c), next to their more usual conditional and temporal uses.

---

have already been entrenched –, children may be more likely to shift relatively infrequent or new constructions towards already existent ones (or mix them up), but this does not mean that their new constructions will necessarily remain beyond childhood and cause the language in general to change (cf. De Smet & Fischer 2017).

27. Another case Hilpert discusses at length (2013: 75–106) involves the development of *mine* and *thine* into *my* and *thy*, where he likewise does not see any analogical influence at work (in spite of the phonological similarity between the two forms, which he duly notes on p. 107), the reason being that first and second person "do not form a natural class" (p. 88). However, analogy *is* very likely here since first and second person *do* form a natural class in discourse terms (cf. e.g. Rice (2000: 182), who notes a major difference between first/second person on the one hand, and third person on the other: first/second person are speech participants, while third person are unspecified actors), and also in terms of animateness. In addition, it is interesting to note that Dutch children and non-standard speakers often change the independent possessives *mijne* 'mine' and *jouwe* 'your' (without any phonological similarity!) into *mijne* and *joune* .

(10) a. Power, although important, is not everything (Hilpert 2013: 156)
b. While a Democrat, he voted for Bush (ibid.: 168)
c. The taste is nice, if a little too salty (ibid.)

To keep the story short, analogy is dismissed because the different parentheticals in (10) are not sufficiently alike enough in the position they take in the sentence, and in the way they collocate with other structural elements such as nominals, adjectives, PPs etc. In other words, there are not enough 'islands of regularity' to make analogy possible.

I see a number of problems with this study, all of which have to be attended to before analogy can be dismissed as an important factor. First, the study considers only other semantically and structurally similar parentheticals that are likewise formed with conjunctions, while it neglects the role played by pragmatically similar adverbs such as *still, yet* and *even*, which also convey an unexpected contrast or circumstance in relation to the main clause; adverbs that, in addition, often co-occur with these same conjunctions, as in (11)c and d:

(11) a. *Even* today, Christians are killed "in the name of God"
b. Yet *still* today, my eyes are wet.
c. *Although* he is dead, he is *still* my protector, guide and mentor (https://twitter.com/marysahl2, retrieved October 2017)
d. *Even if* you don't love me, I'd *still* reach my hand to you. <http://www.searchquotes.com/search/> (retrieved October 2017)

Secondly, Hilpert's investigation makes use of the TIME corpus, which only covers the time space between 1920–2000; older periods are not considered. Thirdly, concessive parentheticals with *if* and *while* are themselves relatively new and far less frequent than the ones with *(al)though* (as Hilpert shows in Figure 5.2 on p. 182). And finally, as far as analogy is concerned, attention is only paid to structurally and positionally quite similar morphosyntactic elements, while other linguistic levels (e.g. discourse, intonation) are not considered.

There is no space to go into any great detail here. I will restrict myself to three observations. First of all, the use of *though* as an *adverb* has not been considered. It is well-known that it can be used in various positions in the clause by itself, just like the fuller parenthetical:

(12) a. The music, *though,* was *still* characterized by the terseness and pungency of expression he had cultivated during the lean years <https://books.google.nl/books?isbn=0199796033> (retrieved June 2015)
b. His band teacher did say he was surprised he was *still* walking *though.* <http://community.cookinglight.com/showthread.php?72589-NCAA-Who-will-win> (retrieved June 2015)

In these cases, it is clear that in semantic-pragmatic terms, the adverb expresses a contrast, something unexpected (as do *still* and *even* in (11) and *though* in (10a)), as is the case in concessives generally. In other words, these adverbs can easily be related to the parenthetical non-finite concessive clause.

Secondly, the use of *though* as both adverb and conjunction is very old; it dates back to Old English. As a conjunction, the OE cognate *þeah* is usually followed by the relative particle *þe* (as in (13));[28] as an adverb it is used by itself or in combination with *swa* (which use is rather similar to *even* or *still* in (11)). Significantly, I found quite a few examples in the Old English Dictionary Corpus[29] with the adverb *þeah* in circumstances similar to the modern construction, showing that the construction may in fact be quite old, see (14)–(17). The meaning of the adverb is always one of contrast (i.e. contrary to expectation) and has been variously translated as 'yet/however/notwithstanding'. Also of interest is the fact that the conjunction occurs with a full clause containing the copula *be*, as in (13). It would be a small step to leave out the copula in clauses like (13), thus also creating a 'modern' parenthetical non-finite clause. (14)-(17) are examples where the adverb *þeah* is used by itself, followed by an adjective or prepositional phrase, which together function very much like clauses such as (13), which contain the verb *be*.

(13) *Þa wearð hyre mod mycclum onbryrd þuruh þa halgen lare,* ***þeah ðe*** *heo þa gyt hæðen wære*[SUBJ]. (ÆLS (Eugenia) 26) 'Then was her mind greatly aroused through the sacred doctrine, though she then was still [a] heathen.'

(14) He *heold his ðeawas swa swa healic biscop. and his muneclice ingehyd* ***swa þeah*** *betwux mannum;* (ÆCHom II, 291.118)
'He observed his moral-behaviour just like [a] holy bishop, and his monastic mindset, even though [being] among men'

(15) *hrepung oððe grapung on eallum limum ac* ***þeah*** *gewunelicost on þam handum* (ÆLS (Christmas)196).
'touching or feeling with all [the] limbs, although [lit. but yet] usually with the hands'

(16) *He folgode þam kasere uncuð him* ***swa þeah*** (ÆLS (Sebastian) 17)
He followed the emperor unknown to him though

(17) *swa þæt ða munecas micclum afyrhte wurdon awrehte ðurh his wodlican stemne, and eodon to uhtsange, ær timan* ***swa þeah*** (ÆLS (Maur) 315) so that

28. In Middle English this relative particle disappears in the conjunctions, making adverb and conjunction *þeah* (ME *theigh, though* etc.) look even more similar.

29. See <http://tapor.library.utoronto.ca/doecorpus/>

the monks, much frightened, were aroused by his furious voice, and went to matins before [it was] time though

Finally, the conjunctions *if* and *though* shared many forms and functions already in Middle English, which may have helped the analogy between them – interestingly, Hilpert (2013: 197–98) also notes that the two conjunctions were still much closer in the 19thC). Some of these forms are indeed still used and interchangeable, such as *as if/as though*, *as though/as if*, *even if/even though*. Somewhat more archaic nowadays are the use of *what though* for *what if*, and possibly the use of the combination *to wonder/doubt though* for *to wonder/doubt if*. Two very usual alternations found in Middle English are now no longer current: *al if/al though* and *if that/though that*, with the loss of *if* in the first case and of *though* in the second.

In brief, the possibility of analogy is dismissed too soon and on too small a basis. It seems more likely in fact that the concessive *if* and *while* parentheticals were formed by analogy on the much earlier (*al*)*though* adverb used in ellipted clausal phrases such as (14)-(17), rather than the other way around as Hilpert assumes. Quite possibly, the analogy between the *if/while* and the *though* constructions was further helped by the fact that all of these constructions are often accompanied by other markers such as *even*, *still* and *yet*, which may have provided additional 'islands of regularity'. This case deserves further investigation.

4.2 Case studies where analogy is given a primary role

I assume that analogy may play a crucial role both before and after constructionalization (pace Traugott & Trousdale 2013; Barðdal & Gildea 2015; and Fried 2013 quoted in Section 2), and that it is our task as historical linguists to find further evidence for or against this by looking at cases of constructionalization in more detail and more broadly than has been done so far. To finish, I will simply point to a number of investigations that show analogy at work. I will not have time to go into any great detail but refer the reader to the published studies I mention below. My point is overall that we should keep an open mind as to this possibility, similar to the way Hofstadter and Sander (2013) have approached the topic of analogy.

In my narrative of the development of HAVE + *to*-infinitive in English from a possessive construction (*I have a book – to read*) into a modal construction of necessity (*I have to read a book*) (Fischer 2015), I argue that there are quite a number of constructions involved where analogical connections in both form and content can be spotted. The argument rests primarily on clear changes in frequencies in a number of construction types and tokens that share lexical elements, on semantic and structural ambiguities that arose through changes in word-order (from SOV/SVO to strict SVO) elsewhere, and on the loss of impersonal constructions which also had an effect on the development of the modal necessity verb HAVE-*to*. In a later article (Fischer & Olbertz in press), we compare the development of HAVE-*to* to what happened in other languages that also have a construction type in which a possessive verb is combined with a marked infinitive. We note that the change did not take place in German and Dutch, which lack the crucial word-order change,[30] but that it did develop in Spanish (which did undergo the word-order change) with the verb TENER followed by *que*, which came to be reinterpreted from a relative pronoun into an infinitival marker. Interestingly enough, we found that Spanish and English share two additional developments which we think were crucial for the development of the full verb into a modal auxiliary, and for the necessity meaning it acquired (factors (i) and (ii) below), both of which are also not found in German and Dutch. In addition, we found a couple of other developments in both languages – (iii) for English and (iv) for Spanish – which they did not share, but which can also be seen as analogically influencing the development of the new modal auxiliary.

i. increasing adjacency of HAVE/TENER and the infinitive marked by *to* and *que* respectively
ii. the very frequent use of a construction involving a possessive verb and a noun meaning 'need' followed by a marked infinitive (*have a need to* + inf./ *aver menester de* + inf.)
iii. a. the frequent use of the noun *need* in other expressions of necessity (*must needs*)[31]
    b. the loss of the impersonal verb *neden* 'need' and BE + *need*, expressing external necessity
    c. the existent possibility to use HAVE as an existential verb with bleached meaning and an inanimate non-agentive subject; all three factors making it possible for *have (a need) to*, to acquire the meaning of external necessity, with the subject functioning as an experiencer rather than an agent.
    d. the loss of the noun *need* in *have (a need) to* just as the noun was lost in *must needs* in (a)
iv. a. the competition between [*aver/haber de*, *tener de*] and [*aver/haber que* and *tener que*], with the latter group taking over the necessity meaning of the former.
    b. the similarity in position (before the inf.) and to some extent also in form between *de* and *que* causing the original relative *que* to be seen as an infinitival marker.

30. Both English and Spanish make use of a very strict SVO word order, unlike Dutch and German.

31. The adverb *nedes* is in fact a noun used in the genitive case.

Another recent study, Noël (2017), discusses the development of the modal expression *be bound to* into an epistemic construction. In traditional grammaticalization studies, this development within modal expressions is usually seen as unidirectional with deontic modals becoming epistemic over time. Noël shows, however, with the help of extensive corpus data and precisely dated frequency counts that the epistemic use of *be bound to* is not a development of an earlier deontic use; rather it acquired its epistemic nature through the fact that *bound* "was already part of a construction expressing speaker certainty" (p. 91), which had been in use for a long time: *I dare/will be bound.* At the same time epistemic *be bound to* was seen as synonymous with epistemic expressions involving adjectives: *be sure to, be certain to*, which also served as analogical models. Noël concludes that "[d]eontic *be bound to* → non-deontic *be bound to* represents an external diachronic reality, in that the use of the former historically precedes that of the latter, but it does not summarize an internal development" (p. 91).

This study shows that a careful analysis of the data, rather than the often global expectations made on the basis of the traditional grammaticalization model helps to see what may really have happened. A similar conclusion was drawn in my own studies (Fischer 1997, 2000) of the development of Germanic infinitival markers, which Haspelmath (1989) had described as a typical and general grammaticalization cline. I argue instead that the development in English diverged from the one in Dutch and German due to the fact that English *to* began to function differently as a result of new infinitival constructions being introduced in late Middle English, which analogically influenced the way *to*-infinitives developed in English.

Further studies providing arguments for the role of analogy can be found in the work of De Smet (2009, 2010, 2012, 2016) and Noël (2016). In addition, the articles in De Smet et al. (2015) indicate that many changes involve multiple constructions rather than unidirectional developments, in which the co-occurring structures may likewise have driven the new construction analogically.

5. A brief conclusion

Analogy in syntactic change may be difficult to prove conclusively because so many different constructions can be involved. But that does not mean that we should not seriously investigate the possibility. Analogy obviously plays a crucial role in learning in general and hence in language acquisition, and it is therefore unlikely that the principle will not remain strongly at work in adult language processing and thus in change. It would also seem strange to deny analogy a place in syntax, when it so clearly plays a role on the phonological, the morphological and the lexical levels, something which all linguists accept. The more we look at historical cases with analogy in mind, and the more we look carefully at what has happened in any particular language with the help of large corpora, the more we may learn about what is probable and what not.

Acknowledgement

I would like to thank audiences at the universities of Rouen and Paris (Sorbonne) for their useful comments and discussion, and two anonymous reviewers for their careful reading of the text, which all helped me to improve it.

References

Auer, Peter & Murray, Robert W. 2015. *Hermann Paul's 'Principles of Language History' Revisited. Translations and Reflections*. Berlin: Mouton de Gruyter.

Bao, Zhiming. 2010. *Must* in Singapore English. *Lingua* 120: 1727–1737. https://doi.org/10.1016/j.lingua.2010.01.001

Barðdal, Jóhanna. 2008. *Productivity. Evidence from Case and Argument Structure in Icelandic* [Constructional Approaches to Language 8]. Amsterdam: John Benjamins. https://doi.org/10.1075/cal.8

Barðdal, Jóhanna, Smirnova, Elena, Sommerer, Lotte & Gildea, Spike (eds). 2015. *Diachronic Construction Grammar* [Constructional Approaches to Language 8]. Amsterdam: John Benjamins. https://doi.org/10.1075/cal.18

Barðdal, Jóhanna & Gildea, Spike. 2015. Epistemological context, basic assumptions and historical implications. In Barðdal, Smirnova, Sommerer & Gildea (eds), 1–50.

Bergs, Alexander & Diewald, Gabriëlle (eds). 2008. *Constructions and Language Change*. Berlin: Mouton de Gruyter. https://doi.org/10.1515/9783110211757

Chalmers, David J., French, Robert M. & Hofstadter, Douglas R. 1992. High-level perception, representation, and analogy: A critique of artificial intelligence methodology. *Journal of Experimental and Theoretical Artificial Intelligence* 4: 185–211. <http://consc.net/papers/highlevel.pdf> https://doi.org/10.1080/09528139208953747

Croft, William. 2000. *Explaining Language Change. An Evolutionary Approach*. London: Longmans.

Croft, William. 2001. *Radical Construction Grammar. Syntactic Theory in Typological Perspective*. Oxford: OUP. https://doi.org/10.1093/acprof:oso/9780198299554.001.0001

De Smet, Hendrik. 2009. Analyzing reanalysis. *Lingua* 119: 1728–1755. https://doi.org/10.1016/j.lingua.2009.03.001

De Smet, Hendrik. 2010. Grammatical interference: Subject marker *for* and the phrasal verb particles *out* and *forth*. In Traugott & Trousdale (eds), 75–104.

De Smet, Hendrik. 2012. The course of actualization. *Language* 88: 601–633. https://doi.org/10.1353/lan.2012.0056

De Smet, Hendrik. 2016. How gradual change progresses: The interaction between convention and innovation. *Language Variation and Change* 28: 83–102.

De Smet, Hendrik & Fischer, Olga. 2017. The role of analogy in language change: Supporting constructions. In *The Changing English Language: Psycholinguistic Perspectives*, Marianne Hundt, Sandra Mollin & Simone Pfenninger (eds), 240–268. Cambridge: CUP.

De Smet, Hendrik, Ghesquière, Lobke & Van de Velde, Freek (eds). 2015. *On Multiple Source Constructions in Language Change* [Benjamins Current Topics 79]. Amsterdam: John Benjamins. https://doi.org/10.1075/bct.79

Deacon, Terence W. 1997. *The Symbolic Species. The Co-Evolution of Language and the Brain*. New York NY: Norton.

Denison, David. 2002. History of the *sort of* construction family. Ms. <http://www.humanities.manchester.ac.uk/medialibrary/llc/files/david-denison/Helsinki_ICCG2.pdf0>

Edwin, E. A. 1973. *Analogy and Association in Linguistics and Psychology*. Athens GA: University of Georgia Press.

Entwisle, Doris R., Forsyth, Daniel F. & Muuss, Rolf. 1964. The syntactic-paradigmatic shift in children's word associations. *Journal of Verbal Learning and Verbal Behavior* 3: 19–29. https://doi.org/10.1016/S0022-5371(64)80055-4

Ervin, Susan M. 1961. Changes with age in the verbal determinants of word-association. *The American Journal of Psychology* 74: 361–372. https://doi.org/10.2307/1419742

Fischer, Olga. 1997. The grammaticalisation of infinitival *to* in English compared with German and Dutch. In *Language History and Linguistic Modelling. A Festschrift for Jaček Fisiak on his 60th Birthday*, Raymond Hickey & Stanisław Puppel (eds), 265–280. Berlin: Mouton de Gruyter. https://doi.org/10.1515/9783110820751.265

Fischer, Olga. 2000. Grammaticalisation: Unidirectional, non-reversable? The case of *to* before the infinitive in English. In *Pathways of Change. Grammaticalization in English* [Studies in Language Companion Series 53], Olga Fischer, Anette Rosenbach & Dieter Stein (eds), 149–169. Amsterdam: John Benjamins. https://doi.org/10.1075/slcs.53.08fis

Fischer, Olga. 2007. *Approaches to Morphosyntactic Change from a Functional and Formal Perspective*. Oxford: OUP.

Fischer, Olga. 2011. Grammaticalization as analogically driven change? In *The Oxford Handbook of Grammaticalization*, Heiko Narrog & Bernd Heine (eds), 31–42. Oxford: OUP.

Fischer, Olga. 2015. The influence of the grammatical system and analogy in processes of language change: The case of the auxiliation of HAVE-TO once again. In *Studies in Linguistic Variation and Change: From Old to Middle English*, Fabienne Toupin & Brian Lowrey (eds), 120–150. Newcastle upon Tyne: Cambridge Scholars.

Fischer, Olga, De Smet, Hendrik & Van der Wurff, Wim. 2017. *A Brief History of English Syntax*. Cambridge: CUP.

Fischer, Olga & Olbertz, Hella. In press. The role played by analogy in processes of language change: The case of English HAVE-to compared to Spanish TENER-que. In *Categories, Constructions and Change in English Syntax* [Studies in English Language Series], Nuria Yáñez-Bouza, Willem B. Hollmann, Emma Moore & Linda Van Bergen (eds). Cambridge: CUP.

Fried, Mirjam. 2013. Principles of constructional change. In Hoffmann & Trousdale (eds), 419–437.

Gentner, Dedre. 2003. Why we're so smart. In *Language in Mind. Advances in the Study of Language and Thought*, Dedre Gentner & Susan Goldin-Meadow (eds), 195–235. Cambridge MA: The MIT Press.

Gentner, Dedre. 2010. Bootstrapping the mind: Analogical processes and symbol systems. *Cognitive Science* 34: 752–775. https://doi.org/10.1111/j.1551-6709.2010.01114.x

Gentner, Dedre, Anggoro, Florencia K. & Klibanoff, Raquel S. 2011. Structure mapping and relational language support children's learning of relational categories. *Child Development* 82: 1173–1188. https://doi.org/10.1111/j.1467-8624.2011.01599.x

Gentner, Dedre, Holyoak, Keith J. & Kokinov, Boicho K. (eds). 2001. *The Analogical Mind. Perspectives from Cognitive Science*. Cambridge MA: The MIT Press.

Gentner, Dedre & Namy, Laura L. 2006. Analogical processes in language learning. *Current Directions in Psychological Science* 15: 297–301. https://doi.org/10.1111/j.1467-8721.2006.00456.x

Gentner, Dedre & Smith, Linsey. 2012. Analogical reasoning. In *Encyclopedia of Human Behavior*, 2nd edn, Vilayanur S. Ramachandran (ed.), 130–136. Oxford: Elsevier. https://doi.org/10.1016/B978-0-12-375000-6.00022-7

Goldberg, Adèle E. 2013. Constructionist approaches. In Hoffman & Trousdale (eds), 15–31.

Hashimoto, Naomi, McGregor, Karla K. & Graham, Anne. 2007. Conceptual organization at 6 and 8 years of age: Evidence from the semantic priming of object decisions. *Journal of Speech, Language and Hearing Research* 50: 161–176. https://doi.org/10.1044/1092-4388(2007/014)

Haspelmath, Martin. 1989. From purposive to infinitive – A universal path of grammaticization. *Folia Linguistica Historica* 10: 287–310.

Hilpert, Martin. 2013. *Constructional Change in English. Developments in Allomorphy, Word Formation, and Syntax*. Cambridge: CUP. https://doi.org/10.1017/CBO9781139004206

Hoffmann, Thomas. 2013. Abstract phrasal and clausal constructions. In Hoffman & Trousdale (eds), 307–328.

Hoffman, Thomas & Trousdale, Graeme (eds). 2013. *The Oxford Handbook of Construction Grammar*. Oxford: OUP. https://doi.org/10.1093/oxfordhb/9780195396683.001.0001

Hofstadter, Douglas. 1995. *Fluid Concepts and Creative Analogies. Computer Models of the Fundamental Mechanisms of Thought*. New York NY: Basic Books.

Hofstadter, Douglas. 2001. Epilogue. Analogy as the core of cognition. In Gentner, Holyoak & Kokinov (eds), 499–538.

Hofstadter, Douglas. 2013. The nature of categories and concepts. *Lecture delivered at Stanford*, March 6, 2013. Made available on Youtube, March 2014.

Hofstadter, Douglas & Sander, Emmanuel. 2013. *Surfaces and Essences: Analogy as the Fuel and Fire of Thinking*. New York NY: Basic Books.

Kalénine, Solène, Peyrin, Carole, Pichat, Cédric, Segebarth, Christoph, Bonthoux, Françoise & Baciu, Monica. 2009. The sensory-motor specificity of taxonomic and thematic conceptual relations: A behavioural and fMRI study. *NeuroImage* 44: 1152–1162. https://doi.org/10.1016/j.neuroimage.2008.09.043

Kaltenböck, Gunther, Heine, Bernd & Kuteva, Tania. 2011. On thetical grammar. *Studies in Language* 35: 852–897. https://doi.org/10.1075/sl.35.4.03kal

Kaltenböck, Gunther & Heine, Bernd. 2014. Sentence grammar vs. thetical grammar: Two competing domains. In *Competing Motivations in Grammar and Usage*, Brian MacWhinney, Andrej Malchukov & Edith Moravcsik (eds), 348–363. Oxford: OUP. https://doi.org/10.1093/acprof:oso/9780198709848.003.0021

Kahneman, Daniel. 2011. *Thinking Fast and Slow*. London: Allen Lane/Penguin.

Kiparsky, Paul. 1974. Remarks on analogical change. In *Historical Linguistics*, Vol. I., John M. Anderson & Charles Jones (eds), 257–275. Amsterdam: North Holland.

Lightfoot, David W. 1979. *Principles of Diachronic Syntax*. Cambridge: CUP.

Malkiel, Yakov. 1993. *Etymology*. Cambridge: CUP. https://doi.org/10.1017/CBO9780511611773

Noël, Dirk. 2016. For a radically usage-based diachronic construction grammar. *Belgian Journal of Linguistics* 30: 39–53. https://doi.org/10.1075/bjl.30.03noe
Noël, Dirk. 2017. Radically usage-based diachronic construction grammar and the development of non-deontic *be bound to*. *Lingua* 199: 72–93. https://doi.org/10.1016/j.lingua.2017.07.012
Paul, Hermann. 1909 [1880]. *Prinzipien der Sprachgeschichte*, 4th edn. Halle: Niemeyer.
Pulvermüller, Friedemann. 2002. *The Neuroscience of Language. On Brain Circuits of Words and Serial Order*. Cambridge: CUP.
Rice, Keren. 2000. *Morpheme Order and Semantic Scope. Word Formation in the Athapaskan Verb*. Cambridge: CUP. https://doi.org/10.1017/CBO9780511663659
Sommerer, Lotte. 2015. The influence of constructions in grammaticalization: Revisiting category emergence and the development of the definite article in English. In Barðdal, Smirnova, Sommerer & Gildea (eds), 107–138.
Steels, Luc. 2011. Introducing Fluid Construction Grammar. In *Design Patterns in Fluid Construction Grammar* [Constructional Approaches to Language 11], Luc Steels (ed.), 3–30. Amsterdam: John Benjamins. https://doi.org/10.1075/cal.11.03ste
Steels, Luc. 2013. Fluid Construction Grammar. In Hoffman & Trousdale (eds), 153–167.
Strong, Herbert Augustus. 1889. *Principles of the History of Language*. New York NY: Macmillan.
Traugott, Elizabeth Closs. 2008a. Grammaticalization, constructions and the incremental development of language. Suggestions from the development of degree modifiers in English. In *Variation, Selection, Development. Probing the Evolutionary Model of Language Change*, Regine Eckardt, Gerhard Jager & Tonjes Veenstra (eds), 219–250. Berlin: Mouton de Gruyter.
Traugott, Elizabeth Closs. 2008b. The grammaticalization of NP *of* NP patterns. In Bergs & Diewald (eds), 23–45.
Traugott, Elizabeth Closs. 2008c. "All that he endeavoured to prove was" …: On the emergence of grammatical constructions in dialogual and dialogic contexts. In *Language in Flux: Dialogue Coordination, Language Variation, Change and Evolution*, Robin Cooper & Ruth Kempson (eds), 143–177. London: Kings College Publications.
Traugott, Elizabeth Closs. 2015. Toward a coherent account of grammatical constructionalization. In Barðdal, Smirnova, Sommerer & Gildea (eds), 51–80.
Traugott, Elizabeth Closs & Trousdale, Graeme (eds). 2010. *Gradience, Gradualness and Grammaticalization* [Typological Studies in Language 90]. Amsterdam: John Benjamins. https://doi.org/10.1075/tsl.90
Traugott, Elizabeth Closs & Trousdale, Graeme. 2013. *Constructionalization and Constructional Changes*. Oxford: OUP. https://doi.org/10.1093/acprof:oso/9780199679898.001.0001
Trousdale, Graeme. 2012. Grammaticalization, constructions and the grammaticalization of constructions. In *Grammaticalization and Language Change. New Reflections* [Studies in Language Companion Series 130], Kirstin Davidse, Tine Breban, Lieselotte Brems & Tanja Mortelmans (eds), 167–198. Amsterdam: John Benjamins. https://doi.org/10.1075/slcs.130.07tro
Trousdale, Graeme. 2016. Construction grammar. In *The Cambridge Handbook of English Historical Linguistics*, Merja Kytö & Pavi Pahta (eds), 65–78. Cambridge: CUP.
Vincent, Nigel & Borjärs, Kersti. 2010. Grammaticalization and models of language. In Traugott & Trousdale (eds), 279–299.
Willems, Klaas. 2016. Georg von der Gabelenz and 'das lautsymbolische gefühl'. A chapter in the history of iconicity research. In *From Variation to Iconicity. Festschrift for Olga Fischer*, Anne Bannink & Wim Honselaar (eds), 439–452. Amsterdam: Pegasus.

Central Southern Guangxi as a grammaticalization area

Yang Huang and Fuxiang Wu
Southwest Jiaotong University / Chinese Academy of Social Sciences

This paper investigates contact-induced grammatical changes that are observed among the Zhuang Tai-Kadai and Sinitic languages in the Central Southern Guangxi Region. Following recent advances in the theoretical analysis of grammaticalization, this paper describes four uncommon grammaticalization processes that represent diffusion from Zhuang into several Sinitic languages. On this basis, we argue that the Central Southern Guangxi Region constitutes a micro-grammaticalization area.

Keywords: Zhuang, Sinitic, language contact, grammaticalization

1. Introduction

Initiated by Boas (1920: 211) and Trubetzkoy (1928), the concept of linguistic area/Sprachbund has been very effective at identifying instances of shared linguistic features that do not fit genetic classifications (cf. Emeneau 1956; Weinreich 1963: 378; Masica 1976; Haspelmath 1998; van der Auwera 1998; Aikhenvald & Dixon 2001; among others). As Thomason (2001: 99) defines it in her introductory book for language contact, "A linguistic area is a geographical region containing a group of three or more languages that share some structural features as a result of contact rather than as a result of accident or inheritance from a common ancestor". In most cases, the shared similarities arise due to diffusion of structural features across linguistic boundaries, eventually producing a convergent spectrum of languages (Campbell 1985: 25).

Meanwhile, recent studies have proposed that linguistic areas (LA) and grammaticalization areas (GA) are related notions that can each be described in terms of areal-linguistic isoglosses. In their classic work, Heine and Kuteva (2005: 216–217) point out that "all LAs are based to some extent on the presence of a corresponding GA, while the opposite does not apply. Even in cases where a proposed

https://doi.org.10.1075/slcs.202.05hua
© 2018 John Benjamins Publishing Company

LA is not widely accepted, it is generally agreed that a GA is involved in some way or other." Since the presence of sprachbunds can perhaps more profitably be reanalyzed as being suggestive of grammaticalization areas, it is not easy to tear them apart (cf. Heine & Kuteva 2005: 210; see also Ramat 2008; Heine 2011; Robbeets 2013).

A wealth of studies have identified Mainland Southeast Asia (MSEA) as a macro linguistic/grammaticalization area on the basis of areal grammaticalization and structural convergence found among the languages of this region (Huffman 1973; Enfield 2005; Goddard 2005: 39–43; Comrie 2007). In this paper it is argued that within this area there is a micro area, referred to as the Guangxi grammaticalization area (Huang & Kwok 2013; Kwok 2014; Huang 2014, 2016). We wish to demonstrate that the Central Southern Guangxi Region (henceforth CS-GXR) is sufficient to characterize a peculiar and exclusive linguistic area on the one hand and a grammaticalization area on the other due to a wide range of specific areal grammaticalization features. Moreover, it is argued that Zhuang, a language group of the Tai-Kadai family, forms a central linguistic bridge between the Sino-Tibetan and the 'exotic' language groups in MSEA.

To begin with, we will deal with the ecological and linguistic context characterizing the Guangxi Region. After that, numerous examples of the area-specific linguistic phenomenon (i.e., the polyfunctional grams 'finish' le:u^{4}, 晒; 'go'去, pai^{1}; 'give' 给, 把, 畀, hɔ:i^{3}; and 'take' 攞, 取, ʔau^{1}) from the Sinitic and Tai-Kadai languages in this region will be displayed. Our concern is exclusively with four areal parallel grammaticalization chains that seem to be cross-linguistically rare, involving the verbs 'finish', 'go', 'give', and 'take'.

In accordance with the findings presented in this study, a tentative Central-Southern Guangxi Grammaticalization Area is established after scrutinizing the diagnostics for a typical grammaticalization area. We further claim that it is the Zhuang Tai-Kadai language group that is responsible for the diffusion of the areal features discussed. The Central-Southern Guangxi Linguistic Area that we propose is part of the broad MSEA linguistic area but differs from other micro areas in exhibiting a set of rare areal features.

2. The ecological context and language diversity

2.1 Geography and history

Characterized by spectacular landscapes, charming natural scenery and diverse ethnic customs, Guangxi Autonomous Region 广西壮族自治区 (GXR) is an impressive area situated in the south of China, facing the Beibu Gulf 北部湾 on the South China Sea and bordering Vietnam to the southwest. Situated in mountainous terrain with an east longitude of 104°26'–112°04' and a north latitude of 20°54'–26°24', Guangxi shares boundaries with a number of Southeast Asian countries. Straddling the Tropic of Cancer, Guangxi has a subtropical monsoon climate, being rainy, warm and humid. July is the warmest month, during which average temperatures range between 23 and 29°C; the coldest time of year is January, with average temperatures between 6 and 16°C. GXR receives 80% of its rain fall between April and September. The region is shaped like a large basin, with higher ground surrounding a lower center.

Central Guangxi has a distinct palaeogeographical framework of isolated carbonate platforms surrounded by deep-water troughs. The carbonate platform deposits are represented by limestones intercalated with coal (Shao et al. 2003). Spectacular caves and fantastic canals (Elephant Trunk Hill 象鼻山, Flute Cave and Yangshuo town 阳朔) are marked on most tourist maps.

Due to its unique geological context and marvelous scenic spots, Guangxi enjoys the status of an economic hub. Since the Tang Dynasty 唐朝 (618–907 C.E), it has also served as a transport hinge, linking China with its neighbors. By the Late Tang, GXR had developed into a full-fledged economic trading hub shaped by the gradual immigration of diverse populations and the interaction of different languages.

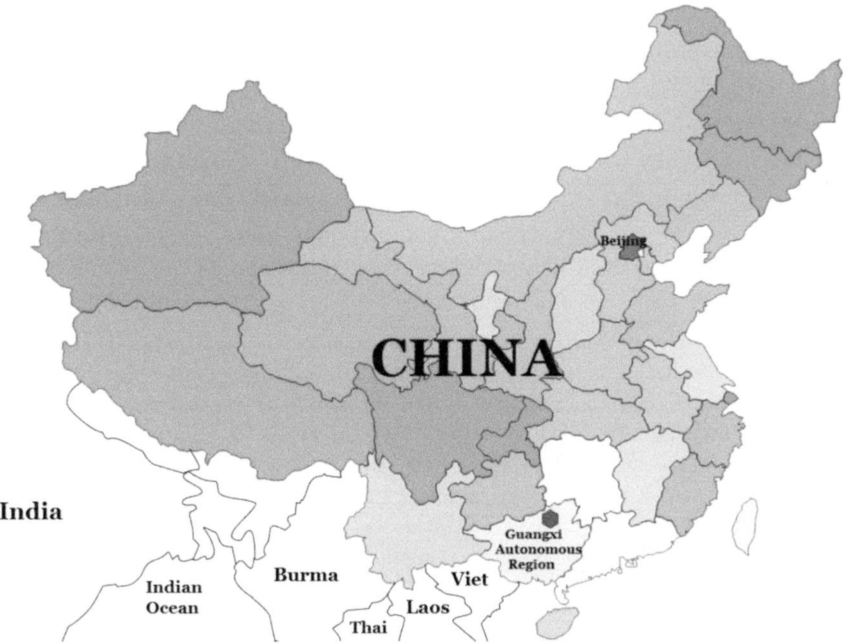

Map 1. Geographic location of the Guangxi Zhuang Autonomous Region

The economic trade and intermarriage also stimulated the convergence of distinct races. The Guangxi Region has had a rich trade relationship with its neighbors since the Early Song Dynasty 宋朝 (approx. 960–1279 C.E). For many years, it served as a favorable trading market connecting Yunnan (云南) and Hunan (湖南) with other Southeast Asian countries. A strong agricultural and manufacturing sector endowed this region with a reputation as a center of foreign trade, into which vast numbers of businessmen and vendors rushed to realize their 'millionaire dream'. However, due to the lack of promising economic development in Guangzhou, the trade in Guangxi was mostly among the local merchants. Economic immigration did not cause as large an influx of new blood as the war movement had (Hong 2004: 108).

2.2 Language profiles

According to the *Language Atlas of China* (Wurm et al. 1987), there are approximately six Chinese dialects and seven minority languages in use in GXR.[1] This complicated language situation is the outcome of mutual influence and convergence amongst a number of related and unrelated languages. Liang and Zhang (1988) and Liu (1998) propose that the indigenous languages of GXR should be historically classified as Tai-Kadai languages rather than Chinese dialects. Cultural assimilation and political integration has accelerated the sinicization of the indigenous languages. Thanks to the retention of an ancient *Baiyue* 百越 linguistic substratum (the Proto-Tai language spoken by the ancient one hundred *Yue* tribes), many Southern Chinese dialects are used by the ethnic tribes as a second language in daily communication. Use of Southern Chinese dialects has been popular in this context since the Early Song Dynasty (Liu 1998: 12). Among all the minority languages spoken in this region, Zhuang is a predominant one undergoing a profound history of contact with its Sinitic companions. Figure 1 displays the genetic affiliations of Zhuang and Chinese dialects spoken in Guangxi:[2]

1. In China, a language spoken by a minority of the population other than the *Han* people 汉人 is termed as a minority language by the government. This definition is exclusively based on the standard of ethnological identification. Languages spoken by the Han people are termed as Mandarin (the lingua franca of China) or Chinese dialects. The six Chinese dialects are Mandarin 官话, Yue 粤语, Min 闽语, Hakka 客家, Gan 赣语, Xiang 湘语; the seven minority languages are Zhuang, Kam, Sui, Lakkja, Maonan, Gelao, Mulam. Whether Pinghua dialect is classified as an individual Chinese dialect is still among debate in Chinese scholars (cf. Li 2007), we therefore keep the question of its genetic status open.

2. Pinghua dialect 平话, also known as Pingsheng 平声, Zheyuan Hua 蔗园话, Tuguai Hua 土拐话 or Tu Baihua 土白话, is a trade language [dialect] spoken in the southern and northern Guangxi Region (Xie et al. 2007). Geographically, it can be divided into two branches, with the

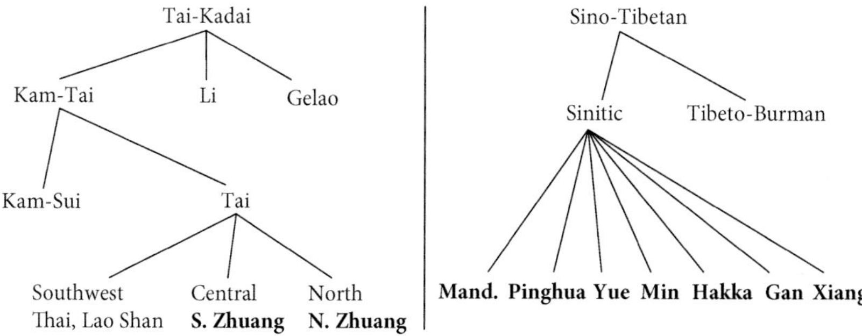

Figure 1. Genetic affiliation of Tai-Kadai and Sinitic languages used in Guangxi

In the remainder of the paper, the following four languages will be discussed: Northern Zhuang (N. Zhuang) of Tai-Kadai, Southwest Mandarin (Fusui 扶绥 and Liujiang 柳江), Pinghua dialects (Binyang 宾阳 and Wutong 五通), and Nanning Yue dialect.

3. Polyfunctionality and versatility

3.1 Polyfunctional 'finish'

Interestingly, a variety of the 'finish' verbs ɬai^{33} 晒, liau^{55} 了 and le:u^{4} demonstrates diverse functions in Nanning Yue, Southwest Mandarin and N. Zhuang (Tai-Kadai) respectively in this region. In the bulk of our data, these morphemes occur after the main verb as well as in sentence-final position, signifying a completed past action or a change of state that is relevant to the preceding situation. This aspectual reading may indicate 'already', 'come to be' or even 'become' (cf. Huang 2016). Alternatively, they have a degree quantifier reading, indicating the maximal degree of a quality when suffixed to the adjectival predicate. This meaning is analogical to 'extremely' in English. In addition, they are parsed as a conjunction indicating the attainment or completeness of a prior event. At the level of discourse, it

northern branch (i.e., Wutong 五通平话, Luocheng 罗城平话, Fuchuan 富川平话, Yongfu 永福平话, etc.) spoken from Guilin to Hexian County, and the southern branch (i.e., Binyang 宾阳平话, Yongning 邕宁平话, Hengxian 横县平话, etc.) extending from Nanning to Baise 百色 or Longzhou 龙州. As has been recorded in many historical documents, Pinghua has enjoyed a much longer history than other Chinese dialects in Guangxi. It was spoken by a large population of Han immigrants during the *Tang* and *Song* Dynasties. While the genetic correlation between the ancestral Pinghua group and the Han Chinese is denied in certain works (Gan et al. 2008), Pinghua has been included in recent dialectal studies in the subgroup of Chinese dialects (Li 2000; Chappell & Li 2016).

also serves to link speech turns. The conjunction 'finish' may stand alone or attach to a pragmatic particle. We will now look at each of the functions in turn.

a. *Universal quantifier*

The 'finish' gram may be interpreted as a universal quantifier when it is postposed to the predicate or occurs in the sentence-final slot in a stative or weakly dynamic context. A mental process verb or existential verb typically accompanies this structure. In this case, the 'finish' gram has scope over the subject at large, denoting a universal quantificational reading.

The items governed by the universal quantifier 'finish' must be number-sensitive and measurable. All bare nouns in our data are understood by default to be plural and divisible in their semantic domain. Here we have Nanning Yue, Southwest Mandarin and Zhuang:

(1) Nanning Yue ɬai^{33} 晒
洞 里边 有 老虎，村民 怕 晒 老虎
tun^{22} li^{24} pin^{55} jɐu^{24} lu^{24}fu^{35} tʃhyn^{55} mɐn^{21} pha^{33} ɬai^{33} lu^{24}fu^{35}
cave inside have tiger villager afraid FINISH tiger
'There is a tiger in the cave, thus all the villagers are afraid of it.'

(2) Zhuang le:u^{4}
po^{6} me^{6} kjai^{2} va^{3} ȵe^{2} ni^{4} le:u^{4}
parents love child this FINISH
'The child's parents both love him [very much].'

b. *Superlative*

There are some contexts where the 'finish' gram co-occurs with degree or gradable adjectives, denoting the meaning of 'extremely'. A superlative 'finish' indicates a situation characterized by an adjective that has attained a maximal degree. Once a divisible subject is available, it may quantify over that subject. As a superlative, the 'finish' gram quantifies over the gradable scale of comparison (Gerner 2013: 293). Similarly there are candidates which display this function as follows:

(3) Nanning Yue ɬai^{33} 晒
园 里 底嘅 花 总 红 晒 至 畀 人 参观
jyn^{22} li^{24} ti^{55}kɛ^{33} fa^{55} ʧuŋ^{35} huŋ^{21} ɬai^{3} tʃi^{33} pi^{3} jɐn^{21} ʧhan^{55}kun^{55}
garden inside TTR follow all red FINISH then CAUS people visit
i. 'The flowers in the garden are not shown to the visitors until they are extremely red.'
ii. 'All the flowers in the garden are shown to the visitors when they are red.'

(4) Zhuang le:u^{4}
ku^{1} ta^{3} θi^{5}ta pja:i^{3} taŋ^{6} min^{2}ta^{4}, ku^{1} kun^{3} pak^{8} le:u^{4}
1SG from PN walk to PN 1SG already tired FINISH
'I was extremely tired after I walked to Guangxi University from Guangxi Minzu University.'

c. *Perfect/perfective aspect marker*

Three quarters of the data show examples of 'finish' as an aspectual marker which is popular in a typological perspective (Cheung 1977; Bybee & Dahl 1989; Cao 1995; Wu 1998). It, as a perfective aspect marker, indicates the completeness of a situation holistically; it can act as a perfect aspect marker to denote the continuing present relevance of a past situation or change to a new state.

(5) Nanning Yue ɬai^{33} 晒
阿个 车司 酒后 开车 捱 警察 罚 晒 钱
a^{33}kɔ^{55} ʧhɛ^{55}ʃi^{55} ʧɐu^{35}hau^{22} hɔi^{55}ʧhɛ^{55} ŋai^{21} keŋ^{35}ʧhat^{3} fat^{2} ɬai^{33} ʧin^{21}
this driver drunk drive PASS police impose FINISH penalty
晒
ɬai^{33}
PRF
'This drunk driver has had a penalty imposed on him by the police.'

(6) Zhuang le^{6}
ka:u^{1} ko:n^{5} ʦa:ŋ^{2} kje^{6}hun^{5} ka:u^{1} ni^{4} tau^{3} ʦi^{6} khe^{6} hun^{5} le^{6}
time last NEG marry time this arrive MOD marry FINISH
'Last time [when I met him] he had not gotten married, but this time [when I met him], he was already married.'

d. *Conjunction*

When verbal 'finish' occurs outside the boundaries of the clause, it usually functions as a discourse conjunction (or linker) to connect a series of clauses that are linearly arranged in the temporal domain. In this use, it seems to be developing into a sequential conjunction in general and contrasting conjunction in particular. The development of this conjunction function occurs at the expense of its verbal function. On the other hand, the verbal meaning of 'finish' is remarkably predominant when it is followed by a pragmatic marker nɛ^{35}. To illustrate:

(7) Nanning Yue ɬai^{33} 晒
我 十岁 来 南宁, 晒-呢, 一直 喺 南宁
ŋɔ^{24} ʃɐp^{2}ɬui^{33} lɔi^{21} nam^{21}neŋ^{22} ɬai^{33}-nɛ^{33} jɐt^{5} ʧek^{2} hɐi^{35} nam^{21}neŋ^{22}
1SG 10 years come PN THEN-PM always be.at PN
'I came to Nanning when I was ten years old, then I lived here for a long time.'

(8) Southwest Mandarin liau^{55} 了
他 买 了 冰箱, 了-嗫, 又再 买 电视
tha^{35} mai^{55} liau^{55} peŋ^{35} ɬiaŋ^{35} liau^{55}- nɛ^{35} iɐu^{21} ʧai^{21} mai^{55} tɛn^{21}ʃi^{21}
3SG buy PFV refrigerator THEN-PM again buy TV set
'He first bought a refrigerator, then he bought a TV set.'

(9) Zhuang le:u^{4}
te^{1} lou^{4} na^{3} ʔan^{1} ɬe:u^{3}ɬi^{5} kei^{3} ja^{5}, le:u^{4}-ne, ʦu^{5} aŋ^{2} lo
3SG hear CL news this already THEN-PM will happy PM
'After hearing this news, he becomes happy.'

There is one context in which the 'finish' combines two clauses that lack a clear temporal connection. In this case, 'finish' truly is a sequential conjunction, which serves to fuse the bi-clausal structure into a mono-clausal one. The conjunction 'finish', in this function, is construed as 'and':

(10) Nanning Yue ɬai^{33} 晒
桂林 天气 好, 晒 水 也 好
kwɐi^{33} lɐm^{21} thin^{55}hi^{33} hu^{35} ɬai^{33} ʃui^{35} ja^{24} hu^{35}
Guiling weather good AND water also good
'The weather in Guilin is nice, and the water is clean.'

(11) Southwest Mandarin liau^{55} 了
他 个人 好爱 吃 猪肉 哦, 了-嗫, 都 还爱
tha^{35} ko^{21}iən^{21} hau^{55}ŋai^{21} ʧhi^{21} ʧəu^{35}iəu^{21} o^{35} liau^{55} -nɛ^{35} tɐu^{35} huan^{21} ŋai^{2}
3SG RECP like eat meat PM AND-PM always also like
吃 鱼 呢
ʧhi^{21} iəu^{21} ɛ^{35}
eat fish PM
'He likes to eat meat and also fish (lit., and he also likes eating fish).'

(12) Zhuang le:u^{4}
va^{3} te^{1} ʔdai^{3} ŋi^{1} ʔdak^{7} θe:u^{5}θi^{3} ni^{4} le^{6}, le:u^{4} ʦai^{2} tai^{1}
3pl PFV hear CL news this PRF AND all cry
'They have heard the bad news, and [they] all cried.'

After that, 晒 /ɬai^{33}/ can link the subordinated clause to the matrix clause in a cause-and-effect sequence. In this use, 晒 /ɬai^{33}/ no longer has any synchronic connection to temporality. I gloss this use as 'thus' in the following examples:

(13) Nanning Yue ɬai^{33} 晒
细鬼 太 懒 晒, 晒, 揾 冇 到 工
ɬɐi^{33}kwɐi^{35} thai^{33} lan^{24} ɬai^{33} ɬai^{33} wɐn^{35} mu^{24} tu^{33} kuŋ^{55}
brother too lazy PM THUS find NEG to work
'[My] brother is too lazy, thus [he] can't find a job.'

(14) Southwest Mandarin liau^{55} 了
今天 是 民歌节 哦, 了-嗫, 口 用 去 读书
kən^{35}thɛn^{35} ʃi^{24} mən^{21}ko^{3} ʧɛ^{21} o^{35} liau^{55}-nɛ^{35} mi^{21} ioŋ^{24} khəɯ^{21} tu^{21} ʃəɯ^{35}
today COP folk song festival PM THUS-PM NEG need go to study
'Today is the folk song festival, thus we don't need to go to school.'

(15) Zhuang le:u^{4}
lok^{8} eŋ^{1} nai^{3} ke^{2} la:i^{1}, le:u^{4}-ne, thok^{8} mi^{2} ʔdai^{3} ta^{3}jo^{2}
child this lazy too THUS-PM study NEG get university
'This child is too lazy, thus he can't [pass the entrance exam] of this university.'

Last but not least, 'finish' markers can link logically contrastive clauses (as 'but'), serving as adversative conjunctions. Note that this use is only found in colloquial conversations rather than literary materials. This usage is restricted to native speakers at age 60 or over[3] in Nanning Yue, Southwest Mandarin and N. Zhuang.

(16) Nanning Yue ɬai^{33} 晒
佢 系 中国人, 晒, 冇 讲 中国话
khy^{24} hɐi^{22} tʃuŋ^{55}kɔk^{3} jɐn^{21} ɬai^{33} mu^{24} kɔŋ^{35} tʃuŋ^{55}kɔk^{3}wa^{22}
3SG COP Chinese people BUT NEG speak Chinese
'He is Chinese, but he cannot speak the Chinese language.'

(17) Southwest Mandarin liau^{55} 了
阿婆 都 已经 八十 了, 了-嗫, 都 口 有 嚜 条
a^{35} p^{h}o^{21} tɐu^{35} i^{55}keŋ^{35} pa^{21}ʃət^{2} lə^{35}, liau^{55}-nɛ^{35} tɐu^{35} mi^{21} iɐu^{55} ɬɐk^{5} t^{h}iau^{21}
grandma MOD already eighty PFV BUT-PM still NEG have any CL
白头发
pəɯ^{21}t^{h}ɐu^{21} fa^{21}
white hair
'[My] grandma is already eighty years old, but she still does not have white hair.'

3. Soon after the Early Qing Dynasty (1685 A. D.), a sporadic migration took place in GXR from Guangdong due to the handicraft industry and economic trade. The Guangdong immigrants took with them their mother language – the early Guangfu Yue dialect – and spread it to the capital city of Guangxi, Nanning. Language contact between Nanning Yue and Zhuang took place in this context, when the indigenous Zhuang people tried to speak the early Guangfu Yue of the immigrants to ensure a better life (Huang 2016). However, contact between modern Nanning Yue and Zhuang is rare and limited due to the widespread use of Putonghua and the influence of the modern Cantonese language. Most young people follow the modern Cantonese speech style, broadening the gap between their modern Yue language and the early Yue spoken about one century ago in Nanning. The traces of contact between Zhuang and Nanning Yue are most clearly evident in the substrate of early Nanning Yue. Hence, in our study, the most grammaticalized item – the conjunction 'finish' – is largely restricted to older generations.

(18) Zhuang le:u^{4}
ka:i^{4}θa:u^{4} pu^{4} swa:i^{4} ko^{5} ha:ŋ^{3} te^{1}, le:u^{4}, te^{1} si^{6} ʔi^{3} ŋ̥wun^{6} ha^{5}
introduce CL handsome boy give 3SG BUT 3SG MOD NEG want marry
'[Her mother has] introduced a handsome boy to her, but she does not want to marry him.'

It is clear from the data that the 'finish' morpheme demonstrates various functions in its diverse grammatical positions and contexts. In the static context, 'finish' has universal quantifier and superlative functions; in dynamic contexts, by contrast, it serves as an aspectual marker and a conjunction. Word order of 'finish' differs according to the languages concerned. Zhuang, which shares a typical word-order characteristics of SVO languages, has a majority of sentence-final 'finish' uses. Table 1 summarizes the property of the polyfunctional 'finish' of this section:

Table 1. An overview of the polyfunctional uses of 'finish'

	Zhuang	NN-Yue	SW Mandarin
Universal quantifier	+	+	
Superlative	+	+	
Aspectual marker	+	+	
Conjunction	+	+	+

The distribution of the features listed in Table 1 is plotted in Figure 2.[4]

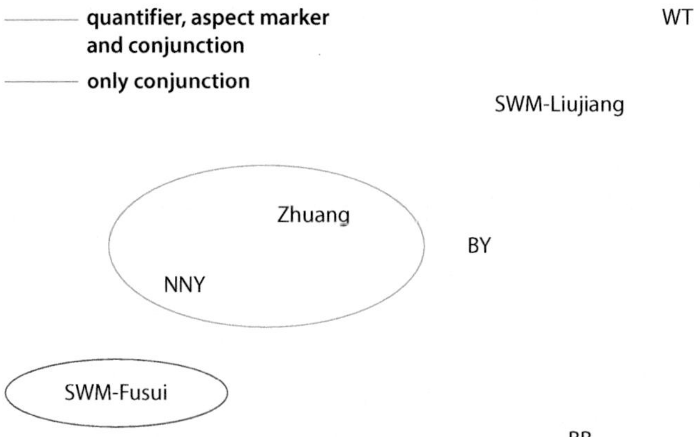

Figure 2. Quantifier, aspect marker and conjunction functions of 'finish' grams

4. We follow van der Auwera (1998) and Haspelmath (1998) to draw the cluster map/quantified isoglosses.

3.2 Polyfunctional 'go'

'Go' verbs in the languages of CS-GXR exhibit peculiarities that are lacking in the adjacent regions of Guangxi. Qin (2012) and Kwok (2014) introduced a polyfunctional scenario and these authors claim that the paradigm of functions expressed by 'go' is shared by a majority of Chinese dialects and Tai-Kadai varieties to be found in this region. Irrespective of the completive and aspectual marker functions best known in the world's languages at large (Bybee et al. 1994: 61; Dahl & Velupillai 2005: 272–281; among others), languages in CS-GXR characterize the sentence-final emphatic particle as well as the imperative and command marker that are typologically scarce (examples are cited from Qin & Qin 2015).

a. *Imperative marker*

Occasionally, 'go' suffixes the resultative and in the context and mood of entreaties and requests, advice and instructions, principles and life mottos, invitations, *etc.* it commonly expresses commanding and quasi-causative notions, covering a basically addressee-oriented interlocution where the addresser commands or causes the addresser to act. I label this category as *imperative marker* 'go' based on its semantic and pragmatic orientation. As represented in (19) and (20), 'go' predicates a request of the addressee, and (21) advice from the speaker to the addressee:

(19) Nanning Yue hy^{33} 去

食饭 饱 去, 冇 系 亲讲 来 六嬢 啲 冇 得

ʃek^{2}fan^{22} pɛu^{35} hy^{33} mu^{24} hɐi^{21} ʧhɐn^{33}kɔŋ^{35} lɐi^{21} luk^{24}nœŋ^{55} ti^{55} mu^{24} tɐk^{5}

eat full GO NEG COP say visit aunt LOC NEG MOD

食饱

ʃek^{2} pɛu^{35}

be-full

'Eat your fill (lit., make yourself full)! Don't say that you are not full when you visit your ant's house.'

(20) Binyang Pinhua hu^{55} 去

讲 齐 去, 你 同样 都 告 冇 赢 政府 嗰

ʧaŋ^{33} ʧɐi^{213} hu^{55} nəi^{22} toŋ^{213} jeŋ^{42} tou^{33} køu^{55} məu^{22} həŋ^{213} ʧəŋ^{55} fou^{33} o^{33}

talk RES GO 2SG same also sue NEG RES government PM

'Whatever you say (lit., go to accuse them of that), you are not able to act against the government.'

(21) Wutong Pinghua həu^{33} 去
口 儿 水 烧开 去 啊 吃 得
khə^{53} ȵi^{34} ʂui^{53} ɕiu^{34}hɐi^{34} həu^{33} ʂau^{53} hiəʔ^{5} tɐʔ^{5}
this QUN water boiled GO PM drink MOD
'[You can] only drink the water when it is boiled!'

(22) Southwest Mandarin khə^{24} 去
放 好 这 凯 钱 去 哦
faŋ^{24} hɔ^{54} tsɿ^{24} kai^{54} tshẽ^{21} khə^{24} o^{21}
put RES this CL money GO PM
'[Go to] keep the money! (lit., put the money well [in your pocket]).'

(23) Zhuang pai^{33}
tɕuŋ^{24} tɕɯ^{11} ŋa:i^{21} tu^{33} nuk^{2} nai^{24} to:t^{55} juŋ^{24} pai^{33}
always COP PASS CL bird this peck mess GO
'[Make this] bird peck [this tree, and make the branch] into a mess, [go!]'
(F.K. Li 1940: 62)

Note that in all the sentences above, the typical commanding and quasi-causative notions are expressed by the 'go' morpheme. When it is omitted, the extra notion disappears, and the whole sentence is semantically ambiguous or pragmatically odd. To witness the data in Nanning Yue and N. Zhuang:

(24) Nanning Yue hy^{33} 去
?食饭 饱, 冇 系 亲讲 来 六孃 啲 冇 得
ʃek^{2}fan^{22} pɛu^{35} mu^{24} hɐi^{21} ʧʰɐn^{33}kɔŋ^{35} lɐi^{21} luk^{24}nœŋ^{55} ti^{55} mu^{24} tɐk^{5}
eat full NEG COP say visit aunt LOC NEG MOD
食饱
ʃek^{2} pɛu^{35}
be-full

i. '[It is time to] eat our fill now. Don't say that you are not full when you visit your aunt's house.' (no suggestive or commanding meaning)
ii. *'We have eaten our fill/eat our fill now. Don't say that you are not full when you visit your aunt's house.' (the binary aspectual reading makes the sentence odd)

(25) Zhuang pai^{33}
?tɕuŋ^{24} tɕɯ^{11} ŋa:i^{21} tu^{33} nuk^{21} nai^{24} to:t^{55} juŋ^{24}
always COP PASS CL bird this peck mess
'[This] bird pecks [this tree, and the branch turns] into a mess.' (only a plain declarative statement, no extra commending meaning. Pragmatically unnatural sentence)

b. *Emphatic particle*

The 'go' morphemes may also be used with a sentence-final emphatic function. In contrast to the perfect marker 'go', which is primarily correlated with the verbal action, the emphatic particle 'go' indicates an intensified mood of certainty and exaggeration. Once the sentence-final 'go' is cancelled, there is no more emphatic notion. While another sentence-final pragmatic marker 啊 (a^{55} in Nanning Yue and a^{33} in Bingyang Pinghua) emphasizes the mood of certainty, it does not usually stand alone (combined with 'go' 去) in these languages. Both the Sinitic and Tai-Kadai groups in this region share this unique function.

(26) Nanning Yue 去
着 食 半 樽 去 啊, 我 食 冇 得 齐
ʃek^{22} ʧœk^{22} pun^{33} ʧɐn^{55} hy^{33} a^{55} ŋɔ^{24} ʃek^{22} mu^{24} tɐk^{55} ʧhɐi^{21}
MOD drink half QUN GO PM 1SG drink NEG MOD RES
'[You need] drink half bottle [of the wine]. I cannot drink [all the wine by myself].'

(27) Binyang Pinghua hu^{55} 去
着 吃 半 瓶 去 啊, 我 吃 冇 得 齐
ʧek^{22} hɐt^{55} pun^{55} piŋ^{213} hu^{55} a^{33} ŋø^{22} hɐt^{55} məu^{22} tɐk^{55} ʧɐi^{213}
MOD drink half QUN GO PM 1SG drink NEG PRM RES
'[I was asked to] drink half bottle of the wine, but I cannot make it!'

(28) Wutong Pinghua həu^{33} 去
有 恁 严重, 掴架 去?
iau^{53} nɐn^{34} in^{31}thieŋ^{53} kuiʔ^{5}ka^{33} həu^{33}
have so serious fight GO
'[Is the problem] so serious that [both of them are angry and] fight with each other?'

(29) Bobai Hakka hi^{42} 去
病 得 咁 严重, 着 住院 去 啊!
phiaŋ^{42} tɛt^{2} kam^{31} ȵiam^{13}tshoŋ^{13} tshɔk^{5} tɕhi^{42}ian^{42} hi^{42} a^{42}
sick PRM SO serious must go-to-hospital GO PM
'[You are] so sick, [you] must go to hospital!'

(30) Southwest Mandarin khə^{24} 去
这 个 娃崽 长 得 高高 的 去
tsɿ^{24} ko^{24} va^{21}tsæ^{54} tsaŋ^{54} tə^{21} kɔ^{33}kɔ^{33} ti^{33} khə^{24}
this CL child grow PRM tall NOM GO
'This child grows very tall!'

(31) Zhuang pai^{1}

ʔdəɯ^{1}	*pa:n*^{3}	*ti*^{3}	*pou*^{4}*θa:i*^{1},	*pou*^{4}*pou*^{4}	*pei*^{2}*pei*^{2}	*pai*^{1}
LOC	classroom	POSS	boys	everyone	fat	GO

'Every boy in the classroom is too fat!'

Table 2. An overview of the functions of 'go' grams*

	Zhuang	NNY	SWM	BY	WT	BB
Imperative maker	+	+	+	+	+	
Emphatic particle	+	+	+	+	+	+

* NNY is the abridged form for Nanning Yue dialect, SWM for Southwest Mandarin, BY for Binyang Pinghua dialect (southern Pinghua branch), WT for Wutong dialect (northern Pinghua branch), BB for Bobai Hakka dialect.

The isoglosses in Figure 3 show the distribution of 'go' functions.

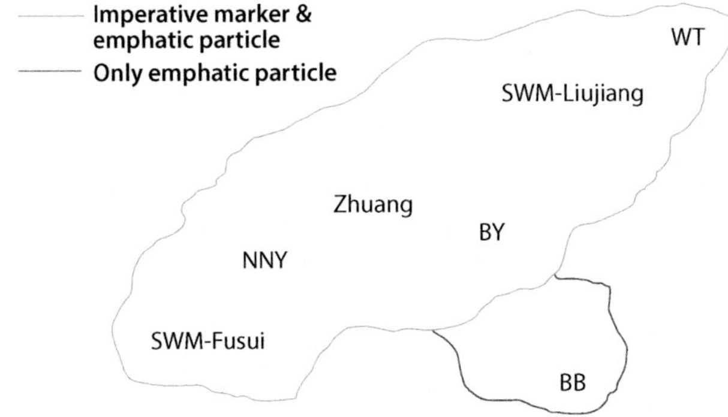

Figure 3. Functions of 'go' grams

3.3 Polyfunctional 'give'

In a similar vein, 'give' verbs in most CS-GXR languages have undergone isomorphic developments. Synchronically, these languages are equipped with polyfunctional 'give' morphemes that encode distinct meanings. As a matter of fact, the various functions of 'give' (ie., dative, benefactive, and malefactive marker) introduced by Qin (2012) are typologically well-known and widespread. However, prefixed cause marker 'give' is seldom reported in the languages in China. Moreover, what distinguishes the scenario in CS-GXR from those found in other regions is the **word order** of the 'give' phrase. Chinese dialects in the Guangxi Region show a popular word order [S-V-O-GIVE], where the 'give' phrase occurs after the main verb. This specific word order differs from the fronting [S-GIVE-V-O] order in Chinese dialectal counterparts outside of GXR at large. Representative languages with these features are shown below:

a. *Benefactive marker*

The benefactive notion in my data is coded by serial verbal constructions with the verb 'give', which loses its original semantics and adds a benefactive/ malefactive/ recipient-like participant into the denoted event. All the languages in question employ the 'give' verb to encode benefaction:

(32) Southwest Mandarin kɐi^{54} 给
哏 少 工资, 哪个 做 给 你?
kɐn^{24} sa^{54} koŋ^{33}tsɿ^{33} na^{54}ko^{24} tsɐu^{24} kɐi^{54} ni^{54}
so less salary who work GIVE 2SG
'[You pay the workers so little]. Who would like to work for you?'

(33) Pinghua pa^{35} 把
你 织 一 件 laŋ^{24}衫 把 我 得 冇?
nei^{22} tsək^{55} jət^{33} kin^{22} laŋ^{35}sam^{35} pa^{35} ŋø^{22} tɐk^{55} məu^{33}
2SG weave one CL clothes GIVE 1SG acquire Q
'Can you weave a piece of cloth for me?'

(34) Zhuang hɔ:i^{3}
khai^{3} təu^{1} hɔ:i^{3} ŋo^{5}
open door GIVE 1SG
'[Please] open the door for me.'

b. *Malefactive marker*

When the situation is unfortunate for the affected argument, the malefactive marker 'give' is employed. Just like the benefactive construction, the malefactive phrase follows the VO unit instead of occupying a preverbal slot.

(35) Southwest Mandarin kɐi^{54} 给
你 还 哏门 犟, 再 犟, 我 就 踢一脚 给
ni^{54} hã^{31} kɐn^{24} mɐn^{31} kiaŋ^{24} tsæ^{24} kiaŋ^{24} ŋo^{54} tɕiɐu^{24} ti^{31}i^{31}kio^{31} kɐi^{54}
2SG MOD so stubborn again stubborn 1SG MOD kick GIVE
你
ni^{54}
2SG
'You are so stubborn! If you are more stubborn [in the future], I will hit you (lit., kick your foot).'

(36) Pinghua pa^{35} 把
你 冇 听话 呢, 啀 就 tsok^{22}一 tsok^{22}把 你
nei^{22} məu^{33} thəŋ^{55} wa^{53} ne^{55} ŋø^{22} təu^{22} tsøk^{22} jət^{33} tsøk^{22} pa^{35} nei^{22}
2SG NEG obey PM 1SG will pat one pat GIVE 2SG
'[If] you don't obey [my orders], I will slap your head.'

(37) Zhuang hɔ:i^{3}
ni^{5} ta:p^{8} te:t^{7} ma:t^{7} ne:u^{2} hɔ:i^{1} te^{1}
2SG box ear CL one GIVE 3SG
'[It seems that] you will box his ears.'

c. *Cause marker*

The semantic interpretation of 'give' as a cause marker is an instance of a pathway whereby a process verb, on account of some salient semantic property, gives rise to a grammatical marker presenting a participant as a cause or source of a change or an event. The language data in SC-GXR, however, show a postposed construction that is barely attested in the Sinitic languages or the adjacent Tai-Kadai languages. For instance:

(38) Southwest Mandarin kɐi^{54} 给
这 个 女的， 哏 鬼 难 搞，我 头昏 给
tsɿ^{24} ko^{24} ny^{54}ti^{33} kɐn^{24} kuɐi^{54} næ^{31} ka^{54} ŋo^{54} thɐu^{31}huɐn^{33} kɐi^{54}
this CL girl so hard deal-with 1SG dizzy GIVE 3SG
她 完
tha^{33} uæ^{31} 去
completely PRF *khə^{24}*
'This girl is so formidable. We are completely dizzy because of her.'

(39) Nanning Yue pi^{35} 畀
我哋 癐 齐 畀 佢 哂
ŋɔ^{24}ti^{22} kwui^{22} ʧhɐi^{21} pi^{35} khy^{24} ɬai^{33}
2PL tired totally GIVE 3SG PRF
'We are totally tired because of him.'

(40) Zhuang hɔ:i^{3}
ŋo^{5} thu^{1} mai^{2} *hɔ:i^{3}* te^{1} le:u^{4} pai^{1}
1SG head hurt GIVE 3SG completely PRF
'My head is completely hurt because of him.'

In a nutshell, the parameter of the multifunctional 'give', though not widely attested in the area, may support the CS-GXR LA hypothesis, given the integrated postverbal word order of the 'give' phrase. We summarize the polyfunctional 'give' scenario in the following table:

Table 3. An overview of the functions of 'give' grams

	Zhuang	BY	NNY	SWM
Postposed benefactive marker	+	+		+
Postposed malefactive marker	+	+		
Cause marker	+		+	+

As a core source, Zhuang diffuses not only its structure of word order (postposed grammatical markers) but also of grammaticalization process ('give' > cause marker) to the adjacent languages. The isoglosses in Figure 4 and 5 show the distribution of 'give' functions:

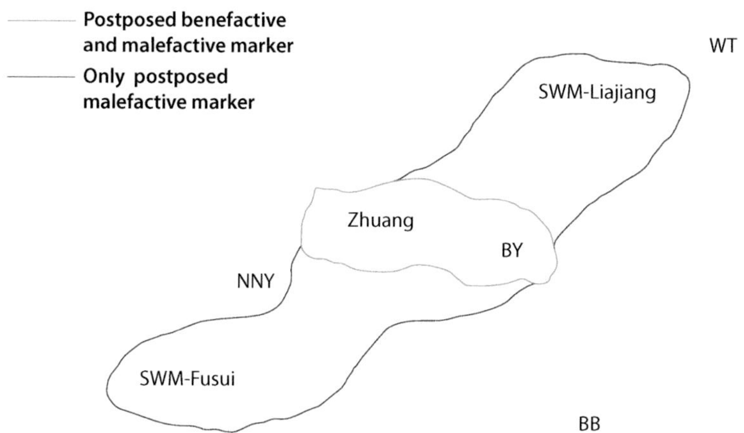

Figure 4. Postposed benefactive and malefactive marker

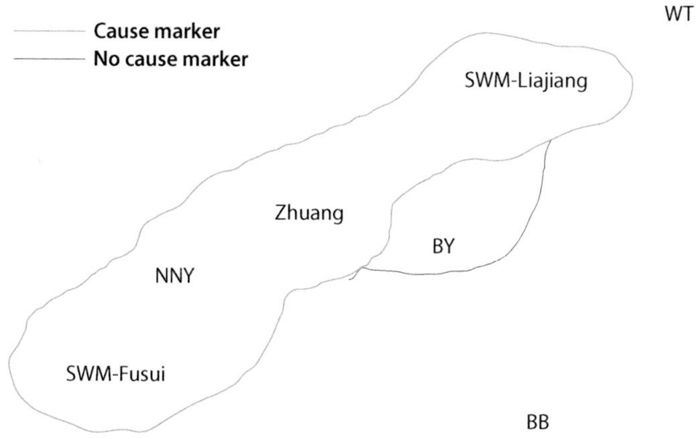

Figure 5. Cause marker

3.4 Polyfunctional 'take'

Huang and Kwok (2013) argue that in most languages of CS-GXR a manner marker, developed from 'take' verb, can be bound with the predicate to signify the manner in which the event takes place. This is an unusual typological feature that is not widely attested beyond the CS-GXR.

(41) Nanning Yue lɔ^{35} 攞
食 鸡蛋 我 钟意 炒 攞 食，冇 钟意 煮 攞 食
ʃek^{22} kɐi^{55}tan^{22} ŋɔ^{24} ʧuŋ^{55} ji^{33} ʧheu^{35} lɔ^{35} ʃek^{22} mu^{24} ʧuŋ^{55} ji^{33} ʧy^{35} lɔ^{35} ʃek^{22}
eat egg 1SG like fry TAKE eat NEG like stew TAKE eat
'I like to cook the eggs by frying instead of stewing.'

(42) Pinghua tshəu^{33} 取
自 己 车 取，冇 是 买
tsok^{22} kei^{53} tshi^{35} tshəu^{33} məu^{22} sei^{22} mai^{22} 取
oneself weave TAKE NEG COP buy TAKE *tshəu^{33}*
'[He] weaved the cloth by himself, but did not buy it [from the shop].'

(43) Zhuang au^{1}
te^{1} pai^{1} ɕa:ŋ^{5}ha:i^{4} naŋ^{3} ho^{4} ɕe^{4} ʔau^{1}
3SG go to Shanghai take train TAKE
'He goes to Shanghai by the way of taking a train.'

Qin (2012) offers a supplementary study on the multifunctionality of 'take' morphemes, and shows that 'take' may ultimately grammaticalize as a selective marker that occurs in pairs of contrasting sentences, where the first clause is negative and the second clause is affirmative. What function the selective marker 'take' encodes can be determined based on the given context. Pragmatically, items in the declarative context win out over those in the negative context:

(44) Pinghua tshəu^{33} 取
今夜 我 冇 凑 叔 睡，我 凑 婶 睡 取
kɐm^{33}ja^{53} ŋø^{22} məu^{22} tshɐu^{55} sok^{55} sø^{53} ŋø^{22} tshɐu^{55} səm^{33} sø^{53} tshəu^{33}
tonight 1SG NEG with uncle sleep 1SG with aunt sleep TAKE
'I won't sleep with my uncle tonight, while instead I will sleep with my aunt [I select to sleep with my aunt].'

(45) Zhuang au^{1}
po:k^{7} kai^{7} ka:i^{5}lau^{2} mi^{2} naŋ^{6} hɔ^{5}ɕe^{5}, naŋ^{6} fəi^{5}ki^{5} au^{1}
time this 1PL NEG take train take plane TAKE
'We don't take the train this time, we will take the plane instead (lit., we select to take the plane).'

Rather than a 'take' verb, many languages employ distinct morphemes to encode the two functions described here. For instance: Hakka (Xinqiao 新桥客家话) ə⁵⁵ɬə⁴², and Southwest Mandarin (Liuzhou) 做 tso²¹/ 做是 tso²¹ si⁵³ can also bear the function of manner and selective marker (Qin 2012: 62–66). Although some of their origins are still unclear, their development parallels that of 'take'. This convergence is likely to have been triggered by language contact, with diffusion from Zhuang infecting the Sinitic languages. The two unique functions are synthesized in Table 4:

Table 4. An overview of the functions of 'take' grams

	Zhuang	BY	NNY	SWM
Manner marker	+	+	+	+
Selective marker	+	+		

The manner marker use exists in all the four linguistic tokens, yet the derived selective marker function is very restricted and merely observed in Zhuang and Binyang Pinghua dialect. The geographic distribution of these markers is shown in Figure 6.

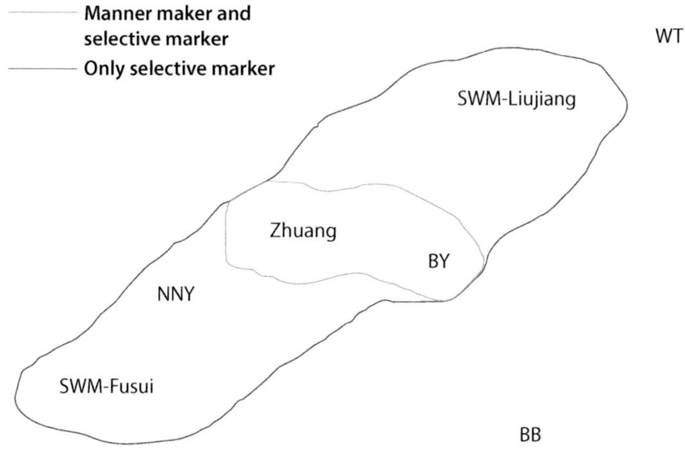

Figure 6. Manner marker and selective marker

3.5 Interim summary

Numerous shared features have been distributed to a wide range of languages in the CS-GXR. While it is probable that those features may be documented somewhere beyond this region worldwide, all the data at hand reflect the fact that languages in the CS-GXR, as opposed to those in other regions of Guangxi, have thoroughly incorporated most of the typical areal features. The Zhuang language is responsible for the directionality of diffusion within this area;[5] although the languages of this region share many traits synchronically, most of them have experienced parallel grammaticalization diachronically. Thus, the CS-GXR should be recognized as a linguistic area in general, where the unrelated language families (Sinitic and Tai-Kadai) have contributed to a distinct Guangxi 'typological profile'.

4. Borrowed grammaticalization

The parameters discussed above may suffice to make a judgment on the area-specific features delimiting CS-GXR. The convergence/isomorphism of linguistic properties in the distinct languages of the region is most likely an outcome triggered by language contact. A large number of areal features, originating from Zhuang, may be viewed as diffuser infecting all the participants in contact. Linguistic area and grammaticalization area are related notions that can each be described in terms of areal-linguistic isoglosses. "Shared features, and especially shared grammaticalization patterns, may result from geographic proximity, contact and borrowing" (Aikhenvald & Dixon 2001: 23). Languages in CS-GXR do not merely share analogic features in a horizontal perspective, but also reveal equivalent grammaticalization stages in a vertical view.

Furthermore, it is reasonable to hypothesize that the impact of Zhuang on Chinese dialects has resulted in creating exclusive, typologically unusual grammaticalization characteristics not found elsewhere in China (Huang 1996; Chappell 2002; Sousa 2012) as well as the abutting MSEA region (Clark 1989;

5. Heine and Kuteva (2005: 33) have proposed a valid diagnostic to identify the instance of contact-induced transfer: If there is a linguistic property *x* shared by two languages M[odel] and R[eplica], and these languages are immediate neighbours and/or are known to have been in contact with each other for an extended period of time, and *x* is also found in languages genetically related to M but not in languages genetically related to R, then we hypothesize that this is an instance of contact-induced transfer, more specifically, that *x* has been transferred from M to R. Geographically, Zhuang speakers and Sinitic speakers have lived together in CS-GXR for centuries, with the result that contact between the Zhuang- and Sinitic-speaking people has penetrated every aspect of daily life. A broad cross-linguistic survey indicates that a certain polyfunctional model discussed in this paper is also found in certain Tai-Kadai languages (e.g., Dai 傣语, Yanghuang 佯僙语) genetically related to Zhuang. Conversely, there is no evidence for any of the models surfacing in Sinitic languages spoken beyond the Guangxi Region other than within the Guangxi Region (cf. Huang 2014). Following Heine and Kuteva's theory, there is thus sufficient information to support our hypothesis that during the contact process, Zhuang was the model language and the Sinitic group is the replica languages. Zhuang appears to have diffused all the polyfunctional models to the neighboring Sinitic varieties.

Bisang 1996; Enfield 2005; Comrie 2007; Bisang & Chappell 2008), resulting in the following shared chains, where Zhuang seems to have provided the model for some Sinitic languages:

i. **'Finish' verb > Universal quantifier > Superlative > Aspectual marker > Conjunction** (Huang & Kwok 2014)

The Zhuang group initially borrowed a fairly common 'finish' verb, *le:u*[4], from Middle Chinese 'finish' 了 (**liɛu*)[6] (Lan 2005: 109; Huang 2014). This is not unusual in this area, since 'finish' verbs in other languages in China and Southeast Asia have grammaticalized functions as aspectual markers and sequential conjunctions (Cao 1995). What is unique to this micro-area is that Zhuang further developed a number of new functions, that is, those of a universal quantifier and a superlative, distinct from those of its Chinese origin in the static context; sequential and contrasting conjunction in the clause-linking context (Huang & Kwok 2014). These grammaticalization chains, absent in other Chinese dialects outside of CS-GXR, have diffused back into their Chinese counterparts of this region in the course of centuries of intensive contact between the Zhuang and Sinitic group. It was the Zhuang type that influenced the geographically adjacent Sinitic groups (cf. Sybesma 2008).

ii. **'Go' > Imperative marker > Emphatic particle** (Qin & Qin 2015)

Another particular example concerns the development of 'go' verbs in these two language groups. Cross-linguistically, it is more likely for a 'go' verb to grammaticalize into a demonstrative or an andative, allative, or tense and aspect marker (Heine & Kuteva 2002: 155–163). Yet a grammaticalization from 'go' verb to emphatic particle via an intermediate stage of imperative marker is rare and uncommon.[7] However, this grammatical chain is widely attested in both the Zhuang and Sinitic group in Guangxi. Most Chinese dialects have grammaticalized the 'go' verb to these markers when it is bounded to the VP in the sentence-final slot. There is hardly any doubt that this unusual development is based on the Zhuang model where the 'go' verb has undergone the polygrammaticalization structure suggested by Kwok (2014).

6. Reconstruction of the Middle Chinese 'finish' 了 is based on Wuyun Pan's online database of Old Chinese phonology (http://www.eastling.org/tdfweb/midage.aspx).

7. While Aikhenvald (2010: 317–325) reports that in certain of the world's languages imperative markers originate from a 'go/to go' etymon, this verbal source is not commonly attested in the relevant literature.

iii. **'Give' verb > Benefactive marker > Malefactive marker > Cause marker** (Qin 2012)

Given that the 'give' verb is inserted between adjectival predicate and object as [ADJ-'GIVE'-O] in Zhuang, it is grammaticalized in Sinitic languages to a cause marker, yielding a quasi-causative reading that 'the object causes the subject to be within the property of the adjective', or 'concerning the object, the subject turns to be in the state described by the adjective'. This grammaticalization occurs in a number of Chinese dialectal groups contiguous to Zhuang.

iv. **'Take' verb > Manner marker > Selective marker** (Huang & Kwok 2013)

The Zhuang 'take' verb has grammaticalized to a manner marker in general when suffixed to individual predicates, and a selective marker in particular when appearing in the sentence-final slot of the contrasting content. Similarly, a block of Chinese dialects (i.e., Nanning Yue, Pinghua, Southwest Mandarin) spoken in the CS-GXR replicated both the syntactic structures and the semantic properties of these two kinds of derived markers from the Zhuang source. This sets the grammaticalization of 'take' verbs within this area off from a wide range of the world's languages, including their Sinitic counterparts beyond this area, where it is common for 'take' verbs to develop a function as a causative, comitative, completive, future, instrument, and patient marker (Heine & Kuteva 2002: 286–289).

Southeast Asia is characterized most of all by a bundle of grammaticalization areas, each characterized by specific processes of grammaticalization (Heine & Kuteva 2005: 203; see also Bisang 1996; Ansaldo 1999; Diller 2001; Enfield 2005). While no reliable information is available on the directionality of diffusion within the Southeast Asian grammaticalization area (cf. Thomason 2001: 90; Heine & Kuteva 2005: 203), it appears to be uncontroversial that Zhuang played a contributing role to the emergence of the micro grammaticalization area of CS-GRX.

The isomorphic features in the languages of CS-GXR differ in the mechanism of their formation during language contact, as we describe below:

i. The distribution pattern from Figure 1 to Figure 6 indicates that most Chinese dialects borrowed the already grammaticalized patterns of versatile 'take', 'finish', 'give' and 'go' through *ordinary grammaticalization* (cf. Heine & Kuteva 2010) from Zhuang, in which the Zhuang shifters transferred the available grammaticalization patterns in their mother language to their secondarily-acquired Chinese dialects. The formation of these categories is based on *indirect diffusion* (Heath 1978: 119–136; Aikhenvald 2003: 237–241) from Zhuang.
ii. The diffusion of the grammaticalized patterns is a two-step process. Zhuang (in the core area) first diffuses its grammaticalized patterns to the languages in its adjacent areas (NNY, BY), and in turn these two Sinitic dialects diffuse the

grammaticalized patterns to their neighboring peripheral languages (SWM, WT, BB). That is for the reason that the languages in the peripheral areas only display the less grammaticalized pattern.

In cautiously defining a GA of CS-GXR, we still do not hesitate to delineate a clear borderline (Emeneau 1956; Campbell 1985; Stolz 2002). Our data in Section 3 propose more reliable information that all the grammaticalization processes occurred within CS-GXR. As Heine and Kuteva (2005: 209) put in their classic study:

> ...while sprachbunds are defined on the basis of clusters of isoglosses, with borders that are notoriously messy and controversial, the boundaries of grammaticalization areas can be defined fairly unambiguously ...

A wide range of Chinese dialects in CS-GXR share more grammaticalizations with the genetically unrelated Zhuang than with other minority languages spoken in this region.[8] We take this to be a result of the relatively large size of the Zhuang community in this region. Prior to the Han expansion, the indigenous inhabitants of the Guangxi Region were ancient Tai (the ancestors of the modern Zhuang). Since at least the Early Qin Dynasty, the Han immigrants were in primary contact with the Zhuang speakers (Li 2002: 134). Among all the other minority groups in this area, the Zhuang were the first to adopt Chinese as their second language in order to ensure more convenient communication with the arriving Sinitic people (Deng 2008: 204). Even in modern ethnic populations, Zhuang makes up a larger proportion of the population (32%) than other minority ethnicities (Yao: 3.3%, Miao: 1.04%, Dong: 0.7%) in the Guangxi Region. Hence, it is Zhuang that becomes the 'diffuser' language, and not the other minority languages.

CS-GXR should exclusively be understood as a typical micro LA in terms of the uncommon convergent linguistic features to be observed in synchrony; and a micro GA in terms of the homogenous grammaticalization paradigms shared by a majority of languages where Zhuang is responsible for the diffusion of all grammaticalization models. The direction of the diffusion is 'Zhuang > Sinitic' and not the other way around, because the grammaticalization patterns (pp. 125–126) in Zhuang (as the model language) are more marked, functional, or grammaticalized (Heine & Kuteva 2003) than in the majority of cases examined in Sinitic.

Some kind of a grammaticalization model exists in all the linguistic data in question, while other models are partially shared by a couple of languages. After computing the quantified isoglosses displayed in Figures 1 to 6 in Section 3, we

8. According to our seven years' fieldwork experience in the Guangxi Autonomous Region, Zhuang is involved in more Sinitic-Tai language contact instances than its Tai counterparts. For the same extrapolation, see Liang & Zhang (1988).

further arrive at the hypothesis that the relation between the core zone and the peripheral zone of this grammaticalization area may be described thus as:

- **Core**: The central southern part of the Guangxi Region, including Nanning 南宁, Chongzuo 崇左, Baise 百色 and the border between Baise and Hechi 河池.
- **Periphery**: The northern part of the Guangxi Region as well as the border area between the central southern part and the southwestern part of this region, including Liuzhou 柳州, Guilin 桂林 and Yulin 玉林.

With this geographic distribution in mind, the scope of the shared grammaticalization model is shown in Map 2.

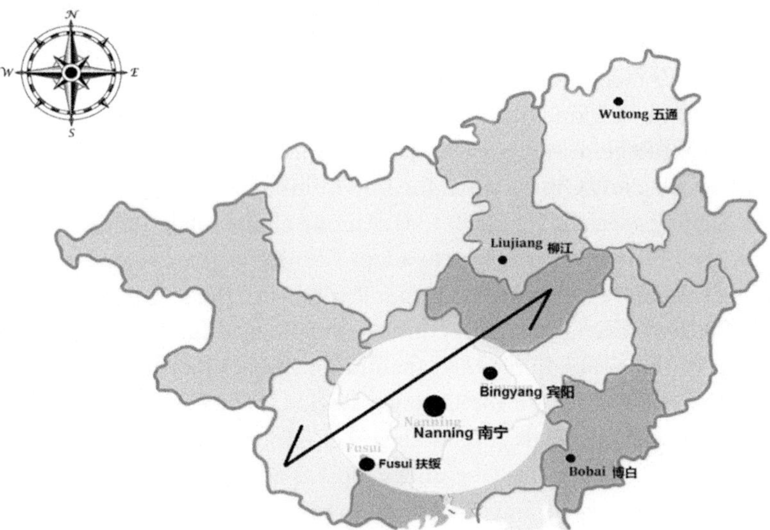

Map 2. Geographic scope of diffused grammaticalization models[9]

As Map 2 shows, it is apparent that all the grammaticalization models providing the source of contact-induced transfer seem to be located in the central southern part of the Guangxi Region, spreading like waves to its neighboring areas from central south to north and southwest. There can be little doubt that this spread is motivated by language contact.

9. The copyright of the vectorgraph belongs to <http://www.oschina.net/>.

5. Conclusion

In his study of areal grammaticalization, Matisoff (1991: 444) concluded that "although many grammatizational tendencies are doubtless universal, there are certainly areal differences of nuance". Numerous languages in MSEA demonstrate striking parallelisms in the way they grammaticalize at large. Yet certain languages still showcase peculiar grammaticalization examples that are typologically and areally rare (Migliazza 1996). This peculiarity may, to some extent, result from intimate contact between distinct language groups of the kind discussed in this paper on contact between Tai-Kadai and Sinitic languages.

Most languages in the Central-Southern Guangxi Region feature a large number of homogeneous linguistic features of phonology, grammar and semantics.[10] Some of them are broadly equivalent with their MSEA counterparts (cf. Sousa 2012), while others are distinctive and unusual. To illustrate this point concretely, we exemplified four patterns of uncommon areal grammaticalization chains exclusively having taken place in CS-GXR.

Unlike previous studies, which were based on a number of similar areal features shared by a cluster of languages in MSEA, we highlighted some disparities that are sufficient to distinguish the CS-GXR from other languages of the MSEA linguistic areas, arguing in favor of a particular CS-GXR grammaticalization area. In this way, we hope to have identified a micro grammaticalization area within MSEA, and to have contributed to a better understanding of areal grammaticalization processes among the languages in MSEA.

Abbreviations

1SG	first person singular	NEG	negative
1PL	first person plural	PASS	passive
2SG	second person singular	PFV	perfective
2PL	second person plural	PM	pragmatic marker
3SG	third person singular	PN	place name
3PL	third person plural	POSS	possessive marker
ATTR	attributive marker	PRF	perfect
CAUS	causative	PRM	postverbal resultative marker

10. Despite of shared grammatical and semantic equivalences, Kwok (2010) also describes a variety of canonical phonological features that have the same distribution as some other features specifically in CS-GXR, such as: long vs. short vowel contrast, complex tone systems, complex consonantal codas (i.e., *-p, -t, -k, -m, -n, -ŋ*), and an abundance of ideophones.

CL	classifier	RECP	reciprocal
COP	copula	RES	resultative
LOC	locative	Q	question marker
MOD	modality marker	QUN	quantifier

Other symbols

The following symbols are used for grammatical description and linguistic changes.

>	grammaticalizes to/develops to
X	items quantified by
X–Y	morpheme boundary between X and Y
?	pragmatically odd
*	unnatural interpretation

This research was supported by the National Social Fund of China 'A Reference Grammar of Muya – A Minority Language Spoken in Southwest China' (16CYY058) and 'Studies on the Semantic Change of Chinese – A Functional-Typological Perspective' (14ZDB098) and the Fundamental Research Funds for the Central Universities 'Language contact in the western Sichuan' (2682018WXTD03). We should first thank the anonymous reviewers for their constructive comments. The first author owes much appreciation to Bernd Heine, Christa Köln, Eric Jackson, Bo Hong, Bit-Chee Kwok, and the participants of the 2nd International Conference on Grammaticalization Theory and Data, Rouen, France, 2016. Any opinions, oversights and errors expressed in this paper are those of the author(s).

References

Aikhenvald, Alexandra Y. & Dixon, Robert M. W. 2001. Introduction. In *Areal Diffusion and Genetic Inheritance: Problems in Comparative Linguistics*, Alexandra Y. Aikenvald & Robert M. W. Dixon (eds), 1–26. Oxford: OUP.

Aikhenvald, Alexandra Y. 2003. *Language Contact in Amazonia*. Oxford: OUP.

Aikhenvald, Alexandra Y. 2010. *Imperatives and Commands*. Oxford: OUP.

Ansaldo, Umberto. 1999. *Comparative Constructions in Sinitic: Areal Typology and Patterns of Grammaticalization*. PhD dissertation, Stockholm University.

Bisang, Walter. 1996. Areal typology and grammaticalization: Processes of grammaticalization based on nouns and verbs in East and Mainland Southeast Asian languages. *Studies in Language* 20(3): 519–597. https://doi.org/10.1075/sl.20.3.03bis

Bisang, Walter & Chappell, Hilary. 2008. Problems with areality-The case of East and Southeast Asian languages. Paper presented at the ESF-OMLL Workshop of 'New Directions in Historical Linguistics', Lyon, France.

Boas, Franz. 1920. The classification of American languages. *American Anthropologist* 22(4): 367–376. https://doi.org/10.1525/aa.1920.22.4.02a00070

Bybee, Joan L. & Dahl, Östen. 1989. The creation of tense and aspect systems in the languages of the world. *Studies in Languages* 13(1): 51–103. https://doi.org/10.1075/sl.13.1.03byb

Bybee, Joan L., Perkins, Revere Dale & Pagliuca, William. 1994. *The Evolution of Grammar: Tense, Aspect, and Modality in the Languages of the World*. Chicago IL: University of Chicago Press.

Campbell, Lyle. 1985. Areal linguistics and its implications for historical linguistics. In *Proceedings of the Sixth International Conference of Historical Linguistics* [Current Issues in Linguistic Theory 34], Jacek Fisiak (ed.), 25–56. Amsterdam: John Benjamins.

Cao, Guangshun. 1995. jìn dài hàn yǔ zhù cí *《近代汉语助词》* (Auxiliaries in the Contemporary Chinese). Beijing: Language and Culture Press.

Chappell, Hilary. 2002. *Sinitic Grammar: Synchronic and Diachronic Perspective*. Oxford: OUP.

Chappell, Hilary & Lan, Li. 2016. Mandarin and other Sinitic languages. In *The Routledge Encyclopedia of the Chinese Language*, Sin-Wai Chan with James Minett & Florence Li Wing Yee (eds), 605–628. London: Routledge.

Cheung, Samuel Hung-nin. 1977. Perfect particles in the bian wen language. *Journal of Chinese Linguistics* 5(1): 55–74.

Clark, Maybeth. 1989. Hmong and Areal South-East Asia. In *Papers in South-East Asian Languages* No. 11: *South-East Asian Syntax* [Pacific Linguistics A77], David Bradley (ed.), 175–230. Canberra: Australian National University.

Comrie, Bernard. 2007. Areal typology of Mainland Southeast Asia: What we learn from the WALS maps. *Manusya Special Issue* 13: 18–47.

Dahl, Östen & Velupillai, Viveka. 2005. Perfective/imperfective aspect. In *World Atlas of Language Structures*, Bernard Comrie, Matthew Dryer, David Gil & Martin Haspelmath (eds), 267–275. Oxford: OUP.

Deng, Yurong. 2008. guǎng xī zhuàng zú zì zhì qū gè mín zú yǔ yán jiān de xiàng hù yǐng xiǎng 广西壮族自治区各民族语言间的相互影响(Mutual Influence between Chinese Dialects and Minority Languages in Guangxi Zhuang Autonomous Region). *fāng yán 《方言》* 3: 204–215.

Diller, Anthony. 2001. Grammaticalization and Tai syntactic change. In *Essays in Tai Linguistics*, M. R. Kalaya Tingsabadh & Arthur S. Abramson (eds), 139–176. Bangkok: Chulalongkorn University Press.

Emeneau, Murray B. 1956. India as a linguistic area. *Language* 32(1):3–16. https://doi.org/10.2307/410649

Enfield, Nicholas J. 2005. Areal linguistics and Mainland Southeast Asia. *Annual Review of Anthropology* 34: 181–206. https://doi.org/10.1146/annurev.anthro.34.081804.120406

Gan, Rui-Jing, Pan, Shang-Ling, Mustavich, Laura F., Qin, Zhen-Dong, Cai, Xiao-Yun, Qian, Ji, Liu, Cheng-Wu, Peng, Jun-Hua, Li, Shi-lin, Xu, Jie-Shun, Jin, Li & Li, Hui. 2008. Pinghua population as an exception of Han Chinese's coherent genetic structure. *Journal of Human Genetics* 53: 303–313. https://doi.org/10.1007/s10038-008-0250-x

Gerner, Matthias. 2013. *A Grammar of Nuosu*. Berlin: Walter de Gruyter. https://doi.org/10.1515/9783110308679

Goddard, Cliff. 2005. *The Languages of East and Southeast Asia*. Oxford: OUP.

Haspelmath, Martin. 1998. How young is standard average European? *Language Sciences* 20(3): 271–287. https://doi.org/10.1016/S0388-0001(98)00004-7

Heath, Jeffrey. 1978. *Linguistic Diffusion in Arnhem Land*. Canberra: Australian Institute of Aboriginal Studies.

Heine, Bernd & Kuteva, Tania. 2002. *World Lexicon of Grammaticalization*. Cambridge: CUP. https://doi.org/10.1017/CBO9780511613463

Heine, Bernd & Kuteva, Tania. 2003. On contact-induced grammaticalization. *Studies in Language* 27(3): 529–572.

Heine, Bernd. 2011. Areas of grammaticalization and geographical typology. In *Geographical Typology and Linguistic Areas, with Special Reference to Africa*, [Tokyo University of Foreign Studies 2], Osamu Hieda, Christa König & Hirosi Nakagawa (eds), 42–66. Amsterdam: John Benjamins. https://doi.org/10.1075/tufs.2.06hei

Heine, Bernd & Kuteva, Tania. 2005. *Language Contact and Grammatical Change*. Cambridge: CUP. https://doi.org/10.1017/CBO9780511614132

Heine, Bernd & Kuteva, Tania. 2010. Contact and grammaticalization. In *The Handbook of Language Contact*, Raymond Hickey (ed.), 86–105. Oxford: Blackwell. https://doi.org/10.1002/9781444318159.ch4

Hong, Bo. 2004. zhuàng yǔ yǔ hàn yǔ de jiē chù shǐ jí jiē chù lèi xíng 壮语与汉语的接触史及接触类型 (The history and characteristic of the language contact between Zhuang and Chinese). In lè zài qí zhōng –wáng shì yuán jiāo shòu qī shí huá dàn qìng zhù wén jí *《乐在其中 –王士元教授七十华诞庆祝文集》* (The Joy of Research: A Festschrift in Honor of Prof. William S-Y. Wang's 70th Birthday), Feng Shi & Zhongwei Shen (eds), 104–120. Tianjin: Nankai University Press.

Huang, Borong. 1996. hàn yǔ fāng yán yǔ fǎ lèi biān *《汉语方言语法类编》*(A Grammatical Compilation of Chinese Dialects). Qingdao: Qingdao Press.

Huang, Yang & Kwok, Bit-Chee. 2013. fāng shì zhù cí zài guǎng xī hàn yǔ fāng yán hé zhuàng dòng yǔ zhōng de kuò sàn: yuán tóu, guò chéng jí qǐ shì 方式助词在广西汉语方言和壮侗语中的扩散:源头、过程及启示 (Diffusions of the manner particles in Chinese dialects and Tai-Kadai languages of Guangxi: Their origins, processes and implications). In dà jiāng dōng qù: wáng shì yuán jiāo shòu bā shí suì hè shòu lùn wén jí *《大江东去:王士元教授八十岁贺寿论文集》* (Eastward Flows the Great River: Festschrift in Honor of Professor William S-Y. WANG on this 80th Birthday), Gang Peng & Feng Shi (eds), 521–540. Hong Kong: City University of Hong Kong Press.

Huang, Yang & Kwok, Bit-Chee. 2014. zhuàng yǔ fāng yán 'wán bì' dòng cí de duō xiàng yǔ fǎ huà mó shì 壮语方言"完毕"动词的多向语法化模式 (Polygrammaticalization of the 'FINISH' verbs in the Zhuang language). mín zú yǔ wén *《民族语文》* 1: 21–32.

Huang, Yang. 2014. Synchronic Variation, Grammaticalization and Language Contact: The Development of the FINISH Morphemes in the Yue-Chinese and the Zhuang Languages in the Guangxi Region. PhD dissertation, City University of Hong Kong.

Huang, Yang. 2016. nán níng yuè yǔ de zhù cí 'shài' 南宁粤语的助词晒(Rethinking of the auxiliary 'ɬai' 晒 in Yue dialect in Nanning, Guangxi Zhuang Autonomous Region). fāng yán *《方言》* 4: 410–419.

Huffman, Franklin E. 1973. Thai and Cambodian: A case of syntactic borrowing? *Journal of the American Oriental Society* 93(4): 488–509. https://doi.org/10.2307/600168

Kwok, Bit-Chee. 2010. yǔ yán jiē chù zhōng de yǔ fǎ biàn huà: nán níng yuè yǔ 'shù yǔ + bīn yǔ + bǔ yǔ' jié gòu de lái yuán 语言接触中的语法变化: 南宁粤语"述语+宾语+补语"结构的来源 (Grammatical change in language contact: On the origin of the 'verb + object + complement' construction in Nanning Yue). *Journal of Chinese Linguistics Monograph* 24: 201–216.

Kwok, Bit-Chee. 2014. nán níng dì qū yǔ yán 'qù' yì yǔ sù de yǔ fǎ huà yǔ jiē chù yǐn fā de 'fù zhì' 南宁地区语言"去"义语素的语法化与接触引发的"复制" (The morpheme GO in three languages of the Nanning region: Paths of grammaticalization and contact-induced 'replication'). *Language and Linguistics* 5: 663–697.

Lan, Qingyuan. 2005. zhuàng hàn tóng yuán cí jiè cí yán jiū 《壮汉同源词借词研究》 (A Study on the Cognates and Loanwords between Zhuang and Han). Beijing: The Minzu University Press of China.

Li, Fang-Kuei. 1940. lóng zhōu tǔ yǔ 《龙州土语》 (The Tai Dialects of Lungchow) [Academia Sinitica]. Shanghai: The Commercial Press.

Li, Lianjin. 2000. píng huà yīn yùn yán jiū 《平话音韵研究》 (A Phonological Study of Pinghua). Nanning: Guangxi People's Publishing House.

Li, Jinfang. 2002. dòng tái yǔ yán yǔ wén huà 《侗台语言与文化》 (The Tai-Kadai Language and Culture). Beijing: The Minzu University Press of China.

Li, Lianjin. 2007. píng huà de fèn qū nèi bù fèn qū jí xì shǔ wèn tí 平话的分区、内部分区及系属问题 (The Classification/Distribution of Pinghua). Fāng yán 《方言》 1: 71–78.

Liang, Min & Zhang, Junru. 1988. guǎng xī zhuàng zú zì zhì qū gè mín zú yǔ yán de xiàng hù yǐng xiǎng 广西壮族自治区各民族语言的相互影响 (The mutual influence of the languages in Guangxi). Fāng yán 《方言》 2: 87–91.

Liu, Cunhan. 1998. guǎng xī de yǔ yán bǎo cáng 广西的语言宝藏 (The values of the languages in Guangxi). wú zhōu shī zhuān xué bào 《梧州师专学报》 14: 12–17.

Masica, Colin P. 1976. *Defining A Linguistic Area-South Asia*. Chicago IL: The University of Chicago Press.

Matisoff, James A. 1991. Areal and universal dimensions of grammaticalization in Lahu. In *Approaches to Grammaticalization*, Vol. 2: *Types of Grammatical Markers* [Typological Studies in Language 19:2], Elizabeth Closs Traugott & Bernd Heine (eds), 383–453. Amsterdam: John Benjamins. https://doi.org/10.1075/tsl.19.2.19mat

Migliazza, Brian. 1996. Mainland Southeast Asia: A unique linguistic area. *Notes on Linguistics* 75: 17–25.

Qin, Dongsheng. 2012. duì guǎng xī sān gè qū yù xìng yǔ fǎ xiàn xiàng de kǎo chá 《对广西三个区域性语法现象的考察》 (On the Three Areal Grammatical Features in Guangxi). PhD dissertation, Hebei Normal University, Shijiazhuang.

Qin, Dongsheng & Fengyu Qin. 2015. guǎng xī hàn yǔ 'qù' hé zhuàng yǔ fāng yán 'pai[1]' de liǎng zhǒng tè shū yòng fǎ-qū yù yǔ yán xué shì jiǎo xià de kǎo chá 广西汉语"去"和壮语方言pai[1]的两种特殊用法—区域语言学视角下的考察 (On the two grammatical properties of the GO morpheme '去' and 'pai[1]' in the Sinitic and Tai-Kadai languages in Guangxi: An areal-typological perspective). mín zú yǔ wén 《民族语文》 2: 68–75.

Ramat, Anna G. 2008. Areal convergence in grammaticalization processes. In *Rethinking Grammaticalization*, Vol. 2: *New Perspectives* [Typological Studies in Language 76], María José López-Couso and Elena Seoane (eds), 129–168. Amsterdam: John Benjamins. https://doi.org/10.1075/tsl.76.08gia

Robbeets, Martine & Cuyckens, Hubert. 2013. Towards a typology of shared grammaticalization, In *Shared Grammaticalization: With Special Focus on the Transeurasian Languages* [Studies in Language Companion Series 132], Martine Robbeets & Hubert Cuyckens (eds), 1–22. Amsterdam: John Benjamins. https://doi.org/10.1075/slcs.132.05rob

Shao, Longyi, Zhang, Pengfei, Gayer, R. A., Chen, Jialang & Dai, Shifeng. 2003. Coal in a carbonate sequence stratigraphic framework: The Upper Permian Heshan formation in central Guangxi, Southern China. *Journal of the Geological Society* 160: 285–298. https://doi.org/10.1144/0016-764901-108

de Sousa, Hilário 2012. The far southern Sinitic languages as part of Mainland Southeast Asia. Paper presented at the Max Planck Institute for Evolutionary Anthropology (MPI) MSEA Workshop, Leipzig, Germany.

Stolz, Thomas. 2002. No Sprachbund beyond this line! On the age-old discussion of how to define a linguistic area. In *Mediterranean Languages: Papers from the MEDITYP Workshop, Tirrenia*, June 2000 [Diversitas Linguarum 1], Paolo Ramat & Thomas Stolz (eds), 259–281. Bochum: N. Brockmeyer.

Sybesma, Rint. 2008. Zhuang: A Tai language with some Sinitic characteristics –Postverbal 'can' in Zhuang, Cantonese, Vietnamese and Lao. In *From Linguistic Areas to Areal Linguistics* [Studies in Language Companion Series 90], Pieter Muysken (eds), 221–274, Amsterdam: John Benjamins. https://doi.org/10.1075/slcs.90.06syb

Thomason, Sarah Grey. 2001. *Language Contact*. Edinburgh: EUP.

Trubetzkoy, Nikolai. 1928. *Proposition 6. Actes du Premier Congrès International des Linguistes*. Leiden: A. W. Sijthoff.

van der Auwera, Johan. 1998. *Adverbial Constructions in the Languages of Europe*. Berlin: Mouton de Gruyter. https://doi.org/10.1515/9783110802610

Weinreich, Uriel. 1963. *Language in Contact: Findings and Problems*, 2nd edn. The Hague: Mouton.

Wu, Fuxiang. 1998. zhòng tán 'dòng + le + bīn' gé shì de lái yuán hé wán chéng tǐ zhù cí 'le' de chǎn shēng 重谈"动+了 + 宾"格式的来源和完成体助词"了"的产生 (Reconsider the origin of the 'V + 了 + C' construction and the emergence of the perfective aspect marker '了'). zhōng guó yǔ wén *《中国语文》* 6: 452–462.

Wurm, Stephen Adolphe. 1987. *Language Atlas of China*. London: Longman.

Xie Jianyou et al. 2007. guǎng xī hàn yǔ fāng yán yán jiū *《广西汉语方言研究》* (Studies on the Han Chinese dialects of Guangxi). Nanning: Guangxi People's Publishing House.

Grammaticalizing connectives in English and discourse information structure

Diana M. Lewis
Aix Marseille University & Laboratoire Parole et Langage

The development of lexical expressions such as VP adverbs, matrix clauses and prepositional phrases into discourse markers and connectives expressing coherence relations has been well explored in the grammaticalization literature, under a broad view of grammaticalization, but there has been less emphasis on how the discourse information structuring functions of markers evolve during these developments. This paper investigates the relationship between discourse coherence marking and information structure by examining two developing discourse connectives: it suggests that the grammaticalization of a lexeme in its construction into a discourse marker may involve acquiring or strengthening discourse-level information structuring functions – indicating relative informational salience – and that (further) grammaticalization of markers may be at least partly directed by information structure.

Keywords: coherence relations, discourse connectives, English, grammaticalization

1. Introduction

The development of lexical expressions such as VP adverbs, matrix clauses and prepositional phrases into discourse markers expressing coherence relations ('discourse connectives' or 'relational discourse particles') has been well explored in the grammaticalization literature, under a broad view of grammaticalization. This work has intersected with recent renewal of interest in parenthetical and peripheral constructions, discourse markers being a major category of 'extra-clausal constituent'. In particular, attention has focused on the extent to which differing positions of markers correlate with different functions. But there has been less emphasis on the discourse information-structuring functions of markers and how these evolve. This chapter investigates aspects of the relationship between English

https://doi.org.10.1075/slcs.202.06lew
© 2018 John Benjamins Publishing Company

discourse connectives and discourse information structure: it suggests that the grammaticalization of a lexeme-in-its-construction into a discourse connective may involve acquiring or strengthening information- structuring functions – foregrounding, backgrounding and structuring units of discourse – and that (further) grammaticalization may be at least partly motivated by information structure (cf. Lehmann 2008). A case study is presented of two English discourse connectives that can occur in different positions relative to the host unit. In each case, the meaning of the discourse connective, in the sense of the coherence relation that it expresses, is similar across initial and final positions but, it is argued, the information structure of the overall 'discourse construction' results at least in part from the discourse connective and its position. If so, there may be implications for how models of discourse structure relate coherence to discourse information structure.

The rest of the chapter is organized into the following sections. The next section sets the study in the context of recent work on the grammaticalization of discourse markers and in particular on the significance of position in the utterance. It also outlines the relationship between coherence relations and information structure. Section 3 presents a case study of the recent evolution of English discourse connectives *after all* and *in fact* in initial and final positions. Section 4 contains a discussion of findings and Section 5 concludes the chapter.

2. Discourse connectives

2.1 Grammaticalization and discourse connectives

The terminological confusion surrounding discourse connectives (or discourse markers, pragmatic markers, linking adverbials, adverbial connectors and so on) reflects uncertainty over their categorial status as well as differing theoretical frameworks. For practical purposes, a discourse connective will be taken as an adverb or adverbial expression characterized by discourse-semantic, structural and lexicalization parameters. ('Lexicalization' is used here in the sense of loss of compositionality: that is, semantic fusion (Bybee 1985: 37) or renunciation of internal analysis (Lehmann 2002: 15).) A discourse connective expresses a coherence relation, is structurally dependent on a host and constitutes a single- or multi-word lexeme (cf. Lewis 2011). This characterization makes no claims about discourse connectives or markers constituting a distinct word class. Insofar as discourse connectives refer back anphorically to a previous idea, they cannot occur discourse-initially (i.e. at the start of a conversation or text, where no ideas have yet been expressed), except, of course, where a non-verbal previous idea is currently activated in the discourse context (cf. Blakemore 1996: 337–8).

The argument that the development of discourse markers, including discourse connectives, is best analysed as a case of grammaticalization dates back at least to Traugott (1995). Since then, grammaticalization scholars have been (increasingly, perhaps) split on whether such developments can be classed as grammaticalization. Roughly speaking, the arguments for viewing discourse marker development as grammaticalization centre around the semantic changes the expressions undergo (desemanticization/bleaching) and the categorial changes from a main constituent such as prepositional phrase (PP) or predicate to some sort of sentence adverb (Brinton & Traugott 2005; Hopper & Traugott 2003). The arguments against tend to focus on the syntactic changes, in particular the fact that emergent discourse markers show increased scope and more flexible positioning, whereas canonical grammaticalization developments show scope decrease, typically involving items becoming affixes. Those who adopt a narrow view of grammaticalization have proposed alternative labels for the type of change that subsumes discourse marking, including 'pragmaticalization' (Erman & Kotsinas 1993; Aijmer 1997) on the grounds that the resultant expressions are 'pragmatic', or 'co-optation' (Heine et al. 2015) on the grounds of sudden scope shift. In this chapter, a broad or extended view of grammaticalization is taken, encompassing changes where items or constructions become more grammatical, whether or not they become more syntactically fixed and more obligatory.

2.2 Positions of discourse connectives

The position of discourse connectives has attracted much recent attention. Questions that have arisen regarding the position of connectives include the frequency and origins of different positions, their motivation and correlations with function. The hypothesis will be put forward in Sections 3 and 4 that the recent increase in English of final position connectives is at least partly motivated by the management of informational salience.

Connectives combine with their host unit and the previous unit (to which they refer back) to form a discourse-level structure of the type [p] [connective [q]] where the connective has scope over the host q. English discourse connectives occur in the three sentence-adverb positions: initial, medial (that is, post first auxiliary or pre-verb if no auxiliary) and final. We will refer to these positions as left periphery (LP), medial and right periphery (RP). The term 'periphery' has been variously used in the functional literature to refer to a structural slot in relation to the clause, to the utterance or to the turn (Beeching & Detges 2014). In the context of discourse connectives, we use the term here in relation to 'host', to refer to a position preceding or following a discourse unit, of any syntactic status, that encodes an idea and acts as the host of a connective.

English discourse connectives are often assumed to occur predominantly in sentence-initial position (e.g. Huddleston & Pullum 2002: 578), but many can occur at both LP and RP. Examples are *actually, after all, anyway, even so, however, in fact, of course, otherwise, rather, really, surely, though, then*. They thus align with 'comment clauses' and deverbal discourse markers such as *I see, I mean, you know, I think, look, mind you, as far as I know*, which have similar positional distribution, as well as with many evaluative sentence adverbs such as *sadly, luckily, curiously* and so on. It has been suggested that only English, among Indo-European languages, has a regular construction with adverbial connectives in final position (Lenker 2010: 198) and that this is "a comparatively recent syntactic change in English, i.e. a new position for adverbial connectors" (2010: 202). And final position (RP) for connectives appears to be increasing. Biber et al. have found that for what they term 'linking adverbials', in the Conversation register initial position is the commonest, medial position is rare, and about 40% of tokens are in final position (1999: 891). Given also the findings that stance adverbials overall occur more frequently in final position in Conversation than in written registers (Biber et al. 1999), it seems safe to infer that RP position is the more recent.[1]

Recent interest in utterance-final particles in general (e.g. Barth-Weingarten & Couper-Kuhlen 2002; Hancil 2014; Hancil, Haselow & Post 2015; Haselow 2012, 2013, 2015; Kim & Jahnke 2011; Mulder & Thompson 2008; Traugott 2012, 2013) has led to hypotheses about the origin and the function of the 'utterance-final slot', and in particular the functional differences that may correlate with position. Final particles have, according to Haselow, "essentially the same function as conjunctions, establishing a two-place relationship between two structural units, conjunctions operating on the sentence-internal level, final particles at utterance-level and

1. A distinction is to be drawn, from the point of view of language change, between discourse markers that have become 'stranded', so to speak, at the end of an utterance due initially to ellipsis of their host unit, and those that occur in end-position immediately following their host unit. The former are exemplified in the concessive constructions of (1). *But still* in (1a) links its host, *that's life*, to *We'll miss each other*, and is at LP. The second conjunct (the host unit) may be ellipted, resulting in occurrences such as (1b) (spoken) and (1c) (written), where the marker is a 'hanging implication' (Thompson & Suzuki 2011: 670). The marker's host unit has at first to be pragmatically inferred, but the marker soon becomes autonomous (in its own tone unit) and ends up at RP. The *but still* of (1a) may then be analysed as being at LP and/or RP.

(1) a. *"We'll miss each other,* ***but still****, that's life".* [1980s, BNC CFY, fiction]
b. *I still can't carry anything heavy in it* ***but still****.* [1980s, BNC-DS KBB, conversation]
c. *Worrying in advance can stave off disaster. Sounds better in Latin, perhaps,* ***but even still****.* [2015, *The Financial Times*, 14/08/2015, feature article]

No claims are made here about 'stranded' markers, other than to point out that over time they can of course become integrated and indistinguishable from markers that have 'moved'.

thus across clause-boundaries" (2015: 210). Aijmer (2002) discusses RP *actually* as differing from LP *actually* in having interpersonal and positive politeness functions. Likewise, in her analysis of *anyway* in varieties of spoken English, Aijmer finds LP *anyway* and RP *anyway* to be distinct constructions with distinct meaning potentials (respectively a resumptive discourse marker or topic closer and modal/intersubjective) (2016: 48–54). In similar vein, RP *though*, is analysed by Lenker as a concessive connector that has been reanalysed as marker of contrast in final position (2010: 186, 196). Others have argued that the left periphery favours subjective meanings, and the right periphery intersubjective meanings (Izutsu & Izutsu 2013;[2] Beeching & Detges 2014). However, counter-evidence has been found for certain English expressions in the peripheries (Traugott 2014, 2016), so that such a functional distribution may at best be a tendency. Not all scholars, however, have found functional differences according to position. In his analysis of Irish English *like*, Schweinberger (2015: 127) finds that the clause-final and clause-medial 'like' share functional properties, despite differing in direction of scope (backwards vs. forwards) and suggests that one is chosen over the other depending on the phrasal constituents that the marker modifies.

Given that a number of connectives can occur in either initial (LP) or final (RP) position in the same context, it is by no means immediately obvious that there are systematic functional differences between them.

2.3 Coherence relations and information structure

Grammaticalization and information structure are linked in at least two ways, according to Lehmann: "[o]n the one hand, information structure is present in the source constructions that undergo grammaticalization and may direct their course. On the other hand, information structure is itself susceptible of grammaticalization" (2008: 207). In the case of discourse connectives, their grammaticalization results in expressions that serve to background (or 'depropositionalize') a discourse relation. Connectives also participate in the information structure[3] of

2. Izutsu and Izutsu (2013: 232) go so far as to suggest that utterance-final position "may be somehow exploitable for (peripheral) intersubjectivity marking in most languages".

3. Information structure is usually taken to involve intrasentential information relations such as theme, rheme, topic, focus, background, contrast and so on. Information relations beyond the clause or sentence have traditionally been dealt with separately and under different labels. Polanyi et al. (2003), among others, distinguish 'information structure' operating at clause level from 'discourse structure' at the level of interclausal information relations. Other labels are 'discourse relations', 'coherence relations' and 'rhetorical structure'. However, the dividing line between sentence and discourse is not so clear-cut: grammar and discourse are interdependent (Mithun 2005, 2016). Many connectives function at the interface between syntactic dependency

the discourse (the sequence of related ideas) they are a part of, to signal the relative salience or informational prominence of adjacent idea units.

Several studies of RP English discourse markers have considered the implications of information structure. In her discussion of how Engish *however* and *though* have developed from subordinators into adverbial connectors, for instance, Lenker claims that "these changes are [...] induced by factors of information structure and may [...] also lead to changes in information structure. In this view, adverbial connectors are – in contrast to subordinators – very strong indicators of a great illocutionary weight of the second connect" (2010: 32). She suggests that information structure accounts for the development of *though* from subordinator (in a hypotactic construction) to sentence-final adverbial connector (in a paratactic construction) thereby changing from a marker of concession to a marker of contrast (2010: 201). The shift of the marker to final position, "a position which clearly differentiates hypotaxis from parataxis", is "triggered by the lack of other distinctive means" (2010: 213). The result is a new slot for connectives, and so a new connective construction.

In his studies of RP *then* and *anyway*, Haselow addresses the relative structural status of the conjuncts, the final position offering "a structural alternative to hypotaxis" (2012: 154), and emphasizing "the paratactic nature of interactive speech" (2015: 227) that gave rise to the construction. Haselow refers to RP *then* as being "based on an implied paratactic conditional construction" (2012: 154) but does not discuss the relative informational salience of the conjuncts.

The next section gives an overview of the development of particular connective functions in *in fact* and *after all*. It will be suggested that, for each adverbial, while the rhetorical relation expressed through occurrences at LP and RP positions does not alter, there is an information structural difference. Initial connectives tend to act as presentatives, foregrounding the host idea that follows them, so that (leaving prosody aside for the moment) it functions as a further utterance carrying as much weight as the previous one. By contrast, final connectives bind their host to the previous idea in a discourse construction where the second conjunct has less informational salience than the first.

---

and discourse structure. Both spoken and written discourse is made up of both units that have 'standard' sentence structure and those that do not, including multi-conjoined clauses or concatenated clause complexes, isolate non-finite clauses and all kinds of fragments that cannot be explained away by ellipsis. Information structure, whether at sentence or discourse level, concerns the relative salience given by speakers to the elements of their discourse, so we will prefer the term (discourse) information structure to 'discourse structure' which sounds analagous to 'sentence structure'.

3. Grammaticalizing discourse connectives and position

3.1 Two recent Engish connectives

In fact and *after all* have followed similar trajectories to become discourse connectives, and have been studied as examples of grammaticalization at discourse level (*v.* Schwenter & Traugott 2000 on *in fact*; Lewis 2007 on *after all*). Both have gone through successive splits: first the prepositional phrase coalesced in some contexts into a complex adverb and later came to express a newer, connective use alongside the older VP-adverbial use. And in each case a further connective use developed, arguably at a more abstract or more subjective level. These developments are typical of grammaticalization and have resulted in polysemy as older, more lexical uses coexist with the newer, more grammatical ones. Both *in fact* and *after all*, as connectives, refer back anaphorically to a previous discourse unit or act as presupposition triggers to evoke an idea that is active in the discourse context. However, these expressions continue to evolve, and may currently be developing further uses.

Discourse connectives are typically multifunctional, and different senses may be differently distributed across syntactic positions. *After all* and *in fact* are interesting in that both initial and final positions, as well as medial position (post-auxiliary) are found for what seems to be one and the same function, although the positional split may also reflect an incipient functional split involving some further grammaticalization.

Section 3.2 looks at the development and current usage of *in fact*; Section 3.3 focuses on *after all*. Section 3.4 summarizes the findings for these two adverbial connectives. Historical data on *in fact* and *after all* are taken from the period 1680–1920s and present-day data from the 1960s and 1980s. The data sources are listed in the appendix. The historical data were chosen to be representative insofar as possible of everyday English in the British Isles and to be as balanced as possible across periods. They consist primarily of personal letters, drama, diaries, and journals. The result is a corpus that provides small numbers of occurrences, and suffers from some 'burstiness' in the data, the stylistic quirks of authors being particularly apparent in usage of idiomatic expressions such as these two. For present-day English examples taken from the British National Corpus the text code is given along with the genre: BNC-CG stands for the contextually-governed part of the spoken section of the corpus, and BNC-DS stands for the demographically-sampled part, i.e. conversation.

3.2 In fact

3.2.1 *Evolution of 'in fact'*

In fact developed into a discourse connective from the prepositional phrase (PP). As a PP used as a VP-adverbial in Early Modern English, *in fact* gradually coalesced into an epistemic adverb emphasizing the veracity of its host. It is found in the eighteenth century in initial, medial and final positions. It often occurred in contexts which contrasted what really was the case 'in fact' with what was thought or said to be the case; its function was thus often epistemic (1) and can be paraphrased by 'in reality'.

(1) *I cannot help thinking .. that Earle's vanity has tempted him to invent the account of her former way of life ... – I dare say she was nothing but an innocent country girl* ***in fact*** . [1799, Austen, personal letter]

From such contexts arose present-day English contrastive *in fact*, illustrated in (2):

(2) *er you mentioned glucose* ***in fact*** *the one that is actually ... produced [...] Dextrose* [1980s, BNC-CG FLY, science lesson]

In fact here has become an adverbial marker of contrast, most frequently in initial position. With the development of the connective function came a move from the sentence-final or medial position typical for VP-adverbials to the initial position typical for connective adverbials.

Further development brought about present-day English elaborative *in fact*, which seems to have arisen during the late eighteenth and early nineteenth centuries from the epistemic 'in reality / in truth' sense, used to increase hearer belief in contexts where some further, potentially surprising claim follows an assertion,[4] as in (3)

(3) a. *The beast [a rhinocerous] .. kept on an even and steady course, which,* ***in fact****, was a kind of pacing*
[1785, Sparrman, *A Voyage to the Cape of Good Hope* translated from the Swedish]

b. *and the accident has vexed me to the heart.* ***In fact****, I could not pluck up spirits to write to you, on account of the unfortunate business.*
[1790, Burns, personal letter]

Such examples seem to have been the immediate precursors to elaborative *in fact*. At this stage *in fact* is unlikely to have had quite the same sense as the present-day

4. Schwenter and Traugott (2000) suggest that elaborative *in fact* developed directly out of contrastive *in fact*, via a reanalysis on to the rhetorical plane where elaborative *in fact* expresses a rhetorical contrast, but our data did not reveal any evidence for this (cf. Lewis 1998); rather, there was evidence of use of the still-epistemic adverb in contexts such as those in (4).

English elaborative discourse connective, but rather to have still been epistemic (cf. *in truth*). But by the late nineteenth century we find occurrences that are more clearly connective (4). An idea is followed by a rhetorically stronger or more specific idea. To say that a state of affairs obtains 'in fact' is to emphasize that one's statement is true, so that hosts of *in fact*, whether expressing a correction of a false claim or an elaboration of the previous claim, carried emphasis. Here, *in fact* functions in much the same way as *indeed*, which had grammaticalized earlier in a very similar way.[5]

(4) You have probably heard – **in fact**, I have told you myself
[1894, Conan Doyle, *The Stark Munro Letters*]

The elablorative use is the most frequent use of *in fact* in present-day English, exemplified in (5). The fact that the host of *in fact* is rhetorically stronger lends it greater informational salience within the discourse.

(5) a. I hate Tech class … I hate Music too .. **in fact** I hate most of my lessons
[1980s, BNC-DS, KPG, conversation]
b. I said do you still have your late night on a Thursday so they said yes he said **in fact** we're open every night now till 6 o'clock
[1980s, BNC-DS, KBC, conversation]

This elaborative construction is shown in (6).

(6) [Claim or stance] [[*in fact*] [Elaboration of claim/stance]]

A further move is beginning to be apparent, whereby *in fact* introduces a discourse unit that has no immediate coherence connection with the preceding one; rather, *in fact* becomes a type of presentative introducing a new idea or topic (7).

(7) *Oh I'll do it myself … hundred and fifty ohm .. think I've got one of them. … yeah …* ***in fact*** *this particular chassis I've never had er … never done any work on* [1980s, BNC-DS, KC1, conversation]

This seems to be a recent shift and it remains to be seen if and how it develops.

5. Fischer (2007: 285) claims that it is likely that the change of *in fact* into a "sentence-adverbial/pragmatic marker was via analogy with *indeed* rather than via any form of grammaticalization, as the suddenness of the development (in comparison to *indeed*) suggests". But Fischer adduces no data to substantiate the suddenness claim, and our data suggest on the contrary that the development was gradual (cf. Lewis 1998). Fischer suggests that a major mechanism for the development of initial-position (LP) pragmatic markers (discourse connectives) is the topicalization (2007: 285, 287, 294–296) of a VP-adverb which later, by analogy with other LP expressions, acquires scope over the following proposition by virtue of its initial position, but she does not discuss final-position (RP) connectives / pragmatic markers.

3.1.2 *Position of* in fact

The earliest occurrences in the data of final *in fact* that cannot plausibly be interpreted as the VP-adverbial, but rather connect back to the previous unit, date from the second half of the nineteenth century (8).

(8) *Well–the truth is–that our firm has got some dealings with these students–a long account* ***in fact****–and as a settlement's approaching…*
[1869, Bernard, *The man of two lives*]

In the data from 1880 to 1920, 13 out of 64 occurrencs of *in fact* are in final position as in (9) and (10).

(9) *they are beginning to bore me horribly those estimable personae of mine. I am very much annoyed* ***in fact*** *– because they have all got (those few who are left) into such a distressfully lofty atmosphere ..* [1889, Dowson, personal letter]

(10) a. *the average man's conscience does not begin work till eight or nine o'clock – not till after breakfast,* ***in fact*** *.*
[1891, Jerome, *Diary of a pilgrimage*]
b. *I came back to-day – finding it supremely triste: did not go near Queen's at all – nowhere* ***in fact****.* [1889, Dowson, personal letter]

It seems likely that RP connective *in fact*, as in (9) and (10), developed not from the epistemic adverb (cf. Example (1)) but after LP and medial uses had acquired a connective sense, or at least strong connective implicatures. We hypothesize that connective *in fact* split into LP and RP constructions only once the elaborative sense had become established. This is because, whereas there is a period when initial and medial uses are vague across epistemic and connective, this does not seem to be the case for RP uses, which are all connective. This hypothesis will need to be tested on a larger corpus , because the present data set is too small to draw any firm conclusions, and with other connectives having a similar history.

In both positions, the host unit seems to bear the same type of relationship to the previous segment, expressing a more accurate, specific or stronger formulation. The different positions may therefore correlate with some other factor. The most noticeable difference is that only one RP occurrence (Example 9) has a full-clause host, the remaining twelve attaching to sub-clausal units as in (10). This finding suggests an association between RP position of the connective and a discourse construction where the second conjunct (the host of the connective) is informationally backgrounded and subordinate to the first conjunt (the previous idea linked back to).

In present-day English, elaborative *in fact* occurs overwhelmingly in initial position. Only 4 occurrences in the LLC corpus are clearly in final position. Of the occurrences in the demographically-sampled section of the BNC (conversation), only 5% are clearly discourse-unit-final (24 occurrences). They occur in contexts where the host of *in fact* can be interpreted as either a greater precision of the previous idea (11) or as a correction of it to a point higher on a scale (12).

(11) a. A -*I will say it's cut shorter at the back*
B -[*unclear*] *sort of waistcoaty* ***in fact***
[1980s, BNC-DS, KBK, conversation]
b. *we went with Traffens one year the first year* ***in fact*** *we went with Traffens*
[1980s, BNC-DS, KE2, conversation]

(12) a. *so come Monday morning Sunday night* ***in fact*** *Noel said gosh …*
[1980s, BNC-DS, KC0, conversation]
b. *they had hundreds in there .. thousands* ***in fact*** *I would say*
[1980s, BNC-DS, KE6, conversation]

In terms of the coherence relation holding between the *in fact* host and the previous unit, again we find very similar relations with LP *in fact* (13). In each case the host expresses a rhetorically stronger idea that elaborates on the previous idea. So that in each case *in fact* introduces a scale on which its host is higher than the idea referred back to.

(13) a. A -*can I have a piece of paper please*
B -***in fact*** *you can have two* [1980s, BNC-DS, KPG, conversation]
b. *lots of people claim ..* ***in fact*** *ever such a lot of people claim that they've got communication with the dead* [1980s, BNC-DS, KBX, conversation]
c. A – *have you got any stamps?*
B -*no I don't think I have ..* ***in fact*** *I know I haven't*
[1980s, BNC-DS, KCX, conversation]
d. *I'm tired .. I'm very tired ..* ***in fact*** *I think I'll go to sleep*
[1980s, BNC-DS, KSV, conversation]

This use is to be distinguished from contrastive *in fact* as in (14), where the host is not stronger, but rather denies the proposition in the previous unit altogether and expresses the contrary.

(14) A -*you were supposed to do six and you only did four!*
B -***in fact*** *erm I'm not supposed to do any number!*
[1980s, BNC-DS, KST, conversation]

While fragments and clauses continue to be connected by final position *in fact* to the previous segment, no examples were found of fragments being connected by initial *in fact*. Examples (15a) and (15c) are both acceptable, while (15b), with initial *in fact*, is odd:

(15) a. *I shouldn't really be here now .. but we had a very quiet surgery ... no one there* ***in fact*** [1993, BNC, JYE, fiction]

b. ??*I shouldn't really be here now .. but we had a very quiet surgery ...* ***in fact*** *no one there* [manipulation of (15a)]

c. *I shouldn't really be here now .. but we had a very quiet surgery ...* ***in fact*** *there was no one there* [manipulation of (15a)]

It seems that the reduced-clause hosts that are compatible with RP *in fact* are designed to be pragmatically dependent on and informationally subordinate to the previous discourse unit. The connective binds its host to the previous unit and marks the end of the sequence. By contrast, initial connectives tend to act by virtue of their position as presentatives to put their hosts into focus.

In positional terms, *in fact* has thus come 'full spiral', so to speak, insofar as its discourse-connective functions have led it from end position (VP-scope) to medial and initial position and thence 'back' to end position but at higher level (wide scope, RP), in a new function. Out of the prepositional-phrase adverbial, an elaborative discourse connective has grammaticalized to host-initial (LP) position and more recently to host-final position (RP). In PDE, *in fact* can function on any of three levels as VP-adverbial (now rare), as epistemic adverb and as discourse connective.

3.3 After all

3.3.1 *Evolution of* after all

In present-day English, adverbial *after all* is found as a temporal VP-adverb, but rarely. It mainly occurs as a sentence adverb encoding counterexpectation (16) and as an adverbial connective signalling a justificative relation (17); that is, its host unit is presented as justifying, or reinforcing the validity of, the previously expressed idea. In this use it expresses 'because' on the speech-act plane.

(16) *oh she's gone to sleep* ***after all*** [1980s, BNC-DS, KBH, conversation]

(17) *Don't get your hopes too high or let yourself get too carried away* ***after all*** *you know what people are like* [1980s, BNC-DS, KBE, conversation]

The typical justificative construction with *after all* can be sketched as in (18).

(18) [Stance or claim] [[*after all*] [Justification]]

Adverb a*fter all* originates in a prepositional phrase (19) that slowly coalesces into an adverb over the sixteenth and seventeenth centuries and eventually becomes connective (Lewis 2007; Traugott 1997).

(19) *doctur Whyt bysshope of Lynkolne dyd pryche at the sam masse; and* ***after all*** *they whent to his plasse to dener* [1555, Machyn, *The diary of Henry Machyn*]
'Doctor White bishop of Lincoln preached at the same mass; and **after all** they went to his place for dinner'

With the grammaticalization of *all* towards determiner status, and its partial replacement by *everything* and *everyone*, the loss of compositionality becomes clearer (cf. also *overall, in all,* etc.) together with semantic narrowing as the adverb acquires implicatures from its typical contexts. Yet it remains in PDE close to its prepositional use. The data for the historical usage includes all occurrences of the sequence *after all*, since there is no discernable dividing line between the prepositional phrase and the emergent adverb (i.e. almost all occurrences are analysable as *after* + NP).

Counterexpectational and justificative senses of *after all* emerge slowly after a period when *after all* has the senses of temporal 'finally' and the more abstract 'in the end' (*cf.* 'when all's said and done'). It acquires a modal-epistemic quality, based on the notion that time (events) produces outcomes, and that over time (after events) firmer judgments can be made about states of affairs. A recurrent context for *after all* in the late seventeenth and eighteenth centuries is following a conjunction and, naturally given its meaning, introducing a topic closure or the end of a turn. Over the period 1680–1839, just under half of occurrences follow a conjunction, equally distributed between addition or reason (*and, for, then*) and contrast (*but, yet, though*) (Table 1). *After all* has no connective sense of its own during the period; it is not tied to any coherence context.

Table 1. Proportions of 'after all' collocating with conjunctions

Period	Proportion	*and, for, then*	*but, yet, though*
1680–1719	11/25	5	6
1720–1759	8/15	3	5
1760–1799	13/32	7	6
1800–1839	21/63	10	11

Both the counterexpectational and the justificative uses develop out of recurrence in contrastive and justificative contexts. The first to emerge is the counterexpectational adverb from contexts typically involving a situation where after some time, effort or activity there is no result or an unexpected result. It emerges from adverbials in initial (20a), final (20b) and medial (20c) positions, this last position being typical for adverb placement.

(20) a. *I have been studying all this Night long to save Charges; but* ***after all****, I find you must be at the Expence of a new Bed*
[c1700, Ward, *The whole pleasures of matrimony*]

b. - *if you are in Earnest you are Undone.*
- *I am afraid not, says he, for I am really afraid she won't have me,* ***after all*** *my Sisters huffing and blustring. I believe I shall never be able to persuade her to it.* [1722, Defoe, *Moll Flanders*]

c. *I have revolved this Sentence in my Mind till I have quite tired myself, but cannot,* ***after all****, find any Meaning in it.*
[1739, Anon, *Review of Hume's 'A treatise of human nature'*]

After all is temporal in these examples, the contrast supplied by *but* or by inference. In contrastive contexts the PP/adverb develops into the modal adverb that it seems to be in (21), where a temporal interpretation makes less sense than a counterexpectational sense of 'despite everything / despite indications to the contrary'.

(21) a. *let not the unhappy Wretch, who,* ***after all****, is your Daughter, want those Necessaries of Life ..*
[c1741, Richardson, *One hundred and seventy-three letters*]

b. *There is no reason to suppose that Miss Morgan is dead* ***after all*** *.*
[1798, Austen, personal letter]

c. *It is more than a fortnight since I left Shanklin chiefly for the purpose of being near a tolerable Library, which* ***after all*** *is not to be found in this place.* [1819, Keats, personal letter]

Although (21a) now looks like a justificative use, there is no evidence that it was used as such at that time; the context might nevertheless invite that inference. (21b) is an early example of the modern counterexpectation usage; *after all* at final position is not in the periphery but it has scope over the whole sentence as it would in initial position, countering a presupposition that there was reason to believe X. Likewise, (21c) counters the presupposition that the writer expected to find a library.

Unambiguous occurrences of connective (justificative) *after all* are found only towards the turn of the twentieth century, as perhaps in (22).

(22) *I would much prefer to get the War completely over than get leave.* ***After all****, in my present job I am not worried by monotony, and I find the work of absorbing interest* [1917, Jones, *War letters of Paul Jones*]

Apparently justificative uses continue in present-day English to be preceded by another connective, usually *'cos/because* (23).

(23) I gave mum thirty five pound because **after all** you know I think she needs it [1980s, BNC-DS, KDN, conversation]

Many occurrences are still vague as to whether the adverb really links back to the previous idea or can be glossed as 'in the end'. These observations are compatible with the justificative *after all* being a recent innovation that is incomplete.

3.3.2 *Position of 'after all'*

Counterexpectation *after all* can no longer occur in initial position, final position being typical (it is not in the periphery, but in end focus). Connective (justificative) *after all* occurs mainly in initial position (24), which suggests a division that would correspond to the polysemy. But the connective also occurs at RP (25).

(24) *Firms will often see merger as an 'easy way out'; **after all**, nobody in business prefers to face competitive pressure* [1990s, public speech]

(25) a. *A: tomorrow*
B: yes OK
*A: why not .. why not you're free **after all*** [1960s, LLC, conversation]
b. *I mean how do you view it? you're a professional **after all*** [1980s, BNC-CG, KRL, radio talk show]

Like RP elaborative *in fact*, RP justificative *after all* is relatively infrequent (fewer than 1 in 10 of occurrences). Unlike RP *in fact*, it does not seem to be acceptable with a sub-clausal host. But it resembles RP *in fact* in that a relationship is unambiguously marked – of justification in the case of *after all* – between the two conjuncts, which is not always so for *after all* in initial position. It is also the case, as for *in fact*, that the LP and the RP occurrences express the same rhetorical relation between the conjuncts that are linked.

3.4 Findings for 'in fact' and 'after all'

The developments so far of *in fact* and *after all* can best be viewed in the light of the broad approach to grammaticalization mentioned in Section 2.1. In this approach, grammaticalization is not restricted to items becoming more fixed and obligatory, but encompasses items becoming more grammatical while undergoing extension and scope expansion. All cases lead to greater abstraction and increased productivity: expansion of the host class, and thereby opportunities for the item to occur, favours increased frequency.

Traugott (2015) argues for a gradient distinction between 'core clause' and periphery. Data on the evolution of *in fact* and *after all* clearly support the gradient hypothesis and a gradual evolution. This suggests they cannot be considered to have undergone 'co-optation' in the sense of Heine (2013).[6] From the perspective of hindsight it appears that a reanalysis occurred, for example, from epistemic VP-adverb *in fact* to (wide-scope) sentence adverb *in fact* with discourse-connective function. Such reanalysis is sometimes discussed as though it progressed incrementally, with increasing frequency of the new analysis as it becomes established alongside the old one. But tracing the evolution 'forwards', so to speak, often reveals, rather, a period of over-extension or over-generalization which only later may settle into a pattern. During the actualization period, both the old and the new analyses obtain simultaneously; that is, "the speaker makes both (or many) analyses" (Harris & Campbell 1995: 82).[7] As has been seen above, *after all* cannot be said to have neatly reanalysed from temporal adverbial to modal adverb and connective. It is not so much that it retains aspects of its origin in its newer uses, as that the older use and the newer one even now can both be seen to obtain in many occurrences. Such dual analysis can persist over many decades or more, and both *in fact* and *after all* illustrate this phenomenon.

4. Grammaticalization and information structure beyond the sentence

Final adverbial discourse connectives are a comparatively recent phenomenon. The earliest, according to Lenker (2010: 200), was *however* in the seventeenth century. Final connective *then* and *though* date from around the same time. Lenker suggests that the construction may be specific to present-day English (2010: 202). The overall RP 'slot' is well established for a range of non-connective but speaker-oriented and interactional discourse markers and comment clauses. So it is plausible that the new connective construction is becoming productive and that further existing connectives are aligning analogically with those early ones. The trajectories of both *in fact* and *after all* from PP to VP-adverb and then modal adverb and connective are similar. And both connectives have recently started to occur at the right periphery of their host unit, where they become 'retrospective' markers. But there are important differences between the two developments. *After*

6. Heine (2013) mentions *in fact*, but cites only one example, which he takes from Traugott (1995). This example is problematic: only the host is given, and when we look at the Hume text, and especially when we take account of other contemporary (mid-eighteenth century) occurrences, it is clear that this occurrence of *in fact* is not connective; nor can it be an example of 'cooptation' in Heine's definition. Indeed, Heine seems to suggest that such connnectives are different from the kinds of declausal expressions with which he illustrates co-optation (2013: 1234).

7. Harris and Campbell (1995: 82–89) discuss three types of evidence that multiple analyses continue in individuals' grammars for some time. See also Hankamer (1977) and Dowty (2003).

all has developed a little more recently than *in fact*. It remains closely linked to its origins as a temporal PP adverbial and retains structural and functional similarity to *after all that, after all's said and done*. In frequency terms, it is overshadowed by its temporal cousin. Moreover, the connective function is not as robust as that of *in fact*, but is often bolstered by, if not carried by, another connective. Connective *in fact*, by contrast, vastly exceeds in frequency VP-adverb *in fact*; and its meaning has now become highly bleached. What are the possible motivations for the development of *in fact* and *after all* as connectives at RP as well as LP? It is suggested that processing and information structure are factors in the emergence of the two patterns, and that the pattern with a RP connective (e.g. [p. q *in fact*]) constitutes a more complex and arguably more grammaticalized construction than the LP pattern.

To explain the linear ordering of main and subordinate clauses in complex sentences, competing motivations have been proposed, including discourse planning advantages for the speaker, ease of processing by the hearer, and the organization of information flow (including thematic structure and relative weight). While 'adverbial clause last' has processing advantages for the speaker (it requires less utterance planning) and hearer (it requires lower memory load), 'adverbial clause first' results in better information flow, because it links back to the previous discourse and provides the ground for the following main idea (Diessel 2005). If we compare now the LP and RP connective constructions, it seems that LP position will have processing advantages for the hearer, insofar as the connective will guide his interpretation of the host unit (Lenker 2010: 198). Final connectives seem to run counter to this natural order, as the hearer must hold the host unit in suspense, only at the end discovering how the speaker makes it relevant to the previous discourse. For the speaker, however, the idea comes first, so that there may be a processing overhead for the LP construction, which is likely to have developed in dialogic contexts where the link is to the previous turn (is the speaker's reaction to her interlocutor's turn).

A second possible factor in the ordering is the speaker's structuring of the discourse information. A number of models of discourse structure address the relationship between coherence relations and discourse-level information structure (relative informational prominence). Some models, such as Rhetorical Structure Theory (RST) (Mann & Thompson 1987), conflate coherence relations with information structure. The early version of RST thus posits two types of coherence relation: symmetrical, relating two discourse units that carry equal prominence, and asymmetrical, where one unit acts as a 'satellite', or support, to the 'nuclear' unit. A large majority of the relations identified by RST are of this second, asymmetrical type. An example is the Justify relation, where a claim (the 'nucleus') is supported by a 'satellite' expressing the speaker's warrant for the claim, thereby increasing the hearer's acceptance of it. In practice, such conflation has been found to be too constraining. To remedy this, Carson and Marcu's (2001) RST model allows some relations to be symmetrical or asymmetrical, and allows some asymmetrical relations to express the relation as nucleus or satellite. Others have gone further to decouple coherence relation from information structure, as in the 'multi-level analysis' model proposed by Stede (2008), where nuclearity is removed from the coherence relation and is redefined in terms of optional support relations between discourse units. Constructions such as those we have seen with *in fact* and *after all* seem to support this last type of model, where relation and relative salience are separate levels, and one relation can co-occur with more than one information contour. As has been seen, LP and RP connectives *in fact* and *after all* each express a particular rhetorical relation, respectively elaboration and justification, independently of position. But the relative informational salience arguably does change. And at RP the connective is more integrated prosodically into the host unit than at LP. These findings are in line with those found, in a rather different rhetorical context, by Gentens et al. (2016) for the develoment of *no wonder*; they also emphasize "the central role played by larger rhetorical structures in the grammaticalization" (2016: 151).

The pattern, or discourse construction, that involves a connective at LP overlaps with the complex sentence construction containing a final-position adverbial clause. Unlike initial adverbial clauses, final ones need not be informationally subordinate to the main clause. Subordinating conjunctions such as *because*, *so that*, *although*, *whereas* and so on, when the clause they introduce follows the main clause, can introduce an idea of equal weight to that of the main clause. In his analysis of finite adverbial clauses, Diessel (2005: 464) finds that "final *because*-clauses … basically function like independent assertions: they tend to provide new information". Connectives like *in fact* and *after all* at LP function very much like *because* in a final adverbial clause. They link their host to the previous idea and at the same time they are points of departure, opening a turn or move or a new idea, and effectively functioning as presentatives that put the following idea(s) into focus. Their hosts are overwhelmingly finite clauses. Like other initial, pre-subject adverbials, these connectives provide grounding for the idea that follows. They have grammaticalized to encode a relatively backgrounded idea (the coherence relation) and they place what follows in focus.

In final position the connectives have the same linking function, but they close a sequence of at least two ideas, the second acting as a comment on the first. It has been seen that RP *in fact* (like some other RP connectives) is found with sub-clausal units which do not occur with LP *in fact*, and which are 'tacked on' to the previous unit, on which they elaborate or comment. Final position may therefore be partly motivated by information structuring. Such a development is arguably to be seen as a further grammaticalization. It results in a 'subordinating discourse construction' that links two units (two independent clauses or a clause and a fragment).

Such a distribution, with both LP and RP positions available for certain connectives, would offer speakers a choice of a presentative or a backgrounding structure. The RP construction is more complex than the LP one in that the host unit seems to be more tightly bound to, or more pragmatically dependent on the previous idea than is the case for hosts of initial connectives. If the two constructions continue to co-exist, over time the LP and RP connectives may start to drift apart towards further polysemy.

5. Conclusion

Discourse-level information structuring involves not only thematic progression (old/new) but also relative informational salience: how information is marked as foregrounded or backgrounded with respect to some other information. Initial position, including the left periphery, has been shown in the past to be associated with particular roles in discourse information structure: it is used for markers of new discourse frames, including topic change, and can also have an attention-seeking and presentational function, serving to place what follows in end-focus position, thereby foregrounding it. By contrast, a connective at RP marks the end of a comment on (or a modification of) an idea that is pragmatically subservient to the previous idea. The hypothesis explored here must be tested on other connective and non-connective peripheral expressions, both of clausal origin such as *I shouldn't wonder* or *mind you* and non-clausal, with a view to better identifying the role of information structure in their development and ongoing evolution.

Many wider questions remain open regarding, first, the interplay between coherence relations and discourse information structure in grammaticalization, and, second, the grammaticalization of information-structuring functions. For future work on the diachrony of English connectives, there is scope for exploring the interactions among their connective, information-structuring and interactional functions.

Appendix. Data sources

Historical English:

The Helsinki Corpus of English Texts (distributed by ICAME).

A Corpus of English Dialogues 1560–1760. 2006. Compiled under the supervision of Merja Kytö (Uppsala University) and Jonathan Culpeper (Lancaster University).

A Corpus of Late Modern English texts, v. 3. Compiled by Hendrik De Smet, Hans-Jürgen Diller & Jukka Tyrkkö.

Archer: A Representative Corpus of Historical English Registers.

London-Lund Corpus of spoken British English (LLC) (distributed by ICAME).

Oxford English Dictionary, 2nd edn.

Additional historical texts C18th-C20th.

Present-day English:

The British National Corpus, v. 2 (BNC World). 2001.

References

Aijmer, Karin. 1997. 'I think' – An English modal particle. In *Modality in Germanic Languages. Historical and Comparative Perspectives*, Toril Swan & Olaf Jansen Westvik (eds), 1– 47. Berlin: Mouton de Gruyter. https://doi.org/10.1515/9783110889932.1

Aijmer, Karin. 2002. *English Discourse Particles: Evidence from a Corpus* [Studies in Corpus Linguistics 10]. Amsterdam: John Benjamins. https://doi.org/10.1075/scl.10

Aijmer, Karin. 2016. Pragmatic markers as constructions. The case of *anyway*. In *Outside the Clause: Form and Function of Extra-Clausal Constituents* [Studies in Language Companion Series 178], Gunther Kaltenböck, Evelien Kreizer & Arne Lohmann (eds), 29–58. Amsterdam: John Benjamins.

Barth-Weingarten, Dagmar & Couper-Kuhlen, Elisabeth. 2002. On the development of final 'though': A case of grammaticalization? In *New Reflections on Grammaticalization* [Typological Studies in Language 49], Ilse Wischer & Gabriele Diewald (eds), 345–361. Amsterdam: John Benjamins. https://doi.org/10.1075/tsl.49.22bar

Beeching, Kate & Detges, Ulrich. 2014. Introduction. In *Discourse Functions at the Left and Right Periphery*, Kate Beeching & Ulrich Detges (eds), 1–23. Leiden: Brill. https://doi.org/10.1163/9789004274822_002

Biber, Douglas, Johansson, Stig, Leech, Geoffrey, Conrad, Susan & Finegan, Edward. 1999. *The Longman Grammar of Spoken and Written English*. Harlow: Longman.

Blakemore, Diane. 1996. Are apposition markers discourse markers? *Journal of Linguistics* 32(2): 325–347. https://doi.org/10.1017/S0022226700015917

Brinton, Laurel J. & Traugott, Elizabeth Closs. 2005. *Lexicalization and Language Change*. Cambridge: CUP. https://doi.org/10.1017/CBO9780511615962

Bybee, Joan L. 1985. *Morphology. A Study of the Relation between Meaning and Form* [Typological Studies in Language 9]. Amsterdam: John Benjamins. https://doi.org/10.1075/tsl.9

Carlson, Lynn & Marcu, Daniel. 2001. *Discourse Tagging Reference Manual*. ISI Tech Report ISI-TR-545, July 2001. https://www.isi.edu/~marcu/discourse/tagging-ref-manual.pdf

Diessel, Holger. 2005. Competing motivations for the ordering of main and adverbial clauses. *Linguistics* 43(3): 449–470. https://doi.org/10.1515/ling.2005.43.3.449

Dowty, David. 2003. The dual analysis of adjuncts/complements in Categorial Grammar. In *Modifying Adjuncts*, Ewald Lang, Claudia Maienborn & Cathrine Fabricius-Hansen (eds), 33–66. Berlin: Walter de Gruyter. https://doi.org/10.1515/9783110894646.33

Erman, Britt & Kotsinas, Ulla-Britt. 1993. Pragmaticalization: The case of *ba'* and *you know*. *Studier i Modern Språkvetenskap* 10: 76–93.

Fischer, Olga. 2007. *Morphosytactic Change. Functional and Formal Perspectives*. Oxford: OUP.

Gentens, Caroline, Kimps, Ditte, Davidse, Kristin, Jacobs, Gilles, Van linden, An & Brems, Lieselotte. 2016. Mirativity and rhetorical structure. The development and prosody of disjunct and anaphoric adverbials with *no wonder*. In *Outside the Clause: Form and Function of Extra-Clausal Constituents* [Studies in Language Companion Series 178], Gunther Kaltenböck, Evelien Keizer & Arne Lohmann (eds), 125–156. Amsterdam: John Benjamins.

Hancil, Sylvie. 2014. The final particle 'but' in British English. In *Grammaticalization – Theory and Data* [Studies in Language Companion Series 162], Sylvie Hancil & Ekkehard König (eds), 235–256. Amsterdam: John Benjamins.

Hancil, Sylvie, Haselow, Alexander & Post, Margje (eds). 2015. *Final Particles*. Berlin: Walter de Gruyter.

Hankamer, Jorge. 1977. Multiple analyses. In *Mechanisms of Syntactic Change*, Charles N. Li (ed.), 583–607. Austin TX: University of Texas Press.

Harris, Alice C. & Campbell, Lyle. 1995. *Historical Syntax in Cross-Linguistic Perspective*. Cambridge: CUP. https://doi.org/10.1017/CBO9780511620553

Haselow, Alexander. 2012. Discourse organization and the rise of final *then* in the history of English. In *English Historical Linguistics 2010* [Current Issues in Linguistic Theory 325], Irén Hegedüs & Alexandra Fodor (eds), 153–175. Amsterdam: John Benjamins.

Haselow, Alexander. 2013. Arguing for a wide conception of grammar. The case of final particles in spoken discourse. *Folia Linguistica* 47(2): 375–424. https://doi.org/10.1515/flin.2013.015

Haselow, Alexander. 2015. Left vs. right periphery in grammaticalization. The case of *anyway*. In *New Directions in Grammaticalization Research* [Studies in Language Companion Series 166], Andrew D. M. Smith, Graeme Trousdale & Richard Waltereit (eds), 157–186. Amsterdam: John Benjamins.

Heine, Bernd. 2013. On discourse markers: Grammaticalization, pragmaticalization, or something else? *Linguistics* 51(6): 1205–1247. https://doi.org/10.1515/ling-2013-0048

Heine, Bernd, Kaltenböck, Gunther & Kuteva, Tania. 2015. Some observations on the evolution of final particles. In *Final Particles*, Sylvie Hancil, Alexander Haselow & Margje Post (eds), 111–140. Berlin: De Gruyter.

Hopper, Paul J. & Traugott, Elizabeth Closs. 2003. *Grammaticalization*, 2nd edn. Cambridge: CUP. https://doi.org/10.1017/CBO9781139165525

Huddleston, Rodney & Pullum, Geoffrey K. 2002. *The Cambridge Grammar of the English Language*. Cambridge: CUP.

Izutsu, Katsunobu & Izutsu, Mitsuko Narita. 2013. From discourse markers to modal/final particles. What the position reveals about the continuum. In *Discourse Markers and Modal Particles: Categorization and Description* [Pragmatics & Beyond New Series 234], Liesbeth Degand, Bert Cornillie & Paola Pietrandrea (eds), 217–235. Amsterdam: John Benjamins. https://doi.org/10.1075/pbns.234.09izu

Kim, Min-Jo & Jahnke, Nathan. 2011. The meaning of utterance-final *even*. *Journal of English Linguistics* 39(1): 36–64. https://doi.org/10.1177/0075424210390798

Lehmann, Christian. 2002. New reflections on grammaticalization and lexicalization. In *New Reflections on Grammaticalization* [Typological Studies in Language 49], Ilse Wischer & Gabriele Diewald (eds), 1–18. Amsterdam: John Benjamins. https://doi.org/10.1075/tsl.49.03leh

Lehmann, Christian. 2008. Information structure and grammaticalization. In *Theoretical and Empirical Issues in Grammaticalization* [Typological Studies in Language 77], Elena Seoane & Marie-José López Couso (eds), 207–229. Amsterdam: John Benjamins. https://doi.org/10.1075/tsl.77.12leh

Lenker, Ursula. 2010. *Argument and Rhetoric. Adverbial Connectors in the History of English.* Berlin: De Gruyter Mouton. https://doi.org/10.1515/9783110216066

Lewis, Diana M. 1998. From modal adverbial to discourse connective: Some rhetorical effects in present-day English. In *Pragmatics in 1998: Selected Papers from the 6th International Pragmatics Conference*, Vol. 2, Jef Verschueren (ed.), 363–375. Antwerp: International Pragmatics Association.

Lewis, Diana M. 2007. From temporal to contrastive and causal: The emergence of connective *after all*. In *Connectives as Discourse Landmarks* [Benjamins Current Topics 92], Agnès Celle & Ruth Huart (eds), 89–99. Amsterdam: John Benjamins. https://doi.org/10.1075/pbns.161.09lew

Lewis, Diana M. 2011. A discourse-constructional approach to the emergence of discourse connectives in English. *Linguistics* 49(2): 415–443. https://doi.org/10.1515/ling.2011.013

Mann, William C. & Thompson, Sandra A. 1987. *Rhetorical Structure Theory: A Theory of Text Organization* [ISI Report RS-87-190]. Marina del Rey, CA: Information Sciences Institute, University of Southern California.

Mithun, Marianne. 2005. On the assumption of the sentence as the basic unit of syntactic structure. In *Linguistic Diversity and Language Theories* [Studies in Language Companion Series 72], Zygmunt Frajzyngier, Adam Hodges & David S. Rood (eds), 169–184. Amsterdam: John Benjamins. https://doi.org/10.1075/slcs.72.09mit

Mithun, Marianne. 2016. Discourse and grammar. In *Handbook of Discourse Analysis*, 2nd edn, Heidi Hamilton, Deborah Schiffrin & Deborah Tannen (eds), 9–41. Oxford: Blackwell.

Mulder, Jean & Thompson, Sandra A. 2008. The grammaticalization of *but* as a final particle in English conversation. In *Crosslinguistic Studies of Clause Combining: The Multifunctionality of Conjunctions* [Typological Studies in Language 80], Ritva Laury (ed.), 179–204. Amsterdam: John Benjamins. https://doi.org/10.1075/tsl.80.09mul

Polanyi, Livia, van den Berg, Martin & Ahn, David. 2003. Discourse structure and sentential information structure: An initial proposal. *Journal of Logic, Language and Information* 12(3): 337–350. https://doi.org/10.1023/A:1024187311998

Schweinberger, Martin. 2015. Comparing 'like' in Irish and British Englishes. In *Pragmatic Markers in Irish English* [Pragmatics & Beyond New Series 258], Carolina P. Amador Moreno, Kevin McCafferty & Elaine Vaughan (eds), 114–134. Amsterdam: John Benjamins. https://doi.org/10.1075/pbns.258.05sch

Schwenter, Scott & Traugott, Elizabeth Closs. 2000. Invoking scalarity. The development of *in fact*. *Journal of Historical Pragmatics* 1(1): 7–25. https://doi.org/10.1075/jhp.1.1.04sch

Stede, Manfred. 2008. Disambiguating rhetorical structure. *Research on Language and Computation* 6: 311–332. https://doi.org/10.1007/s11168-008-9053-7

Traugott, Elizabeth Closs. 1995. The role of the development of discourse markers in a theory of grammaticalization. Paper presented at the *12th International Conference on Historical Linguistics*, University of Manchester, August 1995.

Traugott, Elizabeth Closs. 1997. The discourse connective *after all*: A historical pragmatic account. Paper presented at the *Sixteenth International Congress of Linguists*, Paris, July 1997.

Traugott, Elizabeth Closs. 2012. Intersubjectification and clause periphery. *English Text Construction* 5(1): 7–28. https://doi.org/10.1075/etc.5.1.02trau

Traugott, Elizabeth Closs. 2013. 'I must wait on myself, must I?' at right periphery of the clause in English. Talk given at Lund University, 4 September 2013.

Traugott, Elizabeth Closs. 2014. On the function of the epistemic adverbs 'surely' and 'no doubt' at the left and right peripheries of the clause. In *Discourse Functions at the Left and Right Periphery*, Kate Beeching & Ulrich Detges (eds), 72–91. Leiden: Brill.

Traugott, Elizabeth Closs. 2015. Investigating 'periphery' from a functionalist perspective. *Linguistics Vanguard* 1(1): 119–130. https://doi.org/10.1515/lingvan-2014-1003

Traugott, Elizabeth Closs. 2016. On the rise of types of clause-final pragmatic markers in English. *Journal of Historical Pragmatics* 17(1): 26–54.

PART 2

Case studies

The noun phrase

The grammaticalization of interrogative pronouns into relative pronouns in South-Caucasian languages

Internal development or replica?

Ophelie Gandon
University Sorbonne Nouvelle Paris 3

South Caucasian languages spoken in Caucasus (Georgian, Mingrelian and Svan) resort to finite postnominal relative clauses (henceforth RC) introduced by a relative pronoun as one of their main relativization strategies. The relative pronouns are formally identical to the interrogative pronouns with the addition of a subordinating particle, which suggests that the former has developed from the latter. This paper addresses the issue of whether this is an internal development, or a contact-induced one, more specifically, a case of replica grammaticalization.

Keywords: South Caucasian languages, relative pronouns, interrogative pronouns, grammaticalization, internal development, contact-induced change

1. Introduction

The South Caucasian family is made up of four languages: Georgian, Mingrelian and Svan spoken mainly in South-Western Caucasus, and Laz spoken in North-Eastern Turkey (see Map 1 for the distribution of the four languages). The Figure 1 below represents the genealogical relationships of the family: Svan is the one that differs the most, Mingrelian and Laz are rather close to each other and often considered as two dialects of a same language Zan.

The family has about 5,000,000 speakers, 3,600,000 for Georgian, 380,000 for Mingrelian, 50,000 for Laz and 48,000 for Svan (estimations are from Charachidzé in Blanc et al. 2016).

These languages, especially Georgian, display various relativization strategies, among which are postnominal finite relative clauses introduced by relative pronouns built on interrogative pronouns. This paper discusses whether the

https://doi.org.10.1075/slcs.202.07gan
© 2018 John Benjamins Publishing Company

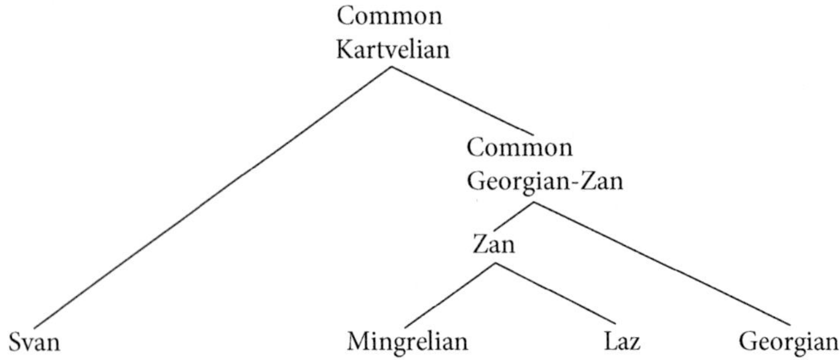

Figure 1. Kartvelian languages (Harris 1991a, 12, inter alia)

grammaticalization of these interrogative pronouns into relative pronouns is an internal development, or a contact-induced phenomenon, more specifically, a case of replica grammaticalization.

2. Postnominal relative clauses introduced by relative pronouns in South Caucasian languages

Georgian, Mingrelian and Svan display finite postnominal relative clauses (henceforth RCs) introduced by relative pronouns as main or among their main relativization strategies, as exemplified below (the RC is between square brackets and the relative pronoun is in bold).[1]

(1) Georgian (Hewitt 1987: 217)
*i-q'o is bič'-i, [**romel-ma-c** gušin amxanag-s*
SV-was that.NOM lad-NOM **who-ERG-SUB** yesterday friend-DAT
scema]
he.hit.him.AOR
'He was that boy who yesterday hit his friend'

(2) Mingrelian (Harris 1991: 383)
*tis, [**namu-še-ti** sinatle iʒiredu-ni]*
that.DAT **which-ABL-SUB** light.NOM show.1SG-SUB
'that (residence), from which a light showed'
(Khubua 1937: 7, 20 in Abesadze 1965: 231–237)

1. Among their main strategies, Georgian and Mingrelian also display a subordinator marked strategy which can appear in pre or postnominal position and which is more specific to the spoken language (Aronson 1972: 139; Hewitt 1987: 187; 1995: 606; 2001: 111; Harris 1991: 384; 1992: 394).

(3) Svan (Tuite 2004: 45)
eǯ ma:re ***[xed-wæ:j*** *ætɣwæč' {< = ad-x-e-ɣwæč'}] gæč-d*
*that man.*NOM ***which.*NOM-SUB** *PV-O3-OBV-pursue.*AOR *knife-ADV*
æd-(i)-sip'-æ:n
*PV-SBV-turn-PASS.*AOR
'The man who was pursuing him turned into a knife'
(Shanidze and Topuria 1939: 110)

(4) Svan (Tuite 2004: 45)
lap'o:r-te:-sga ečxaw e, ***[im-wæ:j*** *ču*
flying-to-in over_there that **where-SUB** down
i-sgwǯ-in-i]
SBV-go:HONORIFIC-PASS-SM
'[It flies up from one place, looking like a lit candle], and flies over there to the place where it descends, and there it goes out'

This strategy is also attested in Old Georgian texts (material for previous states of the other South Caucasian languages is not available):

(5) Old Georgian (Harris 1992: 394)
miugo idua ***[romel-man*** *misca igi]*
he.respond.it Judas **which-ERG** he.give.him him
'Judas, who betrayed him, replied' (Mt 26: 25 AB)

(6) Old Georgian (Fähnrich 1991: 208)
mividoda črdilod mimart, ***[sada-igi*** *iq'o ʒegli igi]*
go.IMPFT.3SG north.INSTR toward **where-SUB** be.AOR.3SG statue ART
'he went toward the north, where the statue was'

However, it is reported to be rare in Laz by Holisky (1991: 419, 457) and Lacroix (2009: 768–69), and is not even mentioned in the grammar of Laz of Pazar (Öztürk & Pöchtrager et al. 2011).[2]

The relative pronouns are based on interrogative pronouns inflected according to the syntactic function of the head noun within the relative clause, plus a subordinating particle (also called subordinating suffix, according to the terminology used by Aronson (1991: 240) and Hewitt (2001: 107)). These particles or suffixes are found as well in subordinating conjunctions, for example in Mingrelian *mutʃ'o* 'how' (*mutʃ'o ret* 'how are you') ➔ *mutʃ'o-t(i)* 'as (soon as)' (Hewitt 2001: 107–10). Some examples are given in the table below:

2. Its presence in Laz could be a calque from Georgian according to Holisky (1991: 457).

(7) Formation of the relative pronouns in South Caucasian languages[3]

	Interrogative pronouns				Relative pronouns
Georgian:	*vin* 'who'	+	*-c*	→	*vinc* 'who'
	ra 'what'	+	*-c*	→	*rac* 'which'
	romeli 'which one'	+	*-c*	→	*romeli-c* 'who, which'
Old Georgian:	*romel* 'which'	+	*-igi*		
	sada 'where'	+	*-igi*		
Mingrelian:	*namu*	+	*-t(i)*	→	*namu-ti*
Svan:	*jer* 'who'	+	*-wæ:j*	→	*jer-wæ:j* 'who'
	ime 'where'	+	*-wæ:j*	→	*im-wæ:j* 'where'
	mä:y 'what'	+	*-wä:y*	→	*mä:y-wä:y* 'which'
	ẋed 'which'	+	*-wä:y*	→	*ẋed-wä:y* 'who, which'

Thus, relative pronouns have obviously developed from interrogative pronouns in the South Caucasian languages. The question arises as to whether this is an internal development, or a contact-induced one. I first consider the possibility of an internal development, and then the possibility of a contact-induced development, more specifically a case of replica grammaticalization (Heine & Kuteva 2003).

3. The possibility of an internal development

In Indo-European languages that display relative pronouns, the latter are often identical or similar to interrogative pronouns: *e.g.* in English, French, Spanish, Russian, Armenian, Modern Greek. Luján (2009: 232) suggests for Indo-European languages that relative pronouns have been grammaticalized from interrogative pronouns via correlative (maximalizing) constructions, in which the semantic of both interrogative and relative match:

> The grammaticalization of **kwi-/*kwo-* in Proto-Indo-European can be best explained as arising from its interrogative value and must have originated in maximalizing relatives. These semantically maximalizing relative clauses introduced by **kwi-/*kwo-* were preposed free and correlative clauses, as shown by Old Latin and Hittite.

Two examples of these correlative constructions quoted by Luján in Latin and Hittite are given below: The relative clause is preposed to the matrix clause, the head noun of the RC (if any) appears within the RC and there is a correlate in the matrix (in bold here), which is coreferent to the head-noun. The semantics in these examples is non-specific, which suggests that interrogative pronouns still

3. Sources: Hewitt 1987: 185; Harris 1991: 332–33; Schmidt 1991: 504; Tuite 2004: 45.

The postposition of the relative clause to the head-noun is quite conceivable, given the fact that in Old Georgian, adjectives used to follow the head noun.[5] [6] So the postposition of the relative to the head noun would be in compliance with the word order.[7]

Besides, one may assume that the insertion of a head noun would be a step toward a more specific meaning, together with a step toward the grammaticalization of the interrogative pronouns into relative ones, by the loss of their interrogative (indefinite) value.

In what follows, I present an argument in support of this scenario based on case attraction, a process frequently found in Old Georgian.

3.3 An argument in support: Cases of case attraction in Old Georgian

Examples of case attraction with regressive assimilation are reported to be frequent in Old Georgian with the finite postnominal relative pronoun strategy (Dondua 1967; Aronson 1972: 128; Hewitt 1987: 198; Harris 1992: 395, *inter alia*): the head noun which is in the matrix clause bears the case that corresponds to its syntactic function within the RC, and not the case dictated by the matrix clause as it would be expected. Two examples are given below: in (15), the head noun *sit'q'ua* 'word' is in the dative case instead of the nominative, and in (16), the head noun *mama* 'father' is in the nominative case when the ergative would be expected.

(15) Old Georgian (Harris 1992: 395)
*sit'q'ua-sa, [**romel-sa** get'q'ude me tkuen], suli ars*
word-DAT **which-DAT** I.tell.it.to.you I you soul be.3SG
'the word which I say to you is spirit' (John 6: 63 Ad)

---

5. Recall that material for previous states of the other South Caucasian languages is not available.

6. Only after an important shift in word order occurred, sometime between Old and Modern Georgian, did adjectives come to precede the nouns they modify, as in Modern Georgian (Harris 2000).

7. Note also that:

- Postposition of the RC seems preferred in languages of the world in general (see among others Dryer 2013: postnominal RCs are much more frequent worldwide than prenominal ones), this possibly for cognitive reasons: one may expect that a postnominal RC will be easier to proceed than a prenominal one (indeed with a prenominal RC, the speaker has to keep in mind the RC until she accedes the noun it modifies).
- Prenominal RCs and relative pronouns seem incompatible; such a combination is not attested worldwide (Downing 1978: 382, 396; Keenan 1985: 149; Creissels 2006, Vol. 2: 240; Andrews 2007: 218; inter alia).

(16) Old Georgian (Harris 1992: 395)
mama-y igi šeni, [romel-i xedavs daparul-sa], mogugos
father-NOM the your **which-NOM** he.see.it secret-DAT he.respond.you
man *šen exadad*
he.ERG you openly
'Your father, who sees in secret, will reward you openly'
(Mt 6: 6 Ad, quoted in (Dondua 1967: 24, 25, 26)

This kind of configuration suggests that the head noun could have belonged to the relative clause in a previous state, just as it is the case in correlative constructions.

Note moreover the presence of a correlate in the matrix in (16) (in bold), specific to this kind of case attraction configuration: "The correlative was infrequent with a relative clause that followed the grammatical norm (that is, that did not have case attraction)" (Harris 1992: 395). Thus, again these constructions with case attraction are quite similar to correlative ones, and could represent an intermediate state in the evolution of correlative relatives into finite postnominal RCs introduced by relative pronouns. Note by the way that such a possibility, besides providing a scenario for the grammaticalization of interrogative pronouns into relative pronouns, also provides an explanation for the frequent occurrences of case attraction in Old Georgian.

Beside these arguments supporting an internal development, a possible influence of some languages in contact must also be considered, a topic which we undertake in the next section.

4. The possibility of a contact-induced development

The influence of some languages in contact in the development of interrogative pronouns into relative pronouns for Georgian, Svan and Mingrelian is conceivable, given the fact that:

- The finite postnominal relative pronoun strategy is almost absent in Laz; Laz is not the language expected to diverge the most in the family (cf. the genealogical tree – Figure 1 – in the introduction), and it is precisely spoken away more in the west in Turkey;
- This finite postnominal relative pronoun strategy is also known to be rare worldwide and specific to languages of Europe (Comrie 1998: 61; Creissels 2006, vol. 2: 228; Hendery 2012: 51);
- Georgian indeed was and still is in contact with some 'European' languages (namely Ancient Greek, Classical Armenian, then Modern Eastern Armenian and Russian; see Section 4.1 and 4.2);

- Relative pronouns built on interrogative pronouns are often calqued or borrowed according to a worldwide study of Hendery (2012: 51) (see also Comrie 1998, 61; Heine & Kuteva 2006: 211–16; Guella 2010; Camilleri & Sadler 2011 for various examples of languages in contact with languages of Europe that have developed relative pronouns built on interrogative pronouns): additional evidence is available both in historical documents (4.1) and in other languages of the Caucasus (4.2).

4.1 'European' languages in contact with Old Georgian

As mentioned above, the only South Caucasian language for which previous states are available is Georgian, a language written since the 5th century AD. Yet several texts from Old Georgian are actually translations from Ancient Greek and Classical Armenian; thus Old Georgian can be considered to have been in contact with both of these languages.

Indeed, both Ancient Greek and Classical Armenian displayed postnominal finite RCs introduced by relative pronouns, as exemplified below:

(17) Ancient Greek (Meyer 2013: 23)

ὁ	*ἀϲτὴρ*	*[ὅν*	*εἶδον*	*προῆγεν*	*αὐτοὺϲ]*
ho	*astḕr*	***hòn***	*eîdon*	*proêgen*	*aὐtoὺc*
DET	star.NOM.SG	**PRO.REL.SG.ACC**	see.AOR.3PL	guide.AOR.3SG	DEM.DAT.PL

'The star that they saw guided them'

(18) Classical Armenian (Meyer 2013: 23)

asteł = n	*[z = **or***	*tesin]*	*ařǰnordeacʿ*	*nocʿa*
star.NOM.SG = DET	ACC = **which.SG**	see.AOR.3PL	guide.AOR.3SG	DEM.DAT.PL

'The star that they saw guided them'

In Ancient Greek, the relative pronoun (*ὅς*) was different from the interrogative pronoun (*τις*) (Luján 2009: 226).[8] Thus, an influence of Ancient Greek in the development of relative pronouns in Old Georgian is not impossible, but it would rather be a case of 'ordinary contact-induced grammaticalization' within the framework of Heine & Kuteva (2003), that is, speakers draw on universal strategies of grammaticalization in order to create a new grammatical category.

In Classical Armenian, on the other hand, relative pronouns where built on interrogative pronouns (Krause, Greppin & Slocum 2016: "The relative pronoun has no distinct forms; rather the forms of the interrogatives are used in this role"). Thus, an Armenian influence is quite likely. Note also that besides translations,

---

8. Thus differently from Modern Greek, in which relative pronouns are formed on interrogative pronouns.

Old Georgian has also possibly been in direct contact with Classical Armenian, as both where (and still are) neighboring languages. Within the framework of Heine & Kuteva (2003), such a contact-induced development would be characterized as a "replica grammaticalization": that is, speakers replicate the grammatical category AND the grammaticalization process they assume to have occurred in the language of contact.

Therefore, an influence of some 'European' languages in contact, especially of Classical Armenian, is conceivable in the development of interrogative pronouns into relative pronouns in Old Georgian. As for other South Caucasian languages, one can note that Georgian, considered as a language of prestige, is known to have exerted an important influence on them (Harris 1991a: 12); thus an influence of Georgian regarding the presence of relative pronouns built on interrogative pronouns in Svan and Mingrelian is also worth considering.[9]

4.2 Other languages of the South Caucasus area displaying postnominal finite RCs introduced by relative pronouns built on interrogative pronouns

An argument in support of such a language-contact influence is the fact that relative pronouns built on interrogative pronouns are often calqued or borrowed across languages (Heine & Kuteva 2006: 211–16; Hendery 2012: 51, inter alia). Indeed, this seems to be especially the case in the South Caucasus area: besides the South Caucasian languages, several other languages spoken in the same area display similar relative pronouns, some of which were clearly produced by language-contact.

Two Indo-European languages spoken in the southern part of the Caucasus display postnominal finite RCs introduced by relative pronouns built on interrogative pronouns: Armenian and Russian, as exemplified below in (19) and (20). Russian is not a first language in the area but it is widespread in all the Caucasus since the second half of the 19th century (Chirikba 2008: 57). Many inhabitants of the Caucasus speak Russian as well, and it can thus be considered as a language of contact in the area.

(19) Eastern Armenian (Dum-Tragut 2009: 479)
łarabałc'i-ner *ēl* *k-an* *[or-onc'* *hamar*
Karabakhian-PL.NOM also exist-PTC.PRS **which-PL.DAT** POST
Samvel-ĕ *heros* *ē]*
Samvel.NOM-the hero.NOM he is
'There are also Karabakhians for whom Samvel is a hero'

9. Indeed Holisky suggests a calque from Georgian for the rare occurrences of the relative pronoun strategy in Laz (Holisky 1991: 457).

(20) Russian
*Мужчина, [**которого** я ждал,] не пришёл*
*mužčina, [**kotopogo** ja ždal,] ne prišël*
man **which.ACC.SGM** I wait.PST NEG come.PST
'The man I was waiting for didn't come'

As this strategy is found in a number of Indo-European languages (English, French, Spanish, Russian, Armenian, etc.), it is likely that its presence in both of these languages is inherited (note that the strategy of Modern Armenian is actually almost the same as the one of Classical Armenian, mentioned in the previous section).

Interestingly, this strategy is also found in some other non-Indo-European languages spoken in South Caucasus: namely Urum and Azeri, two Turkic languages, and Udi and Bats, two North-East Caucasian languages.[10] It is the main strategy for Udi and Urum (Schulze-Fürhoff 1994: 449, 481; Skopeteas 2013), while in Azeri, it is a secondary strategy more specific to spoken language (Babaliyeva 2014). The strategy seems to be well represented in Bats, though no precise indication is given regarding its frequency (Desherijev 1953: 178–79, 292–98; Holisky & Gagua 1994: 176, 205–6). Below are given some examples:

(21) Udi (Schulze-Fürhoff 1994: 503)
*čoban-ĝ-on [**mat' ĝoy-te** eĝel-ux̂ azarru-ne-bak-i] q'eiri*
shepherd-PL-ERG **which.GEN.PL-SUB** sheep-PL ill-3SG-become-AOR other
aš̃-n-ux̂ furu-q'un-p-sa
work-SA-DAT_2 search-3PL-AUX-PRS
'The shepherds whose sheep have become ill look for another job'

(22) Bats (Tsova-Tush) (Desherijev 1953: 295)
*оkхус цıераддина о жагн, [**менух** тха ıамдирахь]*
PRO.3SG he.wrote DEM livre **which_one** today you.read
'He wrote this book that you read today'

(23) Urum (Skopeteas 2013: 351)
*adam, [**angısı-nın ki** it-ın-i ol-dür-du-m],*
man **which_one-GEN SUB** dog-POSS.3SG-ACC die-CAUS-PST-1SG
čıh-ti
go_out-PST
'The man whose dog I killed went out'

---

10. Urum is spoken by Turkish-speaking Pontic Greeks who emigrated from North-East Anatolia to Georgia at the beginning of the 19th century. The number of speakers is estimated at 1,000 to 1,500 (Skopeteas 2013: 335).

(24) Azeri (Babaliyeva 2014)
*25 kitab, [**hansı-lar-ı** **ki**, sən bir il ərzində oxu-yacaq-san]*
25 book **which-PL-ACC SUB** 2SG one year during read-FUT-2SG
'Twenty five books that you will read in one year'

For these languages, this strategy is obviously a later development given the fact that Turkic and North-East Caucasian languages commonly resort to participial prenominal RCs (such as Examples (25) and (26) below), and do not display such postnominal finite RCs with relative pronouns built on interrogative pronouns.

(25) Tabasaran (North-East Caucasian, Babaliyeva 2013: 224)
[mu xu-yi _ ap'-ura-yi] gaf-ar.i-z lig-ay-čva
this dog-ERG make-PRS-PTC word-PL-DAT look-IMP-2PL
'Be careful to the words that this dog says (lit. makes)' (Šahib, p. 84)

(26) Turkish
[_ al-dığ-ın] kitap-lar-ı bul-a-m-ıyor-um
buy-PTC-POSS.2SG book-PL-ACC find-POT-NEG-PROG-1SG
'I cannot find the books you bought'

Interestingly, Udi has been in a long standing contact with Classical Armenian, and is now in contact with Georgian (it is spoken mainly in Georgia and partly in Azerbaijan). Note that Caucasian Albanian, which represents a previous state of Udi, already displayed such a strategy with relative pronouns built on interrogative pronouns (Schulze 2006: 192; Gippert 2011: 228).[11] Thus, the influence for Udi must have occurred a long time ago. Urum has been in contact with Russian, and, for the speakers of the province of Tsalka, also with Armenian; it is now also in contact with Georgian (Skopeteas 2013: 336). Bats is spoken in Georgia and thus has been in contact with at least Georgian (and possibly Russian). Holisky and Gagua (1994) indeed suggest a calque from Georgian for the presence of this strategy in Bats. Azeri finally can also be considered to have been in contact with Russian, as speakers often speak Russian as well (Babaliyeva 2014 indeed suggests an influence of Russian for Azeri).

Consequently, all these languages have been more or less in contact with one or more languages that display postnominal finite RCs introduced by relative pronouns built on interrogative pronouns. The Map 1 below shows the distribution of languages displaying such a strategy (Russian is not represented on the map since it is exclusively a second language): they are all spoken in the same area, in

11. But the material was different: the interrogative pronoun used was *hanay*, and interestingly the subordinating particle corresponded to the Iranian subordinator *-k'e* (Schulze 2006: 192; Gippert 2011: 228).

the southern part of the Caucasus, and thus form a kind of convergence area, that is, where genetically unrelated languages share the same features and may thus diverge from their respective genealogical families in this respect.[12]

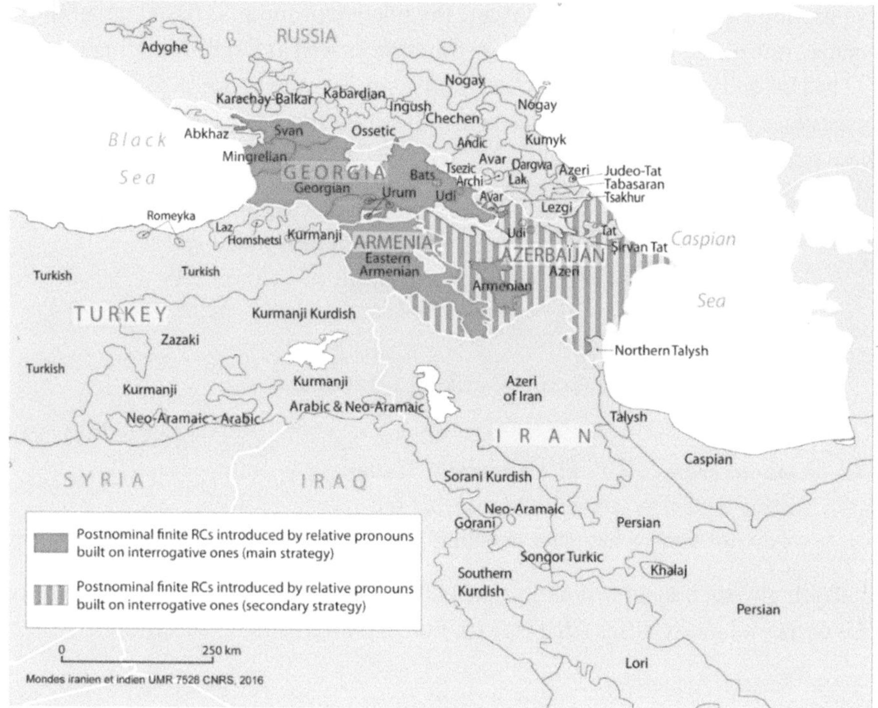

Languages with relative pronouns built on interrogative ones[13]
Map 1.

The fact that Georgian, Svan and Mingrelian are spoken in such an area where relative pronouns built on interrogative pronouns appear to be an easily diffusible feature reinforces the possibility of a calque for these languages.

12. Note that such a relative pronoun strategy is also reported for Judeo-Tat, an Iranian language spoken slightly to the north in the Caucasus, across the northern border of Azerbaijan (Authier 2012: 246, 258–60).

13. This linguistic map has been constructed from the various sources mentioned in the references. Given the difficulty of creating such maps (the impossibility of considering all speakers and villages, the difficulty of deciding which language to represent when several are spoken, the fact that populations may move through time, etc.), an exact delimitation of each language/strategy is not expected; the main purpose here is to give an overall picture of the situation regarding convergence phenomena. I am thankful to Emmanuel Giraudet for his help in the creation of the map.

4.3 The subordinating particle

Finally, it is interesting to note as well the similarity between several of these languages regarding the presence of a subordinating particle in the formation of relative pronouns: in Udi, Urum and Azeri the relative pronoun is based on an interrogative one plus a particle which may function as well as a subordinating particle (*-te* in Udi and *ki* for Urum and Azeri), in a similar way of South Caucasian languages (see Section 2).[14] Examples below illustrate the subordinating function of these particles for Udi and Urum:

(27) Udi (Schulze-Fürhoff 1994: 500)
beĝ-sa-ne [***te*** *iš̃a sa iš̃-en sa gärämzi-n-ax̂ gölö*
see-PRS-3SG **SUB** there one man-ERG one grave-SA-DAT2 very
t'ap'-ne-x̂a
hit-3SG-AUX.PRS
'He sees that a man is heavily striking a grave hard there'

(28) Urum (Skopeteas 2013: 350)
bül-mi-er-ım ***ki*** *petros nä sät-er*
know-NEG-IPFV-1SG **SUB** Petros what sell-IPFV
'I do not know what Peter is selling'

Interestingly, such a subordinating particle is also often present in Armenian in case of free relative clauses (that is, with no head noun and no substitute):

(29) Eastern Armenian (Dum-Tragut 2009: 479)
Es gt-a [***inč'*** ***or*** *du p'ntr-um ēir*]
I.NOM find-AOR.1SG **what.NOM SUB** you.NOM look_for-PTC.PRS you.were
'I found what you were looking for'

The example below illustrates the subordinating function of the particle *or*:

(30) Eastern Armenian (Dum-Tragut 2009: 426)
Vardan-n uz-um ē [***or*** *Vrastan gn-as*]
Vardan.NOM-the want-PTC.PRS he.is **SUB** Georgia.NOM go-SBJV.FUT.2SG
'Vardan wants you to go to Georgia'

14. *-te* in Udi is itself borrowed from Armenian *et'e* (Schulze-Fürhoff 1994: 500), and *ki* in Urum and Azeri has most probably been borrowed from Persian *ki* (possibly promoted by the presence of an interrogative *kim* 'who' in Turkic). Note that interestingly, in Caucasian Albanian (ancestor of Udi) the subordinating particle used combined to interrogative pronouns for forming relative pronouns was the Iranian subordinator *-k'e* (Schulze 2006: 192; Gippert 2011: 228) (see footnote 11).

(Note, however, that besides representing an areal phenomenon, this structure could also represent a typological tendency; thus such combinations are also found for example in colloquial French, *e.g. laquelle qui est arrivée en septembre, c'est Christelle; je trouve pas l'endroit où que t'as mis le livre*, etc.)

5. Conclusion

To conclude, the possibility of an internal development of interrogative pronouns into relative pronouns for Georgian, Svan and Mingrelian, via the evolution of correlative relatives into postnominal ones, is conceivable. The frequent cases of case attraction with regressive assimilation noticed in Old Georgian could represent an intermediate state between both constructions, correlative relatives and postnominal ones, and thus constitute an argument in support of such a scenario.

However, the obvious easy diffusion in this area of relative pronouns built on interrogative pronouns, the fact that the postnominal relative pronoun strategy is otherwise rather rare in non-'European' languages of the world, and the fact that it is absent in Laz, spoken outside the area (at its periphery) suggests that language contact may also have played a role in the grammaticalization of interrogative pronouns into relative pronouns in Georgian, Svan and Mingrelian.

Both phenomena seem equally conceivable and may actually have occurred jointly: one can conceive of a development through correlative constructions promoted by language contact.

Abbreviations[15]

1/2/3	1st/2nd/3rd person	S	subject marker
ABL	ablative	SG	singular
ACC	accusative	OBV	objective version
ADV	adverbial case	OPT	optative particle
AOR	aorist	PASS	passive
AUX	auxiliary	PL	plural
CAUS	causative	POSS	possessive
DAT	dative	POST	postposition
DAT2	dative 2	POT	potentiality
DEM	demonstrative	PRO	pronoun

15. The glosses of some quoted examples have been slightly modified in order to make it uniform, and non-glossed examples have been glossed.

DET	determinant	PROG	progressive
DR	reported speech	PRS	present
ERG	ergative	PST	past
FUT	future	PTC	participle
GEN	genitive	PV	preverb
IMP	imperative	QT	quotative particle
INT	interrogative	S	subject marker
IPFV	imperfective	SA	augment
M	masculine	SBJV	subjunctive
MOD	modal	SBV	subjective version
NEG	negation	SG	singular
NOM	nominative	STI	Set I cross-referencing affix
O	object marker	VAL2	valency operator

References

Abesadze, Nia. 1965. Hip'ot'aksis C'evr-K'avširebi Da K'avširebi Megrulši (Subordinating Conjunctions in Mingrelian), Tbilisis saxelmts'ipo universit'et'is šromebi (Works of Tbilisi State University). *Tbilisis universit'et'is šromebi* (114): 229–257.

Andrews, Avery D. 2007. Relative clauses. In *Language Typology and Syntactic Description*, Timothy Shopen (ed.), 206–236. Cambridge: CUP. https://doi.org/10.1017/CBO9780511619434.004

Aronson, Howard I. 1972. Some notes on relative clauses in Georgian. In *The Chicago Which Hunt: Papers from the Relative Clause Festival*, Paul M. Peranteau, Judith N. Levi & Gloria C. Phares (eds), 136–143. Chicago IL: Chicago Linguistic Society.

Aronson, Howard I. 1991. Modern Georgian. In Harris & Greppin (eds), 219–312.

Authier, Gilles. 2012. *Grammaire Juhuri, ou Judéo-Tat, langue Iranienne des juifs du Caucase de L'est*. Wiesbaden: Reichert.

Babaliyeva, Ayten. 2013. Etudes sur la morphosyntaxe du tabasaran littéraire. PhD dissertation, Ecole Pratique des Hautes Etudes.

Babaliyeva, Ayten. 2014. Les relatives en Azéri. Presented at the Workshop Typologie aréale et stratégies de relativisation, 8–9 december, Paris.

Blanc, André, Charachidzé, Georges, Dubertret, Louis & Serrano, Sylvia. 2016. Caucase. In *Encyclopædia Universalis*. <http://www.universalis-edu.com/encyclopedie/caucase/> (26 February 2016).

Blumgardt, Temo. 2009. Ethnic groups in Caucasus region. Ms.

Bruk, Solomon I. & Apentchenko, V. S. (eds). 1964. *Атлас народов мира*. Главное управление геодезии и картографии, Государственного геологического комитета СССР Институт этнографии им. Н.Н. Миклухо-Маклая Академии Наук СССР. Москва.

Camilleri, Maris & Sadler, Louisa. 2011. Restrictive relative clauses in Maltese. In *Proceedings of the LFG11 Conference*, Miriam Butt & Tracy Holloway King (eds). Stanford CA: CSLI.

Chirikba, Viacheslav A. 2008. The problem of the Caucasian Sprachbund. In *From Linguistic Areas to Areal Linguistics* [Studies in Language Companion Series 90], Pieter Muysken (ed.), 25–93. Amsterdam: John Benjamins. https://doi.org/10.1075/slcs.90.02chi

Comrie, Bernard. 1998. Rethinking the typology of relative clauses. *Language Design* 1: 59–86.

Creissels, Denis. 2006. *Syntaxe générale : Une introduction typologique*, 2 Vols. Paris: Lavoisier.

Desherijev/Дешериев, Ю. Д. 1953. Бацбийский Язык. Фонетика, Морфология, Синтаксис, Лексика / Ответ. Ред. Б. А. Серебренников. Институт языкознания.

Dondua, K'arpez. 1967. Mimartebiti Nacvalsaxelisa Da Misamarti Sit'q'vis Urtiertobisatvis Ʒvel Kartulši (The Relationship between the Demonstrative Pronoun and the Correlative Word in Old Georgian). In *Rčeuli Našromebi* I: 20–29. Tbilisi: Mecniereba.

Downing, Bruce T. 1978. Some universals of relative clause structure. In *Universals of Human Language*, Vol. 4, Joseph H. Greenberg, Charles A. Ferguson & Edith A. Moravcsik (eds), 375–418. Stanford CA: Stanford University Press.

Dryer, Matthew, S. 2013. Order of relative clause and noun. In *The World Atlas of Language Structures Online*, Matthew Dryer & Martin Haspelmath (eds). Leipzig: Max Planck Institute for Evolutionary Anthropology. <http://wals.info/chapter/90> (5 December 2013).

Dumézil, Georges. 1967. *Documents anatoliens sur les langues et les traditions du Caucase, IV: Récits Lazes (Dialecte d'Arhavi)*. Paris: Presses Universitaires de France.

Dum-Tragut, Jasmine. 2009. *Armenian: Modern Eastern Armenian* [London Oriental and African Language Library 14]. Amsterdam: John Benjamins. https://doi.org/10.1075/loall.14

Durand, Marie-Françoise, Martin, Benoît, Placidi, Delphine & Törnquist-Chesnier, Marie. 2007. Atlas de La Mondialisation. Paris: Presses de Sciences Po.

Dzidziguri, Shota. 1969. K'avširebi kartul enaši [Conjunctions in Georgian]. Tbilisi: Tbilisi universit'et'i.

Fähnrich, Heinz. 1991. Old Georgian. In Harris & Greppin (eds), 131–217.

Gandon, Ophélie. 2016. La relativisation dans une perspective aréale: l'Aire caucase – anatolie de l'est – Iran de l'ouest. PhD dissertation, Université Sorbonne Nouvelle.

Gippert, Jost. 2011. Relative clauses in Vartashen Udi. Preliminary remarks. *Iran and the Caucasus* 15: 207–230. https://doi.org/10.1163/157338411X12870596615593

Guella, Noureddine. 2010. On relative clause formation in Arabic dialects of the Maghreb. *Synergies Monde Arabe* 7: 101–110.

Harris, Alice C. 1991a. Overview on the history of the Kartvelian languages. In Harris & Greppin (eds), 9–83.

Harris, Alice C. 1991. Mingrelian. In Harris & Greppin (eds), 315–389.

Harris, Alice C. 1992. Changes in relativization strategies: Georgian and language universals. In *Caucasologie et mythologie comparée, Actes Du Colloque International Du CNRS – IV Colloque de Caucasologie, Sèvre*, 27–29 Juin 1988, Catherine Paris (ed.), 391–403. Paris: Peeters.

Harris, Alice C. 2000. Word order in Georgian. In *Stability, Variation and Change of Word-Order Patterns over Time* [Current Issues in Linguistic Theory 21], Rosanna Sornicola, Erich Poppe & Ariel Shisha-Halevy (eds), 133–163. Amsterdam: John Benjamins. https://doi.org/10.1075/cilt.213.13har

Harris, Alice C. & Greppin, John A. C. 1991. *The Kartvelian Languages* [The Indigenous Languages of the Caucasus 1]. Delmar NY: Caravan Books.

Heine, Bernd & Kuteva, Tania. 2003. On contact-induced grammaticalization. *Studies in Language* 27(3): 529–572. https://doi.org/10.1075/sl.27.3.04hei

Heine, Bernd & Kuteva, Tania. 2006. *The Changing Languages of Europe*. Oxford: OUP. https://doi.org/10.1093/acprof:oso/9780199297337.001.0001

Hendery, Rachel. 2012. *Relative Clauses in Time and Space. A Case Study in the Methods of Diachronic Typology* [Typological Studies in Language 101]. Amsterdam: John Benjamins. https://doi.org/10.1075/tsl.101

Hewitt, Brian G. 1987. *The Typology of Subordination in Georgian and Abkhaz*. Berlin: Mouton de Gruyter. https://doi.org/10.1515/9783110846768

Hewitt, Brian G. 1995. *Georgian. A Structural Reference Grammar* [London Oriental and African Language Library 2]. Amsterdam: John Benjamins. https://doi.org/10.1075/loall.2

Hewitt, Brian G. 2001. Convergence in language change: Morpho-syntactic patterns in Mingrelian (and Laz). *Transactions of the Philological Society* 99(1): 88–145. https://doi.org/10.1111/1467-968X.00075

Holisky, Dee Ann. 1991. Laz. In Harris & Greppin (eds), 395–472.

Holisky, Dee Ann & Gagua, Rusudan. 1994. Tsova-Tush (Batsbi). In Smeets & Greppin (eds), 147–212.

Hourcade, Bernard. 2014. Unité et diversité linguistique de l'Iran. In *Irancarto. Etudes cartographiques sur l'Iran et le monde Iranien*, Bernard Hourcade, Hubert Mazurek, Mohammad-Hosseyn Papoli-Yazdi & Mahmoud Taleghani. <http://www.irancarto.cnrs.fr/record.php?q=SOC-030101&f=local&l=fr> (7 July 2016).

Jijiguri, Šota. 1969. *Ḳavširebi Kartul Enaši*. Tbilisi: Tbilisis Saxelmçipo Universiṭeṭi.

Keenan, Edward L. 1985. Relative clauses. In *Language Typology and Syntactic Description*, Vol. II: *Complex constructions*, Timothy Shopen (ed.), 141–170. Cambridge: CUP.

Khubua, Makar. 1937. *Megruli T'ekst'ebi* (Mingrelian Texts). Tbilisi: Ak'ademia.

Koryakov, Yuri B. 2002. *Atlas of the Caucasian Languages*. Moscow: Institute of Linguistics, Russian Academy of Sciences. <http://www.lingvarium.org/raznoe/publications/caucas/alw_cau_content.shtml> (24 July 2016).

Krause, Todd B., Greppin, John A. C. & Slocum, Jonathan. 2016. *Classical Armenian Online*. <http://www.utexas.edu/cola/centers/lrc/eieol/armol-0.html> (16 June 2016).

Lacroix, René. 2009. Description du dialecte Laze d'Arhavi (Caucasique du sud, Turquie). Grammaire et textes. PhD dissertation, Université Lumière Lyon 2.

Luján, Eugenio, R. 2009. On the grammaticalization of **kʷi-/kʷo-* relative clauses in Proto-Indo-European. In *Grammatical Change in Indo-European Languages. Papers Presented at the Workshop on Indo-European Linguistics at the XVIIIth International Conference on Historical Linguistics, Montreal, 2007* [Current Issues in Linguistic Theory 305], Vit Bubeník, John Hewson, & Sarah Rose (eds), 221–234. Amsterdam: John Benjamins. https://doi.org/10.1075/cilt.305.22luj

Meyer, Robin. 2013. Classical Armenian Relative Clause Syntax. A Comparative Study of Relative Clauses in the Armenian and Greek NT and Other 5th-C. Armenian Texts. MA thesis, University of Oxford.

Öztürk, Balkız & Pöchtrager, Markus A. (eds). 2011. *Pazar Laz*. Munich: Lincom.

Schmidt, Karl H. 1991. Svan. In Harris & Greppin (eds), 475–556.

Schulze, Wolfgang. 2006. A Functional Grammar of Udi. <http://wschulze.userweb.mwn.de/fgusamp.pdf> (28 July 2016).

Schulze-Fürhoff, Wolfgang. 1994. Udi. In Smeets & Greppin (eds), 447–514.

Shanidze, A. & Topuria V. 1939. *Svanuri P'rozauli T'ekst'ebi I: Balszemouri K'ilo* (Svan Prose Texts, I: Upper Bal Dialect). Tbilisi: Mecniereba.

Skopeteas, Stavros. 2013. The Caucasian Urums and the Urum language. *Tehlikedeki Diller Dergisi* (Journal of Endangered Languages) 334–364.

Smeets, Rieks & Greppin, John A. C. (eds). 1994. *North East Caucasian Languages, Part 2* [The Indigenous Languages of the Caucasus 4]. Delmar NY: Caravan Books.

Tuite, Kevin. 2004. A short descriptive grammar of the Svan language. Université de Montréal. <https://www.uni-jena.de/unijenamedia/Downloads/faculties/phil/kaukasiologie/Svan%5Bslightlyrevised%5D.pdf> (6 May 2016).

The verbal phrase

From time to surprise

The case of *será posible* in Spanish[1]

Susana Rodríguez Rosique
University of Alicante

This paper focuses on the meaning and behavior of *será posible* in Spanish. The structure may have two interpretations: a compositional one (*será posible*$_1$), which describes a situation that can hold in the future; and a less transparent one (*será posible*$_2$), related to a negative assessment. The analysis of the different structures invoked by *será posible* proves that *será posible*$_2$ is no longer interpreted as a copula in future plus and adjective, but has been reanalyzed as a mirative marker. Despite its fixed behavior, the mirative value seems to be motivated by the deictic nature of the future. The paper introduces a wide definition of this verb form, based on the deictic instruction of 'distance forward'. Productive, mirative interpretations of the future are analyzed from this perspective and confronted with the mirative *será posible*. More generally, this paper shows that if a wide definition of grammar is assumed, *será posible*$_2$ can be considered a case of grammaticalization.

Keywords: Spanish future, mirativity, distance, information structure

1. Introduction

The present paper focuses on the meaning and behavior of *será posible* in Spanish. This structure has two available readings. On the one hand, it exhibits a compositional meaning which describes a situation that can take place in the future, as seen in (1). Note that this example represents a case of dynamic modality (Nuyts 2008)[2] where the temporal meaning provided by the copula in future tense (*será*)

1. This research is supported by the Ministry of Economy and Competitiveness of Spain, under grant FFI2017-85441-R .

2. According to Nuyts (2008), dynamic modality differs from epistemic and deontic modalities. Unlike the former, which is only used by the speaker in order to describe a state of affairs, epistemic and deontic modalities additionally imply an evaluation of the state of affairs – i.e. questioning it.

https://doi.org.10.1075/slcs.202.08ros
© 2018 John Benjamins Publishing Company

and the sense of root possibility (Sweetser 1990) added by the adjective (*posible*) can be easily recognized.

(1) Esta participación **será posible** a través de un convenio firmado ayer entre la Fundación Santa María la Real [...] y la Universidad de Valladolid
'This participation will be possible through an agreement signed yesterday between Santa María la Real Foundation and the University of Valladolid'
(RAE, *CORPES XXI*)

On the other hand, *será posible* conveys a less transparent meaning which expresses the speaker's negative assessment towards an activated situation, and it can be related to the semantic category of mirativity (DeLancey 1997, 2001), as illustrated in (2) and (3):

(2) Estoy un poco fastidiao. Acabo de recibir una invitación de boda, ya me dirán si o es para estar jodido. **¡Será posible!** ¡Es que se te queda la misma cara que cuando te llega una multa! ¡Hale, a soltar pasta!
'I'm a little pissed off. I've just received a wedding invitation, and tell me if it is not to be fucked. I can't believe it! / Fuck! Your face is the same face as when you get a fine! Geez, time to drop dough!' (RAE, *CORPES XXI*)

(3) ABELARDO. Mira quién fue a hablar ..., que parece un bicho de cazar.
'Look who's talking ... a guy who looks like a beast of prey'
OLVIDO. ¡**Será posible**, este par de carcamales ...!
'I can't believe it! / Such ..., this pair of old fogies ...!' (RAE, *CORPES XXI*)

This latter interpretation of *será posible* (*será posible*$_2$) actually points to the mirative use of the Spanish future in compositional, productive contexts (Squartini 2012; Rodríguez Rosique 2015b), as exemplified in (4):

(4) –A partir de ahora [...] le dices a tu hermana que me llame don Enrique siempre que haya alguien delante [...]. Y se había ido a escape a contárselo a ella, a su hermana Carmen:
'From now on, tell your sister to call me *Don Enrique* whenever there is someone around'. And he had rushed out to tell her, her sister Carmen'
– **¡Será idiota el tonto que tengo por marido!**
'Such an idiot, the stupid that I have as a husband!'
(F. Blanes García, *El cura de Carboneras*. Entrelíneas Editores, 2009, p. 95, from Google Books)

(2)–(3), on one side, and (4), on another, differ in their degree of compositionality or analyzability, though (Traugott & Trousdale 2013). Firstly, the verb may agree with different persons in (4), as shown by (5), something that cannot happen with *será posible* (6). Secondly, a dislocated subject is still identifiable in (4), as (7) highlights. However, if a subject is introduced in (2), the interpretation changes into a dynamic one, as can be seen in (8). Concerning (3), the noun phrase *este par de carcamales* cannot be the syntactic subject due to the caesura represented by the comma, as becomes evident in (9):

Verb agreement

(5) Serán$_{3ps.pl}$ idiotas estos tíos / Seremos$_{1ps.pl}$. idiotas

(6) * Serán posibles / 3a. *Serán posibles estos carcamales

Existence of a syntactic subject

(7) Será idiota el tonto que tengo por marido

(8) #¿Será posible esta situación / esto? (dynamic interpretation in future)

(9) Ø Será posible, este par de carcamales

The aim of this paper consists in showing that *será posible* behaves unitarily as a mirative marker in (2) and (3). However, in spite of its fixed character, the mirative value of the structure is motivated by the deictic nature of the Spanish future. Seeking to find evidence thereof, the paper is organized as follows: Section 2 provides a wide definition of the future based on the deictic instruction of 'distance forward.' Productive, mirative interpretations of the future – as the one displayed by Example (4) – are analyzed from this perspective in Section 3. These productive, mirative uses of the future are compared to the mirative *será posible*. In order to do so, Section 4 offers an analysis where the compositional cases with a temporal location and a dynamic interpretation – Example (1) – are confronted with the fixed cases that have a mirative interpretation. This section also emphasizes the role of the interrogative and that of the information structure in the rise of the mirative *será posible*. Section 5 presents a number of specific and general conclusions derived from the analysis, and poses further questions for future research works.

2. How to deal with the future

Traditionally, tense is considered a grammatical category which codifies time and works deictically (Comrie 1985). From this perspective, the future places the event after the now of the speaker, as Figure 1 shows:[3]

---

3. From a philosophical perspective, both the diagrammatic representation of time in linear terms and the placement of the future in this timeline have constituted controversial issues since ancient times. In fact, it is usually said that the future does not have a linear nature but requires a

Figure 1. Traditional deictic representation of the future

Due to this deictic peculiarity, the future is usually associated with a variety of modal values (Dahl 1985), as shown by Examples (10) to (12). In spite of these modal values, the future still places the event after the now of the speaker:

(10) El próximo fin de semana <u>lloverá</u> en buena parte del país = Prediction
'It will rain in a large part of the country next week'

(11) Mañana te <u>compraré</u> un helado = Promise
'I will buy you an ice-cream tomorrow'

(12) <u>Entregarás</u> el proyecto la semana que viene = Request, order
'You will hand in the paper next week'

More interestingly, though, the future may occur in non-posteriority contexts, as (13) exemplifies. In such cases, this verbal form has been related both to inferential evidentiality – insofar as the speaker makes an estimate or a conjecture – and to epistemic modality – since the speaker evaluates the proposition as probable:

(13) A: ¿Qué hora es?
'What time is it?'
B: Serán las cuatro
'It must be four' (Bello [1847] 1970: 236)

The modal values adhered to Examples (10)–(12) along with the possibility for the future to occur in non-posteriority contexts has provoked some controversy concerning its status. According to some authors (Bertinetto 1979; Giannakidou & Mari 2012), the future is essentially a modal form, which explains both the modal values in (10)–(12) and its presence in cases such as (13). For others (Sthioul 1998; de Saussure & Morency 2012; de Saussure 2013), the future is essentially a temporal form, even in examples such as (13), which can be explained in perspectival terms, as a kind of meta-representation that justifies the change from expressing a state of affairs to convey the verification of that state of affairs. Broader approaches – such as the philosophical view (Jaszczolt 2009) or the Cognitive proposal

ramified structure precisely because of its nature. A summary of the different perspectives and a general approach to this discussion can be seen in works such as that of Weinrich ([1964] 1974) or – more recently – the one written by De Brabanter, Kissine and Sharifzadeh (2014). From a conceptual perspective, however, the conception of time as a notional structure which derives from perceptual processing mechanisms and provides a set of articulated metaphors (Evans 2003) may justify the deictic function of tenses.

(Langacker 1991: 240–281; Brisard 1997) – also defend the modal nature of the future; they specifically argue that the future is modal because tense – and even time, in general – is a modal notion. More recently (Escandell 2010, 2014), the future in Spanish has been defined as what Aikhenvald's (2004) calls a 'grammatical evidential'; from this perspective, it is claimed that the future always codifies that the source of information is a speaker's inner process.

When it seemed that the debate on the future focused on the prevalence of the modal value over the temporal one – or vice versa –, or on which analytical tool – either modality or evidentiality – was wider for its definition, attention has been moved in another direction: the discursive uses (Rodríguez Rosique 2018). In fact, (14)–(16) provide evidence that the future can play several roles in discourse and eventually in the communicative situation as a whole. Note that the utterance introduced by the future in (14) is presented as a necessary conclusion following from a previous argument, which becomes a persuasive mechanism that ultimately turns out to be highly productive in interaction (Rodríguez Rosique 2017). This verbal form may also introduce a weak counter-argument, as in the case of the concessive future represented by (15), thus highlighting the strength of the opposite conclusion (Rodríguez Rosique 2015a). Additionally, as already presented above, the future can be used with a mirative purpose, whereby it comes to convey a kind of evaluation or assessment –a pattern already observed in (4) and now, once again, in (16).

(14) Era la primera posibilidad que se daba a los periodistas para hacer cursos académicos. **Entonces, comprenderás$_{\text{fut}}$ que no pude dejar ya el periodismo y tuve que hacerlo**
'It was the first opportunity given to journalists so that they could attend academic courses. Then you have to understand that I was not able to leave journalism any more, and I had to do so' (RAE, *CREA*, Oral, sf)

(15) <T4>: Porque piensan que así, consintiéndoles, lo mismo están más felices [...]
'Because they think that, in that way, spoiling them, they could even feel happier'
<T8>: **Sí, a los niños los harán$_{\text{fut}}$ muy felices pero no es eso lo que les interesa.**
'Yes, they may make children very happy, but that is not what they need'
(Azorín 2002: 374)

(16) – A partir de ahora [...] le dices a tu hermana que me llame don Enrique siempre que haya alguien delante [...]. Y se había ido a escape a contárselo a ella, a su hermana Carmen:
– **¡Será$_{\text{fut}}$ idiota el tonto que tengo por marido!**

> 'From now on, tell your sister to call me *Don Enrique* whenever there is someone around. And he had rushed out to tell her, her sister Carmen:
> – Such an idiot, the stupid that I have as a husband!'
> (F. Blanes García, *El cura de Carboneras*. Entrelíneas Editores, 2009, p. 95, from Google Books)

These discursive uses represent a new challenge for the definition of the future. In fact, they have recently been explained from different perspectives. For instance, Squartini (2012) focuses on the concessive future (15) and relates it to Nuyts' notion of intersubjectivity. According to Nuyts (2001, 2012), an utterance is subjective when it appears as the speaker's exclusive responsibility – i.e. the speaker is the only source. By contrast, an utterance is intersubjective when it emerges as a responsibility shared by both the speaker and the addressee. For Squartini, the notion of intersubjectivity – represented by the concessive future – emerges vis-à-vis that of mirativity – represented by the mirative future: both notions point to a shared source. Squartini's analysis is attractive since it calls for information which remains 'in the air' in order to explain the discursive uses of the future. However, Nuyts' notion of intersubjectivity seems more appropriate to explain the persuasive future (14) than the concessive one, since the latter shows a speaker who does not seem to share responsibility but he rather distances himself from the addressee's perspective. Furthermore, it will be necessary to specify the connection between the concessive and the mirative future. Rivero (2014) has also recently focused on the concessive future (15), which she considers a case of mirativity. According to her, the future behaves here as a weak modal operator through which the speaker does not show himself as responsible for the uttered information – and he may even deny it. Rivero does not analyze cases such as (16), though.

A unitary form of explaining the discursive uses of the future and simultaneously relating them to its temporal and epistemic values is through a reformulation of its deictic nature (Rodríguez Rosique 2015a, in press). The future in Spanish always invokes a deictic instruction of 'distance forward' (Fleischman 1989). This instruction can be projected upon a subjectivity axle (Traugott 1989, 2010; Schwenter 1999) which comes across the different levels of meaning established by Sweetser (1990) due to successive scope widenings (Bybee, Perkins & Pagliuca 1994; Traugott & Dasher 2002), as illustrated by Figure 2. In this way, polysemy does not count as a bunch of unrelated meanings; instead, it emerges as a unitary and systematic way of accounting for the different pictures of the future mentioned above.

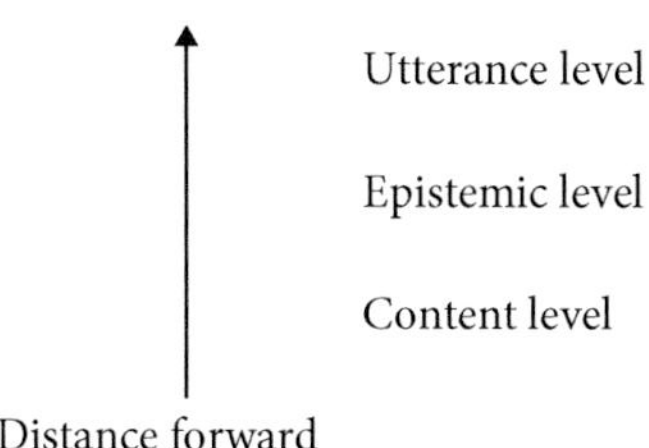

Figure 2. A deictic definition for future

At the content level, the future works inside the proposition: the deictic instruction of distance forward is projected upon the event, subsequently being interpreted as posteriority. As for the epistemic level, the deictic instruction is projected over the proposition and can thus be interpreted both in modal and in evidential terms. From a modal point of view, unlike what happens with past forms, the distance forward is interpreted in a positive way; in other words, it places the proposition somewhere between hypotheticality and certainty (Akatsuka 1985; Rodríguez Rosique 2011; de Saussure 2013). From an evidential perspective, the speaker expresses an event as the result of an inference, an estimate or a conjecture. The distance forward can thus be justified either because the event is subject to a subsequent corroboration (Pérez Saldanya 2002; de Saussure 2013), or because a deduction is always subsequent to its evidence (Langacker 2011; Martines 2017). There is a *sine qua non* requirement for the future to operate at this level: the future must be dislocated – or expressed differently, extracted from its natural context of posteriority (Rojo & Veiga 1999). At the utterance level, the distance is projected upon the speech act, so the future may play several interpersonal roles (Pérez Saldanya 2002) somehow linked to Traugott's notion of intersubjectivity (1989, 2010). Once again, a requirement must be fulfilled so that this can happen: the information occurring in the future must have been previously activated.

Activation constitutes an orthogonal notion of the dichotomy *new vs. old* information. Old information, understood as Common Ground (CG) or shared knowledge, is the set of knowledge, beliefs and assumptions that the speaker and the addressee share when they are involved in an interaction (Stalnaker 1978; Lewis 1979; Heim 1983; Clark 1996). In order to organize his discourse, the speaker advances hypotheses (Gutiérrez Ordóñez 1997) about what the CG between him and his addressee would be according to a number of shared bases, such as cultural communities – in turn determined by nationality, education, politics, ethnicity, gender, etc. – as well as according to perceptual experiences and joint actions (Clark 1996). CG is updated as communication proceeds, but this cannot happen unless information is admitted by the speaker and the addressee alike. Nevertheless, information may be discussed before being incorporated into CG (Ginzburg 2015). Activation emerges as a useful notion at this point. Activated or salient information is the one that the speaker assumes to be profiled in the addressee's mind at the moment of the interaction (Chafe 1976, 1994; Prince 1992; Dik 1997; Lambrecht 1994; Dryer 1996). This information can be activated either discursively or situationally. Furthermore, since activation is a notion related to short-term memory, information lies along a continuum which has as one of its extremes the activation focus, or to put it in another way, the information that we pay special attention to. This continuum also includes semi-deactivated information, that is, the one which has been activated but is becoming less prominent. Accessible information, or the one which has not been activated as such but has to do with previously activated information, lies in this continuum as well. At the opposite side of them all, we find non-activated information. Figure 3 below represents the activation continuum.

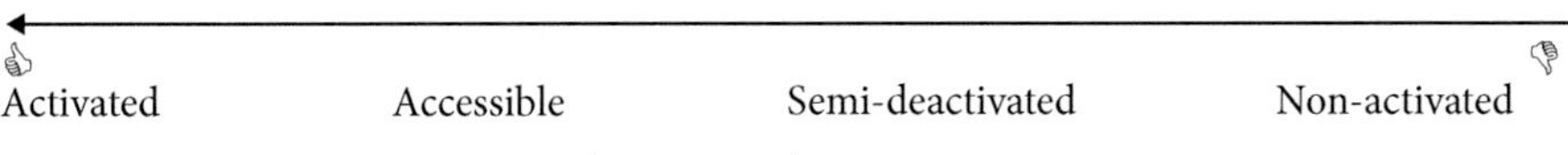

Figure 3. Activation continuum (Dryer 1996)

3. The mirative future

When information occurring in the future has been activated in advance, the deictic 'distance forward' instruction may be projected upon the utterance. Among the values played by the future in these cases stands out the mirative one, as can be seen in a repetition of (16):

(16) – A partir de ahora [...] le dices a tu hermana que me llame don Enrique siempre que haya alguien delante [...]. Y se había ido a escape a contárselo a ella, a su hermana Carmen:
– **¡Será$_{\text{fut}}$ idiota el tonto que tengo por marido!**
'From now on, tell your sister to call me *Don Enrique* whenever there is someone around. And he had rushed out to tell her, her sister Carmen:
– Such an idiot, the stupid that I have as a husband!'

Mirativity is a universal category (DeLancey 1997, 2001 vs. Lazard 1999; Hill 2012) which marks the status of a proposition with respect to the speaker's general knowledge structure. It has to do with a natural tendency that languages have to draw a distinction between the information that forms part of the speaker's integrated picture about the world and any new information not belonging to that integrated picture. Then, it does not only concern the information structure but also contains an evaluative component. In fact, it is assumed that the core meaning of mirativity has to do with surprise as well as with Aksu and Slobin's (1986) notion of *unprepared mind* (Aikhenvald 2012; Peterson 2013). The connection between mirativity and new information is not exempt from controversy, though. For instance, according to Peterson (2013), new information is a necessary – but not sufficient – condition for mirativity, since many cases expressing new information are not mirative. Furthermore, Aikhenvald (2012) argues that, in the case of mirativity, information may be new for the speaker, new for the addressee, or new for the audience; and along the same lines, Hengeveld and Olbertz (2012) consider that mirativity may include new information for the speaker – in most cases – or new information for the addressee. Rather than to new information, the mirative uses of the future are here related to activated information.

Once the notion of mirativity has been outlined, the question about the role of the future in cases such as (16) arises. First, note that the information occurring in future has been activated beforehand; more specifically, the future introduces accessible or deducible information from a previously activated one: the assessment *será idiota* arises as a result or a consequence[4] of a previously activated situation (the husband's arrogant behavior). Since the information occurring in future has been activated in advance, the 'distance forward' instruction is projected upon the utterance and turns it into a *distanced evaluation*, which in turn triggers a negative effect of criticism or rejection. In fact, the mirative future always occurs with negative terms – in other words, it is always depreciatory –, which explains the anomaly found in (17) as well as the relevant interpretation of suspended structures such as (18), where a negative qualification is expected (Rodríguez Rosique 2015b).

(17) *Será simpática
'Such a nice girl'

(18) Serás …
'Such a …'

Beyond the well-known and controversial relationship with evidentiality, mirativity is also connected with exclamation and exclamativity (Hengeveld & Olbertz 2012; Rett 2012). Exclamation is a type of expressive speech act which can be associated to certain grammatical constructions – exclamatives (Michaelis 2001; Castroviejo 2008, 2010) – or can be triggered exclusively as a result of intonation

4. In fact, it could represent a peculiar case of *bridging* as Clark (1977) understands it. According to him, bridging arises when a discursive segment is presented as a consequence or a result from another previous one. Note that in cases such as (11) an *assessment* arises as a consequence or a result of a previously activated *situation*, which explains why the discursive role turns into a kind of expressive one.

(Potts 2007). This mirative future precisely alternates both with exclamatives[5] and with attributive structures that contain an emphatic indefinite article *un* (Portolés 1993; Fernández Leborans 1999; Suñer 1999):

(19) a. ¡Será idiota!
b. ¡Qué idiota (es)! [Exclamative]
c. Es un idiota [Attributive structure with emphatic *un*]

As opposed to these compositional cases, the mirative *será posible* cannot alternate with the structures in (19), as shown in (20), where the exclamative and the construction with emphatic *un* are excluded:

(20) a. ¡Será posible! (mirative interpretation)
b. *¡Qué posible (es)! [Exclamative]
c. *Es un posible [Construction with emphatic *un*]

Then, the question about how the mirative *será posible* works arises.

4. Analysis: *Será posible* in contemporary Spanish

An analysis of the occurrences of *será posible* in *CORPES XXI* (*Corpus del Español del siglo XXI*), compiled by Real Academia Española and available on line <http://www.rae.es/recursos/banco-de-datos/corpes-xxi>, has been carried out with the aim of answering the question asked at the end of the previous section.

Out of 304 occurrences obtained, 244 are still compositional structures, where the schema formed by a copula in future tense (*será*) plus an adjective (*posible*) can be easily identified. Furthermore, most of these occurrences convey a dynamic interpretation, since they denote a situation that can take place in the future. In this sense, a strong tendency exists for the occurrence of phrases insisting on the means for the situation to occur, such as *a través de* (21), *con* (22), *gracias a* (23), etc. The structure also admits a great variety of syntactic subjects, including noun phrases (21), (23), (24), infinitive clauses (22), (27), *que* + subjunctive clauses (25), or pronouns (26), and can be accompanied even by a participant involved in the accomplishment of the situation – i.e. a benefactive –, as in (27):

5. The connection between the future and exclamativity extends beyond this alternation. In fact, the relation between the future and a kind of exclamative construction with *si* is usually assumed in the literature (Alarcos 1994; Iglesias Recuero 2000; González Calvo 1997; Alonso 1999; RAE 2009; Hernanz 2012; Sánchez López 2015; Bosque 2017): *¡Si sera idiota!* This option is also excluded for *será posible*: #*¡Si será posible!*

(21) Esta participación **será posible** a través de un convenio firmado ayer entre la Fundación Santa María la Real [...] y la Universidad de Valladolid
'This participation will be possible through an agreement signed yesterday between Santa María la Real Foundation and the University of Valladolid'

(22) ¡Con el nuevo almacén del agua **será posible** incluso llevar a cabo paradas técnicas de mayor duración!
'With the new water store it will be possible even to get longer technique stops!'

(23) Esa recuperación **será posible** [...] gracias a unas políticas macroeconómicas adecuadas [...]
'That recovery will be possible [...] thanks to some appropriate macroeconomic policies [...]'

(24) "Esta misma mañana hemos tenido una reunión. Seguimos trabajando y **será posible** el acuerdo", dijo
'"We have just had a meeting this very morning. We keep working and the agreement will be possible", he said'

(25) Así, el profesorado puede conocer en todo momento el listado de su alumnado matriculado en las asignaturas que imparta, e incluso **será posible** que visualice los datos contenidos en las fichas digitales de todos aquellos estudiantes que posean la tarjeta
'Thus, teachers can know at all times the list of students enrolled in the courses that they impart, and it will even be possible for them to see the data in the digital records of all students who have the card'

(26) Tanto González como Morlán han asegurado que estas actuaciones permitirán garantizar la seguridad de ciudadanos y trabajadores y restablecer cuanto antes el servicio de Cercanías, si bien no han querido precisar la fecha en que esto **será posible**
'Both Gonzalez and Morlán have assured that these actions will help ensure the safety of citizens and workers and restore the *Cercanías* [Suburban Train] service as soon as possible, although they did not want to specify the date when this will be possible'

(27) Con ellos podremos ponernos muy cerca del sujeto, por muy grande que sea, y sin embargo nos **será posible** incluirlo por completo en la foto
'With these devices we will be able to stand really close to the subject, however large it is, and yet we will be able to include it completely in the picture'

Será posible as a compositional structure with a dynamic interpretation can be affected both by negation and by an interrogative, as (28), on the one hand, and (29)–(30), on the other, respectively show:

(28) Y, paradójicamente, esta ratificación no **será posible** hasta que los mismos parlamentos nacionales no hayan ratificado el Convenio revisado de Eurocontrol
'And paradoxically, this ratification will not be possible until the actual national parliaments have not ratified the revised Eurocontrol agreement'

(29) He de darte la razón, hija, pero **¿será posible** encontrar a algún hombre capaz de haber llegado a semejante grado de perfección?
'I have to agree with you, my daughter, but will it be possible to find a man who could have reached such a degree of perfection?'

(30) Sin embargo, sabemos también que lo deseable es que la sociedad civil pueda gestionar todo aquello para lo que sea capaz de auto organizarse. **¿Será posible** que encontremos el equilibrio y la colaboración necesaria entre el sistema público de cultura y la iniciativa cultural privada, tanto la social y sin ánimo de lucro como la empresarial?
'However, we also know that it is desirable for civil society to be able to manage everything for which it can organize itself. Will it be possible for us to find the necessary balance and collaboration between the public system and private cultural initiative, both the social and non-profit one as the business-oriented one?'

Note how (28) denotes that a certain situation will not take place in the future. Concerning (29)–(30), the speaker uses the question to ask about the possibility for an alluded situation to occur in the future.

Nevertheless, interrogatives play an important role for the appearance of the mirative *será posible*. In fact, it is in these environments that we find the necessary ambiguity for the change to occur, so they can be considered *bridging contexts* (Heine 2002; Diewald 2002; Smirnova 2015). Interrogatives actually allow the future to exhibit a value other than the temporal one, as can be seen in (31), where the future does not place the event after the now of the speech, but its use allows the speaker to *speculate* about the possibility of an ongoing situation: the deictic 'distance forward' instruction is then projected upon the epistemic level.

(31) A Gaspar se le aceleró el corazón y se le puso un nudo en el estómago. El mismo que había notado dos días antes. "¿**Será posible** que a mi edad todavía me pasen estas cosas?"

'Gaspar felt his heart race and a knot in the stomach. The one which he had noticed two days earlier. "Can it be possible that these things still happen to me at my age?"'

The cases illustrated by (32)–(33) are a bit different, however. The future neither works at the temporal level nor at the epistemic one, but the 'distance forward' is now projected upon the utterance level, and, as a consequence, the speaker distances himself from his speech act. In fact, the interrogatives in (32)–(33) are *marked* or *exclamative* (Escandell 1999; Alonso 1999), since they do not expect an answer but rather emphasize previously activated information.

(32) De seriedad, ni gota para un remedio. Se afanan por convertir asuntos de poca monta en cuestiones de principios. ¿**Será posible** que el Tripartito no tenga ocupaciones más urgentes que las selecciones deportivas?
'Not a single drop of seriousness. They strive to turn small matters into key issues. How can it be possible that the Tripartite has no more urgent occupations than the national sport teams?'

(33) Frente al supermercado de Sant Andreu, la gente comenzó a arremolinarse junto a los héroes de la tragedia. Había familiares y curiosos, y mucho dolor. "¡Dios mío! ¿**Será posible** que hayan sido capaces de poner una bomba aquí dentro?"
'Opposite Sant Andreu's supermarket, people began to swirl alongside the heroes of the tragedy. There were relatives and onlookers, and a lot of pain. "My God! How can it be possible that they managed to plant a bomb in here?"'

As explained above, one requirement that needs to be fulfilled for the deictic 'distance forward' instruction to be projected upon the utterance is that the information occurring in the future must have been previously activated. Note that the speaker has just stated that "they [the political parties] make an effort to turn small matters into key issues" in (32), and similarly the speaker in (33) has just described the macabre scene after a bomb explosion. In this sense, it deserves to be highlighted that the syntactic subject in (32)–(33) is represented by a subordinate clause introduced by *que* plus the subjunctive mood. Note that the Spanish subjunctive is the mood for non-assertion (Lunn 1989) through which information is placed at a second level of discourse, either because it is not certain or – more relevantly here – because it has already appeared and there is no need to activate it again. Both (32) and (33) show *será posible* introducing a situation as 'something that is happening but is difficult to conceive as possible.'

Nevertheless, (31)–(33) are still compositional structures where the schema [copula in future (*será*) + an adjective (*posible*)] continues to be easily identified, and an evidence for this is provided by the fact that they admit a syntactic subject – they often do occur with it. The peculiarity is that the future does not play a temporal role here, but a discursive one in the most significant cases (32)–(33).

The next step becomes visible in cases such as (2) – repeated below as (34) –, and (35), where the non-compositional structure with a mirative value appears:

(34) Estoy un poco fastidiao. Acabo de recibir una invitación de boda, ya me dirán si no es para estar jodido. **¡Será posible!** ¡Es que se te queda la misma cara que cuando te llega una multa! ¡Hale, a soltar pasta!
'I'm a little pissed off. I've just received a wedding invitation, and tell me if it is not to be fucked. I can't believe it! / Fuck! Your face is the same face as when you get a fine! Geez, time to drop dough!'

(35) –No nos ha tocado nada, pero lo importante es que haya salud
'–We haven't won anything, but the important thing is that we stay healthy'
–¡Pues eso faltaba! Que encima de que no me toca la lotería me atropelle un camión. **¿Será posible?**
'–That's the last straw! In addition to not winning the lottery, I could get run over by a truck. I can't believe such a …'

Semantically, these examples express an evaluative distance towards an activated situation; more precisely, they convey the speaker's rejection or criticism. Formally, *será posible* cannot be interpreted as a copula in future tense (*será*) plus an adjective (*posible*) anymore. In fact, the situation triggering the speaker's assessment cannot be embedded as a syntactic subject – at least not without also rendering a change of interpretation. Concerning (34), note that "I've just received a wedding invitation" cannot be interpreted as the syntactic subject of *será posible*: if it were assumed, the mood in the subordinate clause should be subjunctive, and a similar reading to (32) and (33) would be obtained, as shown in (36).[6] Instead, the most plausible rephrasing of (34) seems to be a structure such as that in (37), where the situation that triggers the evaluation is reintroduced as an utterance-level causal clause which justifies the expressive speech act played by *será posible*, as the preceding comma and the indicative mood of the subordinate clause suggest:

(36) #¿Será posible que acabe de recibir una invitación de boda?
'How can it be possible that I have just received a wedding invitation?'

(37) Será posible, que acabo de recibir una invitación de boda
'I can't believe it / Fuck! I say so because I've just received a wedding invitation'

6. An epistemic reading would be more difficult to justify in this case: for instance, we would need to assume that someone does not know how a wedding invitation is and that he is making some conjectures about it.

On other occasions, it is not so easy to isolate the clause representing the situation that triggers *será posible*'s assessment in the surrounding discourse. This is what happens in (35), where the assessment has a previous interlocutor's speech act as scope. A possible paraphrase is highlighted in (38):

(38) Será posible, que dices que no nos ha tocado nada pero que lo importante es que haya salud
'I can't believe such a … I say so because you have just said that we haven't won anything, but the important this is that we stay healthy'

Further evidence for the impossibility of *será posible* to occur with a subject is provided by (3), now repeated in (39), where the lack of agreement between the noun phrase and *será*, as well as the existence of the caesura, confirm the absence of a syntactic subject.

(39) ABELARDO. Mira quién fue a hablar …, que parece un bicho de cazar.
'Look who's talking … a guy who looks like a beast of prey'
OLVIDO. ¡**Será posible**, este par de carcamales …!
'I can't believe it! / Such …, this pair of old fogies …!'

Note that in cases such as (39) the speaker attitude is extended from the situation to the people involved therein; in other words, the speaker expresses his rejection or criticism towards *someone* involved in the activated situation through the use of *será posible*, which is compatible with the negative term used to refer to them (*este par de carcamales* 'this pair of old fogies').

The impossibility to introduce a syntactic subject in examples such as (34) and (35), or the occurrence of *será posible* with a noun phrase that cannot be analyzed as its syntactic subject – as it happens in (39) – confirms their status as conventionalization cases (Heine 2002); or, expressed differently, *será posible* appears in new contexts where it is neither compatible with the original meaning nor with the compositional interpretation.

This non-compositional mirative *será posible* (*será posible*$_2$) also constitutes a marked structure in prosodic terms. In fact, speakers usually doubt about how to transcribe it, whether with question marks or with exclamation marks – 'exclamative questions,' in the words of Alonso (1999) –, or even with ellipsis or dots.

All the samples of *será posible*$_2$ found in *CORPES XXI* come from oral discourse or from literary texts pretending to use an informal register – that explains the small number of occurrences compared with the compositional cases. The colloquial register is actually less representative in *CORPES XXI* than the formal one. Different data are obtained when taking a glance at an oral corpus, such as *Alicante Corpus del Español (ALCORE)*, where all the cases found correspond precisely to the non-compositional mirative type – that is, *será posible*$_2$ –, as exemplified in (40):

(40) Porque ella decía: "Yo un día me voy a Campoamor, pongo una paradita y vendo todo mi dote". **¡Será posible!**
'Because she said: "One day I will go to Campoamor, put up a stall and sell all my dowry". I can't believe it / Such …!' (Azorín 2002)

5. Conclusions

This paper has demonstrated that *será posible* is associated with synchronically different structures, representing a case of 'layering' as defined by Hopper (1991). On the one hand, it may behave as a compositional structure; in most of these cases, *será posible* is interpreted as describing a root possibility – i.e. the possibility for the state of affairs to hold in the future. However, some of these cases show the future playing a role other than the temporal one, something which tends to happen in interrogatives, which can thus be considered bridging contexts. More specifically, the future can operate at the epistemic level – introducing a conjecture – or, more significantly, it may indicate the speaker's distance towards his utterance and, by extension, towards the situation which that utterance points to. This latter case can only apply if the information occurring in future has been previously activated, triggering a kind of exclamative or marked question. Both the examples where the future works at the epistemic level and those where the deictic 'distance forward' instruction is projected upon the utterance represent a case of semantic change – or subjectification (Traugott & Dasher 2002) –, but the structure remains compositional, since the schema integrated by a copula in future tense (*será*) plus an adjective (*posible*) can still be recognized.

On the other hand, *será posible* may behave as a fixed structure. Semantically, *será posible*$_2$ conveys the speaker's evaluative distance towards an activated situation – i.e., a kind of expressive meaning that can fall under the label of mirativity. Formally, it is no longer interpreted as a compositional structure but has been reanalyzed as a mirative marker. In fact, a syntactic subject cannot be embedded, no verb agreement exists, and it is associated with a marked intonation. Furthermore, *será posible*$_2$ has restrictions as far as register is concerned; more precisely, it appears more often in colloquial, informal discourses, something that is compatible with its new interpersonal, intersubjective role (Traugott 2010) – i.e. showing the speaker's negative assessment towards an activated situation which looks for the addressee's acquiescence. *Será posible*$_2$ thus represents a case of grammaticalization through which it has abandoned the field of sentence grammar to enter the sphere of discourse grammar (Kaltenböck, Heine & Kuteva 2011; Heine, Kaltenböck, Kuteva & Long 2013).

The specific analysis of *será posible* carried out in the present paper poses some challenges for further research. The identification of questions as the bridging contexts for the emerging of *será posible*$_2$ when some informational circumstances are met actually suggests the need to deal with the links between the future and interrogatives. Similarly, the diachronic relationship and synchronic interferences between *será posible* and the productive mirative future also arise as a fruitful area for future research. While *será posible* seems to have become specialized for criticizing situations, the productive mirative future appears to be used to reject human attitudes; however, examples such as (3) – or (37) – require a closer examination, perhaps in the light of analogical thinking (Traugott and Trousdale 2013).

References

Aikhenvald, Alexandra Y. 2004. *Evidentiality*. Oxford: OUP.

Aikhenvald, Alexandra Y. 2012. The essence of mirativity. *Linguistic Typology* 16: 435–485. https://doi.org/10.1515/lity-2012-0017

Akatsuka, Noriko. 1985. Conditionals and the epistemic scale. *Language* 61(3): 625–639. https://doi.org/10.2307/414388

Aksu-Koç, Ayhan & Slobin, Dan. 1986. A psychological account of the development and use of evidentials in Turkish. In *Evidentiality: The Linguistic Coding of Epistemology*, Wallace Chafe & Johanna Nichols (eds), 159–167. Norwood NJ: Ablex.

Alarcos, Emillio. 1994. *Gramática de la lengua española*. Madrid: Espasa-Calpe.

Alonso, Ángel. 1999. Las construcciones exclamativas. In Bosque & Demonte (eds), 3993–4050.

Azorín, Maria Dolores. 2002. *ALCORE. Alicante Corpus del Español*. Alicante: Universidad de Alicante

Bello, Andrés. [1847]1970. *Gramática de la lengua castellana destinada al uso de los americanos*. Buenos Aires: Sopena.

Bertinetto, Pier Marco. 1979. Alcune ipotesi sul nostro futuro (con osservazioni su *potere* e *dovere*). *Rivista di Grammatica Generativa* 4 (1–2): 77–138.

Bosque, Ignacio. 2017. Spanish exclamatives in perspective: A survey of properties, classes, and current theoretical issues. In *Advances in the Analysis of Spanish Exclamatives, Ignacio* Bosque (ed.), 1–52. Columbus OH: The Ohio State University Press.

Bosque, Ignacio & Demonte, Violeta (eds). 1999. *Gramática descriptiva de la lengua española*. Madrid: Espasa-Calpe.

Brisard, Frank. 1997. The English tense-system as an epistemic category: The case of futurity. In *Lexical and Syntactical Constructions and the Construction of Meaning* [Current Issues in Linguistic Theory 150], Marjolijn Verspoor, Kee Dong Lee & Eve Sweetser (eds), 271–285. Amsterdam: John Benjamins. https://doi.org/10.1075/cilt.150.20bri

Bybee, Joan, Perkins, Revere Dale & Pagliuca, William. 1994. *The Evolution of Grammar. Tense, Aspect, and Modality in the Languages of the World*. Chicago IL: The University of Chicago Press.

Castroviejo, Elena. 2008. Deconstructing exclamations. *Catalan Journal of Linguistics* 7: 41–90.

Castroviejo, Elena. 2010. An expressive answer. Some considerations on the semantics and pragmatics of *wh-* exclamatives. *Proceedings from the Annual Meeting of the Chicago Linguistic Society* <http://elena-castroviejo-miro.cat/papers/cls44-castroviejo-DEF.pdf>.

Chafe, Wallace. 1976. Givenness, contrastiveness, definiteness, subjects, topics, and point of view. In *Subject and Topic*, Charles N. Li (ed.), 25–55. New York NY: Academic Press.

Chafe, Wallace. 1994. *Discourse, Consciousness, and Time. The Flow and Displacement of Conscious Experience in Speaking and Writing*. Chicago IL: The University of Chicago Press.

Clark, Herbert H. 1977. Bridging. In *Thinking: Readings in Cognitive Science*, Philip N. Johnson-Laird & Peter Cathcart Wason (eds), 411–420. London: CUP.

Clark, Herbert H. 1996. *Using Language*. Cambridge: CUP. https://doi.org/10.1017/CBO9780511620539

Comrie, Bernard. 1985. *Tense*. Cambridge: CUP. https://doi.org/10.1017/CBO9781139165815

Cornillie, Bert. 2009. Evidentiality and epistemic modality. On the close relationship between two different categories. *Functions of Language* 16(1): 44–62. https://doi.org/10.1075/fol.16.1.04cor

Dahl, Östen. 1985. *Tense and Aspect Systems*. Oxford: Basil Blackwell.

De Brabanter, Phillipe, Kissine, Mikhail & Sharifzadeh, Saghie. 2014. Future tense vs. future time: An introduction. In *Future Times, Future tenses*, Phillipe De Brabanter, Mikhail Kissine & Saghie Sharifzadeh (eds), 1–25. Oxford: OUP.

De Saussure, Louis. 2013. Perspectival interpretations of tenses. In *Time. Language, Cognition and Reality*, Kasia Jaszczolt & Louis de Saussure (eds), 46–72. Oxford: OUP. https://doi.org/10.1093/acprof:oso/9780199589876.003.0004

De Saussure, Louis & Morency, Paul. 2012. A cognitive-pragmatic view of the French epistemic future. *Journal of French Language Studies* 22: 207–223. https://doi.org/10.1017/S0959269511000445

DeLancey, Scott. 1997. Mirativity: The grammatical marking of unexpected information. *Linguistic Typology* 1(1): 33–52. https://doi.org/10.1515/lity.1997.1.1.33

DeLancey, Scott. 2001. The mirative and evidentiality. *Journal of Pragmatics* 33: 369–382. https://doi.org/10.1016/S0378-2166(01)80001-1

Diewald, Gabriele. 2002. A model for relevant types of contexts in grammaticalization. In *New Reflections on Grammaticalization* [Typological Studies in Language 49], Ilse Wischer & Gabriele Diewald (eds), 103–120. Amsterdam: John Benjamins. https://doi.org/10.1075/tsl.49.09die

Dik, Simon. 1997. *The Theory of Functional Grammar*. Berlin: Mouton de Gruyter.

Dryer, Matthew. 1996. Forms, pragmatic presupposition, and activated propositions. *Journal of Pragmatics* 26: 475–523. https://doi.org/10.1016/0378-2166(95)00059-3

Escandell, Maria Victoria. 1999. Los enunciados interrogativos. Aspectos semánticos y pragmáticos. In Bosque & Demonte (eds), 3929–3991.

Escandell, Maria Victoria. 2010. Futuro y evidencialidad. *Anuario de Lingüística Hispánica* 26: 9–34.

Escandell, Maria Victoria. 2014. Evidential futures: The case of Spanish. In *Future Times, Future Tenses*, Phillipe De Brabanter, Mikhail Kissine & Saghie Sharifzadeh (eds), 219–246. Oxford: OUP.

Evans, Vyvyan. 2003. *The Structure of Time. Language, Meaning and Temporal Cognition* [Human Cognitive Processing 12]. Amsterdam: John Benjamins.

Fernández Leborans, Maria Jesús. 1999. La predicación. Las oraciones copulativas. In Bosque & Demonte (eds), 2357–2461.

Fleischman, Suzanne. 1989. Temporal distance: A basic linguistic metaphor. *Studies in Language* 13(1): 1–50. https://doi.org/10.1075/sl.13.1.02fle

Giannakidou, Anastasia & Mari, Alda. 2012. The future of Greek and Italian: An epistemic analysis. *Proceedings of Sinn und Bedeutung* 17: 255–270. <http://semanticsarchive.net/Archive/Dk3NGEwY/GiannakidouMari.pdf>

Ginzburg, Jonathan. 2015. *The Interactive Stance. Meaning for Conversation*. Oxford: OUP.

González Calvo, José Manuel. 1997. Estructuras exclamativas en español. In *IV Jornadas de Metodología y Didáctica de la Lengua Española: Sintaxis*, José Manuel González Calvo & Jesús Terrón González (eds), 143–177. Cáceres: Universidad de Extremadura.

Gutiérrez Ordóñez, Salvador. 1997. *Temas, remas, focos, tópicos y comentarios*. Madrid: Arco Libros.

Heim, Irene. 1983. On the projection problem for presuppositions. *WCCFL* 2: 114–125.

Heine, Bernd. 2002. On the role of context in grammaticalization. In *New Reflections on Grammaticalization* [Typological Studies in Language 49], Ilse Wischer & Gabriele Diewald (eds), 83–101. Amsterdam: John Benjamins. https://doi.org/10.1075/tsl.49.08hei

Heine, Bernd, Kaltenböck, Gunther, Kuteva, Tania & Long, Haiping. 2013. An outline of discourse grammar. In *Reflections on Functionalism in Linguistics*, Shannon Bishoff & Carmen Jeny (eds), 155–206. Berlin: Mouton de Gruyter.

Hengeveld, Kees & Olbertz, Hella. 2012. Didn't you know? Mirativity does exist! *Linguistic Typology* 16(3): 487–503. https://doi.org/10.1515/lity-2012-0018

Hernanz, Maria Llouisa. 2012. Sobre la periferia izquierda y el movimiento: El complementante *si* en español. In *El movimiento de constituyentes*, José M. Brucart & Ángel Gallego (eds), 151–171. Madrid: Visor.

Hill, Nathan. 2012. Mirativity does not exist: ḥdug in "Lhasa" Tibetan and other suspects. *Linguistic Typology* 16 (13): 389–434.

Hopper, Paul. 1991. On some principles of grammaticization. In *Approaches to Grammaticalization*, Vol. 1: *Theoretical and Methodological Issues* [Typological Studies in Language 19:1], Paul Hopper & Elizabeth Closs Traugott (eds), 17–35. Amsterdam: John Benjamins. https://doi.org/10.1075/tsl.19.1.04hop

Iglesias Recuero, Silvia. 2000. Propiedades interpretativas y discursivas de la estructura ¡(Si) será bobo! In *Cien años de investigación semántica: De Michel Bréal a la actualidad*, Marcos Martínez Hernández et al. (eds), 529–542. Madrid: Ediciones Clásicas.

Jaszczolt, Kasia. 2009. *Representing Time: An Essay on Temporality as Modality*. Oxford: OUP.

Kaltenböck, Gunther, Heine, Bernd & Kuteva, Tania. 2011. On thetical grammar. *Studies in Language* 35(4): 852–897. https://doi.org/10.1075/sl.35.4.03kal

Lambrecht, Knud. 1994. *Information Structure and Sentence Form. Topic, Focus and the Mental Representations of Discourse Referents*. Cambridge: CUP. https://doi.org/10.1017/CBO9780511620607

Langacker, Ronald W. 1991. *Foundations of Cognitive Grammar*, Vol 2. Stanford CA: Stanford University Press.

Langacker, Ronald W. 2011. The English present: Temporal coincidence vs. epistemic immediacy. In *Cognitive Approaches to Tense, Aspect and Epistemic Modality* [Human Cognitive Processing 29], Adeline Patard & Frank Brisard (eds), 45–86. Amsterdam: John Benjamins. https://doi.org/10.1075/hcp.29.06lan

Lazard, Gilbert. 1999. Mirativity, evidentiality, mediativity, or other. *Linguistic Typology* 3: 91–109. https://doi.org/10.1515/lity.1999.3.1.91

Lewis, David. 1979. Scorekeeping in a language game. *Journal of Philosophical Logic* 8: 339–359. https://doi.org/10.1007/BF00258436

Lunn, Patricia. 1989. Spanish mood and the prototype of assertability. *Linguistics* 27: 687–702. https://doi.org/10.1515/ling.1989.27.4.687

Martines, Josep. 2017. L'émergence des futurs épistémiques romans. L'exemple du catalan médiéval du XIIIème siècle. In *Le futur dans les langues romanes*, Laura Baranzini (ed.). Berne: Peter Lang.

Michaelis, Laura. 2001. Exclamative constructions. In *Language Typology and Language Universal: An International Handbook*, Martin Haspelmath (ed.), 1038–1050. Berlin: De Gruyter.

Nuyts, Jan. 2001. Subjectivity as an evidential dimension in epistemic modal expressions. *Journal of Pragmatics* 33: 383–400. https://doi.org/10.1016/S0378-2166(00)00009-6

Nuyts, Jan. 2008. Qualificational meanings, illocutionary signals, and the cognitive planning of language use. *Annual Review of Cognitive Linguistics* 6: 185–207. https://doi.org/10.1075/arcl.6.09nuy

Nuyts, Jan. 2012. Notions of (inter)subjectivity. *English Text Construction* 5(1): 53–76. https://doi.org/10.1075/etc.5.1.04nuy

Pérez Saldanya, Manuel. 2002. Les relacions temporals i aspectuals. In *Gramàtica del català contemporani*, Joan Solà, Maria Rosa Lloret, Joan Mascaró & Manuel Pérez Saldanya (eds), 2567–2662. Barcelona: Empúries.

Peterson, Tyler. 2013. Rethinking mirativity: The expression and implication of surprise. Ms, University of Toronto. <http://semanticsarchive.net>

Portolés, José. 1993. Atributos con un enfático. *Revue Romane* 28(2): 218–236.

Potts, Christopher. 2007. Into the Conventional-Implicature dimension. *Philosophy Compass* 4(2): 665–679. https://doi.org/10.1111/j.1747-9991.2007.00089.x

Prince, Ellen. 1992. The ZPG letter: Subjects, definiteness, and information status. In *Discourse Description: Discourse Analyses of a Fundraising Text* [Pragmatics & Beyond New Series 16], William C. Mann & Sandra A. Thompson (eds), 295–325. Amsterdam: John Benjamins. https://doi.org/10.1075/pbns.16.12pri

Real Academia Española [RAE]. 2009. *Nueva gramática de la lengua española*. Madrid: Espasa-Calpe.

Real Academia Española [RAE]. Banco de datos (CREA). Corpus de Referencia del Español Actual. <http://www.rae.es>

Real Academia Española [RAE]. Banco de datos (CORPES XXI. Corpus del Español del siglo XXI. <http://www.rae.es>

Rett, Jessica. 2012. Expressing exceeded expectations in exclamatives and other constructions. *Second Cornell Workshop in Linguistics and Philosophy.*

Rivero, Maria Luisa. 2014. Spanish inferential and mirative futures and conditionals: An evidential gradable modal proposal. *Lingua* 151: 197–215. https://doi.org/10.1016/j.lingua.2014.04.009

Rodríguez Rosique, Susana. 2011. Valores epistémicos de las categorías verbales. Cuando la pragmática se integra en la gramática. *Verba. Anuario Galego de Filoloxia* 38: 243–269.

Rodríguez Rosique, Susana. 2015a. Distance, evidentiality and counter-argumentation: Concessive future in Spanish. *Journal of Pragmatics* 85: 181–199 https://doi.org/10.1016/j.pragma.2015.03.017

Rodríguez Rosique, Susana. 2015b. Spanish future in evaluative contexts. *E-Humanista/IVITRA* 8: 500–516.

Rodríguez Rosique, Susana. 2017. The future of necessity in Spanish: Modality, evidentiality and deictic projection at the crossroads. In *Evidentiality and Modality in European Languages: Discourse-pragmatic Perspectives*, Juana I. Marín-Arrese, Julia Lavid, Marta Carretero, Elena Domínguez Romero, Maria Victoria Martín de la Rosa & Maria Pérez Blanco (eds), 57–86. Frankfurt: Peter Lang.

Rodríguez Rosique, Susana. 2018. Tenses in interaction: Beyond evidentiality. In *Perspectives on Evidentiality in Spanish: Evidentiality and Genre* [Pragmatics & Beyond New Series 290], Adrián Cabedo Nebot & Carolina Figueres Bates (eds). Amsterdam: John Benjamins. https://doi.org/10.1075/pbns.290.10rod

Rojo, Guillermo & Veiga, Alexandre 1999. El tiempo verbal. Los tiempos simples. In Bosque & Demonte (eds), 2867–2934.

Sánchez López, Cristina. 2015. Dos tipos de oraciones exclamativas totales en español. In *Studium grammaticae. Homenaje al profesor José A. Martínez*, Alfredo I. Álvarez, Ramón de Andrés, Álvaro Arias, Félix Fernández de Castro, Teresa Fernández, Serafuba García, Hortensia Martínez, Antonio J. Meilán, Ana I. Ojea, Javier San Julián & Juan Carlos Villaverde (eds), 711–730. Oviedo: Universidad de Oviedo. <https://www.researchgate.net/publication/311993708_Studium_grammaticae_Homenaje_al_profesor_Jose_A_Martinez> (30 April 2018).

Schwenter, Scott. 1999. *Pragmatics of Conditional Marking*. New York NY: Garland.

Smirnova, Elena. 2015. Constructionalization and constructional changes. The role of context in the development of constructions. In *Diachronic Construction Grammar* [Constructional Approaches to Language 18], Jóhanna Barðdal, Elena Smirnova, Lotte Sommerer & Spike Gildea (eds), 81–106. Amsterdam: John Benjamins. https://doi.org/10.1075/cal.18.03smi

Squartini, Mario. 2008. Lexical vs. grammatical evidentiality in French and Italian. *Linguistics* 46(5): 917–947. https://doi.org/10.1515/LING.2008.030

Squartini, Mario. 2012. Evidentiality in interaction: The concessive use of the Italian future between grammar and discourse. *Journal of Pragmatics* 44: 2116–2128. https://doi.org/10.1016/j.pragma.2012.09.008

Stalnaker, Robert C. 1978. Assertion. In *Syntax and Semantics*, 9: *Pragmatics*, Peter Cole (ed.), 315–332. New York NY: Academic Press.

Sthioul, Bertrand. 1998. Temps verbaux et point de vue. In *Le temps des événements, Jacques Moeschler* (ed.), 197–220. París: Kimé.

Suñer, Avelina. 1999. *La aposición y otras relaciones de predicación en el sintagma nominal*. In Bosque & Demonte (eds), 523–564. Madrid: Espasa-Calpe.

Sweetser, Eve. 1990. *From Etymology to Pragmatics: Metaphorical and Cultural Aspects of Semantic Structure*. Cambridge: Cambridge University Press. https://doi.org/10.1017/CBO9780511620904

Traugott, Elizabeth Closs. 1989. On the rise of epistemic meanings in English: An example of subjectification in semantic change. *Language* 65(1): 31–55. https://doi.org/10.2307/414841

Traugott, Elizabeth Closs. 2010. (Inter)subjectivity and (inter)subjectification: A reassessment. In *Subjectification, Intersubjectification and Grammaticalization*, Kristin Davidse, Lieven Vandelanotte & Hubert Cuyckens (eds), 29–71. Berlin: Walter de Gruyter. https://doi.org/10.1515/9783110226102.1.29

Traugott, Elizabeth Closs & Dasher, Richard B. 2002. *Regularity in Semantic Change*. Cambridge: Cambridge University Press.

Traugott, Elizabeth Closs & Trousdale, Graeme. 2013. *Constructionalization and Constructional Changes*. Oxford: OUP. https://doi.org/10.1093/acprof:oso/9780199679898.001.0001

Weinrich, Herald. [1964]1974. *Estructura y función de los tiempos en el lenguaje*. Madrid: Gredos.

C-gravitation and the grammaticalization degree of "present progressives" in English, French, and Dutch

Naoaki Wada
University of Tsukuba

This paper aims to explain the differences of grammaticalization degree among the "present progressives" in English, French, and Dutch by introducing the notion of "C-gravitation" (i.e., gravitation toward the consciousness of the speaker) into their grammaticalization process. Hirose (1995, 2000) & Hasegawa and Hirose (2005) proposed a general theory of linguistic comparison in which public-self-centered languages, such as English, are distinguished from private-self-centered languages, such as Japanese, in terms of the notions of "public self" (i.e., the subject of communicating) and "private self" (i.e., the subject of thinking), based on which I developed two types of C-gravitation in Wada (2008) to explain differences concerning tense and mood among public-self-centered languages, including English, French, and Dutch. The above differences will be explained along these lines from a broader perspective.

Keywords: C-gravitation, present progressives, public self, grammaticalization degree

1. Introduction

Studies on tense, aspect, and modality in terms of grammaticalization have been conducted extensively in recent years (e.g., Traugott & Heine 1991; Heine 1993; Hopper & Traugott 1993, 2003; Bybee, Perkins & Pagliuca 1994; Pagliuca 1994; Bybee & Fleischman 1995; Dahl 2000; Joseph & Janda 2003; Narrog & Heine 2011; Nicolle 2012). Included in these are studies of "progressives" in European languages (e.g., Bertinetto 2000 for Romance progressives and Ebert 2000 for Germanic progressives).[1] In grammaticalization studies, the cross-linguistic

1. I use the term *progressive* in the sense of "progressive form" in this study.

https://doi.org.10.1075/slcs.202.09wad
© 2018 John Benjamins Publishing Company

perspective is inevitable, but the detailed, language-specific perspective is also important (Bybee, Perkins & Pagliuca 1994). On this basis, contrastive analyses of progressives between two European languages in terms of grammaticalization degree have been presented, but as far as I know, such studies are relatively few in number. For example, Boogaart (1999) compares the English progressive (i.e., the form *be* + *-ing*) and Dutch "progressives", including the forms of *aan het* + infinitive + *zijn*, postural verb + *te* + infinitive, and *bezig* + *zijn* + *{te/met}* + infinitive; De Wit & Patard (2013) and De Wit, Patard & Brisard (2013) compare the English progressive and the French "progressive" (i.e., the form *être* + *en train de* + infinitive); Mortier (2008) compares the French and the Dutch progressives with grammaticalization principles, making a passing reference to the English progressive. Comparison of two languages only determines which of the two has more grammaticalized progressives. To offer a more general picture, we need to compare at least three languages on the common ground from a general-theoretic perspective–an attempt that few previous studies have made.

In this paper, I will, along the lines mentioned above, explain the differences of grammaticalization degree of the present progressives in English, French, and Dutch. To be specific, I will develop Mortier's grammaticalization principle-based study and introduce the notion of "C-gravitation", i.e., a notion proposed in Wada (2008) to explain different grammatical behaviors among "public-self-centered" languages, such as English, French, Dutch, and German, which is based on the theory of "public/private self" and "public/private expression" (Hirose 1995, 2000; Hasegawa & Hirose 2005), a general theory of linguistic comparison. I will confine myself to present progressives because, as De Wit, Patard & Brisard (2013) indicate, present and past "progressives" behave differently in many respects and should be treated separately; we can thereby not only motivate the differences of grammaticalization degree of the present progressives in the three languages, but also offer a broader picture of the grammaticalization behaviors of those present progressives and other tense forms from a unified point of view.

2. Previous studies

2.1 Boogaart (1999)

Let us start by surveying (a) Boogaart (1999), (b) De Wit & Patard (2013) and De Wit, Patard & Brisard (2013), and (c) Mortier (2008) as representative studies.

First, Boogaart observes that the progressives in Dutch are optional and much more restricted in use than the English progressive.[2]

(1) a. He is talking with a flutist.
b. *Hij praat met een fluitist.*
he talks with a flutist
'He is talking with a flutist.' [the intended reading]

(2) a. Mary was being a good teacher. (Boogaart 1999: 174)
b. ?*Mary was een goeie lerares aan het zijn.*
Mary was a good teacher on the be (Boogaart 1999: 175)
c. ?*Mary zat een goeie lerares te zijn.*
Mary sat a good teacher to be (Boogaart 1999: 175)

(3) a. The paper was being read. (Boogaart 1999: 179)
b. **De krant lag gelezen te worden.*
the paper lay read to become (Boogaart 1999: 178)
c. **De krant was gelezen aan het worden.*[3]
the paper was read on the become (Boogaart 1999: 179)

(4) a. In those days they were eating breakfast in the dining room. (Boogaart 1999: 185)
b. #*In die tijd waren ze aan het ontbijten in de eetkamer.*
in that time were they on the breakfast in the dining room (Boogaart 1999: 185)
c. #*In die tijd zaten ze te ontbijten in de eetkamer.*
in that time sat they to breakfast in the dining room (Boogaart 1999: 185)

(5) a. (Yesterday it seemed like I would leave tomorrow at two, but) I am now leaving tomorrow at three o'clock. (Boogaart 1999: 188)
b. **Ik ben nu morgen om drie uur aan het vertrekken .*
I am now tomorrow at three hours on the leave (Boogaart 1999: 189)

2. In this study, the target forms are underscored.

3. According to Boogaart (1999: 179), the *aan het* sentence containing *worden* in the passive form can be used if it expresses gradual change in a non-agentive interpretation, as in (i):

(i) *Je bent oud aan het worden*
you are old on the become
'You're getting old.' (Boogaart 1999: 179)

As shown in (1), the progressive form is required to refer to an ongoing event in English, but the simple form is allowed for that purpose in Dutch. As exemplified in (2), the English progressive can coincide with temporary state predicates, but, essentially, the Dutch progressives cannot. The English progressive allows the passive form, as in (3a), receives a habitual reading, as in (4a), or gains a futurate reading, as in (5a); this is not the case with Dutch, as illustrated in (3b), (3c), (4b), (4c), and (5b). Based on these data, Boogaart gives a detailed comparison of the progressives in English and Dutch in relation to the lexical aspect of verbs and concludes that the Dutch progressives are less grammaticalized than the English progressive. However, this conclusion should be considered from and supported by a wider perspective.

2.2 De Wit & Patard (2013) and De Wit, Patard & Brisard (2013)

Next, De Wit & Patard (2013) observe, in a corpus-based study, that the French progressive is also optional and is more restricted in use and lower in frequency than the English progressive. Let us look at several linguistic phenomena supporting this.[4]

(6) a. *Il parle avec une flûtiste.*
he talks with a flutist
'He is talking with a female flutist.' [the intended reading]

b. *Il est en train de parler avec une flûtiste.*
he is in movement of talk with a flutist
'He is talking with a female flutist.'

(7) a. *Ça fait un an que je suis en train de faire un truc qui est incroyable.*
it makes a year that I am in movement of do a thing that is incredible
'For a year I've been doing this incredible thing.'
(De Wit & Patard 2013: 121)

b. So then, and then, he sort of pulled the paper aside, and he's still staring at you. (De Wit & Patard 2013: 116)

(8) a. I'm leaving tomorrow. (De Wit & Patard 2013: 122)

b. * *Je suis en train de partir demain.*
I am in movement of leave tomorrow
(De Wit & Patard 2013: 122)

4. French glosses in this sub-section are mine.

(9) a. *Dès qu'ils ont une place apparemment ils* *sont en train*
as soon as.they have a place apparently they are in movement
d'mettre des des immeubles de bureaux. J'sais pas si vous avez
of.put ART;PL ART;PL buildings of offices I know NEG if you have
remarqué.
noticed
'As soon as they have space apparently they're putting in office buildings. I don't know if you've noticed.' (De Wit & Patard 2013: 122)

b. Everywhere we've been, in the past several years, everybody's talking about how, the weather just isn't normal. (De Wit & Patard 2013: 118)

First, (6) suggests that in French, it is not obligatory to use the progressive form to describe an ongoing event. Second, De Wit & Patard found in their corpora only one instance of the limited-duration use of the French progressive, as in (7a), but 16 instances of the English progressive, including (7b). Third, the French progressive does not have a futurate use, but the English progressive does, as indicated by (8). Fourth, both progressives allow a habitual reading, as shown in (9). From these data, they conclude that the French progressive is less grammaticalized than the English progressive.

De Wit, Patard & Brisard (2013: 860–869) attribute this difference mainly to whether the two languages have an aspectual distinction (i.e., perfective vs. imperfective) in the past-tense paradigm. According to them, the distinction by means of the aspectual prefix system had disappeared by the end of the Old English period, and Middle English was in the state of "aspectual vacuum" (i.e., lack of the formal distinction between the two aspects). In their analysis, progressives in this state of English developed to finally become entrenched in the present-tense paradigm as dedicated forms to denote ongoing events in the present, which brought about the "perfectivization" of the simple present. By contrast, they continue, the opposition between the *imparfait* (past imperfective) and the *passé simple* (past perfective) had already established in the Middle French period, and unlike English, French did not have any powerful motivation for the development of the past progressive and, hence, the present progressive. For this reason, the French progressive is not grammaticalized as highly as the English progressive.

Their explanation itself is convincing, but a question arises as to why the present progressive in French has grammaticalized to some extent despite there being no powerful motivation. In addition, their idea cannot be applied to a direct comparison among the English, French, and Dutch present progressives.[5]

5. De Wit, Patard & Brisard (2013: 862) state that the lower degree of grammaticalization of the progressives in Dutch and German may be due to the survival of the aspectual prefix system and the encroachment of the present perfect forms into the function of past perfective, which

English and were finally combined into the ancestor of the *be* + *-ing* form. I take this observation as indicating that English has undergone Specialization, a process during which the number of the forms available for referring to ongoing events decreases. In addition, although English once allowed the simple present to describe ongoing events, in Present-Day English the progressive form is basically the only dedicated form to refer to ongoing events. These observations suggest that the English progressive has undergone not only Specialization but also Obligatorification and therefore has almost completely taken the place of the simple form to refer to ongoing events.[8] We can thus conclude that with respect to the progressives, English has reached a further stage in the grammaticalization process than have French and Dutch.

To give a wider picture of the grammaticalization process, we also need to consider the correlation between the variety of uses/functions and the degree of grammaticalization. As we observed in Sections 2.1 and 2.2, the Dutch progressives have fewer uses/functions than the French progressive, which has fewer uses/functions than the English progressive. For example, the French progressive has a habitual use, as in (9), but the Dutch progressives do not, as in (4); the French and Dutch progressives have more limited uses than the English progressive, because, for example, they do not have a futurate use (constituting another functional category "future"), as shown in (5) and (8). These differences can also be explained in terms of the degree of grammaticalization because it is often the case that as a (tense-aspect-mood) form is further grammaticalized, it develops more uses/functions (De Wit & Patard 2013: 126). This phenomenon is often referred to as semantic enrichment, as illustrated in, say, the grammaticalization of *be going to* through metaphorical and metonymical inferences (cf. Hopper & Traugott 2003: 93).

The increase of the uses/functions of a grammaticalized form is due to *secondary grammaticalization* (cf. Givón 1991). Secondary grammaticalization is defined as "the development of further grammatical functions by an already grammaticalized construction" (Nicolle 2012: 372) or means that "the construction acquires a more fixed grammatical meaning and enters paradigmatic relations with alternative grammatical forms" (Kranich 2010: 7). It is in general a relatively later phase of the grammaticalization process than *primary grammaticalization*, i.e., "the development from lexical to grammatical status" (Nicolle 2012: 372). Primary and secondary grammaticalization constitute a continuum called the *grammaticalization chain* (Nicolle 2012: 384). This chain enables us to make the following claim: The fact that the French progressive has developed more uses/functions than Dutch progressives implies that the former is more grammaticalized, whereas the fact

8. See Kranich (2010) for a comprehensive, diachronic analysis of the English progressive.

that the English progressive has developed more uses/functions than the French progressive implies that the former is far more grammaticalized.

A question, then, arises as to what motivates the different degrees of grammaticalization of the present progressives in English, French, and Dutch. In fact, Nicolle (2012: 390) asks a similar question as to why "some [languages] seem to grammaticalize new [tense and aspect] markers more rapidly than others." In the first place, what was a driving force to facilitate the grammaticalization process of the progressive form? If we restrict ourselves to the present progressives, we can answer the questions from a broader perspective.

3. C-gravitation

To this end, I will introduce the notion of "C-gravitation", i.e., gravitation toward the consciousness of the speaker, proposed in previous work (Wada 2008). This notion was intended to provide a common ground to explain (synchronic) differences of grammatical phenomena with respect to deictic categories (especially tense and mood) in "public-self-centered" languages – including English, French, Dutch – i.e., languages characterized by the notion of "public-self-centeredness", which is based on the theory of "public/private self" and "public/private expression", i.e., a general theory of linguistic comparison, proposed by Hirose (1995, 2000) and Hasegawa & Hirose (2005). The introduction of C-gravitation into the developed version of Mortier's grammaticalization principle-based analysis provides a broader picture of the grammaticalization behaviors of the present progressives of the three languages from a general-theoretic perspective.

3.1 Background to C-gravitation

Let us start by clarifying what public-self-centeredness is. Hirose contends that English is a public-self-centered language and Japanese is a private-self-centered language, on the assumption that the speaker is dissolved into two aspects, i.e., the public and the private self. The public self is the subject of communicating, i.e., the speaker who faces an addressee or has one in mind; the private self is the subject of thinking or consciousness, i.e., the (potential) speaker who has no addressee in mind. Generally speaking, language has two major functions, i.e., the function of representing what the speaker thinks about or is conscious of and the function of communicating it to the hearer (cf. Searle 1983: 165). The two functions correspond respectively to the levels of private and public expression in Hirose's terminology, and the private self and public self are the subjects of private and public expression, respectively. On this basis, he provides a new perspective of linguistic comparison in terms of whether the unmarked deictic center of a language is in the public self or private self. This perspective characterizes languages in terms of which aspect (i.e., self) of the speaker their grammatical phenomena are oriented to or centered around. These observations underlie the above contention.

A question naturally arises as to which self the grammatical phenomena of languages other than English and Japanese are oriented to or centered around. In Wada (2008), I have argued, using four criteria, that – in addition to English – German, Dutch, French, Spanish, and Swedish are basically public-self-centered languages. I will show in what sense we can state this, using three out of the four criteria in (15) to which public-self-centered languages provide affirmative answers.

(15) a. The existence of a special word for the public self. (Criterion A)[9]
b. The existence of a marked grammatical device (i.e., the subjunctive mood) to express private expression. (Criterion B)
c. The existence of tense morphemes integrated with person, number, and mood (other deictic categories). (Criterion C)

Criterion A presupposes Hirose's (1995) hypothesis that direct speech is a quotation of public expression and indirect speech is a quotation of private expression (this hypothesis will be justified in Section 3.2). Given this, (16) shows that in the English direct speech complement (a quotation of the original utterance as it is, i.e., public expression) the first-person pronoun *I* is used to refer to the speaker as public self, irrespective of who is talking to whom; on the other hand, in the English indirect speech complement (a quotation of the original thought or the mental representation of the original speaker, i.e., private expression) personal pronouns "are diverted to represent the private self, depending on whether the subject of the private expression in question is the first, second, or third person" (Hirose 2000: 1630).

(16) a. {I/You/Ryoko} said to {Ken/the boss/Mother}, "I am lonely."
b. {I/You/Ryoko} thought that {I/you/she} {was/were} lonely.

In Hirose's theory, this suggests that English has a special word for the public self (i.e., *I*) but not one for the private self and is, therefore, a public-self-centered language.

As for Criterion B, we presuppose Curme's (1977: 216) statement that the subjunctive mood is a grammatical device that represents a situation as a conception of the mind. Given Hirose's theory of the public/private self and public/private expression, the subjunctive is a grammatical device reflecting the perspective (i.e., way of thinking or viewing) of the private self (i.e., conceptualizer) involved.

9. This criterion is based on a series of works by Yukio Hirose.

Considered along these lines, it may be safe to assume that in linguistic environments where both the indicative and subjunctive moods are potentially available, if the subjunctive represents the private self's perspective, then the indicative is a grammatical device reflecting the perspective of the public self, i.e., the reporting speaker (we will return to this matter in Section 3.2). It might appear that the use of the subjunctive mood is redundant in the indirect speech complement, for its use bothers to show that the relevant perspective is that of the original speaker as private self in his/her private expression. Nevertheless, the subjunctive is available here as a marked grammatical device (cf. Quirk et al. 1985: 155–158). These observations paradoxically imply that English, as a public-self-centered language, by default requires public-self-centeredness (i.e., orientation toward the reporter) even in a quotation of private expression (i.e., indirect speech), and it is therefore necessary to use the subjunctive as a grammatical device to "feature" the private self's perspective in this linguistic environment. This is exemplified by, for example, a mandative-subjunctive sentence like *The committee {proposes/ proposed} (that) Mr Day be elected* (Quirk et al. 1985: 156).

Finally, Criterion C is based on my claim that an English finite verb – which has a tense inflection integrated with other deictic categories such as person, number, and mood – has a tense structure (i.e., structured grammatical time information) reflecting public-self-centeredness, i.e., orientation toward the speaker at speech time, at which the speaker as public self "faces" a hearer in the speech situation (see Wada 2001, 2013). This explains why, as implied in (16), when a direct speech sentence is paraphrased into an indirect speech one, a situation in the present relative to the time of the original utterance (at which is located the private self's perspective) is changed into a situation in the past relative to the time of reporting the whole sentence (at which is located the public self's perspective).

With respect to these criteria, German, Dutch, French, Spanish, and Swedish show essentially the same behaviors as English and are therefore public-self-centered languages.[10] However, these public-self-centered languages do not

10. Japanese is classified as a private-self-centered language because it provides negative answers to these criteria. For example, finite predicates in Japanese, as a private-self-centered language, do not have tense inflections integrated with person, number, and mood, and thus in indirect speech they are chosen with the time of the original utterance (at which is located the private self's perspective) being the base time, as in (i), which makes a sharp contrast with the English case (16b).

(i) {Watasi/Anata/Ryooko}-wa (zibun-wa) samisi-i to omot-ta.
{I/You/Ryoko}-TOP (self-TOP) be.lonely-PRS QUOT think-PST
'{I/You/Ryoko} thought that {I/you/she} {was/were} lonely.'

The two types of C-gravitation adopted in this study do not apply to non-public-self-centered languages.

necessarily show uniformity with respect to a variety of linguistic phenomena concerning deictic categories such as tense and mood. This is why I introduced the notion of C-gravitation.

3.2 Two types of C-gravitation

The consciousness involved in C-gravitation (i.e., gravitation toward the consciousness of the speaker) is defined as part of the mind of the speaker as public self that is operative when he/she does mental activities including uttering and thinking;[11] it is, by definition, always in existence at speech time (usually the utterance time of the whole sentence) in the speech situation consisting of speaker and hearer, as well as here and now. Even if both the public and private self of the same speaker exist at speech time, especially in independent or main clauses, the public self is, by default, given priority over the private self in public-self-centered languages because they have the characteristics of public-self-centeredness. The public self therefore serves as the unmarked deictic center (or egocentricity) of tense and mood phenomena in public-self-centered languages. Speech time, or the speech situation, is distinctive in that it is the locus that the speaker as public self and the hearer can always share, thereby playing a crucial role in communication.

With this background information, C-gravitation is assumed to be a process in which the consciousness of the speaker as public self at speech time augments its power of influence in the grammatical system of public-self-centered languages, and as a result, linguistic phenomena featuring orientation to the consciousness of the public self come to the fore. C-gravitation is a gradual notion, and the more tense/mood phenomena with a higher degree of C-gravitation a public-self-centered language has, the higher degree of public-self-centeredness it shows. The relevant tense/mood phenomena are represented by the following two cases: (a) A public-self-centered language further develops the grammaticalization of specialized forms referring to the speech situation and (b) the tense forms whose semantic range (i.e., the "maximal scope" of the semantic value) includes speech time develop more semantic uses or functions strongly oriented to speech time or allow their reference range (i.e., target part of the semantic range) to cover the time span including speech time. Metaphorically speaking, in public-self-centered languages, as the power of influence of the consciousness of the public self augments, the time span including speech time – or the speech situation – comes to form a "magnetic pole" in their grammatical system, and the use of relevant tense/mood forms and their semantic uses/functions may be likened to materials like iron that gravitate toward the magnetic pole.

11. My notion of "consciousness" might be comparable to Bühler's (1982) "origo".

In Wada (2008), I employed C-gravitation to consider a number of tense/mood phenomena of English, German, Dutch, French, Spanish, and Swedish as public-self-centered languages. I included aspect forms such as finite progressive and perfect forms in "tense forms" because they involve a tense, and I take the same stance here. The findings of that study were that as a general tendency, the degree of public-self-centeredness is highest in English, lowest in German, and the other languages are located in between; the more grammatical phenomena concerning deictic categories (including tense and mood) with a higher degree of C-gravitation a language has, the higher degree of public-self-centeredness the language shows. However, with respect to individual tense-mood phenomena, it was sometimes the case that for one phenomenon, the degree of C-gravitation of a language is higher than that of another language, but for another phenomenon, the former is lower than the latter. This "twist" state applied especially to the languages located in the middle of the "public-self-centeredness scale".

As I have already shown in the above part of this section, I argued there that C-gravitation is embodied in two ways: (a) the C-gravitation concerning the use of relevant tense/mood forms and (b) the C-gravitation concerning the semantic functions/uses of tense forms. Let us first briefly survey the latter type, which is defined in (17):

(17) If tense forms whose semantic range includes speech time develop more semantic functions/uses "foregrounding" (the time span including) speech time, then the degree of C-gravitation is higher.

The term *foreground* is used to cover both strong orientation to speech time and restriction of the reference range to the time span including speech time. This type of C-gravitation is, for instance, employed to explain the differences among the present perfect forms–whose semantic range includes speech time because the finite verb is present–in English, Dutch, and German: The present perfect in English develops more uses foregrounding the time span including speech time than that in Dutch, which in turn develops more such uses than that in German. For example, the English perfect, unlike the Dutch and German perfects, has the continuative use, i.e., a use whose reference range covers speech time, whereas the English and Dutch perfects, unlike the German perfect, do not allow an imperfective-past reading, i.e., a "pure"-past-viewpoint reading (Boogaart 1999: 160). These differences are accounted for by hypothesizing, based on (17), that the degree of this type of C-gravitation is highest in English, lowest in German, and in-between in Dutch with respect to the semantic uses/functions of the present perfect (Wada 2015), which is in keeping with the general tendency of the degree of public-self-centeredness stated above.

I turn now to the C-gravitation concerning the use of tense/mood forms, which is directly relevant to this paper, defined in (18):

(18) If tense/mood forms featuring reference to the public self's perspective at speech time develop in linguistic environments where they are not necessarily needed, then C-gravitation is in operation.

This type of C-gravitation, for example, explains why the indicative mood, i.e., the grammatical device featuring the public self's perspective at speech time (the time of reporting), develops in the indirect-speech complement of public-self-centered languages.

Recall that indirect speech complements are quotations of the original speaker's private expression, i.e., the thought or mental representation of the original speaker as private self, including his/her perspective (cf. Vandelanotte 2009). When the original utterance, as in the direct-speech complement of (19a), is reported in the form of indirect speech, not only must the reporter change grammatical elements into those reflecting his/her own perspective, as in (19b), but he/she can also change wordings as long as the original (or reported) speaker's intention is preserved, as in (19c) (Quirk et al. 1985: 1025).

(19) a. John said, "I feel so bad."
b. John said that he felt so bad.
c. John said that he was sick.

This suggests that indirect speech complements represent the original speaker's private expression, i.e., the level of thought or mental representation of the original speaker, which the reporter reconstructs from the original communicative utterance.

As we saw in the discussion about Criterion B above, the fact that the indicative mood is used in indirect speech indicates the public-self-centeredness of the language involved within our framework. In fact, the indicative mood is available in the complement clause of verbs of saying in German, as in (20d), and basically obligatory in the complement clauses of verbs of saying in English, French, and Dutch, as in (20a)–(20c).

(20) a. John said that Mary was sick.
b. *John a dit que Mary était malade.*
John has said that Mary be-PST.IND sick
c. *John zei dat Mary ziek was.*
John said that Mary sick be-PST.IND
d. *Emily sagte, dass sie krank {sei/ist}.*[12]
Emily said that she sick be-PRS.{SBJV/IND}

12. The German indicative present *ist* in indirect speech can refer to a situation in the present relative to the time of the original utterance in the past. This is different from the English,

Curme (1977: 216) states that the indicative mood represents a situation as a fact. In indirect speech complements, however, indicative forms do not always represent a real fact, so I take the situation involved as a fact from the reporter's perspective. For this reason, as I stated above, indicative forms in indirect speech are regarded as grammatical means reflecting the perspective of the reporter as public self at speech time (i.e., the time of reporting). In the present analysis, the fact that the indicative mood is usually obligatory in the complements of verbs of saying in English, French, and Dutch implies that with respect to the mood phenomenon in indirect speech, the degree of this type of C-gravitation is higher in the three languages than in German, which also allows the subjunctive mood, as illustrated by (20d). In what follows, I will concentrate on the C-gravitation concerning the use of tense/mood forms, using simply "C-gravitation" to refer to this type of C-gravitation.

4. Explanation

With these observations in mind, let us show what kind of role C-gravitation plays in explaining the different behaviors of the present progressives in English, French, and Dutch. To be specific, I will make a hypothesis about the degree of C-gravitation with respect to the use of present progressives in the three languages – defined in (21) below – which is compatible with the general tendency of the degree of public-self-centeredness observed above, and introduce it into the grammaticalization chain (seen in Section 2.4) to function as a driving force for further developing the primary grammaticalization of the present progressive, thereby influencing their secondary grammaticalization indirectly.

(21) The degree of C-gravitation is highest in English, lowest in Dutch, and in-between in French.[13]

French, and Dutch cases in (20a)–(20c). Although we need more discussion to arrive at a final conclusion, I tentatively assume that this is also a consequence of the different degrees of public-self-centeredness among these languages. Since German has the lowest degree of public-self-centeredness, even the tense-form choice can be based on the time of the original utterance at which is located the private self's perspective, not on the time of reporting at which is located the public self's perspective.

13. The general tendency of the degree of public-self-centeredness shown in the main text implies that German is located at a lower position than Dutch on the scale of the degree of C-gravitation with respect to the use of present progressives. This gives an answer to the question addressed in note 5, i.e., why the degree of grammaticalization of the present progressive is higher in Dutch than in German. In connection with this, Anthonissen, De Wit & Mortelmans

Before going to our explanation, however, let us confirm one premise: In order to strengthen the corresponding relationship between forms (signs) and meanings (values) in the grammatical system of a language, it is easier to minimize the number of relevant grammaticalized forms corresponding to the value (or semantic range) involved and finally create a dedicated form. This premise, supported by a cognitive-linguistic perspective, lies in the observation that the development of grammaticalization involves Specialization followed by Obligatorification, as shown in Sections 2.3 and 2.4.

Now, let us proceed to our explanation. First, the three languages in question have the simple present, i.e., the more general form to describe situations obtaining not only at speech time but also in a wider time range including the present. In French and Dutch, even in the case of non-stative verbs, the simple presents can be used to cover the semantic range of the present progressives, i.e., the specialized forms referring primarily to ongoing events at speech time. In English, the simple present was once used to cover the semantic range of the present-progressive form of non-stative verbs, but this is largely not the case now.[14] These observations imply that the present progressive is or was not necessarily needed in this linguistic environment. Nevertheless, the three languages have developed present progressives. I argue that C-gravitation triggers the further development of primary grammaticalization of the present progressives, i.e., the tense forms that can inherently depict an ongoing event at speech time and feature reference to the consciousness of the speaker as public self at speech time. Given hypothesis (21), we can therefore claim that since the degree of C-gravitation is higher in French than in Dutch, the reduction of the number of periphrastic forms to describe ongoing events proceeds more in French (Specialization); since the degree of C-gravitation

(2016) state that although the *am* + infinitive + *sein* form, i.e., a German progressive form, was once said to be restricted to some regions like the Rhineland, its use is now expanding in spoken language. This observation also supports our analysis based on C-gravitation. Spoken language presupposes the speaker as a typical kind of public self because he/she definitely faces the hearer in this environment, so it is an appropriate environment for the operation of C-gravitation. C-gravitation serves as a "facilitator" for the German progressive form to further grammaticalize and thus spread in spoken language.

14. It is certain that even in Present-Day English, the simple present can be used to refer to ongoing events at speech time in such cases as sports commentaries or to events happening in front of the observer in the form of so-called *there*-constructions, e.g., *Here comes the bus!* (pointed out to me by a reviewer). However, these cases are special, and such uses of the simple present are only possible when the perfective characteristic of the simple present in Present-Day English is not contradictory to the instantaneous characteristic of speech time (see Langacker 2001 for details).

is still higher in English than in French, the present progressive has essentially been established as the dedicated form in English (Obligatorification).

C-gravitation is also relevant to the secondary grammaticalization of the present progressives in such a way that it propels their further development on the grammaticalization chain and indirectly induces the development of uses/functions.[15] Due to C-gravitation, they establish a more fixed position in the grammatical system. By combining C-gravitation with the three grammaticalization principles observed in Section 2, we can now present the whole picture of the grammaticalization process (i.e., the grammaticalization chain) of the present progressives in English, French, and Dutch.

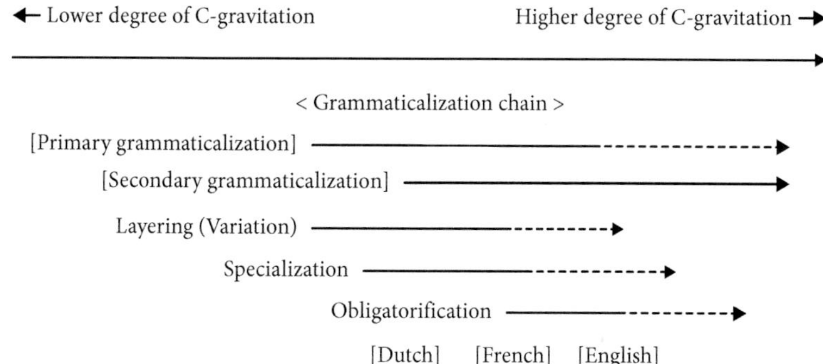

Figure 1. The grammaticalization chain and the degree of C-gravitation of the present progressives in English, French, and Dutch

Figure 1 briefly shows the relationship between the degree of C-gravitation, the relevant sub-processes (stages) of grammaticalization principles, and the location of the present progressives of the three languages on the grammaticalization chain (i.e., the whole process of grammaticalization). C-gravitation is a driving force for propelling the further grammaticalization of the present progressive; the higher the degree of C-gravitation is, the further the grammaticalization proceeds. The solid-line portions of the arrows symbolize the "foreground" ranges of the sub-processes involved in the grammaticalization principles. The broken-line parts indicate the "background" ranges of the relevant sub-processes. In the whole process of grammaticalization, Layering is the presupposition for Specialization, and Obligatorification occurs toward the end of Specialization. After the primary grammaticalization proceeds to some extent, the secondary grammaticalization

15. It might appear that this is not compatible with hypothesis (17) because some of the developed uses/functions do not appear to foreground speech time, e.g., the futurate use. However, we are not arguing that C-gravitation is responsible for every change in the grammaticalization chain. Other factors are also crucially relevant to the expansion of the uses/functions of this form.

begins and proceeds in parallel with it, during which the grammaticalized forms acquire a more fixed grammatical status, developing more uses/functions. We are assuming that the foreground ranges of the sub-processes are not mutually exclusive but can co-exist during some period of time (Nicolle 2012: 386; cf. Bybee, Perkins & Pagliuca 1994), so they show a relative positional relationship (cf. Mortier 2008: 8). This co-existence is a general assumption in grammaticalization studies.

Since English has the highest degree of C-gravitation, it has undergone Specialization/ Obligatorification, and the English present progressive has entered deeply into the secondary grammaticalization. In this way, C-gravitation indirectly induces the expansion of uses/functions of the English present progressive, e.g., the futurate, passive-voice, and habitual-aspect uses. French has not undergone Specialization/Obligatorification completely, because the simple present can still be used to describe ongoing events. The French present progressive has not entered so deeply into the secondary grammaticalization, because it has not yet established a fixed grammatical status and has developed fewer uses than has the English present progressive. For example, it cannot represent the futurate use, as shown in (8) above. As far as the progressives are concerned, Dutch has not proceeded to a further stage in Specialization in comparison with French, because it still has three periphrastic forms. The Dutch progressives are, at best, located around the beginning stage of secondary grammaticalization, developing the limited number of uses/functions. For example, they do not allow the futurate, passive-voice, and habitual-aspect uses, as we saw in Section 2.1. From these observations, I conclude that the higher the degree of C-gravitation is, the smaller the number of forms to refer to events ongoing at speech time will be and the more uses/functions the present progressives will develop.[16]

5. Consequence

As a consequence of the above analysis, we can explain the grammaticalization degree of the so-called GO-futures in English, French, and Dutch. First, it seems safe to assume that the primary future forms of English, French, and Dutch are,

16. In Wada (2008), I argued that the degree of C-gravitation is higher when the target language has more present progressive forms. However, considering the discussion on the grammaticalization of the progressive forms by such studies as Mortier (2008), I came to assume that the higher degree of C-gravitation matches up with the lower number of the present progressives. This might affect one of the findings there, namely, that the degree of public-self-centeredness is a little higher in Dutch than in French (Wada 2008: 292), but it does not affect the general tendency of the degree of public-self-centeredness.

respectively, the *will*-form, simple future, and *zullen*-form, all of which refer to the future in a more neutral fashion and in a wider range than their GO-future counterparts, which are illustrated in (22).[17]

(22) a. It is going to rain tomorrow.
b. *Il va pleuvoir demain.*
it goes rain tomorrow
c. *Morgen gaat het regenen.*
tomorrow goes it rain

Therefore, the GO-futures are not necessarily needed in future time reference in these languages, as far as temporal reference is concerned. In fact, German, which has the primary future form *werden* + infinitive, does not have a GO-future (Eckardt 2006: 95):

(23) a. *Morgen wird es regnen.*
tomorrow becomes it rain
'It will rain tomorrow.'
b. **Morgen geht es regnen.*
tomorrow goes it rain
'It is going to rain tomorrow.' [the intended reading]

As is often said, the GO-futures in English, French, and Dutch represent present-oriented future in comparison with the primary future forms (Larreya 2001; van Olmen & Mortelmans 2009). The GO-future sentences in (22) above therefore imply a cause or omen at speech time that leads to the actualization of a future situation, whereas the primary-future sentences in (24) below do not indicate such present-orientation.

(24) a. It will rain tomorrow.
b. *Il pleuvra demain.*
it rain-FUT tomorrow
c. *Morgen zal het regenen.*
tomorrow shall it rain

The observations so far enable us to argue that the development of GO-futures, i.e., present-oriented future forms, is a reflection of the operation of C-gravitation in these languages. The GO-futures have developed in such a way to feature reference to the consciousness of the speaker as public self in a linguistic environment

17. It is usually said that the French GO-future tends to be restricted to the spoken register or refer to the definite, nearer future; the Dutch GO-future is more developed in (West) Flemish, but not so much in Northern Dutch (van Olmen & Mortelmans 2009).

in which such forms are not necessarily needed because the primary future forms are available.

Now, let us examine whether hypothesis (21) above works here. First, the English GO-future is higher in the degree of C-gravitation than the GO-futures in French and Dutch because the former is in the progressive form while the latter are not. As we have seen, the present progressive is a specialized form to depict an ongoing event at speech time, and the establishment of such a form in the grammatical system of public-self-centered languages is due to the higher degree of C-gravitation.

Second, the English GO-future has developed more uses/functions than the French and Dutch GO-futures. This is exemplified by the examples in (25)–(27), which show that the English GO-future has fully developed the simple-future use,[18] but the French and Dutch GO-futures have not:[19]

(25) a. I'm going to be forty in a few years.
(S. Sheldon, *Master of the Game*, p. 204)
b. He is going to be two tomorrow.
c. (?)Tomorrow is going to be Sunday.[20]
d. There is going to be a public holiday on Friday.

(26) a. ?*Je vais avoir quarante ans dans quelques années.*[21]
I go have forty years in a few years

---

18. The term *simple future* used in my study (e.g. Wada 2001) refers to the case in which the situation involved is judged by the speaker to be absolutely certain to occur or obtain in the future.

19. The examples in (25)–(27) have been judged by at least two native speakers of each language. The question mark enclosed by parentheses in (25c) means that the judgment differs from informant to informant (see note 20). The question mark in (26a) means that the two French informants judged the sentence to be a little odd (see note 21). The question marks in (27) mean that two out of the four Dutch informants I consulted judged the sentence to be bad or questionable; the double question mark in (27b) means that three out of the four Dutch informants judged the sentence to be bad or questionable. Those who accepted the Dutch sentences in (27) are children.

20. With respect to (25c), Kevin Moore (personal communication), North American, comments: "A possible context would be that we have to get everything ready tonight so that we will be ready for something special that will happen on Sunday." Kashino (1993: 178) notes that of the five informants he asked, one found the sentence acceptable, one unacceptable, and the other three marginal.

21. The low acceptability of this sentence seems to be due to a restriction to the effect that the French GO-future tends to refer to the definite, nearer future (see note 17). Thus, as the acceptability of (26b) implies, the French GO-future itself can basically refer to a simple-future use describing human age.

b. *Il <u>va</u> <u>avoir</u> deux ans demain.*
he goes have two years tomorrow

c. **Demain, ça <u>va</u> <u>être</u> dimanche.*
tomorrow it goes be Sunday

d. **Ça <u>va</u> <u>être</u> férié vendredi.*
it goes be public holiday Friday

(27) a. ?*Ik <u>ga</u> over enkele jaren veertig <u>zijn</u>.*
I go about a few years forty be

b. ??*Hij <u>gaat</u> morgen twee (jaar oud) <u>zijn</u>.*
he goes tomorrow two year old be

c. ?*Morgen <u>gaat</u> het zondag <u>zijn</u>.*
tomorrow goes it Sunday be

d. ?*Vrijdag <u>gaat</u> het een feestdag <u>zijn</u>.*
Friday goes it a holiday be

These data suggest that in English, the GO-future, as well as the present progressive, reflects the highest degree of grammaticalization; in my analysis, this is due to the highest degree of C-gravitation. However, comparing (26) with (27) does not clearly indicate whether French is more grammaticalized and thus higher in the degree of C-gravitation than Dutch with respect to the behavior of GO-futures;[22] we need to investigate more relevant phenomena to show that the statements about French and Dutch in hypothesis (21) hold for the GO-futures as well. However, the above observations about the French and Dutch GO-futures are at least not incompatible with the general tendency of the degree of public-self-centeredness observed in Section 3.2.

6. Conclusion

In this paper, I have provided an analysis of the differences of grammaticalization degree of the present progressives in English, French, and Dutch from a broader perspective. Specifically, I argued that C-gravitation is in operation in the three languages, but its degree is different, which motivates the different degrees of grammaticalization of the present progressives of the three public-self-centered languages.

One might say, as a reviewer has pointed out, that my analysis cannot apply to the grammaticalization of past progressives. However, as we mentioned

22. This might be due to the fact that the GO-futures in French and Dutch are not in the progressive form.

in Section 1, the present and past progressives should be considered separately because they behave differently in many respects (De Wit, Patard & Brisard 2013: 847–848). The most crucial point for this treatment is the fact that in the case of non-stative situations, the English present progressive almost obligatorily refers to a situation ongoing at speech time (i.e., the time of orientation in the case of present progressives), while the English past progressive does not obligatorily refer to a situation ongoing at a past time of orientation. My analysis offers a straightforward explanation: C-gravitation is not in operation in the use of the past progressive, which is not a tense form featuring reference to the public self's perspective at speech time.

Acknowledgments

I would like to thank Prischilla Ishida and Kevin Moore for English data; Benoît Leclercq and Pierre-Chauveau Thoumelin for French data; and Bert Cappelle and his family for Dutch data. Special thanks go to Yukio Hirose as well as two reviewers for their comments and criticism on earlier versions of this paper and Sylvie Hancil for her editorial work.

References

Anthonissen, Lynn, De Wit, Astrid & Mortelmans, Tanja. 2016. Aspect meets modality: A semantic analysis of the German *am*-progressive. *Journal of Germanic Linguistics* 28(1): 1-30.

Bertinetto, Pier Marco. 2000. The progressive in Romance, as compared with English. In Dahl (ed.), 559-604.

Boogaart, Ronny. 1999. *Aspect and Temporal Ordering: A Contrastive Analysis of Dutch and English*. The Hague: HAG.

Bühler, Karl. 1982. The deictic field of language and deictic words. In *Speech, Place, and Action: Studies in Deixis and Related Topics*, Robert J. Jarvella & Wolfgang Klein (eds), 9-30. New York NY: John Wiley & Sons.

Bybee, Joan & Fleischman, Suzanne. 1995. *Modality in Grammar and Discourse* [Typological Studies in Language 32]. Amsterdam: John Benjamins. https://doi.org/10.1075/tsl.32

Bybee, Joan, Perkins, Revere Dale & Pagliuca, William. 1994. *The Evolution of Grammar: Tense, Aspect, and Modality in the Languages of the World*. Chicago IL: The University of Chicago Press.

Curme, George O. 1977. *A Grammar of the German Language*. New York NY: Frederick Unger.

Dahl, Östen. 2000. *Tense and Aspect in the Languages of Europe* [Empirical Approaches to Language Typology EUROTYP 20–6]. Berlin: Mouton de Gruyter. https://doi.org/10.1515/9783110197099

De Wit, Astrid & Patard, Adeline. 2013. Modality, aspect and the progressive: The semantics of the present progressive in French in comparison with English. *Languages in Contrast* 13: 113-132. https://doi.org/10.1075/lic.13.1.06wit

De Wit, Astrid, Patard, Adeline & Brisard, Frank. 2013. A contrastive analysis of the present progressive in French and English. *Studies in Language* 37: 846-879.

Ebert, Karen H. 2000. Progressive markers in Germanic languages. In Dahl (ed.), 605-653.

Eckardt, Regine. 2006. *Meaning Change in Grammaticalization: An Enquiry into Semantic Reanalysis*. Oxford: OUP. https://doi.org/10.1093/acprof:oso/9780199262601.001.0001

Fischer, Olga. 1992. Syntax. In *The Cambridge History of the English Language*, Vol. II: 1066-1476, Norman Blake (ed.), 207-408. Cambridge: CUP. https://doi.org/10.1017/CHOL9780521264754.005

Givón, Talmy. 1991. The evolution of dependent clause morpho-syntax in Biblical Hebrew. In *Approaches to Grammaticalization*, Vol. II: *Types of Grammatical Markers* [Typological Studies in Language 19:2], Elizabeth Closs Traugott & Bernd Heine (eds), 257-310. Amsterdam: John Benjamins. https://doi.org/10.1075/tsl.19.2.14giv

Hasegawa, Yoko & Hirose, Yukio. 2005. What the Japanese language tells us about the alleged Japanese relational self. *Australian Journal of Linguistics* 25(2): 219-251. https://doi.org/10.1080/07268600500233019

Heine, Bernd. 1993. *Auxiliaries: Cognitive Forces and Grammaticalization*. Oxford: OUP.

Hirose, Yukio. 1995. Direct and indirect speech as quotations of public and private expression. *Lingua* 95(4): 223-238. https://doi.org/10.1016/0024-3841(94)00006-8

Hirose, Yukio. 2000. Public and private self as two aspects of the speaker: A contrastive study of Japanese and English. *Journal of Pragmatics* 32(11): 1623-1656. https://doi.org/10.1016/S0378-2166(99)00111-3

Hopper, Paul J. 1991. On some principles of grammaticization. In *Approaches to Grammaticalization, Vol. I: Theoretical and Methodological Issues* [Typological Studies in Language 19:1], Elizabeth Closs Traugott & Bernd Heine (eds), 17-35. Amsterdam: John Benjamins. https://doi.org/10.1075/tsl.19.1.04hop

Hopper, Paul J. & Traugott, Elizabeth Closs. 1993. *Grammaticalization*. Cambridge: CUP.

Hopper, Paul J. & Traugott, Elizabeth Closs. 2003. *Grammaticalization*, 2nd edn. Cambridge: CUP. https://doi.org/10.1017/CBO9781139165525

Joseph, Brian D. & Janda, Richard D. 2003. *The Handbook of Historical Linguistics*. Malden MA: Blackwell. https://doi.org/10.1002/9780470756393

Kashino, Kenji. 1993. *Imiron kara Mita Gohoo* (Usage as Seen from Semantics). Tokyo: Kenkyusha.

Kranich, Svenja. 2010. *The Progressive in Modern English: A Corpus-Based Study of Grammaticalization and Related Changes* [Languages and Computers: Studies in Practical Linguistics 72]. Amsterdam: Rodopi. https://doi.org/10.1163/9789042031449

Langacker, Ronald W. 2001. The English present tense. *English Language and Linguistics* 5(2): 251-271. https://doi.org/10.1017/S1360674301000235

Larreya, Paul. 2001. Modal verbs and the expression of futurity in English, French and Italian. In *Modal Verbs in Germanic and Romance Languages* [Belgian Journal of Linguistics 14], Johan van der Auwera & Patrick Dendale (eds), 115-129. Amsterdam: John Benjamins.

Lehmann, Christian. 1985. Grammaticalization: Synchronic variation and diachronic change. *Lingua e Stile* 20(3): 303-318.

Mortier, Liesbeth. 2008. An analysis of progressive aspect in French and Dutch in terms of variation and specialization. *Languages in Contrast* 8(1): 1-20. https://doi.org/10.1075/lic.8.1.02mor

Narrog, Heiko & Heine, Bernd. 2011. *The Oxford Handbook of Grammaticalization*. Oxford: OUP.

Nicolle, Steve. 2012. Diachrony and grammaticalization. In *The Oxford Handbook of Tense and Aspect*, Robert I. Binnick (ed.), 370-397. Oxford: OUP.

van Olmen, Daniël & Mortelmans, Tanja. 2009. Movement futures in English and Dutch: A contrastive analysis of *be going to* and *gaan*. In *Studies on English Modality*, Anastasios Tsangalidis & Roberta Facchinetti (eds), 357-386. Berlin: Peter Lang.

Pagliuca, William. 1994. *Perspectives on Grammaticalization* [Current Issues in Linguistic Theory 109]. Amsterdam: John Benjamins. https://doi.org/10.1075/cilt.109

Quirk, Randolph, Greenbaum, Sidney, Leech, Geoffrey & Svartvik, Jan. 1985. *A Comprehensive Grammar of the English Language*. London: Longman.

Searle, John R. 1983. *Intentionality: An Essay in the Philosophy of Mind*. Cambridge: CUP. https://doi.org/10.1017/CBO9781139173452

Traugott, Elizabeth Closs & Heine, Bernd. 1991. *Approaches to Grammaticalization*, 2 Vols [Typological Studies in Language 19]. Amsterdam: John Benjamins.

Vandelanotte, Lieven. 2009. *Speech and Thought Representation in English: A Cognitive-Functional Approach* [Topics in English Linguistics 65]. Berlin: Mouton de Gruyter. https://doi.org/10.1515/9783110215373

Wada, Naoaki. 2001. *Interpreting English Tenses: A Compositional Approach*. Tokyo: Kaitakusha.

Wada, Naoaki. 2008. Kootekiziko Tyuusinsei no Doai to Seioosyogo no Hoo/Zisei Gensyoo no Sooi (The degree of public-self-centeredness and differences of mood and tense phenomena in West-European languages). In *Kotoba no Dainamizumu* (The Dynamism of Language), Yu-ichi Mori, Yoshiki Nishimura, Susumu Yamada & Mitsu-aki Yoneyama (eds), 277-294. Tokyo: Kurosio.

Wada, Naoaki. 2013. A unified model of tense and modality and the three-tier model of language use. *Tsukuba English Studies* 32: 29-70.

Wada, Naoaki. 2015. *Differences in the semantic range of the English, Dutch, and German perfects and C-gravitation*, paper presented at ICLC 13, Northumbria University, UK.

The avertive and proximative grams in Maltese using the auxiliary *għodd*

Maris Camilleri
University of Essex

Maltese has grammaticalised an avertive construction involving a perfective lexical verb in combination with the auxiliary *għodd*; itself a grammaticalisation from a lexical verb, which as in the rest of the Arabic vernaculars means 'count', but which in Classical Arabic also means 'counter-to-fact'. *Għodd* is synchronically also used to build one of the proximative constructions available in the language. The lexical verb in the proximative construction can be either imperfective or perfective, and it is only the verb's lexical semantics that can disambiguate between an avertive or proximative reading when it is a perfective verb that combines with *għodd*. The focus in this paper is the syntax of these constructions, where the auxiliary is essentially analysed as a raising predicate. Additional data is however provided to highlight the auxiliary's further development and grammaticalisation, where we observe the loss of its PRED-value, i.e. its semantic associations, as it comes to function as a feature-bearing auxiliary at the syntactic level.

Keywords: avertive, proximative, grammaticalisation, auxiliation, Maltese

1. Introduction

Little work on grammaticalisation has been done on Maltese, except for notable exceptions such as Borg (1988), Vanhove (1993), Vanhove et al. (2009), Camilleri (2016a) and Camilleri & Sadler (2017). In this paper we will be focusing on the verb-form *għodd* in Maltese, lit meaning 'count.IMP.SG'. We will for the first time discuss this form in detail from the domain of grammaticalisation. As a result of changes in the morphosyntax, changes in the subcategorisation-frame associated with the verb *għodd*, occur. Coupled with additional dependencies between the morphosyntax of the verb and the lexical semantics of other elements in

https://doi.org.10.1075/slcs.202.10cam
© 2018 John Benjamins Publishing Company

the syntactic environment, *għodd* comes to demonstrate distinct functions and contributes distinct interpretations to the construction built.

Għadd is the lexical verb meaning 'count' in Maltese. This verb has itself grammaticalised and taken on an auxiliary-like function with the meaning 'almost'. This change from the lexical use of the verb-form, to what we will here be arguing to function as an auxiliary has been accompanied by a change in the inflectional paradigm. *Għodd*, which we here gloss as 'almost', is not a canonical verb-form, but rather forms part of what the literature on Maltese and Arabic refers to as the class of pseudo-verbs (Comrie 1991, 2008; Brustad 2000; Peterson 2009). Essentially, as we will see below, such pseudo-verbs inflect non-canonically with the use of ACCUSATIVE morphological forms (Camilleri 2014), and take a PRESENT TENSE interpretation (Spagnol 2009). These morphosyntactic differences that obtain between the lexical verb and the grammaticalised form that originates from it, also entail a distinct argument-structure/subcategorisation frame. The lexical verb 'count' is transitive, and takes two nominal arguments, which map onto SUBJECT and OBJECT grammatical functions, while the 'almost' counterpart obligatorily requires a complement that is either a verbal predicate that is lexical or functional, or a non-verbal predicate.

As the lexical verb grammaticalised into what we will argue to function as an auxiliary, the grammaticalisation of an analytic construction has taken place. The construction's interpretation at the semantic domain varies depending on the morphological form of the lexical verb. As will be presented in this paper, depending on the morphological form and the value of the morphosemantic features involved, we seem to be either dealing with an avertive or a proximative construction, in the sense of Kuteva (2001) and Kuteva et al. (2015).[1] In the earliest discussions on *għodd*, which include Aquilina (1965: 106) and Cremona (1966: 76), as cited in Vanhove (1993: 208–209), reference is only made to the IMMINENCE value expressed by this auxiliary. In this paper we will therefore be illustrating how in fact, this is only one of the two values which *għodd* is able to project.

Before delving into the Maltese data facts, we here introduce both the terminology and the analytic constructions under study in this paper. Kuteva et al. (2015: 4) define the avertive construction (or affix) 'as a linguistic expression standing for a verb situation which was on the verge of taking place but did not take place'. More specifically it is representative of the 'counterfactuality of the realization of an imminent, past situation where the verb situation is viewed as a whole (i.e. perfective)' (p. 2). The meaning associated with this interpretation is: 'was on

1. The fact that one and the same auxiliary form will be here shown to build two distinct constructions is not unheard of. Precisely in the discussion of parallel constructions to be discussed here, Kuteva (2001: 102–103) mentions how in Nahuatl, the same affix expresses the interpretations associated with both the avertive and proximative constructions.

the verge of V-ing but did not V' (Kuteva, 2001: 77), i.e. an 'expression of an action that was potentially imminent but did not ultimately get realized' (p. 78)… i.e. 'the action was on the point of occurring, yet did not occur'. The meaning is thus the one we otherwise get through the use of 'almost', 'nearly' or 'just about' in English. (1)–(2) illustrate two instances of such avertive constructions.

(1) *Štjax* *da padna*
want.1SG.IMPV to fall.down.PFV.1SG.PRES
'I nearly fell down.' Bulgarian: Kuteva et al. (2015: 4)

(2) *I liketa had a heart attack*
'I almost had a heart attack.' Southern American English: Kytö and Romaine (2006) cited in Kuteva et al. (2015: 4)

(3) demonstrates the Maltese equivalent, which, as the main thrust of this paper is to posit, represents the grammaticalisation of an avertive construction.

(3) *Għodd-ni* *x-xarrab-t*
count.IMP.SG-1SG.ACC REFL-CAUSE.wet.PFV-1SG
'I almost got wet.' Maltese: Camilleri (2016b).

The interpretational characteristics which Kuteva (2001: 84) and Kuteva et al. (2015: 3) attribute to the avertive construction are:

Imminence
Perfectivity
Pastness
Counterfactuality

Under this understanding, such grammaticalised constructions make reference to the domains of ASPECT (grammatical and lexical), TENSE and MOOD. As a result of this, Kuteva et al. (2015: 3) view the avertive not merely as an avertive construction, but also as a 'semantically elaborate grammatical category' in itself.

When it comes to the proximative construction, we have an analytic expression of this phasal ASPECTUAL value (Brinton 1988) that refers to 'a temporal phase located close before the initial boundary of the situation described by the main verb', i.e. implying that the event is 'close' to happening (Heine & Kuteva 2002: 24). Kuteva (2001) provides the Nandi example in (4) as an instantiation of a proximative construction, demonstrating the grammaticalisation of the volitional verb 'want' and its function in the construction of a proximative construction.

(4) *mâ-ko-rárak-tà así:s(ta)*
want-3-fall-ITV sun(NOM)
'The sun is about to set.' Nandi: Kuteva (2001: 125)

(5) is illustrative of the proximative construction in Maltese using the same item *għodd*.

(5) *Għodd-ha* *ħa* *t-a-għmel* *ix-xita*
count.IMP.SG-3SGF.ACC PROSP 3F-FRM.VWL-do.IMPV.SG DEF-rain.SGF
'It's almost going to rain.' Maltese: Camilleri (2016b).

When using the same means to express the different functions, as we see in Maltese, when comparing (3) and (5), Kuteva (2001: 92, 103) specifically states that the proximative function and structure is derived from the avertive one. This comes about as a result of the gradual loss of the TENSE and MOOD interpretations associated with the avertive structure, such that the proximative only comes to maintain relevance to the ASPECTUAL domain, where the IMMINENCE interpretation is maintained.

With this introductory foundation, we are now in a position to dig in the avertive and proximative structures, built with the auxiliary *għodd* in Maltese. In §2 we consider the meanings and morphosyntax of the form *għodd*, and in §3 the avertive and proximative grams are discussed in detail, and an analysis of the construction involving *għodd* and the lexical verb is provided. §4 then discusses and accounts for what seems to be a further grammaticalisation of the auxiliary. §5 then provides a further discussion and §6 concludes this paper.

2. Għodd

The form *għodd* used to build avertive and proximative constructions is morphologically the Imperative 2SG form of the lexical verb *għadd* 'count' (Aquilina 1965: 106) as in the other Arabic vernaculars.[2] It should here be mentioned that the cognate form in Standard Arabic also means 'counter-to-fact', apart from 'count', which interpretation, however, is no longer maintained in the vernaculars, including Maltese. Having said this, the South-Western Arabic dialect, for one, has in fact grammaticalized the use of the verbal form as an Avertive-constructing item (field notes). When we look carefully at the use of *għodd* in the avertive construction, We will find how it appears that while the 'counter-to-fact'/counterfactual interpretation is no longer associated with the lexical verb (if it ever was, at least in Maltese), this underlying interpretation is what resonates in the pseudo-verbal use of *għodd*. If this is indeed the case, then it is quite interesting that this

2. Note that the imperative is built off the imperfective, and hence the imperfective stem is the same form. Note that in some more Modern registers of Standard Maltese, the perfective form is in fact *għodd*.

pseudo-verbal grammaticalisation parallels the situation of the pseudo-verbs *donn* 'as though' and għad 'still'; 'anymore' (when negated), which are both maintained in the grammar, even if the associated lexical verbs are obsolete. It seems therefore that pseudo-verbs, albeit their further grammaticalisation at the morphosyntactic level, happen to at the same time preserve the older or the more original/conservative traits, at the semantic level.[3] The lexical verb meaning 'count' is a typical transitive predicate which takes on the usual canonical morphosyntactic associations as any other lexical predicate in Maltese, inflecting for perfective and imperfective forms, and is then able to combine with the relevant auxiliaries to build the analytic constructions expressing a number of TENSE and ASPECT interpretations (see Aquilina (1973), Fabri (1995) and Camilleri (2016a) for more detail).

(6) *Għaddej-t-hom kollha*
count.PFV-1SG-3PL.ACC all.PL
'I counted them all.'

The form *għodd*, which builds the avertive and proximative constructions differs from the lexical counterpart, both with respect to its morphosyntax as well as its subcategorisation frame. In the prototypical avertive and proximative constructions built with the use of *għodd*, one finds a verbal complement predicated of it. While morphologically-derived out of the lexical verb, it syntactically functions as a MOOD- or ASPECT-realizing auxiliary, as will become clearer in this paper. *Għodd* is referred to as a pseudo-verb, which is a class of verb-like items, as referred to in the traditional literature of Maltese and Arabic, which are characterised by the fact that these verb-like functioning items are derived from an array of stems, including synchronic/diachronic imperatives, prepositions, nouns and quantifiers (Brustad 2000; Comrie 2008). As part of this verb's participation in the pseudo-verb class, Spagnol (2009: 17) mentions how these class of verbs 'denote stative situations related to notions such as possession, inclusion, appearance, and mental states', and crucially are always interpreted in the PRESENT TENSE. At the syntactic level, pseudo-verbs are verb-like in the sense that in most contexts,

3. It should here be mentioned that we will be concentrating on the Standard variety, as in certain dialects, e.g. the North Eastern *Naxxari* spoken by the author, the same *għodd* takes on an additional function, and may be used to substitute the pseudo-verbs *qis* and *donn*, which while derived from the imperative forms meaning 'measure' and (obsolete) 'think' respectively, now mean 'as though'. The dialectal use and function of *għodd*, which goes beyond its use in avertive and proximative constructions is represented in (i) below. We will here have nothing more to say on this additional function which *għodd* takes in certain dialectal varieties.

(i) *Hawn għodd-ok qtaj-t xagħr-ek!*
Here count.IMP.SG-2SG.ACC cut.PFV-2SG hair-2SG.GEN
'It's as though you've cut your hair!'

they appear to function as verbal predicates, such that they can subcategorise for a SUBJ and a clausal argument, particularly when taking on auxiliary-like functions that realize/express a number of morphosemantic/morphosyntactic features (Comrie 1982; Vanhove 1993).

The morphosyntactic defining characteristic of pseudo-verbs is how their inflection differs from that of canonical verbs. These essentially obligatorily inflect through the use of bound ACC or GENITIVE pronominal forms which are otherwise in the language used to express the OBJ, OBLIQUE OBJ and POSSESSIVE grammatical functions, and which on the contrary, are not obligatory, in the sense that these pronominal forms can be substituted by NPs (albeit a number of other constraints at times). This is not the case when such pronominal forms attach onto pseudo-verbs, where essentially, as argued for in Camilleri (2014, 2016a, 2018), they come to function as non-canonical SUBJ realizations which are in an allomorphic relation with the canonical NOMINATIVE inflection present on non-pseudo-verb verbal forms, be them with a lexical or grammatical function. Arguing for such an analysis aligns these verbs with a crosslinguistic characteristic of predicates that take a number of experiencer type properties, such as those denoting physiological states, 'have'-type predicates, propositional attitude verbs, and modality predicates (Haspelmath 2001), which commonly express their SUBJs through non-canonical means. To illustrate the inflectional difference, as well as the paradigmatic variation more broadly, Table 1 represents the paradigms of the verbal and pseudo-verbal paradigms of *għadd* and *għodd* respectively.

Table 1. The paradigmatic representations of the lexical verb *għadd* 'count' and the pseudo-verb *għodd* 'almost'

Morphosyntactic features	*għadd* 'count'*		*għodd* 'almost'
	perfective	imperfective	PRESENT-interpretation
1SG	għaddej-t	n-għodd	għodd-ni
2SG	għaddej-t	t-għodd	għodd-ok
3SGM	għadd	j-għodd	għodd-u
3SGF	għadd-et	t-għodd	għodd-ha
1PL	għaddej-na	j-għodd-u	għodd-na
2PL	għaddej-t-u	t-għodd-u	għodd-kom
3PL	għadde-w	j-għodd-u	għodd-hom

* Refer to the rest of the paradigm in Camilleri (2014) for the full set of distinct forms in the paradigm associated with the lexical verb *għadd* 'count', given the display of overabundant behaviours in some cells.

Although seemingly quite distinct from the canonical verbal paradigm, *għodd* does indeed function as a verb. Furthermore, although not using the usual NOM inflection, the ACC pronouns bound on the stem still realize SUBJ inflection, as we will be demonstrating. Evidence in favour of a verbal analysis of the pseudo-verb comes from the expression of negation, which in Maltese is quite a robust test for verb-hood, although not without its exceptions (see Lucas (2014); Camilleri & Sadler (2016)). First let's consider the contrast in (7). There we observe that while the prepositional function of *għand* 'at' takes pronominal negation, which is broadly not otherwise used to negate verb-forms (but see Spagnol (2009); Camilleri (2016a) for a discussion on the use of pronominal negation with Imperfective forms when these realize a PROGRESSIVE ASPECTual value as opposed to a HABITUAL one; see also McNeil (2017) for similar behaviour in Tunisian), the pseudo-verbal counterpart, which functions as a possessive predicate as well as a modal auxiliary (Vanhove et al. (2009); Camilleri submitted), is negated just as though it belonged to the category of canonical verbs, and the *ma …-x* circumfixal negation strategy is used instead.

(7) a. *Il-ktieb* *mhux* *għand-i*
DEF-book.SGM COP.NEG.3SGM at-1SG.GEN
'The book is not at my place.' Prepositional function of *għand*.

b. *M'għand-i-x* *ktieb*
NEG.have-1SG-NEG book
'I don't have a book.' Verbal function of *għand*.

In parallel to this prepositional vs. pseudo-verbal realization of NEG in the case of *għand*, while the pseudo-verb *għodd* used to build the avertive and proximative constructions under discussion is morphologically derived from the imperative form, it is not negated in the same way other imperative forms are. Consider the contrast in (8) below.

(8) a. *(La) t-għodd-x* *ħażin!*
NEG 2-count.IMP.SG-NEG bad
Don't count wrongly. Negating the Imperative *għodd*.

b. *Issa hawn m'għodd-ok-x* *qtil-t-ni!*
now here NEG.almost-2SG.ACC-NEG kill.PFV-2SG-1SG.ACC
Now here (don't you see that) you almost killed me!
Negating the pseudo-verb *għodd*.

Primarily, as illustrated through (8a), the lexical imperative counterpart is negated through the obligatory *-x* suffix attached onto the 2SG imperfective form, along with an optional PROHIBITIVE *la*. On the other hand, as illustrated in (8b), the pseudo-verb is negated with the *ma …-x* circumfixal negation strategy.

The evidence which we can use to enhance the claim that we are indeed dealing with a SUBJ-realization expressed by ACC bound forms on *għodd* comes from a number of syntactic behaviours. See also Camilleri (2016a: 154–161; 2018; submitted) for more detail. In discussing evidence related to SUBJhood, we will at the same time also be providing evidence in favour of a raising analysis for *għodd*, i.e. where the auxiliary synchronically functions as a raising predicate, which in turn implies that the avertive and proximative constructions to be discussed in more detail in §3 cannot be treated as merely periphrastic structures that fill a cell in a paradigm. Rather, the evidence points towards a structure that is bi-clausal, i.e. one where while *għodd* takes an auxiliary function, it functions as the syntactic and semantic head of the clause, with the lexical predicate then functioning as the semantic head of an embedded clause that is predicated of the auxiliary.[4]

The first evidence we can provide in favour of our claim that the pronominal ACC inflection realizes a SUBJ grammatical function comes from the agreement displayed on the PAST TENSE auxiliary *kien* 'be', when the avertive or proximative constructions built with *għodd* need to be shifted in a PAST time reference.

(9) *Huma kien-u għodd-hom waqgħ-u/nixf-u*
they be.PFV.3-PL almost-3PL.ACC fall.PFV.3-PL/dry.PFV.3-PL
'They had almost fell/dried.'

This is not all there is to say about the agreement expressed on *kien*, however. Just as the pseudo-verb need not display agreement with the embedded SUBJ of the lexical verb, as in (10a), where it defaults to a 3SGM form, the auxiliary *kien* may itself display a default form, independent of whether the pseudo-verb itself displays agreement or a default form.

(10) a. *Għodd-u għosfr-ot*
almost-3SGM.ACC disappear.PFV-3SGF
'She almost disappeared.'

b. *Kien/kien-et għodd-u/-ha*
be.PFV.3SGM/be.PFV-3SGF almost-3SGM.ACC/-3SGF.ACC
għosfr-ot
disappear.PFV-3SGF
'She had almost disappeared.'

The full agreement in (9) vs. the default agreement displayed by *għodd* in (10a) vs. could be taken to be indicative of a SUBJ-to-SUBJ raising – It-extraposition type of alternation. The presence of a default 3SGM *kien* in (10b), even when *għodd* displays agreement with the SUBJ of the lexical verb, is here understood to be possible

4. An anonymous reviewer rightly questions how does this periphrastic analysis then resolve with the fact that we are still providing an auxiliary analysis for *għodd*? We are basing our description within the Lexical Functional Grammar (LFG) framework, which in fact allows for a two-fold analysis for auxiliaries (Falk 2008), as we will see further below.

as a consequence of the fact the SUBJ predicated of *għodd* is non-canonically realized. (Refer to Onishi (2001) and the references therein for other crosslinguistic parallels, where the non-canonical realization of grammatical functions results in the presence of default strategies elsewhere in the structure). Other agreement behaviours which further suggest a bi-clausal analysis, but which for reasons of space we do not delve in, include the presence of copy raising (see Camilleri et al. 2014; Camilleri 2017, submitted) displayed by the presence of a SUBJ in the *għodd* clause that is anaphorically-bound to a non-SUBJ GF predicated of the lexical verb in the embedded clause, which is expressed by a pronominal form.[5] Furthermore, the very presence of default agreement on the PAST TENSE auxiliary *kien* (as in (10b)) implies that the SUBJ agreement on the lexical verb is not available to control the agreement on *kien*, precisely because of the fact that *kien* is not in the local clause as the lexical predicate itself. The presence of a 3SGM agreement on *kien* in the absence of *għodd* in 10b would have resulted in agrammaticality.

Further evidence in favour of a raising analysis, is the fact that the SUBJ can itself be inanimate (11a), a meteorological DP (11b) or an idiom chunk (11c) that retains its idiomatic interpretation. Such data illustrates how we are dealing with a predicate that does not impose any thematic constraints on its SUBJ. This is after all the expected behaviour if we are here also claiming that *għodd* has grammaticalised into an auxiliary (Heine 1993; Vanhove 1993).

(11) a. *Għodd-hom t-kemmx-u l-ħwejjeġ*
almost-3PL.ACC REFL-wrinkle.PFV.3-PL DEF-clothes
'The clothes almost got wrinkled.'

b. *Dis-sħana kollha għodd-ha*
DEM.SGF.DEF-heat.SGF all.SGF almost-3SGF.ACC
sturdie-t-ni
make.dizzy.PFV-3SGF-1SG.ACC
'All this heat almost made me dizzy.'

c. *Naħqa ta' ħmar għodd-ha telgħ-et is-sema!*
bray.SGF of donkey almost-3SGF.ACC climb.PFV-3SGF DEF-sky
Lit: 'A donkey's bray almost climbed/made it to heaven.'
'The call of the poor/downtrodden almost made it to places of more power! (But didn't).'

5. An illustration of such an example is the following in (i), where the SUBJ of the matrix is anaphorically-bound with the resumptive pronoun in the OBJ position of the lexical verb in the embedded clause.

(i) *Dit-tifla għodd-ha waqqgħ-u-ha*
DEM.SGF.DEF-girl.SGF almost-3SGF.ACC fall.CAUSE.PFV.3-PL-3SGF.ACC
'The girl's like they almost made her fall.'

Further evidence in favour of the SUBJ status of the ACC pronouns comes from the usual SUBJ-to-SUBJ raising exhibited when the avertive or proximative construction headed by *għodd* is itself embedded under a prototypical raising predicate, such as *deher* 'seem' or one of the pseudo-verbs *qis/donn* 'as though'. (Alotaibi et al. 2013; Camilleri et al. 2014; Camilleri 2016a, 2018)

(12) a. *It-tfal qis-hom għodd-hom kien-u Qed*
DEF-children as.though-3PL.ACC almost-3PL.ACC be.PFV.3-PL PROG
j-i-ġ-ġield-u
3-EPENT.VWL-RECIP-quarrel.IMPV-PL
'The children seem as though they were about to start fighting.' Avertive

b. *Marija dehr-et għodd-ha ħa t-aqa'*
Mary appear.PFV-3SGF almost-3SGF.ACC PROSP 3F-fall.IMPV.SG
'Mary appeared almost about to fall.' Proximative

From the above discussion, one observes how the item which itself builds the avertive and at least one type of proximative construction (as will be illustrated in §3.2 and §5) has itself grammaticalised out of a lexical verbal item which itself synchronically means 'count', and which in the mother language also means 'counter-to-fact'. So far we have discussed this item's grammaticalisation and its syntactic function, synchronically. While in § 3.4 we will have more to say on the actual grammatical contributions expressed by the auxiliary in terms of morphosyntactic feature-projections, we have up till now established that we seem to be dealing with an auxiliary that syntactically functions like a raising predicate. If this syntactic account is on the right track, then the avertive and proximative constructions under discussion here are bi-clausal, where the auxiliary *għodd* behaves as a semantic predicate that subcategorises for a clausal complement that maps onto IP or VP constituents. From the data facts presented, *għodd* is however shown to not be an obligatory SUBJ-to-SUBJ raising auxiliary.

The analysis here is couched within the Lexical Functional Grammar (LFG) framework (Bresnan 1982; Bresnan et al. 2016), also the theoretical framework underlying the description presented in this paper. We here seem to be compelled to take advantage of the theory's flexibility in its analysis of auxiliaries, which can indeed be analysed either as pure feature bearers, or as predicates that themselves take an argument-list, and which in their majority are of the raising-type (Falk 1984, 2008).

In what follows we will look into detail at the specifics of the avertive and proximative structures built with the use of the auxiliary *għodd* in Maltese.

3. The avertive and proximative constructions headed by *għodd*

In this section we discuss the morphosyntactic specifics of the individual constructions. Before we do so, however, we primarily present the morphological array of verbal predicates that can appear after *għodd* and which themselves syntactically head the clausal complement. As clearly illustrated from the paradigm in Table 1, canonical verb-forms in Maltese inflect for perfective and imperfective forms in the indicative MOOD. (13a) involves a perfective verb-form. From the contrast between (13b, c) vs. (13d) it becomes clear that a bare imperfective form is not possible. Rather, the imperfective form must take one of the PROSPECTIVE or IMMINENCE auxiliaries (see Saydon 1935; Vanhove 2000; Camilleri 2016a) or the PROGRESSIVE auxiliary *qed/qiegħed* (see Borg 1988; Camilleri 2016a; Camilleri & Sadler 2017).[6]

(13) a. *Il-Milied għodd-u wasal*
DEF-Christmas.SGM almost-3SGM.ACC arrive.PFV.3SGM
'Christmas almost arrived.' (Aquilina 1965: 106)

b. *Għodd-hom ħa/sa/se/ser j-i-tilq-u*
almost-3PL.ACC PROSP/IMMINENCE 3-FRM.VWL-leave.IMPV-PL
'They are almost about to/going to leave.'

c. *Hawn għodd-ni qed n-a-ra doppju*
here almost-1SG.ACC PROG 1-FRM.VWL-see.IMPV.SG double
'Here I am almost seeing double.'

d. **Għodd-hom j-i-tilq-u*
almost-3PL.ACC 3-FRM.VWL-leave.IMPV-PL
Intended: 'They are almost leaving.'

6. Note that in the dialect, it is possible to have active participial forms as in (i). Yet, when this is the case, the meaning is no longer 'almost', but 'as though':

(i) *Kien għodd-u*
be.PFV.3SGM almost-3SGM.ACC
ġej/riesaq/miexi lej-na
go.ACT.PTCP.SGM/get.close.ACT.PTCP.SGM/walk.ACT.PTCP.SGM towards-1PL.GEN
'He was as though he's coming/walking towards us.'

With this same interpretation, an imperfective verb-form is also possible.

(ii) *Ghodd-ok t-kellm-u kuljum*
almost-2SG.ACC 2-talk.IMPV.SG-3SGM.ACC everyday
'It's as though you talk to him everyday.'

Apart from the contexts where an imperfective form is marked with PROG, PROSP, or IMMINENCE particles, the imperfective can also be used in the context of another pseudo-verbal form, e.g. *għandi* in (14).

(14) *Għodd-ni* *għand-i* *n-e-rġa'* *m-mur*
almost-1SG.ACC at-1SG.GEN 1-FRM.VWL-repeat.IMPV.SG 1-go.IMPV.SG
Lit: 'Almost at-me I repeat I go.'
'I almost have to go again.'

From the set of data in (13)–(14) it is clear that the embedded clause cannot map onto a CP at the constituent-structure, in the sense that the embedded clause is never introduced by a complementiser, and neither can a discourse function such as a TOPIC or FOCUS come in between *għodd* and the lexical verb. The complement clause can be a VP, as illustrated through the data in (13), or an IP, as illustrated through the data in (14) and (15).

(15) a. *Għodd-hom/–u* *kien* *qabad-hom*
almost-3PL.ACC/–3SGM.ACC be.PFV.3SGM catch.PFV.3SGM-3PL.ACC
in-ngħas
DEF-sleepiness.SGM
'They were almost overcome by sleepiness.'
b. *Għodd-ha* *kel-l-ha*
almost-3SGF.ACC be.PFV.3SGM-have-3SGF.GEN
t-e-rġa' *t-i-bda*
3F-FRM.VWL-repeat.IMPV.SG 3F-FRM.VWL-start.IMPV.SG
'She almost had to start again.'

The question to consider now is whether it is possible to morphosyntactically identify an avertive structure from a proximative one. This is what we discuss in §3.1–§3.2 below.

3.1 The morphosyntax of the avertive construction

At first glance, it seems that avertive constructions, represented by the data in (16) below, all involve a perfective verb-form.

(16) a. *Il-ħwejjeġ* *għodd-hom* *t-kemmx-u*
DEF-clothes almost-3PL.ACC REFL-wrinkle.PFV.3-PL
'The clothes almost got wrinkled.'
b. *Għodd-na* *ħbat-na*
almost-1PL.ACC crash.PFV-1PL
'We almost crashed.'

c. *Għodd-ha x-xarrb-et, Marija*
almost-3SGF.ACC REFL-get.wet.PFV-3SGF Mary
'Mary almost got wet.'

The data facts so far appear to corroborate further to Kuteva et al.'s (2015: 4) claim that in languages that display perfective vs. imperfective morphological distinctions, 'the main verb slot in the avertive structure is filled out by a perfective verb'. On the basis of this fact, they define the construction as a 'structure which stands for a bounded verb situation – viewed as a whole – which was on the verge of taking place in the past, but didn't' (p. 4). In fact it is specifically the presence of *għodd* which is rendering the 'averted' meaning. If we contrast the data in (17) with the mere use of the perfective verb-form, we end up with actual instantiated and bound events, characteristic of the perfective morphology of the lexical verb.

(17) a. *Għodd-u waqaj-na*
almost-3SGM.ACC fall.PFV-1PL
'We almost fell (but we didn't).' Avertive construction

b. *Waqaj-na*
fall.PFV-1PL
'We fell.' Perfective morphology

Given how the avertive construction is associated with the culmination of interpretations which bring together Imminence, Perfectivity, Pastness and Counterfactuality, I here wish to contrast the avertive construction with another analytic construction, as provided in the data paradigm in (18), i.e. the PAST PROSPECTIVE-realizing structure. The aim is to be able to disentangle the contribution which is specific to the auxiliary *għodd* in the construction, as opposed to the overall accumulative morphosyntactic and morphosemantic interpretations associated with *għodd* along with the perfective lexical verb which together build the avertive construction. The specific contributions of the auxiliary seem to be the Counterfactuality and Imminence interpretations. The additional morphosyntactic and morphosemantic interpretations associated with what constitutes the avertive are realized by the very interpretations associated with the perfective lexical verb-form. Consider the following:

(18) a. *Għodd-ni xtraj-t libsa*
almost-1SG.ACC buy.PFV-1SG dress
'I almost bought a dress.' Avertive – PRESENT TENSE anchoring

b. *Kon-t għodd-ni xtraj-t libsa*
be.PFV-1SG almost-1SG.ACC buy.PFV-1SG dress
'I had almost bought a dress.' Avertive – PAST TENSE anchoring

c. *Kon-t ħa n-i-xtri libsa*
be.PFV-1SG PROSP 1-FRM.VWL-buy.IMPV.SG dress
'I was going to buy a dress.'
PAST PROSPECTIVE. Camilleri (2016a: 210)

While overlapping semantic interpretations exist across the constructions presented in (18), what's crucial is that the means with which the shared interpretations are realized at the syntactic level differ. When comparing (18b-c), we observe how both constructions make reference to a past event. The dress-buying event has definitely not taken place in (18b) and (18a), as expressed through the avertive construction. On the other hand, a counterfactual interpretation with respect to this event's actualization/instantiation in the construction expressing a PAST PROSPECTIVE is likely, but not necessary. Moreover, while the perfective interpretation in the avertive construction is expressed by the lexical verb, in (18c), it is only the auxiliary 'be' that is perfective in form. Additionally, when comparing between the PRESENT TENSE-anchored avertive in (18a) as opposed to the PAST PROSPECTIVE construction in (18c), while the semantic interpretation of both is in the Past, at the syntactic level, however, it is only the structure in (18c) that expresses PAST TENSE. The avertive construction in (18a) is anchored in a Present time reference. It is therefore only through the presence of the auxiliary *kien* that we get a PAST TENSE feature-value projected at the syntactic level.

3.2 The morphosyntax of the proximative construction

The proximative construction is meant to 'define a temporal phase located close before the initial boundary of the situation described by the main verb', and semantically 'only' denotes the 'imminence' of the situation. Given the contrast in the interpretations found between the avertive and the proximative constructions, where there is essentially a loss of attributes associated with the latter construction, Kuteva (2001: 103) proposes that the latter function comes out of the former as a result of the loss of 'particular specificities of its meaning, namely the counterfactual as well as the pastness element', which is why for her the proximative only maintains a relevance to ASPECT, more specifically, the IMMINENCE interpretation. As discussed in Kuteva et al. (2015: 5), Heine (1992) identified the Proximative as an "almost"-ASPECT, which can be thought of as another means with which to view the IMMINENCE of the eventuality's instantiation.

Proximative constructions built out of the presence of *għodd* along with either of the PROSP- or IMMINENCE-marked imperfective forms of the lexical verb would be the most straightforward expected combination to express the set of interpretations associated with the proximative.

(19) a. *Milli qed n-a-ra, għodd-hom ħa*
from.COMP PROG 1-FRM.VWL-see.IMPV.SG almost-3PL.ACC PROSP
j-i-rbħ-u
3-FRM.VWL-win.IMPV-PL
'From what I am seeing, they are almost going to win.' PROXIMATIVE

b. *(Kien/kien-et) għodd-ha ħa*
be.PFV.3SGM/be.PFV-3SGF almost-3SGF.ACC PROSP
t-a-għmel ix-xita
3F-FRM.VWL-do.IMPV.SG DEF-rain.SGF
'Rain was/is almost going to fall.' (PAST) PROXIMATIVE

Once again, the actual proximation of the eventuality denoted by the lexical verb is a result of the presence of *għodd*, since in contrast to (19b), removing *għodd*, as in (20), yields a general PROSPective interpretation without the additional reference to the actual closeness or imminence of when the prospective event is to happen.

(20) *ħa t-a-għmel ix-xita*
PROSP 3F-FRM.VWL-do.IMPV.SG DEF-rain.SGF
'It's going to rain/It will rain.' PROSPECTIVE

The facts associated with the proximative construction do not stop there. They appear to become further complicated with the fact that synchronically, the interpretations associated with the proximative structure can be expressed by the very combination of *għodd* and a perfective lexical verb, as illustrated through the examples in (21).

(21) a. *Il-Milied għodd-u wasal*
DEF-Christmas.SGM almost-3SGM.ACC arrive.PFV.3SGM
'Christmas almost arrived.' (Aquilina 1965: 106)[7]

b. *Għodd-u/–hom nixf-u l-ħwejjeġ*
almost-3SGM.ACC/–3PL.ACC dry.PFV.3-PL DEF-clothes
'The clothes almost got dry.'

What is crucial for us to consider is that these constructions, although involving a perfective morphological form, do not have any PAST TENSE reference or counterfactual modal interpretations associated with them (as opposed to what we get in the case of the perfective form in the avertive). Rather, what is being

7. Changing the structure with the inclusion of the adjunct *fil-ħin* 'on time' results in an avertive construction once again, however.

(i) *Għodd-u wasal fil-ħin*
almost-3SGM.ACC arrive.PFV.3SGM in.DEF-time
'He almost arrived on time (but didn't).'

highlighted in this construction is the near completion or closeness of completion of the bounded event denoted by the same verb-form. As a matter of fact, although in principle the combination in (21b) could have yielded an avertive reading, this is not the case, as there is no PAST TENSE reference involved. On the other hand, the structure in (22), whose only difference from (21b) is that it involves the PAST TENSE-realizing auxiliary, renders a clear unambiguous avertive reading, in parallel to (18b).

(22) *Kien/kien-u* *għodd-u/-hom* *nixf-u*
be.PFV.3SGM/be.PFV.3-PL almost-3SGM.ACC/-3PL.ACC dry.PFV.3-PL
l-ħwejjeġ
DEF-clothes
'The clothes had almost got dry (but didn't).' Avertive construction

As things stand at the moment, the combination of *għodd* and a perfective lexical verb in principle yields to an ambiguous structure, which only seems to be able to be disambiguated on the basis of the verb's lexical semantics. A question we are faced with at this point is what to do with the fact that Maltese *għodd* + perfective constructions do not simply yield an avertive interpretation, in line with the expected behaviour which Kuteva et al. (2015) discuss with respect to those languages which display a perfective-imperfective split in their grammar. Furthermore, while the interpretational bleaching seems to suggest that the proximative may indeed be a derivation from the avertive, in terms of morphosyntax, it becomes somewhat unclear to see how this is possible, in a context where the combination with a perfective can indeed yield either an avertive or a proximative interpretation. The question is whether the *għodd* + perfective combination has always been simultaneously an avertive and a proximative construction, or whether this structural combination started out first as an avertive construction and then developed as a proximative.

3.3 The POLARITY feature and the avertive and proximative constructions

Another morphosyntactic difference which obtains when analyzing avertive and proximative structures is what one observes when considering facts related to negation. What we appear to have, although not considered elsewhere, is an interplay with polarity, morphological form, and interpretation.

Let us first consider the contrast in (23). Essentially we here observe an avertive construction which in (23a) involves a positive verb-form in the embedded clause, and a negative counterpart in (23b).

(23) a. *Għodd-ni għamil-t kollox*
almost-1SG.ACC do.PFV-1SG everything
'I almost did everything.'

b. *Għodd-ni m'għamil-t-x kollox*
almost-1SG.ACC NEG.do.PFV-1SG-NEG everything
'I almost didn't do everything (but I did).'

The contrast in (23) is the expected behaviour. For completeness one should add that negating the auxiliary instead of the lexical predicate results in a distinct interpretation, as illustrated through (24).

(24) *M'għodd-ok-x għamil-t kollox, mhux vera!*[8]
NEG.almost-2SG.ACC-NEG do.PFV-2SG everything NEG true
'It's not true! You didn't almost do everything!'

When we then consider the proximative construction, once again the main interest is what happens in the context of a perfective lexical verb. Consider the contrast below, between a perfective positive form in (25a) and a negative form in (25b)/(25c).

(25) a. *Għodd-hom nixf-u*
almost-3PL.ACC dry.PFV.3-PL
'They are soon about to dry.' Positive proximative

b. *Għodd-u ma wasal-x fil-ħin*
almost-3PL.ACC NEG arrive.PFV.3SGM-NEG in.DEF-time
'He almost didn't arrive on time (but he did).' Negative avertive

c. *Ghodd-hom ma nixf-u-x*
almost-3PL.ACC NEG dry.PFV.3-PL-NEG
Cannot mean: 'They will almost not dry.' *Negative proximative
'They have almost not dried (i.e. were on the verge of not drying but they have).' Negative avertive

What this appears to be demonstrating, therefore, is that if the perfective lexical verb internal to the proximative constructions subcategorized by *għodd* is negated, then the construction shifts its interpretation in a way that it can no longer be understood as a proximative construction. Rather, the construction is interpreted

8. In exclamative structures such as (i) below, we can have a negated form of the auxiliary *għodd* which however does not impart any NEGATIVE interpretations.

(i) *Issa dik m'għodd-hie-x qatl-it-ni?!*
now DEM.SGF NEG.almost-3SGF.ACC-NEG kill.PFV-3SGF-1SG.ACC
Lit: Now that not almost she killed me?
Hadn't she almost killed me?! / Now don't you see how she almost killed me!

as an avertive; hence the contrast between (21a) and (25b). On the other hand, the proximative construction that involves a prospective verb-form, i.e. an imperfective form with *ħa* or *se* retains the same interpretation and is not affected by NEG-marking. NEG counterparts to the positive (26a) involve NEG-marking on either the lexical verb (26b), or on the auxiliary (26c), and a distinct interpretation obtains, which in turn provides us with additional support for the bi-clausal construction which we have argued for in §1.

(26) a. *Għodd-u* *ħa* *j-i-fdal* *xi* *ħaġa*
almost-3SGM.ACC PROSP 3M-FRM.VWL-remain.IMPV.SG some thing
'There's almost going to be something left.'

b. *Għodd-u* *m'hu* *ħa* *j-i-fdal*
almost-3SGM.ACC NEG.3SGM PROSP 3M-FRM.VWL-remain.IMPV.SG
xejn
nothing
'There's almost not going to be anything left.'

c. *M'għodd-u* *ħa* *j-i-fdal* *xejn*
NEG.almost-3SGM.ACC PROSP 3M-FRM.VWL-remain.IMPV.SG nothing
'There's not almost going to be anything left.'

Contra the view in Kuteva et al. (2015) where the avertive structure is essentially some sort of 'elaborate grammatical category' that cuts across the domains of tense, aspect and mood, I would rather view the avertive structure as itself the output of a cumulation of distinct TENSE, ASPECT and MOOD interpretations which come about from the semantic and syntactic contributions of *għodd* along with the lexical verb which heads the embedded clause which the auxiliary subcategorises for. Given the data presented so far, and given that auxiliaries in LFG can either project a PRED value along with an argument-list, where they syntactically and semantically head the *f*-structure, or simply express a grammatical feauture, I here posit that *għodd* is a PRED-bearing auxiliary that also projects a grammatical contribution to the *f*-structure.

In Camilleri (2016a: 211), it was argued that at least with respect to the avertive use of *għodd*, the auxiliary's function is to signal some sort of pragmatic force/effect that conveys to the hearer that an eventuality almost took place, but didn't. Therefore, an analysis involving a feature in the *f*-structure, along the lines of a feature-based analysis which denotes that a clause type is interrogative or exclamative and so on, was employed. *Għodd* was associated with a (↑CLAUSE TYPE) = AVERTIVE feature-value in its lexical entry, which was meant to associate the semantic interpretations that cut across the domains of TENSE, ASPECT and MOOD. This association was constrained to be the case when a perfective verb (that can in fact be NEG-marked) is present in the complement clause, whose lexical semantics coupled by the appropriate ADJs allow for such interpretations. The function of the auxiliary in the proximative construction was on the other hand taken to be one that expresses the ASPECTual value: PROXIMATIVE.

Here I do not resort to the same analytical detail, however, in the case of the avertive construction. While the avertive and proximative constructions are indeed bi-clausal structures, i.e. where the auxiliary and the lexical verb head their own separate *f*-structure and *għodd* is an auxiliary that functions as a non-obligatory raising verb, the features expressed by *għodd* at the *f*-structure level when building the avertive construction differ. I here take *għodd* to be primarily an auxiliary that in combination with a perfective verb-form whose lexical semantics allows for an avertive interpretation, expresses the feature-values: MOOD = COUNTERFACTUAL and DISTANCE = IMMINENCE.[9] The rest of the interpretations which characterise an avertive construction I take to be derived at the semantic level as a result of the very syntax combining an auxiliary that realizes this set of morphosyntactic features together with a perfective verb-form with its associated semantic interpretations.

A representative partial lexical entry for the auxiliary *għodd* in its function and contribution in the avertive construction is provided below:

għodd V: (↑PRED) = 'almost<XCOMP|COMP>SUBJ'
(↑SUBJ) = {(↑XCOMP SUBJ)|3SGM}
(↑XCOMP|COMP PRED VFORM) = Perfective ^ POL = {NEG|POS} →
(↑MOOD) = COUNTERFACTUAL ^ (↑DISTANCE) = IMMINENCE
.
.
.

4. Further development of the auxiliary *għodd*

In what follows we consider what seems to be an additional grammaticalisation of the auxiliary *għodd*. Synchronically, it seems that the auxiliary, in certain avertive and proximative constructions has developed into a feature-denoting auxiliary as opposed to its function as a PRED-bearing auxiliary in the constructions discussed so far. Consider the data in (27) below. Here we find structures that parallel

9. For reasons of space I will here not go into any detail as to why I identify the value IMMINENCE as pertaining to DISTANCE, in Maltese, as opposed to say ASPECT, as Kuteva (2001) and Kuteva et al. (2015) do. For more detail see Camilleri (2016a).

verb-less constructions, and where instead of a subcategorized clausal argument, we have different predicate types, including NPs; PPs; and APs (given an appropriate lexical semantic interpretation of these predicates). Removing the auxiliary renders a usual avertive-less interpretation.

(27) a. *Dan ħodd-u isem ta' tifla*
DEM.SGM almost-3SGM.ACC name.SGM of girl
'This is almost a girl's name (but isn't).' Avertive with NP PRED.

b. *Daqt ħodd-ok ġewwa*
soon almost-2SG.ACC inside
'You're almost inside.' Proximative with PP PRED.

c. *Kien/kon-t ħodd-ok fix-xifer*
be.PFV.3SGM/be.PFV-2SG almost-2SG.ACC in.DEF-edge
'You were almost at the edge (but not quite).' Avertive with PP PRED.

d. *Kien-et ħodd-ha isbaħ mill-bieraħ*
be.PFV-3SGF almost-3SGF.ACC COMPAR.beautiful from.DEF-yesterday
'She was almost better than yesterday.' Avertive with AP PRED.

Stronger evidence that it is the auxiliary/copula-like *ħodd* in (27) which is rendering the avertive and proximative interpretations is demonstrated from the contrast that obtains in (28). Primarily, the proximative construction with *ħodd* in (28a) parallels the construction including the adjunct *kważi* 'almost' (28b). On the other hand, removing either of these items, as in (29), results in a construction which does not syntactically denote any IMMINENCE or proximative readings.

(28) a. *Il-Milied/Mejju ħodd-u magħ-na*
DEF-Christmas/May.SGM almost-SGM.ACC with-1PL.GEN
'Christmas/May is almost with us, i.e. is close to being here.'
Proximative.

b. *Il-Milied/Mejju kważi magħ-na*
DEF-Christmas/May.SGM almost with-1PL.GEN
'Christmas/May is almost with us, i.e. is close to being here.'

(29) *Il-Milied/Mejju magħ-na*
DEF-Christmas/May.SGM with-1PL.GEN
'Christmas/May is with us.'

One could possibly argue that this data may be indicative of a potential synchronic 'end point' in the grammaticalisation and evolvement of *ħodd*, where the auxiliary is in a state where it clearly seems to have started losing its PRED value, developing as a copula/feature-bearing auxiliary, predicative verbless structures. As things stand, therefore, *ħodd* has a dual syntactic behaviour as an auxiliary in Maltese. It functions as an auxiliary that can be both endowed with a PRED feature and morphosyntactic and morphosemantic features, which features and their values vary, as determined in §3.1–§3.4, depending on whether the construction is an avertive or a proximative. It can in other syntactically-determined contexts function as a feature-bearing auxiliary, in parallel with the behaviour of other copulas in Maltese.

5. Discussions and conclusions

In this paper we have specifically highlighted how one and the same structure may itself provide us with either a 'be about to do something (irrespective of whether the context is past or non-past) or else was just about to do something but never did it in past contexts … this is an ambiguity characteristic of the so called "functional overlap" stage, where a historically earlier and a historically later function for the same form coexist' (Kuteva 2001: 108). Here we have specifically illustrated how overarching this fact is that *għodd*, with a distinct morphosyntax and argument-structure is itself a lexical verb in the language. In this respect, *għodd* overalaps its function both between an auxiliary and a lexical verb, as well as in its function as an auxiliary, where as identified in this study, *għodd* builds avertive and proximative structures.

The grammaticalisation of pseudo-verbs in Maltese, as well as the grammaticalisation of analytic constructions built out of these, is not a one-off instance related with *għodd* in Maltese. In parallel to the trajectory of *għodd*, Camilleri (2016) finds that for example the (grammaticalised) pseudo-verbs *il* lit. 'to' and *għad* 'still, yet/just', when in combination with a lexical verb, analytically express different PERFECT ASPECTual values (see also Camilleri 2016a, submitted). Furthermore, another common trait is that just as the morphosyntactic- and morphosemantic-feature values realized by *għodd* vary depending on the morphology and lexical semantics of the lexical verb (or on other predicate type), in the case of the pseudo-verb *għad*, the value of the PERFECT expressed by the construction differs, or becomes ambiguous depending on the morphological form of the lexical verb, apart from other interactions with the syntax, such as the presence of the complementiser *kemm* (or *kif*), as illustrated in the contrast in (30) below.

(30) a. *Għad-ni* *n-i-kteb* *l-ittra*
still-1SG.ACC 1-FRM.VWL-write.IMPV.SG DEF-letter
'I am still writing the letter.' CONTINUATIVE
'I have just written the letter.' PERFECT of RECENT PAST

References

Alotaibi, Yasir, Alzaidi, Muhammad, Camilleri, Maris, ElSadek, Shaimaa & Sadler, Louisa. 2013. Psychological predicates and verbal complementation in Arabic. In *Proceedings of the LFG13*, Miriam Butt & Tracy Holloway King (eds), 6–26. Stanford CA: CSLI.

Aquilina, Joseph. 1973. *The Structure of Maltese: A Study in Mixed Grammar and Vocabulary*. Msida: Royal University of Malta.

Aquilina, Joseph. 1965. *Teach yourself Maltese*. London: Paul's House.

Borg, Albert. 1988. *Ilsienna*. Malta: Has Sajjied.

Bresnan, Joan. 1982. Control and complementation. In *The Mental Representation of Grammatical Relations*, Joan Bresnan (ed.), 282–390. Cambridge MA: The MIT Press.

Bresnan, Joan, Asudeh, Ash, Toivonen, Ida & Wechsler, Stephen. 2016. *Lexical-functional Syntax*. Oxford: Wiley-Blackwell.

Brinton, Laurel. 1988. *The Development of English Aspectual Systems: Aspectualizers and Post-verbal Particles*. Cambridge: CUP.

Brustad, Kristen. 2000. *The Syntax of Spoken Arabic*. Washington DC: Georgetown University of Press.

Camilleri, Maris. 2014. The Stem in Inflectional Verbal Paradigms in Maltese. PhD dissertation, University of Surrey.

Camilleri, Maris. 2016a. Temporal and Aspectual Auxiliaries in Maltese. PhD dissertation, University of Essex.

Camilleri, Maris. 2016b. The grammaticalisation of an avertive and proximative construction using the pseudo-verb *għodd-* in Maltese. Paper presented at the Gramm2 Conference, Rouen, France.

Camilleri, Maris. 2018. On raising and copy raising in Maltese. In *The Languages of Malta*, Patrizia Paggio & Albert Gatt (eds), 171–201Berlin: Language Science Press.

Camilleri, Maris. submitted. On the syntax and development of a Universal Perfect construction in Arabic.

Camilleri, Maris & Sadler, Louisa. 2016. *Xejn* in Maltese. Paper presented at the 2nd Form for Arabic Linguistics. York, UK.

Camilleri, Maris & Sadler, Louisa. 2017. Posture verbs and Aspect: A view from vernacular Arabic. In *Proceedings of LFG17*, Miriam Butt & Tracy Holloway King (eds). Stanford CA: CSLI.

Camilleri, Maris, ElSadek, Shaimaa & Sadler, Louisa. 2014. Perceptual reports in (varieties of) Arabic. In *Proceedings of LFG14*, Miriam Butt & Tracy Holloway King (eds), 179–199. Stanford CA: CSLI.

Comrie, Bernard. 1982. Syntactic-morphological discrepancies in Maltese sentence structure. *Communication and Cognition* 15: 281–306.

Comrie, Bernard. 1991. On the importance of Arabic for general linguistic theory. In *Perspectives on Arabic Linguistics III* [Current Issues in Linguistic Theory 80], Bernard Comrie & Mushira Eid (eds), 3–30. Amsterdam: John Benjamins.
https://doi.org/10.1075/cilt.80.04com

Comrie, Bernard. 2008. Pseudoverb. In *Encyclopaedia of Arabic Language and Linguistics*, Vol. III, 739–740. Leiden: Brill.

Cremona, Anthony. 1966. The phraseological use of the verbs 'qies', 'għodd', and 'dann'. *Journal of Maltese Studies* 3: 75–78.

Fabri, Ray. 1995. The tense and aspect system of Maltese. In *Tempussysteme in europaeischen Sprachen* II, Rolf Thieroff (ed.), 327–343. Tübingen: Niemeyer.

Falk, Yehuda. 1984. The English auxiliary system: A lexical-functional analysis. *Language* 60(3): 483–509. https://doi.org/10.2307/413988

Falk, Yehuda. 2008. Functional relations in the English auxiliary system. *Linguistics* 46(4): 861–889.

Haspelmath, Martin. 2001. Non-canonical marking of core arguments in European languages. In *Non-canonical Marking of Subjects and Objects* [Typological Studies in Language 46], Alexandra Y. Aikhenvald, Robert M. W. Dixon & Masayuki Onishi (eds), 53–84. Amsterdam: John Benjamins. https://doi.org/10.1075/tsl.46.04has

Heine, Bernd. 1992. Grammaticalization chains. *Studies in Language* 16(2): 335–368.

Heine, Bernd. 1993. *Auxiliaries: Cognitive Forces and Grammaticalization*. Oxford: OUP.

Heine, Bernd & Kuteva, Tania. 2002. *World Lexicon of Grammaticalization*. Cambridge: CUP. https://doi.org/10.1017/CBO9780511613463

Kuteva, Tania. 2001. *Auxiliation: An Enquiry into the Nature of Grammaticalization*. Oxford: OUP.

Kuteva, Tania, Aarts, Bas, Popova, Gergana & Abbi, Anvita. 2015. *The grammar of "counter-to-fact"*. Ms, SOAS, London.

Kytö, Merja & Romaine, Suzanne. 2006. Adjective comparison in nineteenth-century English. In *Nineteenth-Century English*, Merja Kytö, Mats Ryden & Erik Smitterberg (eds), 194–214. Cambridge: CUP.

Lucas, Chris. 2014. Indefinites and negative concord in Maltese: Towards a dynamic account. In *Perspectives on Maltese Linguistics*, Albert Borg, Sandro Caruana & Alexandra Vella (eds), 225–248. Berlin: Akademie Verlag.

Onishi, Masayuki. 2001. Non-canonically marked subjects and objects: Parameters and properties. In *Non-canonical Marking of Subjects and Objects* [Typological Studies in Language 46], Alexandra Y. Aikhenvald, Robert M. W. Dixon & Masayuki Onishi (eds), 1–50. Amsterdam: John Benjamins. https://doi.org/10.1075/tsl.46.03oni

Peterson, John. 2009. 'Pseudo-verbs': An analysis of non-verbal (co-)predication in Maltese. In *Introducing Maltese Linguistics* [Studies in Language Companion Series 113], Bernard Comrie, Ray Fabri, Elizabeth Hume, Manwel Mifsud, Thomas Stolz & Martine Vanhove (eds), 181–205. Amsterdam: John Benjamins. https://doi.org/10.1075/slcs.113.13pet

Saydon, Pietru P. 1935. Il-Kelmiet *sa, ħa, qed*. *Il-Malti* 11: 44–45.

Spagnol, Michael. 2009. Lexical and grammatical aspect in Maltese. *Ilsienna* 1: 51–86.

Vanhove, Martine. 1993. *La langue maltaise: Etudes syntaxiques d'un dialectearabe 'périphérique'*. Wiesbaden: Harrassowitz.

Vanhove, Martine. 2000. Future, injunctive and purpose subordinating conjunctions: The case of Maltese *ħalli, ħa* and *biex*. In *Proceedings of the Third International Conference of AÏDA, Association Internationale de Dialectologie Arabe, 1998, Malta*, Manwel Mifsud (ed.), 235–240. Valetta: Salesian Press.

Vanhove, Martine, Miller, Catherine & Caubet, Dominique. 2009. The grammaticalisations of modal auxiliaries in Maltese and Arabic vernaculars of the Mediterranean area. In *Grammaticalization of Modal particles*, Johan van der Auwera (ed.), 325–362. Berlin: Mouton de Gruyter.

Discourse markers

Pragmatic uses of *nu* in Old Saxon and Old English

Elise Louviot
Université de Reims Champagne-Ardenne – CIRLEP

The Proto-Germanic temporal adverb **nū* has developed pragmatic uses in most Present-Day Germanic languages, as a modal particle and/or as a discourse marker. Synchronically, the two categories are usually considered distinct, but they have much in common, especially in terms of function. Diachronically, it is unclear whether they typically develop independently or constitute two different steps in the same evolutionary pathway. This paper examines two closely related early Germanic corpora (Old English and Old Saxon verse) to determine whether uses of *nu* matching the formal and functional features typically associated with modal particles and discourse markers respectively can be identified there. It finds that many of the pragmatic uses found in Present-Day Germanic languages can already be observed to some extent in those corpora, especially in Old English, but that there is still too much continuity between the various pragmatic uses of *nu* (and indeed between lexical, grammatical and pragmatic uses of *nu*) in Old English and Old Saxon to consider that such uses reflect the existence of truly distinct markers.

Keywords: Old English, Old Saxon, pragmatics, discourse markers, modal particles, poetry, *nu*, now

1. Preliminaries

1.1 Theoretical background

Since the 1980s, linguists have paid an increasing amount of attention to small words and phrases occurring very frequently in speech, usually unstressed, which do not contribute to the syntactic structure or propositional content of the sentence, but which seem to play a crucial role in discourse and interaction. Such words and phrases are difficult to categorize and have accordingly received many different labels: pragmatic markers, discourse markers, utterance particles and

https://doi.org.10.1075/slcs.202.11lou
© 2018 John Benjamins Publishing Company

modal particles are among the most common ones. The labels are not interchangeable, but neither do they correspond to a neat subclassification.

Modal particles (MPs) correspond to a relatively closed class of markers 'restricted to a specific distributional position (generally the middle field in Germanic languages)'[1] (Degand et al. 2013: 7) and whose function is primarily (inter)subjective. They have a relatively fixed scope (though that scope is variously identified with the clause, the sentence, the speech-act or the utterance) and tend to be regularly associated with certain types of illocutionary forces (Degand et al. 2013; Waltereit & Detges 2007).

Discourse markers (DMs), on the other hand, correspond to a much more nebulous category which, when it is understood in its broadest sense, encompasses both markers primarily oriented towards text-organisation and markers of (inter) subjectivity,[2] and which has no fixed distributional features, though sentence-initial position is often regarded as typical (Schiffrin 1987: 328; Brinton 2010: 285–6; Degand et al. 2013: 5–6). They are either unstressed or an independent intonation group, they are typically poorly integrated syntactically and they have variable scope, potentially operating at either a local or global level of discourse.

In other words, MPs and DMs differ in two main interrelated respects. Formally, MPs differ from DMs in that they are typically clause-internal and unstressed, whereas DMs are often clause-initial and may carry stress if they occur as an independent tone unit. Functionally, both types of markers are very close in that both may have (inter)subjective functions, but DMs are more likely to contribute directly to text-organization, precisely because they typically occur in initial position. Linguists who focus primarily on function are therefore more likely to treat both categories as one, whereas those focusing on form are more likely to treat them as very distinct categories (Auer & Maschler 2016).

Diachronically, the development of such markers is even more problematic, both in terms of how they fit into grammaticalization from a theoretical standpoint and in terms of how their pathways intersect.

First, if grammaticalization is understood in the most basic way possible, as the transformation of a referential item into a functional item, then the development of MPs and DMs must be seen as part of it. However, as shown by Ocampo (2006: 316), DMs fit some of the criteria for grammaticalization (e.g. movement

1. For van Gelderen (2001), English MPs do not follow the same distributional pattern and are more likely to be found in the periphery, but several of the examples she provides have been considered DMs elsewhere (e.g. *then, well, like*).

2. Some authors favour the term 'pragmatic markers' for markers of intersubjectivity and only use the term 'discourse marker' with respect to textual organization. In practice, however, the same markers often display both types of function simultaneously.

towards more abstraction, relational function, frequent phonological attrition) but not all (e.g. belonging to a closed class, being part of morphology and syntax, reduced scope). MPs are slightly less problematic (they may be said to belong to a closed class and their scope is potentially narrower than that of DMs), without being a perfect fit either (they are also outside syntax and they still have a large scope).

As a consequence, there is currently no consensus among linguists regarding whether the development of DMs and MPs should be treated as part of grammaticalization (provided grammaticalization is understood more broadly, see in particular Traugott 1995; Lenker 2000; Traugott & Trousdale 2013: 96–112), as a subtype of grammaticalization (Wischer 2000) or as a distinct phenomenon called pragmaticalization (Erman & Kotsinas 1993; Aijmer 1997; Günthner & Mutz 2004; Dostie 2004; Ocampo 2006). Solving that issue is much beyond the scope of the present paper and very much depends on what we call grammar and what place, if any, pragmatics has in it.

In this paper, I assume that the transformation of existing linguistic items into items with pragmatic functions (such as MPs and DMs) is connected closely enough to the process of grammaticalization that it cannot be studied without any reference to that theoretical background, but that it is distinct enough to justify focusing more particularly on new pragmatic uses of a given marker instead of treating all new uses (including grammatical ones) on the same footing.

Second, given that many markers may have both MP and DM uses, it is worth wondering whether such uses develop independently from the same root or whether they may derive from each other and if so in what direction. Traugott initially claimed that grammaticalization tended to follow a path from propositional to textual to subjective/expressive meanings (Traugott 1982), before hypothesizing two concurrent tendencies towards more metatextuality and more subjectivity (itself followed by a movement towards more intersubjectivity, Traugott 1989 and 2003), but has more recently argued that an adverb was more likely to evolve first into an MP and then only into a DM (Traugott 2007), which would suggest that metatextual meanings arise after (inter)subjective ones after all.[3] This paper will try to determine whether the data observed in the selected corpus suggests a particular direction in the development of new pragmatic functions.

3. Conversely, Aijmer (2002: 95) considers that, in English, *now*'s use as a modal particle 'represents the end-point of grammaticalisation from a deictic source' and thus comes after its use as a discourse marker.

1.2 Object[4]

As noted above, it is not uncommon for the same marker to have both DM and MP uses. Proto-Germanic **nū* and its descendants constitute a particularly interesting case. Originally a temporal adverb with reference to the moment of utterance ('now', 'presently'),[5] **nū* has developed pragmatic (and grammatical) uses in all Present-Day Germanic languages where it survives.

In English, *now* can be used as a subordinator, but also as a discourse marker signalling transition to a new topic or a new attitude to the topic at hand (Schiffrin 1987; Lenker 2010) or as a modal particle signalling the speaker's attitude (Aijmer 2002: 57–96).

In (High) German, *nu(n)* can be used as a subordinator, but also as an interjection or as a filler inviting the hearer to go on. It can also be used as a text-structuring device (which may behave like a regular adverb or like a DM prosodically and syntactically) signalling a new step in the ongoing discourse, related to, yet distinct from what comes before in some way. It can also be used pragmatically (usually behaving like an MP prosodically and syntactically, but sometimes like a DM), to signal relevance or to appeal to knowledge shared by the participants in order to overcome a perceived objection or obstacle. *Nun* is also frequently combined with other markers: *nun (ein)mal, nun gut, nun ja*, etc. (Pérennec 1995; Metrich et al. 1998; Golato 2016).

In Dutch, *nu* is primarily used as a temporal adverb and occasionally as a subordinating conjunction, but the (originally dialectal) form *nou* has further uses: as a modal particle, it is most often used to intensify the action meaning of directives, questions and requests and, as a discourse marker, it can be used to signal a new stage in ongoing discourse or, at the beginning of a new turn of speech, to signal that the speaker's response may not meet the hearer's expectation (Mazeland 2016).

In Icelandic, *nú* can be used as a discourse marker, either to signal a shift to a new topic in an ongoing discourse or to express reservation or surprise regarding what the other speaker has just said (not entirely unlike Dutch then, though not quite identical). It can also be used as a modal particle, often to show that the speaker is explicitly addressing the previous turn, but disaligning themselves from it in some way. It also often expresses a strong affective stance, with the

4. My thanks to Peter Auer, Yael Maschler, Andrea Golato, Mirja Saari and Hanna Lehti-Eklund who have given me access to their papers (still in press at the time this work was written), which proved very helpful for this section.

5. Auer and Maschler (2016) also mention the possibility that *nū* had a resultative meaning in Proto-Germanic, in addition to the temporal one.

speaker attempting to get the hearers to do something or pay attention to something (Hilmisdóttir 2011).

In Swedish, *nu* has developed textual (to introduce a new topic or create a connection with an earlier action or utterance) and (inter)subjective meanings (for instance with imperatives or rhetorical questions, to express the speaker's affective stance) over time, but its use has declined sharply in Sweden-Swedish and mostly survives in fixed phrases and in Finland-Swedish (Saari & Lehti-Eklund 2016).

Generally speaking, while there are genuine differences across languages, Auer and Maschler (2016) identify a number of core pragmatic functions shared by most cognates of *now* (and of the related marker *nå*/*na*) in many European languages. They can be summed up so: textually, the marker points both forward (signalling a new step) and backwards (expressing a contrast with or a consequence of what came before); (inter)subjectively, the marker can express various attitudes to the utterance or to the addressee such as impatience, emotional involvement or some kind of non-alignment.

So far, not that much is known concerning possible MP and DM uses of *now*'s cognates in ancient Germanic languages, but several studies have shown that text-structuring functions, at least, could be discerned relatively early on (see Fries 1993: 540; Defour 2007: 202–217 and Lenker 2010: 61–64 for Old English; Betten 1992, for Middle High German; Saari & Lehti-Eklund 2016, for Old Swedish).

Identifying MP and DM uses of a marker in ancient texts is a challenge for obvious reasons: such markers are particularly typical of spontaneous oral interaction and their correct interpretation is often dependent on such factors as prosody, facial expression and posture, context and of course a good (native or near-native) mastery of the language and of the cultural context.

That being said, earlier studies (in particular Abraham 1991 and Brinton 1990 & 2010) have shown that the task was challenging but not impossible. Brinton (1990: 58–59) makes a particularly important point regarding the orality of Old English poetry: while it is likely that spontaneous oral features, once borrowed into another medium, change to some extent (and potentially acquire metacommunicative meanings), it is undeniable that oral features are very much present in Old English poetry, which means that DMs and MPs can be found there, even if it can be more difficult to identify their precise functions than it would be in a contemporary corpus.

Some scholars distrust the reliability of poetry as a source of linguistic data, especially where syntax is concerned (see for instance Gardner 1971: 15; McLaughlin 1983: 66; Molencki 1991: 15), but evidence seems to contradict such views: as shown by Cichosz (2010), poetry is in fact the only Old English text type showing syntactic structures that are relatively free of foreign (mostly Latin) influences. One may add two important facts: Old English poetry is rich in dialogues, i.e. in represented interaction (unlike the earliest Old Swedish texts, for instance, which are collections of laws for the most part) and it can provide us with some information on prosody, through metrical stress.

As a consequence, it makes sense to try and locate DM and MP uses in that corpus. For the present study, I have chosen to compare Old English and Old Saxon verse. The two corpora are very closely related, both generically and linguistically, which means that they offer the same benefits and which makes comparison easier.[6] On the other hand, they are somewhat contrasted in terms of syntax: while word order is still fairly flexible in both languages (which means that the existence of a recognizable middle field is not always self-evident in either), Old English is much freer with the verb-second rule than other (ancient) Germanic languages, including Old Saxon.

For Old Saxon, I have looked at every occurrence of *nu* in *Heliand* and *Genesis* individually (155 occurrences). For Old English, which is a larger corpus, I have looked at every occurrence of *nu* in the four main poetic codices (423 occurrences), which represent roughly 60% of all extant occurrences in poetic texts (712).[7] Most instances of *nu* occur in dialogue, though some can also be found in narratorial comments to the audience or in genres such as riddles, or elegies, which suppose a speaker addressing an audience.

1.3 Method and outline

The fact that Brinton (1990 and 2010) focuses on DMs in Old English, whereas Abraham (1991) is more interested in MPs in the history of German and closely related languages is no coincidence: those choices reflect different amounts of scholarly interest (and, to some extent, of evidence) for DMs and MPs in Present-Day English and Present-Day German respectively. However, there is no reason a priori to think that DM uses are more likely to be found in Old English and MPs more likely to be found in Old Saxon. There is no reason either to suppose that the pragmatic functions identifiable in those two corpora will necessarily match closely those found in Present-Day Germanic languages (be it English, Low German or others).

6. It must be noted, though, that the Old Saxon poetic corpus is made up of only two poems (*Heliand* and *Genesis*) and therefore not comparable with its Old English counterpart in terms of quantity and diversity of texts.

7. Out of the 289 instances not considered here, 150 come from Psalms and 62 from *Boethius' Meters*. The rest corresponds to short prayers, charms and fragments. Examples from those texts have been included occasionally but they are excluded from the quantitative data.

As much as possible, the present study attempts to look at *nu* in Old English and Old Saxon verse without any preconception regarding its uses. To that aim, I have used form as a starting point: instead of looking for occurrences matching certain predetermined functions (for instance those attested for cognates of *nu* in Present-Day Germanic languages), I have looked for occurrences appearing to match the formal features typical of DMs or MPs. This, in itself, creates its own problems, because there is no reason to suppose emerging DMs or MPs will already have all of the formal features associated with them today. However, using form as a starting point has the important benefit of being less open to subjective bias, whereas it is only too easy to unintentionally read an anachronistic meaning into a text.

Then, I have looked for recurring patterns potentially indicative of emerging DM or MP uses. The underlying assumption is this: lexical items can have pragmatic uses in context, but such uses will have little in common with each other; conversely, if a pragmatic function becomes conventionalized, i.e. if it becomes inherent to a given item, then we can expect some noticeable regularities.

The approach chosen here is mostly qualitative, even though some quantitative data are provided. All instances of *nu* have been classified according to their word order and all instances corresponding to a given word order have been examined in detail to try and uncover their specificities.

The most common word orders are as follows:[8] pre-initial *nu* (*nu* + X + finite verb), pre-verbal *nu* (*nu* + finite verb), conjunctive *nu* (*nu*… finite verb in final position), post-verbal *nu* (*nu* immediately after the finite verb) and medial or late *nu* (*nu* occurring later than immediately after the finite verb or somewhere inside a subordinate clause).

Table 1. Word order for clauses with *nu* in old English and old Saxon verse

	Old English		Old Saxon	
pre-initial *nu*	32	8%	0	0%
pre-verbal *nu*	45	11%	50	32%
conjunctive *nu*	103	24%	32	21%
post-verbal *nu*	112	26%	20	13%
medial or late *nu*	76	18%	46	30%
other	55	13%	7	5%
total	423	100%	155	100%

8. Other word orders include ambiguous instances (for instance when a verb can be interpreted as final or as occurring in second or third position in a short clause) and instances where *nu* immediately follows a conjunction.

For our purpose, the most interesting word orders are pre-initial *nu* (which is an interesting candidate for DM uses) and post-verbal *nu* (a good candidate for MP uses). However, such patterns have to be examined in comparison with others, so as to have a full picture of the multiple ways in which *nu* can be used in Old English and Old Saxon.

In this paper, I first discuss briefly lexical and conjunctive uses of *nu*, before moving on to potential MP and DM uses themselves.

2. Multiple uses of *nu* in Old English and Old Saxon

2.1 Lexical use of *nu*: Temporal (and contrastive) adverb

2.1.1 *Formal features*

As a temporal adverb, *nu* is syntactically integrated, which means that, in Old English (OE) and Old Saxon (OS), it will typically be found in initial/pre-verbal (1) or medial (2) and (3) position (corresponding respectively to the front field, i.e. before the finite verb, and to the middle field, i.e. inside the verbal bracket, inasmuch as the topological model is applicable to those languages). In initial position, *nu* cannot carry metrical stress due to Kuhn's Law (Kuhn 1933). In medial position, it can carry metrical stress (3), depending on its position in the verse.

(1) (OS) '**nu** habað thit lioht [afgeben]', quað he,
'Erodes [the] cuning; he uuelde is âhtien giu,
frêson is ferahas. **Nu** maht thu [an] [friðu] lêdien
that kind undar euua cunni... (*Heliand* 771b–774a)[9]

Now King Herod has given up this light, he said, he always wanted to hunt him down, to take his life violently. ***Now*** *you can lead the child in peace to your clan...*

(2) (OE) Forþon se mon ne þearf
to þisse worulde wyrpe gehycgan,
þæt he us fægran gefean bringe
ofer þa niþas þe we **nu** dreogað (*Guthlac A* 46b–49a)

Therefore, a person does not need to rely on this world for an improvement, that it will bring us sweet happiness instead of the troubles that we ***now*** *endure.*

9. All quotations from Old Saxon are taken from Behaghel & Taeger's editions (1984 and 1996) and all quotations from Old English are taken from the Anglo-Saxon Poetic Records (Dobbie 1942 and 1953; Krapp & Dobbie 1936; Krapp 1931, 1932a and 1932b). All translations are my own.

(3) (OS) Mi is an handun **nu**
uuîti endi uunderquâle, thea ik for thesumu uuerode scal,
tholon [for thesaru thiodu]. (*Heliand* 4567b–4569)

Punishment and terrible torture are ***now*** *at hand for me, that I will have to endure in front of this troop, in front of this people.*

Both the initial (pre-verbal) position and the medial position are more frequent in Old Saxon verse (50 and 37 occurrences out of 155, or 32% and 24% respectively) than in Old English verse (45 and 55 out of 423, or 11% and 13% respectively).[10]

Old English and Old Saxon verse also show the possibility of having a number of lexical elements in late position, after the end field (for instance after a participle or after an infinitive), including the adverb *nu*. In that case, it will carry metrical stress (4).

(4) (OE) To hwon sculon wit weorðan **nu**? (*Genesis B* 815b)[11]

What will become of us ***now?***

That pattern is relatively rare: 5% of all clauses with *nu* in Old English (21 out of 423) and 6% in Old Saxon (9 out of 155).

2.1.2 *Meaning*

Semantically, *nu* is used to refer to a time period including the moment of utterance, but such overdetermination of the reference to the present moment (which is already marked by the verbal tense) is usually justified by the fact that there is something special about that present moment: it is recognized as differing in some way from what came before. As such, there is often a notion of contrast with a past moment (1), and/or of the beginning of a new stage or era (1), (3), (4). We see here the basis for many of the pragmatic meanings that *nu* has developed in various Germanic languages over time: a marker that looks both backward and forward, and a notion of contrast or discrepancy with what came before.

2.2 Grammatical use of *nu*: From adverb to conjunction

Both Old English and Old Saxon have developed a use of *nu* as a subordinating conjunction translatable as 'since' or 'now that', with a temporal and causal

10. The figures do not include instances of *nu* located immediately after the finite verb, which are examined separately below (Section 2.3).

11. The equivalent passage in the Old Saxon text reads *te hui sculun uuit uuerdan nu*, with the same meaning.

meaning.[12] As with other conjunctions, it may be used alone (5) or in correlation with another instance of the same marker behaving like a regular adverb (6). As the conjunction appears in initial position in the clause, it will always be unstressed (see 2.1.1 above).

(5) (OE) Siþþan we motan
anmodlice ealle hyhtan,
nu we on þæt bearn foran breostum **starIað**. (*Christ I* 339b–341)[13]

Then we may rejoice, all of us together, ***since*** *we* ***will be looking*** *at the child on your lap.*

(6) (OS) **Nu** uuêt ik that ik scal an thînum heti libbian,
forđ an thînum fîundscepi, **nu** ik mi thesa firina **gideda**
(*Genesis* 649b–650)[14]

Now *I know that I shall live in your hatred, henceforth in your enmity,* ***now*** *I* ***have done*** *this crime.*

That grammatical use is often recognizable from the specific word order of subordinate clauses in Old English and Old Saxon (with the conjunction in initial position and the finite verb in final or late position, see 5 and 6). That pattern (with the finite verb beyond the third position) is relatively frequent in both languages with 32 occurrences in Old Saxon (21%) and 103 (24%) in Old English. While various elements can occur after the finite verb (including a non-finite verbal form), the typical word order in such clauses is SOV.

However, the connection between that word order and subordination is not systematic, whether in verse or in prose.[15] The word order typical of subordinate

12. The shift from temporality to causality is a very common type of semantic change, often encountered in a process of grammaticalization as a marker acquires a more and more abstract meaning (Heine, Claudi & Hünnemeyer 1991: 257; Abraham 1991: 370).

13. It is worth noting that *nu* cannot be translated here by 'now' since that moment has not yet come to pass: the original lexical meaning of *nu* is bleached to some extent (though it would be possible to retain the notion of temporality if *nu* is translated by 'when'). For other instances, see for example *Elene* 635, *Christ I* 82 and 247 (OE) and *Heliand* 150 (OS).

14. For other instances using correlation, see for example *Genesis B* 403b–404a, *Beowulf* 426b–430, *Daniel* 291–295a (OE), *Heliand* 3253–3256, *Genesis* 569–570(OS).

15. Cichosz's study of word order in Old English and Old High German shows that in those languages the finite verb in subordinate clauses (especially noun clauses and adverbial clauses) is found after the second position in most cases, typically (but not always) in final position. The trend is particularly strong for adverbial clauses in poetry, where the verb is postponed in about

clauses may be found when there is no notion of causality (7) and the notion of causality may be found with an SVO order (8).

(7) (OS) … thu uurdi thines bruođar bano. **Nu** he bluodig **ligit**,
uundun uuorig thes ni habda he eniga geuuuruhte te thi,
sundae, gisuohta thoh thu ina nu aslagan hebbias… (*Genesis* 634–636)[16]

… you became your brother's killer. ***Now*** *he* ***lies*** *bloody, sore with wounds; in this he has not sought from you repayment for any deed or injury (= he had done nothing to deserve this), though you have now slain him…*

(8) (OE) Miltsa ðu me, meahta walden, **nu** ðu **wast** manna geðohtas,
help ðu, hælend min, handgeweorces
þines anes, ælmehtig god,
efter þinre ðære miclan mildhiortnesse. (*Psalm 50* 31–34)[17]

Have pity on me, master of powers, ***now*** *you* ***know*** *the thoughts of men, help, my saviour, with your own handiwork, almighty God, according to your great compassion.*

As a consequence, whether a particular instance of *nu* in initial position should be interpreted as a temporal/causal conjunction or not depends not merely on purely formal (syntactical) criteria, but also on how the reader interprets the meaning of a particular sentence. The border between adverb and conjunction can thus sometimes be somewhat fuzzy, hence the frequent designation of such markers as adverbs/conjunctions, following Mitchell (1985: § 2418).[18]

80% of all clauses in both languages. As for the direct object, when there is one, it is located after the subject and before the finite verb in more than 80% of all adverbial clauses in poetry (Cichosz 2010: 174–192).

16. For other instances with that word order without any notion of causality, see for example *Beowulf* 1818 and 2053–2054, *Elene* 813 (OE), *Heliand* 4007b and 5756 (OS).

17. For other instances with an apparently similar causal/temporal meaning, but with an atypical word order, see for example *Judgment Day II* 68–70, *Exodus* 420, *Genesis B* 836b–837a (OE), *Genesis* 655, *Heliand* 3854b6–3855 (OS). It must be noted that in most instances the verb is not in final position, but does not appear in initial or second position either: it appears relatively late in the clause but can be followed by various phrases, and even with verbal elements as in *Genesis B* 836b–837a, where the finite verb is followed by the direct object and a past participle.

18. Lenker (2010: 49) interestingly notes that conjunctions and adverbs with connective functions were not perceived as different categories by grammarians until the 18th century.

2.3 Possible MP uses

MPs in Germanic languages are typically located in the middle field, i.e. within the verbal bracket. As seen above, this is also a place where lexical uses of an adverb can be expected. However, unlike lexical adverbs, MPs are typically unstressed and they occupy a relatively fixed position within the middle field. In our corpus, there is one syntactic position that matches those criteria: the position immediately following the finite verb. In Old English, that position is very common for *nu* and typically occurs when the finite verb is in initial position: 112 occurrences in total (or 26% of all clauses, which makes it the most common position for *nu* in that corpus), 99 of which have their finite verb in initial position.[19] It is also a very common position for *þa* ('then'), whose pragmatic uses are well-established (Enkvist & Wårvik 1987; Enkvist 1994; Wårvik 1994, 2011; Kim 1992) and for several other short words with connective functions such as *eft*, *þonne* or *þeah* (see Lenker 2010, appendix B).[20] In Old Saxon, the position is attested, though it is much less common: 20 occurrences in total (or 13% of all clauses, which makes it only the fourth most common position for *nu* in that corpus), only 7 of which have their finite verb in initial position.

2.3.1 *Following imperatives*

The post-verbal position is very common with imperatives. In Old English, 48 of the 112 relevant clauses have an imperative (or 43%) and 48 of the 51 imperatives found in the same clause as *nu* use that syntactic pattern (or 94%). Imperatives are especially frequent when the verb occurs in initial position (V1) and is immediately followed by *nu*. They can also be found in slightly modified forms of that pattern, but the further from the dominant pattern a form is, the less frequent imperatives become. In Old Saxon, only 4 of the 20 post-verbal uses of *nu* follow an imperative (20%) and 4 of the 5 imperatives found in the same clause as *nu* follow that pattern (80%). The few existing occurrences seem to occur in the same constructions as in Old English.

19. Those figures include 91 occurrences where the finite verb is immediately followed by *nu* and 21 where a personal pronoun is inserted between the finite verb and *nu*. Those occurrences have been included because they are very similar in terms of contents and thus seem to correspond to the same pattern.

20. Lenker examines what she calls the 'post-first-position', wherever the connector occurs after the first position, whether that position is occupied by a verb or by another element such as a noun phrase. However, in the corpus studied here, there are only two occurrences of *nu* in 'post-first-position' after an element other than the finite verb in Old English (none in Old Saxon), and only a few more if clauses where the 'first' element is preceded by *hwæt* or by a negation are included.

Table 2. Use of the imperative in clauses where the finite verb is (almost) immediately followed by *nu*

	Old English	Old Saxon
V1 *nu*	41 out of 80 (51%)	2 out of 3 (67%)
V1 personal pronoun *nu*	6 out of 19 (32%)	2 out of 4 (50%)
V2 *nu*	1 out of 11 (9%)	0 out of 6 (0%
V2 personal pronoun *nu*	0 out of 2 (0%)	0 out of 7 (0%)
Total	43% (48/112)	4 out of 20 (20%)

(9) (OE) **Temað nu** and wexað, tudre fyllað (*Genesis A* 196)

Grow now and increase, fill with progeny...

(10) (OE) Weorð me **nu** milde, meotud ælmihtig (*Andreas* 902)

Be *kind to me* ***now****, almighty ruler...*

(11) (OS) **Hôriad nu** huô thie blindun (*Heliand* 3661a)

Hear now *how the blind...*

(12) (OS) ac **îli** thu **nu** ofstlîco endi them erlon cûði (*Heliand* 5935)

but ***hasten*** *(you)* ***now*** *quickly and reveal to the earls...*

In such instances, the lexical verb in the imperative typically carries metrical stress and *nu* is thus located in the dip between the two metrical stresses.[21] The extent to which the temporal value of *nu* is retained in that use is uncertain and probably varies a great deal from one instance to another. With an imperative, *nu*'s temporal meaning comes across as expressing urgency ('do it now rather than later'), which is indeed perceptible in some cases (12; see also OS *Heliand* 5863 and OE *Andreas* 936, *Elene* 313 and *Beowulf* 3101).

However, there are instances where the idea of urgency would seem almost incongruous (9) and in many, if not most of them, it seems as if something more is conveyed, though the nature of that something very much depends on the relationship between speaker and addressee.

When the speaker is in a position of authority, it rather seems as if *nu* is used by them to show they are taking charge (of the general situation or of the conversation in particular, as in 11). When the speaker is not in a position of authority (which does not occur in the few Old Saxon instances we have), it seems that they

21. There are exceptions to that pattern, however: 7 of the 48 relevant Old English imperatives are apparently unstressed, and 1 or 2 of the 4 relevant Old Saxon imperatives (depending on how the hypermetric verse is scanned) is/are similarly unstressed.

are still trying to impose their will through different means, and that the use of *nu* contributes to that strategy. It can come across as expressing some form of affective intensity (10) and/or as connected to a notion of causality: such orders or requests may appear after the mention of a fact justifying the legitimacy of the action required (13)[22] or be supplemented by a clause of justification itself introduced by the conjunction *nu* (14).

(13) (OE) þu eart gescyldend wið sceaðan wæpnum,
ece eadfruma, eallum þinum;
ne læt **nu** bysmrian banan manncynnes,
facnes frumbearn, þurh feondes cræft
leahtrum belecgan þa þin lof berað. (*Andreas* 1291–1295)

You are a protector against the enemy's weapons, eternal origin of bliss, for all your worshippers; **now** *do not let the bane of mankind, the first child of wickedness, through the devil's craft, mock and accuse of shameful acts those who bear your praise.*

(14) (OE) Geþenc **nu**, se mæra maga Healfdenes,
snottra fengel, **nu** ic eom siðes fus,
goldwine gumena, hwæt wit geo spræcon (*Beowulf* 1474–1476)

Think **now**, *illustrious kinsman of Healfdene, wise prince,* **now** *that I am ready for this expedition, gold-giving friend of men, of what we said earlier...*

It might be tempting, in such cases, to translate *nu* by 'as such' or 'so' (comparable with French *donc* in similar contexts). The implication seems to be that it is not only the speaker who requires the action suggested, but the present situation itself.

It is worth noting that there are some instances in Old English (none in Old Saxon, probably due to the small number of imperatives overall) where an imperative is followed by an instance of *nu* which carries metrical stress. There are 2 instances in post-verbal position (15) and (16) and 3 further in the clause, see (17) and (18), where *nu* has to receive metrical stress because of its syntactic position.[23]

22. There is one very similar instance in Old Saxon (*Heliand* 879), except in that case *nu* appears in initial position before the verb and not in typical MP position. That pattern in only found once in the Old Saxon corpus and none at all in the Old English one.

23. Kuhn's First Law requires adverbs such as *nu* to occur in the first unstressed portion of the clause when they are unstressed themselves; if they occur later, they have to be stressed (Kuhn 1933).

(15) (OE) 'Onhicgað **nu** halige mihte,
wise wundor godes! (…)' (*Daniel* 472–473a)

'Consider ***now*** *the holy power, the wise miracle of God! (…)'*

(16) (OE) Geþinga us **nu** þristum wordum
þæt he us ne læte leng owihte
in þisse deaðdene gedwolan hyran (*Christ I* 342–344)

Intercede for us ***now*** *with bold words, so that he does not leave us any longer in this valley of death to obey a wicked one*

(17) (OE) Cyð ricene **nu**
hwæt ðu þæs to þinge þafian wille. (*Elene* 607b–608)

Make known quickly ***now*** *what you will consent to in this matter.*

(18) (OE) Wes þissum leodum **nu**
and mægburge minre arfæst (*Genesis A* 2825b–2826)

Be kind to these people ***now*** *and to my tribe…*

Metrical stress is usually found on lexical items. However, in terms of meaning and context, how such instances differ from those examined above (9)–(14) is not obvious. In one case (17), there is a sense of urgency compatible with *nu*'s temporal meaning, but in the others, (15), (16) and (18), such a temporal meaning is not particularly prominent, certainly not more prominent than in some of the other examples quoted above (see in particular 10, 13 and 14, which express similar ideas). In fact, one of these quotations (15) has a better claim than most to a text-connective use of *nu*: the speaker asks the audience to consider the power of God at the beginning of a speech concerned with that very topic. While *nu* is stressed in all four examples, it is possible that it is perceived as more lexical in the latter two (17) and (18), where its syntactic (and not just metrical) position is more typical of a lexical item. In any case, the existence of such examples suggests a continuity between typical lexical uses and what does appear as a convincing MP use: in such uses, *nu* carries pragmatic meanings that go beyond its original semantic content, but it is probably not perceived as a wholly distinct word.

2.3.2 *Other post-verbal uses of* nu

It is difficult to find other uses of *nu* showing both formal and functional characteristics of MPs. In Old Saxon, the prevalence of the verb 'to be' with post-verbal *nu* is striking at first sight,[24] but closer examination shows a clear temporal meaning in most instances and the apparent homogeneousness is belied by the great variety of syntactic patterns, including two questions and one hypothetical clause.

The Old English evidence is more plentiful as there are many post-verbal instances of *nu* in assertive clauses (61, to be precise), most of them (50, or 82%) with the verb in initial position. A handful of them are actually very similar in function to the instances studied above: they do not use the imperative, but they still convey an injunction.

(19) (OE) Scealt **nu** dædum rof,
æðeling anhydig, ealle mægene
feorh ealgian (*Beowulf* 2666b–2668a)

You must ***now****, renowned for your deeds, a resolute nobleman, defend your life with all your strength.*

(20) (OE) Nu is sæl cumen,
þrea ormæte, is **nu** þearf mycel
þæt we wisfæstra wordum hyran. (*Andreas* 1165b–1167)

Now that this fate has come, an extraordinary calamity, there is ***now*** *great need that we should listen to the words of the wise.*

The existence of such sentences is interesting, because it suggests that *nu* has an affinity with a certain type of pragmatic function (injunctions) and not merely with a certain verb form. However, there are only 3 instances in total, so this is a marginal pattern in our corpus.

As with Old Saxon, the verb 'to be' is strikingly common (28 instances, or 46% of assertive clauses with post-verbal *nu*). That verb is almost always unstressed and its presence at the beginning of a clause seems to be attracting other potentially unstressed words such as *nu*. This hypothesis is confirmed by the fact that the verb 'be' is very rare in clauses where *nu* occurs later in the clause (7 of 76 clauses or 9%), but very common when *nu* occurs in initial position just before it (31 of 45 clauses or 69%). It thus seems likely that, in some instances at least, metrical factors influence the decision to select a particular pattern.

While metre is definitely a factor, it is not the only one. Metrically, *nu is* and *is nu* are strictly equivalent, for instance, and both word orders are found in our corpus. Functionally, both word orders are commonly used to introduce a new state of affairs, sometimes with pathetic overtones. Formally, the two patterns show some differences in the type of subjects they favour. Pre-verbal *nu* is sometimes

24. It is used in 11 of the 20 occurrences of the pattern and its variants: V1 *nu* (1/3), V1 personal pronoun *nu* (2/4), V2 *nu* (6/6), V2 personal pronoun *nu* (2/7).

found with the first person, very rarely with the second,[25] and extremely often with the third (18, 2 and 80% respectively). With post-verbal *nu*, the first person is present in a similar proportion (16%), and the third is also dominant (67%), but the second person is more common (16%). Most instances are confrontational to some extent: the speaker typically requires the addressee to examine their own self or their own behaviour in some way.

(21) (OE) Eart ðu **nu** dumb ond deaf, ne synt þine dreamas awiht.
(*Soul & Body I* 65)

You are **now** dumb and deaf; all your joys are nothing.

(22) (OE) and þu lignest **nu** þæt sie lifgende,
se ofer deoflum dugeþum wealdeð. (*Daniel* 763–764)

and **now** you deny that the one who rules above the armies of devils is alive.

It is interesting that the pattern favoured for imperatives (and other injunctions) is also apparently favoured by other utterances oriented towards the addressee, where the speaker tries to control the behaviour of the addressee in some way. Differences between the types of meaning conveyed by post-verbal and pre-verbal *nu* are not so marked as to suggest the existence of two distinct markers, but this apparent affinity of post-verbal *nu* with the second person could be fertile ground for the development of a genuine marker of intersubjectivity.

Another interesting formal feature of post-verbal *nu* is how often the subject is implicit. In Old English, personal pronoun subjects are much more likely to be found before the finite verb than after (Cichosz 2010: 98–103). Therefore, personal pronouns subjects are relatively rare with post-verbal *nu* (which usually has its finite verb in initial position, see above) and pre-verbal *nu* (when *nu* is immediately before the finite verb), especially in the third person.[26] In our corpus, all 36 instances of pre-verbal *nu* with a third-person subject have an expressed subject, usually a noun phrase. On the other hand, the subject is implicit in 12 of the 41 instances of post-verbal *nu* with a third-person subject.[27] This means there must

25. There is only one instance in our corpus (out of 45 clauses), where the pronoun is attached to the verb (*Christ and Satan* 57b).

26. With pre-verbal *nu*, 3 of the 8 first-person subjects are expressed and so is the only instance of a second-person subject. There is only one third-person pronominal subject. With post-verbal *nu* in assertive clauses, 4 of the 10 first-person and 6 of the 10 second person subjects are pronominal, and there is only 1 instance of a third-person pronoun, in a sentence where the finite verb is not in initial position.

27. And in several of the clauses with first- and second-person subjects, see footnote above.

be some continuity with what precedes, as the referent of the subject has to be recoverable. As a consequence, the pattern is more likely to be found as a form of conclusion, to state the new state resulting from previous actions.

The lack of an expressed subject also automatically focuses the attention on the predicate, which tends to be the newest information. This could reinforce the impression that a radically new state of affairs is presented. It must be noted that the use of the verb in initial position itself already conveys that idea (Petrova 2006: 159), so it is difficult to pinpoint what exactly post-verbal *nu* contributes to the pattern. Since in many cases a notion of temporality (and often of contrast with an earlier state) is still present and since in Old Saxon, where the finite verb is rarely found in initial position, no recognizable pattern of this type seems to exist for assertive clauses, it seems very likely that the pragmatic function initially came from the fronting of the finite verb at least as much as from *nu*'s lexical (temporal) meaning and that post-verbal *nu* absorbed part of that function through its close association with the verb.

2.3.3 *Concluding remarks on potential MP uses*

The available evidence suggests that the patterns we have identified as potential MP uses have evolved from the conjunction of several factors: imperative mood, verb in initial position and presence of the temporal adverb *nu*. It seems that the association of the imperative mood with the other two factors has become conventionalized enough that it is legitimate to talk of a new construction or new usage (which can be called 'MP').

In Old English, even without the imperative mood, the marked word-order contributes to the impression of prominence or added intensity, while the actualizing properties of temporal *nu* tie the utterance more closely to the situation of utterance and the speaker. Together, those two factors have the potential to enhance the forcefulness and the legitimacy of an utterance. Interestingly (perhaps as the result of contamination from the pattern using the imperative), a number of those sentences are explicitly oriented towards the addressee, conveying a form of judgment on the speaker's part.

However, in such cases the evidence for conventionalization is not so strong: it might be fairer to treat such instances as the type of adverbial uses allowing pragmatic inference from which the MP use was able to emerge than as MP uses as such.

2.4 Possible DM uses

In verse, it is impossible for a marker not to be integrated prosodically at all. It is certainly impossible for a word like *nu* to appear as a separate intonation group, so such a criterion cannot apply here. Additionally, clause boundaries tend to coincide with verse boundaries and Kuhn's Law predicts that a word like *nu* will have to receive metrical stress (and will thus be more likely to be interpreted as a lexical element) if it is found at the end of a verse. As a consequence, the only peripheral position where one might expect to find a DM in Old English and Old Saxon is the initial position. Old English and Old Saxon differ significantly in how they handle that position, however, so they will have to be examined separately.

2.4.1 *Possible DM uses in Old Saxon*

Like most Germanic languages, Old Saxon is a verb-second language, which means that if *nu* occurs in initial position it will normally be followed by the finite verb immediately (negations do not count).[28] Such a position is quite typical for an adverb, so no formal feature can differentiate adverbs from potential DMs in that position.

The pre-verbal position is the most common in the Old Saxon corpus, representing about a third of all occurrences of *nu* (50 out of 155 or 32%). There are almost as many occurrences of *nu* late in the middle field (i.e. not immediately after the finite verb) or beyond the verbal bracket (37 and 9 respectively, representing 30% of all occurrences together). Since the late position is almost certainly lexical, it is interesting to compare the two, to see if the pre-verbal position is associated with different functions.

One important difference concerns predominantly temporal and/or pathetic uses. In the late position, those meanings are clearly present in 43% and 26% of occurrences respectively (sometimes together).[29] In the pre-verbal position, such meanings can still be found, but less often: 12% of occurrences for each. Very often (in 28 occurrences out of 50 or 56%), pre-verbal *nu* is used to draw attention to a new state of affairs (23). In that case, the speaker is taking responsibility for pointing to the new fact, but that fact is often available to the addressee in some way, either because it is the consequence of what happened or was said just before (24) or, more frequently, because that fact is perceptible in the situation.

(23) (OS) 'ic scal eu', [quað] [he], 'liobara thing,
[suîðo] uuârlîco uuilleon seggean,
cûðean craft mikil: **nu** is Krist geboran
an theser*o selbun naht, sâlig barn godes,
an [thera] Dauides burg, drohtin the gôdo. (*Heliand* 397b–401)

28. Unless, of course, the finite verb occurs in final position, which is usually the position expected for subordinate clauses, though poetry shows some exceptions to that trend, see 2.2. above.

29. Since the same instance of *nu* can combine two meanings (temporal value and presentation of new fact or temporal and pathetic value, for instance), some instances are counted twice in this paragraph.

I am going to tell you, he said, very truly and eagerly, about something more pleasant, to reveal a great power: ***now*** *Christ is born on this very night, the blessed child of God, in David's city, the good lord.*

(24) (OS) Thuo an forahtun uuarđ
Kain aftar them quidiun drohtinas, quađ that hie uuisse [garoo,]
that is ni mahti uuerđan [uualdand] uuiht, an [uueroldstundu]
dâdeo bidernid, 'sô ik is nu mag drûbundian hugi,' quađ he,
'beran an mînun breostun, thes ik mînan bruođar sluog
thuru mîn handmegin. **Nu** uuêt ik, that ik scal an thînum heti libbian,
forđ an [thînun] fîundscepi, nu ik mi thesa firina gideda
(*Genesis* 646b–650)[30]

Then, Cain grew afraid after the words of the lord, he said that he knew completely that none of his deeds could ever be hidden from the ruler: 'So I can now bear in my heart', he said, 'his grieving mind, because I slew my brother with the power of my hands. ***Now*** *I know that I shall live in your hatred, henceforth in your enmity, now I have done this crime...'.*

The fact that it is perceptible may even be made explicit (25). In such cases, it seems as if the point of the utterance is not so much to impart new information as to call onto the addressee to acknowledge the new state of affair. Indeed, there are even cases where the speaker is pointedly drawing attention to a fact that is very well-known to the addressee, but is considered jarring or unexpected enough to deserve pointing out (26, especially the second instance).

(25) (OS) **nu** maht thu sie sehan standen hêr
an sundiun bifangan: saga huat thu [is] uuillies.' (*Heliand* 3854b–3855)[31]

'... ***now*** *you can see her standing here, snared with sins: say of it what you will.'*

(26) (OS) **Nu** sint thîna gesti sade,
sint thîne druhtingos druncane suîðo,
is thit folc [frômôd]: **nu** hêtis thu hîr forð dragan
alloro lîðo lofsamost (*Heliand* 2060b–2063a)

Now *your guests have had their fill, the members of your retinue are very drunk, this crowd is cheerful:* ***now*** *you order to have brought forth the best fruit-wine of all....*

30. See also *Genesis* 656, which is very similar.

31. See also *Genesis* 557.

Such uses of *nu* show a complex overlay of functions and meanings. The temporal meaning may have receded in the background, but it is still valid (most obviously in (23), which, of the examples quoted here, is closest to a 'simple' temporal meaning), and it is difficult to separate *nu*'s connective and intersubjective functions. It clearly points forward, to something that is both a new fact and a new topic for conversation, but that new element does not appear out of nowhere. It is typically connected to the pre-existing situation in some way (as its result or, on the contrary, as a challenge). The intersubjective value of *nu* is based on that very dynamic: on the one hand, the speaker is taking charge, stirring the conversation in a new direction and deciding what is worth commenting on in the present situation, but on the other hand, they are also trying to legitimize that move through an appeal to some common ground, something both interactants can agree on (because they both know it or see it, for instance).

Another common use of pre-verbal *nu* (19 instances or 38%) is to express the intent of the speaker, either as a protagonist (27) or specifically as a speaker (28) and (29).

(27) (OS) **Nu** uuilliu ik thi an helpun uuesen (*Heliand* 2956b)[32]
Now I want to be of help to you…

(28) (OS) '**Nu** scal ik is thi biddean', quað he (*Genesis* 814a)
'**Now** I shall ask you for it', he said…

(29) (OS) **Nu** seggiu ik iu te uuârun thoh (*Heliand* 5092b)
Now I say to you however truly….

Such examples show obvious similarities with those already commented on: they allow the speaker both to connect a new stage in the discourse with what precedes and to adopt a particular stance as the one in charge of where the conversation is going. The pragmatic meanings observed are consistent enough and recurring often enough that it seems legitimate to consider they are already conventionalized to a certain extent. At the same time, the lack of identifiable distinctive formal features and of traces of genuine semantic bleaching (all instances are compatible with *nu*'s temporal meaning, even if that meaning may not seem predominant)[33] suggest that *nu*'s transformation into a genuine DM, distinct from the temporal adverb, is still under way.

32. See also *Genesis* 770b–772a. In most cases, the utterance actually concerns what the speaker wants the addressee to do rather than what they want to do themselves: see *Heliand* 704b–705, 879b–880, 1359b–1360, 1888b and 2824b–2825a.

33. On that topic, see further Louviot (forthcoming).

2.4.2 *Possible DM uses in Old English*

The Old English situation is made more complex by the fact Old English obeys the verb-second rule less strictly than other Germanic languages (in verse as in prose), which means that it is not uncommon for more than one element (but rarely more than two) to be found before the finite verb, even when the verb is not in final position. When *nu* occurs before a non-final finite verb, it will be in initial position (not taking into account conjunctions such as *and*), which means that two word orders are possible: *nu* + verb and *nu* + X + verb. In our corpus, there are 45 instance of pre-verbal *nu* (11%) and 32 instances of pre-initial *nu* (8%).

It is worth considering whether those two options behave similarly from a pragmatic point of view or whether there are noticeable differences between the two patterns. This is all the more tempting as, X + verb being the expected word order in a V–2 language, *nu* + X + verb suggests that *nu* is in a particularly peripheral position, somehow outside the regular boundaries of the clause, i.e. exactly where one would expect to find a DM (hence our label 'pre-initial').

2.4.2.1 *Syntactic differences between the two patterns.* Examination of the Old English poetic corpus reveals that there are a number of syntactic differences (beyond word order) between the two patterns, which means that the choice between them may not be based exclusively (or primarily) on pragmatic criteria. The most striking difference resides in the nature of the subject. As stated above, pronominal subjects are much more likely to be found before the finite verb than after in Old English (Cichosz 2010: 98–103). As a consequence, pronominal subjects are very rare with pre-verbal *nu*: one example is found in *Christ and Satan* (57b–58), where the pronoun is cliticized (*earttu* for *eart þu*, 'you are') and six occurrences are found in *Genesis B*, which is translated from (and thus influenced by) Old Saxon. The only genuine example I have found in Old English poetry is *Riddle 40* 98–99 (*Nu hafu ic in heafde*, 'Now I have on my head').

By contrast, pronominal subjects are very common with pre-initial *nu*. The element inserted between *nu* and the finite verb is the subject in most cases (27 out of 32 instances or 84%) and that subject is almost always pronominal (24 out of 27 instances or 89%). Some scholars interpret such pronouns as clitics (see in particular generative works such as van Kemenade 1987 and Pintzuk 1996) and would thus see *nu* as occupying the initial, rather than the pre-initial position. Whatever the pertinence of the clitic interpretation regarding Old English syntax more generally (and it is much beyond the scope of this paper to venture an opinion on it), it must be granted that it cannot account for all cases of pre-initial *nu*.

In our corpus, there are 3 instances where the position between *nu* and the finite verb is filled by a lexical subject (*Beowulf* 939b, *Riming Poem* 43, *Husband's Message* 43), 2 where it is filled by a pronominal object (*Exodus* 421 and *Genesis B*

816a), 1 where it is filled by a lexical object (*Riddle 93* 28), and 2 where it is filled by an adverbial phrase (*Andreas* 66b and *Guthlac B* 1298b). It may also be the case that the pronominal subject is supplemented by another element such as the pronominal element *self* (30) or a name in apposition (31), in which case the clitic interpretation seems harder to maintain.

(30) (OE) **Nu** þu sylfa meaht
on sefan þinum soð gecnawan (*Juliana* 341–342)[34]
Now you can acknowledge the truth yourself in your mind...

(31) (OE) **Nu** ðu, Andreas, scealt edre geneðan in gramra gripe.
(*Andreas* 950–951a)[35]
Now you Andreas shall venture at once within the grasp of angry people.

Such examples suggest that there really is a syntactic position that can be filled between *nu* and the finite verb, even if that syntactic position is more available to some elements than others.

2.4.2.2 *Pragmatic differences between the two patterns.* As noted above (2.3.2), pre-verbal *nu* is very often found with the verb 'to be' (31 instance out of 45 or 69%). Examination of the actual clauses shows a pragmatic use of *nu* very similar to what has already been observed for Old Saxon (2.4.1) and for some of the Old English instances of post-verbal *nu* in assertive clauses (2.3.2): whether the finite verb is 'to be' or not, the speaker is typically calling attention, not to an action that is ongoing at the time of utterance, but rather to a new state of affairs, sometimes even to the beginning of a new era (32).

As with Old Saxon, the information presented is not necessarily a new, as yet unknown fact that the speaker chooses to impart to the addressee. In many cases, the speaker is actually calling attention to something that is already known or perceptible in some way (to the speaker, but also to the addressee and/or the audience), a fact which may be made explicit (33).

(32) (OE) **Nu** sceal sincþego ond swyrdgifu,
eall eðelwyn eowrum cynne,
lufen alicgean; (*Beowulf* 2884–2886a)

Now the receiving of treasure and the giving of swords, all the enjoyment of a native land, the beloved homeland of your people shall cease.

34. See also *Andreas* 340 and *Elene* 1120. *Christ I* 149b is also similar, but it has not been included here because it is ambiguous in that the verb could be interpreted as occurring in final position.

35. See also *Genesis A* 1906b–1907, which could not be included because the verb could be interpreted as final.

(33) (OE) **Nu** is undyrne
werum æt wine hu þa wihte mid us,
heanmode twa, hatne sindon. (*Riddle* 42 15b–17)[36]

Now it is revealed to men at their wine how the creatures, the two abject ones, are called among us.

Such utterances display undeniable, yet rudimentary pragmatic features. The speaker uses *nu* to introduce a new object of interest in the conversation, which means that it contributes both to structuring the speaker's discourse and to establishing the speaker as a witness or as a guide pointing to what needs witnessing. *Nu*'s position at the beginning of the clause seems to facilitate this text-structuring function: while, in our corpus, pre-verbal *nu* is slightly less common than post-verbal *nu* in an assertive clause and while both positions can be used to introduce a new state of affairs, pre-verbal *nu* is much more often used at the very beginning of a speech than post-verbal *nu* (9 out of 45 or 20% against 3 out of 61 or 5%).

However, in many instances, pre-verbal *nu*'s temporal meaning is still very much present and the new element pointed to is usually a new element in the world and not a new element in discourse. *Riddle 42* (quote 33 above) is actually quite exceptional in that here, for once, *nu* seems to refer to the time of the riddle's utterance as such: it comes at the end of the riddle, when the audience is expected to be able to solve the mystery.

Pre-initial *nu* is different from pre-verbal *nu* in that its intersubjective dimension is much more pronounced. Whereas pre-verbal *nu* and post-verbal *nu* in assertive clauses are predominantly found with third-person subjects, such subjects are a minority here (8 out of 32 clauses or 25%). Interestingly, only one of those third-person subjects is pronominal, even though pronominal subjects are the norm for this pattern.[37] The type of verbs encountered is also different: the verb *beon* is still relatively common (8 clauses out of 32, 5 of which with the 1st person singular pronoun *ic*), but modals (especially *magan*, 'be able to', 10 instances) and verbs of perception (sensory or intellectual, 11 instances in total) are very characteristic of that pattern.

Three main uses of pre-initial *nu* may be identified. First, with the verb *beon* and the first person, there are a few instances where the pattern is used to call attention to the (pathetic) state of the addressee (34).

36. Similar instances include *Andreas* 1602 and *Christ and Satan* 228 and 439.

37. Lexical third-person subjects are found both after the finite verb (when another element is inserted between *nu* and the finite verb) and before it: in that case, they are relatively short: *min hreþer* ('my heart', *Rhyming Poem* 43a), *scealc* ('a soldier', *Beowulf* 939b) and *se mon* ('the man', *Husband's Message* 43b).

(34) (OE) **Nu** ic eom orwena
þæt unc se eðylstæf æfre weorðe
gifeðe ætgædere. Ic eom geomorfrod! (*Genesis A* 2224b–2226)[38]

Now I am without hope that to us together a family support will ever be granted. I am old with sadness!

Such instances are not radically different from those observed in verb-second clauses, except for the fact the new information presented is perhaps more obviously emotionally charged (something which, incidentally, also brings them closer to lexical, pathetic uses of *nu* in medial position).

Second, as in Old Saxon, there are a number of instances expressing the speaker's intent regarding the addressee, especially what they allow or want them to do (35).

(35) (OE) **Nu** ðu, Andreas, scealt edre geneðan
in gramra gripe. (*Andreas* 950–951b)[39]

Now you Andreas must at once venture into the grasp of cruel ones.

There is a strong intersubjective dimension in such examples, which is not very different from that observed in possible MP uses of *nu* after imperatives.

Third, there are quite a few instances (typically with 2nd person pronouns associated to the modal *magan* and a lexical verb of sensory or intellectual perception) where a new fact is presented, but the emphasis has shifted from the fact itself to its availability to the addressee (36) and (37).

(36) (OE) **Nu** ðu miht gehyran, hæleð min se leofa,
þæt ic bealuwara weorc gebiden hæbbe,
sarra sorga. (*Dream of the Rood* 78–80a)

Now you can hear, my dearest man, that I, the work of criminals, have endured harsh pains.

38. See also *Christ and Satan* 155b–158 and 176, and, with an additional adverb of intensity, *Guthlac B* 1268–1269.

39. See also *Judgment Day II* 82, *Maldon* 175, *Resignation* 41, *Guthlac A* 6 and *Beowulf* 395, and, to some extent, *Christ III* 1327 and *Andreas* 1179–1180a. It is worth noting that whereas *sculan* ('shall') has an epistemic value when it is used with the first pattern, it has a deontic value here (see also *Judgment Day* II 82).

(37) (OE) **Nu** ðu miht gecnawan þæt þe cyning engla
gefrætwode furður mycle
giofum geardagum þonne eall gimma cynn. (*Andreas* 1517–1519)[40]

Now you can perceive/understand that the king of angels has adorned you in days of old with graces much superior to all the family of gems.

Such instances occur after an explanation or a narrative and, to some extent, demand from the addressee that they acknowledge common ground with the speaker, that they recognize that they accept the truth and validity of what has just been said. It is striking that the verb of choice is *gehyran* and not *geseon*:[41] the speaker is not referring to events the addressee has witnessed directly, but to information conveyed through discourse. Of all the uses of *nu* examined in this paper, those probably have the strongest connection to the level of discourse.

It seems then that there is a genuine difference between the two possible word orders, but that it is not a simple matter of adverbial vs. DM use or less pragmatic vs. more pragmatic use. When *nu* is used in initial position in Old English poetry, it tends to express conventional pragmatic meanings that go beyond mere temporality, whether the verb occurs in second position or not. However, the pre-verbal pattern is typically used in less intersubjective contexts, to draw attention to a new object of interest that usually lies outside discourse, whereas the pre-initial pattern is typically used in very intersubjective contexts, which may be concerned with the speaker and addressee as actors in the world (expressing the speaker's state of mind or trying to influence the addressee in some way) or with the speaker and addressee as discourse interactants (demanding acknowledgement of what has just been said).

It is quite possible that the difference between the two patterns originates from a simple difference in the syntactical behaviour of pronominal and lexical subjects, but it seems likely that the differentiation has conventionalized beyond syntax: if syntax was still the only factor at play, we would expect to see more instances

40. Similar examples include *Andreas* 340–341a, 595 and 811, *Elene* 511, *Juliana* 341b–342 (quote 30 above). See also (without *magan*) *Resignation* 25–26, *Genesis A* 916 and *Psalm 50* 31, as well as (with a plural) *Andreas* 1197 and 1558.

41. I have found only one similar instance with *geseon* in Old English poetry (*Elene* 1120, without *magan* and with a first person plural pronoun as subject). The Old English prose corpus shows a dozen prototypical instances of the same pattern and there too the verbs of choice are *gehyran* and verbs of more abstract perception and understanding (*ongitan, tocnawan* and *oncnawan*), with only two instances of *geseon*.

where a 3rd person pronoun is used with pre-initial *nu*,[42] or more instances of verbs other than *beon* in clauses with pre-verbal *nu*.

That being said, it must be noted that, as with Old Saxon, the emergence of *nu* as a full DM is still underway: while some pragmatic uses of *nu* are clearly already conventionalized to some extent, they remain compatible with *nu*'s temporal meaning and in most cases reference is made to events outside discourse itself.

2.4.3 *Concluding remarks on potential DM uses*

Whether in Old English or in Old Saxon, the use of *nu* in initial position inherently favours the development of connective functions: located at the boundary between two clauses, *nu* allows the speaker to introduce a new object of interest in the conversation. Usually, that object does not come out of the blue: in the same way that temporal uses are oriented towards the present and/or the future while also implying some kind of contrast with the past, pragmatic uses of *nu* in initial position are oriented towards the new topic, but usually imply some form of connection between that topic and what has been said or done before.

In both languages, such uses of *nu* also have an intersubjective dimension: the speaker is claiming the right to take the conversation in a new direction and can appeal to the hearer's perception to justify the (present) relevance of the new topic. Both languages also use *nu* in initial position to reinforce utterances where the speaker expresses an intent to act on the addressee in some way: in terms of function, such utterances have much in common with the potential MP uses of *nu* with imperatives.

However, in the (admittedly much smaller and less diversified) Old Saxon corpus, more obviously intersubjective uses of *nu* are not characterized by any distinctive formal feature and few utterances focus on discourse as such. By contrast, Old English shows a differentiation between two possible word orders, pre-verbal *nu* being used to present new events (usually in the world and not in discourse) and pre-initial *nu* for more obviously intersubjective utterances. One pattern (*nu* + 2nd person pronoun + *magan* + verb of perception) is especially interesting in that it is used specifically to refer to the preceding discourse: such phrases have a strong argumentative dimension that can be glossed as 'now that I have said all that, you can (you must?) understand that X is true.' In a sense, the speaker is trying to force the addressee to acknowledge common ground.

42. Admittedly, 3rd person pronouns are often omitted in Old English poetry, but they do occur and the same differentiation between 3rd person and 1st/2nd person uses does not appear with other markers such as *þa*: the pattern *þa* + 3rd person pronoun + V is very rarely encountered, but so is *þa* + 2nd/1st person pronoun + V.

3. Conclusion

Two main conclusions can be drawn from the data observed. First, it is clear that, in Old English and Old Saxon verse, there is a continuum between the various meanings and functions of *nu*. Not only is the original temporal meaning still present to some extent in almost all uses of the marker, but there are some signs of continuity between uses of *nu* as a conjunction and potential pragmatic uses, as well as continuity among those pragmatic uses. It is also worth noting that many of the uses identified in of Present-Day Germanic languages are already present: introducing a new topic related yet distinct from what precedes, appealing to knowledge shared by the participants, intensifying directive speech acts.

Second, there is a complex interplay between form and meaning: the existence of a distinctive word order (no matter what its original function is) favours the emergence of recognizable patterns regularly associated with the same pragmatic function. In Old English, the loosening of the verb-second rule leads to more varied word orders, which may have favoured the emergence of distinctive patterns. Over time, such distinctive patterns can lead to the emergence of truly distinct markers (that we may call DMs or MPs for instance), but it is probably premature to consider such markers already exist as separate words in the corpora examined here. It rather seems that we are faced with a single marker showing great versatility in its possible uses.

This could lead us to reconsider the diachronic evolution of DMs and MPs more widely. It may not be a question of determining whether DMs develop from MPs, MPs from DMs, or whether the two develop independently from each other. A fourth scenario is quite possible whereby a single marker develops a variety of more or less conventionalized pragmatic uses, which, for a long period, still show important similarities and can likely still influence each other, but which may eventually become distinct enough (both formally and functionally) to deserve different labels.

References

Primary sources

Behaghel, Otto & Taeger, Burkhard (eds). 1984. *Heliand und Genesis*. Tübingen: Max Niemeyer [*Heliand*].

Behaghel, Otto & Taeger, Burkhard (eds). 1996. *Heliand und Genesis*. Berlin: De Gruyter [*Genesis*].

Dobbie, Elliott Van Kirk (ed.). 1942. *The Anglo-Saxon Minor Poems* [Anglo-Saxon Poetic Records 6]. New York NY: Columbia University Press; London: Routledge and Kegan Paul.

Dobbie, Elliott Van Kirk (ed.). 1953 *Beowulf and Judith* [Anglo-Saxon Poetic Records 4]. New York NY: Columbia University Press.

Krapp, George Philip & Dobbie, Elliott Van Kirk (eds). 1936. *The Exeter Book* [Anglo-Saxon Poetic Records 3]. New York NY: Columbia University Press; London: Routledge and Kegan Paul.

Krapp, George Philip (ed.). 1931. *The Junius Manuscript* [Anglo-Saxon Poetic Records 1]. New York NY: Columbia University Press; London: Routledge and Kegan Paul.

Krapp, George Philip (ed.). 1932a. *The Paris Psalter and the Meters of Boethius* [Anglo-Saxon Poetic Records 5]. New York NY: Columbia University Press; London: Routledge and Kegan Paul.

Krapp, George Philip (ed.). 1932b. *The Vercelli Book* [Anglo-Saxon Poetic Records 2]. New York NY: Columbia University Press.

Secondary sources

Abraham, Werner. 1991. The grammaticization of the German modal particle. In *Approaches to Grammaticalization, Vol. II: Types of Grammatical Markers* [Typological Studies in Language 19:2], Elizabeth Closs Traugot & Bernd Heine (eds), 331–380. Amsterdam: John Benjamins. https://doi.org/10.1075/tsl.19.2.17abr

Aijmer, Karin. 1997. I think: An English modal particle. In *Modality in Germanic Languages. Historical and Comparative Perspective*, Toril Swan & Olaf Jansen Westvik (eds), 1–47. Berlin: Mouton de Gruyter. https://doi.org/10.1515/9783110889932.1

Aijmer, Karin. 2002. *English Discourse Particles: Evidence from a Corpus* [Studies in Corpus Linguistics 10]. Amsterdam: John Benjamins. https://doi.org/10.1075/scl.10

Auer, Peter & Maschler, Yael. 2016. The family of NU and NÅ across the languages of Europe and beyond: Structure, function, and history. In Auer & Maschler (eds), 1–47.

Auer, Peter & Maschler, Yael (eds). 2016. *NU & NÅ: A Family of Discourse Markers across the Languages of Europe and Beyond*. Berlin: Walter de Gruyter.

Betten, Anne. 1992. Sentence connection as an expression of medieval principles of representation. In *Internal and External Factors in Syntactic Change*, Marinel Gerritsen & Dieter Stein (eds), 157–174. Berlin: Mouton de Gruyter. https://doi.org/10.1515/9783110886047.157

Brinton, Laurel J. 1990. The development of discourse markers in English. In *Historical Linguistics and Philology, Jacek Fisiak* [Trends in Linguistics, Studies and Monographs 46], 45–71. Berlin: Mouton de Gruyter. https://doi.org/10.1515/9783110847260.45

Brinton, Laurel J. 2010. Discourse markers. In *Historical Pragmatics*, Andreas H. Jucker & Irma Taavitsainen (eds), 285–314. Berlin: Mouton de Gruyter.

Cichosz, Anna. 2010. *The Influence of Text Type on Word Order of Old Germanic Languages: A Corpus-based Contrastive Study of Old English and Old High German* [Studies in English Medieval Language and Literature 27]. Frankfurt: Peter Lang.

Defour, Tine. 2007. A Diachronic Study of the Pragmatic Markers *Well* and *Now:* Fundamental Research into Semantic Development and Grammaticalisation by Means of a Corpus Study. PhD dissertation, University of Gent.

Degand, Liesbeth, Cornillie, Bert & Pietrandrea, Paola (eds). 2013. *Discourse Markers and Modal Particles: Categorization and Description* [Pragmatics & Beyond New Series 234]. Amsterdam: John Benjamins. https://doi.org/10.1075/pbns.234

Dostie, Gaétane. 2004. *Pragmaticalisation et marqueurs discursifs: Analyse sémantique et traitement lexicographique*. Brussels: De Boeck.

Enkvist, Nils Erik & Wårvik, Brita. 1987. Old English *þa*, temporal claims, and narrative structure. In *Papers from the 7th International Conference on Historical Linguistics* [Current Issues in Linguistic Theory 48], Anna Giacolone Ramat, Onofrio Carruba & Giuliano Bernini (eds), 221–237. Amsterdam: John Benjamins. https://doi.org/10.1075/cilt.48.17enk

Enkvist, Nils Erik. 1994. Problems raised by Old English *þa*. In *Writing vs Speaking: Language, Text, Discourse, Communication* [Tübinger Beiträge zur Linguistik 392], Světla Čmejrková, František Daneš & Eva Havlová (eds) 55–62. Tübingen: Gunter Narr.

Erman, Britt & Kotsinas, Ulla-Britt. 1993. Pragmaticalization: The case of *ba'* and *you know*. *Studier i Modernspråkvetenskap* 10: 76–93.

Fries, Udo. 1993. *Towards a description of text deixis in Old English*. In *Anglo-Saxonica. Hans Schabram zum 65. Geburtstag*, Klaus R. Grinda & Claus-Dieter Wetzel (eds), 527–540. Munich: Wilhelm Fink.

Gardner, Faith F. 1971. *An Analysis of Syntactic Patterns of Old English*. The Hague: Mouton.

Golato, Andrea. 2016. Nu(n) in standard German: Its functions as a temporal adverbial, as an adverbial structuring discourse, and as a modal particle and discourse marker. In Auer & Maschler (eds), 320–355.

Günthner, Susanne & Mutz, Katrin. 2004. Grammaticalization vs. pragmaticalization? The development of pragmatic markers in German and Italian. In *What Makes Grammaticalization? A Look from its Fringes and its Components*, Walter Bisang, Nikolaus P. Himmelmann & Björn Wiemer (eds), 77–107. Berlin: Mouton de Gruyter.

Heine, Bernd, Claudi, Ulrike & Hünnemeyer, Friederike. 1991. *Grammaticalization: A Conceptual Framework*. Chicago IL: The University of Chicago Press.

Hilmisdóttir, Helga. 2011. Giving a tone of determination: The interactional functions of *nú* as a tone particle in Icelandic conversation. *Journal of Pragmatics* 43: 261–287. https://doi.org/10.1016/j.pragma.2010.07.020

Kim, Taejin. 1992. *The Particle 'þa' in the West-Saxon Gospels: A Discourse-Level Analysis* [Europäische Hochschulschriften 14, Angelsächsische Sprache und Literatur 249]. Bern: Peter Lang.

Kuhn, Hans. 1933. Zur Wortstellung und -betonung im Altgermanischen. *Beiträge zur Geschichte der Deutschen Sprache und Literatur* 57: 1–109. https://doi.org/10.1515/bgsl.1933.1933.57.1

Lenker, Ursula. 2000. *Soþlice* and *witodlice*: Discourse markers in Old English. In *Pathways of Change. Grammaticalization in English* [Studies in Language Companion Series 53], Olga Fischer, Anette Rosenbach & Dieter Stein (eds), 229–249. Amsterdam: John Benjamins. https://doi.org/10.1075/slcs.53.12len

Lenker, Ursula. 2010. *Argument and Rhetoric: Adverbial Connectors in the History of English* [Topics in English Linguistics 64]. Berlin: Mouton de Gruyter. https://doi.org/10.1515/9783110216066

Louviot, Elise. Forthcoming. Semantic bleaching of *Nu* in Old Saxon. *Folia Linguistica Historica*.

Mazeland, Harrie. 2016. The positionally sensitive workings of the Dutch particle *nou*. In Auer & Maschler (eds), 377–408.

McLaughlin, John. 1983. *Old English Syntax: A Handbook*. Tübingen: Niemeyer. https://doi.org/10.1515/9783111411590

Metrich, René et al. 1998. Les Invariables Difficiles : Dictionnaire allemand-français des particules, connecteurs, interjections et autres « mots de la communication », vol. 3. Richardmenil: Association des Nouveaux Cahiers d'Allemand.

Mitchell, Bruce. 1985. *Old English Syntax*. Oxford: Clarendon Press. https://doi.org/10.1093/acprof:oso/9780198119357.001.0001

Molencki, Rafał. 1991. *Complementation in Old English*. Katowice: Uniwersytet Śląski.

Ocampo, Francisco. 2006. Movement towards discourse is not grammaticalization: The evolution of *claro* from adjective to discourse particle in spoken Spanish. In *Selected Proceedings of the 9th Hispanic Linguistics Symposium*, Nuria Sagarra & Almeida Jacqueline Toribio (eds), 308–319. Somerville MA: Cascadilla Proceedings Project.

Pérennec, Marcel. 1995. Von Zeitdeiktika zu Text-und Diskurskonnektoren: Überlegungen zur sprachlichen Temporalität. In *Rand und Band: Abgrenzung und Verknüpfung als Grundtendenzen des Deutschen, Festschrift für Eugène Faucher zum 60*. René Metrich and Marcel Vuillaume (eds), 299–314. Tübingen: Gunter Narr.

Petrova, Svetlana. 2006. A discourse-based approach to verb placement in early West-Germanic. In *Interdisciplinary Studies on Information Structure* 5, Shinichiro Ishihara, Michaela Schmitz & Anne Schwarz (eds), 153–185. Potsdam: Universitätsverlag.

Pintzuk, Susan. 1996. Cliticization in Old English. In *Approaching Second: Second Position Clitics and Related Phenomena*, Aaron L. Halpern & Arnold M. Zwicky (eds), 375–409. Stanford CA: CSLI.

Saari, Mirja & Lehti-Eklund, Hanna. 2016. The Swedish *nu*: A historical perspective. In Auer & Maschler (eds), 409–441.

Schiffrin, Deborah. 1987. *Discourse Markers*. Cambridge: CUP. https://doi.org/10.1017/CBO9780511611841

Traugott, Elizabeth Closs & Trousdale, Graeme. 2013. *Constructionalization and Constructional Changes*. Oxford: OUP. https://doi.org/10.1093/acprof:oso/9780199679898.001.0001

Traugott, Elizabeth Closs. 1982. From propositional to textual and expressive meanings: Some semantic-pragmatic aspects of grammaticalization. In *Perspectives on Historical Linguistics* [Current Issues in Linguistic Theory 24], Winfred P. Lehman & Yakov Malkiel (eds), 245–271. Amsterdam: John Benjamins. https://doi.org/10.1075/cilt.24.09clo

Traugott, Elizabeth Closs. 1989. On the rise of epistemic meanings in English: An example of subjectification in semantic change. *Language* 65: 31–55. https://doi.org/10.2307/414841

Traugott, Elizabeth Closs. 1995. The role of the development of discourse markers in a theory of grammaticalization. Paper presented at the ICHL XII, Manchester. Version of 11/97. <http://www.stanford.edu/~traugott/ect-papersonline.html>

Traugott, Elizabeth Closs. 2003. From subjectification to intersubjectification. In *Motives for Language Change*, Raymond Hickey (ed.), 124–139. Cambridge: CUP. https://doi.org/10.1017/CBO9780511486937.009

Traugott, Elizabeth Closs. 2007. Discussion article: Discourse markers, modal particles, and contrastive analysis, synchronic and diachronic. *Catalan Journal of Linguistics* 6: 139–157.

van Gelderen, Elly. 2001. The syntax of mood particles in the history of English. *Folia Linguistica Historica* 22(1–2): 301–330.

van Kemenade, Ans. 1987. *Syntactic Case and Morphological Case in the History of English*. Dordrecht: Foris.

Waltereit, Richard & Detges, Ulrich. 2007. Different functions, different histories: Modal particles and discourse markers from a diachronic point of view. *Catalan Journal of Linguistics* 6: 61–80.

Wårvik, Brita. 1994. Participants tracking narrative structure: Old English *þa* and topicality. In *Topics and Comments: Papers from the Discourse Project* [Anglicana Turkuensia 13], Sanna-Kaisa Tanskanen & Brita Wårvik (eds), 115–139. Turku: University of Turku.

Wårvik, Brita. 2011. Connective or 'disconnective' discourse marker? Old English *þa*, Multifunctionality and narrative structuring. In *Connectives in Synchrony and Diachrony in European Languages* [Studies in Variation, Contacts and Change in English 8], Anneli Meurman-Solin & Ursula Lenker (eds). <http://www.helsinki.fi/varieng/journal/volumes/08/warvik/>

Wischer, Ilse. 2000. Grammaticalization vs. lexicalization. "methinks" there is some confusion. In *Pathways of Change. Grammaticalization in English* [Studies in Language Companion Series 53], Olga Fischer, Anette Rosenbach & Dieter Stein (eds), 355–370. Amsterdam: John Benjamins. https://doi.org/10.1075/slcs.53.17wis

(Inter)subjectification and paradigmaticization

The case study of the final particle *but*

Sylvie Hancil
University of Rouen

This paper proposes a diachronic analysis of final *but* in a corpus of Northern English, a dialect where final particles represent a characteristic feature of the grammar. Recently, much emphasis was given to the study of *but* from a synchronic perpective in American and Australian English. This investigation closes the gap and is pursued in Northern English in the DECTE corpus, extending over a 50 years' span (1960–2010). The various semantico-pragmatic values are studied diachronically. It is shown that final *but* undergoes the process of paradigmaticization as it enters into the paradigm of final particles by enriching it with lexical and structural persistence. Besides, the subjective values are evaluated on Traugott and Dasher's (2002) subjectivity cline.

Keywords: final particle, Northern English, paradigmaticization, persistence, subjectification

1. Introduction

Since the time of Saussure grammar has often been considered to be an internally coherent structure and a self-contained system. But with the advent of interactional linguistics, this perspective has evolved since the mid-1970s and the understanding of grammar has become dynamic, taking into account the role of the co-speaker and more generally the organization of social life. Recently, the growing interest in the study of final particles in non-Asian languages (see, for instance, Hancil, Haselow & Post 2015) has acknowledged the importance of linguistic expressions that cannot be explained by traditional grammar but by interactional grammar.

https://doi.org.10.1075/slcs.202.12han
© 2018 John Benjamins Publishing Company

This study is situated within this tradition and offers a diachronic analysis of the final particle *but* in the *Diachronic Electronic Corpus of Tyneside English (*DECTE) corpus over a 50-year period (1960–2010). After presenting the previous literature and the data, it explains how the various semantico-pragmatic values have evolved over the periods considered, thereby contributing to not only enriching the spectrum of the traditional contrastive value of *but* but also enlarging the host class of the construction, which corresponds to the definition of grammaticalization by Himmelmann (2004). The analysis shows how the notion of lexical persistence introduced by Hopper (1991) is complemented by the notions of structural persistence (Breban 2009) and procedural persistence for the implicit structure X *but* Y (Hancil 2014). The study also addresses the processes of subjectification and intersubjectification and discusses the hierarchy proposed by Traugott's (2010) subjectivity cline. In addition, there is a need to rehabilitate the notion of paradigm in non-morphological contexts (Nørgård-Sørensen & Heltoft 2015) to comprehend how the final particle *but* is inserted in the grammatical paradigm of final particles and to understand how paradigmaticization partakes of grammaticalization.

2. Previous literature

The phenomenon of final particles has been relatively understudied in European languages. In English, it is the final particle *but* that has attracted the attention of researchers such as Mulder and Thompson (2008) and Mulder, Thompson and Williams (2009) in American and Australian English. Only Hancil (2014, 2015, 2016) has focused her attention on British English. The presence of discourse markers in final position is attested in Northern Englishes, as confirmed by Trudgill (2004) and Clarke (2010), or more recently by Beal, Burbano and Llamas (2012):

> Sentence-final *but*, as in *I don't like it but*, is well known in colloquial Australian English. It does not occur in England, except in Tyneside, but is common in Ireland and Scotland. (Trudgill 2004: 19)

> Sentence-final *but* has been linked to British (particularly northern), Scottish, Irish and Australian English. (Clarke 2010: 153)

> There are a number of sentence-final features that are characteristic of North-Eastern dialects. *But*, for example, may be used in sentence-final position to mean 'though' (e.g. *I'll manage but*), in addition to its standard usage as a conjunction. Such use of *but* has been attested not only in Tyneside but also in Wearside. (Beal, Burbano-Elizondo & Llamas 2012: 92)

Relying on conversation-based corpora of American English and Australian English, Mulder and Thompson (2008: 180) study the behaviour of final *but* and argue for the grammaticalization cline in (1):

(1) Initial *but* >Janus-faced *but* > final *but*
IU-initial conjunction IU-final discourse particle.
IU stands for Initial Unit.

Mulder and Thompson (2008: 195) distinguish six stages on the grammaticalization pathway, which are syntactically described as in (2a–f), respectively. Square brackets indicate an intonation unit, and X and Y semantically conflict each other through a contrast or concessive relationship. The initial and Janus 1 *buts* begin, but the others end, an intonation unit.

(2) a. Initial: X [but Y]
b. Janus 1: X [but,] Y
c. Janus 2: [X but]
d. Final 1 (final hanging): [X but]
e. Indeterminate: [X/Y but]
f. Final 2 (final particle): [Y but]

Janus *buts* are "between" the initial and final buts, and are called "Janus" because they have properties of both "initial" and final *buts*, and can be interpreted as either.

Mulder and Thompson (2008) show that *but* follows a grammaticalization pathway that starts as an "initial *but*" as illustrated in (3a) and becomes "Janus-faced *but*" as exemplified in (3b)-(c) to "final *but*" as shown in (3d)–(f).

(3) a. So he got another radio this summer, but of course that got rippled off also. (Initial)
b. I don't know what the real story is, but, ... it sounded kinda neat. (Janus 1)
c. ...we would charge (H) ...five-hundred fifty dollars on an- on an account, it would be five-hundred dollars, it's really kind of switch around but. (H) what...what that would-...I think it would be good for (H) ...the five or six of us, (H) to have Galino down here, (H) can kind of explain what products, ...we can offer from the bank side, ~ Matt needs to know that, and ... and we all need to know that, (H) and then, we can figure out how ~ Matt's, ... the products that LCL's gonna offer will plug into that. (Janus 2)
d. W'l now Didier – makes his money by going to Atlantic City but –. (Final 1)
e. "Yep. They are now any way." "Um...my mum doesn't think so – but," (Indeterminate)

f. "You sounded funny @@(H)" "I know. Sounded like an alright person but." (Final 2) (cited from Izutsu and Izutsu 2014)

In the initial Example (3a), initial *but* begins an Intonation Unit and the contrasting value is provided with the preceding sentence (for more details, see Schiffrin (1987) among others).

In the Janus 1 Example (3b), prosodically it can be assimilated as a final *but* upon its production, but in reality the speaker immediately gives further contrasting material in the same turn, which transforms it into an introducer. In the Janus 2 Example (3c), the speaker continues his turn and there is no evidence that the subsequent material stands in contrast with that preceding the *but*; it is used in fact as introducing a social action.

A final particle is a discourse marker that occurs at the end of an interactional unit, whether a turn, a turn unit, or a prosodic unit, and indexes certain pragmatic stances. (Mulder and Thompson 2008: 183). While American English and Australian English have final hanging *but*, only Australian English has final particle *but*.

In the final 1 Example (3d), there is a clear implication left "hanging" such that the clause with *but* is open to being interpreted as a concession. This *but* tells the hearer that there is an implication and invites the hearer to infer what it is and to continue the interaction appropriately given that implication. The Example (3e) is an in-between case, where *but* can be interpreted as a final 1 or a final 2 instance. It is said to be indeterminate. In the final 2 Example (3f), the semantically contrastive material is given in the IU ending with the final *but* particle. The particle closes a construction which conveys the semantically contrasting content.

The main differences of Southern English andTyneside English with American and Australian English final *but* are: there are no Janus[1]-types of *but* in the two corpora of Southern English and Tyneside English examined and the particle has developed meanings other than the contrastive semantic value, as shown in Hancil (2014, 2015). In addition, just like American and Australian English, the prosody of the final particle is associated with a low-flat contour, as displayed by the contour of an occurrence from DECTE (P1) in Figure 1:

1. See Section 4 for a full description.

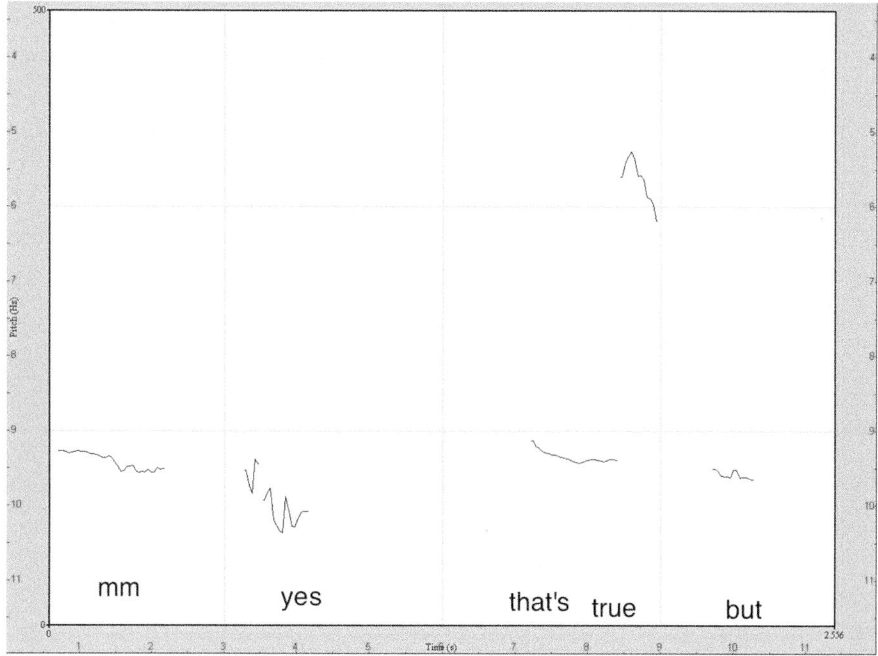

Figure 1. Intonational contour of final *but* in the corpus

3. Presentation of the data

It was shown in a synchronic study of final *but* (Hancil 2014) that the highest figures for the use of final *but* were identified in the north of Britain. So it was decided to work in a diachronic corpus of the same dialect. The Diachronic Electronic Corpus of Tyneside English (DECTE) is a collection of text transcriptions and audio files of interviews with a wide variety of people from the North East of England. It extends from the late 1960s to the early 2000s and includes three subcorpora (and consequently three periods named P1, P2, and P3).

The first subcorpus comprises 37 interviews and 229,909 words. It dates back to the late-60s-early70s; the *Tyneside Linguistic Survey* (TLS) project includes Tyneside speakers talking about their life stories and their attitudes to the local dialect.

The second subcorpus was compiled in 1994: the *Phonological Variation and Change in Contemporary Spoken English* (PVC) project comprises dyads of Tyneside friends and relatives talking about a large variety of topics. 18 interviews were conducted and there are 208,295 words.

The third subcorpus NECTE2 was created in 2007–2011 with 44 interviews. There are 366,062 words. Like those in PVC, these interviews each record two informants who are usually friends or relatives and therefore similar in age or social background, or both. The conversations generally last from 30 to 70 minutes and cover a wide range of topics, with different degrees of participation and direction from the different student interviewers involved.

For each period, because the figures are relatively low, it was chosen to provide normalized figures for 200,000 words per period. All the examples were checked by native speakers of the dialect.[2]

4. Diachronic evolution of semantico-pragmatic meanings in the corpus

Three categories of semantico-pragmatic meanings associated with the final particle *but* may be found in the DECTE corpus: textual, attitudinal and social.

A textual value can be described as a discourse-building component, which creates textual coherence within a series of propositions. An attitudinal value reflects the attitude of the speaker. A social value mirrors the rules of the etiquette in society, especially in social interaction.[3]

4.1 Textual values

Two types of textual values are identified: contrast and anaphor/cataphor.

The first type of textual value to be found in the DECTE corpus is related to the expression of contrast, which can be paraphrased by *though*, as shown in Table 1:

Table 1. Evolution of contrastive values in DECTE

Period **Meaning**	**P1**	**P2**	**P3**
Contrast	9	18	21

According to Table 1, the number of contrastive values extends from 9 occurrences in P1 to 18 in P2 (+ 100%) and it slightly augments from P2 to P3 (21 occurrences, + 16.7%). Contrast can be illustrated in (4) and (5):

2. Special thanks go to Karen Corrigan and her students, University of Newcastle, for the interpretation of the data, along with Caroline Oates.

3. In Hancil (2014), I distinguished two categories, namely discourse values and attitudinal values, but I believe that this three-partite classification better reflects the meanings associated with final *but*.

(4) A: uhhuh there's the park down the bank
B: that's right aye <unclear /> what
A: not much of it there now like **but**
B: yeah they're going to build a school or something aren't they
A: they've built a school
B: oh i see aye
A: it's up now (DECTE, P1)

(5) A: I like Yorkshire accent, Irish accent and southern accent and Italian accent and Geordie accent.
B: Does a person's accent affect what you think of them?
A: Yeah.
B: On what basis?
A: If they're from Newcastle, I actually do judge them more. I'm a total snob sometimes, to be fully honest. I know that's bad but yeah, but then, no I am.
B: What about you?
A: What, do I judge people on their accents?
B: Mm
A: Err I really I don't know sorry. I might do **but.**
B: you're not aware of it.
A: Yes.
B: Have you ever been aware that you sound really different to someone else?
A: Yes. (DECTE, P3)

In (4), A speaks about the building near the bank and makes a contrast between what is there and what is not there near a park by adding the final particle *but*, concluding that there is not much of it there now. In (5), by using final *but*, speaker A makes a contrast between the proposition *I might judge people on their accents* and the preceding comment further back *I know it's bad*. Final *but* can be paraphrased by *though*.

The second type of textual values in the DECTE corpus has to do with anaphor/cataphor, as illustrated in Table 2:

Table 2. Evolution of anaphoric and cataphoric values in the DECTE corpus

Period Meaning	P1	P2	P3
Anaphor	0	10	7
Cataphor	4	8	10

Table 2 displays the figures for the anaphoric and cataphoric values in the DECTE corpus. It is only in P2 that we first find anaphoric values (10 occurrences) and the figures slightly decrease in P3 (7 occurrences, −30%). They can be paraphrased by *you know* and can be shown in (6) and (7):

(6) A: you were the only one that came down
B: and you like an idiot said go I'll buy you three pints at dinnertime if you go from the very top. I nearly killed myself
A: <laughter>
B: I think I threw them in the river
A: aye that was that playing centre that was that was opposite <unclear>
B: god i landed right on the base of my spine at the bottom of the bank <pause > i think i could have done with a little professional instruction before <unclear > < "laughter" >
A: <laughter> we had some canny we had some canny days up there **but**
B: <unclear /> remember when we did get to the pub i tried to play darts and my eyes were still watering (DECTE, P2)

(7) A: but if we go clubbing we don't we don't drink, he drives, so it's generally
B: I don't take pills when I'm driving I might add, well I don't take pills at all <pause> I'm a speed boy! Always have been, always will be **but**
A: <laughter> What – like tell me about the funniest thing that's ever happened <pause> on B: <sigh> (DECTE, P3)

In (6), speaker B remembers an episode of his life when he threw pints in the river and fell down on his back. By using final *but,* he points to these nice days of his youth ('canny' is a term of endearment in the North). In (7), Speaker B uses final *but* to point to the previous co-text in which he mentions he takes drugs and shows he loves taking speed: *always have been, always will be.*

According to Table 2, cataphoric values were already employed in P1 (4 occurrences) and doubled in P2 (8 occurrences) and finally stabilized in P3 (10 occurrences). Examples (8) and (9) illustrate this usage that can be paraphrased by *you know*:

(8) A: i divn't know <pause /> i could see them doing it just because Brazil were easily the better team because you see every now and again you get the odd
B: yeah **but**
A: shock

B: they haven't played that well throughout the world cup I don't think (DECTE, P2)

(9) A: Aye that's right
B: If you've got the money that is you know <interruption> I mean er
A: That's it
B: That's the big er the whole back the money
A: That's right
B: Shut up
A: But er
B: You'll probably get that on the mic as well <laughter> the bird chirping
A: Aye
B: It's all right
A: Aye
B: No we used to have a budgie when I was em when I was little and he didn't last long I think he only lived about five six year **but**
A: Aye
B: You couldn't you'd go through basically you couldn't shut him up but then you'd go for days without him saying anything
A: Aye (DECTE, P3)

In (8), A and B speak about soccer teams and A emphasizes how Brazil is normally good. B uses final *but* to point to the following co-text, which announces that Brazil was not as good as expected at the world cup. In (9), B speaks about the days when he got a little bird and with final *but*, he anticipates more of what he is about to say about this bird: *you couldn't shut him up.*

4.2 Attitudinal values

Attitudinal values are also present in the DECTE corpus. Two types are distinguished: intensity and doubt. The first type of attitudinal values is the intensifying value, which can be paraphrased by *really*, as shown in Table 3:

Table 3. Evolution of attitudinal values in the DECTE corpus

Period Meaning	P1	P2	P3
Intensifier	28	9	21
Doubt	0	6	2

Table 3 shows that P1 is the period where there are the most numerous values of the intensifying value (28 occurrences). In P2 the figures are nearly divided by 3 (9 occurrences) and in P3 the figures increase again dramatically (21 occurrences, + 133.3%). They can be illustrated in Examples (10) and (11):

(10) A: yeah <unclear> yeah I remember you only got a week when we were
B: that's right a week
A: young you got a week's holiday
B: aye
A: <unclear /> yeah
B: yes it's a far cry **but**
A: mm
B: you see i think what's tending to happen there's probably people still doing the same sort of thing harry but we've been lucky you know and we've moved on (DECTE, P2)

(11) A: Don't do anything <laughter>
B: Okay, can you tell me where you see yourself in twenty years?
A: Nice house, possibly kids, I really do want children **but**
B: Twenty years yes, I'd see myself with kids.
A: I love children.
B: And a secure job, married, happy. (DECTE, P3)

In (10), speakers A and B compare the length of their holidays now and back in their youth. By using final *but*, B emphasizes how short the holiday was in the old days. In (11), the speakers talk about their life project in twenty years' time. A, by using final *but*, emphasizes she really wants to have children.

The second type of attitudinal values is the value of doubt, which can paraphrased by *I doubt it*. There is no occurrence with a meaning of doubt in P1. It is only in P2 that the value of doubt is employed (6 occurrences). And in P3, the figures are rare (2 occurrences). Examples (12) and (13) illustrate this value:

(12) A: yeah I know it stops it yeah I couldn't I was trying to think what the prizes would be for if they weren't the subject ones like last year I because I thought they can't be the subject ones because the GCSE results aren't in because we got our prizes for ours
B: mm
A: and the others got theirs for theirs but eh
B: i don't know
B: i think they might keep a couple **but**
A: glad ours wasn't on prediction or we'd've got now <vocal desc = "laughter" />
B: you'd have got more of them (DECTE, P2)

(13) A: I don't think you can just expect to get a < interruption> degree and then just get a job you've got to be.
B: No 'Cause a lot now it's do with experience but how can you have – you cant really have both can you it's
A: You can do some volunteer work and stuff.
B: Yeah I suppose **but.**
A: So how do feel about people that say like <pause> being a student it's like – there's no point in getting a degree anymore it's like you may as well just go get work experience and life experience it's more important. Do you agree with that?
(DECTE, P3)

In (12), A and B talk about the possible end of prizes after their exam. By using final *but*, B expresses some doubt and confirms that the teachers might keep a couple of prizes. In (13) A and B speak about the difficulty of getting a job when you are a student; by employing final *but*, B shows some doubt about the experience you can get through volunteer work.

4.3 Social value

There is another type of value that is identified in the corpus and it is the social value of a filler, according to which the marker is devoid of semantic meaning. The speaker uses it purely for social reasons to render the conversation more lively and keep the conversation entertaining. The evolution of this value is displayed in Table 4:

Table 4. Evolution of the filler value in the DECTE corpus

Period Meaning	P1	P2	P3
Filler	2	4	9

Even though the figures are relatively low they are worth considering. They extend from 2 occurrences in P1 to 4 occurrences in P2, and finally to 9 occurrences in P3. The figures are doubled in each period. They can be exemplified as in (14) and (15):

(14) A: mm <unclear > I think he wants to well <pause > obviously more <pause > qualifications you get the better it'll be <unclear >
B: mm
A: making more money in there and so <pause > I think like **but**

B: yeah
A: so <pause /> i don't think he wants do he only wants to do like two sciences <pause /> and he's asking which (DECTE, P2)

(15) A: Really <pause> bloody hell. Right em <laughter> crunches, I love Crunchies, they're great they're my favourite <pause> you like Twirls don't you?
B: Love twirls, but I also love toffee-crisps but I kind of like can't really am stopping eating Nestle now for moral
A: <interruption> ooo why?
B: reasons <pause> Coca-cola as well 'cause Nestle are em part of this group that em make formula milk and they're like trying to er badly promote it in Africa, but in places where they don't have em access to sanitary water so they just making
A: yeah **but**
B: and yeah obviously it's not, and they're using like water from a cesspit. And the babies are getting ill
A: That's really bad (DECTE, P3)

In (14) A and B discuss about the necessity of having good qualifications to get a good pay. A employs final *but* to keep the conversation going without adding any semantic meaning to the utterance. In (15) A and B speak about how successful Nestle is in the world but they note that in Africa they have difficulty in using proper water. A uses final *but* to fill the gap and keep the conversation rolling.

So, among the three categories distinguished, it appears that the textual values of final *but* are the most prominent in the data, especially the values of contrast throughout the periods. I shall now have a look at the notion of persistence.

5. Lexical, procedural and structural persistence

Since Hopper's (1991) seminal work on grammaticalization processes have often been referred as being determined by the lexical meaning of the item undergoing grammaticalization lexical persistence was said to be at work. In her historical study on adjectives of difference, Breban (2009) added a novel facet of persistence in grammaticalization, namely structural persistence, which she showed came into play, relying on the idea that individual lexical items typically occur as part of larger structural units. I would like to add another facet of persistence and speak about procedural persistence to refine the notion of lexical persistence: the idea hinges on the fact that a linguistic expression has a semantically abstract invariant that illustrates the underlying mechanism of the particle and constrains its evolution. I would like to show that the three types of persistence play a part in the grammaticalization of the final particle *but*.

According to Table 1, it was clear that the original value of constrast persisted all over the periods and reached a climax in P3 (20.9% of all the values in P1 vs. 30% of all the values in P3). Structurally, the final particle (FP) can be associated with Figure 2:

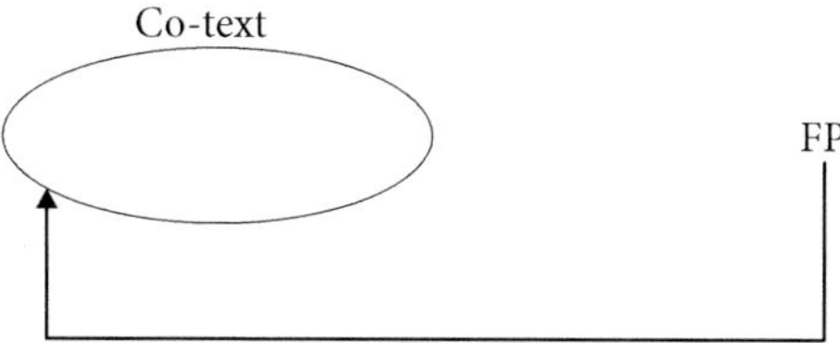

Figure 2. Constructional schema of the final particle *but*

To understand in what way the constructional schema has been present since period P1, it is important to delineate the procedural persistence and see how it goes hand in hand with the original structure.

In Hancil (2014) I showed that that the particle could be associated with spatial dissociation since the beginning. It is a well-established fact that from a diachronic point of view, *but* started its life as a complex preposition OE *be* + *útan/ bútan* composed of OE *be* 'near, at the side of' and OE *útan* 'out, outside, beyond the limits of'. Hence the combination meant 'on the outside of'. With *but*, the located element is opposed to the spatial locator; there is a spatial dissociation between the located element and the locator, as shown in (16):

(16) The dog is but the house.
'The dog is outside the house'.

The located element *The dog* is located in relation to the preposition *outside*. The locator is explicitly expressed by *the house*; and the preposition *outside* shows that the located element is spatially dissociated from the locator *the house*.

In the case of final *but*, which has the structure 'X-*but*-Y' (see Hancil 2014), X is the preceding discourse and Y is present implicitly. The various meanings attached to the final particle *but* can be derived from its fundamental spatial value. In the value of contrast within the construction 'X *but*', the speaker indicates with the use of the dissociative marker that the located clause X is situated in relation to an implicit clause Y indicating the non-validation of the proposition X. The value of final *but* as doubt proceeds from the same mechanism. As for the use of final *but* as an anaphor/cataphor, the speaker goes "out" of the proposition to look for a referent and makes a link with this referent. No mention of the locator is explicitly made and it ends up being understood in light of the preceding context; hence the value of anaphor/cataphor. The difference between anaphor and cataphor lies in the fact the speaker looks at the previous co-text for the case of anaphor and at the following co-text in the case of cataphor. In the case of final *but* being used as an intensifier, the value of high degree can be linked to the value of spatial dissociation in the original meaning. With the high degree, you move away from a typical value towards a completely different value: a possibility is to extract the high value.[4] With the use of final *but* as a filler, the speaker wants to say something else (the original meaning of dissociation persists) and places the final particle in the conversation to keep it going.

Consequently, the three phenomena of persistence, whether it be lexical, procedural or structural, are all at work together in the process of grammaticalization of the final particle *but*.

6. (Inter)subjectification and Traugott's (2010) subjectivity cline

Traugott (2010: 35) has proposed a subjectivity cline to encapsulate the notions of subjectivity and subjecification in the theory of semantic change:

non- / less subjective > subjective > intersubjective.

where "Subjectification is the semasiological process whereby Speakers/Writers come over time to develop meanings for L[exeme]s to encode or externalize their perspectives and attitudes as constrained by the communicative world of the speech event, rather than by the so-called "real-world" characteristics of the event or situation referred to" (Traugott & Dasher 2002: 30). And intersubjectification takes place "in instances where meanings come explicitly to index and acknowledge SP/Ws attitude toward the Adressee/Reader in the here and now of the speech event" (Traugott & Dasher 2002: 31). Let us note that the presence of intersubjectivity presumes the existence of subjectivity: "there cannot be intersubjectification without some degree of subjectification" (Traugott & Dasher 2002: 31), which imposes a hierarchy in semantic change.

Table 5 shows the evolution of the number of intersubjective meanings. It has constantly increased over the three periods in DECTE: There were 43 occurrences in P1, then 55 in P2 (+ 27.9%) and finally 70 in P3 (+ 27.3%) overall there is a 62.8% increase over a 60-year period. If we consider the classification of the previous section, the distribution is as follows in Table 6:

4. According to Culioli's theory of enunciative operations, a gradable expression has prototypically an interior and exterior with a prototypical value p and a highest value on the up-scale of degrees.

Table 5. Overall distribution of intersubjectivity in DECTE

Period	**P1**	**P2**	**P3**
Nb of occurrences	43	55	70

Table 6. Detailed distribution of intersubjective meanings in DECTE

Period **Meaning**	**P1**	**P2**	**P3**
Textual	13	36	38
Attitudinal	28	15	23
Social	2	4	9

The three types of meanings are connected with intersubjectivity since they all solicit the attention of the hearer. Among the three intersubjective meanings distinguished, the textual meanings have been leading since P2, the contrastive meaning coming first, the attitudinal meanings coming second and the social meaning coming third. Interestingly, there was a re-modeling of the intersubjective meanings between P1 and P2, as the attitudinal meanings that were used the most in P1 were outnumbered in P2. The presence of the slight increase in social meaning (from 2 occurrences in P1 to 9 occurrences in P3) shows that the co-enunciator is less actively participating in the intersubjectivity process as there seems to be a little shift from intersubjectivity to "interactiveness" (Fitzmaurice 2004: 427), whereby the final particle *but* is just used to "keep the conversation going" (Fitzmaurice 2004: 438). So Traugott's cline can be supplemented and the final *but* in DECTE follows the following cline:

Intersubjectivity> interactivity.

Besides, the intersubjectivity meanings were present from the beginning in DECTE. One way to explain this is to refer to the speaker's discourse strategy that uses the particle *but* in final position due to interactional terms. Indeed, the genre of the text (dialogue) directly influences its communicative goal: informal conversations involve exchanges between interlocutors, so they are interlocutor-oriented. The syntax, i.e. the linear order of constituents, adapts itself to these interactional forces. Various studies in discourse analysis have long established that the ideal place for the interlocutor to manifest his point of view about the speaker's sentence is at the end of the speaker's sentence (see Sacks et al. 1974: 707–708; Pomerantz 1984, *inter alia*). Postpossible completion is one of the structurally provided and recurrently exploited positions for initiating "repair, i.e., "transition-space repair"" (Schegloff 1996: 91):

> And there is a variety of usages which have post-possible completion as one of their environments of possible occurrence – such as address terms, courtesy terms, and the like. (Schegloff 1996: 91)

Consequently, final *but* complements the list of interactional markers and there was no shift from subjectivity to intersubjectivity in the corpus studied, which echoes Ghesquière et al.'s (2012) remarks about a looser network of relations between subjectivity and intersubjectivity. Moreover, this present study underlines the importance of textual relations in historical change, which supports the claim of Breban (2006), Ghesquière (2010) and Narrog (2016) that argue that discourse-orientation needs to be reconsidered. In her analysis of historical changes in English adjectives, Ghesquière (2010, 308) contends that Traugott's earlier 1982 pathway was more to the point:

> Traugott's (1982) pathway of semantic change is semantically more fine-grained than her later cline of intersubjectification ans seems to capture better the semantic development of the adjectives of completeness. (Ghesquière 2010: 308)

Narrog (2016) agrees with this point and "does not believe that a fixed order of changes can be established" (Narrog 2016: 41). Besides, Narrog (2016: 41) thinks discourse-orientation is commonly associated with a later stage in grammaticalisation, but the present study shows that textual relations were present right from the start of P1 in the case of final *but* in DECTE. So it is necessary to revise the cline and postulate a looser network of relations between subjectivity and intersubjectivity, and *a posteriori* between textual meanings, attitudinal and social meaning with tendencies only.

7. Paradigmaticization

Because the final position in an utterance is crucial in the study of the final particle, word order will be studied through the prism of grammaticalization and the notion of paradigms will be rehabilitated in non-morphological contexts to see how final *but* can be said to generate a grammatical paradigm. Following Nørgård-Sørensen and Heltoft (2015), it is shown that paradigmatic organization is not restricted to morphology and can be extended to word order and constructional syntax.

7.1 Word order, grammaticalization and paradigms

Word order change has been recurrently considered to be an epiphenomenon of grammaticalization, as underlined by Sun and Traugott (2011), who mention

Heine & König's (2010) study of word order in ditransitive constructions as being a consequence of the grammaticalization of communicative strategies.

> Word order is a fairly fundamental means for speakers to structure discourses, but its ontological status is a matter of much debate in some linguistic theories. Suffice it to draw attention to two contrasting opinions that have been voiced in formal frameworks on the ordering of ditransitive objects. Whereas some treat linear order as a distinct category in their theory (Barss & Lasnik, 1986; Jackendoff, 1990), others maintain that linear order is derivative of other syntactic phenomena (Larson, 1988). The kind of data looked at in this paper suggests that linearization of R[ecipient-like argument] and T[heme argument] is neither a syntactic primitive nor can it be explained satisfactorily in terms of syntactic phenomena; rather, it is *derivative of the grammaticalization of communicative strategies.*
>
> The present paper was about the grammaticalization of functional principles; it was meant to demonstrate that linearization of ditransitive objects can best be accounted for *in terms of a small set of communicative strategies.* [...] The communicative strategies that we proposed [...] are of different kinds; they relate on the one hand to the speaker's goal to map events to be observed in the "real world" onto linguistic discourse (iconicity), on the other hand they concern the pragmatics of presenting arguments, by proposing either distinctions of salience or topicality attributed to referents (prominence) or of relative grammatical complexity (weight). (Heine & König 2010: 117)(the italics are mine)

But, as demonstrated by Nørgård-Sørensen et al. (2011) and Nørgård-Sørensen & Heltoft. (2015), it is possible to re-consider the picture if one takes into account paradigmatic organization:

> Once we adopt and develop the paradigmatic dimension as an essential criterion for identifying grammaticalised categories, word order changes per se need no longer be excluded from the realm of grammaticalisation. The relevant topological oppositions are the expression system (form system) of the paradigm; information structural contrasts – or illocutionary contrasts, as shown above – are frequent examples of possible content oppositions (the semantic contrasts) of a topological paradigm. (Nørgård-Sørensen & Helthoft. 2015: 281)

For instance, in her analysis of descriptive adjectives becoming intensifiers and quantifiers, Breban (2008) shows that the change of function is related to a change in position, thereby underlining the fact that semantic change hinges on word order only. Breban successfully shows that Adamson's (2000) claim about word order in the NP is verified: grammaticalization in the NP goes hand in hand with movement of the grammaticalizing adjective to more leftward positions in the premodifying string. She concludes that:

> The adjectives of difference have been going through a double process of grammaticalization and subjectification from a lexical attribute use to the grammaticalized postdeterminer use and in a second stage from the postdeterminer to a quantifier use. [...]these three functions have been associated with three typical positions in the English NP." (Breban 2008: 300)

The attribute use of adjectives of difference is exemplified in (17):

(17) Billy starred as a drug dealer in the hard-hitting Robert Carlyle drama Looking After Jo Jo. That was after he played the sleazy nightclub owner George Skelly in Taggart. Then there were two episodes of The Bill as *two completely different characters.* (Breban 2008: 266)

The postdeterminer use of the adjectives of difference is illustrated in (18):

(18) The cards, from Futera, will put you on the wave of popularity rugby. union is riding after the excitement of the World and Bledisloe Cups. There are 110 *different* cards in the series featuring past and present rugby. greats including Tim Horan, Jason Little and Campese Ken Catchpole, Roger Gould and Andrew Slack. (Breban 2008: 288)

And finally, the quantifier use of the adjectives of difference is displayed in (19):

(19) A criminal was branded, during my stay here, for the third offence; but. the relief he received made him declare that the judge was one of the best. men in the world. I sent this wretch a trifle, at *different* times, to take with. him into slavery. (Breban 2008: 287)

So, the semantic change from descriptive adjective via distributional function to quantifier function goes hand in hand with a positional change. Post-determiners stand after the determiner position, but they are placed before evaluators and descriptive adjectives, as illustrated in (20):

(20) a. Several lovely kind women
b. the same lovely kind women (Nørgård-Sørensen & Heltoft 2015: 279)

So word order here can be considered grammatical as it forms paradigmatic oppositions between topological patterns.

Another example of a topological change is the change in Danish from an alternation Mod N vs N Mod to the current situation where only Mod N is permitted. In the 13th century, adjectival modifiers and demonstratives are practically always preposed but possessive pronouns and genitives are not reanalyzed as determiners and follow the paradigm (21):

(21) Marked focus vs Unmarked

POSS N	N POSS	
fæ sit	sit fæ	
'cattle his'	'his cattle'	(Nørgård-Sørensen & Heltoft 2015: 280)

According to Heltoft (2010), genitives and possessives are later reanalyzed as determiners, which leads to the loss of the option N POSS, since determiners are now before the N. The paradigmatic contrast is lost through a combination of further grammaticalization and degrammaticalization. So this is an instance of word order that can be said to be grammatical as it is an integrated, obligatory part of the expression system of a grammatical category.

Consequently, topological positions can enter into the realm of grammaticalization if they express a grammatical category. The grammatical paradigm can be delineated through a list of defining features, as summarized by Nørgård-Sørensen & Heltoft. 2015:

> First, the grammatical paradigm is a *closed set* of items, the number of members being fixed at a given language stage.
> Second, for every paradigm one must specify its *domain*, i.e. the syntagmatic context where it applies.
> Third, a paradigm has a semantic *frame*, i.e. a common semantic denominator within which the content of the individual members is defined in opposition to each other. [...]
>
> Fourth, the choice between the members is *obligatory*. In the given syntagmatic context defining the domain of the paradigm speakers cannot avoid picking one or the other member. The choice can be free or bound, but must be made.
> Fifth, a paradigm is asymmetric, distinguishing marked and unmarked members, possibly in a hierarchical structure (especially in the case of multi-membered paradigms). (Nørgård-Sørensen & Helthoft 2015: 262–263)

I shall test these defining features of a grammatical paradigm in the next section.

7.2 Final *but* and paradigmaticization

Let us see in what way the grammaticalization of final *but* is an instance of paradigmaticization.

It might be tempting to classify final *but* as being the result of cognitive forces. Extracting a linking adverbial from its usual position (initial or medial) creates syntactic tensions that are motivated by the speaker's pragmatic discourse strategy (Ochs, Schegloff & Thompson 1996). In the text-strategic chain, sentence-final constructions are identified as markers of afterthought. The postposing of the construction will typically be interpreted by the hearer as the speaker signalling that his sentence is not semantically complete, which justifies the sentence-final elaboration. In this sense, it is a specific illustration of the repair mechanism to which the speaker resorts when he wants to correct unplanned spoken discourse (cf. Schegloff et al. 1977: 377). In final *but*, its use by the speaker in sentence-final position can be explained by the speaker attempting to guide the interlocutor's interpretation of the situation when he takes the floor.

But the consideration of cognitive forces is not enough a criterion to define final *but* and it underestimates the nature of grammatical relations the particle creates. Let us review the defining features that are characteristic of the grammatical paradigm the particle is likely to generate.

First, final *but* is part of the relatively closed set of final particles in English such as *like, though, anyway, so* and *then*. Second, the domain of the paradigm is the right periphery of an utterance and has to do with word order. Third, the semantic frame of the paradigm is related to the reference by the speaker to the common ground between speaker and co-speaker and its evaluation in order to guide the hearer in the interpretation of the utterance. In the case of final *but*, the semantic frame was shown to be a marker of dissociation. Fourth, the choice between the members is communicatively obligatory (Diewald 2011): the communicatively compulsory presence of final *but* shows that grammar should be extended beyond the level of a classical set of morphosyntactic rules governing the skeleton of a sentence in order to incorporate all aspects of communication. Fifth, the paradigm is asymmetric: the marked member when it encodes a contrast is final *but*, *though* being the unmarked member; the marked member when it has an anaphoric/cataphoric meaning is final *but*, whereas the marker *you know* is the unmarked member; the marked member when it has an intensifying member is final *but* while the adverb *really* is the unmarked member; the marked member is final *but* when it fulfils the role of a filler, whereas the absence of an adverb is the unmarked member. Consequently, final *but* can be said to create a grammatical paradigm and to undergo a process of paradigmaticization along the lines described by Nørgård-Sørensen & Heltoft (2015).

8. Conclusion

In this diachronic analysis, it was shown that final *but* could be associated with lexical, procedural and structural persistence and the particle was undergoing a process of increasing intersubjectification, accompanied by a process of interactification which turned the role of the co-speaker from active to passive in the exchange between interlocutors. Because intersubjectivity was present from the beginning in the Northern English corpus it was claimed, following Ghesquière's

(2010) and Narrog's (2016) arguments, that it was necessary to loosen the relations between subjectivity and intersubjectivity and not to postulate a hierarchy between the two. Besides, it was underlined that it was necessary to rehabilitate the notion of paradigms in non-morphological contexts, as was clearly demonstrated by Nørgård-Sørensen et al. (2011) and Nørgård-Sørensen & Heltoft (2015), in order to fully understand the linguistic phenomenon of final particles that are fully integrated in oral discourse.

This study brings out supplementary evidence that grammar cannot be defined traditionally in morphosyntactic terms and it must encapsulate all the parameters necessary for comprehension: from phonology, syntax, morphology, cognitive processes, and all the interactional information, whether it be explicit or implicit, that contributes to the coherence and cohesion of discourse (see, f.i., Traugott 2003; Haselow 2013 and Hancil (2016). Many a linguist has become convinced that "the only way to fully understand linguistic structure is to consider it as an adaptive response to recurrent habits in the way people talk to each other" (Ford & Thompson 1996: 172).

References

Adamson, Sylvia. 2000. A lovely little example: Word order options and category shift in the premodifying string. In *Pathways of Change: Grammaticalization in English* [Studies in Language Companion Series 53], Olga Fischer, Anette Rosenbach & Dieter Stein (eds), 39–66. Amsterdam: John Benjamins. https://doi.org/10.1075/slcs.53.04ada

Beal, Joan & Burbano Elizondo, Lourdes & Llamas, Carmen. 2012. *Urban North-Eastern English: Tyneside to Teeside*. Edinburgh: EUP.

Breban, Tine. 2006. Grammaticalization and subjectification of the English adjectives of general comparison. In *Subjectification: Various Paths to Subjectivity*, Angeliki Athanasiadou, Costas Canakis & Bert Cornillie (eds), 241–278. Berlin: Mouton de Gruyter.

Breban, Tine. 2008. Grammaticalization, subjectification, and leftward movement of English adjectives of difference in the noun phrase. *Folia Linguistica* 42(3): 259–305.

Breban, Tine. 2009. Structural persistence: A case based on the grammaticalization of English adjectives of difference. *English Language and Linguistics* 13(1): 77–96. https://doi.org/10.1017/S1360674308002888

Clarke, Sandra. 2010. *Newfoundland and Labrador English*. Edinburgh: EUP. https://doi.org/10.3366/edinburgh/9780748626168.001.0001

Diewald, Gabriele. 2011. Pragmaticalization (defined) as grammaticalization of discourse functions. *Linguistics* 49: 365–390. https://doi.org/10.1515/ling.2011.011

Fitzmaurice, Susan. 2004. subjectivity, intersubjectivity and the historical construction of interlocutor stance: From stance markers to discourse markers. *Discourse Studies* 6: 427–448. https://doi.org/10.1177/1461445604046585

Ford, Cecilia & Thompson, Sandra A. 1996. Interactional units in conversation: Syntactic, intonational, and pragmatic resources for the management of turns. In *Interaction Grammar*, Elinor Ochs, Emanuel A. Schegloff & Sandra A. Thompson (eds), 14–164. Cambridge: CUP. https://doi.org/10.1017/CBO9780511620874.003

Ghesquière, Lobke. 2010. On the subjectification and intersubjectification paths followed by the adjeectives of completeness. In *Intersubjectification and Grammaticalization* [Topics in English Linguistics 66], Kristin Davidse, Lieven Vandelanotte & Hubert Cuyckens (eds), 277–314. Berlin: De Gruyter. https://doi.org/10.1515/9783110226102.3.277

Ghesquière, Lobke, Brems, Liselotte & Van de Velde Freek,. 2012. Intersubjectivity and intersubjectification: Typology and operationalization. *English Text Constructioni* 5(1): 128–152. https://doi.org/10.1075/etc.5.1.07ghe

Hancil, Sylvie. 2014. The final particle *but* in British English: An instance of cooptation and grammaticalization at work. In *Grammaticalization – Theory and Data* [Studies in Language Companion Series 162], Sylvie Hancil & Ekkehard König (eds), 235–255. Amsterdam: Benjamins.

Hancil, Sylvie. 2015. *Grammaticalization of final but: From discourse connective to final particle*. In Hancil, Haselow & Post (eds), 157–172.

Hancil, Sylvie. 2016. Périphérie droite et macro-grammaire. In *Modèles Linguistiques*, Isabelle Gaudy-Campbell & Héloïse Parent (eds), 133–154. Paris: Éditions des Dauphins.

Hancil, Sylvie, Haselow, Alexander & Post, Margje. 2015. *Final Particles*. Berlin: De Gruyter.

Haselow, Alexander. 2013. Arguing for a wide conception of grammar: The case of final particles in spoken discourse. *Folia Linguistica* 47(2): 375–424. https://doi.org/10.1515/flin.2013.015

Heine, Bernd & König, Christa. 2010. On the linear order of ditransitive objects. *Language Sciences* 32: 87–131. https://doi.org/10.1016/j.langsci.2008.07.002

Heltoft, Lars. 2010. Paradigmatic structure in a usage-based theory of grammaticalisation. In *Language Usage and Language Structure*, Kasper Boye & Elizabeth Engberg-Pedersen (eds), 145–166. Berlin: Mouton de Gruyter.

Himmelmann, Nikolaus P. 2004. Lexicalization and grammaticization: Opposite or orthogonal? In *What Makes Grammaticalization? A Look from its Fringes and its Components*, Walter Bisang, Nikolaus P. Himmelmann & Björn Wiemer (eds), 21–42. Berlin. Mouton de Gruyter.

Hopper, Paul J. 1991. On some principles of grammaticization. In *Approaches to Grammaticalization*, Vol. 1: *Theoretical and Methodological Issues* [Typological Studies in Language 19:1], Traugott, Elizabeth Traugott & Bernd Heine (eds), 17–35. Amsterdam: Benjamins. https://doi.org/10.1075/tsl.19.1.04hop

Izutsu, Mitsuko N. & Katsunobu, Izutsu. 2014. Truncation and backshift: Two pathways to sentence-final coordinating conjunctions. *Journal of Historical Pragmatics* 15: 1, 62–92.

Mulder, J. & Thompson, S. A.. 2008. The grammaticization of but as a final particle in English conversation. In Laury R. *Aspects of Grammaticalization. (Inter)subjectification and Directionality. The multifunctionality of conjunctions*, 179–204. Amsterdam, Benjamins.

Mulder, J., Thompson, S.A. & Williams, C. P.. 2009. Final but in Australian English conversation. In Peters, P., Collins, P. & Smith, A. (eds.), *Comparative Studies in Australian and New Zealand English*, 339–359. Amsterdam. Benjamins.

Narrog, Heike. 2016. Three types of subjectivity, three types of intersubjectivity, their dynamicization and a synthesis. In *Aspects of Grammaticalization. (Inter)subjectification and Directionality*, Hubert Cuyckens, Lobke Ghesquière & Dan Olmen (eds), 19–46. Berlin: De Gruyter.

Nørgård-Sørensen, Jens & Heltoft, Lars. 2015. Grammaticalization as paradigmatisation. In *New Directions in Grammaticalization Research* [Studies in Language Companion Series 166], Andrew D. M. Smith, Graeme Trousdale & Richard Waltereit (eds), 261–292. Amsterdam: John Benjamins.

Nørgård-Sørensen, Jens, Helthoft, Lars & Schøsler, Lene. 2011. *Connecting Grammaticalization* [Studies in Functional and Structural Linguistics 65]. Amsterdam: John Benjamins. https://doi.org/10.1075/sfsl.65

Ochs, Elinor, Schegloff, Emanuel A. & Thompson, Gail (eds). 1996. *Interaction and Grammar*. Cambridge: CUP. https://doi.org/10.1017/CBO9780511620874

Pomerantz, Anita. 1984. Agreeing and disagreeing with assessments: Some features found in preferred/dispreferred turn shapes. In *Structures of Social Action*, J. Maxwell Atkinson & John Heritage (eds), 232–254. Cambridge: CUP.

Sacks, Harvey, Schegloff, Emanuel A. & Jefferson, Gail. 1974. A simplest systematics for the organization of turn-taking for conversation. *Language* 50: 696–735. https://doi.org/10.1353/lan.1974.0010

Schegloff, Emanuel A. 1996. *Turn organization: One intersection of grammar and interaction*. In Ochs, Schegloff & Thompson (eds), 52–133. https://doi.org/10.1017/CBO9780511620874.002

Schegloff, Emanuel A., Jefferson, Gail & Harvey Sacks 1977. The preference for self-correction in the organization of repair in conversation. *Language* 53(2): 361–382. https://doi.org/10.1353/lan.1977.0041

Schiffrin, Deborah. 1987. *Discourse Markers*.Cambridge: CUP https://doi.org/10.1017/CBO9780511611841

Sun, Chaofen & Traugott, Elizabeth. 2011. Grammaticalization and word order change. In *The Oxford Handbook of Grammaticalization*, Heike Narrog & Bernd Heine (eds), 378–388. Oxford: OUP.

Traugott, Elizabeth Closs. 2003. Constructions in grammaticalization. In *The Handbook of Historical Linguistics*, Brian Joseph & Richard Janda (eds), 624–647.Oxford: Blackwell. https://doi.org/10.1002/9780470756393.ch20

Traugott, Elizabeth. 2010. (Inter)subjectivity and (inter)subjectification: A reassessment. In *Intersubjectification and Grammaticalization* [Topics in English Linguistics 66], Kristin Davidse, Lieven Vandelanotte & Hubert Cuyckens (eds), 29–71. Berlin: De Gruyter. https://doi.org/10.1515/9783110226102.1.29

Traugott, Elizabeth & Dasher, Richard B. 2002. *Regularity in Semantic Change*. Cambridge: CUP.

Trudgill, Peter. 2004. *New Dialect Formation: The Inevitability of Colonial Englishes*. Edinburgh: EUP.

The development of three classifiers into degree modifier constructions in Chinese

Yueh Hsin Kuo
University of Edinburgh

This paper is a constructionalisation case study on how a post-head degree modifying (sub)schema arose, which generalises over three constructions that are classifiers in origin: *yi xie* 'some', *yi dian* 'one bit', and *yi xia* 'one downward motion'. Two factors underlie their developments: diminutive semantics, and pragmatically motivated syntactic contexts. Their diminutive semantics is general enough for them to be used as degree modifiers, while their postverbal and sentence-final positions, created by a specific topic-comment structure and zero anaphora, enable them to function as degree modifiers and even hedges. Despite similarities, they also display idiosyncrasies, such as collocational preferences.

Keywords: constructionalisation, classifier, degree modifier, Chinese

1. Introduction

There has been much work done on the development of degree modifier (DM) constructions from binominal constructions in English, including *a sort of*, *a bit*, and *a lot of*, especially from the perspective of construction grammar (e.g. Traugott 2007, 2008; Brems 2011; Trousdale 2012). These binominal constructions have the structure NP_1 *of* NP_2 in which NP_1 is the head, while their DM counterparts do not have NP_1 as their heads. For example, *a lot of* is originally a partitive (i.e. *a lot of land* 'part of the land') in which *a lot* is the head, but gradually developed first into a quantifier (i.e. *a lot of land* 'much land') in which *a lot* is no longer the head, and then a DM (i.e. in *a lot happier*, *a lot* boosts the degree of *happier*).[1] Traugott (2008) observes that the development of *a lot of* NP_2 is characterised

1. Traugott (2007, 2008) among others consider NP_1 *of* NP_2 as a DM when NP_2 has a scalar reading, so *a lot* in *a lot of fun/hysteria* are DMs. In this study DMs are more strictly defined as adverbial.

https://doi.org.10.1075/slcs.202.13kuo
© 2018 John Benjamins Publishing Company

functionally by the fact that partitives imply quantity, and quantity in turn invokes degree or scalarity. Formally, there are a loss of integrity and rebracketing: *a lot of* has become crystallised as a unit in which *a* and *of* are decategorised (no longer an indefinite article and a preposition, respectively), and the syntactic head shifts to the following NP_2 or AP so that only NP_2 triggers agreement. Trousdale (2012) shows that some other DMs originating from binominal constructions, called 'the H-constructions', have different histories. *Helluva* and its relatives (*helluv*, *hella*, *hecuv* and *hecka*) developed not from partitive binominal constructions, but evaluative binominal constructions *a hell/heck of* NP_2. Evaluative binominal constructions (e.g. *that jackass of a plumber, a sod of a car*), unlike *a lot of*, do not invoke inferences of quantity. However, Trousdale notes that what enables the H-constructions to develop into DM constructions is that they 'have the necessary semantics (*hell* and *heck* are far more semantically generally than *jackass*) and may invite the necessary inferences for a quantifier reading' (2012: 181) in contexts where NP_2 contains an adjective. For example, *a hell of a short journey* represents a bridging context (Heine 2002) in which evaluative and DM readings are possible: the speaker may mean 'the journey was unbearable, though short' (the evaluative reading), or 'it was surprisingly short' (Traugott and Trousdale 2010: 36).

A developmental pathway similar to *a lot of* or the H-constructions can also be found in Chinese: it involves general semantics and syntactic environments where inferences of degree are invited. Two classifier constructions, *yi xie* and *yi dian*, underwent the development and acquired degree modifying functions. (1) demonstrates their original function of quantification. In (2) they are DMs, signalling a low intensity or short duration.

(1) chi yi xie/dian fan
eat one some/bit rice
'Eat some rice/eat a bit of rice'.

(2) shui yi xie/dian[2]
sleep one some/dot
'(Please) sleep for a bit; take a nap.'

A hedging function is also present in (2). Another similar classifier is *yi xia*, usually described as a verbal classifier as it counts the occurrence of an action and literally means 'one time'. It has also developed into a DM akin to (2), which can be used as hedge.

2. *Shui yi xie* may not be grammatical synchronically, but diachronically so. See also Section 4.3.

(3) feng yi xia
sew one time
'to sew a bit; sew for a short while.' (taken from Paris 2013: 260)

Despite their forms as classifiers, (1)–(3) deviate from typical classifiers in two ways. Formally they only take an invariant numeral *yi* 'one', while typical classifiers can take any numeral. Functionally, *yi* does not have a literal, cardinal number reading. That is, *yi* 'one' is decategorised, not unlike *a* in *a lot of* (cf. Chen 2015's 'fixed one-phrase', Ahrens and Huang 2016's 'approximate measure words', and Paris 2013's 'weak classifiers'). This study accounts for how these classifiers developed the adverbial functions found in (2) and (3).

In the same spirit as previous research on binominal constructions in European languages (e.g. Verveckken 2012 on Spanish, De Clerck & Colleman 2013 on Flemish Dutch), this paper also adopts a constructional approach to the DMs' development. Previous studies have argued a constructional perspective is needed to account for DM constructions because, first, they are idiosyncratic with respect to their original binominal structures; second, it is the entire construction that grammaticalises, as evidenced by the fact that it is the whole binominal NP_1 *of* NP_2 that has developed degree modifying functions. The Chinese DM constructions under investigation are also idiosyncratic with respect to their source structures, and it is the entire *yi* + classifier construction that has changed. Another parallel with the H-constructions is that the development of the DM constructions is characterised by general semantics and specific syntactic environments inviting inferences of degree modification.

The paper is organised as follows. Section 2 outlines the constructionalisation framework. Section 3 presents *yi xie*'s history and analysis. Section 4 focuses on *yi dian* and *yi xia*. Section 5 concludes this paper. Data were retrieved from the Chinese Centre of Chinese Linguistics (CCL) Corpus, chosen for its unparalleled diachronic coverage.[3]

2. Constructions and constructionalisation

The version of diachronic construction grammar adopted herein is proposed by Traugott and Trousdale (2013; henceforth T&T), based on Goldberg (1995, 2006). In this framework, constructions, defined as form-meaning pairings, are the basic units of linguistic organisation and analysis. At first, idiosyncrasy was essential to the postulation of constructions (Goldberg 1995); however, it has been recognised

3. <http://ccl.pku.edu.cn:8080/ccl_corpus/>

that frequency alone motivates users to store forms and functions as constructions (Goldberg 2006). This study is qualitative; frequency is not the central focus. However, the fact that the DM constructions under investigation are not compositional (i.e. their classifier forms do not predict them to be DM constructions) qualifies them as constructions. The following formalism by Booij (2010; also followed by T&T) is adopted: [[F]] < –> [[M]], where the arrow associates F (for Form) and M (for Meaning) together, and the whole structure represents a construction. Four levels of constructions are recognised: constructs, micro-constructions, subschemas and schemas. Constructs are actual instances of use. Micro-constructions are abstractions over constructs and subschemas over micro-constructions. Schemas are the highest level of abstractions.

For example, consider again the binominal constructions. Actual instances of them (e.g. *I had a lot of food today*) are constructs, while *a lot of NP* are micro-constructions, over which we can propose two subschemas: large size (*a lot/bunch of*) and small size (*a bit/shred of*). A binominal quantifier schema then represents the most general, schematic information that abstracts over all the specific micro-constructions: [[[NP_1 of] NP_2] < –> [quantity –$entity_2$]] (modified and taken from T&T: 25). The constructionalisation framework also distinguishes two types of change: constructional changes and constructionalisation. Constructional changes involve just formal or functional change, in a given construction, while constructionalisation is more specifically defined as 'the creation of $form_{new}$-$meaning_{new}$ (combinations) of signs' (T&T: 22). Three parameters are proposed to model constructionalisation: compositionality, schematicity and productivity. Compositionality is related to how predictably form and meaning can be matched. Schematicity refers to how abstract, formally or functionally, a construction is, or how many lower-level constructions it abstracts over. There are two types of productivity: type and token productivity. The former concerns how many new micro-constructions a (sub)schema sanctions, while the latter is related to the frequency with which a construction is used.

In T&T procedural ('grammatical') constructionalisation is the creation of new grammatical construction and involves increases in schematicity and productivity and decreases in compositionality. Take for example the development of [NP_1 *of* NP_2] > [[NP_1] ADJ]. It has become more schematic because it no longer just quantifies nouns, but also modifies adjectives, and degree modification is a more abstract function than quantification; more type-productive because overtime it has sanctioned more micro-constructions (e.g. *a lot/bunch/bit/shred of*). It has become less compositional because the original binominal structure predicts NP_1 is the head, while in the DM construction, NP_1 is no longer the head, making it an idiomatic phrase that has a less transparent form-meaning mapping. In constructional terms, what this study analyses thus is: 'how do the post-verbal degree modifying (sub)schema (an abstraction over instances like Examples 2 and 3) arose?'

3. The history and analysis of *yi xie*

In this section the history of *yi xie* is reconstructed, based on the CCL corpus, followed by the analysis of its development, which will be shown to overlap the histories of *yi dian* and *yi xia*.

3.1 The history of *yi xie*

Yi xie's origin can be traced back to the early *Tang* Dynasty (circa 7th c.) in the forms of *xiexie* and *xiezi*, both of which are quantifiers meaning 'a small amount of; some'. Formally, *xiexie* is reduplicated, while *xiezi* contains a diminutive suffix 子-*zi*, originally meaning 'child'.

(4) 縱有些些理，無煩說短長[4]
zong you xiexie li, wu xu shuoduanchang
even.though have some.RDP reason NEG need criticise
'Even though you may be right, there is no need to criticize anyone.'
王梵志 *Wang Fanzhi* (?- circa 670)

(5) 方有些子語話分
fang you xiezi yuhua fen
then have some.DIM word share
'… then have some words to share.' 悟本禪師 *Wuben Chanshi* (807–869)

Xiexie and *xiezi* were general in its semantics; they quantified abstract or concrete nouns. For example, 紕縵*piman* 'loose fabric', 時光 *shiguang* 'time', and 管弦 *guanxian* 'music'.

Xiexie or *xiezi* used as a DM can be found in the *Wu Dai* and early *Song* Dynasty section of the corpus (circa late 9th - early 10th c.). As a DM, *xiexie* or *xiezi* indicates 'to a small extent or low degree; slightly'. For example,

4. The following abbreviations are used: 1SG = first person singular; 2SG = second person singular; 3SG = third person singular; AGN = agent nominaliser; ASP = aspect; COM = comparative marker; COP = copular; DIM = diminutive; FP = final particle; LOC = locative; NEG = negation; GEN = genitive; PRO = prohibitive; RDP = reduplication.

(6) 諸人莫鬧, 聽說些些
zhuren mo nao, tingshuo xiexie
people PRO fuss, listen.up slightly
'You people stop the fuss, listen up for a second.'
王敷 *Wang Fu* (mid. 8th-late 10th c.)

In addition to *xiexie* and *xiezi*, 一些 *yi xie*, 些兒 *xier* and 一些兒 *yi xier* are attested. *Yi* means 'one'. *-Er* is also a diminutive suffix, originally meaning 'child'. Both the quantifier and DM uses have coexisted and survived into Modern Chinese. As *yi xie* in Modern Chinese is categorised as a classifier (Chao 1968; Li & Thompson 1981) on the basis that it takes *yi* 'one' and quantifies nouns, it is by this period that we may say *xie* had become a classifier from a quantifier. *Xie* alone as a quantifier or DM also began appearing independently in this period. As a DM, *xie* is frequently found in resultative or comparative constructions where it indicates that the degree of the resultant state, or the compared quality, is low. For example,

(7) 要放寬些
yao fang kuan xie
have.to release wide slightly
'You must relax it a bit.' 朱子語類 *Zhuzi Yulei* (1270)

(8) 禹又比顏子粗些
yu you bi Yanzi cu xie
Yu even COM Yanzi rough slightly
'Yu is even slightly more uncouth than Yanzi.' *Zhuzi Yulei* (1270)

In (8) *fang kuan* is a resultative compound where *kuan* 'wide; widen' can be analysed as an adjective or stative verb indicating the resultant state of *fang* 'release'. (8) is an instance of the comparative construction with the comparative marker 比 *bi*. It has the form [NP_1 *bi* NP_2 AP] and meaning [NP_1 is more AP than NP_2], in which *xie* is part of the AP.

In the *Yuan* Dynasty (1271–1368) section of the corpus, *xie* can be found as a hedge, or more specifically, a sentence final particle used in giving requests or commands. It is not always easy to distinguish DM and final particle *xie*. It can have either reading in (9). But in the same period, some instances of *xie* also show the DM reading does not hold, such as (10).

(9) 休言語, 靠後些
xiu yanyu, kao hou xie
PRO speak lean back slightly/FP
'Do not speak, lean back (a little).' by 王實甫 *Wang Shifu* (1260–1336)

(10) (咱同母親尋三哥屍首去來。) 母親行動些
muqin xingdong xie
mother move FP
'(Let's go find third brother's corpse with mother). Mother, come (please).'
關漢卿 *Guan Hanqing* (1241–1320)

In (10), the urgency of the context (a corpse is at stake) does not make it felicitous to say the mother is only asked to 'move a little bit'. This indicates *xie* has evolved into a final particle.

In the 16th c. *xie* began achieving more independence from the comparative marker *bi* to the point that in some instances it alone suggests comparative degree:

(11) 好是好, 就是淡些, 再熬濃些更好了
hao shi hao, jiushi dan xie, zai ao nong xie geng hao le
good COP good but mild slightly again brew thick slightly even better ASP
'(This tea) is good, but somehow a bit mild; if brewed a bit thicker it would be even better.'
紅樓夢 *Hong Lou Meng* (1791)

In Standard Chinese, *xie* cannot take a standard of comparison (i.e. NP_2 in the comparative construction described above), and in general there is no unambiguous instance where *xie* is solely a comparative marker, not a DM. Only in some routine expressions like 快些*kuai xie* 'faster (used imperatively; similar to *hurry up*!)' and 好些*hao xie* 'better; *hao*: good' does *xie* more unambiguously encode comparative degree. Hence, *xie*'s comparative meaning in (10) can be considered a pragmatic extension of degree modification. Apart from the final particle all functions of *xie* have survived into Standard Chinese (but in some non-standard varieties it has survived and even evolved; see Li 2008 on final particle 唦 *sha*, derived from *xie*).

3.2 The analysis of *yi xie*

Based on (4)–(6) we can observe that there are two micro-constructions involving *xie* and its variants: quantifier *xiexie* [[*xiexie* NP] < –> [some NP]], and DM *xie* [[VP/AP *xie*] < –> [slightly VP/AP]] (henceforth *xie* and its variants used as quantifiers will be labelled as *xiexie*; as DMs, *xie*). Not only the syntactic category, but also the head-modifier order has changed. *Xiexie* precedes the head, while *xie* follows the head. This is an instance of 'rebracketing', a type of reanalysis that leads to a new representation with a different syntactic configuration (Hopper & Traugott 2003: 50–51). A similar instance has been observed in the shift of headhood from NP1 to NP2 in the development from binominal to DM constructions (cf. Traugott 2007, 2008), motivated by the pragmatic implicature that a unit/part implies quantity and degree. There are two types of ambiguous structure that motivated the parsing of quantifier *xiexie* as DM *xie*: a specific use of topic-comment structure and zero anaphora.

Topic and comment are crucial in explaining sentence structure in Chinese (Chao 1968; Li & Thompson 1981; LaPolla 1993). Following Li and Thompson (1981), in a Chinese topic-comment structure, an initial NP is the topic and the following VP is the comment on it, while the NP does not have to be an argument selected or subcategorised for by the verb.[5] In a specific kind of topic-comment structure, analogous to object fronting, the topical NP may leave its modifier *xiexie* behind, resulting in the separation of *xiexie* from its head, and an ambiguous sequence that allows the reading that *xiexie* does not modify the NP, but the verb, due to its proximity to the verb. This is represented as: [[V *xiexie* NP_i] < –> [V some NP_i]] - > [[NP_i V *xiexie*] < –> [NP_i, V some (of it_i)]]. On the left hand side is a sequence where the NP is not topical, as found in (4)–(5); On the right hand side, the NP modified by *xiexie* is in topical and in initial position, hence distant from *xiexie*. (12) is an early example:

(12) 佛法薄會些些
fofa bu hui xiexie
Buddhist.doctrines NEG know some.RDP
'Buddhist doctrines, I don't know any.'
盧山遠公話 *Lushan Yuangong Hua* (circa 972)

(12) has the structure [NP V *xiexie*] in which *xiexie* modifies the NP. On hearing a construct like (12), users may 'bracket' *xiexie* and the verb together, as *xiexie* is closer to the verb.

The other type of ambiguous sequence that enabled the emergence of DM *xie* is the use of zero anaphora. In Chinese, anaphora can be left unexpressed when they can be understood from the context (see Li & Thompson 1979; LaPolla 1993; Tao 1996). When *xiexie* is postverbal and modifies a zero anaphor, it also results in a sequence where *xiexie* seems to modify the verb. This is represented as [V *xiexie* NP] vs. [V *xiexie* ∅] where *xiexie* on the right-hand side modifies a zero anaphor. (13) is an early instantiation of the structure:

(13) 紅腮隱出枕函花,有些些
hong sai yin chu zhenhan hua, you xiexie
red cheek subtly emerge pillowcase flower, have some.RDP
'From the red cheeks emerge subtly the pillow case's floral patterns; there are some (of the floral patterns).'
張泌 *Zhang Bi* (circa 842–941)

5. There is no consensus in the functional literature on whether Chinese has 'subject' or whether topic must be selected by the verb (i.e. if Chinese has 'dangling' topic), the details of which should not concern this study.

On hearing constructs like (13), users may reanalyse *xiexie* as adverbial, due to the proximity between *xiexie* and the verb. Consider (14), where *xie* does not quantify *jing* 'mirror', but modifies *mo* 'to polish', as at the very start the speaker explicitly says 'just like *a* mirror':

(14) 如一鏡然,今日磨些,明日磨些,不覺自光
ru yi jing ran, jinri mo xie, mingri mo xie, bu jue
like one mirror so, today rub slightly tomorrow rub slightly NEG notice
zi guang
naturally shine
'Just like the way (you polish) a mirror, if you polish it bit by bit every day, it will shine without you noticing.' *Zhuzi Yulei* (1270)

(6)–(8) and (14) show that it is not possible to assign a non-adverbial reading to *xie*, as there is no topical NP from which it is separated, or an anaphor that allows us to reconstruct what NP *xie* quantifies. These examples suggest that constructionalisation has happened: a new form and meaning pairing, the DM *xie*-micro construction [[V *xie*] < –> [V slightly]], has been created, from [[V *xiexie* NP] < –> [V a bit of NP]], via contexts such as [V *xiexie* ∅] and [NP V *xiexie*]. These structures are pragmatically motivated as the use of zero anaphora or topical NPs is discourse-dependent. The participation of DM *xie* in resultative constructions also enabled it to modify adjectives, as the resultant state of a resultative compound can be analysed as a stative verb or adjective (see 7). Note that the DM *xie*-micro construction later took on *yi*. It is not a case of constructionalisation, but a formal constructional change.

Furthermore, the placement of quantity adverbials in Chinese and the semantics of *xie* also motivated the change. Quantity adverbials are postverbal (Li & Thompson 1981: Ch. 8.5) and as noted above, *xie* can quantify practically any type of noun, therefore is general. The general semantics of *xie* allows it to be taken as a 'pro-adverb' (i.e. it can stand in for quantity adverbials; see Schachter 1985: 34) when it is postverbal. For example, in (15) *gongchi* 'meter' and *fenzhong* 'minutes' specify the extent and duration of *pao* 'run':

(15) wo pao le shi gongchi/ fengzhong
I run ASP ten meter; minute
'I ran ten meters/minutes.'

They can be replaced by *xie* (*wo pao le xie* 'I ran a bit'), which obscures the specific content of the adverbials, but indicates more generally the small extent or short duration of *pao*.

DM constructions in Chinese typically are pre-head (e.g. [[*hen* AP] < –> [very AP]]), except for those involving an item of verbal origin with the semantics of 'arriving; reaching' that indicates degree (e.g. [[AP *zhiji*] < –> [extremely AP]]; *zhi ji* 'lit. reach limit'), or an auxiliary (e.g. [[AP/VP$_1$*de* VP$_2$] < –> [So AP/VP$_1$ that VP$_2$]]; Lamarre 2004). Thus, the creation of the *xie*-micro construction involves decreases in compositionality: a post-head position previously was not associated with a degree modifying, simplex item of a quantifier or classifier origin. Its development involves higher schematicity, as its adverbial function is more abstract than quantification. Based on the contrast between *xie* and other pre-head constructions, we can identify the *xie*-micro construction as being sanctioned by a post-head degree modifying subschema that also includes more specific, contentful modifiers such as quantity adverbials. This subschema is part of the degree modifying schema, comprised of both post-head and pre-head degree modifying subschemas. After *xie*, more similar expressions can be found in the post-head degree modifying position, thus indicating increases in type productivity of the subschema, exemplified by *yi dian* and *yi xia* below.

Xie's diminutive semantics also motivated its development into a final particle. Its source semantics 'small' carries over to its quantifier and degree modifying functions ('a small amount of' and 'to a small extent'). That lends it easily to be used as a hedge. Diminutive expressions are commonly used as hedges as they can effectively attenuate the illocutionary force of the speaker or establish a friendly tone. In giving commands or requests, using the diminutive may also make it sound easier, less important or obligatory to perform the task, thereby minimizing the imposition on the addressee (see Leech 1983: 148 on hedges such as *a bit* and *a little* (*bit*); Jurafsky 1996: 557–558 for a brief review on diminutives as hedges crosslinguistically). Notably, DM *xie*'s postverbal, thus frequently final, position also renders it suitable for intersubjective use, as the final position hosts a wide variety of particles with intersubjective meaning (see Chao 1968; Li & Thompson 1981).

4. The histories and analyses of *yi dian* and *yi xia*

This section recounts the histories of *yi dian* and *yi xia*. It will then proceed to show that their developments highly resemble that of *yi xie*. Hong (2013) also presents a detailed analysis of *yi dian*, which differs from, but complements the analysis proposed here.

4.1 The history of *yi dian*

Dian means 'point, dot'. *Yi dian* is a classifier, meaning 'one dot (of)'. Similar to *xie* and its variants, *yi dian* can be reduplicated (*yi dian dian*) or suffixed with *–zi* or *–er*.

(16) 一點水墨
yi dian shuimo
one dot ink
'A dot of ink.' 五燈會元 *Wudeng Huiyuan* (1152)

(17) 中間只有一兩點子光
zhongjian zhi you yi liang dianzi guang
middle only have one two dot.DIM light
'There's only one or two dots of light in the middle.' *Zhuzi Yulei* (1270)

As 'one dot' invites inferences of 'a small quantity', the meaning of *yi dian* later generalised to 'a bit of; few; little' (cf. 18). At that stage *yi* became decategorised; it did not mean 'one' dot. Even later, *yi dian* occurred in post-head position and modified adjectives or verbs (cf. 19 and 20). Similar to *xie*, in some instances *yi dian* can resemble a comparative marker (cf. 21).

(18) 我若吃一點酒
wo ruo chi yi dian jiu
1SG if eat one bit wine
'If I drink a bit of wine.' *Guan Hanqing* (c. 1241–1320)

(19) 可惜遲了一點兒
kexi chi le yi dianr
pity late ASP one bit.DIM
'It's a pity that it's a bit little.' *Hong Lou Meng* (1791)

(20) 錯我一點兒, 管不得誰....一例清白處治
cuo wo yi dianr, guanbude shei yili qingbai chuzhi
mistreat 1SG one bit.DIM no.matter who without.exception justly punish
'If you mistreat me even by a little, whoever you are, I will deal out justice.'
Hong Lou Meng (1791)

(21) 這孩子命裡不該早娶, 等大一點兒再定罷。
zhe haizi ming li bu gai zao qu, deng da yi dianrzai ding
this kid life LOC NEG should early marry wait big one bit.DIMthen decide
ba
FP
'This kid is not destined to marry early; let's wait until he gets a bit older, then we will make a decision.' *Hong Lou Meng* (1791)

It is also possible to find *dian* without *yi*, especially in routine expressions where, like *xie*, *dian* resemble a comparative marker, as shown in (22). It can be used as a hedge, as in (23):

(22) 快點進去
kuai dian jinqu
fast bit enter
'Hurry up, get in there.' 醒世姻緣 *Xingshi Yinyuan* (circa 1700)

(23) 放尊重一點
fang zunzhong yi dian
put respect one bit
'Be (a bit more) respectable!' (taken from Hong 2013: 55)

4.2 The history of *yi xia*

Xia is highly polysemous: it can mean 'low; below; descend'. In its classifier use, it is a verbal classifier: it quantifies downward hitting motions, typically that of hitting, striking or knocking. Therefore, it is used prototypically with transitive verbs. For example,

(24) 行者敲弓一下
xing zhe qiao gong yi xia
walk AGN knock bow one time
'Those who walk (foot soldiers) should give their bows a knock.'
通典 *Tongdian* (801)

Later *yi xia* generalised to 'for a short duration; in a second'. For example, in (25) *yi xia* does not have the literal meaning of 'one strike', but simply indicates a short duration:

(25) 紹聞略遲疑一下
Shaowen lue chiyi yi xia
Shaowen slightly hesitate one time
'Shaowen slightly hesitated a bit.' 岐路燈 *Qiludeng* (1749)

Similar to *yi xie* and *yi dian*, *yi xia* has variants that are reduplicated (*yi xia xia*) or suffixed with *–zi* or *–er*. However, it began attracting *–zi* and *–er* later *yi xie* or *yi dian*: while *–er* and *–zi* attached to *yi xie* and *yi dian* as early as the *Song* Dynasty, the earliest examples of *yi xiezi* are found in the *Yuan* Dynasty section of the corpus. *Yixia* also prefers *–zi* over *–er* (e.g. 26). *Yi xia* can also be used as a hedge, especially in collocation with 等 *deng* 'wait':

(26) 你揀那大棒子打著，一下子打死了他
ni jian na da bangzi da zhe yi xia.zi da si le ta
2SG pick that big club hit ASP, one time.DIM hit die ASP 3SG
'You picked up that big club and kept hitting him. you killed him instantly.'
抱妝盒 *Baozhuang He* (circa 1271–1368)

(27) 只好委屈你多等一下
zhihao weiqu ni duo deng yi xia
without.choice do.wrong 2SG more wait one time
'We are without any choice but to trouble you to wait a bit longer.'
八仙得道 *Baxian Dedao* (mid.-late 19th c.)

4.3 The analyses of *yi dian* and *yi xia*

Both *yi dian* and *yi xia* have undergone similar developmental processes. First, it involved generalisation of meaning from a small unit of measurement (*yi dian* 'a dot'; *yi xia* 'one strike') to a small quantity or short duration in general ('a bit of'; 'for a short duration'). Second, they were used in ambiguous sequences where they might be 'bracketed' with the verb, similar to those involving *xiexie*: topic-comment structure and zero anaphora. The generalised semantics of *yi dian* and *yi xia* also aided in the reanalysis: like *xie*, they could be taken as 'pro-adverbs', paraphrasing their lexical counterparts, quantity adverbials.

For example, *yi dianr* in (28), similar to *xie* in (12), is also closer to the verb than the NP in topic position. In (29), it modifies a zero anaphor, resulting in a structure where it is adjacent to the verb, but distant from the NP:

(28) 萬丈水不教泄漏了一點兒
wan zhang shui bu jiao xielou le yi dianr
ten.thousand measurement.unit water NEG let leak ASP one bit.DIM
'Ten thousands *zhang* of water, I don't let leak a bit.'
白樸 *Bai Pu* (1226–1306)

(29) 你說的話，我牢牢的記著，要違背一點兒…
ni shuo de hua, wo laolaode ji zhe, yao weibei yi dianr
2SG say GEN word 1SG firmly remember ASP if disobey one bit.DIM
'What you said, I will remember. If you don't follow a bit (of what you said)'.
Xingshi Yinyuan (circa 1700).

Constructs like (28) and (29), reminiscent of (12) and (13), allow the reanalysis that *yi dian* is a postverbal DM, especially (29). As the head-modifier relation between the head NP ('what you said') and *yi dianr* may be more opaque due to the relative long distance in (29), users might bracket the verb and *yi dianr* together rather than the NP and *yi dianr*.

Yi xia is slightly different from *yi xie* and *yi dian*, as it does not modify adjectives, but verbs. But in a sequence where the verb takes a zero anaphor as its postverbal argument, *yi xia* is immediately after the verb, resulting again in a structural context where the verb and *yi xia* may be analysed together. For example,

(30) 有幾件粗糙東西，煩整理一下
you ji jian cucao dongxi fan zhengli yi xia
have some items rough thing please sort.out one time
'There is some rubbish, please sort (it) out a bit.' *Qiludeng* (1749).

In (30), *cucao dongxi* 'rubbish' can be identified as the zero postverbal argument of *zhengli* (*zhengli cucao dongxi* 'sort out the rubbish'). As it is coded as zero, *yi xia* can be taken as modifying the verb. This, again, is reminiscent of (13), where *xiexie* modifies a zero anaphor.

Examples like (19)–(23) and (25) suggest that *yi dian* and *yi xia* have developed into DMs. *Yi dian* in *cuo wo yi dianr* 'mistreat me a bit' or *da yi dianr* 'a bit bigger' cannot be said to modify an NP, whether zero or not, while *yi xia* in *chiyi yi xia* 'hesitate a bit' modifies a non-transitive verb, and it may not necessarily signal just a short duration, but also a small extent. For example, *xiang yi xia* 'think a bit' can also indicate the extent to which *xiang* 'think' goes. Therefore, following the constructionalisation of *xie*, we can identify two more micro-constructions under the post-head degree modifying subschema: *yi dian*- and *yi xia*-micro-constructions, [[V (*yi*) *dian/xia*] < –> [V slightly]]. Their forms and functions overlap with *xie*-micro construction: formally, they are post-head, and can take *yi* and be reduplicated or suffixed with *–er* or *–zi*; functionally, they signal a low degree or intensity.[6]

At the subschema level, there are increases of schematicity and productivity: the subschema abstracts over and sanctions more micro-constructions. Its compositionality decreases: even though a high number of members in the subschema might help predict a postverbal classifier as a DM, the micro-constructions have obvious differences that make it difficult to predict exact form-function correspondences. For example, the post-head and final position *yi dian* and *yi xia* occupy, combined with their general, diminutive semantics, also facilitate their pragmatic use as hedges. But unlike final particle *xie*, *yi dian* and *yi xia* does not seem to have semanticised this function in final position; whenever they are used as hedges,

6. Interestingly, according to 'the dictionary, 汉语方言大词典 Hanyu Fangyan Dacidian (Xu & Gongtian 1999: 208)', *xia* in the variety spoken in 安溪 *Anxi* is synonymous with *xie* in its quantifier sense, further highlighting their similarities.

their source semantics of 'doing something a bit' can be identified. Formally, *yi* is more likely to be preserved in *yi dian* and *yi xia* than *yi xie*, which can be attributed to the fact that *yi dian* and *yi xia* originated as classifiers, while *xie* acquired *yi* after it had evolved into a DM. Some collocational preferences also distinguish these DMs. While typically they modify activity verbs, some verbs appear to prefer one or two of them. *Deng (yi) xie* 'wait for a while' is attested diachronically (e.g. in 野叟曝言 *Yesou Puyan*, 1779), but synchronically not nearly as idiomatic as *deng yi xia* (cf. 27). *Shui xie* 'sleep a bit' diachronically is possible (e.g. in the work of 馬致遠 *Ma Zhiyuan*, 1250–1321), but rare, if not impossible, nowadays.

Finally, the post-head degree modifying subschema accounts for novel constructs: the subschema must be a pattern users can recognise and thus model novel expressions on. For example, (31) was retrieved from a Taiwanese online forum. It contains a classifier 一滴 *yi di* 'one drop' used innovatively as a post-head DM. *Yi* is decategorised and *di* does not literally mean 'drop'. *Di* is also triplicated, supposedly to signal an even lesser degree than *yi di*:

(31) 今天逼自己稍微早一滴滴滴起來
jintian bi ziji shaowei zao yi di di di qilai
today force self slightly early one drop drop drop get.up
'Today I forced myself to get up just a teeny-weeny bit earlier.'
<https://www.dcard.tw/f/talk/p/26264> (22 October 2017)

5. Conclusion

This study has demonstrated that the constructionalisation of post-head degree modifiers originated from specific contexts where particular, pragmatically motivated syntactic configurations led to the reanalysis of *yi xie*, *yi dian*, and *yi xia* as DMs. The semantics of *yi xie*, *yi dian*, and *yi xia* also facilitated their developments as their general meaning could easily be taken as paraphrasing quantity adverbials, their more specific, lexical counterparts.

T&T remark that one of the advantages of a constructional approach is that it allows the researcher 'to see how networks, schemas, and micro-constructions are created or grow and decline, as well as the ability to track the development of patterns at both levels' (233); that is, to think in terms of both the concrete (constructs; micro-constructions) and the abstract (schemas). This study has capitalised on this advantage by proposing the post-head degree modifying subschema, which abstracts over the functional and formal similarities of *yi xie/dian/xia*. Novel usage such as (31) can thus be explained.

References

Ahrens, Kathleen & Huang, Chu-Ren 2016. Classifiers. In *A Reference Grammar of Chinese*, Chu-Ren Huang & Dingxu Shi (eds), 169–198. Cambridge: CUP.

Bernd, Heine. 2002. On the role of context in grammaticalization. In *New Reflections on Grammaticalization* [Typological Studies in Language 49], Ilse Wischer & Gabriele Diewald (eds), 83–101. Amsterdam: John Benjamins.

Booij, Geert. 2010. *Construction Morphology*. Oxford: OUP.

Brems, Lieselotte. 2011. *Layering of Size and Type Noun Constructions in English*. Berlin: Mouton de Gruyter. https://doi.org/10.1515/9783110252927

Chao, Yuen Ren. 1968. *A Grammar of Spoken Chinese*. Berkeley CA: University of California Press.

Chen, I-Hsuan. 2015. *The Diachronic Development and Syncrhonic Distribution of Minimizers in Mandarin Chinese*. PhD dissertation, University of California at Berkeley.

De Clerck, Bernard & Colleman, Timothy. 2013. From noun to intensifier: Massa and massa's in Flemish varieties of Dutch. *Language Sciences* 36: 147–160. https://doi.org/10.1016/j.langsci.2012.04.005

Goldberg, Adele E. 1995. *Constructions: A Construction Grammar Approach to Argument Structure*. Chicago IL: University of Chicago Press.

Goldberg, Adele E. 2006. *Constructions at Work the Nature of Generalization in Language*. Oxford: OUP.

Hong, Po-Yao. 2013. The Grammaticalization of Post-verbal yidian 'yi dian' in Mandarin Chinese. MA thesis, National Chiao Tung University.

Hopper, Paul J. & Traugott, Elizabeth Closs. 2003. *Grammaticalization*, 2nd edn. Cambridge: CUP. https://doi.org/10.1017/CBO9781139165525

Jurafsky, Daniel. 1996. Universal tendencies in the semantics of the diminutive. *Language* 72: 533–578. https://doi.org/10.2307/416278

Lamarre, Christine. 2004. Verb complement constructions in Chinese dialects: Types and markers. In *Sinitic Grammar: Synchronic and diachronic Perspectives*, Hilary Chappell (ed.), 85–120. Oxford: OUP.

LaPolla, Randy J. 1993. Arguments against 'subject' and 'direct object' as viable concepts in Chinese. *Bulletin of the Institute of History and Philology* 63: 759–813.

Leech, Geoffrey N.. 1983. *Principles of Pragmatics*. New York NY: Longman.

Li, Charles N. & Thompson, Sandra A. 1979. Third person pronouns and zero-anaphora in Chinese discourse. In *Syntax and Semantics*, Vol. 12: *Discourse and Syntax*, Talmy Givon (ed.), 311–336. New York NY: Academic Press.

Li, Charles N. & Thompson, Sandra A. 1981. *Mandarin Chinese: A Functional Reference Grammar*. Berkeley CA: University of California Press.

Li, Xiaojun. 2008. The generation of modal particle Sha and its dialectal variants. *Linguistic Sciences* 7: 398–405.

Paris, Marie-Claude. 2013. Verbal reduplication and verbal classifiers in Chinese. In *Breaking Down the Barriers: Interdisciplinary Studies in Chinese Linguistics and Beyond*, (eds), 257–278. Taipei: Academica Sinica.

Schachter, Paul 1985. Parts-of-speech systems. In *Language Typology and Syntactic Description: Clause Structure*, Vol. 1, Timoty Shopen (ed.), 3–61. Cambridge: CUP.

Tao, Liang. 1996. Topic discontinuity and zero anaphora in Chinese discourse: cognitive strategies in discourse processing. In *Studies in Anaphora* [Typologial Studies in Language 33], Barbara Fox (ed.), 487–514. Amsterdam: Benjamins. https://doi.org/10.1075/tsl.33.15tao

Traugott, Elizabeth Closs. 2007. The concepts of constructional mismatch and type-shifting from the perspective of grammaticalization. *Cognitive Linguistics* 18(4): 523–557. https://doi.org/10.1515/COG.2007.027

Traugott, Elizabeth Closs. 2008. Grammaticalization, constructions and the incremental development of language: Suggestions from the development of degree modifiers in English. In Variation, Selection, Development- Probing the Evolutionary Model of Language Change, Regine Eckardt, Gerhard Jäger & Tonjes Veenstra (eds), 219–250. Berlin: Mouton de Gruyter.

Traugott, Elizabeth Closs & Trousdale, Graeme. 2010. *Gradience, Gradualness and Grammaticalization* [Typological Studies in Language 90]. Amsterdam: John Benjamins. https://doi.org/10.1075/tsl.90

Traugott, Elizabeth Closs & Trousdale, Graeme. 2013. *Constructionalization and Constructional Changes*. Oxford: OUP. https://doi.org/10.1093/acprof:oso/9780199679898.001.0001

Trousdale, Graeme. 2012. Grammaticalization, constructions, and the grammaticalization of constructions. In *Grammaticalization and Language Change: New Reflections* [Studies in Language Companion Series 130], Kristin Davidse, Tine Breban, Liselotte Brems & Tanja Mortelmans (eds), 167–198. Amsterdam: Joh Benjamins. https://doi.org/10.1075/slcs.130.07tro

Verveckken, Katrien. 2012. Towards a constructional account of high and low frequency binominal quantifiers in Spanish. *Cognitive Linguistics* 23: 421–478. https://doi.org/10.1515/cog-2012-0013

Xu, Baohua & Gongtian, Yilang. 1999. Hanyu Fangyan Dacidian 汉语方言大词典. Beijing: Zhonghua Book Company.

From the inside to the outside of the sentence

Forming a larger discourse unit with *jijitsu* 'fact' in Japanese

Reijirou Shibasaki
Meiji University

This study examines the development of the projector *jijitsu* 'the fact is, in fact' from the earlier nominal predicate *jijitsu-nari/dearu/da/desu/dearimasu* (fact-copulative verb) in Modern through Present-day Japanese. Evidence from corpus studies suggests that *jijitsu* undergoes both formal and functional changes from the inside of the sentence as a nominal predicate to the outside of the sentence as a projector, connecting preceding and following information, forming a larger discourse unit. This change is characteristic of 'constructionalization' in the sense of Traugott and Trousdale (2013). The nominal predicate use of *jijitsu* inside the sentence also goes through several formal changes in the choice of copulative verbs over time, i.e. 'constructional changes'. Constructionalization attested in the history of *jijitsu* echoes the historical processes of similar constructions in European languages, which means that language users have the potential to make 'discourse-pragmatic' sense of a given context, and such a newly emergent sense is likely to be formally realized at the edge of a sentence.

Keywords: constructionalization beyond the sentence, constructional changes, projectors, discourse and grammar

1. Introduction

Pragmatic markers (PMs) have received broad attention from functionally-oriented researchers and accordingly been named in a variety of ways due to their wide range of discourse-pragmatic functions and specific morpho-syntactic forms, e.g. 'comment clauses' (Quirk et al. 1985), 'shell nouns' (Schmid 2000), 'parentheticals' (e.g. Huddleston & Pullum 2002), 'epistemic phrases' (Wierzbicka 2006), 'projector constructions' (Hopper & Thompson 2008) or simply 'formulaic' expressions (Wray 2009) (e.g. Brinton 2010 for a useful summary). In recent years, the

https://doi.org.10.1075/slcs.202.14shi
© 2018 John Benjamins Publishing Company

sequential relation of PMs to either preceding or following information in both written and spoken language has started to be extensively examined in several languages with increased attention to the left periphery (LP henceforth) and the right periphery (RP henceforth) of an utterance (e.g. Beeching & Detges 2014; Traugott 2015). Since expressions used at both LP and RP are often fixed forms with distinctive functions (e.g. turn-taking, focalizing, etc. at LP, while turn-yielding, modalizing, etc. at RP), it is likely that some researchers associate the emergence of such PMs at the LP and RP with grammaticalization. More broadly, Traugott (2003: 624) states that "...early in grammaticalization, lexemes grammaticalize only in certain highly specifiable morphosyntactic contexts, and under specifiable pragmatic conditions."

In the history of Japanese, PMs that have developed from clausal connectives such as *-keredomo* 'although' and *-dakara* 'because' into connective particles *(da) ke(re)do(mo)* 'but' and stand-alone *dakara* 'so' are well attested; they serve at the LP to frame the upcoming main message (e.g. Onodera 2004; Higashiizumi 2015). In addition to those well-studied connectives, sets of free-standing nominals can be used as discourse connectives usually at the LP as in (1). Note that data sources will be explained in Section 3.

(1) *Kekkon nanteno mo, hitori no ningen o shoyuu.suru toiu*
marriage so-called also one person GEN human ACC possess.do so-called
koto ni naru no-daroo ka. Jijitsu, kekkon o shinaku temo
COMP PT become NML-may.be QP fact marriage ACC do.not even.if
nagaku tsukiatte-iru to otoko wa oubou-ni-naru.
long go.together if man TOP high-handed-PT-become
'Speaking of marriage, (I wonder if it means) that one is in the possession of another. In fact, even if (people) do not get married, men become high-handed if (they) go together for a prolonged period.'
(2004 *Hebi ni Piasu*; BCCWJ)

On the other hand, *jijitsu* 'fact' can be used as part of a nominal predicate as in (2).

(2) *Dejitaru-ni-natte, shigoto no haba ga hirogatta-no wa jijitsu-desu.*
digital.PT-become job GEN range NOM widen.PST-NML TOP fact-COP.POL
Tada, amari hiroge sugiru to betsuno genba no shigoto ni
but too broaden a.bit.much if another field GEN job PT
hurete-shimau.
be.an.obstacle-AUX
'In the digital era, (it) is the fact that the range of (our) jobs became wider. Yet if (we) increase the range (of our jobs) too much, it turns out that (such increased workload) will bring about obstacles to jobs in another field.'
(2001 *The art of spirited away*; BCCWJ)

A Google search of the LP use of *jijitsu* (i.e. PM) and the sentence-final use of *jijitsu-desu* (i.e. part of a predicate) results in 92,200,000 and 39,300,000 entries respectively (accessed: Nov. 26, 2016), which shows that these expressions, especially the PM function of *jijitsu*, seem to be commonly used in a formulaic way.

Many researchers have investigated nominal predicates as in (2) and adverbialized nominals as in (1) from either historical or discourse-pragmatic perspectives (e.g. Horie 2012; Shin'ya 2014; Narumi 2015). However, the diachronic relation between the two functionally different uses of an expression such as *jijitsu* 'fact' has yet to be demonstrated. Narumi (2015) pays special attention to the adverbialized functions of erstwhile nominal forms; however, as Kawase (2016: 146) points out, the kind of morpho-syntactic conditions (or rather discourse-sequential relations) that facilitate the degree of adverbialization is not clearly specified there. To the best of my knowledge, Takahashi and Higashiizumi (2014) take a pioneering role in the diachronic study of adverbialized nouns in Japanese with respect to discourse-syntactic structures (see Section 5.1), although their theoretical considerations are not fully developed.

It seems that PM uses of these independent nominals have developed from their erstwhile nominal-predicate uses as in (2), which is presumably triggered by analogy with the structurally and functionally similar development of connective particles such as *(da)ke(re)do(mo)* 'but' and stand-alone *dakara* 'so', i.e. from clause-final predicate uses to clause-initial PM uses (LP). Therefore, the purpose of the current paper is to uncover the historical pathway of the functional expansion of *jijitsu* and to explain how it changes in certain discourse contexts in terms of constructionalization (Traugott & Trousdale 2013). While this study deals with the development of the PM *jijitsu* with regard to constructionalization, it does not underestimate the achievements in grammaticalization research. Rather, a constructionalization approach comes to terms with or acts synergistically with a grammaticalization approach, because the development under discussion gives support to the statements that "constructions (elements in context) and not individual lexical items are the proper domain of grammaticalization" (Himmelmann 2004: 31) and that "the reinterpretation of grammaticalization in terms of constructions" helps researchers to have a more accurate grasp of form-function pairings (Smith et al. 2015: 1; see Traugott 2003 above). Note that in this study, a set of expressions that introduce the speaker's upcoming statement, signaling to the interlocutor to get ready for it, are regarded as 'projectors' (Hopper & Thompson 2008: 105; see Section 5.1 for further discussion).

This current paper is organized as follows. In Section 2, I will give a brief account of the history of *jijitsu* and a short synopsis of the studies on *jijitsu*. In Section 3, I will present the corpora used for this study, while in Section 4,

I will provide the survey results based on the corpora. Section 5 is devoted to the summary and discussion of the constructionalization of *jijitsu*.

2. Background

2.1 A short history of *jijitsu*

According to Kitahara (2006), the most comprehensive dictionary of the Japanese language, *jijitsu* is considered to have started its life as part of a nominal predicate in the early eleventh century as in (3) and (4), while its adverbial use is witnessed about nine centuries later as in (5).

(3) *Udaiben kitari-te iwaku, Saiin no jijitsu-nari…*
duty.position come-and say place.name GEN fact-COP
'Udaiben came (over here) and said (what happened at) Saiin Palace (i.e. theft) is a fact.' (c.1017 [July 2] *Midookanpakuki*; Kitahara 2006, Vol. 6: 655)

(4) *Udaishoo no tokoro tikaki ni aru niyori, annai wo tofa.simu.*
duty.position GEN place nearby PT exist because guide ACC ask.make
Jijitsu-nari.
fact-COP
'Since Udaishoo's Palace is in the vicinity (of my place), (I) ordered (my subordinates) to guide (me). (It) is the fact.'
(c.1017 [July 7] *Midookanpakuki*; Yamanaka 1985: 133)

(5) *Soshite jijitsu, tookyoo de wakai ookuno onna no o-tomodachi mo oari*
and fact Tokyo in young many female GEN PREF-friend too exist
no koto de atta.
GEN COMP COP PST
'And in fact, (it) turned out that (he) has lots of young girlfriends in Tokyo.'
(c.1914 *Inaka Ishi no Ko*; Kitahara 2006, Vol. 6: 655)

It is obvious that the development of the adverbial use of *jijitsu* took a fair amount of time. Since these examples of speech are widely separated in time, I referred to some unabridged dictionaries and reference books for successive periods between the eleventh and late nineteenth centuries (Maeda 1974; Doi et al. 1980; Morita 1989; Okubo & Kinoshita 1991; Ebara 2008), as well as several historical corpora of particular genres, i.e. *Sharebon* (gay-quarter novelettes) and *Ninjoobon* (love stories) in the eighteenth and nineteenth centuries (Ichimura 2015 and Fujimoto & Takada 2015), respectively. However, only a couple of hard-to-find examples emerged as in (6), and even those examples turned out to comprise part of the nominal predicate construction as in (3) and (4).[1]

(6) *jijitsu tara.ba kidai.fusigi no daimoku nari.*
fact AUX.if rare.wonder GEN instance COP
'If (this) is a fact, (it should) be a rare occurrence.'
(?late 14C, *Meitokuki*; Doi 1994, Vol. 3: 273)

The survey results tell us that while the nominal predicate of *jijitsu* dates back to the early eleventh century, the number of instances of *jijitsu* seems to be extremely sparse in the eleventh through nineteenth centuries. Furthermore, all the examples found in these periods are used as part of the nominal-predicate construction as in (3), (4) and (6). Judging from these observations, we feel compelled to state that the adverbial usage of *jijitsu*, usually occurring at the LP of sentence, is only developed later in the late nineteenth century and gains in increasing popularity in the early twentieth century.[2]

In the following two periods, Meiji (c.1868–1912) and Taisho (c.1912–1926), both nominal and adverbial uses of *jijitsu* begin to show an upward trend according to the results of my corpus surveys (see Section 4 for details). What is characteristic of these modern times is an integration of written and spoken styles called *genbun icchitai*, which in general is considered to begin in these periods (e.g. Onodera 2004: 23). On the other hand, Tatsuno (2007: § III.7) suggests that it already started in the Edo period (c.1603–1867), specifically in 1843 when *Musuidokugen*, a life story written in a colloquial style by a bohemian Kokichi Katsu, was published, which he believes to facilitate *genbun icchitai* in later periods.

1. Furuhashi et al. (2012) provide another example of *jijitsu* from a diary called *Rakushishanikki* (18C?) in the Edo period (c. 1603–1867) as in (i); however, the usage is clearly nominal-oriented.

(i) *Shinseki-no Rakushisha-no tanzaku ni sensei no jijitsu ichijiku o*
the.real-GEN proper.name-GEN a.strip.of.paper PT teacher GEN/NOM fact all? ACC
chojutushi-te okuraru.
write-and send.HON
'On a strip of authentic Rakushisha tanzaku, the teacher wrote a long list of facts and sent (it).'
(18C? *Rakushishanikki*; Furuhashi et al. 2012: 157)

2. Onodera (2004: 89–90) considers the language in the (late) Muromachi period (c. 1336–1573) as the earliest origin of the present-day Tokyo Japanese; the earlier texts are treated separately from the later texts to uncover the natural process of language change. Her claim can be supported by the survey results in Shibasaki (2010), albeit from a different perspective. Note that dividing the history of Japanese still seems to be controversial, which means that linguistic periods and political periods/events do not necessarily coincide with each other (cf. Onodera 2004: 238–240; Shibatani 1990: 119–120; and Frellesvig 2010: 1–3); similar issues are often discussed in relation to the historical division of the English language (Curzan 2017).

Building on these observations, the adverbialized *jijitsu* in the late nineteenth century onward seems to have stemmed from the impact of the spoken mode on the written mode, reformulating discourse sequential relations (cf. Tabor & Traugott 1997 and Traugott & Dasher 2002: Chap 4; Keizer 2016; see Mair 2006 for a similar observation under the name of 'colloquialization' in English). In fact, the adverbial use of *jijitsu* at the LP can be qualified as a kind of discourse marker, a stance marker (cf. Morimoto 1994 for the term SSA (the speaker's subjective attitude) adverbs) or clause-medial connector (cf. Fujiwara 2011; Saegusa 2013), all of which show some features of spoken-ness even when used in written discourse (cf. Noguchi 2016). I will thus lay emphasis on the incipient and extensive stages of *jijitsu* in the Meiji and Taisho periods, and the contemporary use of *jijitsu* in the last few decades, respectively.

2.2 Overview of research on *jijitsu*

2.2.1 *A commentary inductive adverb at sentence-initial position*

Watanabe (1971) introduces the term *chuushakunoyuudoo fukushi* 'commentary inductive adverbs (lit.)' based on their discourse-pragmatic functions, which he defines as follows: they take a lead and serve to anticipate what comes next (p. 318). A set of adverbs he includes in this specific category are *mochiron* 'of course', *muron* 'take it for granted that…', *jijitsu* 'in fact, the fact is (that)', and *jissai* 'in fact, practically'. Take a look at (7).

(7) a. *Jijitsu kono booshi wa sumaato-da.*
fact this hat TOP smart-COP
'In fact, (one looks) smart in the hat.'

b. *Mochiron gensho o yomu.*
of.course original.edition ACC read
'Of course, (I) will read the original edition (not the translation).'
(Watanabe 1971: 317–318)

What qualifies Watanabe (1971) as an insightful study is that he states that (7) can be rephrased as (8a). Note that this is suggested but not provided in Watanabe (1971: 319) and I made the constructed Example (8a) based on his suggestion.

(8) a. *Kono booshi ga sumaato-na no wa jijitsu da*
this hat NOM smart-COP NML TOP fact COP
'(One) looks smart in the hat. That's the fact. (lit. That (one) looks smart in the hat is the fact.)'

b. *Gensho o yomu no wa mochiron-da.*
Original.edition ACC read NML TOP of.course-COP

'(I) will read the original edition (not the translation), of course. (lit. That (I) will read the original edition is a sure thing.)'
(both examples from Watanabe 1971: 318–319)

Watanabe (1971) does not take any contemporary discourse-pragmatic approach to the choice of the sentence-initial adverbial *jijitsu* or the sentence-final predicate use of *jijitsu*. Nevertheless, as I tried to pick up his real intention in the translation, his sharp observation on the syntactic realization of *jijitsu* either at LP or at the sentence-final predicate position is worthy of attention in light of constructionalization (but see Section 5.1 for further discussion).[3]

2.2.2 *A kind of adverbial connector between sentences*

Takeuchi (1973: 140) suggests that the discourse function of commentary inductive adverbs should serve to add sentence-external information at the discourse level to the sentence-internal information in the *jijitsu*-prefaced clause. In other words, for a better understanding of the functions of commentary inductive adverbs, we need to widen our view from the sentence level to the discourse level, which means that it is necessary to consider the preceding context (see also Fujiwara 2011 and Saegusa 2013 below).

Consider the following examples.

(9) *Dare demo ii kara atamakazu ga hosii no kamo. Jijitsu,*
anybody even okay from number NOM want NML FP fact
hitomukashimae ni kurabe tara ninki mo ochi-mashita-shi.
decade.ago PT compare if popularity PT fall-POL-because
'(They) don't mind who (but they) want to get enough people maybe. In fact, (such TV programs) are less popular now than a decade ago.'
(2005 *Yahoo Chiebukuro*, Entertainment; BCCWJ)

(10) *Tabako suu koto de, honno.wazukana jikan demo,*
tobacco smoke COMP by a.small.fraction.of time even
kaihoos-are-ru to omotte-ita-shi, jijitsu, sooiu kimochi ni
emancipate-PAS-PRES COMP think-PST-and fact like.that feeling PT
natte-imashi-ta.
become-POL-PST
'By smoking, (I) thought (I) could be released (from agony) even for a small amount of time, and in fact, (I) felt like that.' (2008 *Yahoo Blog*: BCCWJ)

In these examples, the clause or sentence following *jijitsu* provides a piece of evidence for, or additional information to, the clause or sentence preceding *jijitsu*.

3. For the functions of nominal predicates in contemporary Japanese see Shin'ya (2014).

That is, commentary inductive adverbs associate part of the preceding information with the following statement. In this regard, Morimoto (1994) and Fujiwara (2011) provide similar observations as to the discourse-pragmatic functions of *jijitsu*. Otake (2009: 149) also touches on the usage of *jijitsu* and *jijitsu wa* (TOP) 'in fact, the fact is (that)'; however, his description is restricted to the relation of *jijitsu* to the following clause but not to the preceding sentence, as marked NA (not available) in Table 1 below.[4]

Table 1. Discourse sequence of *jijitsu* (based on Shibasaki 2017: 112)*

	Discourse sequence		
Form	[X $_{\text{sentence 1}}$]	*jijitsu*	[Y $_{\text{sentence 2}}$]
Function	NA		anticipate what comes next (Watanabe 1971: 317–319)
	statement		evidence for the statement (Takeuchi 1973: 137–140)
	proposition		evidence for the proposition (Morimoto 1994: 142–143)
	NA		actual condition (to X?) (Otake 2009: 149)
	common belief		information that is congruent with the common belief but is unexpected to the speaker (Fujiwara 2011: 52–53)
	preceding context		evidence for the preceding context (Saegusa 2013: 54)

* They use different data. For example, Takeuchi (1973) seems to use examples from some preceding studies and constructed examples. Morimoto (1994) attempts a qualitative analysis of a variety of "speaker's subjective attitude" adverbs based on questionnaires, while Fujiwara (2011) uses open-access resources on the search engines of Google and goo.

Table 1 summarizes the sequential relation of *jijitsu* based on the descriptions and observations mentioned above. While commas are sometimes inserted between *jijitsu* and the following sentence, they do not necessarily mean any intonational break or pause especially in the written texts; rather, it seems to reflect the writer's own preference for particular punctuation styles.

Regardless of their terminological differences, the function of the *jijitsu*-prefaced sentence seems to have one distinctive feature, that of producing evidence for the preceding sentence as in Table 1, which means that *jijitsu* cannot be used as a PM without any relevant preceding context (Saegusa 2013: 52; see Section 5.1 for relevant discussions). In fact, the following example sounds strange because Speaker B does not accept the evidence of Speaker A's utterance.

4. Otake (2009: 149) compares the bare form *jijitsu* and the form accompanied by the topic maker *jijitsu wa*, and states that the latter is upgraded to the main clause without solid evidence. However, it is not likely that *jijitsu wa* can always perform a main clause function as far as has been hither to observed.

(11) A: *kotoshi no fuyu wa yuki ga ooi toiu yohoo*
this.year GEN winter TOP snow NOM be.ample so-called forecast
deshi-ta.
COP-PST
'The weather forecast told (us) that (we would) have much snow this winter.'

B: *(??Jijitsu) mada zenzen futteimasen.*
in fact yet not.at.all fall.POL.NEG
(??In fact), (we) have so far had no snow (this year).'
(Morimoto 1994: 142)

On the other hand, Morimoto (1994: 147) suggests that (as an adverb), *jijitsu* is not likely to appear at sentence-final position as in (12), presumably because it cannot serve to introduce evidence for the preceding utterance. In fact, the corpora used for this study do not include any such examples as (12).[5]

(12) ??*Isshuukan de taiin shimashita, jijitsu.*
one.week PT hospital.discharge do.PST fact
'(I could) leave the hospital in a week, in fact.' (Morimoto 1994: 147)

2.2.3 *Boundary between written and spoken languages*

Some language users are acutely aware of language change. Noguchi (2016: 62–63) keeps a sharp eye on the stand-alone forms of such adverbialized nouns as *kihon* 'basically' (<*kihon-teki-ni* [basis-SUF-PT] 'basically'), *gensoku* 'in principle' (<*gen-soku-toshite* [principle-as]), *kekka* 'as a result' (<*sono kekka* [that.medial result]) and *shoojiki* 'to be frank' (<*shoojiki-ni-itte* [truth-PT-saying]) and clearly states that these reduced forms can be used only in spoken language but not in written language. While she makes no mention of the independent use of *jijitsu*, it comes within the range of her pedagogical or prescriptive vision. In the case of *kekka* 'as a result', however, the stand-alone usage appears to be conventionalized even in written language as clearly shown in Takahashi and Higashiizumi (2014). It thus seems that the written-spoken boundary has become more obscure in recent years (see Section 4 for actual uses of *jijitsu*).

2.3 Interim summary

As shown in the previous subsections, the discourse functions of the adverbialized *jijitsu* have been addressed in a variety of descriptive and theoretical frameworks. On the whole, the adverbial or PM use of *jijitsu* is found to introduce evidence

5. In (12) another adverb *jissai* 'in fact' can be used grammatically at sentence-final position.

or justification for the preceding context. On the other hand, such findings are confined to the usage, written or spoken, of *jijitsu* exclusively in contemporary Japanese; how *jijitsu* has been functionally expanded from nominal predicate to adverb is yet to be demonstrated. Therefore, I will place particular emphasis on its historical development, giving a comparative survey of the data from the Meiji and Taisho periods with those from the past couple of decades, based on the corpora shown in Section 3.

3. Corpora

As explained in Section 2.1, there is an extended interval of time between the first appearance of the nominal-predicate *jijitsu* and that of the adverbial *jijitsu*: the former appears in the early eleventh century, while the latter appears in the early twentieth century. I will thus focus on its development from the Meiji period (c.1868–1912) onwards, based on the examples from the following corpora in Table 2. Table 3 exhibits the number of words for each period in *Taiyo Corpus* based on Tanaka (2012).

Table 2. Modern Japanese Corpora**

Corpus (period)	Number of words
Meijrokuzasshi (1874–1875)	approx. 180,000 words
Kokuminnotomo (1887–1888)	approx. 1 mil. words
Kindai Josee Zasshi (1894–1895, 1909, 1925)†	approx. 2.1 mil. letters
Taiyo Corpus (1895, 1901, 1909, 1917, 1925)	approx. 5.34 mil words (see Tanaka 2012)
Balanced Corpus of Contemporary Written Japanese (= BCCWJ) (1971–2005)††	approx. 62.7 mil. words

† This corpus consists of the following three magazines: *Josee Zasshi* (1894/95), *Jogaku Sekai* (1909) and *Fujin Kurabu* (1925).
†† Only the genre of book is accessed for the current study.
** Several paths of grammaticalization from clause-final predicates to clause-initial discourse markers in the history of Japanese have been attested in Onodera (2004) and Higashiizumi (2015). Note that the very similar discourse sequence of sentences is also confirmed in the development of the *no wonder* construction (Gentens et al. 2016: 133–135)

Table 3. Details of *Taiyo Corpus* (based on Tanaka 2012)

Period	Number of words
1895	approx. 1.3 mil. words
1901	approx. 1.2 mil. words
1909	approx. 1.0 mil. words
1917	approx. 0.97 mil. words
1925	approx. 0.87 mil. words

4. Survey results

In order to ensure consistency with the following discussion, I will keep the focus on the issue at hand, namely, the development of the PM use of *jijitsu* at the LP of sentence from its erstwhile nominal predicate use at the sentence-final position. Examples (1) and (2) are repeated here for clarification as (13) and (14), respectively. Note that in the analysis of the PM use of *jijitsu*, I will focus only on the free-standing form of *jijitsu* without any particles and modifiers as in (13).

(13) *Jijitsu, kekkon o shinaku temo nagaku tsukiatte-iru to otoko wa*
fact marriage ACC do.not even.if long go.together if man TOP
oubou-ni-naru.
high-handed-PT-become
'In fact, even if (couples) do not get married, men become high-handed if (they) go together for a prolonged period.' (2004 *Hebi ni Piasu*; BCCWJ)

(14) *Dejitaru-ni-natte, shigoto no haba ga hirogatta-no wa jijitsu-desu.*
digital.PT-become job GEN range NOM widen.PST-NML TOP fact-COP.POL
'In the digital era, (it) is the fact that the range of (our) jobs became wider.'
(2001 *The art of spirited away*; BCCWJ)

What should be further mentioned about the predicate use of *jijitsu* is that there are four forms of copulative verbs attached to *jijitsu*. The following dates for the first appearance of each form are based on Kitahara (2006). The oldest form *-nari* can be found as early as the eighth century; two examples of *jijitsu-nari* from the eleventh century are illustrated in (3) and (4). The second oldest form *-dearu* is witnessed in the thirteenth century, although its historical development is open to debate and some controversial hypotheses have been proposed (Kitahata 2006, Vol. 9: 529). Another form *-da* appears in the fifteenth century, while the other form *-desu* is considered to come into use in the late Muromachi period (c.1336–1573). All of these forms continue to be used up until the second half of the twentieth century, but the proportional frequencies of these forms vary according to the historical stages in Tables 2 and 3 (see Table 5 in Section 4.1). Note that one variant form *-dearimasu* (a polite form for *dearu*) is also found in the corpora.

4.1 Modern Japanese periods

Tables 4 and 5 summarize both LP and sentence-final predicate uses of *jijitsu* with their raw frequencies (N = number). In these tables, LP examples mean that they are adverbialized PMs at the initial position of the sentence, while sentence-final (S-final) predicate examples mean that they are used as part of the sentence-final predicate, followed by period.

Table 4. The adverbial and predicate uses of *jijitsu* in the *Meijrokuzasshi, Kokuminnotomo,* and *Kindai Josee Zasshi* corpora

Adverbial use (LP)			**Predicate use (S-final)**	
	N (rel. freq.%)	**% (norm. freq.)†**	**N (rel. freq.%)**	**% (norm. freq.)**
1874–75	0 (0%)	0%	3 (100%)	1.7%
1887–88	0 (0%)	0%	13 (100%)	1.3%
1884–95	0 (0%)	N.A.	3 (100%)	N.A.
1909	0 (0%)	N.A.	10 (100%)	N.A.
1925	1 (14.3%)	N.A.	6 (85.7%)	N.A.

† The normalized frequency is calculated per 1,000 words in Table 4.

Table 5. The LP and the S-final predicate uses of *jijitsu* in the *Taiyo* corpus

Adverbial use (LP)			**Predicate use (S-final)**	
	N (rel. freq.%)	**% (norm. freq.)†**	**N (rel. freq.%)**	**% (norm. freq.)**
1895	0 (0%)	0%	12 (100%)	0.9%
1901	1 (3%)	0.08%	28 (97%)	2.3%
1909	0 (0%)	0%	67 (100%)	6.7%
1917	2 (2%)	0.2%	95 (98%)	9.8%
1925	9 (9%)	1.0%	90 (91%)	10.3%

† The normalized frequency is calculated per 1,000 words in Table 5.

The normalized frequency in each table is calculated per 1,000 words, except for the *Kindai Josee Zasshi* corpus. As shown in Table 2, the size of this corpus is described in terms of the number of letters, not words; therefore I left their normalized frequencies in Table 4 (and Table 6) unspecified (N.A.). Note that all the ambiguous examples and non-sentence-initial uses are excluded; S = sentence; N (rel. freq.) stands for the relative frequency of one usage in relation to the other at one synchronic stage. In the approximately 50 years covered by these corpora, the adverbial use of *jijitsu* is not yet established in terms of frequency, although it seems to show a slowly increasing trend in frequency in the last four stages. Notice that the first appearance of the adverbial *jijitsu* in these corpora is in 1901, which is mostly consistent with that of Kitahara (2006), the first example shown in (5). The predicate use of *jijitsu*, on the other hand, becomes conventionalized as seen in the increasing normalized frequency.

The variant forms of copulative verbs following *jijitsu* are illustrated in Tables 6 and 7. The total number of the predicate use of *jijitsu* demonstrates an upward trend, which is clearer in the normalized frequencies; however, the preferred forms at each historical period exhibit substantial changes. For example, after the turn of the twentieth century, the *-nari* form sharply decreases in number while the *-dearu* form seems to replace it; both *-da* and *-desu* forms begin to gradually increase in the twentieth century. Note that one example of *jijitsu-deseu* 'will be a fact' in 1909 is counted as one variant of *-desu* in Table 6.

Table 6. The copulative forms attached to *jijitsu* in the *Meijrokuzasshi*, *Kokuminnotomo*, and *Kindai Josee Zasshi*

	-nari	*-dearu*	*-dearimasu*	*-da*	*-desu*	Total
	N (RF%)	N (RF%)	N (RF%)	N (RF%)	N (RF%)	
	[NF%]	[NF%]	[NF%]	[NF%]	[NF%]	
1874–75	3 (100%)	0	0	0	0	3 (100%)
	[1.7%]					
1887–88	12 (92%)	1 (8%)	0	0	0	13 (100%)
	[1.2%]	[0.1%]				
1884–95	3 (100%)	0	0	0	0	3 (100%)
	[NA]					
1909	0	6 (60%)	1 (10%)	1 (10%)	2 (20%)	10 (100%)
		[NA]	[NA]	[NA]	[NA]	
1925	0 (1%)	1 (16.7%)	4 (66.6%)	0 (0%)	1 (16.7%)	6 (100%)
		[NA]	[NA]	[NA]		

† The normalized frequency is calculated per 1,000 words in Table 6.

Table 7. The copulative forms attached to *jijitsu* in the *Taiyo* corpus

	-nari	*-dearu*	*-dearimasu*	*-da*	*-desu*	Total
	N (RF%)	N (RF%)	N (RF%)	N (RF%)	N (RF%)	
	[NF%]	[NF%]	[NF%]	[NF%]	[NF%]	
1895	39 (95.1%)	0	2 (4.9%)	0	0	41 (100%)
	[3.0%]		[0.2%]			
1901	64 (85.3%)	8 (10.7%)	3 (4%)	0	0	75 (100%)
	[5.3%]	[0.7%]	[0.3%]			
1909	30 (39.5%)	34 (44.7%)	0	11 (14.5%)	1 (1.3%)	76 (100%)
	[3%]	[3.4%]		[1.1%]	[0.1%]	
1917	16 (15.2%)	73 (69.5%)	1 (0.9%)	11 (10.5%)	4 (3.8%)	105 (99.9%)
	[1.6%]	[7.5%]	[0.1%]	[1.1%]	[0.4%]	
1925	1 (1.0%)	72 (77.4%)	1 (1.0%)	14 (15.1%)	5 (5.4%)	93 (99.9%)
	[0.1%]	[8.3%]	[0.1%]	[1.6%]	[0.6%]	

† The normalized frequency is calculated per 1,000 words in Table 6.

4.2 Present-day Japanese periods

Table 8 summarizes both LP and sentence-final predicate uses of *jijitsu* from 1971 to 2005. Each usage seems to have been highly conventionalized, showing an approximate ratio of 40% (adverbial) to 60% (nominal predicate) from the mid-1980s onwards.

On the other hand, Table 9 shows a huge shift in the choice of copulative verbs in PDJ. For example, the *-nari* form becomes old-fashioned almost completely, and the *-dearimasu* form remains very infrequent probably due to its over-polite connotation. While the *-dearu* form continues to increase from Modern Japanese

Table 8. The LP and sentence-final predicate uses of *jijitsu* in the *BCCWJ* corpus (in the genre of book)

	Adverbial use (LP)		Predicate use (S-final)	
	N	%	N	%
1971–1974	0	0%	0	0%
1975–1979	7	37%	12	63%
1980–1984	3	18%	14	82%
1985–1989	50	40%	74	60%
1990–1994	101	42%	137	58%
1995–1999	101	36%	179	64%
2000–2005	351	38%	573	62%

Table 9. The copulative forms attached to *jijitsu* in the *BCCWJ* corpus (in the genre of book)

	-nari	*-dearu*	*-dearimasu*	*-da*	*-desu*	Total
	N (%)	N (%)	N (%)	N (%)	N (%)	N (%)
1971–74	0	0	0	0	0	0
1975–79	1 (8%)	7 (58%)	0	4 (33%)	0	12 (99%)
1980–84	0	8 (57%)	0	2 (14%)	4 (29%)	14 (100%)
1985–89	0	58 (78%)	1 (1%)	6 (8%)	9 (12%)	74 (99%)
1990–94	0	87 (64%)	2 (2%)	22 (16%)	26 (18%)	137 (100%)
1995–99	0	96 (54%)	3 (2%)	37 (20%)	43 (24%)	179 (100%)
2000–05	0	309 (54%)	2 (0.3%)	104 (18.2%)	158 (27.5%)	573 (100%)

(ModJ) periods, the other two forms *-da* and *-desu* begin to be used in growing numbers from the mid-1980s. Note that the number of words in each stage of BCCWJ is not specified; accordingly, the normalized frequencies are not shown in the tables.

What is worth mentioning is the fact that the adverbial usage at the LP has become common in PDJ, which means that *jijitsu* underwent a radical structural change in the last century. The nominal-predicate use at the sentence-final position continues to take the same abstract form i.e. *jijitsu* + copulative verb since the eleventh century, although the preferred forms of copulative verb have shifted in accordance with the changes in the times.

5. Summary and discussion

5.1 From the inside to the outside of the sentence for a larger discourse unit

As explained in Section 2.1, the older usage of *jijitsu* is the nominal-predicate construction, *jijitsu*-copulative verb, which is still more frequent than the PM use in PDJ as shown in Section 4. Let us think again about the structure with (14), repeated here as (15).

(15) *Dejitaru-ni-natte, shigoto no haba ga hirogatta-no wa jijitsu-desu.*
digital.PT-become job GEN range NOM widen.PST-NML TOP fact-COP.POL
'In the digital era, (it) is the fact that the range of (our) jobs became wider.'
(2001 *The art of spirited away*; BCCWJ)

As clearly seen in this typical example, the nominalized clause is topicalized by the topic marker *wa* and immediately followed by the nominal predicate with *jijitsu* (see (2) and (8)); structurally, the *jijitsu*-predicate is inside the bi-clausal sentence. Pragmatically, on the other hand, the thematic clause is accompanied by the rhematic *jijitsu*-predicate. This complex clause sentence structure has been in use since the eleventh century.

In the early twentieth century, however, the adverbialized *jijitsu* emerged at the LP of the following sentence; it performs a dual function that links to previous discourse and guides the hearer's expectations for the subsequent stretch of discourse. (1) is repeated here as (16).

(16) *Kekkon nanteno mo, hitori no ningen o shoyuu.suru toiu*
marriage so-called too one.person GEN human ACC possess.do so-called
koto ni naru no-daroo ka. Jijitsu, kekkon o shinaku temo
COMP PT become NML-may.be QP fact marriage ACC do.not even.if
nagaku tsukiatte-iru to otoko wa oubou-ni-naru.
long go.together if man TOP high-handed-PT-become
'Speaking of marriage, (I wonder if it means) that one is in the possession of the other. In fact, even if (couples) do not get married, men become high-handed if (they) go together for a prolonged period.'
(2004 *Hebi ni Piasu*; BCCWJ)

The first sentence provides one idea (a rhetorical question in this example), while the second sentence prefaced by *jijitsu* provides justification for the idea (also see (9)). This newly emergent usage of *jijitsu* appears to go beyond one sentence structure and into a larger discourse unit, connected by *jijitsu* appearing between the sentences.[6] Nevertheless, the sequence of information structure remains the same as schematized in Figure 1. S = sentence. Note that the clause-linking function of the *jijitsu* predicate in (ii) is discussed in the next subsection.

In Figure 1, the term 'projector' stands for a set of expressions that anticipate upcoming discourse (Hopper & Thompson 2008: 105) and that relate it to the preceding information (Shibasaki 2014a, 2014b and 2018). What Figure 1 tells us about this structural change is that the theme-rheme relation realized in one sentence becomes discourse-driven over history, putting together both thematic and rhematic sentences in this specifiable sequential relation. In a nutshell, the syntactic change of *jijitsu* involves an increase in structural scope, i.e. from a bi-clausal sentence to a sequenced-sentence construction, in a very similar way as suggested in Tabor & Traugott (1998) and Traugott & Dasher (2002: 152–189).

6. In addition to the corpora in Table 2, I have checked the examples from *The Radio Drama Transcripts* broadcast from 1937 to 1945 (Endo et al. 2004) and conversation transcripts from Gendai Nihongo Kenkyuukai (2011) recorded in 1993. However, neither nominal nor adverbial use of *jijitsu* can be found in these transcripts.

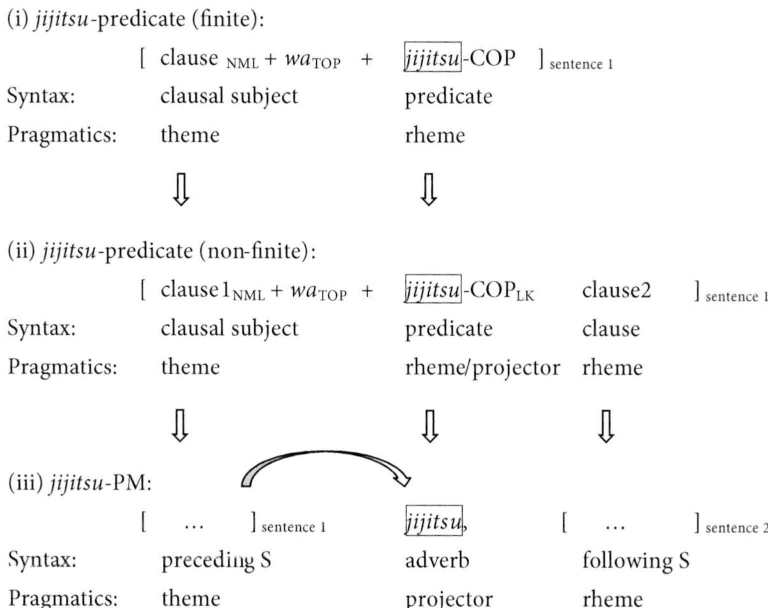

Figure 1. Constructionalization beyond sentence with *jijitsu* 'fact' (based on Shibasaki 2017: 119)

One anonymous reviewer receives the impression that the change from the sentence-final predicate to the sentence-initial projector is a radical change in syntax, which seems to be a fair statement if one addresses language change within the purview of sentence grammar. However, if we broaden our outlook to how to combine sentences in a stretch of discourse, such a radical structural change would not be unusual. In fact, Narrog and Heine (2017: 22) point out that "the focus in CG [Construction Grammar] has been on identifying and describing individual constructions, especially those apparently not well captured through traditional phrase structures, and not on systematically describing the clause structure (or more generally, grammatical structure) of any language" (see Section 5.2 for Hilpert's 2013: 210 relevant opinion). Radical changes in the syntax of *jijitsu* proceed from the inside to the outside of the sentence and cannot fully be explained in the framework of traditional approaches including grammaticalization. Conversely, Construction Grammar (or constructionalization in this particular case) may give a better account of this phenomenon (see Section 5.2).

On reconsidering the matter summarized in Table 1 (Section 2.2.2), all preceding research grasps the essentials of the PM use of *jijitsu*; the sequential relations of information in Table 1 and in Figure 1 (iii) are basically the same. That being said, no preceding studies on the PM *jijitsu* succeed in directing our attention to the discourse-sequential expansion in Figure 1, which is presumably triggered by discourse-pragmatic pressures. I view this process here as 'constructionalization beyond the sentence.'[7]

5.2 Why constructionalization works

Traugott (2014) defines 'constructionalization' as follows.

(17) *Constructionalization* is the development of form$_{new}$-meaning$_{new}$ pairs, i.e. constructions. (Traugott 2014: 89)

As discussed in Section 5.1, *jijitsu* undergoes the formal change from a nominal predicate to an adverb and the functional change from a rhematic predication in one sentence to a projecting connector serving between sentences (cf. Lenker 2015). That is, the direction of change from (i) to (iii) in Figure 1 turns out to be a typical case of constructionalization (Cxzn). The increasing degree of spoken-ness in the written mode in the nineteenth century (discussed in Section 2.1) may have played a role in widening the scope of information structure, subsequently giving rise to the adverbialized *jijitsu*.

Before we go any further, it will be appropriate here to explain why this study adopts a constructionalization perspective rather than a grammaticalization perspective. While this study mainly focuses on the change from a nominal predicate (finite) to an adverbial use of *jijitsu*, the *jijitsu* predicate with the continuous form of the copulative verb can serve a clause-chaining function situated in the middle of the change as in Figure 1 (ii). Let us consider the following example.

(18) *Cha no kisetsu wa niseki no teikisen nomi toshite.wa, unpanryoku*
tea GEN season TOP two.CL GEN liner.ship only TOP carrying.capacity
ni fusoku o tuguru wa jijitsu-dea-tte, sitagatte Dagurasusen shinnyuu
PT lack ACC tell TOP fact-COP-LK therefore Douglas.ship intrusion
no yochi o sonsuru koto to naru o motte (…) isseki no senpaku
GEN room ACC exist COMP PT become ACC by one.CL GEN vessel
o kuwae…
ACC add
'(It) is true (that) in the season of tea, only two liner ships cannot provide sufficient carrying capacity; therefore (we need to) add one (more) shipping vessel by considering (that fact) that there is some room susceptible for the ship Douglas…' (1909 *Nanshinkooromondai*; Taiyo)

7. Needless to say, this view is partially related to 'rhetorical structure theory' proposed by Mann and Thompson (1988). One anonymous reviewer comments that the theme-rheme structure is usually applied to the clause or clause-complex; I am grateful for his/her comment. Since *jijitsu* develops out of a complex clause sentence as in Figure 1, the case of *jijitsu* is not inconsistent with the reviewer's view.

In this example, the conjunction *sitagatte* 'therefore' can be omissible as briefly shown in (19a), because the linking form of *jijitsu-dea-tte* itself fulfils its role in introducing the following statement. Or if one should try to manipulate the sentence, s/he might change *jijitsu-dea-tte* (fact-be-linking.form (lit.)) either into the sentence-end form *jijitsu-dearu* (fact-be-end.form) as in (19b) or into *jijitsu* without a copulative verb in an extreme case as in (19c), accompanied by a period (as discussed in Section 5.3), because the conjunction *sitagatte* 'therefore' can be used sentence-initially to introduce the following strategy, i.e. how to cope with the vessel scarcity problem. As a result, the function of *jijitsu* in this case cannot fully be defined either as a projector or as a predicate; in other words, this usage of *jijitsu* is situated on a predicate-projector continuum.

(19) a. … *o tuguru wa jijitsu-dea-tte, Dagurasusen shinnyuu no…*
b. … *o tuguru wa jijitsu-dearu. Sitagatte Dagurasusen…*
c. … *o tuguru wa jijitsu. Sitagatte Dagurasusen…*

With regard to the relation of grammaticalization to Construction Grammar (CG), Narrog and Heine (2017: 22) state that "while for grammaticalization, the distinction between lexical and grammatical, and less vs. more grammatical, categories has been definitional, the denial of such a distinction is central to common versions of CG." If languages with plenty of historical documents like Japanese are examined, a lexical category is likely to turn into a grammatical category over an extended period of time. On the other hand, once a category is scrutinized over a short period of time as in this study i.e. about fifty years in Table 4 and about thirty years in Table 8, the lexical-grammatical division is not practical; rather, elements appear to be on a lexical-grammatical cline as is seen in the case of *jijitsu*. Note in passing that even specialists in grammaticalization studies state that "it [grammaticalization] challenges the discreteness of linguistic categories, even that between grammar and the lexicon" (Wischer 2006: 130).

This view of grammar or language change seems not to strike wide of the mark. For example, Langacker (2008: 20) states that "What the linguistic data seems to be trying to tell us is that lexicon and grammar form a gradation instead of being sharply dichotomous", which can be considered to be a central tenet of Cognitive Grammar. In the same vein, Halliday and Matthiessen (2014: 64) stress "the unity of lexis and grammar, as the two poles of a single cline" in the framework of Systemic Functional Grammar; the same is applied to Construction Grammar in which the distinction between lexical and grammatical categories is blurred because grammar is regarded as "the structuring and symbolization of semantic content" there (Langacker 1987: 12). It is true that Noël (2007: 185) argues that "grammaticalization, as a change from lexical to grammatical, is not an issue in CG [Construction Grammar]: construction grammatical units can by definition not become more grammatical." Nevertheless, the view of grammar on a lexical-grammatical cline without division seems to be more realistic especially from a diachronic perspective, i.e. constructionalization, and in fact it serves well as a way to get a grip on the phenomenon of grammar in use, inter alia, in the case of *jijitsu* (see Narrog & Heine 2017: 22–23 for further discussion).

Goldberg (2006: 5) regards 'constructions' as follows:

(20) All levels of grammatical analysis involve constructions: learned pairings of form with semantic or discourse function, including morphemes or words, idioms, partially lexically filled and fully general phrasal patterns. (Goldberg 2006: 5)

Constructions are ubiquitous; the reinterpretation of language change in terms of constructions is a principled approach (Traugott 2003: 624; Himmelmann 2004: 31; Smith et al. 2015: 1). However, as appropriately remarked in Hilpert (2013: 210), research into the realm of discourse especially from a diachronic perspective is relatively underdeveloped partially due to the absence or scantiness of textual resources (but see Tabor & Traugott 1998 and Traugott & Dasher 2002). Considering such a research imperative, the current study on the constructionalization of *jijitsu* beyond the realm of the sentence serves to contribute to Construction Grammar.

5.3 Local changes inside the sentence

Since Traugott (2014: 89) introduces another related phenomenon, 'constructional changes' (CCs), I will touch on the issue briefly. CCs are defined as follows:

(21) *Constructional changes* are changes to features of constructions, such as semantics (e.g. *wif* 'woman' > 'married woman') or morphophonology (e.g. *had* > *'d*). Such changes precede or follow constructionalization. (Traugott 2014: 89)

That is, either semantic or formal (but not both) changes to the construction in point are considered a CC. In the case of the nominal-predicate use of *jijitsu*, copulative verbs attached to *jijitsu* represent substantial changes as in Tables 7 and 9, while the whole constructional template i.e. *jijitsu* + copulative verb undergoes no major changes; the basic rhematic meaning or function is retained.[8] I thus argue that such a shift in the choice of predicate forms represents constructional changes.

8. The copulative verbs can take several clause-combining forms, which implies another case of constructionalization from sentence-final to sentence-medial changes, formally and functionally, of the nominal predicate with *jijitsu*. I cannot address the issue here due to space limitation.

Figure 2 is based on Figure 1 (i), with the addition of the five types of copulative verbs as a case of CC. The order of the forms is roughly from the oldest form *jijitsu-nari* to the newer but the most infrequently used form *jijitsu-dearimasu*. The constructions there can form a more schematic construction '*jijitsu*-COP' as in Figure 2. All the copulative forms have been used so far regardless of their lower or higher frequency in comparison to the others. On the other hand, the copula-less use of the sentence-final *jijitsu* can be sporadically found as in (22), sometimes with sentence-final particles as in (23).

(i) *jijitsu*-predicate:

	[clause $_{\text{NML}}$ + *wa*$_{\text{TOP}}$	+ *jijitsu*-COP	{ *jijitsu-nari* / *jijitsu-dearu* / *jijitsu-da* / *jijitsu-desu* / *jijitsu-dearimasu* / *jijitsu*-X }] $_{\text{sentence 1}}$
Syntax:	clausal subject	predicate	
Pragmatics:	theme	predicate	

Figure 2. Local changes inside the sentence

(22) *Bii-gumi no hito-tachi ga ano kaaten o yorokondeiru no*
B-class GEN people-PL NOM that curtain ACC become.happy NML
wa jijitsu.
TOP fact
'(It is a) fact that people in B class are happy with that curtain.'
(1989 *Akai Kutsu Tanteidan*; BCCWJ)

(23) *Shuuto demo, daijini-suru koto wa jijitsu ne.*
mother-in-law even esteem.highly COMP TOP fact FP
'(It is a) fact that (I) care for even (my) mother-in-law.'
(2001 *Nippon'ichi Yuukiaru Yome*; BCCWJ)

In (22), *jijitsu* appears to be used at the sentence-final position with no copulative verb; that is, *jijitsu* can be used as part of the *jijitsu*-Ø construction. In (23), *jijitsu* is used with the final particle *ne* but not accompanied by any copulative verb, which

On the other hand, an anonymous reviewer has an interest in the choice of copulative verbs for which I am grateful to her/him. One needs to consider period-specific factors (as in Note 3), generation-specific factors (e.g. younger vs. older generations) or interactional factors (e.g. power relations) to uncover clues to solving this mystery. I will leave this issue unexplained for my future study.

implies that *jijitsu* itself can play a role as a predicate without any copulative verb.[9] That is why I chose to use '*jijitsu*-X' as a representative of new sub-constructions with different parts of speech from copulative verbs. Once a network of '*jijitsu*-COP' is established, a cluster of constructions may potentiate another cluster of constructions such as '*jijitsu*-X' as in (22) and (23). One might wonder whether low-frequency constructions such as *jijitsu-dearimasu* can serve to form a cluster of constructions. However, Bybee (2015: 40) states that "it is not currently known exactly how to determine what is low and what is high" in frequency (see Shibasaki 2018 for further discussions). The history of *jijitsu* exemplifies this process.

What is worth mentioning here is Du Bois's (2003: 49) view of discourse and grammar, which I argue can promote awareness and understanding of constructionalization from a synchronic perspective.

(24) Theoretical assumptions about discourse and grammar:
  a. Speakers exploit available grammatical structures to realize their goals in speaking;
  b. The aggregate sum of what speakers do in discourse exhibits recurrent patterning beyond what is predicted by rules of grammar;
  c. Grammatical structure tends to evolve along lines laid down by discourse pattern: grammars code best what speakers do most.

(Du Bois 2003: 49)

The first assumption (24a) is very important in that language users make full use of available grammatical resources for the purpose of achieving a goal. No projector constructions can emerge from nothing; they are reused for facilitating better communication within the acceptable range of grammaticality, resulting in broadening the permissible scope of information structure; *jijitsu* is no exception.[10] Recurrent discourse patterning through repeated use in (24b) and (24c) can be witnessed in Tables 4–7 in Section 4. Furthermore, what Du Bois (2003) emphasizes in (24c) is the speaker's role in the formation of discourse pattern. His view of discourse and grammar is also reflected in the emergence of projector constructions in Figure 1: grammatical descriptions therein appear to be based on the speaker's role in contextual expansion in tandem with constructional changes and constructionaliza-

9. Presumably, the constructional template [… $_{\text{NML/COMP}}$ + *wa*$_{\text{TOP}}$ + *jijitsu*-COP] has been reduced and conventionalized as [… $_{\text{NML/COMP}}$ + *wa*$_{\text{TOP}}$ + *jijitsu*] without copulative verbs in recent years.

10. While Keizer (2016) takes a Functional Discourse Grammar (FDG) approach, her view of language in discourse seems to be consistent with what has hitherto been discussed in the current paper. Izutsu and Izutsu (2016) propose an exaptational approach to what otherwise is difficult to explain; what is examined there is very close to what is addressed here and in Gentens et al. (2016).

tion. That is, theory and practice can be harmonized as reciprocal reinforcement for understanding of how languages change.

Acknowledgements

The earlier version of the present paper was presented at *the Third Meeting of Kyoto Pragmatics Colloquium (KPC-3)*, Kyoto Institute of Technology, Kyoto, Japan, 13 March 2016. I would like to express my profound gratitude to Hiroaki Tanaka for his inviting me to such an exciting meeting and to the audience, especially Hiroshi Ohashi, Kaoru Horie, Kojiro Nabeshima, and Kazuyo Murata, for their insightful questions and support. Special thanks go to Heather Oumounabidji for her last-minute input, Kiyoko Toratani for her constructive advice at the *Gramm2*, and my two anonymous reviewers for their forward-looking discussion with me on the issues. Any remaining errors are my own. Note that this study is part of my Grant-in-Aid for Scientific Research (C) project (No. 16K02781) supported by the Japan Society for the Promotion of Science.

Abbreviations

ACC	accusative	PAS	passive
AUX	auxiliary	PM	pragmatic marker
CL	noun classifier	POL	polite
COMP	complementizer	PREF	prefix
COP	copulative verb	PRES	present tense
FP	final particle	PST	past tense
GEN	genitive	PT	particle
HOM	honorific	QP	question particle
LK	linking form of verb	S	sentence
NML	nominative	SUF	suffix
NEG	negative	TOP	topic

References

Corpora

Balanced Corpus of Contemporary Written Japanese (BCCWJ). <http://www.kotonoha.gr.jp/shonagon/>

Kindai Josee Zasshi Corpus. Asuko Kondo, Yoko Mabuchi & Noriko Hattori (eds). 2012. Tokyo: National Institute for Japanese Language and Linguistics. <http://pj.ninjal.ac.jp/corpus_center/cmj/woman-mag/>

Kokuminnotomo Corpus. Asuko Kondo (ed.). 2014. Tokyo: National Institute for Japanese Language and Linguistics <http://pj.ninjal.ac.jp/corpus_center/cmj/kokumin/>.

Meijroku zasshi Corpus. Asuko Kondo, Yoko Mabuchi & Noriko Hattori (eds). 2012. Tokyo: National Institute for Japanese Language and Linguistics. <http://pj.ninjal.ac.jp/corpus_center/cmj/meiroku/>

Ninjoobon. Akari Fujimoto & Tomokazu Takada (eds). 2015. Tokyo: National Institute for Japanese Language and Linguistics.

Sharebon. Taro Ichimura (ed.). 2015. Tokyo: National Institute for Japanese Language and Linguistics <http://pj.ninjal.ac.jp/corpus_center/chj/edo.html>.

Taiyo Corpus (CD-ROM). 2005. Tokyo: Hakubunkan Shinsha.

Text references

Gappon Josei no kotoba, dansei no kotoba: Shokuba-hen. (CD-ROM) (*Composite Volume Female and Male Languages at Place of Work*). 2011. Gendai Nihongo Kenkyuukai (ed.). Tokyo: Hituzi Syboo Publishing.

Midookanpakuki Zen Chuushaku, Kaneigannen (An Annotated Edition of Midookanpakuki, Kaneigannen [c. 1017]). 1985. YutakaYamanaka (ed.). Tokyo: Kokushokankookai.

Senjichu no hanashi kotoba, razio dorama daihon kara (CD-ROM) (*Spoken Language during Wartime: Radio Drama Transcripts*). 2004. Orie Endo, Taku Kimura, Takashi Sakurai, Chieko Suzuki, Haruko Hayakawa & Toshiaki Yasuda (eds). Tokyo: Hituzi Syboo Publishing.

Dictionaries

Daijiten (An Unabridged Dictionary of the Japanese Language). 1994 [1936]. Vol. 12. reprinted edn. Tokyo: Heibonsha.

Doi, Tadao (editor in chief). 1994. *Jidaibetsu Kokugojiten Muromachi Jidai-hen San* (The Historical Japanese Dictionary, Muromachi Period III). Tokyo: Sanseido.

Doi, Tadao, Morita, Takeshi & Chonan, Minoru (eds). 1980. *Hooyaku Nippo Jisho* (The Japanese Version of Vocabulario da Lingoa de Iapam). Tokyo: Iwanami.

Ebara, Taizo. 2008. *Edogo Daijiten* (An Unabridged Dictionary of the Edo Language), Tsutomu Ogata (ed.). Tokyo: Kadokawa

Kitahara, Yasuo (editor in chief). 2006. *Nihon Kokugo Daiijiten* (The Dictionary of the Japanese Language). Tokyo: Shogakkan.

Maeda, Isamu (ed.). 1974. *Edogo Daijiten* (An Unabridged Dictionary of the Edo Language). Tokyo: Kodansha.

Morita, Takeshi (ed.). 1989. *Hooyaku Nippo Jisho Sakuin* (Indices to the Japanese Version of *Vocabulario da Lingoa de Iapam*).

Okubo, Tadakuni & Kinoshita, Kazuko (eds). 1991. *Edogo Jiten* (A Dictionary of the Edo Language). Tokyo: Tokyo-do.

Secondary sources

Aijmer, Karin. 2007. The interface between discourse and grammar: *The fact is that*. In *Connectives as Discourse Landmarks* [Pragmatics & Beyond New Series 161], Agnès Celle & Ruth Huart (eds), 31–46. Amsterdam: John Benjamins. https://doi.org/10.1075/pbns.161.05aij

Beeching, Kate & Detges, Ulrich. 2014. Introduction. In *Discourse Functions at the Left and Right Periphery*, Kate Beeching & Ulrich Detges (eds), 1–23. Leiden: Brill. https://doi.org/10.1163/9789004274822_002

Brinton, Laurel J. 2010. Discourse markers. In *Historical Pragmatics*, Andreas H. Jucker & Irma Taavitsainen (eds), 285–314. Berlin: De Gruyter Mouton.

Bybee, Joan L. 2015. *Language Change*. Cambridge: CUP.

Curzan, Anne. 2017. Periodization in the history of the English language. In *The History of English: Historical Outlines from Sound to Text*, Laurel J. Brinton & Alexander Bergs (eds), 8–35. Berlin: De Gruyter Mouton.

Du Bois, John W. 2003. Discourse and grammar. In *The New Psychology of Language*, Vol. 2, Michael Tomasello (ed.), 47–88. Mahwah NJ: Lawrence Erlbaum Associates.

Fujiwara, Hirofumi. 2011. On the formation of adverbs that introduce true information (written in Japanese). In *Aspects of Grammatical Descriptions*, Chuo University Institute of Humanities (ed.), 41–64. Tokyo: Chuo University.

Furuhashi, Nobuyoshi, Suzuki, Tai & Ishii, Hisao (eds). 2012. *Gendaigo kara Kogo o Hiku* (Look up Ancient Words by Modern Words). Tokyo: Kawadeshoboo.

Frellesvig, Bjarke. 2010. *A History of the Japanese Language*. Cambridge: CUP. https://doi.org/10.1017/CBO9780511778322

Gentens, Caroline, Kimps, Ditte, Davidse, Kristin, Jacobs, Gilles, Van linden, An & Brems, Lieselotte. 2016. Mirativity and rhetorical structure: The development and prosody of disjunct and anaphoric adverbials with *'no' wonder*. In *Outside the Clause. Form and Function of Extra-Clausal Constituents* [Studies in Language Companion Series 178], Gunther Kaltenböck, Evelien Keizer & Arne Lohmann (eds),125–156. Amsterdam: John Benjamins.

Goldberg, Adele E. 2006. *Constructions at Work*. Oxford: OUP.

Higashiizumi, Yuko. 2015. Periphery of utterance and (Inter) subjectification in Modern Japanese: A case study of competing causal conjunctions and connective particles. In *New Directions in Grammaticalization Research* [Studies in Language Companion Series 166], Andrew D. M. Smith, Graeme Trousdale & Richard Waltereit (eds), 135–156. Amsterdam: John Benjamins.

Himmelmann, Nikolaus P. 2004. Lexicalization and grammaticalization: Opposite or orthogonal? In *What Makes Grammaticalization? A Look from its Fringes and its Components*, Walter Bisang, Nikolaus P. Himmelmann & Björn Wiemer (eds), 21–42. Berlin: Mouton de Gruyter.

Hilpert, Martin. 2013. *Constructional Change in English*. Cambridge: CUP. https://doi.org/10.1017/CBO9781139004206

Hopper, Paul J. & Thompson, Sandra A. 2008. Projectability and clause combining in interaction. In *Cross-Linguistic Studies of Clause Combining: The Multi-Functionality of Conjunctions* [Typological Studies in Language 80], Ritva Laury (ed.), 99–123. Amsterdam: John Benjamins. https://doi.org/10.1075/tsl.80.06hop

Horie, Kaoru. 2012. The interactional origin of nominal predicate structure in Japanese: A comparative and historical pragmatic perspective. *Journal of Pragmatics* 44: 663–679. https://doi.org/10.1016/j.pragma.2011.09.020

Huddleston, Rodney & Pullum, Geoffrey K. 2002. *The Cambridge Grammar of the English Language*. Cambridge: CUP.

Izutsu, Katsunobu & Izutsu, Mitsuko N. 2016. Exaptation and adaptation: Two historical routes to final particles in Japanese. In *Exaptation and Language Change* [Current Issues in Linguistic Theory 336], Muriel Norde & Freek Van de Velde (eds), 377–402. Amsterdam: John Benjamins.

Kawase, Suguru. 2016. Review of Narumi (2015). *Nihongo no Kenkyu* 12(3): 141–148.

Keizer, Evelien. 2016. The *(the) fact is (that)* construction in English and Dutch. In *Outside the Clause. Form and Function of Extra-Clausal Constituents* [Studies in Language Companion Series 178], Gunther Kaltenböck, Evelien Keizer & Arne Lohmann (eds), 59–96. Amsterdam: John Benjamins.

Kerr, Betsy. 2014. Left dislocation in French. In *Perspectives on Linguistic Structure and Context. Studies in honor of Knud Lambrecht* [Pragmatics & Beyond New Series 244], Stacey Katz Bourns & Lindsy L. Myers (eds), 223–240. Amsterdam: John Benjamins. https://doi.org/10.1075/pbns.244.11ker

Langacker, Ronald W. 1987. *Foundations of Cognitive Grammar*, Vol 1: *Theoretical Prerequisites*. Stanford CA: Stanford University Press.

Langacker, Ronald W. 2008. *Cognitive Grammar: A Basic Introduction*. Oxford: OUP. https://doi.org/10.1093/acprof:oso/9780195331967.001.0001

Lenker, Ursula. 2015. Knitting and splitting information: Medial placement of linking adverbials in the history of English. In *Contact, Variation, and Change in the History of English* [Studies in Language Companion Series 159], Simone E. Pfenninger, Olga Timofeeva, Anne-Christine Gardner, Alpo Honkapohja, Marianne Hundt & Daniel Schreier (eds), 11–38. Amsterdam: John Benjamins.

Mann, William & Thompson, Sandra A. 1988. Rhetorical structure theory: Toward a functional theory of text organization. *Text* 8: 243–281. https://doi.org/10.1515/text.1.1988.8.3.243

Morimoto, Junko. 1994. *Hanashite no Shukan o Arawasu Hukshi nitsuite* (On Japanese Adverbs of the Speaker's Subjective Attitude). Tokyo: Kuroshio.

Narrog, Heiko & Heine, Bernd. 2017. Grammaticalization. In *The Cambridge Handbook of Historical Syntax*, Adam Ledgeway & Ian Roberts (eds), 7–27. Cambridge: CUP.

Narumi, Shinichi. 2015. *Nihongo ni okeru Kango no Hen'yoo no Kenkyu: Hukushi-ka o Chuushin to shite* (Studies in the Japanization of Chinese Loanwords: Focusing on Adverbialization). Tokyo: Hituzi Syobo Publishing.

Noël, Dirk. 2007. Diachronic construction grammar and grammaticalization theory. *Functions of Language* 14(2): 177–202. https://doi.org/10.1075/fol.14.2.04noe

Noguchi, Keiko. 2016. *"Hobo-hobo" "Ima-ima?"!: Kuizu Okashina Nihongo* ("Approximate-approximate Now-now?"!: Funny Japanese Quizzes). Tokyo: Kobunsha.

Onodera, Noriko O. 2004. *Japanese Discourse Markers. Synchronic and Diachronic Discourse Analysis* [Pragmatics & Beyond New Series 132]. Amsterdam: John Benjamins. https://doi.org/10.1075/pbns.132

Onodera, Noriko O. & Traugott, Elizabeth Closs (eds). 2016. *Diachronic and Cross-Linguistic Approach to Form-Function-Periphery (LP and RP) Mapping*. Special issue of the *Journal of Historical Pragmatics* 17(2).

Otake, Yoshio. 2009. *No da ni Taioosuru Eigo no Koobun* (The Japanese No da-Construction and the Corresponding English Constructions). Tokyo: Kuroshio.

Quirk, Randolph, Greenbaum, Sidney, Leech, Geoffrey & Svartvik, Jan. 1985. *A Comprehensive Grammar of the English Language*. London: Longman.

Saegusa, Reiko. 2013. Meishi kara hukushi, setsuzokushi e (From nouns to adverbs and conjunctions). *Department Bulletin Paper* 4: 49–61. Tokyo: Hitotsubashi University.

Schmid, Hans-Jörg 2000. *English Abstract Nouns as Conceptual Shells: From Corpus to Cognition*. Berlin: Walter de Gruyter. https://doi.org/10.1515/9783110808704

Shibasaki, Reijirou. 2010. Frequency as a cause of semantic change. In *Formal Evidence in Grammaticalization Research* [Typological Studies in Language 94], An Van linden, Jean-Christophe Verstraete & Kristin Davidse (eds), 225–244. Amsterdam: John Benjamins.

Shibasaki, Reijirou. 2014a. On the development of *the point is* and related issues in the history of *American English. English Linguistics* 31(1): 79–113.

Shibasaki, Reijirou. 2014b. On the grammaticalization of *the thing is* and related issues in the history of American English. In *Studies in the History of the English Language: Evidence and Method in Histories of English*, Michael Adams, Robert D. Fulk & Laurel J. Brinton (eds), 99–122. Berlin: De Gruyter Mouton.

Shibasaki, Reijirou. 2017. Danwakoozoo no kakuchoo to koobunka nitsuite (Expansion of discourse-syntactic structures and constructionalization). In *Nihongo Goyooron Fooramu* 2 (Japanese Pragmatics Forum 2), Shigehiro Kato & Masato Takiura (eds), 107–133. Tokyo: Hituzi Syobo.

Shibasaki, Reijirou. 2018. Sequentiality and the emergence of new constructions. In *Explorations in English Historical Syntax* [Studies in Language Companion Series 198], Hubert Cuyckens, Hendrik De Smet, Liesbet Heyvaert & Charlotte Maekelberghe (eds), 285–308. Amsterdam: John Benjamins.

Shibatani, Masayoshi. 1990. *The Languages of Japan*. Cambridge: CUP.

Shin'ya, Teruko. 2014. *Studies on Noun Orientation of Japanese Language* (*written in Japanese*). Tokyo: Hituzi Syobo.

Smith, Andrew D. M., Trousdale, Graeme & Waltereit, Richard. 2015. Introduction. In *New Directions in Grammaticalization Research* [Studies in Language Companion Series 166], Andrew D. M. Smith, Graeme Trousdale & Richard Waltereit (eds), 1–8. Amsterdam: John Benjamins.

Tabor, Whitney & Traugott, Elizabeth Closs. 1998. Structural scope expansion and grammaticalization. In *The Limits of Grammaticalization* [Typological Studies in Language 37], Anna Giacalone Ramat & Paul J. Hopper (eds), 229–272. Amsterdam: John Benjamins. https://doi.org/10.1075/tsl.37.11tab

Takahashi, Keiko & Higashiizumi, Yuko. 2014. Usage of *kekka* in Modern Japanese Corpora (written in Japanese). *Proceedings of the Sixth Corpus Japanese Linguistics Workshop*, 103–112. Tokyo: National Institute for Japanese Language and Linguistics (NINJAL).

Takeuchi, Michiko. 1973. Hukushi to wa nanika (What adverbs are). In *Rentaishi, hukushi* (Adnominal nouns and adverbs), Kazuhiko Suzuki & Ooki Hayashi (eds), 71–146. Tokyo: Meijishoin.

Tanaka, Makiro. 2012. Meijikooki kara Taishooki no goi no reberu to goshu (Levels and types of words from Late Meiji to Taisho eras). Tokyo: National Institute for Japanese Language and Linguistics. <http://pj.ninjal.ac.jp/corpus_center/cmj/doc/09Tanaka.pdf>

Tatsuno, Kazuo. 2007. *Bunshoo no Migakikata* (How to Polish One's Writing). Tokyo: Iwanami.

Traugott, Elizabeth Closs. 2003. Constructions in grammaticalization. In *The Handbook of Historical Linguistics*, Brian D. Joseph & Richard D. Janda (eds), 624–647. Oxford: Blackwell. https://doi.org/10.1002/9780470756393.ch20

Traugott, Elizabeth Closs. 2014. Toward a constructional framework for research on language change. In *Grammaticalization – Theory and Data* [Studies in Language Companion Series 166], Sylvie Hancil & Ekkehard Köning (eds), 87–105. Amsterdam: John Benjamins.

Traugott, Elizabeth Closs. 2015. Investigating 'periphery' from a functionalist perspective. *Linguistics Vanguard* 1(1): 119–130. https://doi.org/10.1515/lingvan-2014-1003

Traugott, Elizabeth Closs & Dasher, Richard B. 2002. *Regularity in Semantic Change*. Cambridge: CUP.

Traugott, Elizabeth Closs & Trousdale, Graeme. 2013. *Constructionalization and Constructional Changes*. Oxford: OUP.

Watanabe, Minoru. 1971. *Kokugo Koobunron* (A Syntactic Theory of Japanese). Tokyo: Hanawa-shobo.

Wierzbicka, Anna. 2006. *English: Meaning and Culture*. Oxford: OUP. https://doi.org/10.1093/acprof:oso/9780195174748.001.0001

Wray, Alison. 2009. Identifying formulaic language: Persistent challenges and new opportunities. In *Formulaic Language*, Vol. 1: *Distribution and Historical Change* [Typological Studies in Language 82], Roberta Corrigan, Edith A. Moravcsik, Hamid Ouali & Kathleen M. Wheatley (eds), 27–52. Amsterdam: John Benjamins. https://doi.org/10.1075/tsl.82.02ide

Wischer, Ilse. 2006. Grammaticalization. In *Encyclopedia of Language and Linguistics*, Vol. 5, 2nd edn, Keith Brown (ed.), 129–135. Oxford: Elsevier. https://doi.org/10.1016/B0-08-044854-2/00192-9

The development of the Chinese scalar additive coordinators derived from prohibitives

A constructionist perspective

Bing Zhu and Kaoru Horie
Kwansei Gakuin University / Nagoya University

In this paper, we trace from a constructionist perspective the diachronic development of the Chinese scalar additive coordinators meaning roughly 'let alone' derived from a prohibitive expression 'don't say'. We argue that a construction schema formed by the combination of a prohibitive marker with a SAY verb conveying the scalar additive meaning may have been established in Ancient Chinese. This construction schema analogically sanctioned more forms of such pattern into scalar additive coordinators over time, including *biéshuō* in Contemporary Chinese. The development of the scalar additive coordinators derived from the prohibitives is more likely to be considered as a case of constructionalization. Crucially, it is the entire construction that has spread over time. The present study demonstrates that prohibitives can also serve clause combining functions.

Keywords: scalar additive coordinator, prohibitives, constructionalization, *biéshuō*

1. Introduction

Cross-linguistically, imperatives can serve to form complex sentences such as conditionals and concessives (e.g., Heine et al. 1991: 191; Haspelmath & König 1998; Dobrushina 2008; Aikhenvald 2010: 235–241; Narrog 2012a). For example, the English imperative clause 'make a move' in (1) can invoke a conditional interpretation. The imperative form of the Japanese verb *suru* 'do', i.e., *seyo* in (2), functions as a concessive connective conveying the meaning of 'whether it is X or Y'.

(1) *Make a move* and I'll shoot. (Quirk et al. 1985: 832; emphasis added)

https://doi.org.10.1075/slcs.202.15zhu
© 2018 John Benjamins Publishing Company

(2) *Neko ni* ***seyo,*** *inu ni* ***seyo,*** *okoru taimingu ga*
cat DAT do.IMP dog DAT do.IMP get angry.NPST timing NOM
muzukashii.
difficult.NPST
'*Whether* cats *or* dogs, the right timing for getting angry with them is difficult.' (Narrog 2012a: 43; translation by the original author)

Both of the imperatives above have lost their typical directive meaning and have obtained the text-building function of creating textual coherence (Narrog 2012a: 37–38).

Similarly, in Contemporary Chinese the combination of a prohibitive (or negative imperative) marker *bié* (别) with a SAY verb *shuō* (说), which literally means 'don't say', has grammaticalized into a connective.[1] *Biéshuō* conveys a scalar additive meaning, similar to 'let alone' or 'not to mention', as in (3).

(3) a. 别说每天跑1000米,就是跑3000米,对他而言也是小菜一碟。
Biéshuō *měitiān pǎo 1000 mǐ, jiùshì pǎo 3000 mǐ duìtāéryán*
PROH-say every day run 1000 meter even run 3000 meter for him
yě shì xiǎocài-yīdié.
also COP a piece of cake
'Even running 3000m every day is just a piece of cake for him, *let alone* 1000m.'

b. 他连高中都没上过,更别说大学了。
Tā lián gāozhōng dōu méi shàng guo, gèng ***biéshuō*** *dàxué le.*
he even high school even NEG go to PRF even PROH-say university CRS
'He has never even been to high school, *let alone* university.'
(by the authors)

The syntactic and semantic properties of the connective *biéshuō* have been adequately described by previous studies (e.g., Xing 2001: 237; Dong 2007; Han 2008; Yin 2009; Zhou 2013, 2014). The connective *biéshuō* typically arises in a complex syntactic structure generalized as (4).[2]

1. The prohibitive in Chinese is typically expressed by some special negations conveying the negative imperative meaning (e.g., *bié, búyào*) (Li & Thompson 1981: 455–456; van der Auwera & Lejeune 2013).

2. The unit Q can be marked by various particles which usually convey a concessive conditional meaning, such as *jiùshì, jiùsuàn, lián* 'even (if)'. According to Yin's (2009: 114) corpus investigation of Contemporary Chinese, *jiùshì* is most frequently (65.93%) used together with *biéshuō*. It should be noted, however, that the concessive conditional marker may be omitted occasionally.

Besides, Zhou (2013) regards the *biéshuō* occurring at the beginning of the sentence (3a) and at the back position (3b) as different connectives. Indeed, the adverb *gèng* 'even' with an emphatic meaning often appears before the *biéshuō* occurring at the back position as in (3b),

(4) ***Biéshuō*** P ($NP_1/VP_1/S_1$), *jiùshì* Q ($NP_2/VP_2/S_2$) VP_0.

P and Q, which can be NPs, VPs or sentences syntactically, usually share the single VP_0. The two units in combination with the VP_0 represent two events belonging to a shared domain but showing different degrees of realizability. The speaker takes the occurrence of P as given and then adds another unit Q which is more difficult to realize than P. *Biéshuō* introduces the unit P, while Q is typically introduced by a concessive conditional marker such as *jiùshì*. For example, in (3a), *pǎo 1000mǐ* 'running 1000m' (P) and *pǎo 3000 mǐ* 'running 3000m' (Q) share the same domain of the distance he runs every day. However, *pǎo 1000 mǐ* 'running 1000m' is easier to realize than *pǎo 3000 mǐ* 'running 3000m'. In other words, even the more difficult event can and will be made to happen (i.e., even running 3000m every day is just a piece of cake for him), let alone the easier one (i.e., running 1000m is of course easy for him). The speaker takes advantage of the scalar contrast to praise "his" running ability. As for (3b), the speaker is talking about "his" low level of education. Generally speaking, *shàng dàxué* 'going to university' is more difficult to realize than *shàng gāozhōng* 'going to high school'. However, due to the negative predicate, the situation reverses, and what is compared here is the "difficulty" of "not going to high school" (Q) and "not going to university" (P). Although *biéshuō* occurs at the back position of the complex sentence, it still introduces the unit of lower degree in the domain, that is "not going to university" is easier to realize or more likely to occur than "not going to high school". In sum, there is always a step-up of degree from P to Q.

In traditional Chinese linguistics, *biéshuō* is categorized as a *Dìjìn Liáncí* 'step-up connective' which is a subtype of coordination (Xing 2001: 237). English *let alone* is also labeled as a coordinator by some scholars (Fillmore et al. 1988; Huddleston & Pullum 2002: 1319). Furthermore, in König's (1991: 42) semantic classification of focus particles, *let alone* is situated in the group of scalar additive particles, similar to *even* and *also*. Chinese *biéshuō* and English *let alone* show

---

but it seems to be optional (3b′). In addition, as in (3b″), the *biéshuō* clause can also be moved to the front position and it doesn't influence the truth condition of the original sentence.

(3) b′. *Tā lián gāozhōng dōu méi shàng guo, Ø biéshuō dàxué le.*
he even high school even NEG go to PRF PROH-say university CRS
'He has even never been to high school, *let alone* university.'

b″. *Biéshuō dàxué le, tā lián gāozhōng dōu méi shàng guo.*
PROH-say university CRS he even high school even NEG go to PRF
'He has even never been to high school, *let alone* university.'

Therefore, we don't distinguish them as different connectives here and take (4) as the general syntactic structure where the connective *biéshuō* arises.

some differences syntactically. While *biéshuō* can occur at the beginning and in the middle of a sentence as in (3) (see also footnote 2), for instance, *let alone* usually occurs sentence-medially, leading the second clause. However, both of the two particles are used to add one measurement to another and combine two units of different degrees in a shared domain. Therefore, we call them scalar additive coordinators (henceforth SAC for short) in this paper.[3]

There has been a growing body of literature on the development of the SAC *biéshuō* (e.g., Dong 2007; Hou 2009; Zhou 2014). They commonly assume that *biéshuō* derived from the syntagmatic combination and grammaticalization of the prohibitive marker *bié* with the SAY verb *shuō*. In other words, the SAC *biéshuō* has been considered to mainly have evolved as a result of the reanalysis of the prohibitive expression *bié shuō* 'don't say' via pragmatic inference. However, a key problem with the previous studies on the development of *biéshuō* is that they are mainly based on synchronic presumptions and reconstructions in the absence of much diachronic investigation. Moreover, the mechanism of the semantic change (e.g., pragmatic inference, abduction) has been discussed a lot, while the crucial context that led to the emergence of *biéshuō* hasn't received sufficient attention.[4] In contrast to these works, Yin (2009) points out that *biéshuō* may derive from the analogical extension of *mòshuō* (莫说) in Ancient Chinese. *Mòshuō* is formed by a prohibitive marker *mò* and a SAY verb *shuō*, which is morphologically similar to *biéshuō*. It grammaticalized into a connective conveying the scalar additive meaning in the Song Dynasty (960–1279 CE).

Yin's (2009) assumption provides us with an important clue to the diachronic development of *biéshuō*. As there existed multiple prohibitive markers (e.g., *mò* (莫), *xiū* (休)) and SAY verbs (e.g., *dào* (道), *yán* (言)) similar to *bié* and *shuō* in Ancient Chinese, there may have been more than one combined form (e.g., *mòdào, mòyán, xiūdào*) that grammaticalized into an SAC before the emergence of *biéshuō*. If so, we can hypothesize that the schema shown in (5) may have already

3. Actually, some other scalar particles such as Chinese *jiushi* 'even (if)', English *even, also* can also be regarded as scalar additive coordinators (SAC) as we define here. However, in the current paper this term is only used to refer to the ones derived from the combination of a prohibitive marker with a SAY verb.

4. For instance, Dong (2007) hypothesizes that there is an intermediate stage of 'don't need to say' between the prohibitive meaning and the scalar additive meaning, and advances a two-step process of abduction as the mechanism of this semantic change. Chen (2017: 40 footnote 6) notes that "Elizabeth Traugott (p.c.) points out that the conjunction *bieshuo* seems conceivably to convey 'ignoring/not saying' and suggests that it is grammaticalized from its negative imperative use."

been established in Ancient Chinese, and it subsequently sanctioned new SACs including *biéshuō* by analogy over time.[5]

(5) [[prohibitive marker + SAY verb] $_{\text{COORDINATOR}}$ ↔ [scalar additive]]

In other words, the emergence of the SAC *biéshuō* may not merely depend on the syntagmatic combination and reanalysis of the prohibitive marker *bié* with the SAY verb *shuō*, but have also been influenced by some earlier forms of similar pattern.

The current paper aims to propose a diachronic and constructionist account of the development of the Chinese scalar additive coordinators deriving from prohibitives such as *biéshuō*. This paper is organized as follows: Section 2 briefly introduces the constructional approach to grammatical change. Section 3 outlines the diachronic development of the SAC from the prohibitives. Section 4 explores the diffusional change of the SAC. Section 5 states the conclusion.

2. The constructional approach

In grammaticalization research, the crucial role of linguistic context has been widely recognized (e.g., Bybee et al. 1994; Lehmann 1995; Heine 2002; Diewald 2002; Hopper & Traugott 2003 among others). For example, Bybee et al. (1994: 11) argue that "it is the entire construction, and not simply the lexical meaning of the stem, which is the precursor, and hence the source of the grammatical meaning". Similar to this point of view, in recent years there has been considerable interest in applying the framework of Construction Grammar (e.g., Goldberg 1995, 2006; Croft 2001) to grammatical change, which is often referred to as Diachronic Construction Grammar (e.g., Noël 2007; Gisborne & Patten 2011; Trousdale 2012; Hilpert 2013; Traugott & Trousdale 2013; Barðdal et al. 2015). Briefly speaking, a unit is considered to obtain new grammatical functions not as a single morpheme, but as a whole construction including the linguistic context where it is embedded.

In the present paper, we mainly employ Traugott & Trousdale's (2013) framework of constructionalization. A construction is understood to be a form-meaning pairing and a speaker's language knowledge is regarded as a network that consists of constructions with different levels of abstraction (Goldberg 1995, 2006; Croft 2001). According to Traugott and Trousdale (2013: 22), constructionalization (Cxzn) is "the creation of a form$_{\text{new}}$-meaning$_{\text{new}}$ (combinations) of signs. It forms

5. We mainly refer to the formalism for construction schemas used by Booij (2010) and Traugott & Trousdale (2013). The left side is the form and the right side is its meaning. The form and meaning are linked by a double-headed arrow which indicates the construction is a form-meaning pairing.

new type nodes, which have new syntax or morphology and new coded meaning, in the linguistic network of a population of speakers". On the other hand, a constructional change (CC) is "a change affecting one internal dimension of a construction. It does not involve the creation of a new node" (Traugott & Trousdale 2013: 26). Typical constructional changes include expansion of pragmatics, semanticization of those pragmatics and mismatch between form and meaning, which may lead to constructionalization. In turn, there may be some further constructional changes after a constructionalization and these constructional changes may enable a new constructionalization to take place. The succession of changes can be summarized as (6).

(6) CCs ➡ Cxzn ➡ CCs (➡ Cxzn_{new})
(Traugott & Trousdale 2013: 28; partially modified)

As for the SAC such as *biéshuō*, the constructional meaning of scalar additive can not be strictly predicted from its components of the prohibitive marker and the SAY verb (cf. Goldberg 1995: 4). Its scalar additive meaning is not derivable from the individual components, but from the combination as a whole. Furthermore, as illustrated based on (3) and (4) in Section 1, the functional realization of the SAC largely rests on the interaction between the two units of P and Q. In other words, the complex syntactic structure shown in (4) can be considered as the primary discourse context where the SAC arises. This observation implies that the development of the SAC may also be intimately connected with the discourse contexts where the source structure, i.e., the combination of the prohibitive marker and the SAY verb, used to occur. Therefore, in the following section we will trace the constructionalization process of the SAC with a particular focus on the context in which the construction emerged.

3. The diachronic development of the SAC

3.1 The discourse contexts giving rise to the SAC

In this section, we will first observe the discourse contexts in which the combination of a prohibitive marker with a SAY verb used to occur prior to the emergence of the SAC. According to our diachronic corpus investigation, until the Tang Dynasty (618–907 CE), such combinations appeared to convey only the directive meaning 'don't say', as in (7).[6]

6. We use the Ancient Chinese data of the CCL Corpus (Center for Chinese Linguistics, Peking University; http://ccl.pku.cn:8080/ccl_corpus/index.jsp). We selected the combinations of the

(7) a. 匪言勿言,匪由勿语。
Fēiyán ***wù yán****, fēiyóu* ***wù yǔ****.*
improper words PROH say unreasonable words PROH say
'*Don't say* improper and unreasonable words.'
Shījīng (诗经 11th–6th c. BCE)

b. 莫言尔贱,而不受命。
Mò yán *ěr jiàn, ér bú shòumìng.*
PROH say you humble so NEG accept the order
'*Don't say* that you are humble and so you don't accept the order.'
Quánliángwén (全梁文 6th–7th c. CE)

Besides the examples of prohibitive clause alone like (7), we can also observe some examples in which an additional clause (II) follows the prohibitive clause as in (8). Clause II can be understood as asserting a reason for the prohibitive and the two clauses form a casual relation in the speech-act domain (Sweetser 1990: 76–86).[7]

(8) a. 莫言贫贱即可欺,人生富贵自有时。
Mò yán *pínjiàn jì kě qī,* (I) *rénshēng fùguì zì yǒu shí.* (II)
PROH say poor so can tease life get rich originally have time
'*Don't say* that the poor can be teased, (*because*) everybody may get rich at some time.' Cuī Hào (崔颢 704–754 CE) *Cháng'ān dào* (长安道)

following common prohibitive markers and SAY verbs in the history of Chinese (cf. Jiang 1991; Wang 2003) as the search keys.

Prohibitive markers	SAY verbs
wù (毋), *wù* (勿), *mò* (莫), *xiū* (休), *búyào* (不要), *bié* (别)	*yuē* (曰), *huà* (话), *yún* (云), *dào* (道), *yán* (言), *yǔ* (语), *jiǎng* (讲), *lùn* (论), *shuō* (说), *shuōdào* (说道), *wèi* (谓)

The corpus data are divided by political dynasties (but without the precise yearly specifications). We will refer to the time of the data mainly using the periodization of Chinese dynasties instead of the periodization of written Chinese (e.g., Wang 1958; Peyraube 1996). This is because the development of the SAC did not cover so large a span of the history and also because the periodization of the Chinese dynasties with a smaller span of time may help us illustrate this process more accurately.

7. It seems to be not unusual to add a reason for a speech act such as prohibitive and there may have existed examples of this pattern ('Don't say P, because Q.') before the Tang Dynasty. However, such examples were first attested only from the Tang Poems in the corpus and not previously.

b. 别君莫道不尽欢,悬知乐客遥相待。
Bié jūn ***mò dào*** *bú jìnhuān,* (I) *xuánzhī lèkè yáo*
leave you PROH say NEG enjoy oneself guess pleasant thing distant
xiāngdài. (II)
wait
'*Don't say* that I can't enjoy myself any more when I leave you, (*because*) I guess there are many pleasant things waiting for me in the distance.'
Lǐ Bái (李白 701–762 CE) *Xiàtú guī shímén jiùjū* (下途归石门旧居)

If we examine the semantic relation between the two clauses, we can find that Clause II usually includes a contrastive content Q to the prohibited content P in Clause I. In (8a), *pínjiàn jì kě qī* 'the poor can be teased' (P) contrasts with *rénshēng fùguì zì yǒu shí* 'everybody may get rich at some time' (Q); in (8b), *bú jìnhuān* 'I can't enjoy myself any more' (P) contrasts with *lèkè yáo xiāngdài* 'many pleasant things wait in the distance' (Q). In other words, the speaker asserts the validity of the prohibitive by presenting a contrastive statement immediately thereafter.

Another crucial discourse context attested from the Tang Dynasty is exemplified by (9). In these examples, the combination of a prohibitive marker with a SAY verb can be interpreted as a concessive marker besides the literal prohibitive meaning.

(9) a. 莫言长有千金面,终归变作一抄尘。
Mò yán *zhǎngyǒu qiānjīn miàn,* (I) *zhōngguī biànzuò yī chāo*
PROH say have noble face after all change to one CLF
chén. (II)
dust
'*Don't say* that she has a noble face, (*because even so*) it will turn to a handful of dust eventually (i.e., she will eventually die some day).'
'*Although* she has a noble face, it will turn to a handful of dust eventually (i.e., she will eventually die some day).'
Zhāng Zhuó (张鷟 660–740 CE) *Yóuxiānkū* (游仙窟)

b. 勿言分寸铁,为用乃长兵。
Wù yán *fēncùn tiě,* (I) *wéi yòng nǎi chángbīng.* (II)
PROH say small iron PASS use COP powerful weapon
'*Don't say* that it's only a small iron (in the arrow), (*because even so*) if it can be adequately used, it will be a powerful weapon.'
'*Although* it's only a small iron in the arrow, if it can be adequately used, it will be a powerful weapon.'
Bái Jūyì (白居易 772–846 CE) *Jiànzú* (箭镞)

c. 莫道无语,其声如雷。
Mò dào wú yǔ, (I) *qí shēng rú léi.* (II)
PROH say NEG say his voice like thunder
'*Don't say* that he said nothing, (*because even so*) his voice was in fact like the thunder (i.e., his silence meant much).'
'*Although* he said nothing, his voice was in fact like the thunder (i.e., his silence meant much).'
Zǔtáng jí (祖堂集 circa. 10th c. CE)

Similar to (8), there exists a contrastive relation between the propositional contents P and Q of the two clauses in (9) as well: *zhǎngyǒu qiānjīn miàn* 'she has a noble face' (P) vs. *biànzuò yī chāo chén* 'it will change to a handful of dust' (Q) (9a); *fēncùn tiě* 'it's a small iron' (P) vs. *nǎi chángbīng* 'it can be a powerful weapon' (Q) (9b); *wú yǔ* 'he said nothing' (P) vs. *qí shēng rú léi* 'his voice was like the thunder' (Q) (9c). The reason why (9) can invoke a concessive interpretation while (8) can not seems to be mainly associated with the factuality of P. In (9a), the noble face implies her high social position, and the utterance is on the assumption that the speaker has known her high social position. In (9b), it is an objective fact that the iron in the arrow is small. As for (9c), according to the prior context, it is the speaker's response to his disciple who told the speaker that "he said nothing". In sum, it can be inferred that the speakers have recognized P as a real fact in each utterance. When P is judged to be a fact and at the same time shows a semantic contrast to the declarative content Q, a concessive relation between the two clauses can be easily invoked. At this time, the combination of the prohibitive marker with the SAY verb can be regarded as a concessive marker.[8]

Besides the concessive interpretation, the original prohibitive and causal interpretations are still available in (9). However, when P is limited to a fact, there is a pragmatic meaning rising. As the English translation "even so" shows, Clause II can entail a concessive conditional meaning. Concretely speaking, even though P is a fact, if the speaker doesn't want to admit or highlight it, he/she may choose to

8. Although the concessive marker use of the combination of a prohibitive marker with a SAY verb has disappeared from Contemporary Chinese, we can attest such examples like the following one continually till the Yuan Dynasty (1271–1368 CE) in about the 14th century.

休道黄金贵,安乐最值钱。
Xiū dào huángjīn guì, ānlè zuì zhíqián
PROH say gold expensive happiness most valuable
'*Don't say* that gold is worth much, (*because even so*) it is happiness that is the most valuable thing.'
'*Although* gold is worth much, it is happiness that is the most valuable thing.'
Qiànnǚ líhún (倩女离魂 13th–14th c. CE)

prohibit the interlocutor from mentioning it and explain the reason for the prohibition by first conceding that it is true and then providing a contrastive fact to declare his/her own assertion. The concessive conditional meaning may not be verbalized, but it can be naturally included as a part of the speaker's declarative strategy and pragmatically implied in the discourse.

As we will explain in detail in 3.2, the discourse patterns described above provides the crucial contexts for the emergence of the SAC in the subsequent period.

3.2 The rise of the SAC

In the 10th century of the Five Dynasties & Ten Kingdoms (907–960 CE) period, the combination of the prohibitive marker *mò* with the SAY verb *dào* was first attested as an SAC from a Buddhism text *Zǔtáng jí*, as in (10).[9]

(10) a. 莫道不会,设使会得,也只是左之右之。
Mòdào bú huì, shèshǐ huì dé, yě zhǐshì
PROH-say NEG understand even if understand get also only
zuǒzhīyòuzhī.
roughly
'Even if you could, you can only understand it roughly, *much less* you can't understand it at all.'

b. 莫道是骨,皮也不识。
Mòdào shì gǔ, pí yě bù shí.
PROH-say COP bone fur also NEG recognize
'You can't even recognize the fur, *let alone* the bone.'

Zǔtáng jí (祖堂集 circa. 10th c. CE)

In (10a), *bú huì* 'you can't understand it at all' (P) and *huì dé* 'you can understand it' (Q) form a positive–negative polarity relation, and they share the same domain of describing one's ability to understand. Generally, one needs to make efforts in order to understand something that he/she couldn't understand before. In other words, there is an increase of the reliazablity from P to Q. As for (10b), the speaker is talking about the interlocutor's visual capability. Although the fur of an animal is usually easier to recognize than the bone, due to the negative predicate, the shared domain here should be the "unrecognizability" of the parts of an animal.

9. The judgments of the SAC examples seems to be unambiguous as they are relatively unequivocal. The prohibitive marker with the SAY verb can hardly be interpreted as the prohibitive or concessive meaning any more. Instead, the scalar additive meaning is obviously the natural interpretation. Syntactically, as illustrated in Section 1, there is usually a concessive conditional marker (e.g., *shèshǐ* 'even if' in (10a)) and/or an additive marker (e.g., *yě* 'also' in (10a) and (10b)) occurring in the following clause.

As the event "can not recognize the bone" (P) is more likely to occur than the event "can not recognize the fur" (Q), there is also a step-up of the degree from P to Q. In either example, P is introduced by the SAC *mòdào*. The speaker takes the occurrence of the event represented by P as a given fact and then adds another unit Q which is more difficult to realize in order to emphasize the interlocutor's low ability to understand and discriminate respectively.

From the 12th century in the Southern Song Dynasty (1127–1279 CE), the scalar additive examples became common and more combinations of such pattern functioned as SACs such as *mòshuō*, *mòshuōdào*, *xiūdào* appeared, as shown in (11). *Biéshuō* was first attested as an SAC from the novel *Xǐngshì yīnyuán zhuàn* published in the 17th century between the end of the Ming Dynasty (1368–1644 CE) and the beginning of the Qing Dynasty (1644–1911 CE).

(11) a. 莫说十日,只读得一日,便有功验。
__Mòshuō__ shírì, zhì dú dé yírì, biàn yǒu gōngyàn.
PROH-say ten days only read get one day then have effect
'Even if you could read for only one day, it will affect, *let alone* ten days.'
Zhūzǐ yǔlèi (朱子语类 circa. 12th c. CE)

b. 学者最怕因循,莫说道一下便要做成。
Xuézhě zuì pà yīnxún, __mòshuōdào__ yīxià biàn yào zuò chéng.
scholar most fear cling PROH-say at a time then want do succeed
'Scholars shouldn't stick to the old way of thinking, *let alone* want to achieve results at a time.' *Zhūzǐ yǔlèi* (朱子语类 circa. 12th c. CE)

c. 休道是小生,便是铁石人也意惹情牵。
__Xiūdào__ shì xiǎoshēng, biànshì tiěshírén yě yìrěqíngqiān.
PROH-say COP young man even if hardhearted man also lingering
'Even a hardhearted man would be lingering, *let alone* a young man.'
Xīxiāng jì (西厢记 13th–14th c. CE)

d. 别说娘不去,就是娘去,我也是要拦的。
__Biéshuō__ niáng bú qù, jiùshì niáng qù, wǒ yě shì yào lán de.
PROH-say mom NEG go even if mom go I also COP will prevent NMLZ
'Even if mom would go, I will prevent her, *much less* she won't go.'
Xǐngshì yīnyuán zhuàn (醒世姻缘传 circa. 17th c. CE)

In Examples (10) and (11), the combinations of the prohibitive markers with the SAY verbs can hardly be interpreted as the prohibitive or concessive meaning like the Examples (8) and (9) in 3.1. Instead, they function as a connective as a whole conveying the scalar additive meaning. In other words, a form_{new}-$\text{meaning}_{\text{new}}$ pairing has been created and the constructionalization of the SAC has occurred.

We argue that the SAC formed by the combination of a prohibitive marker with a SAY verb is likely to arise in the discourse contexts illustrated in 3.1. The main evidence can be attributed to the continuity of the contextual properties between the discourse patterns where the prohibitive combinations used to appear and the complex structure in which the SACs arise. Recall the schematic structure (4) which is exemplified by (3), (10) and (11). Three remarkable properties can be observed from the structure: (i) two units of P and Q are combined together and in terms of they form a contrastive relation on the difficulty of realization; (ii) P which is introduced by the SAC represents an event which is easier to realize or more likely to occur than Q, and the occurrence of P is taken as a given fact by the speaker in the utterance; (iii) the unit Q is generally marked by a concessive conditional marker. Before the emergence of the SAC, similar contextual properties were already observed from the discourse patterns in which the prohibitive combinations used to appear, especially the ones exemplified by (9). In this connection, example (9c) is repeated as (12).

(12) 莫道无语,其声如雷。
Mò ***dào*** *wú yǔ, qí shēng rú léi.*
PROH say NEG say his voice like thunder
'*Don't say* that he said nothing, (*because even so*) his voice was in fact like the thunder (i.e., his silence meant much).'
'*Although* he said nothing, his voice was in fact like the thunder (i.e., his silence meant much).' *Zǔtángjí* (祖堂集 circa. 10th c. CE)

A declarative clause follows the prohibitive clause, and it introduces a propositional content *qí shēng rú léi* 'his voice was like the thunder' (Q) which contrasts with another propositional content *wú yǔ* 'he said nothing' (P) in the prohibitive clause. Furthermore, the propositional content P "he said nothing", which was told by the interlocutor, should have been recognized as a fact by the speaker. Otherwise, instead of declaring a direct conflict statement after the prohibitive clause, the speaker is more likely to explain why he doesn't believe "he said nothing". Meanwhile, as a part of the speaker's declarative strategy, a pragmatic meaning of concessive conditional, i.e., "*even if* he had said nothing, his voice was in fact like the thunder" can be inferred from the discourse. In addition, in such a discourse context, the two clauses can also be interpreted as a concessive relation as shown by the second translation. At this time, the combination of the prohibitive marker *mò* with the SAY verb *dào* can be regarded as a concessive marker as a whole. In fact, cross-linguistically, there is a close association between concessive and scalar additive meanings. According to a semantic map for additives (Figure 1) based on a sample of 42 languages proposed by Forker (2016), there are 30 languages in which the additives are also used to mark concessive and scalar additive meanings. This cross-linguistic tendency highlights the close conceptual association between the two categories.

concessive —— scalar additive —— additive —— constituent coordination

Figure 1. A semantic map for additives (part) (Forker 2016: 87 Figure 1; partially modified)

Therefore, we hypothesize that it is in the discourse contexts illustrated in 3.1 that the combination was reanalyzed into the SAC. Specially, the concessive interpretation of the combination seems to be an intermediate phase that led to the emergence of the SAC.

4. The diffusional change of the SAC construction

In Section 3, we sketched the diachronic development of the SAC from the combination of a prohibitive marker with a SAY verb, especially the crucial discourse contexts that triggered the change. In this section, we will focus on the mechanism that led to the emergence of different SAC forms including *biéshuō* introduced in Section 1.

After the first SAC *mòdào* appeared in about the 10th century, more and more combinations of prohibitive markers and SAY verbs functioning as SACs came to be attested in the subsequent periods. Table 1 lists the SAC forms and their frequencies in each period.

Table 1 is constructed as follows. The second line of "PROH + SAY" shows the total token frequencies of the combinations of the prohibitive markers with the SAY verbs in each period. The third line of "SAC (TK)" illustrates the frequencies of the SAC tokens attested in each period. The percentages shown in the fourth line of "SAC (%)" represent the proportion of the SAC tokens in the total "PROH+SAY" tokens. The fifth line of "SAC (TP)" shows the number of the SAC forms, i.e., the type frequencies in each period.[10] The concrete forms and their token frequencies attested in each period are listed from the sixth line. The relative frequency of each form to the total SAC tokens in that period is indicated by the

10. Due to the variation in the data amount of each period, we chose to compare the proportion of the SAC tokens in the total PROH+SAY tokens, i.e., the relative frequency of the SAC tokens in each period here. Besides the literal prohibitive use and SAC use, *biéshuō* has also acquired a discourse marker use in the early 20th century (e.g., Dong 2007; Chen 2017). As we mainly focus on the development of the SAC use in the present study, the distribution of the discourse marker use was not investigated in detail here.

In addition, we randomly selected subsets of the examples of the Qing Dynasty for our analysis due to the large volume of the data from that period. Therefore, it may not be an exhaustive list in Table 1. However, we can still observe a rough tendency of significant increase on both type and token frequencies of the SACs over time.

Table 1. The SAC forms and frequencies attested in the CCL Corpus

	Five Dynasties & Ten Kingdoms (907–960 CE)	Northern Song (960–1127)	Southern Song (1127–1279)	Yuan (1271–1368)	Ming (1368–1644)	Qing (1644–1911)	Republic of China (1912–1949)
PROH-SAY	52	49	257	65	679	381	671
SAC (TK)	5	3	30	27	267	187	281
SAC (%)	9.62%	6.12%	11.67%	41.54%	39.32%	49.08%	41.88%
SAC (TP)	1	2	3	7	9	6	7
mò-dào	5 (100%)	2 (66.67%)	12 (40.00%)	—	2 (0.75%)	—	—
xiū-dào	—	1 (33.33%)	—	5 (18.52%)	7 (2.62%)	1 (0.53%)	1 (0.36%)
mò-shuō	—	—	16 (53.33%)	9 (33.33%)	171 (64.04%)	40 (21.39%)	146 (51.96%)
mò-shuōdào	—	—	2 (6.67%)	1 (3.70%)	—	—	—
mò-yán	—	—	—	1 (3.70%)	3 (1.12%)	—	1 (0.36%)
xiū-shuō	—	—	—	7 (25.93%)	41 (15.36%)	42 (22.46%)	18 (6.41%)
xiū-shuōdào	—	—	—	3 (11.11%)	1 (0.37%)	1 (0.53%)	—
xiū-yán	—	—	—	1 (3.70%)	5 (1.87%)	—	—
mò-jiǎng	—	—	—	—	1 (0.37%)	—	2 (0.71%)
búyào-shuō	—	—	—	—	36 (13.48%)	13 (6.95%)	70 (24.91%)
bié-shuō	—	—	—	—	—	90 (48.13%)	43 (15.30%)

percentage in the bracket. The mark "–" means that the form wasn't observed in the data of that period.

From Table 1, we can observe a significant increase both in the number of the combined SAC forms (type frequency) and in their token frequency relative to the 'genuine' prohibitive tokens from the Yuan Dynasty. We thus hypothesize that the construction schema in (13) (repetition of (5) in Section 1) may have been established in about the 12th to 14th centuries and have come to sanction more forms during the subsequent periods. In other words, the construction has spread over time.

(13) [[prohibitive marker + SAY verb] $_{\text{COORDINATOR}}$ ↔ [scalar additive]]

The spreading of the construction can be seen as a case of diffusional change based on analogy. As the new combinations of prohibitive markers and SAY verbs conveyed the meaning of 'don't say' similar to the old ones, speakers became able to match the new forms to the construction schema as well. As a result, it has expanded its range of application to other combinations and yielded new SACs.

As for *biéshuō*, it can also be regarded as a "product" of this diffusional change. We can not completely exclude the possibility that pragmatic inference played a part in the development of the scalar additive meaning from the prohibitive meaning in *biéshuō* (see [11]). However, we couldn't find much diachronic evidence in the current data. Instead, *biéshuō* has unambiguously and frequently been used to convey the scalar additive meaning since the early period. See Table 1 as well as examples (11d) in 3.2 and (14).

(14) a. 别说是钦差,就是皇上圣旨,我也不遵!
Biéshuō shì qīnchāi, jiùshì huángshang shèngzhǐ,
PROH-say COP imperial commissioner even emperor imperial decree
wǒ yě bù zūn!
I also NEG obey
'Even if it's the imperial decree from the emperor, I will not obey it, *let alone* the imperial commissioner's order.'
Shīgōng'àn (施公案 circa 18th c. CE)

11. For instance, Dong (2007) hypothesizes that there is an intermediate stage of 'don't need to say' between the prohibitive meaning and the scalar additive meaning, and advances a two-step process of abduction as the mechanism of this semantic change. Chen (2017: 40 footnote 6) notes that "Elizabeth Traugott (p.c.) points out that the conjunction *bieshuo* seems conceivably to convey 'ignoring/not saying' and suggests that it is grammaticalized from its negative imperative use."

b. 他原行的正走的正,你行动便有个坏心,连我也不放心,别说他了。
Tā yuán xíng de zhèng zǒu de zhèng, nǐ xíngdòng
he inherently do NMLZ upright walk NMLZ upright you act
biàn yǒu ge huài xīn, lián wǒ yě bú fàngxīn, ***biéshuō*** *tā le.*
even if have CLF bad heart even I also NEG feel relieved PROH-say he CRS
'As he is inherently a man of integrity, if you conduct yourself inappropriately,
even I will worry about you, *let alone* he.'
Hónglóu mèng (红楼梦 circa. 18th c. CE)

On the other hand, analogy is likely to have played an important role in the development of *biéshuō*. According to Jiang (1991), the prohibitive marker *bié* was first observed in the literature of the Yuan Dynasty in about the 14th century and became commonly used in about the 17th century. When *bié* became a conventionalized prohibitive marker, it participated in the diffusional change. As a result of the analogical extension of the construction schema in (13), *bié shuō* was sanctioned as a new SAC. It can be presumed that some frequently used forms in Ming and Qing periods such as *mòshuō*, *xiūshuō* and *búyàoshuō* acted as the immediate analogues.

Although the construction schema in (13) showed a high productivity and sanctioned a number of new SACs over time, in view of the low token frequencies and the appearance in limited periods, some forms such as *mòshuōdào, mòjiǎng* may have merely appeared as temporary combinations and may not have become conventionalized. On the other hand, some forms such as *mòshuō*, *xiūshuō* and *búyàoshuō* seem to have become conventionalized in the history as they were frequently used for a long period of time. However, with the obsolescence of the old prohibitive markers (e.g., *mò, xiū*) and SAY verbs (e.g., *dào, yán*), the SACs consisting of these forms disappeared. Consequently, only *búyàoshuō* and *biéshuō* have survived into Contemporary Chinese.[12] That is to say, although the construction is non-compositional semantically, it is still highly analyzable morphosyntactically (cf. Traugott & Trousdale 2013: 121).

5. Conclusion

From a constructionist perspective, the present paper has addressed the diachronic development of the Chinese scalar additive coordinators (SAC) with meaning similar to 'let alone', which derived from prohibitives. We argued that

12. The prohibitive marker *mò* still exists in some dialects of Chinese such as Sichuan dialects (Wang et al. 1989: 236). Although *mòshuō* as an SAC has disappeared from the Standard Contemporary Chinese, it can still be used in the Sichuan dialects (p.c. Yang Huang).

a construction schema formed by a combination of a prohibitive marker with a SAY verb conveying the scalar additive meaning may have been established in the history of Chinese. The emergence of the SAC *biéshuō* in Contemporary Chinese was greatly influenced by the analogical extension modeled on the construction, instead of merely depending on the direct syntagmatic combination and grammaticalization of the prohibitive marker *bié* with the SAY verb *shuō* via pragmatic inference. In addition, we examined the crucial discourse contexts that arguably gave rise to the new construction. The development of the SACs derived from the prohibitives is more likely to be considered as a case of constructionalization. Crucially, it is the entire construction that has spread over time.

Finally, we would like to briefly remark on the typological implications of this expansion path from prohibitive to scalar additive coordination in Chinese. As mentioned at the beginning of this paper, imperatives are observed to obtain textual functions and serve to combine clauses cross-linguistically. The present case study of Chinese demonstrates that prohibitive (or negative imperative) expressions can also serve clause combining functions and provides a rarely discussed pathway of change, i.e., prohibitive > scalar additive. Furthermore, the development of textual functions in such inherently intersubjective expressions (see also examples in (1) and (2)) challenges the applicability of the unidirectional hypothesis of (inter)subjectification (Traugott 1995, 2003, 2010) in semantic change. Instead, there seems to be an increasing orientation towards text/discourse especially at the late stage of grammaticalization (Narrog 2012a, b). A diachronic constructional investigation of the textual functions of imperatives and prohibitives across languages is in our next agenda.

Acknowledgements

Part of this work is supported by the grant from the Japan Society for the Promotion of Science (#22520384; PI: Kaoru Horie). We thank the organizer and the audience of the Second International Conference on Grammaticalization (Gramm 2) held in Rouen, France, in April 2016. Our thanks also go to the anonymous reviewer and Yueh Hsin Kuo for their insightful comments on earlier versions of this paper. Any remaining errors are solely our own.

Abbreviations

COP	Copula	NOM	Nominative
CLF	Classifier	NPST	Non-past
CRS	Currently relevant state	PASS	Passive

DAT	Dative	PRF	Perfect
IMP	Imperative	PROH	Prohibitive
NEG	Negation		
NMLZ	Nominalizer		

References

Aikhenvald, Alexandra Y. 2010. *Imperatives and Commands*. Oxford: OUP.

Barðdal, Jóhanna, Smirnova, Elena, Sommerer, Lotte & Gildea, Spike. 2015. *Diachronic Construction Grammar* [Constructional Approaches to Language Series 18]. Amsterdam: John Benjamins. https://doi.org/10.1075/cal.18

Booij, Geert. 2010. *Construction Morphology*. Oxford: OUP.

Bybee, Joan, Pekins, Revere Dale & Pagliuca, William. 1994. *The Evolution of Grammar. Tense, Aspect, and Modality in the Languages of the World*. Chicago IL: The University of Chicago Press.

Chen, Jiajun. 2017. Dialogicity in dialogue. Deriving Chinese discourse marker *bieshuo* from the negative imperative. *Journal of Pragmatics* 110: 34–49.

Croft, William. 2001. *Radical Construction Grammar. Syntactic Theory in Typological Perspective*. Oxford: OUP. https://doi.org/10.1093/acprof:oso/9780198299554.001.0001

Diewald, Gabriele. 2002. A model for relevant types of contexts in grammaticalization. In *New Reflections on Grammaticalization* [Typological Studies in Language Series 49], Ilse Wischer & Gabriele Diewald (eds), 103–120. Amsterdam: John Benjamins. https://doi.org/10.1075/tsl.49.09die

Dobrushina, Nina. 2008. Imperatives in conditional and subordinate clauses. In *Subordination and Coordination Strategies in North Asian Languages* [Current Issues in Linguistic Theory Series 300], Edward J. Vajda (ed.), 123–141. Amsterdam: John Benjamins. https://doi.org/10.1075/cilt.300.13dob

Dong, Xiufang. 2007. Cihuihua yu huayubiaoji de xingcheng (Lexicalization and the formation of discourse markers). *Shijie Hanyu Jiaoxue* (Chinese Teaching in the World) 1: 50–61.

Fillmore, Charles J., Kay, Paul & O'connor, Mary Catherine. 1988. Regularity and idiomaticity in grammatical constructions. The case of *let alone*. *Language* 64(3): 501–538. https://doi.org/10.2307/414531

Forker, Diana. 2016. Toward a typology for additive markers. *Lingua* 180: 69–100.

Gisborne, Nicolas & Patten, Amanda. 2011. Construction grammar and grammaticalization. In *The Oxford Handbook of Grammaticalization*, Heiko Narrog & Bernd Heine (eds), 92–104. Oxford: OUP.

Goldberg, Adele E. 1995. *Constructions. A Construction Grammar Approach to Argument Structure*. Chicago IL: University of Chicago Press.

Goldberg, Adele E. 2006. *Constructions at Work. The Nature of Generalization in Language*. Oxford: OUP.

Han, Lei. 2008. Lianci "bieshuo" gongneng tanxi (On the function of the connective *bieshuo*). In *Xiandai Hanyu Xuci Yanjiu yu Duiwai Hanyu Jiaoxu* (The study of grammatical words in Contemporary Chinese and teaching Chinese as a foreign language), Vol. 2, Huyang Qi (ed.), 121–134. Shanghai: Fudan University Press.

Haspelmath, Martin & König, Ekkehard. 1998. Concessive conditionals in the languages of Europe. In *Adverbial Constructions in the Languages of Europe* [Empirical Approaches to Language Typology 20–3], Johan van der Auwera & Donall Baoill (eds), 563–640. Berlin: Mouton de Gruyter. https://doi.org/10.1515/9783110802610.563

Heine, Bernd. 2002. On the role of context in grammaticalization. In *New Reflections on Grammaticalization* [Typological Studies in Language Series 49], Ilse Wischer & Gabriele Diewald (eds), 83–101. Amsterdam: John Benjamins. https://doi.org/10.1075/tsl.49.08hei

Heine, Bernd, Claudi, Ulrike & Hünnemeyer, Friederike. 1991. *Grammaticalization. A Conceptual Framework*. Chicago IL: The University of Chicago Press.

Hilpert, Martin. 2013. *Constructional Change in English. Developments in Allomorphy, Word-Formation and Syntax*. Cambridge: CUP. https://doi.org/10.1017/CBO9781139004206

Hopper, Paul J. & Traugott, Elizabeth Closs. 2003. *Grammaticalization*, 2nd edn. Cambridge: CUP. https://doi.org/10.1017/CBO9781139165525

Hou, Ruifen. 2009. "Bieshuo" yu "bieti" (*Bieshuo and bieti*). *Zhongguo Yuwen* (Studies of the Chinese Language) 2: 131–140.

Huddleston, Rodney & Pullum, Geoffrey K. 2002. *The Cambridge Grammar of the English Language*. Cambridge: CUP.

Jiang, Lansheng. 1991. Jinzhici "bie" kaoyuan (Explore the source of the prohibitive marker *bie*). *Yuwen Yanjiu (Linguistic Research)* 1: 42–47.

König, Ekkehard. 1991. *The Meaning of Focus Particles. A Comparative Perspective*. New York NY: Routledge.

Lehmann, Christian. 1995. *Thoughts on Grammaticalization*. Munich: Lincom.

Li, Charles N. & Thompson, Sandra A. 1981. *Mandarin Chinese. A Functional Reference Grammar*. Berkeley CA: University of California Press.

Narrog, Heiko. 2012a. Beyond intersubjectification. Textual uses of modality and mood in subordinate clauses as part of *speech-act* orientation. *English Text Construction* 5(1): 29–52. https://doi.org/10.1075/etc.5.1.03nar

Narrog, Heiko. 2012b. *Modality, Subjectivity and Semantic Change. A Cross-linguistic Perspective*. Oxford: OUP. https://doi.org/10.1093/acprof:oso/9780199694372.001.0001

Noël, Dirk. 2007. Diachronic construction grammar and grammaticalization theory. *Functions of Languages* 14(2): 177–202. https://doi.org/10.1075/fol.14.2.04noe

Peyraube, Alain. 1996. Recent issues in Chinese historical syntax. In *New Horizons in Chinese Linguistics*, James C-T. J. Huang & Yen-Hui Audrey Li (eds), 161–213. Dordrecht: Kluwer. https://doi.org/10.1007/978-94-009-1608-1_6

Quirk, Randolph, Greenbaum, Sidney, Leech, Geoffrey & Jan, Svartvik. 1985. *A Comprehensive Grammar of the English Language*. London: Longman.

Sweetser, Eve E. 1990. *From Etymology to Pragmatics. Metaphorical and Cultural Aspects of Semantic Structure*. Cambridge: CUP. https://doi.org/10.1017/CBO9780511620904

Traugott, Elizabeth Closs. 1995. Subjectification in Grammaticalisation. In *Subjectivity and Subjectification*, Dieter Stein & Susan Wright (eds), 31–54. Cambridge: CUP. https://doi.org/10.1017/CBO9780511554469.003

Traugott, Elizabeth Closs. 2003. From subjectification to intersubjectification, In *Motives for Language Change*, Raymond Hickey (ed.), 124–139. Cambridge: CUP. https://doi.org/10.1017/CBO9780511486937.009

Traugott, Elizabeth Closs. 2010. Inter subjectivity and (inter)subjectification. A reassessment. In *Subjectification, Intersubjectification and Grammaticalization*, Kristin Davidse, Lieven Vandelanotte & Hubert Cuyckens (eds), 29–71. Berlin: Mouton de Gruyter. https://doi.org/10.1515/9783110226102.1.29
Traugott, Elizabeth Closs & Trousdale, Graeme. 2013. *Constructionalization and Constructional Changes*. Oxford: OUP. https://doi.org/10.1093/acprof:oso/9780199679898.001.0001
Trousdale, Graeme. 2012. Theory and data in diachronic Construction Grammar. The case of the *what with* construction. *Studies in Language* 36(3): 576–602. https://doi.org/10.1075/sl.36.3.05tro
van der Auwera, Johan & Lejeune, Ludo (with Valentin Goussev). 2013. The prohibitive. In *The World Atlas of Language Structures Online*, Matthew S. Dryer & Martin Haspelmath (eds). Leipzig: Max Planck Institute for Evolutionary Anthropology. <http://wals.info/chapter/71> (29 October 2017).
Wang, Li. 1958. *Hanyushi Lunwenji* (Paper collection on the history of Chinese). Beijing: Science Publishing.
Wang, Weihui. 2003. Hanyu "shuolei ci" de lishi yanbian yu gongshi fenbu (The historical change and synchronic distribution of the Chinese SAY verbs). *Zhongguo Yuwen* 4: 329–342.
Wang, Wenhu, Zhang, Yizhou & Zhou, Jiayun. 1989. *Sichuan Fangyan Cidian* (Dictionary of Sichuan Dialects). Chengdu: Sichuan People's Publishing House.
Xing, Fuyi. 2001. *Hanyu Fuju Yanjiu* (Research on the Chinese complex sentences). Beijing: The Commercial Press.
Yin, Hailiang. 2009. Xiandai Hanyu "bieshuo" de pianzhang xianjie gongneng jiqi yufahua (Study on the cohesive function of *bieshuo* in Contemporary Chinese and its grammaticalization). *Xi'nan Nongye Daxue Xuebao* (Journal of Southwest Agricultural University) [*Social Science Edition*] 7(4): 111–116.
Zhou, Li. 2013. Qianhou fenju zhong butong de lianjie chengfen "bieshuo" (*Bieshuo* as different connectives in the front and back clause). *Shijie Hanyu Jiaoxue* (Chinese Teaching in the World) 4: 498–511.
Zhou, Li. 2014. Lianci "bieshuo" yu "budan" (The conjunction *bieshuo* and *budan*). *Yuyan Yanjiu* (Studies in Language and Linguistics) 34(3): 52–58.

Cross-varietal diversity in constructional entrenchment

The final-tag construction in Irish and American English

Mitsuko Narita Izutsu and Katsunobu Izutsu
Fuji Women's University / Hokkaido University of Education

The present study analyzes clauses with final tags as a construction, i.e., a symbolic form-meaning pairing, which is formulated as [[ANCH$_i$ FT$_j$] ↔ [S conclude verbalization of proposition$_i$ with attitude$_j$]] (ANCH: Anchor, FT: Final Tag, S: Speaker). The final-tag construction is observed in most varieties of English. However, a comparison of two spoken corpora of English (SPICE-Ireland and the Santa Barbara Corpus) reveals that the degree of the constructional entrenchment of this symbolic unit differs markedly between Irish and American English. Our analysis illustrates that both type and token frequencies of final tags are higher in Irish English than American English. Interpreting the results in terms of the three characteristics of grammatical constructionalization: increase in schematicity, increase in productivity, and decrease in compositionality (Traugott & Trousdale 2013), our study concludes that the final-tag construction is more entrenched in the minds of Irish English speakers than American English speakers. This observation points to a greater development of the construction in Irish English, where the final position has become a more accommodating slot of broader versatility in which the speakers can put a wider variety of expressions for emotive and/or interactive purposes. In addition to conceivable motivations (sub- and superstrate influences) responsible for the development, the constructional approach can also illustrate the impact of a well-entrenched schema on incremental language use.

Keywords: constructionalization, entrenchment, final tag, Irish English, American English

https://doi.org.10.1075/slcs.202.16izu
© 2018 John Benjamins Publishing Company

1. Introduction

While final particles are known to be common in head-final languages such as Japanese and Korean, some recent studies (e.g., Hancil et al. 2015) have shown that sentence-final or right-peripheral position is similarly exploited for interactive, discourse-pragmatic purposes in head-initial languages, too. English, for example, has question tags (e.g., *isn't it* and *do you*) and has also developed "non-concordant" tags such as *is it* and *isn't it/innit* (Allerton 2009: 310). Recent research subsumes various types of sentence/clause-final expressions under the category of final particles such as conjunctions, adverbials, focus particles, and others (see Hancil et al. 2015 for a classification of final particles). From a diachronic perspective, Traugott (2016) demonstrates that pragmatic markers have been available in right-peripheral position from Old English onwards with the number of types used expanding over time. At the end of her discussion on the rise of clause-final pragmatic markers in English, Traugott (2016: 49) poses several areas of potential open inquiry to be resolved, one being "what differences there are among varieties of English."

A growing interest in variational pragmatics (e.g., Schneider & Barron 2008; Fried et al. 2010) has already attempted to provide some answers to this question. For example, Tottie & Hoffmann (2006) investigate so-called "canonical" tag questions (*It's raining, isn't it/is it?, It's not raining, is it/isn't it?*) in a spoken subpart of the British National Corpus and the Longman Spoken American Corpus, and determine that the frequency of tag questions in the British database is more than nine times as high as in the American corpus. This is in accordance with Algeo's observation that Americans think of tag questions as "characteristically British" (2006: 296). A heavier use of tag questions in British English is also corroborated by Barron et al. (2015), who contrast British English with Irish English on the basis of an analysis of spontaneous conversations in ICE-corpora (ICE-GB and ICE-Ireland). They find tag questions in ICE-GB to be about 1.8 times more frequent than in ICE-Ireland. Allerton (2009: 323) suggests that the avoidance of canonical tags in American English may be related to its preferential use of other final tags such as *right*. Barron et al. (2015: 520–521) similarly consider that the less frequent use of tag questions in Irish English relative to British English may be ascribable to the heavier use of "typically Irish" tags (2015: 521) such as *like, sure it can't, so she is*, and others.

For other kinds of final tags, Lucek (2011) makes a comparison of "invariant" tags (e.g., *right, you know, you see, is it*) across six varieties of English, contrasting the data set of the face to face conversations in SPICE-Ireland with the result of Columbus' (2009a) analysis of invariant tags in the five varieties. The comparison reveals that Irish English occupies the third place in the total number of invariant tags, following Singapore and Indian English but ahead of New Zealand, Hong Kong, and British English. However, since Columbus' (2009a) study does not include utterance-final *like*, a very common tag in Ireland, Lucek (2011: 104) argues that "[i]f the 'like' tags are included, Irish English now becomes the variety with the most utterance-final tags." The study also reports that, of the 17 invariant tags examined, utterance-final *you know*, *yeah*, and *yes* are more frequently used in Irish English than in the other varieties.

Many other studies have focused on the cross-varietal distribution of a single pragmatic marker. Siemund et al. (2009) investigate the positional distribution of *like* across non-standard varieties of English (Irish, Indian, Philippine and East African English), using the spoken components of ICE-corpora. They observe that Irish English and Indian English employ *like* at the margins of clauses more frequently than the other varieties, but Irish English displays a preference for its use in clause-final position while Indian English favors clause-initial position. Schweinberger (2015) compares the use of *like* in Irish English and south-eastern British English, and demonstrates that clause-final *like* is significantly more frequent in Irish English, representing its most favored positional variant. Kallen (2013: 190–192) also observes a similar difference in the use of final *like* between Irish English and British English.

Clancy & Vaughan (2012), comparing the Limerick Corpus of Irish English with the British National Corpus, observe that Irish English shows a greater frequency of the non-temporal, pragmatic use of *now*. Their analysis shows that it often occupies utterance-final position, which signifies "one fundamental difference" between the two varieties (2012: 239). For pragmatic markers less known as final tags, Kirk & Kallen (2010) attest clause-final *but* or "the adverbial tag use of *but*" (Aitken 1979: 109) in SPICE-Ireland and observe its similarity to the use in Scottish English.

As seen from the above, final tags have recently been drawing much scholarly attention. The main focus of these studies is on the discourse-pragmatic functions or the socio-linguistic diversities of individual final pragmatic markers or a particular group of tags (e.g., invariant tags). However, few studies have ever attempted to investigate final tags from an overarching perspective. The present study seeks to take a step in that direction and attempts to conduct a more comprehensive study of final tags, not only looking at canonical tags but other pragmatic markers in final position.

We will compare American English and Irish English, two varieties less often studied with respect to final tags. To incorporate a broad range of pragmatic markers into a comparative frame of analysis, we will take a constructional approach (Traugott & Trousdale 2013) to final tags, where clauses with final tags are viewed as a construction, which is a symbolic form-meaning pairing (e.g., Goldberg

1995: 1; Langacker 1987: 58). This approach enables us to investigate to what extent the two varieties show the constructional entrenchment of final-tagged structures (i.e., structures with final tags). The result of analysis is able to illuminate an oft-neglected force for the development of linguistic structures, i.e., an influential effect of a highly entrenched constructional schema on language use. As a constructional template becomes more schematic and more deeply entrenched in the minds of speakers, it can come to serve as an important motivation that facilitates further uses of pragmatic markers in final position and, over time, encourages a further development of the final-tag construction in a given variety of a language.

2. Data

The data investigated in this study were taken from a spoken corpus of each variety: the SPICE-Ireland corpus (Kirk et al. 2011) and the Santa Barbara Corpus of Spoken American English (DuBois et al. 2000, 2003, 2004, 2005). The SPICE corpus is the annotated version of the spoken portion of ICE-Ireland (the Ireland component of the International Corpus of English). It provides the annotations of discourse-pragmatic and prosodic features of spoken language. Specifically important to this study is that sentence tags are assigned the annotation @ in the corpus. As for American English data, since ICE does not have the spoken component of the variety, we employed the Santa Barbara Corpus (SBC) of Spoken American English, which was originally designed to represent the spoken material of ICE-US. The two corpora, however, are not parallel in key respects. SBC consists of 60 files and contains about 249,000 words in total. The much larger SPICE-Ireland contains 626,597 words and 15 text categories. We thus selected the following three text categories from SPICE, which would match SBC as closely as possible both in size and variety.

The Santa Barbara Corpus (SBC 1–60):	c.249,000 words
SPICE-Ireland:	186,266 words
– Face to face conversation (P1A-001 to P1A-090)	20,239 words
– Telephone conversation (P1A-091 to P1A-100)	43,007 words
– Classroom discussion (P1B-001 to P1B-020)	
TOTAL	249,512 words

For SPICE, the files numbered P1A-001 to P1A-045, P1A-091 to P1A-095, and P1B-001 to P1B-010 represent texts from Northern Ireland (NI), and the other files constitute the corpus material from the Republic of Ireland (ROI).

The identification of sentences in SPICE was based on the notation indicating a speech unit <#> , which corresponds roughly to a sentence (Kallen & Kirk 2012: 19). The spontaneous nature of conversation allows us to consider that sentences include speech units "which are not full or well-formed grammatical sentences" (Kallen & Kirk 2012: 19), as shown in the units initiated by <#> below:[1]

(1) A: <#> <dir> Who's in goals for ye </dir>
B: <#> <rep> Uh Packie Bonner </rep>
A: <#> <rep> Oh* funny </rep> <#> <dir> Ah-no* who's in goals </dir>
B: <#> <rep> David Ryan </rep> (P1A-087 *Line dancing*)

On the other hand, it is much more difficult to identify a sentence in SBC. Since sentences as units are regarded as less essential to the analysis of conversations than other units such as turns and intonation units, the corpus does not have any special notations for indicating a sentence. For the present purpose, we decided to regard a sentence as a sequence of words that can be both grammatically and prosodically separated from the following word. For example, *isn't it* in (2) constitutes an intonation unit independent of its anchor clause (Huddleston & Pullum 2002: 891), but is regarded as forming a sentence with the anchor because it is not preceded by a significantly long pause.[2]

(2) WALT: It's a good reason to be afraid,
Isn't it? (SBC021 *Fear* 486.210–487.630)

The unit of a sentence thus defined delimits the maximum range of a linguistic structure where final tags can possibly occur.

3. Final tags

3.1 Final tags as retrospective types of pragmatic markers

The present study defines final tags as pragmatic markers deployed for interactive purposes at grammatical completion points (see 3.2 for details). For pragmatic markers, there has been no consensus about the definition of and membership in the category (e.g., Schiffrin 1987; Brinton 1996; Fraser 1996; Fischer 2006; Aijmer 2002,

1. SPICE-Ireland also provides speech act notations such as <dir> (directive) and <rep> (representative). Since such notations are not directly pertinent to the present discussion, we will not discuss them in any further detail.

2. A final tag is attached to its anchor. The term "anchor" is adopted from Huddleston & Pullum (2002: 891). Other terms such as "host" or "main/matrix clause" are avoided, because they are oft-used in other phenomena such as affixation/cliticization and subordination.

2013). We regard them as a broader category basically in line with Amador-Moreno et al. (2015: 5), who include question tags and vocatives in the category of pragmatic markers (see also Fraser 1996; Andersen 2001). Since this study focuses on the interactive or discursive use of pragmatic markers, subjective modal adverbs (e.g., *maybe, perhaps*) and adverbs of frequency (e.g., *generally, commonly*) were excluded.

Further excluded from our analysis was the prospective type of pragmatic markers. It must be noted at this juncture that the discussion of final pragmatic markers is in fact inherently problematic. As we argued elsewhere (Izutsu & Izutsu 2014), there are two types of pragmatic markers which occupy final position: those with prospective scope and with retrospective scope (cf. Corrigan 2015: 52–53; Haselow 2016: 95). For example, final *but*s in Australian English (Mulder & Thompson 2008; Mulder et al. 2009) exhibit such two types, as exemplified in (3) and (4). The prospective type of final *but* (Mulder & Thompson's "final hanging *but*") has "an implication left 'hanging'" (2008: 179), inviting an interlocutor's inference about a further continuation of the utterance. The structure obtains as a result of cutting [Y] off the underlying compound sentence "X *but* Y," as shown in (5a). On the other hand, the retrospective type (Mulder & Thompson's "final particle *but*") involves placing the conjunction after Y, combining the two preceding units [X] and [Y], as illustrated in (5b).[3] Notice that in (4) the sentence *Sounded like an alright person but* can be replaced by *But (I) sounded like an alright person.* (See also (42) and (43) for Irish English examples of the retrospective type of *but*.)

(3) "Final hanging *but*"
Karen: W'l now Didier –makes his money by going to Atlantic City **but**- (1.7)
Charles: hhh hhh HAH HAH HAH HAH
(Mulder & Thompson 2008: 186)

(4) "Final particle *but*"
Kylie: You sounded funny @@ (H)
Diana: I know.
Sounded like an alright person **but**.
(Mulder & Thompson 2008: 191)

3. The prospective and retrospective types are respectively referred to as the truncation- and backshift-types in our previous studies (e.g., Izutsu & Izutsu 2014). The present study employs the terms "prospective" and "retrospective" in order to include pragmatic markers whose unmarked positions are not restricted to clause-initial position (e.g., adverbial connectors and comment clauses). However, the term "prospective" is still misleading, because the *but* in [X, *but*] does not only have a prospective orientation, anticipating an implication which would ensue, but also has a retrospective scope over the preceding element [X]. We employ the term "prospective" simply for the sake of disambiguation from the "retrospective" type.

(5) a. PROSPECTIVE TYPE: X, *but* Y. > X, *but.* "final hanging *but*"
b. RETROSPECTIVE TYPE: X, *but* Y. > X, Y *but.* "final particle *but*"

Similar differences are observed in the following examples. The pragmatic markers *so* in (6) and *you know* in (7) belong to the prospective type. In (6), D's third utterance *both are open so* suggests an implication: '(so) you can have whichever you like.' In (7), *you know,* following an incomplete utterance, invites an inference about traffic conditions, which is later stated explicitly as *the traffic isn't bad*:

(6) D: <#> <dir> Now* <,> who wants what to drink </dir>
B: <#> <dir> I would love a glass of white wine </dir>
D: <#> <com> Right </com> <#> <dir> Uhm Sarah </dir>
A: <#> <rep> I'll drink red or white <,> whatever you're </rep>
D: <#> <rep> Well* I-mean* both are open **so** </rep>
A: <#> <dir> I'll have a glass of white then as well please if <{> <[> that's okay </[> </dir>

(SPICE P1A-019 *Clothes*)

(7) C: <#> <rep> No* 1I wouldn't 1mAke% I've never <unclear> 2 sylls </unclear> make it in five </rep> <#> <rep> On a 1SAturday of course% it's it's 1rEAlly quick% <,> because the traffic isn't **you-know@***</rep> <#> <rep> I'd be going in at maybe like* <,> like* half 1twElve% and the 1trAffic isn't <{> <[> 1bAd% </[> </rep>

(SPICE P1A-065 *America trip 2*)

On the other hand, *so* in (8) and *you know* in (9) represent a retrospective type. Hickey (2007: 371) mentions that "[s]*o* is used in sentence-final position to indicate consent or acquiescence," citing the following example: "I'm just putting on the kettle." "I'll have a cup of tea **so**." *So* in final position has a meaning similar to *then* (Christensen 1996: 119) or *in that case* (Dolan 2012: 233). In (8), *so* is used to form a retrospective relation with A's utterance (*I'm not really into clubs*), such as 'what kind of music do you like (then/in that case)?'[4] *You know* in (9) is slightly different; it is not used to refer back to the information mentioned in the previous discourse but to confirm the speakers' shared understanding that they didn't discuss the topic before.[5]

4. Although the *so* in (8) is placed in clause-final position, not sentence or utterance-final one, such an example was included in our study because final position in the present research is identified as a grammatical completion point, not the very end of a sentence or an utterance, as will be discussed in 3.2.

5. The asterisk (*) attached to words or phrases indicates that they are treated as discourse markers (Kallen & Kirk 2012: 42).

(8) A: <#> <rep> Uhm I do </rep> <#> <rep> I go to the pub until about twelve and I might go up to a party afterwards or <{> <[> something but I'm not really into clubs </[> </rep>
B: <#> <icu> <[> Oh right yeah yeah </[> </{> <,> yeah <,> yeah </icu> <#> <dir> And <,> what kind of music do you like **so*** <,> <{> <[> if </[> you don't like the music they play in the clubs </dir>
(SPICE P1A-057 *Studying 2*)

(9) B: <#> <rep> Well* 1thAt's the 2imprEssion I got% </rep> <#> <rep> I'm not 2sUre now%@* </rep> <#> <rep> We 1dIdn't 2discUss it% **you-2knOw%@*** </rep>
A: <#> <rep> Well* it 1sOUnds like more 2mOney% </rep>
(SPICE P1A-001 *Riding*)

This study focuses upon the retrospective type of final pragmatic markers. One reason for the exclusion of the prospective type is that final pragmatic markers of this type are in fact the potential initial element of an implicit continuation. It does not indicate the end of a self-contained unit of conversation *per se* but requires an interlocutor's inference to fully understand the speaker's intended meaning. Since final tags are generally used "at the end of a unit of talk that is already potentially complete" (Haselow 2016: 78), pragmatic markers which do not mark such completion cannot be regarded as relevant examples of final tags.

This criterion of final tags as elements attached to a self-contained unit allows us to exclude general extenders such as *and stuff like that* in (10) from the group of final tags (see also Denis & Tagliamonte 2016 for a similar differentiation).

(10) MICHAEL: (H) I mean he va- basically invented the radio,
<% **and stuff like that,**
(SBC017 *Wonderful Abstract Notions* 719.445–723.210)

Since general extenders are understood to refer to "a category 'in the air'" (Aijmer 2013: 127), the interlocutors are required to "infer additional or alternate members [...] of the category the speaker has in mind" (Overstreet 1999: 47). This requirement of a further inference aligns general extenders with the prospective type of pragmatic markers.

We must admit, however, that the exclusion of the prospective type was not an easy task (see also Denis & Tagliamonte 2016: 91–95) mainly because of the ambiguity between the two types of final pragmatic markers.[6] All such ambiguous examples were submitted to native speakers of the varieties for their judgment.

6. Note that the decision in SPICE-Ireland is not consistent, either. Some final tags of the prospective type, which were excluded in this study, are assigned the tag annotation @ as in (7), though not in (6).

However, there were still cases where even native speakers found it difficult to resolve uncertainties, because in such cases it is only a speaker of an utterance who ultimately knows whether a pragmatic marker is used retrospectively or prospectively. Such examples were treated as "unclear" in our analysis.

3.2 Final tags as pragmatic markers at grammatical completion points

In SPICE, a final tag is characterized as "a structurally-defined notational category which refers to an adjunction at the end of a sentence of spoken discourse" (Kallen & Kirk 2012: 56). In most cases the tag annotation is only given to a pragmatic marker occurring at the very final position (or right-most peripheral position) of a sentence, as indicated by @ in (11):[7]

(11) E: <#> <rep> You can't 2cAll yourself Ph_2D yet% </rep> <dir> **2cAn-you%@** </dir> <#> <dir> Or 2cAn you% </dir>
(SPICE P1A-002 *Dinner chat 1*)

However, this definition excludes obvious examples of final tags. In (12), for example, only *Joelle*, a vocative, is indicated as a tag, but *isn't it*, which is the second to last phrase, does not receive the tag annotation @. Also, since only very final elements are identified as tags in the SPICE corpus, possible candidates for tags like *is she* in (13) are not coded as tags, either.

(12) A: <#> <rep> That's good </rep> <dir> **isn't-it** Joelle@ </dir>
(SPICE P1A-022 *Pizza*)

(13) A: <P1A-067$A> <#> <dir> Oh* she's going 1bAck% **2Is-she%** <{> <[> for 1gOOd% </[> </dir> (SPICE P1A-067 *Apprenticeship*)

Such lack of consistency and adequacy was resolved by manually choosing all the possible final pragmatic markers in the two corpora. When ambiguity arose in interpretation, native speakers of the varieties were consulted.

Since final tags not only appear at the very end of a sentence but also occur in other positions, we regarded "grammatical completion points" (Clancy et al. 1996: 366–367, see also Ford & Thompson 1996: 143–145) as possible positions

7. However, the corpus annotation was not consistent across the texts. Some texts contain more than one tag symbol in a sentence:

B: <#> <rep> Aye* that 's a video there <,> **so-it-is@** <,> **hey@** </rep> <&>laughter </&>
(SPICE P1A-080 *Motorbikes*)

for the occurrences of final tags.[8] A grammatical completion point is defined as "a point at which the speaker could have stopped and have produced a grammatically complete utterance" (Clancy et al. 1996: 366). The notion of grammatical completion point allows an incremental understanding of the completion of a coherent conversation unit, as Ford & Thompson (1996: 143) put it: "[s]yntactically complete utterances can always be extended through further additions, so points of grammatical completion may be incremental." For example, consider (14), which contains a series of grammatical completion points as indicated by slashes:

(14) They just went out/ to Chisera=,/
.. to go out/ to the river./

(Clancy et al. 1996: 367)

Ford & Thompson (1996: 143) explain that an utterance can be viewed as a grammatically complete clause "with an overt or directly recoverable predicate," which is a view basically in line with Kallen & Kirk's (2012: 19) idea of sentences noted in Section 2. This view allows us to include the following kind of example, where a final tag is attached to a non-clausal anchor. The complete utterance meaning is easily retrieved from the prior discourse: '(They went on vacation) one time, yeah.'[9]

(15) SHERI: Oh did they go on vacation?
STEVEN: <X One time,
yeah X>.

(SBC058 *Swingin' Kid* 1402.438–1404.864)

8. Grammatical completion is also called "syntactic completion" in Ford & Thompson (1996: 143–145).

9. Note that when a final pragmatic marker has its scope over only a part of the preceding clause, i.e., a part which does not have an independent illocutionary force as in: *This is why I didn't wanna take the job* ***to begin with*** (SBC053 *I Will Appeal* 807.817–810.586), where *to begin with* is a modifier within the preceding subordinate clause rather than having a scope over the overall sentence. Such examples were excluded from the analysis. However, as Schweinberger points out, the scope of pragmatic markers (notably *like*) is ambiguous without "meta-linguistic information or pause-indicators" (2012: 186). For example, in the sentence *I just went up to say hello* ***like*** (P1A-008 *Rock bands*), the *like* may be interpreted as sentence-final or may have its scope over only *hello* (or *to say hello*). Such pragmatic markers were included with a view to the possibility of their having a scope over a whole clause.

4. Results

4.1 Type and token frequencies

Table 1 summarizes the token frequencies of final tags in the two corpora: SPICE-Ireland contains 3,472 occurrences of final tags, while the Santa Barbara Corpus (SBC) finds only 1,617. That is, the actual occurrences of final tags in SPICE are more than twice as frequent as those in SBC ($\chi^2 = 676.17$, df = 1, p-value < 2.2e-16).[10]

Table 1. Token frequencies in the two corpora

Irish English (SPICE-Ireland)	3,472 occurrences of final tags (128 unclear uses)
American English (SBC)	1,617 occurrences of final tags (72 unclear uses)

Table 2 shows the type frequencies of final tags: SPICE contains 111 types of final tags but only 74 types were found in SBC. It is clear that SPICE shows a greater type variety of final tags than SBC ($\chi^2 = 7.4$, df = 1, p-value = 0.006522).

Table 2. Type frequencies in the two corpora

Irish English (SPICE-Ireland)	111 types of final tags
American English (SBC)	74 types of final tags

A detailed breakdown of final tags in each corpus is given in Appendices A and B, where some of the groupings are adopted from Allerton (2009: 309-312). Furthermore, the present study classified final tags into three main types: auxiliary-centered tags (AUX-tags), morphologically fixed tags (FIX-tags), and vocative tags (VOC-tags). AUX-tags (e.g., *is it, don't you, has he*) consist of an auxiliary verb and a pronominal subject. Their forms are mostly variable, depending on the subject and (auxiliary) verb of the anchor. FIX-tags (e.g., *you know, I think, right, yeah*) do not exhibit such morphological variability; their forms are fixed irrespective of the subject and verb forms of the anchor clauses. AUX-tags are clausal as they are regarded as elliptical clauses, and FIX-tags are of two types: clausal and lexical tags.

AUX-tags and FIX-tags roughly correspond to the familiar dichotomies such as "canonical" and "invariant" tags (Andersen 2001: 103–104), "concordant" and "non-concordant" tags (Allerton 2009: 310), "variable" and "non-variable" tags (Kallen & Kirk 2012: 55–57), respectively. The invariant or non-concordant tags imply "non-adherence to the rules of subject-verb concord" (Andersen 2001: 105)

10. We used R for the statistical analysis (R Development Core Team 2016).

between an anchor and the tag. The term "invariant" has been introduced to group the non-concordant use of *is it/isn't it* with final tags such as *you know* and *right* despite their different formal make-ups. Note, however, that the "non-adherence to the rules of subject-verb concord" is not in fact clear-cut. There were BE-type tags which display partial adherence to the rules, as in (16) and (17), where the tags agree with their anchors in tense but not in subject and verb type, and as in (18), which shows concordance in tense and subject, but not in verb type. Thus, this study does not employ terms such as "invariant" or "non-concordant" for the classification of final tags but treats the non-canonical use of BE-type tags as AUX-tags together with canonical tags because it necessarily contains a form of the auxiliary *be* as well as the pronominal subject (see also Axelsson 2011: 4, who similarly includes *innit* into a group of question tags because it originates from *isn't it* or *ain't it*).[11]

(16) D: <#> <rep> Ha you've to go earlier and spend quality time with mother </rep> <dir> **is-it@** </dir> <&> laughter </&>
(SPICE P1A-042 *Photos*)

(17) A: <#> <rep> I met him at the <,> met him at the match </rep> <dir> **was-it@** </dir>
(SPICE P1A-069 *Christmas trees*)

(18) D: <#> <rep> Something happened to her in Twohey's </rep> <dir> **wasn't-it@** </dir>
(SPICE P1A-053 *Student grants 1*)

Furthermore, the distinction between "variable" and "non-variable" tags (Kallen & Kirk 2012) was not adopted either in order to avoid terminological confusion. What Kallen & Kirk (2012: 55–56) regard as "variable" tags include "comment clauses" (e.g., *you know* and *I think*), which many other studies treat as "invariant" tags (e.g., Columbus 2009a, b; Lucek 2011; Barron et al. 2015: 499).[12]

11. The following example also illustrates a difficulty in using grammatical concord as a criterion for differentiating the types of question tags.

(i) NICK: I'm wrapping up tight,
aren't I ~Bill. (SBC057 *Throw Me* 205.391–206.927)

The incongruence between the verb forms of the anchor and the tag is due to the avoidance of the negative contraction *amn't* (Quirk et al. 1985: 129), not resulting from the "invariabilisation (grammaticalisation) process" (Andersen 2001: 100), in which tags such as *is it* and *innit* come to be used in wider grammatical environments.

12. Kallen & Kirk regard comment clauses as "variable" tags, because they vary "in relation to the preceding clause or with speaker and interlocutor status" (2012: 56).

Figure 1 represents the proportion of final tags by major category. While the total number of final tags in Irish English is about 2.1 times greater than that in American English, the four types of AUX-tags (BE-, DO-, HAVE-, and MODAL-tags) and lexical FIX-tags (e.g,. *right, okay*) are even far more frequent in Irish English, which, compared to American English, employs a 3.3 times greater number of the AUX-tags and a 2.7 times larger number of lexical FIX-tags. Clausal FIX-tags (e.g., *you know, you see*) do not mark such a great difference, but still those tags are 1.6 times more frequent in Irish English. Despite the overall infrequency of final tags, only vocatives are as common in American English as in Irish English (383 in IrE and 365 in AmE); this difference is statistically insignificant ($\chi^2 = 0.43316$, df = 1, p-value = 0.5104).

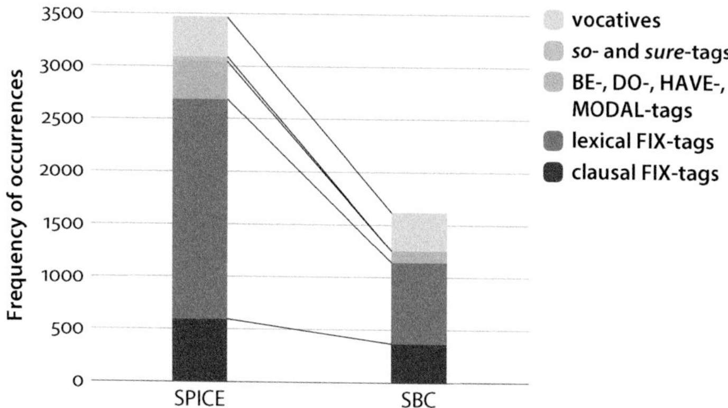

Figure 1. Proportion of final tags by major category, based on total frequency

Figures 2 and 3 summarize the top five final tags in each corpus, ranked by frequency. The yellow column represents the total occurrences of final tags in each corpus. In SPICE, *like* appears most frequently, followed by *you know*, vocative tags, and *yeah*, and final tags with BE (*is it? isn't it?*) rank fifth. On the other hand, in SBC, vocative tags occupy the first place in the ranking, followed by *you know*, *right*, *yeah*, and the connective *though* comes to the fifth place. Vocative tags, *you know* and *yeah* rank in the top five in both corpora.

Murphy (2015: 74), investigating *the Corpus of Age and Gender – Irish English (CAG-IE)*, examines the frequency of Irish pragmatic markers, irrespective of the positions where they occur, and finds that *like* is the most frequent pragmatic marker (7,972 tokens), followed by *sure* (3,045), *now* (3,028), *anyway* (2,705), *well* (2,017), etc. A comparison with our result suggests that *like* favors final position in Irish English, as will be detailed below, but the position is less suitable for the

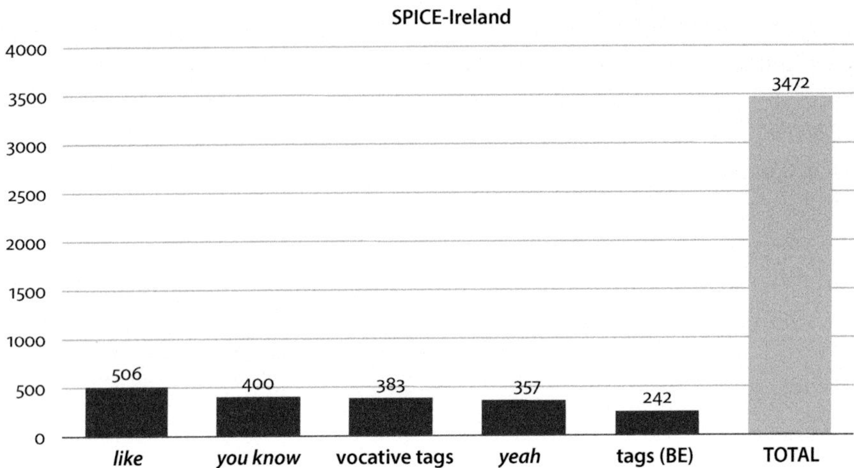

Figure 2. The top five final tags in SPICE

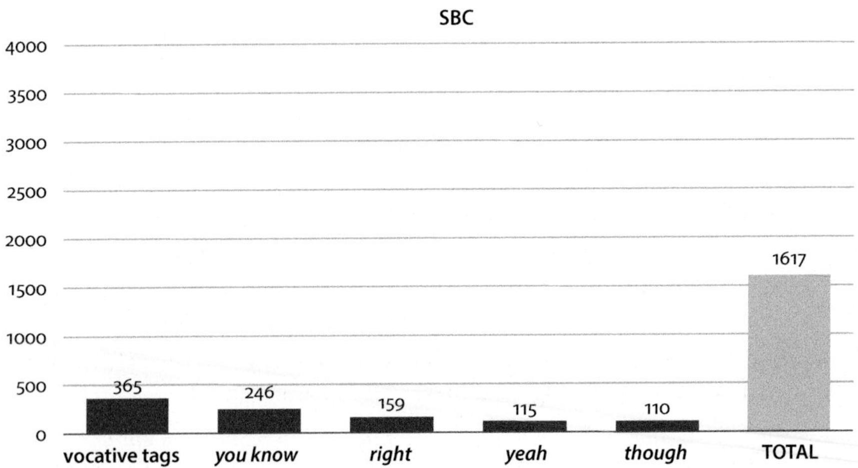

Figure 3. The top five final tags in SBC

occurrences of *sure* and *well*, the frequencies of which are low or non-existent (11 tokens for *sure* and none for *well*) in our study.

4.2 Some notable differences between the two varieties

4.2.1 *AUX-tags*

SPICE finds 6 types and 403 tokens of AUX-tags, while SBC contains only 4 types and 109 tokens. Irish English has two unique forms of AUX-tags: *so*-tags and *sure*-tags, as given in (19)–(20) and (21)–(22), respectively. These two types of tags are often seen as prominent features of Irish English (Hickey 2007: 277; Kallen 2013: 268; Barron 2015: 203–204; Barron & Pandarova 2016: 123).

(19) D: <#> <rep> <[1> Not at all </rep> <#> <rep> He's not that age </[1> </{1> </rep>
F: <#> <rep> <[2> That's 2rIght% </rep> <#> <rep> He did a lot of subbing 2thEre **so-he-did%@** </[2> </{2> </rep>
(SPICE P1A-002 *Dinner chat 1*)

(20) B: <#> <rep> Ah* 1shE went back to 1bEd for a while there%@* </rep>
C: <#> <rep> Jesus* I've 1nO messages at 1All now **so-I-haven't%@** </rep>
(SPICE P1A-016 *Catching up*)

(21) C: <#> <dir> You're not interested in anything but music **sure-you're-not@** </dir>
(SPICE P1A-067 *Apprenticeship*)

(22) A: <#> <com> Mm I'll think about it </com>
B: <#> <rep> You still haven't decided yet </rep> <dir> **sure-you-haven't@** </dir>
(SPICE P1A-093 *Motorbikes*)

There were 41 occurrences of *so*-tags: 18 tokens in the data set of Northern Ireland (NI) and 23 tokens in that of the Republic of Ireland (ROI). This regional distribution slightly contrasts with the result of the analysis by Walshe (2016: 335–336), where *so*-tags are more frequently used in NI (19 tokens) than in ROI (6 tokens). The number of *sure*-tags found in our data is very small: 3 tokens in NI and 1 token in ROI. This is different from Barron's study of an IrE retail corpus (2015: 222), where she finds a relatively high number of *sure*-tags in the smaller database.

Irish English indicates a greater frequency of the other AUX-tags, too. SPICE contains 358 tokens (BE-type 242, DO-type 60, HAVE-type 17, MODAL-type 39), while SBC finds only 109 tokens (BE-type 48, DO-type 45, HAVE-type 5, MODAL-type 11). In particular, the BE-type tags are fare more numerous in Irish English. This is partly due to the comparatively high frequency of the non-canonical use of BE-type tags (e.g., *is it*, *isn't it*) ("non-paradigmatic use" in Andersen 2001). There were 20 examples of such uses in SPICE as in (23) and (24) (see also (16)–(18) above), but only one example found in SBC as in (25).[13] No examples of *innit*,

13. This result is incongruent with that of Lucek (2011), where he found 32 invariant examples of *is it* and 42 examples of *isn't it* despite the fact that his data set (P1A-001 to P1A-90 in SPICE-Ireland) is smaller than ours (P1A-001 to P1A-100 and P1B-001 to P1B-020). Although he does not give a precise definition of invariant tags, he seems to have included examples of *is it?/isn't it?*, which cannot be regarded as clear cases of non-concordance. His invariant tags probably

which is reported to be found in British English (Andersen 2001: Chapter 4; Tottie & Hoffman 2006; Axelsson 2011), were found in either corpus.

(23) A: <#> <dir> Why why would you close it **is-it@** </dir>
(SPICE P1A-055 *Hospitals*)

(24) D: <#> <rep> They're going to Rome <,> </rep> <dir> **isn't-it@**
(SPICE P1A-088 *Therapy inaugural*)

(25) EVELYN: a- a- Wilcox made his money.
Wasn't it? (SBC023 *Howard's End* 561.335–564.230)

A greater variety of AUX-tags in Irish English is also shown by the use of declarative tags (Biber et al. 1999: 139–140).[14] There were 11 examples of declarative tags in Irish English as in (26), but American English again finds only one example as in (27):

(26) A: <#> <rep> She's only in her late fifties **she-is@** </rep>
(SPICE P1A-040 *Family banter*)

(27) LANCE: … Now are we still required to w- –
write,
like,
the Empires that coming in through the gates VFR?
.. Don't they?
.. **We are?** (SBC022 *Runway Heading* 247.060–252.451)

Also, there were four examples of tags with non-enclitic negation in SPICE as in (28), and one example in SBC as in (29). Quirk et al. (1985: 810) associate this usage with "informal English in Northern BrE dialects" as well as "formal English" (also see Axelsson 2011: 99). The Irish English occurrences of these tags may be subject to an influence from Northern BrE dialects, and the example of American English may pertain to the genre specific formality of the discourse, namely, a lecture on the history and theology of Martin Luther as in (29):

(28) B: <#> <rep> I'm sure you're pleased </rep> <dir> **are-you-not@** </dir>
(SPICE P1A-019 *Clothes*)

(29) FOSTER: there are passages in the Scriptures,
.. **are there not?**
(SBC 025 *The Egg which Luther Hatched* 364.873–367.823)

---

subsume many examples which were not counted as non-canonical uses in this study, e.g., question tags with verbless anchors (e.g., *A fallacy,* ***is it***, P1A-052).

14. Declarative tags are also referred to as "reinforcement tags" (Hewings & Hewings 2005: 98).

One feature only found in American English is a final tag characterized by "an emphatic change of subject" (Siertsema 1980: 299, also see Axelsson 2011: 32), as in (30) and (31). SBC finds four examples, but no examples were found in SPICE.[15]

(30) NATHAN: ... I don't even know how you start this one,
do you? (SBC009 *Zero Equals Zero* 1484.5–1487.11)

(31) MARCIA: ... I wouldn't see why we couldn't send her home tonight,
would you? (SBC018 *Vet Morning* 225.220–227.165)

4.2.2 *Clausal FIX-tags*

For the final-tag use of clausal pragmatic markers ("comment clauses" in Brinton 2008 and Quirk et al. 1985 or "parentheticals" in Huddleston & Pullum 2002), SPICE contains 37 types and 595 tokens, and SBC has 29 types and 370 tokens. One of the most remarkable differences is the use of clausal pragmatic markers with *say* in final position: SPICE has 7 types and 28 tokens, but SBC finds no occurrences. The frequency in SPICE may be partly due to the preference in Southern Ireland. Of 28 tokens of clausal pragmatic markers with *say* in final position, 22 tokens were observed in ROI and 6 tokens in NI. Kallen (2005: 61) reports that *I'd say* in general is "a highly salient discourse marker in southern Irish English." His observation is extended to our analysis of its final-tag use. *I'd say* is more preferred in Southern Ireland than in Northern Ireland (ROI: 17 tokens and NI: 3 tokens). It is also worth noting that *say* is sometimes preceded by other modal auxiliaries like *have to* and *must*:

(32) B: <#> <rep> Mmm <,> I like the oul brand names now* <{> <[> **I'd have to** </[> **say myself** I-do@ </rep> (SPICE P1A-090 *Designer clothes*)

(33) A: <#> <exp> I-mean* I do I really like it now **I must say** </exp>
(SPICE P1A-006 *Girls' chat 1*)

In both varieties, *you know* represents the most frequent clausal FIX-tags. In disregard of positional variation, Jucker & Smith (1998: 176) report that *you know* is the most favored of all the clausal pragmatic markers in their data of American conversations, and Kallen (2005: 63–65) observes a preferential use of *you know* relative to *I mean* in Irish English. For the use of *you know* in final position, our analysis reveals that Irish English uses final *you know* to a greater extent than American English (400 tokens in SPICE and 246 in SBC). This result, in tandem

15. This type of tag is generally excluded from an analysis of question tags (Siertsema 1980: 299; Axelsson 2011: 32) for lack of co-reference with the subject of the anchor. However, we included it in the category of AUX-tags because it consists of an auxiliary verb and a pronominal subject like other AUX-tags.

with Lucek's (2011) observation of the predominance of final *you know* in Irish English over the other varieties investigated, further indicates a strong preference of final *you know* in Irish English.

A similar difference is observed with other clausal FIX-tags. For example, there were 48 occurrences of *you see* in SPICE but only 11 in SBC, and 44 occurrences of *I think* in SPICE but 28 in SBC. American English speakers seem to prefer *I guess*, which occurs more frequently in SBC than in SPICE (18 tokens in SBC and 1 in SPICE). This result conforms to a general view of *I guess* as "almost exclusively American" (Algeo 2006: 139, see also Biber et al. 1999: 983).

4.2.3 *Lexical FIX-tags*

A prevalence of final tags in Irish English was also documented in the category of lexical pragmatic markers. Lucek (2011) observes that utterance-final *like*, *yeah*, and *yes* show a greater frequency in Irish English than in the other five varieties of English (British, New Zealand, Singapore, Indian, and Hong Kong English). Our study reveals that their marked prevalence in Irish English was also attested in comparison with the lower frequencies in American English. In addition to these pragmatic markers, the following sections discuss several others that merit special attention from comparative perspectives (*now*, *but*, *so*, *right*, adverbs of factuality and totality, and non-word phonological sequences).

4.2.3.1 *Like.* Final *like* is one of the most remarkable features in Irish English. It appeared as the most frequent pragmatic marker in SPICE (506 tokens), yet there were no examples in SBC.[16] *Like* is not only attached to declarative sentences as in (34) but to exclamatory and interrogative sentences as in (35) and (36):

(34) C: <#> <rep> I <{> <[> went </[> up to him last night and he was sitting there **like@** </rep> <#> <rep> And I just went up to say hello **like@** </rep> <#> <rep> It was grand </rep> <#> <dir> How're you getting on </dir>

16. Schweinberger (2014: 221) found one example of final *like* in SBC as in (i), suggesting that it "focuses or emphasizes a new piece of information."

(i) RICKIE: And he' [2s like2] balding [3**like**3],
REBECCA: [2Yeah2].
[3You3] can come in the courtroom.
(SBC008 *Tell the Jury That* 933.90–936.85)

As we listened to the recording, we did not interpret this as an example of final *like*. It is more natural to consider that Rickie's utterance was cut off by the following utterance by Rebecca: *You can come in the courtroom.* Rickie's final word *like* was overlapped by the first word *you*, as indicated by the square brackets indexed with number 3. Rickie's intention to continue her speech is also detectable from the continuing intonation of her utterance, which is signaled by a comma.

<#> <dir> How're you getting on </dir> <#> <rep> It's always the usual craic **like@** </rep> (SPICE P1A-068 *Rock bands*)

(35) A: <#> <rep> <[> What the stupid **like@** </rep> <#><icu> I know </[> </{> </icu> (SPICE P1A-005 *Masons*)

(36) D: <#> <dir> Is this supposed to be true **like@** </dir>
B: <#> <rep> I don't know </rep> (SPICE P1A-051 *Clothing dad*)

Unlike initial or medial *like*, the final-tag *like* has a retrospective orientation with its scope, "which does not encompass elements to its right, but to its left" (Schweinberger 2015: 121; also see Kallen 2006: 12). Various functions have been pointed out for this final *like*: "a hedge" (Amador-Moreno 2010: 121) or "mitigation" (Corrigan 2015: 51), indicating "the end of old information" (Corrigan 2015: 51) or marking "post opinion/fact" (Columbus 2009b), and others. The present result corroborates the claim of previous research that clause-final *like* is much more frequent in Irish English than in other varieties of English, where fewer, if any, examples of final *like* were attested: British English (Lucek 2011; Kallen 2013; Schweinberger 2015), Singapore, Indian, New Zealand, and Hong Kong English (Lucek 2011), Philippine, Indian and East African English (Siemund et al. 2009). A comparison with American English reveals the starkest contrast. Tagliamonte (2012: 172) notes that "the clause-final use of *like* is not among the attested uses of discourse *like* in the current literature on North American varieties of English" (see also Schweinberger 2015: 127, n.6 for a similar account). Indeed, no examples of the final-tag *like* were found in SBC. The corpus only contains the prospective type of final *like*, which could have had its scope over elements on its right, as shown in (37):

(37) DORIS: ... (H) Take .. one of the capsules,
and two of the white.
... Las- .. Lazex?
Or [something **like**] --
SAM: [Lazix=]? (SBC011 *This Retirement Bit* 1045.66–1054.48)

Although the pragmatic marker *like* in general is often associated with younger speakers in varieties of English (e.g., Andersen 2001: Chapter 5; Tagliamonte 2005: 3.1; D'Arcy 2007: 388), the final-tag use of *like* in Irish English is widespread across "speakers of all ages" (Kallen 2013: 191, see also Corrigan 2010: 100). It represents a "robust" feature of Irish English (Kallen 2006: 14), commonly used "in a wide variety of informal and relatively more formal contexts" (Kallen 2013: 191).[17]

17. In his statistical analysis of the ICE-Ireland data, however, Schweinberger (2012) finds out that clause-final *like* is age and gender specific: it is more readily used by male speakers older than 50 years of age.

4.2.3.2 *Now.* Another distinctive feature of Irish English is the final-tag use of the pragmatic marker *now*. Final *now* occurred 167 times in SPICE, as opposed to 24 times in SBC. American English only exhibits the following kinds of the non-temporal use of final *now* (Schiffrin 1987: Chapter 7):

(38) CYNTHIA: <VOX Coyote,
... come on **now**,
(SBC054 *'That's Good', Said Tiger* 239.804–241.550)

(39) JO: I knew=.
... I [said to ~Wess],
WESS: [What'd I do with my] hearing aid
JO:
(SBC059 *You Baked* 15.963–19.366)

Now in final position is employed as "a hearer-oriented intensifier" (Aijmer 2002: 93) as in (38) or used for a "topic change," for example, indicating a change "from the main topic [...] to an aside" (Aijmer 2002: 87) as in (39).

However, Irish English contains clause-final uses which are less likely available in other varieties of English (Clancy & Vaugham 2012: 239, 242). For example, the final *now* in (40) is used as a hedge (Hickey 2015: 24; Migge 2015: 398), which mitigates "the illocutionary force of an utterance, allowing the speaker to weaken his/her commitment to its propositional content" (Clancy & Vaugham 2012: 237). In (41), *now* co-occurs with a mental state predicate and functions as "a marker of affect intensification" (Migge 2015: 403):

(40) C: <#> <rep> I don't know **now@*** </rep> (SPICE P1A-032 *Art –Football*)

(41) B: <#> <rep> It was it was I enjoyed it **now@*** </rep>
(SPICE P1A-033 *Singers*)

4.2.3.3 *But.* In Irish English, some connectives are placed in final position and retrospectively used to conclude the preceding clause. One such case is the connective *but*, as in:

(42) B: <#> <dir> Did they </dir> <&> laughter </&> <#> <rep> Och* that's easy to do **but** </rep> <dir> isn't-it@ </dir>
(SPICE P1A-042 *Photos*)

(43) D: <#> <rep> Something happened to her in Twohey's </rep> <dir> wasn't-it@ </dir> <#> <rep> And she just moved suddenly </rep>
A: <#> <rep> It's <,> all that it is Janie it's muscular spasm **but** </rep><#> <rep> It's literally from being bent over and constant writing </rep>
(SPICE P1A-053 *Student grants 1*, also in Kallen 2013: 184)

The *buts* in these examples indicate some kind of opposition between the two clauses preceding the connective or between the preceding clause and contextually given information (see also 5.3 below). Kallen (2013: 183) states that the final use of *but* in Irish English is not part of "elliptical sentences." That is, it is not the prospective (final hanging) type of *but*, but corresponds to the retrospective (final particle) type of *but* in Australian English (Mulder & Thompson 2008; Mulder et al. 2009; Izutsu & Izutsu 2014) (see 3.1 above). Although this final usage has often been seen as a well-noted feature of Irish English (Hickey 2007: 257, 375; Kallen 2013: 182–185), the number of its occurrences was comparatively small in the present result, i.e., nine tokens in SPICE.[18] No examples of the final tag *but* were attested in our American English data, as likewise observed by Mulder & Thompson (2008: 192) and Mulder et al. (2009: 350).

4.2.3.4 *So.* Unlike Australian English, Irish English also has the final-tag use of *so*, as in (44) and (45). As noted in 3.1, this final *so* has a retrospective scope, meaning closer to 'then' or 'in that case' (Christensen 1996: 119; Dolan 2012: 233).

(44) B: <#> <rep> I got up in the middle of the night and everything to look out to see where the alarm was </rep> <#> <rep> I was <,> you-know* I'd laid there for about quarter of an hour like* listening to this alarm doing de doing <,> and there was a blue light flashing in the window and everything </rep> <#> <rep> So I said there was <{> <[> probably a fire </[> </rep>
C: <#> <dir> <[> It was you </[> </{> opened the curtains **so@*** </dir>
B: <#> <rep> Yeah </rep>
C: <#> <rep> You didn't close them properly after you and this morning at seven o'clock <,> there was a light shining in my face <,> </rep>
(SPICE P1A-050 *Fireworks*)

(45) B: <#> <icu> <[> Oh right yeah yeah </[> </{> <,> yeah <,> yeah </icu> <#> <dir> And <,> what kind of music do you like **so*** <,> <{> <[> if </[> you don't like the music they play in the clubs </dir> (= 8)

Although the final-tag use of *so* is often described as a notable feature of Irish English (Hickey 2007: 371, 375, 2015: 22; Amador-Moreno 2010: 123), the occurrences in our data were not so frequent (eight tokens) as generally assumed.

18. For the analysis of final *but*, we referred to the study of Kirk & Kallen (2010: 2.8). However, the finding of our analysis is slightly different from theirs because of differences in data size and tag identification. Kirk and Kallen dealt with the whole spoken component of ICE-Ireland, whereas we only used three of the spoken categories as noted in Section 2. And we also included final tags occupying positions other than the very end of sentences as in (42). As Kirk and Kallen argue, the final tag *but* is another feature shared by Ireland and the northern part of Great Britain (e.g., Scotland).

Binchy (2005) demonstrates that this usage of *so* is common in price statements by Irish service providers:

(46) C: Pine Needle please.
S: That's only one eighty eight **so** please. (Binchy 2005: 330)

Often followed by *please*, it functions as a politeness marker "to soften the server's demand for money" (Binchy 2005: 319). It seems that the *so* expresses the service provider's reasoning process involving the calculation of the price charged in a transaction: 'You want to buy pine needle, so it will be one eighty eight.' Adding a marker of causal inference as a buffer makes the service provider's utterance less direct than the point-blank statement of price: *That's one eighty eight.*[19]

4.2.3.5 *Adverbs of factuality.* Adverbs of factuality such as *really* and *actually* were also more common in Irish English. While SBC has 5 types and 36 occurrences, SPICE finds 7 types and 172 occurrences, among which *really* and *actually* were predominant. Although these adverbs have "discourse-marking" and "non-discourse marking" (genuine adverbial) uses (Kallen 2015: 141), we did not make such a strict distinction between the two functions, assuming that most final examples were used for discourse-marking functions.

Irrespective of positional variation, Biber et al. (1999: 869) observe a slightly stronger preference of *actually* in American English than in British English, while Aijmer (2013: 104) reports the opposite tendency: *actually* occurred 166 times per 100,000 words in ICE-GB, as compared with only 49 times in SBC. Kallen (2015) compares the spoken material from ICE-Ireland with the relevant ICE databases of four varieties of English (Great Britain, New Zealand, Canada and Jamaica), and observes that Irish English is relatively high in the total number of occurrences of *actually*, though lower than New Zealand and British English.

The present result points to a much greater use of final *actually* in Irish English (81 tokens) than in American English (9 tokens). Many of the examples were used as a kind of "softener" (Aijmer 2013: 114) or to "hedge statements" (Carter & McCarthy 2006: 29). The examples of *actually* in (47) are used to soften the assertive force of each sentence, which could be implicated without the use of the final tag (cf. Aijmer 2013: 115):

(47) A: […] <#> <rep> And then we went over to to <unclear> 2 sylls </unclear> and uh it was fine **actually@*** </rep> <#> <rep> I was half sort-of* expecting it was going to be like uh a murder picture <,> but it was grand </rep> <#> <rep> It was really fine </rep> <#> <rep> And it's so nice cos

19. We are indebted to Fergus O'Dwyer (personal communication) for this observation.

everything's there <{2> <[2> and then </[2> if you have to get a few bits and pieces in Sainsbury's you're grand <,> you can park the car </rep> <#> <rep> It was great **actually@*** </rep> <#> <rep> It was really good </rep>
(SPICE P1A-007 *Girls' chat* 2)

Kallen (2015: 136) remarks that the use of *actually* "does not bear any obvious connection to the Irish language" and "has not generally been seen as a distinctive feature of Irish English," but his study of *actually* in ICE-Ireland as compared with other ICE-corpora (Great Britain, New Zealand, Canada and Jamaica) reveals that its use in conversations manifests itself as "a robust feature of Irish English discourse" (2015: 152). The present data, restricted to *actually* in final position, provides further support for his result in light of comparison with American English.

Really in final position is also a pragmatic marker more strongly associated with Irish English. We found 78 instances of final *really* in SPICE, but only 20 instances in SBC. The final use is often described as a "stance adverbial" (Biber et al. 1999: 857) or an epistemic marker of "truth attesting" (Paradis 2003: 3.1). Paradis (2003: 211) suggests that final *really* has "pragmatic flexibility [...] both in the direction of intensifying and attenuating the level of certainty expressed over and above the statements." *Really* in (48) is used to reinforce the speaker's alignment with the addressee's opinion, whereas the pragmatic marker in (49) has "a hedging function" (Paradis 2003: 209) or a "softening or cajoling effect" (Stenström 1986: 157) in the "context where the opposite is presupposed" (Paradis 2003: 198). The two functions were observed in both varieties of English.

(48) E: <#> <rep> <[> Yeah </[> </{> <,> and that's about all </rep>
A: <#> <rep> I-think* that's about it **really** </rep>
(SPICE P1A-082 *Kissogram*)

(49) A: <#> <rep> No </rep> <#> <exp> At the end of the day I'm not very interested in examinations to be honest with you </exp> <#> [...] <#> <rep> The exam I-mean* <,> I don't think the exams are are important **really** <,> </rep> <#><rep> Uhm <,> they are well* they are important from your point of view I-suppose* they are </rep> <#>
(SPICE P1B-013 *Industrial policy 1*)

4.2.3.6 *Adverbs of totality.* Although the number of occurrences is not high, the final use of adverbs of totality as in (50) should also be worth noting, because they were only found in Irish English.

(50) D: <#> <icu> 8RIght% </icu> <#> <rep> That's 1Only like* ten minute 2wAlk then% from <,> 1Ormeau <{> <[> Road 2tOO% </[> </rep>

C: <#> <rep> <[> From the </[> </{> 2Ormeau Road% **2tOtally%** 2yEAh%@* (SPICE P1A-091 *Haircut –Mortgage*)

Eight tokens (2 tokens for *absolutely*, 4 for *totally*, 2 for *completely*) were identified in SPICE, but none in SBC.

4.2.3.7 *'Yes' or 'no' words.* The final-tag use of words meaning 'yes' or 'no' also reveals some remarkable features of Irish English. Lucek (2011: 101) reports that yeah is the third most frequent "invariant" tag in the face-to-face-conversation category of SPICE. The present analysis yields the same result as seen in Figure 2; yeah comes to the third place among FIX-tags (i.e., with the exclusion of vocatives). The Irish English data finds 357 tokens of final yeah, which contrast with 115 tokens in the American English data. Interestingly, Irish English not only favors the final tag yeah, but also prefers to use yes and no in final position as in (51) and (52). There were 32 occurrences of the final-tag use of yes in SPICE, while SBC has only 8 occurrences. The final-tag use of no occurred 65 times in SPICE, but only 5 times in SBC.

(51) C: <#> <rep> Flashback <,> with uh Dennis Hopper </rep>
B: <#> <rep> That was good **yeah@*** </rep>
C: <#> <rep> Ah* that's very good </rep>
A: <#> <rep> It's very good <,> </rep>
B: <#> <dir> Is it a new one **no@** </dir> <&> banging noise </&>
(SPICE P1A-052 *Buttermilk*)

(52) B: <#> <rep> <[1> Oh* that'd be great **yes@*** <,> </rep> <#>
(SPICE P1A-013S *Student chat 2*)

In addition to such marked frequencies, what is of more interest with Irish English is that it employs other variants associated with 'yes'/'no' words, as noted by Kallen & Kirk (2012: 107), such as *aye* (a dialectal variant of *yes*) as in (53) and the repetitive use of *yeah* and *no* as in (54) and (55):

(53) C: <#> <rep> <[4> He doesn't say anything </[4> </{4> **aye@*** </rep>
(SPICE P1A-032 *Art-Football*)

(54) D: <#> <rep> That's it **yeah-yeah@*** </rep> <#>
(SPICE P1A-090 *Designer Clothes*)

(55) C: <#> [...] <#> <rep> He 1wOUldn't deal with 1thAt% <,> **no-no@*** </rep>
(SPICE P1A-067 *Apprenticeship*)

A summation over all kinds of 'yes'/'no' words in final position yields a far greater frequency in SPICE (512 tokens) than in SBC (128 tokens).

4.2.3.8 *Non-word phonological sequences.* One of the characteristic features of American English is a predilection for "non-word phonological sequences" (Allerton 2009: 310). SBC finds 5 types and 69 tokens (*huh, hunh, unhunh, hm, oh*), while SPICE contains 6 types and 19 tokens (*ah, eh, oh, huh, uh-huh, hey*). Although type variation is slightly smaller in American English, the greater token frequency in SBC is specifically linked to a preferential use of *hunh* (59 tokens). This form was not found in SPICE, and its variant (*huh*) appears only once. *Hunh* occurs in "appeal" or question intonation as indicated by a question mark in (56) or in final-falling intonation as marked by a period in (57) (Du Bois et al. 1993: 54–55):

(56) DAN: [2You gotta do some2]thing over there,
hunh?
JENNIFER: … <WH Yeah WH>. (SBC024 *Risk* 496.790–499.645)

(57) SHERI: [Was it hard s]itting in the back of their truck,
They gotta pretty small truck,
hunh.
STEVEN: … Well,
.. Shred said,
… <VOX I wanna sit back the=re VOX>.
(SBC058 *Swingin' Kid* 1261.900–1268.131)

Our result mostly conforms to a prevalent view of *hu(n)h* as a marker especially common in the United States (Norrick 1995: 689; Biber et al. 1999: 1089).

4.2.3.9 *Right. Right* often tends to be strongly associated with Irish English, as is known for its distinctive pronunciation spelled *roysh.*[20] As Amador-Moreno (2015: 372) notes, it is "elaborate linguistically and would require deep familiarity with IrE" for its thorough understanding. In her analysis of a fictional corpus, Amador-Moreno explains that *right* is a frequently occurring word, which occupies the 13th place out of all the words in the corpus (2015: 375), and observes that it tends to be placed in clause-final position, often "in collocation with *like* to the left" (e.g., "There's *like*, total silence, *roysh*, and …") (2015: 377).

However, a comparison with American English shows that the final-tag use of *right* is not a unique feature of Irish English. In fact, final *right* was more common in American English (159 tokens in SBC as opposed to 101 tokens in

20. Allerton (2009: 310–312) considers that *right* can belong to two different lexical groups: "words meaning '(be) true/truth'" and "words meaning '(be) in order.'" However, since *right* is often "ambiguous between the two interpretations" (Allerton 2009: 313), we classified it into the latter lexical group, considering its affinity with *alright* (see Appendices A and B).

SPICE), occupying the third place in the frequency ranking as in Figure 3 above. Considering the smaller total number of final tags found in SBC, we can see a great reliance on *right*, along with *hu(n)h*, in American English, as shown in (58) (see also Allerton 2009: 312 for the popularity of the final tag *right* in American English).

(58) SHARON: (H) First they're like,
.. first I only had fifteen kids.
right?
.. And the,
(H) legally you have to have eighteen.
.. HISD rules has it that you have to have at least eighteen.
right? (SBC004 *Raging Bureaucracy* 502.19–510.99)

5. A constructional account of final-tagged structures

Although some distinctive features have been attested in each variety of English, there is an overall tendency for Irish English to more strongly favor final pragmatic markers than American English. This fact does not merely represent varietal differences, but can also be viewed as manifesting different degrees of constructional entrenchment of final-tagged structures.

5.1 Grammatical constructionalization (Grammatical Cxzn)

The model of constructionalization represents one of the recent constructional approaches to language changes (*inter alia* Noël 2007; Fried 2008; Hilpert 2013; Traugott & Trousdale 2013). It is grounded on the basic assumption that a construction is "a conventional symbolic unit" (Langacker 1987: 58) of form and meaning (Gisborne & Patten 2011: 93; Traugott & Trousdale 2013: 11). Traugott & Trousdale (2013: 22) define constructionalization (Cxzn) as "the creation of a form_{new}-$\text{meaning}_{\text{new}}$ pairing," i.e., "the development of a new sign," which may follow or precede a sequence of relevant constructional changes, i.e., changes in meaning or form, but not both of them (Traugott & Trousdale 2013: 26–29).

In accordance with various disciplines of Construction Grammar (Fillmore et al. 1988: 501; Goldberg 1995: 4; Croft 2001: 17), constructions are considered to range in size from clausal structures down to phrasal and morphological ones. This broad view of construction entails the classification of constructionalization into two types: grammatical and lexical constructionalization, i.e., "changes that result in constructions that are primarily procedural in function […] and primarily contentful" (Traugott & Trousdale 2013: 94), respectively. Final-tagged structures discussed in this study encode procedural meaning, signaling how and to what degree of illocutionary strength a speaker intends to conclude the verbalization of information.

Traugott & Trousdale (2013: 1.4.2 and 3.3) argue that grammatical constructionalization is characterized by three factors: increase in schematicity, increase in productivity, and decrease in compositionality. The schematicity of a construction is viewed as gradable and hence hierarchical, ranging from a schema at the highest level down to subshemas and then to micro-constructions (construction-types), which are instantiated by constructs (actual tokens). Schematicity increases when a schema becomes abstract and open enough to sanction more (sub)types and tokens.

Traugott & Trousdale (2013: 117–118, also see Traugott 2014: 91–93, Traugott 2015: 65–73) illustrate the rise of the auxiliary *be going to* from the purposive expression as an example of increasing schematization.[21] Its examples as a future tense marker, a marker of "relative, prospective future" (Traugott 2015: 68), were available in the early seventeenth century but mostly with animate, hence volitional, subjects. They consider that *be going to* was constructionalized as a tense auxiliary in the early eighteenth century, when it occurred in syntactic contexts which were unlikely to yield the interpretation of "motion-with-a-purpose" (Traugott 2015: 68), such as its use with inanimate subjects and its occurrence in raising constructions (e.g., *there is going to be…*) (Traugott & Trousdale 2013: 118). It is when *be going to* with temporal interpretation manifested such syntactic properties of auxiliaries that constructionalization as the creation of a form_{new}-$\text{meaning}_{\text{new}}$ pairing was testified. As the construction expanded to sanction more verb types as infinitival complements, such as the motion verb *go* (*be going to go*) and stative verbs (e.g., *be going to like*) (Hopper & Traugott 1993: 3; Traugott & Trousdale 2013: 118), it developed a more general schema that can provide a more abstract template for accommodating a larger number of types and instances, hence leading to increase in productivity.

Traugott (2014: 90) looks at productivity in terms of two dimensions: "the extent to which a schema sanctions other less schematic constructions (type productivity) and the frequency with which a construction is used (token productivity)." The increase in these two kinds of productivity is often gauged by frequency: "expansion both of construction-types (type-frequency) and of constructs (token-frequency)" (Traugott & Trousdale 2013: 113). A linguistic item of

21. Traugott and Trousdale (2013: 116) make a distinction between two types of increase in schematicity: the increasing schematization of micro-constructions (instantiated by actual linguistic instances) and that of schemas (which represent linguistic entities abstracting over micro-constructions).

high token frequency is likely to be "entrenched (or stored as a unit)" (Traugott & Trousdale 2013: 48). Through its repeated use, such a unit can lose compositionality due to the process of automatization or routinization (e.g., Hopper & Traugott 1993: 64–65; Haiman 1994), and, as a whole, become highly accessible and easily produced. It has also been pointed out in studies of language acquisition and language change (e.g., Brooks et al. 1999; Bybee 2007) that frequently occurring items become so deeply entrenched that they are likely to exhibit resistance to change. One oft-cited example is the irregular past tense forms of verbs with high token frequency like *kept*, which are less likely to be overgeneralized by children and to be changed in history to the regular past tense form **keeped* (e.g., Bybee 2007: Chapters 5 and 12). As will be argued below, this "conserving effect" (Bybee 2007: 271) of token frequency may contribute to the retention of a final tag uniquely found in Irish English.

While token frequency generally contributes to the entrenchment of a micro-construction (i.e., a construction type instantiated by actual tokens), type frequency is specifically responsible for entrenchment at more abstract levels, namely, (sub)schemas (cf. Evans & Green 2006: 118–120), as Croft (2001: 28) puts it clearly: "productivity, represented by the entrenchment of a more abstract schema, is a function of its type frequency." For example, the regular past tense schema [V-*ed*] is productive, because it sanctions so many verb types that it becomes well entrenched in the minds of English speakers. The well-entrenched schema is highly accessible to the speakers and hence increases its applicability to newly incoming verbs like *googled* (Bybee 2007: 14–15). In other words, the greater number of types are used, the more productive and, therefore, the more entrenched a schema becomes. Such a highly entrenched schema is cognitively salient enough to accommodate further types, lending itself to the creation of a more abstract schema. As Traugott & Trousdale (2013: 18) note, increased collocational range as exemplified by Himmelmann's (2004: 32) "host-class expansion" is "a hallmark of increased productivity." In sum, a construction, if it is higher in both type and token frequencies, can be considered to be more "entrenched as a form-meaning pairing in the mind of the language user" (Traugot & Trousdale 2013: 1) and be more productive than otherwise.

Decrease in compositionality is "reduction of transparency in the link between meaning and form" (Traugott & Trousdale 2013: 113) or "mismatch between aspects of form and aspects of meaning" (Traugott & Trousdale 2013: 19). When a sequence of forms is associated with a new meaning, the older formal make-up becomes less transparent as it is obfuscated by the new collocational meaning. A mismatch between form and meaning remains until there emerges morphosyntax features associated with the new semantic category. In the case of *be going to*, a mismatch occurred in an earlier stage of the development where a new, future meaning was not yet accompanied by the emergence of morpho-syntactic features characteristic of prototypical auxiliaries (e.g., their occurrence with all types of subjects including inanimate as well as animate ones). The mismatch was later resolved with the emergence of a form$_{new}$-meaning$_{new}$ pairing (Traugott 2014: 92), as in the sentence *it's gonna rain tonight.*

5.2 Constructionalization and final-tagged structures

The constructionalization of final-tagged structures can be traced back to the time when pragmatic markers started to be used in final position, having their retrospective scope over an overall proposition to which they add some discourse-pragmatic meanings. Lenker (2010: 200) argues that the final use of adverbial connectors is "a comparatively recent phenomenon" in English, identifying occurrences of sentence-final *however* in the early ModE as one of the earliest examples.

On the other hand, Traugott (2016) finds that final pragmatic markers were already attested in OE in her recent study of the development of pragmatic markers at RP (Right-Periphery). Some pragmatic markers all translated as 'truly' (*witodice, soðlice, cuðlice* and *gewislice*) were used in clause-final position to reinforce the truthfulness of the preceding proposition. Traugott (2016: 33) thus concludes that "in OE there was a position 'outside' the clause at RP," although type and token frequencies were relatively low. Final position already available in OE has been "expanded" (Traugott 2016: 35) in the history of English to sanction more various types of pragmatic markers, chronologically characterized by the appearance of final comment clauses (e.g., *I wene* 'I think') in ME, the progressive spread of final adverbial connectors from ME onwards (also Lenker 2010; Haselow 2012), and the constant increase of question tags in the early ModE onwards (e.g., *have thay, dyd I not*) (also Tottie & Hoffmann 2009).[22]

This historical sketch of the development of final pragmatic markers leads us to consider that final-tagged structures were already available in OE with the rise of a form$_{new}$-meaning$_{new}$ pairing, which could be formulated as in the following constructional schema:[23]

22. Traugott (2016: 42) considers that final *then* "was rare before later EModE" in retrospective contrastive reading. However, since Haselow (2012: 169) documents "the relatively high frequency of occurrence of *then* as a final connector in late ME," we interpret final adverbial connectors as already existing in ME.

23. This formulation follows the basic template for the description of a symbolic constructional unit adopted by Traugott and Trousdale (2013: 8): [[F] ↔ [M]], where F stands for Form and M for Meaning and the outer brackets represent a conventionalized symbolic unit with a link between form and meaning, which is indicated by the double-headed arrow.

(59) [[ANCH$_i$ FT$_j$] ↔ [S conclude verbalization of proposition$_i$ with attitude$_j$]][24]

The form [ANCH$_i$ FT$_j$] indicates that the speaker concludes the verbalization of a proposition designated in the anchor with an emotive and/or interactive attitude associated with a final tag, such as strengthening an assertion, seeking agreement, mitigating the force of an utterance, and others.

Constructionalization occurs in the sequences of "constructional changes," the relevant semantic or morphophonological/syntactic changes. The changes that precede constructionalization are referred to as "pre-constructionalization constructional changes" (PreCxzn CCs), and those that follow it as "post-constructionalization constructional changes" (PostCxzn CCs) (Traugott & Trousdale 2013). For example, the constructionalization of *be going to* as a tense auxiliary is preceded by PreCxzn CCs including the semantic change to prospective future and is followed by PostCxznCCs including "morphological and phonological reduction" like *be gonna* and "expansion of collocations" (Traugott & Trousdale 2013: 27) like the expansion of infinitival complements to include the motion verb *go* or verbs that do not have the meaning of purposeful motion (e.g., stative verbs like *be* and *have*). Traugott & Trousdale (2013) represent a relationship between constructionalization (Cxzn) and constructional changes (CC) as sketched in (60):

(60) PreCxzn CCs
↓↓
Cxzn
↓↓
PostCxzn CCs

(Traugott & Trousdale 2013: 28)

Considering that the final-tag construction was already observed in the period of OE, we can assume that it is now undergoing the stage of PostCxzn CCs in both varieties of English. Just as the construction *X be going to do* was expanded to include a wider range of subjects and verbs, so is the final-tag construction described in (59) expanding its collocational range, allowing more types of final tags (FT) and consequently increasing token frequency as well. Since type and token frequencies are responsible for entrenchment at abstract/schematic and concrete levels, respectively (cf. Croft 2001: 28; Evans & Green 2006: 118–120), the differences in the type and token frequencies of final tags between the two varieties of

24. S and H stand for Speaker and Hearer, respectively, ANCH signifies an anchor, FT represents a final tag, and a subscript ($_i$ or $_j$) indicates a form-meaning correspondence. While Traugott and Trousdale (2013) generally use major grammatical categories such as N, V, or ADJ in the form pole, we employ ANCH and FT for notational convenience. This study included elliptical clauses as the anchors of final tags if they were recoverable in context (e.g., *One time, yeah*), as discussed in 3.2.

English can be seen as revealing different degrees of entrenchment of the final-tag construction in (59). The constructional schema is entrenched to a greater extent as the lower levels of subschemas as well as micro-constructions are activated through repeated uses of various final-tagged sentences.[25] In other words, Irish and American English differ in the degrees of constructional entrenchment, as will be demonstrated in the following section.[26]

5.3 Constructional entrenchment of final-tagged structures in Irish and American English

The three factors (increase in schematicity, increase in productivity and decrease in compositionality) illustrate the development of the final-tag construction in the two varieties of English. As seen in Section 4, a comparison of the two corpora reveals that both type and token frequencies of final tags are higher in Irish English than in American English. This result clearly indicates that the category of the final-tag construction is more schematic and productive in Irish English than in American English. Irish English finds 37 more types (or "micro-constructions") of final pragmatic markers (111 types in SPICE and 74 types in SBC) including several kinds of variety-specific final tags: clausal pragmatic markers with *say* (e.g.,

25. However, the relation between frequency and entrenchment should be considered carefully. Frequency in a corpus reveals a numeral tendency of linguistic data retrieved from a speech community, hence inherently social, while entrenchment is concerned with the cognitive activation of a linguistic unit in the mind of a single speaker. As Schmid (2010: 101–103, 115–117) aptly argues, the relation has long been unquestioned by many cognitive linguists (see also Blumenthal-Dramé 2013: Chapter 3). Reflecting upon his own "from-corpus-to-cognition-principle" (2000: 39), Schmid stresses that "an additional logical step" (2010: 117) is required to link between the two notions. Of two types of frequency he proposes, Schmid argues that "absolute frequency" has a correlation with the strength of entrenchment, because "frequency of occurrence in discourse relates to frequency of processing in the minds of the members of the speech community" (2010: 119). However, such a correlation is less obvious in the case of "relative frequency," e.g., the frequency of a unit relative to other units in the same discourse environment or to its occurrences in other environments. Since our analysis is based on absolute frequency, we can assume that the discussion of entrenchment is supported by the data, given the following rationale provided by Schmid (2016):

> [F]requencies of occurrence in large, balanced corpora can not only serve as an approximation of the kind of repetitiveness that the average speaker produces and is typically exposed to, but actually provide clues as to the potential effects of this exposure on the cognitive systems of individual speakers. (2016: 14)

26. We owe the term "constructional entrenchment" to an anonymous reviewer of this article, who suggested how the extent or degree of language changes should be treated in the framework proposed by Traugott & Trousdale (2013).

I'd say), lexical pragmatic markers such as *like* and *but*, two kinds of AUX-tags (*so*-tags and *sure*-tags), and others. The number of the higher-level groupings subsuming these is also greater in Irish English, as shown in Appendices A and B. In SPICE, clausal FIX- tags contain 18 verb types (KNOW, THINK, MEAN, etc.) and FIX lexical tags consist of 13 higher-level groupings (expressions meaning '(be) in order,' words for 'yes' and 'no,' etc.) excluding OTHERS, whereas in SBC, clausal FIX- tags include 12 verb types and lexical FIX- tags consist of 11 higher-level groupings. As seen in 5.1, the more types of pragmatic markers are recruited in the final-tag construction, the greater number of higher-level groupings, or "subschemas," are likely to be created, which contributes to the further expansion of superordinate categories (clausal FIX-tags, lexical FIX-tags, etc.).[27] The constructional network thus formed results in a more schematic structure. In this respect, the final-tag construction in Irish English can be viewed as having formed a more schematic category than American English.

The higher type frequency in Irish English also points to a greater increase in productivity (type productivity), as Bybee notes: "type frequency is a major factor determining the degree of productivity of a construction" (2007: 14, see also Traugott & Trousdale 2013: 113). A construction that sanctions a greater number of types is more amenable or open to newer types ("host-class expansion" in Himmelmann 2004: 32). Take, for example, clausal FIX-tags. SPICE finds 18 verb types in this group of pragmatic markers, but SBC has only 12 verb types. The larger number of verb types in Irish English suggests a greater latitude in verb choice, as we can even find *hear* (*do you hear*), *agree* (*I agree*), and *admit* (*I must admit*), which occurred only once in SPICE but were not found in SBC. Furthermore, type productivity is also increased by a greater syntactic variation. For example, as seen in 4.2.2, the clausal pragmatic marker with *say* appears in manifold forms: *I'd say*, *I must say*, *I'd have to say*, *I should say*, and others.

The increased productivity of final-tagged structures is also evidenced by token frequency (token productivity). We have found that Irish English shows a far greater token frequency than American English (3,472 tokens in SPICE and 1,617 in SBC). This greater token frequency is partly explained by the types of final tags unique to Irish English, (e.g., *like*, *so*, *but*, etc.), but it is also attributed to final tags found in the two varieties. For example, Irish English is higher in the occurrences, for example, of the four common AUX-tags (BE, DO, HAVE and MODAL; 358 in SPICE and 109 in SBC), *you know* (400 in SPICE and 246 in SBC), and *yeah* (357 in SPICE and 115 in SBC). The repeated use of a given pragmatic marker in final position results in the reinforcement or entrenchment of its use as a final tag, and

27. These superordinate categories may also be viewed as higher-level subschemas, which suggests that "subschemas" in Traugott & Trousdale's (2013) framework are multilayered.

encourages its further use with less cognitive effort. As mentioned in 5.1, linguistic forms of high token frequency are likely to be consolidated as a unit. In the present case, utterances, as units, are often concluded by pragmatic markers, some of which are more deeply entrenched as final tags and thus become a more integral part of each utterance and more easily accessible to speakers.

The fact that Irish English shows higher frequencies in both type and token suggests that the schema of the final-tag construction is expanding in two contrasting directions: preservation and innovation. Repeated occurrences of forms contribute to preserving or retaining pragmatic markers that already exist as final tags ("the conserving effect" of token frequency in Bybee 2007: 271) as is the case of the persistent use of final *like*, which continues to be used in the face of its decline in use in more standardized varieties of English, as will be seen below. On the other hand, high type frequency serves to create a more schematic or abstract network, which allows an increasing number of new types to enter into the construction, as is the case of clausal FIX-tags in Irish English. It is with respect to these two frequencies that the final-tag construction in Irish English has developed into a more schematic and productive category, which can accommodate a wider variety of types and produce a larger amount of instances.

The third characteristic of constructionalization ("decrease in compositionality") is well illustrated by the final-tag use of connectives. Traugott & Trousdale (2013: 121) explain that "decrease in compositionality typically arises when there is a mismatch between the older morpho-syntax and a newer meaning." The development of final *but* describes how such a mismatch occurs in final-tagged structures.[28] The older morpho-syntax of a connective, or a coordinator in particular, normally forms a three-part construction with two elements combined by a connective in-between, as shown in (61a):

(61) a. three-part construction: X, *but* Y

↓

b. three-part construction: X, Y *but*

↓

c. three-part construction?: (X), Y *but* (X: implicitly given)

↓

d. two-part construction: Y *but*

In Irish English as well as Australian English (Mulder & Thompson 2008; Mulder et al. 2009), *but* can be shifted back to clause-final position, having the form of

28. This analysis of final *but* is different from Mulder & Thompson's (2008: 195), who take a "continuum" view of the development. It rather follows the analysis of the retrospective type of final *but* as shown in (5b). See Izutsu & Izutsu (2014) for the detailed discussion.

[X, Y *but*] as in (61b), where the coordinator has a retrospective scope, combining the two preceding elements (X and Y). The first element (X) is sometimes implicit and contextually given, and the resulting structure may be difficult to see as a three-part construction as in (61c). When the coordinator weakens its force to combine the two elements and is more likely to be interpreted as having its scope over the immediately preceding clause, the structure may be viewed as a two-part construction as in (61d), which corresponds to an unmarked structure of final tags. Notice here that the original three-part construction is less transparent in light of the semantics of final-tagged structures, since the new meaning does not presuppose the presence of the first conjunct (X). Here, we can see decrease in the compositionality originally required by the syntax of the coordinator *but*. The mismatch between the older syntax and the newer meaning seems to be resolved in the minds of Irish English speakers, who use *but* in syntactic contexts where coordinators are not normally expected as in *Och that's easy to do* **but** *isn't it* in (42), but it is still felt only as a coordinator by native English speakers of some other varieties, notably American English speakers. A similar account is possible for final *so* in Irish English.[29]

A consideration of the corpus results in terms of the three characteristics of constructionalization leads us to conclude that Irish English displays a greater degree of the entrenchment of the final-tag construction [[ANCH$_i$ FT$_j$] ↔ [S conclude verbalization of proposition$_i$ with attitude$_j$]] than American English. Thus, by comparison, the construction is more easily accessible to Irish English speakers and hence more likely applicable to a wider variety of pragmatic markers.

It is worthy to note that since Irish English speakers have such a highly entrenched final-tag construction with a broader application potential, we found some cases where no fewer than three pragmatic markers are used together in final position, as in (62) and (63). Such triple occurrences of final tags were not observed in SBC.

(62) A: <#> <rep> Oh* that's crucial **aye* so-it-is you-know@** * </rep> <#>
(SPICE P1A-045 *Fish*)

(63) B: <#> <rep> Mmm <,> I like the oul brand names **now*** <{> <[> **I'd have to** </[> **say myself I-do@** </rep> (SPICE P1A-090 *Designer clothes*)

29. In other words, if the use of *but* or *so* as a final tag is viewed as a micro-construction sanctioned by the final-tag constructional schema in (59), it is considered that Irish English speakers possess such micro-constructions and a subschema subsuming them in their linguistic knowledge, but American English speakers do not.

5.4 Motivating factors for the development of the final-tag construction in Irish English

One might consider that the abundance of final tags in Irish English reflects substrate influences of Irish Gaelic. There are some clause-final uses of pragmatic markers, which may be considered to be transferred from Irish Gaelic. For example, Hickey (2007: 371) explains that clause-final *so* may be regarded as "an equivalent to Irish *más ea* 'if-that-is so' which is also found sentence-finally: *Beidh cupán tae agam más ea*, lit. 'will-be cup tea-at-me if-that-is so.'" Similarly, the frequent use of the final tag *is it* may be associated with the general question tag ***an ea?*** 'is it?,' as Hickey (2007: 277) again puts it: "[t]he Irish model for such usage is the general question tag *an ea?* 'is it?' which can be placed at the end of a sentence or phrase, e.g., *Níl sé agat, an ea?* [is-not it at-you, is it] 'You don't have it, is it?'"

However, not all the clause-final pragmatic markers can be traced back to lexical equivalents of Irish Gaelic. For example, Hickey (2015: 24) remarks that the pragmatic marker *like*, the final-tag use of which is the most frequent in our data, "does not have a direct formal equivalent in Irish" (Hickey 2015: 24). Indeed, D'Arcy (2005: 4) notes that final *like* is "the 'traditional British' use of *like*" (see also Andersen 2001: 226), which dates back to the late eighteenth and early nineteenth centuries, as documented in OED.[30] Schweinberger (2014: 76) posits the most possible scenario for its development: "clause-final LIKE spread from southern parts of England outward to Ireland and Scotland" (see also Corrigan 2015: 49).[31] It thus seems illegitimate to assume a direct transfer of final *like* from a lexical equivalent in Irish Gaelic.

Rather than ascribing each type of final tag to a particular lexical item or grammatical feature of the substrate language, the development of the final-tag construction should be viewed as more complex. In addition to the presence of direct parallels in Irish Gaelic (e.g., *más ea* 'if-that-is so,' *an ea* 'is it'), some other contributing forces from Irish Gaelic may be simultaneously operating on the notable development of the final-tag construction in Irish English. For example, one of the related, if not direct, substrate contributions would be the influence of the

30. The final-tag use of *like* is often seen as a varietal feature specifically found in the northern part of the British isles (Hedevind 1967: 237, cited in Schweinberger 2012: 187, Miller & Weinert 1995: 368). However, final *like* is also reported to be found in the Southeast (Anderwald 2004: 192–193) and Northeast (Beal 2004: 136) of England.

31. D'Arcy also suggests that final *like* "must have been transplanted to North America," because they are sporadically found in the speech of older generation in Canadian English: e.g., *We need to smarten it up a bit* ***like*** (75 year-old female speaker) (D'Arcy 2005: 68). However, this usage is now "extremely rare" (D'Arcy 2007: n.5) in North American English even within the cohort of speakers over the age of 60.

Irish response style on the greater use of AUX-tags (e.g., *do you*, *won't you*). Irish Gaelic "has no words for *yes* and *no*"; an answer repeats the verb of the question "in either the affirmative or the negative" (Hickey 2007: 159). Hickey (2007: 160) suggests that this response style "is in connection with tag questions" in that both are formed on the basis of a similar repeating pattern. It could also be possible that some other indirect influences from the substrate language are similarly in place.

Furthermore, superstrate contributions, i.e., impacts of English, are not negligible either. As mentioned above, final *like* preserves a pattern of British usage in the late eighteenth and early nineteenth centuries, which is thus seen as a case of "the retention of superstrate features which have either disappeared from standard usage or have always been restricted to non-standard dialects" (Harris 1991: 209). In other words, the continuing influences of the sub- and superstrate languages may be operative in the development of final-tagged structures. As Harris (1991: 209) puts it, "[r]ather than seeking a unique substratal or superstratal source for a particular linguistic feature, it is often more illuminating to regard the two as mutually reinforcing."

However, one last question we need to ask: are they the only possible motivating forces for the greater use of final tags in Irish English? In addition to such contributing sources, this research can propose one more influential factor for the development of linguistic systems in languages, i.e., the impact which the entrenchment of a constructional schema has on incremental language use. Recall that many pragmatic markers are used clause-finally both in Irish English and American English (*you know*, *you see*, *yeah*, *really*, *actually*, etc.). Only with reference to sub- and superstrate influences, we could not explain why Irish English speakers conspicuously prefer to use these markers in final position. Also, we have seen that the final use of adverbs of totality (*absolutely*, *totally*, *completely*) were attested in SPICE, but not in SBC, although these adverbs are frequently used in other positions in American English. We may want to ask again why Irish English speakers are more likely to use these adverbs in final position than American English speakers.

Considering the magnitude of the development of final tags in Irish English, it is reasonable to assume that this developmental process is also stimulated by a motivating force inherent in the well-entrenched schema of the construction. We have argued that the final-tag construction is more firmly entrenched in the minds of Irish English speakers, which suggests that they have a stronger feeling to indicate the closure of their utterances with some linguistic means, like speakers of languages with final particles (e.g., Japanese, Korean, etc.). As mentioned in 5.1 above, the productivity of a construction is associated with the entrenchment of abstract schemas as well as the reinforcement of linguistic units. Our constructional approach to final tags is able to demonstrate that the schematic final-tag construction as described in (59) represents a constructional template available for English speakers when they want to conclude a unit of talk with a certain emotive and/or interactive attitude. As the constructional template becomes more entrenched and more cognitively salient to speakers of a language variety, it provides them a stronger impetus for further uses of pragmatic markers in final position. The present analysis based on the two corpora reveals that this situation is more remarkable in Irish English, where final position has developed into a more productive slot of broader versatility.

6. Conclusion

The present study regards clauses with final tags (*isn't it, will you, you know, right,* etc.) as a symbolic construction with a slot for pragmatic markers in final position. A comparison of the two corpora (SPICE-Ireland and SBC) reveals that both type and token frequencies of final tags are higher in Irish English than in American English. These high frequencies lead us to conclude that the final-tag construction is more firmly entrenched in the minds of Irish English speakers (as comparable with speakers of some Asian languages like Japanese and Korean). In other words, the construction in Irish English forms a more schematic and entrenched category, which can accommodate a wider variety of types and produce a larger amount of instances.

This marked development of the final-tag construction in Irish English can be attributed to several motivations including sub- and superstrate influences. However, it is important to note that such preference for final tags is not simply due to the total summation of the two influential forces, but rather it is also subject to another influential force of the highly entrenched schema of the final-tag construction. A constructional account of language change as proposed by Traugott & Trousdale (2013) suggests that increases in both type and token frequencies serve to contribute to the entrenchment and expansion of the constructional category. The greater variety of final tags is used in greater frequency, the more schematic and entrenched the category network becomes, which then spurs on greater exploitation of final position for an interactive, discursive purpose. This recurrent process will continue unless there is a social or linguistic hindrance to this development.

We believe that our holistic and comparative approach to the final-tag construction will help to unravel our intuitive and naïve question of why speakers of some varieties often strike us as somewhat "foreign" in the way of closing utterances. The present result suggests that the final position of a clause or a sentence is not equally exploited in the two varieties of English. Speakers of Irish English seem to have a stronger desire to end their utterances with some kind of pragmatic marker, feeling more need to linguistically encode discourse-pragmatic functions such as softening or intensifying their own utterances, questioning or confirming the interlocutor's knowledge state, and facilitating a further interaction. On the other hand, Americans seem to be less inclined to do so. One might assume that prosodic marking may play a more important role than the verbal coding of final tags in some varieties. Also, given some previous observations (e.g., Algeo 2006; Tottie & Hoffmann 2006) on a heavier use of tag questions by British people, one might even conjecture that the greater frequencies of final tags could be an areal phenomenon of British Isles with some influence of language contact. Investigation of these issues will have to await further research.

Acknowledgment

We are deeply indebted to Fergus O'Dwyer and Martin J. Murphy for their very kind help in analyzing a large amount of data. We are also thankful to Charles Mueller and Paddy Hall for data consultation. We are grateful to Yukako Ishii for statistical support. We would like to thank Bernd Heine, Ekkehard König, Eijiro Shibasaki and other participants at Gramm 2 for their insightful comments and suggestions. We are also indebted to two reviewers for their constructive criticism and theoretical advice. Our final thanks go to Hancil Sylvie, who gave us an opportunity to present an earlier version of this paper at the conference. All remaining errors and shortcomings are of course ours. This research was supported by JSPS KAKENHI Grant Number 16K02637.

References

Aijmer, Karin. 2002. *English Discourse Particles. Evidence from a Corpus* [Studies in Corpus Linguistics 10]. Amsterdam: John Benjamins. https://doi.org/10.1075/scl.10

Aijmer, Karin. 2013. *Understanding Pragmatic Markers. A Variational Pragmatic Approach*. Edinburgh: EUP.

Aitken, Adam Jack. 1979. Scottish speech: A historical view, with special reference to the Standard English of Scotland. In *Languages of Scotland*, Adam Jack Aitken & Tom McArthur (eds), 85–118. Edinburgh: W. & R. Chambers.

Algeo, John. 2006. *British or American English? A Handbook of Word and Grammar Patterns*. Cambridge: CUP. https://doi.org/10.1017/CBO9780511607240

Allerton, David J. 2009. Tag questions. In *One Language, Two Grammars?* Günter Rohdenburg & Julia Schlüter (eds), 306–323. Cambridge: CUP. https://doi.org/10.1017/CBO9780511551970.017

Amador-Moreno, Carolina P. 2010. *An Introduction to Irish English*. London: Equinox.

Amador-Moreno, Carolina. P. 2015. "There's, like, total silence again, roysh, and no one says anything": Fictional representations of "new" pragmatic markers and quotatives in Irish English. In Amador-Moreno, McCafferty & Vaughan (eds), 370–389.

Amador-Moreno, Carolina. P., McCafferty, Kevin & Vaughan, Elaine. 2015a. Introduction. In Amador-Moreno, McCafferty & Vaughan (eds), 1–16.

Amador-Moreno, Carolina. P., McCafferty, Kevin & Vaughan, Elaine (eds). 2015b. *Pragmatic Markers in Irish English* [Pragmatics & Beyond New Series 258]. Amsterdam: John Benjamins. https://doi.org/10.1075/pbns.258

Andersen, Gisle. 2001. *Pragmatic Markers and Sociolinguistic Variation. A Relevance-Theoretic Approach to the Language of Adolescents* [Pragmatics & Beyond New Series 84]. Amsterdam: John Benjamins. https://doi.org/10.1075/pbns.84

Anderwald, Lieselotte. 2004. The varieties of English spoken in the Southeast of England: Morphology and syntax. In *A Handbook of Varieties of English*, Vol. 2: *Morphology & Syntax*, Bernd Kortmann, Kate Burridge, Rajend Mesthrie, Edgar W. Schneider & Clive Upton (eds), 175–195. Berlin: Mouton de Gruyter.

Axelsson, Karin. 2011. Tag Questions in Fiction Dialogue. PhD dissertation, University of Gothenburg.

Barron, Anne. 2015. "And your wedding is the twenty-second <.> of June is it?" Tag questions in Irish English. In Amador-Moreno, McCafferty & Vaughan (eds), 203–228.

Barron, Anne & Pandarova, Irina. 2016. The sociolinguistics of language use in Ireland. In *Sociolinguistics in Ireland*. Raymond Hickey (ed.), 107–130. London: Palgrave Macmillan.

Barron, Anne, Pandarova, Irina & Muderack, Karoline. 2015. Tag questions across Irish and British English: A corpus analysis of form and function. *Multilingua* 34(4): 495–525. https://doi.org/10.1515/multi-2014-0099

Beal, Joan. 2004. English dialects in the North of England: Morphology and syntax. In *A Handbook of Varieties of English*, Vol. 2: *Morphology & Syntax*, Bernd Kortmann, Kate Burridge, Rajend Mesthrie, Edgar W. Schneider & Clive Upton (eds.), 114–141. Berlin: Mouton de Gruyter.

Biber, Douglas, Johansson, Stig, Leech, Geoffrey, Conrad, Susan & Finegan, Edward. 1999. *Longman Grammar of Spoken and Written English*. London: Longman.

Binchy, James. 2005. *Three forty two so please*: Politeness for sale in Southern-Irish service encounters. In *The Pragmatics of Irish English*, Anne Barron & Klaus P. Schneider (eds), 313–335. Berlin: Mouton de Gruyter. https://doi.org/10.1515/9783110898934.313

Blumenthal-Dramé, Alice. 2013. *Entrenchment in Usage-Based Theories. What Corpus Data Do and Do Not Reveal about the Mind*. Berlin: Mouton de Gruyter.

Brinton, Laurel J. 1996. *Pragmatic Markers in English. Grammaticalization and Discourse Functions*. Berlin: Mouton de Gruyter. https://doi.org/10.1515/9783110907582

Brinton Laurel J. 2008. *The Comment Clause in English. Syntactic Origins and Pragmatic Development*. Cambridge: CUP. https://doi.org/10.1017/CBO9780511551789

Brooks, Patricia J., Tomasello, Michael, Dodson, Kelly & Lewis, Lawrence B. 1999. Children's tendency to overgeneralize their argument structure constructions: The entrenchment hypothesis. *Child Development* 70: 1325–1337. https://doi.org/10.1111/1467-8624.00097

Bybee, Joan L. 2007. *Frequency of Use and the Organization of Language*. Oxford: OUP. https://doi.org/10.1093/acprof:oso/9780195301571.001.0001

Carter, Ronald & McCarthy, Michael. 2006. *The Cambridge Grammar of English*. Cambridge: CUP.

Christensen, Lis. 1996. *A First Glossary of Hiberno-English*. Odense: Odense University Press.

Clancy, Brian & Vaughan, Elaine. 2012. "It's lunacy now": A corpus-based pragmatic analysis of the use of 'now' in contemporary Irish English. In *New Perspectives on Irish English* [Varieties of English around the World G44], Bettina Migge & Máire Ní Chiosáin (eds), 225–245. Amsterdam: John Benjamins. https://doi.org/10.1075/veaw.g44.11cla

Clancy, Patricia M., Thompson, Sandra A., Suzuki, Ryoko & Tao, Hongyin. 1996. The conversational use of reactive tokens in English, Japanese, and Mandarin. *Journal of Pragmatics* 26: 355–387. https://doi.org/10.1016/0378-2166(95)00036-4

Columbus, Georgie. 2009a. A corpus-based analysis of invariant tags in five varieties of English. In *Corpus Linguistics. Refinements and Reassessments*, Antoinette Renouf & Andrew Kehoe (eds), 401–414. Amsterdam: Rodopi. https://doi.org/10.1163/9789042025981_022

Columbus, Georgie. 2009b. Irish *like* as an invariant tag: Evidence from ICE-Ireland. Paper presented at American Association for Corpus Linguistics (AACL) 2009. Edmonton, Canada. <http://www.ualberta.ca/~aacl2009/PDFs/Columbus2009AACL.pdf> (27 September 2015).

Corrigan, Karen P. 2010. *Dialects of English. Irish English*, Vol. 1: *Northern Ireland*. Edinburgh: EUP.

Corrigan, Karen P. 2015. "I always think of people here, you know, saying like after every sentence": The dynamics of discourse-pragmatic markers in Northern Irish English. In Amador-Moreno, McCafferty & Vaughan (eds.), 37–64.

Croft, William. 2001. *Radical Construction Grammar. Syntactic Theory in Typological Perspective*. Oxford: OUP. https://doi.org/10.1093/acprof:oso/9780198299554.001.0001

D'Arcy, Alexandra. 2005. LIKE: Syntax and Development. PhD dissertation, University of Toronto.

D'Arcy, Alexandra. 2007. LIKE and language ideology: Disentangling the fact from fiction. *American Speech* 82(4): 386–419. https://doi.org/10.1215/00031283-2007-025

Denis, Derek & Tagliamonte, Sali A. 2016. Innovation, right? Change, you know? Utterance-final tags in Canadian English. In *Discourse-Pragmatic Variation and Change in English. New Methods and Insights*, Heike Pichler (ed.), 86–112. Cambridge: CUP.

Dolan, Terence P. 2012. *A Dictionary of Hiberno-English*, 3rd edn. Dublin: Gill & MacMillan.

Du Bois, John W., Schuetze-Coburn, Stephan, Cumming, Susanna & Paolino, Danae. 1993. Outline of discourse transcription. In *Talking Data. Transcription and Coding in Discourse Research*, Jane A. Edwards & Martin D. Lampert (eds), 45–89. Hillsdale, NJ: Lawrence Erlbaum Associates.

Du Bois, John W., Chafe, Wallace L., Meyer, Charles & Thompson, Sandra A. 2000. *Santa Barbara Corpus of Spoken American English*, Part One. Philadelphia, PA: Linguistic Data Consortium. <http://www.linguistics.ucsb.edu/research/santa-barbara-corpus>

Du Bois, John W., Chafe, Wallace L., Meyer, Charles, Thompson, Sandra A. & Martey, Nii. 2003. *Santa Barbara Corpus of Spoken American English*, Part Two. Philadelphia, PA: Linguistic Data Consortium. <http://www.linguistics.ucsb.edu/research/santa-barbara-corpus>

Du Bois, John W. & Englebretson, Robert. 2004. *Santa Barbara Corpus of Spoken American English*, Part Three. Philadelphia, PA: Linguistic Data Consortium. <http://www.linguistics.ucsb.edu/research/santa-barbara-corpus>

Du Bois, John W. & Englebretson, Robert. 2005. *Santa Barbara Corpus of Spoken American English*, Part Four. Philadelphia, PA: Linguistic Data Consortium. <http://www.linguistics.ucsb.edu/research/santa-barbara-corpus>

Evans, Vyvyan & Green, Melanie. 2006. *Cognitive Linguistics. An Introduction*. Edinburgh: EUP.

Fillmore, Charles J., Kay, Paul & O'Connor, Mary Catherine. 1988. Regularity and idiomaticity in grammatical constructions. *Language* 64: 501–538. https://doi.org/10.2307/414531

Fischer, Kerstin (ed.). 2006. *Approaches to Discourse Particles*. Oxford: Elsevier.

Ford, Cecilia E. & Thompson, Sandra A. 1996. Interactional units in conversation: Syntactic, intonational, and pragmatic resources for the management of turns. In *Interaction and Grammar*, Elinor Ochs, Emanuel A. Schegloff & Sandra A. Thompson (eds), 134–184. Cambridge: CUP. https://doi.org/10.1017/CBO9780511620874.003

Fraser, Bruce. 1996. Pragmatic markers. *Pragmatics* 6(2): 167–190. https://doi.org/10.1075/prag.6.2.03fra

Fried, Mirjam. 2008. Constructions and constructs: Mapping a diachronic process. In *Constructions and Language Change*, Alexander Bergs & Gabriele Diewald (eds), 47–79. Berlin: Mouton de Gruyter.

Fried, Mirjam, Östman, Jan-Ola & Verschueren, Jef. 2010. *Variation and Change. Pragmatic Perspectives*. Amsterdam: John Benjamins. https://doi.org/10.1075/hoph.6

Gisborne, Nikolas & Patten, Amanda. 2011. Construction grammar and grammaticalization. In *The Oxford Handbook of Grammaticalization*, Heiko Narrog & Bernd Heine (eds), 92–104. Oxford: OUP.

Goldberg, Adele E. 1995. *Constructions. A Construction Grammar Approach to Argument Structure*. Chicago, IL: The University of Chicago Press.

Haiman, John. 1994. Ritualization and the development of language. In *Perspectives on Grammaticalization*, William Pagliuca (ed.), 3–28. Amsterdam: John Benjamins. https://doi.org/10.1075/cilt.109.07hai

Hancil, Sylvie, Haselow, Alexander & Post, Margje. 2015. *Final Particles*. Berlin: Mouton de Gruyter.

Harris, John. 1991. Conservatism versus substratal transfer in Irish English. In *Dialects of English. Studies in Grammatical Variation*, Peter Trudgill & Jack K. Chambers (eds), 191–212. London: Longman.

Haselow, Alexander. 2012. Discourse organization and the rise of final *then* in the history of English. In *English Historical Linguistics 2010. Selected Papers from the Sixteenth International Conference on English Historical Linguistics (ICEHL 16), Pécs, 23–27 August 2010* [Current Issues in Linguistic Theory 325], Irén Hegedűs & Alexandra Fodor (eds), 153–175. Amsterdam: John Benjamins.

Haselow, Alexander. 2016. A processual view on grammar: Macrogrammar and the final field in spoken syntax. *Language Sciences* 54: 77–101.

Hedevind, Bertil. 1967. *The Dialect of Dentdale in the West Riding of Yorkshire*[Studia anglistica upsaliensia 5]. Uppsala: University of Uppsala.

Hewings, Ann & Hewings, Martin. 2005. *Grammar and Context. An Advanced Resource Book*. London: Routledge.

Hickey, Raymond. 2007. *Irish English. History and Present Forms*. Cambridge: CUP. https://doi.org/10.1017/CBO9780511551048

Hickey, Raymond. 2015. The pragmatics of Irish English and Irish. In Amador-Moreno, McCafferty & Vaughan (eds), 17–36.

Hilpert, Martin. 2013. *Constructional Change in English. Developments in Allomorphy, Word Formation, and Syntax*. Cambridge: CUP. https://doi.org/10.1017/CBO9781139004206

Himmelmann, Nikolaus. 2004. Lexicalization and grammaticalization: opposite or orthogonal? In *What Makes Grammaticalization. A Look from its Fringes and its Components*, Walter Bisang, Nikolaus P. Himmelmann & Björn Wiemer (eds), 21–42. Berlin: Mouton de Gruyter.

Hopper, Paul J. & Traugott, Elizabeth Closs. 1993. *Grammaticalization*. Cambridge: CUP.

Huddleston, Rodney & Pullum, Geoffrey K. 2002. *The Cambridge Grammar of the English Language*. Cambridge: CUP.

Izutsu, Mitsuko N. & Izutsu, Katsunobu. 2014. Truncation and backshift: Two pathways to sentence-final coordinating conjunctions. *Journal of Historical Pragmatics* 15(1): 62–92. https://doi.org/10.1075/jhp.15.1.04izu

Jucker, Andreas H. & Smith, Sara W. 1998. And people just you know like 'wow': Discourse markers as negotiating strategies. In *Discourse Markers. Descriptions and Theory* [Pragmatics & Beyond New Series 57], Andreas H. Jucker & Yael Ziv (eds), 171–201. Amsterdam: John Benjamins. https://doi.org/10.1075/pbns.57.10juc

Kallen, Jeffrey L. 2005. Silence and mitigation in Irish English discourse. In *The Pragmatics of Irish English*, Anne Barron & Klaus P. Schneider (eds), 47–71. Berlin: Mouton de Gruyter. https://doi.org/10.1515/9783110898934.47

Kallen, Jeffrey L. 2006. *Arrah, like, you know*: The dynamics of discourse marking in ICE-Ireland. Presented at the Sociolinguistics Symposium 16, University of Limerick, 6–8 July 2006. <http://www.tara.tcd.ie/bitstream/handle/2262/50586/Arrah%20like%20y%27know.pdf?sequence=1&isAllowed=y> (29 September, 2015).

Kallen, Jeffrey L. 2013. *Irish English*, Vol. 2: *The Republic of Ireland*. Berlin: Mouton de Gruyter.

Kallen, Jeffrey L. 2015. "Actually, it's unfair to say that I was throwing stones": Comparative perspectives on uses of *actually* in ICE-Ireland. In Amador-Moreno, McCafferty & Vaughan (eds), 135–155.

Kallen, Jeffrey L. & Kirk, John M. 2012. *SPICE-Ireland. A User's Guide*. Belfast: Cló Ollscoil na Banríona.

Kirk, John M. & Kallen, Jeffrey L. 2010. How Scottish is Irish Standard English? In *Northern Lights, Northern Words. Selected Papers from the FRLSU Conference, Kirkwall 2009*, Robert McColl Millar (ed.), 178–213. Aberdeen: Forum for Research on the Languages of Scotland and Ireland. <https://www.abdn.ac.uk/pfrlsu/documents/Kirk%20and%20Kallen,%20How%20Scottish%20is%20Irish%20Standard%20English.pdf> (25 August 2015).

Kirk, John M., Kallen, Jeffrey L., Lowry, Orla, Rooney, Anne & Mannion, Margaret. 2011. *The SPICE-Ireland Corpus. Systems of Pragmatic Annotation for the Spoken Component of ICE-Ireland*. Version 1.2.2. Belfast: Queen's University Belfast and Dublin: Trinity College Dublin.

Langacker, Ronald W. 1987. *Foundations of Cognitive Grammar*, Vol. 1: *Theoretical Prerequisites*. Stanford, CA: Stanford University Press.

Lenker, Ursula. 2010. *Argument and Rhetoric. Adverbial Connectors in the History of English*. Berlin: Mouton de Gruyter. https://doi.org/10.1515/9783110216066

Lucek, Stephen. 2011. "I came up and I seen this haze of smoke, like": How Irish are invariant tags? *Trinity College Dublin Journal of Postgraduate Research* 18: 95–108.

Migge, Bettina. 2015. *Now* in the speech of newcomers to Ireland. In Amador-Moreno, McCafferty & Vaughan (eds), 390–407.

Miller, Jim & Weinert, Regina. 1995. The function of LIKE in dialogue. *Journal of Pragmatics* 23: 365–393. https://doi.org/10.1016/0378-2166(94)00044-F

Mulder, Jean & Thompson, Sandra A. 2008. The grammaticization of *but* as a final particle in English conversation. In *Crosslinguistic Studies of Clause Combining* [Typological Studies in Language 80], Ritva Laury (ed.), 179–204. Amsterdam: John Benjamins. https://doi.org/10.1075/tsl.80.09mul

Mulder, Jean, Thompson, Sandra A. & Penry Williams, Cara. 2009. Final *but* in Australian English conversation. In *Comparative Studies in Australian and New Zealand English. Grammar and Beyond* [Varieties of English around the World G39], Pam Peters, Peter Collins & Adam Smith (eds), 339–359. Amsterdam: John Benjamins. https://doi.org/10.1075/veaw.g39.19mul

Murphy, Bróna. 2015. A corpus-based investigation of pragmatic markers and sociolinguistic variation in Irish English. In Amador-Moreno, McCafferty & Vaughan (eds), 65–88.

Noël, Dirk. 2007. Diachronic construction grammar and grammaticalization theory. *Functions of Language* 14: 177–202. https://doi.org/10.1075/fol.14.2.04noe

Norrick, Neal R. 1995. *Hunh*-tags and evidentiality in conversation. *Journal of Pragmatics* 23: 687–692. https://doi.org/10.1016/0378-2166(94)00045-G

Overstreet, Maryann. 1999. *Whales, Candlelight, and Stuff Like That. General Extenders in English Discourse*. Oxford: OUP.

Paradis, Carita. 2003. Between epistemic modality and degree: The case of *really*. In *Modality in Contemporary English*, Roberta Facchinetti, Manfred Krug & Frank Palmer (eds), 191–220. Berlin: Mouton de Gruyter. https://doi.org/10.1515/9783110895339.191

Quirk, Randolph, Greenbaum, Sidney, Leech, Geoffrey & Jan, Svartvik. 1985. *A Comprehensive Grammar of the English Language*. London: Longman.

R Development Core Team. 2016. *R: A Language and Environment for Statistical Computing*. Vienna: R Foundation for Statistical Computing. <http://www.r-project.org>

Schiffrin, Deborah. 1987. *Discourse Markers*. Cambridge: CUP. https://doi.org/10.1017/CBO9780511611841

Schmid, Hans-Jörg. 2000. *English Abstract Nouns as Conceptual Shells. From Corpus to Cognition*. Berlin: Mouton de Gruyter. https://doi.org/10.1515/9783110808704

Schmid, Hans-Jörg. 2010. Does frequency in text instantiate entrenchment in the cognitive system? In *Quantitative Methods in Cognitive Semantics. Corpus-Driven Approaches*, Dylan Glynn & Kerstin Fischer (eds), 101–133. Berlin: Mouton de Gruyter.

Schmid, Hans-Jörg. 2016. A framework for understanding linguistic entrenchment and its psychological foundations. In *Entrenchment and the Psychology of Language Learning. How We Reorganize and Adapt Linguistic Knowledge*, Hans-Jörg Schmid (ed.), 9–35. Berlin: Mouton de Gruyter.

Schneider, Klaus P. & Barron, Anne. 2008. *Variational Pragmatics. A Focus on Regional Varieties in Pluricentric Languages* [Pragmatics & Beyond New Series 178]. Amsterdam: John Benjamins. https://doi.org/10.1075/pbns.178

Schweinberger, Martin. 2012. The discourse marker LIKE in Irish English. In *New Perspectives on Irish English* [Varieties of English around the World G44], Bettina Migge & Máire Ní Chiosáin (eds.), 179–201. Amsterdam: John Benjamins. https://doi.org/10.1075/veaw.g44.09sch

Schweinberger, Martin. 2014. The Discourse Marker LIKE: A Corpus-based Analysis of Selected Varieties of English. PhD dissertation, University of Hamburg.

Schweinberger, Martin. 2015. A comparative study of the pragmatic marker *like* in Irish English and in south-eastern varieties of British English. In Amador-Moreno, McCafferty & Vaughan (eds), 114–134.

Siemund, Peter, Maier, Georg & Schweinberger, Martin. 2009. Towards a more fine-grained analysis of the areal distributions of non-standard features of English. In *Language Contacts Meet English Dialects. Studies in Honour of Markku Filppula*, Esa Penttilä & Heli Paulasto (eds), 20–45. Newcastle upon Tyne: Cambridge Scholars.

Siertsema, Berthe. 1980. Sidelights on tag questions. In *The Melody of Language*, Linda R. Waugh & Cornelis H. van Schooneveld (eds), 299–314. Baltimore, MD: University Park Press.

Stenström, Anna-Brita. 1986. What does *really* really do? Strategies in speech and writing. In *English in Speech and Writing. A Symposium*, Gunnel Tottie & Ingegerd Bäcklund (eds), 149–163. Stockholm: Almqvist & Wiksell International.

Tagliamonte, Sali A. 2005. *So* who? *Like* how? *Just* what?: Discourse markers in the conversations of young Canadians. *Journal of Pragmatics* 37: 1896–1915. https://doi.org/10.1016/j.pragma.2005.02.017

Tagliamonte, Sali A. 2012. *Roots of English. Exploring the History of Dialects*. Cambridge: CUP. https://doi.org/10.1017/CBO9781139046718

Tottie, Gunnel & Hoffmann, Sebastian. 2006. Tag questions in British and American English. *Journal of English Linguistics* 34(4): 283–311. https://doi.org/10.1177/0075424206294369

Tottie, Gunnel & Hoffmann, Sebastian. 2009. Tag questions in English: The first century. *Journal of English Linguistics*. 37(2): 130–161. https://doi.org/10.1177/0075424209332962

Traugott, Elizabeth Closs. 2014. Toward a constructional framework for research on language change. In *Grammaticalization –Theory and Data* [Studies in Language Companion Series 162], Sylvie Hancil & Ekkehard König (eds), 87–105. Amsterdam: John Benjamins.

Traugott, Elizabeth Closs. 2015. Toward a coherent account of grammatical constructionalization. In *Diachronic Construction Grammar* [Constructional Approaches to Grammar 18], Jóhanna Barðdal, Elena Smirnova, Lotte Sommerer & Spike Gildea (eds), 51–79. Amsterdam: John Benjamins. https://doi.org/10.1075/cal.18.02tra

Traugott, Elizabeth Closs. 2016. On the rise of types of clause-final pragmatic markers in English. *Journal of Historical Pragmatics* 17(1): 26–54.

Traugott, Elizabeth Closs & Trousdale, Graeme. 2013. *Constructionalization and Constructional Changes*. Oxford: OUP. https://doi.org/10.1093/acprof:oso/9780199679898.001.0001

Walshe, Shane. 2016. Irish society as portrayed in Irish film. In *Sociolinguistics in Ireland*, Raymond Hickey (ed.), 320–343. London: Palgrave Macmillan.

Appendix A. A list of final tags in SPICE-Ireland

FIX-tags	clausal tags	KNOW	you know	400
			do you know	8
			don't you know	1
			I know	3
			I don't know	6
		THINK	I think	44
			I don't think	2
			do you think	4
		MEAN	I mean	10
			you mean	3
			does that mean	1

		SUPPOSE	I suppose	14
		GUESS	I guess	1
		WONDER	I wonder	1
		UNDERSTAND	I don't understand	1
		REMEMBER	do you remember	1
		SEE	you see	48
			I see	1
		HEAR	do you hear	1
		SAY	I'd say (I would say)	20
			I must say	2
			I should say	1
			I'd have to say (myself)	2
			I have to say	1
			we'll say	1
			shall we say	1
		TELL	I'll tell you	2
			I can tell you	1
			(I) told you	1
			let me tell you	1
		BET	I bet	2
		AGREE	I agree	1
		SEEM	it seems (to me)	3
		ADMIT	I must admit	1
		BE + Adj.	I'm afraid	1
			I'm sure	3
		MIND (imp.)	mind you	1
FIX-tags	lexical tags	expressions meaning '(be) in order'	okay	37
			right	101
			alright	34
			oh-right	1
		words for 'yes' or 'no'	yeah	357
			yeah-yeah	15
			oh-yeah	2
			yes	32
			aye	39

(*continued*)

		no	65
		no-no	2
	deictic expressions	now	167
		then	129
		there	9
		that	8
	personal pronouns	yourself	2
		myself	1
		him	1
	approximative markers	like	506
		kind of	2
		sort of	2
	non-word phonological sequences	ah	1
		eh	2
		oh	3
		huh	1
		uh-huh	9
		hey	3
	adverbs of factuality	really	78
		actually	81
		indeed	8
		in fact	1
		to tell you the truth	1
		truthfully	1
		no doubt	2
	adverbs of consent	(of) course	16
		sure	11
		surely	6
		certainly	3
		definitely	2
		exactly	3
	adverbs of totality	absolutely	2
		totally	4
		completely	2

		adverbs of sincerity	seriously	2
			to be honest (with you)	11
			honestly	2
			quite frankly	1
		connectives	but	9
			so	8
			though	90
			however	1
			nonetheless	1
			by the way	1
			in other words	1
			anyway(s)	159
			anyhow	4
			first of all	2
			in the first place	8
		expressions of completion	finito	1
			full stop	1
		expressions of God	God	3
			Jesus	4
			oh-(my)-God	2
			for goodness sake	1
			for God's sake	1
		others	just	2
			please	24
AUX-tags	clausal tags	reduced clauses	tags (BE)	242
			tags (DO)	60
			tags (HAVE)	17
			tags (MODAL)	39
			tags (so)	41
			tags (sure)	4
vocative tags (VOC-tags)				383
TOTAL				3472

Appendix B. A list of final tags in SBC

FIX-tags	clausal tags	KNOW	you know	246
			do you know	3
			I know	3
			I don't (really) know	12
		THINK	I think	28
			I would think	1
			I don't think	1
			you think	4
			do you think	1
			don't you think	1
		MEAN	I mean	1
			you mean	4
		REMEMBER	remember	6
			I can't remember	1
		GUESS	I guess	18
		PRESUME	I presume	1
		WONDER	I wonder	1
		SEE	you (can) see	11
			see	8
			I see	5
		TELL	I (can) tell you	2
			I'm telling you	1
			I told you	1
		SEEM	it seems (to me)	3
			he seems to be	1
		BET	you bet	1
			bet you	1
		BE SURE	I'm sure	3
			I'm not sure	1
FIX-tags	lexical tags	expressions meaning '(be) in order'	okay	85
			right	159
			alright	33
		words for *yes* and *no*	yeah	115

	yes	8
	no	5
deictic expressions	now	24
	then	47
	there	2
	that	1
approximative markers	kinda	1
non-wordphonological sequences	huh	4
	hunh	59
	unhunh	2
	hm	2
	oh	2
adverbs of factuality	really	20
	actually	9
	indeed	4
	in fact	2
	to tell you the truth	1
adverbs of consent	of course	4
	why not	2
	sure	1
	for sure	2
adverbs of sincerity	to be honest (with you)	2
	all honesty	1
connectives	anyway(s)	24
	anyhow	2
	though	110
	by the way	2
	in other words	1
	on one hand	2
	first of all	1
expressions of completion	period	5
expressions of God	Jesus (Christ)	5
	(My) God	5
	goodness	1

(*continued*)

		others	please	17
			would you please	1
AUX-tags	clausal tags	reduced clauses	tags (BE)	48
			tags (DO)	45
			tags (HAVE)	5
			tags (MODAL)	11
vocative tags (VOC-tags)				365
TOTAL				1617

Subject index

G

H

I

L

M

N

O

P